GANG INJUNCTIONS AND ABATEMENT

Using Civil Remedies to Curb Gang-Related Crimes

GANG INJUNCTIONS AND ABATEMENT

Using Civil Remedies to Curb Gang-Related Crimes

Matthew D. O'Deane

CRC Press
Taylor & Francis Group
Boca Raton London New York

CRC Press is an imprint of the
Taylor & Francis Group, an **informa** business

CRC Press
Taylor & Francis Group
6000 Broken Sound Parkway NW, Suite 300
Boca Raton, FL 33487-2742

First issued in paperback 2018

ISBN-13: 978-1-4398-6787-7 (hbk)
ISBN-13: 978-1-138-37455-3 (pbk)

Library of Congress Cataloging-in-Publication Data

O'Deane, Matthew David.
Gang injunctions and abatement : using civil remedies to curb gang-related crimes / author, Matthew D. O'Deane.
p. cm.
Includes bibliographical references and index.
ISBN 978-1-4398-6787-7
1. Gang prevention--Law and legislation--United States. 2. Injunctions--United States. I. Title.

KF9375.O34 2011
347.73'77--dc23 2011019275

Visit the Taylor & Francis Web site at
http://www.taylorandfrancis.com

and the CRC Press Web site at
http://www.crcpress.com

Contents

List of Figures

List of Tables

About the Author

Dr. Matthew O'Deane has been a California police officer since 1992 when he was hired by the National City Police Department in southern California.

From 1992 to 2002 he investigated gang and narcotics cases on a daily basis. In May of 2002, he was hired as an Investigator for the San Diego County District Attorney's Office in the Bureau of Investigations where he has worked since, the majortity of the time working cases while assigned to the Gang Prosecution Unit.

Dr. O'Deane earned his Ph.D. in Public Policy in 2007. He also has a master's degree in Public Administration, and bachelor's degree in Criminal Justice. Currently Dr. O'Deane is a professor for Kaplan University in the Masters of Criminal Justice Program and is also a professor for National University in the Criminal Justice Program.

He has also been a featured presenter at numerous national and international law enforcement and academic conferences speaking on the topic of gangs. This is the third book by Dr. O'Deane on the topic of gangs. He published the *Gang Investigator's Handbook* with Paladin Press in 2007 and *Gangs: Theory, Practice* and *Research with* LawTech Custom Publishing in 2010. Dr. O'Deane has also published articles for *Law Officer Magazine*, *Police Magazine*, and the *FBI Law Enforcement Bulletin* in the past several years.

Dr. O'Deane created this book to help understand the dynamics of using civil laws to address the gang problem facing many of our communities. For more on the injunctions, including maps, photos, and research, go to http://www.crcpress.com/product/isbn/9781439867877

1

Introduction

As gang crime continues across the country, police, prosecutors, and community members seek methods to reduce the spread of gang-related criminal activity. The use of civil gang injunctions has become a growing feature of crime control strategies across the nation. At the same time, these injunctions have also raised constitutional controversies over restrictions on speech and assembly. Despite the debate, the use of injunctions has consistently increased on an annual basis since they were first utilized. In 2010, the State of California surpassed the 150-gang-injunction plateau since they started to be implemented more than 25 years ago. One of the questions I wanted to answer in this book is: Do these civil remedies help curb gang violence in the communities in which they were implemented? In addition to understanding the impact or level of effectiveness, I also wanted to explore what makes any given injunction or abatement effort more or less effective, and what variables impact gang injunction effectiveness to help make future gang injunctions more effective. While the book speaks specifically about laws and issues in California and only a few other locations, lessons learned can be applicable in any other U.S. areas where the appropriate civil remedies and gang problems exist.

The immense costs of gangs to our society, and the legal and policy issues relating to gang injunctions and abatement, make the policy worthy of study and review. In large part, our criminal justice system and our police forces are reactive, in that they seek to punish individuals for past actions that violated existing criminal laws. Because of this, crime prevention strategies generally rely on prevention through deterrence. The government either deploys the police where they will deter crime, or seeks to use the consequences of the criminal justice system as a deterrent to commit criminal acts. However, some legal tools have been expressly designed to prevent future crime through the imposition of restrictions, such as those contained in gang injunctions. Such civil mechanisms or remedies seek to impose a set of circumstances on a gang or an individual before, rather than after, a crime has been committed. Like any tool, such as a hammer, the tool of gang injunctions can be used for constructive purposes or as a clumsy bludgeon; it often depends on the skill with which it is wielded.

Many people feel helpless against crime, because crime is often seen as an inevitable part of our society. It has been said, "If a criminal wants to get you, they will get you." This belief leads to helplessness, fear, and apathy. Apathy is one of the most dangerous elements in society today. When law-abiding citizens refuse to go outside after dark, they have voluntarily turned over their neighborhoods to the ones who commit the crimes. Many times, a community will not fight against gangs and crime because its members feel they will not be successful.

Often, people view dangerous gang members like large rocks that cannot be moved, or even budged. I know, however, from first-hand experience that gang members are not like rocks; they are more like weeds. Unlike an inanimate rock, a weed will grow. As a weed grows, it roots, sprouts, and chokes out healthy plants. A single weed quickly overtakes an entire garden. When criminal gang activity is allowed to flourish, the effect is the same.

The typical law enforcement approach to crime is reactive. Once a crime has been committed, law enforcement responds, writes a report, and begins the preliminary investigation. It is certainly more humane and cost-effective to prevent a crime from occurring. Crime prevention is the proactive side of law enforcement. Crime prevention is more desirable because it addresses the potential for crime before it becomes a serious problem. Unfortunately, many people do not address crime situations until it is too late. A good example is a burglary victim who suddenly becomes interested in home security systems (locks, alarms, security screens, etc.). Once a crime problem has become too large, it is often easier to run away from it than face it. Equate a gang problem to killing a vicious bear. The easiest way to kill a bear is while it is a cub. If the bear has had the opportunity to grow, it becomes progressively harder to defeat. The same is true about criminal activity and gangs.

The use of civil laws and procedures to target these gangs oftentimes takes the form of gang injunctions or gang abatement projects in known gang neighborhoods and at known gang hangouts. According to the Los Angeles Police Department, approximately 60% of all gang crimes that occur in the city limits do so at 10% of all properties or locations in Los Angeles. This is a significant fact that many police agencies overlook; this fact supports the view that the police should take the location or the area into account as a significant factor in fighting gang crime.

The purpose of gang injunctions and gang abatement is to target the properties or neighborhoods where gang members engage in activity that destroys the quality of life for the law-abiding citizens, where gang members are repeatedly contacted or arrested by the police; however, despite police efforts, criminal activities nonetheless persist. Rather than responding to the same location over and over again and simply making arrests, civil remedies attempt to stop, or at least lessen, the impact of the gang, at the specific location or identified target area.

Proponents say that obtaining a gang injunction or abating a gang singles out the bad actors, the gangsters, and puts them on notice that they will be held liable for violations. This policy does have more than its fair share of *legal controversies.* Concerns have been raised over the legal precedents that gang injunctions and abatement create. Specifically, these concerns relate to whether gang injunctions go too far in restricting the speech and assembly rights of persons who have not yet committed crimes, or that they violate constitutional rights such as due process or the right to representation by counsel.

CRIMINAL LAW VERSUS CIVIL LAW

When you think of criminal laws, think of Perry Mason, the judge and jury. When you think of civil laws, think of Judge Wapner and *The People's Court.* The issues and the procedures are quite different. In criminal law, the police must have probable cause to arrest someone. Suspicion is not enough. Probable cause is where a deputy knows that a crime happened, and believes the perpetrator is the one being detained. When a deputy begins to question the person who was just arrested, he must tell the suspect about his or her Miranda rights. Law enforcement cannot search an apartment without a warrant, which is not easy to obtain. If the officer is able to build enough evidence to arrest a suspect, there is still no guarantee the prosecutor's office will file charges. If charges are filed, there is no guarantee the person will be brought to a jury trial. If the person is brought to a jury trial, there is no guarantee the jury will convict. If the jury convicts, there is no guarantee the person will go to prison. If the person goes to prison, there is no guarantee that he will stay there very long. In many cases, plea bargains are made, probation is given, and in some situations, the charges are just dropped. In most cases, the people who are arrested at rental properties do not go to prison. They are released very soon after being arrested, and they go back home to their apartment.

In civil law, the procedure is much different. Civil court does not represent the typical courtroom scenario. In criminal cases, a jury must be convinced beyond a reasonable doubt. In civil law, the judge only needs to see a preponderance of evidence. A preponderance of evidence is much less than proof beyond a reasonable doubt. A preponderance of evidence needs only to be 51% to adjudicate. Proof beyond a reasonable doubt requires virtually 100% to convict the accused.

PUBLIC NUISANCES

Prosecutors and police obtain gang injunctions and abate gangs by applying the law of public nuisance to the particular harms criminal street gangs cause. We normally associate a nuisance with minor annoyances, and indeed the nuisance law originally developed out of the need to address minor offenses. However, the nuisance doctrine applies equally to the serious activities of criminal street gangs, and is an effective tool for tackling gang violence as well.

Historically, public nuisances were addressed via the common law doctrine. In common law public nuisance came to cover relatively minor offenses that involved some interference with the interests of the community at large, and were recognized as rights of the general public and hence were entitled to protection.

Both gang injunctions and gang property abatements are nuisance abatement actions. However, they seek different remedies. A gang injunction is a lawsuit against an entire gang or specific members of a local gang. A gang property abatement focuses on a specific property and targets the property owners and the specific gang members who are creating or allowing the nuisance at that specific location. A gang injunction focuses on a geographic area (often called a safety zone or target area) within which the gang's activities are restricted. Among other things, gang injunctions typically prohibit two or more gang members from associating in public view in the safety zone if they were served with the order. Gang property abatements, on the other hand, target a specific property regardless of whether it is located in a safety zone and seek to stop criminal activity from occurring there.

Public nuisances can include a wide array of issues; for example, the nuisance may interfere with the public's health, as in the case of keeping diseased animals on one's property or an unkept swimming pool, which can potentially breed malarial mosquitoes. A public nuisance may also interfere with the public safety, such as your neighbor storing explosives in his or her backyard shed in the midst of the city or the shooting of fireworks on public streets, which could harm or kill innocent people or set your neighbors' houses on fire.

A public nuisance may also interfere with public morals, such as houses of prostitution or indecent exhibitions which people passing by may have to observe. A public nuisance may also interfere with the public peace, such as a loud gang party with music keeping neighbors awake into the morning hours. A public nuisance may also interfere with a public convenience, such as the obstruction of a public street or sidewalk or blocking access to businesses on a particular street.

In each of these instances the interference with the public right is typically found to be unreasonable and can constitute a criminal offense as well as a tort, or a civil violation.

When gangsters operate out of rental property, for example, neighborhoods suffer and landlords and community members pay a high price. That price may include a decline in property values, particularly when the activity begins affecting the reputation of the entire neighborhood. Property damage can arise from the gang conduct, via retaliation, or neglect; damage can be caused by police raids. Property value can also be affected by civil penalties, including temporary closure of the property or even property seizure, loss of rent during the eviction and repair periods, fear and frustration when dealing with dangerous and threatening gang-affiliated tenants, and increased resentment and anger between neighbors and property managers.

It is widely recognized that gang enforcement alone will never solve the gang problem. Enforcement must be just one component of a balanced approach, which includes suppression, intervention, and prevention, if a truly long-term gang solution is to be reached. Focusing on solely one or the other of the big three approaches (suppression, intervention, prevention) while neglecting the others typically undermines the effectiveness of each, individually and combined. Gang abatement and injunctions are unique in that they can actually be considered prevention, intervention, or suppression, depending on the context in which you view the problem.

While suppression efforts are needed to hold gangsters accountable for their actions, this suppression is not necessarily going to solve the problem at entrenched gang locations. Gang members highly value these locations, and when one person is arrested, another is frequently willing to quickly fill the void and resume the criminal activity. When local or federal law enforcement officers or agents determine that arrests will not stop criminal gang activity at a private property, they refer the property to prosecutors for possible nuisance abatement.

It is hard for a gang to sell drugs out of a house if the house is demolished because the owners did not control the gang members on their property. This is why civil remedies can be a very powerful tool against gangs, and if owners do not help solve the problem, they are undoubtedly part of the problem. Who can be sued as a civil remedy? Owner(s) of real property the gangs live at, owner(s) of the businesses the gangs hang out at, lessees/renters of the properties that allow gangs to engage in crime, managers of the properties that fail to take action, management companies, the real property itself (*in rem* suit), or any combination of the above.

WHAT IS AN INJUNCTION OR ABATEMENT?

A gang injunction is an order of a court directing gang members to refrain from an act or acts. Gangs are often breaking the law because the activity they engage in constitutes a public nuisance under the California Civil Code, or a similar code for the state in which you reside. The nuisance abatement action seeks to improve conditions at the property or neighborhood so that gang members will not be able to use the property to conduct business without increased risk. Gang injunctions and property abatements are a critical, but sometimes overlooked, weapon in law enforcement's arsenal against gangs. When gang abatement extends beyond the scope of a specific property like an apartment complex, for example, and impacts an entire neighborhood, gang injunctions are often sought.

Gang injunctions allow the police to contact and arrest gang members they know or suspect to be on the order, in some cases before they have the opportunity to commit a crime. Gang abatement allows the police to target the property owners that allow gangsters to use the property as a gang hangout without taking precautions to protect residents in the area, and gives the police the added authority to remove the gang members from the property. Injunctions and abatement are proactive tools that give the police the ability to arrest gang members simply for being together in public view, displaying a gang hand sign, wearing gang-specific clothing within the target area, or for being on a property where they should not be.

The concept behind the use of injunctions or abatement laws that force property owners or gang members to make changes or face sanctions is one of the fundamental powers of the judiciary. The court must be specific in the orders that it issues. The people bound by the order must be identified either individually or as an identifiable group, and the things that are mandated or prohibited by the order must be defined. The injunction must address the specific problem the court is attempting to remedy. However, because a judge issuing an injunction is seeking to remedy a specific problem caused by particular people or groups, the judge can prohibit those people from doing things that the legislature could not make illegal by passing a law or municipal code. This is true because injunctions are remedies imposed by the judge for specific violations (or threatened violations) of the law.

Injunctions differ from statutes and ordinances in that they are much narrower as to whom and what they apply to, despite popular media reports that once an injunction is granted, it applies to everyone in the neighborhood, or even everyone in the gang, which is not the case. There is a well-known saying that "ignorance of the law is not a defense." This is true of statutes, which everybody must obey. This is why visitors to states where it is illegal to make a right turn against a red light still get tickets even though they didn't know the rule.

In contrast, in order to be bound by an injunction, a person must be "on notice" of the injunction and its terms. Because it is a special order that applies only to certain people or groups of people, those people must have been notified of the injunction before they can be found to have violated it. Gang injunctions seek to level the playing field and restore balance to the communities. When gang members gather together, they promote their gang's activities, they encourage each other to commit crimes on behalf of the gang, and they become targets for rival gang members. The more visible the gang is, the stronger the gang becomes, and the more fear it is able to instill in the community.

For this reason, the gang's presence is a major factor when evaluating its ability to harass, intimidate, and commit crimes in its territory. When a gang injunction is granted, all members that are served with the order are subject to it. Any individual gang member who is notified of the injunction is from then on subject to the restrictions of the injunction, which aim to keep gang members from controlling a specific geographic area. Therefore, the injunction will only be effective in achieving these aims if the problematic members in the specific area have been identified and served, and the order is enforced. A gang's strength is in its numbers; gang injunctions attempt to undermine a gang's ability to commit crime by reducing the number of active members that can be in public view in these areas. Although media accounts of gang injunctions tend to focus on controversy or conflict, when residents of the gang-plagued area are interviewed by police and academics alike, the reactions are typically favorable. Civil gang injunctions can play an important role in the intervention, prevention, *and* suppression of gang activities.

The efficacy of gang injunctions is clearer today than it was 10 or 15 years ago, but many critics feel that their efficacy still remains unclear. This is potentially problematic, as the use of such injunctions has increased since their inception. Responsible public policy dictates that policy decisions are evaluated empirically to determine their level of effectiveness and to formulate and implement effective policies. Reducing crime is important to any civil society; regardless if specific injunctions are found to be effective or ineffective, responsible public policy dictates a review of significant policies implemented to ensure the best use of public resources.

THE GANG PROBLEM

Chapter 16 seeks to answer several questions, primarily what exactly is the size and scope of the gang problem in California, where there are an estimated 350,000 gang members and over 6,300 different street gangs engage in crime on a daily basis. Law enforcement estimates that unregistered or undocumented numbers could be two to four times higher than the numbers of known members in some jurisdictions.

Street gangs are not a new problem in the United States; gangs have been terrorizing America's communities at least since the early 1800s. Law enforcement has had to deal with these criminals over the years, primarily using traditional arrests for violations of a criminal statute that does little to prevent the emergence of street gangs, either on the individual or on the collective group level.

The evidence for inclusion as a gang member in an injunction typically includes a complete historical background check of the members named in the order, including every arrest report, field interview, and police contact that tends to support the law enforcement position that the individual served is a member of the gang and that they are part of the public nuisance. Supporting evidence typically includes examples of recent crimes committed by the gang, a description of the gang's territory, the history of the gang, the characteristics of the gang, and how the group meets the legal definition of a gang (Penal Code Section 186.22).

Gang injunctions are fertile ground for civil rights groups to challenge the validity of the technique. Therefore it is extremely important that proposed injunctions be tailored to attack the gang behavior causing the public nuisance, but be no broader than necessary.

The restrictions outlined in gang injunctions only apply to members of the enjoined gang who engage in specific acts prohibited by the civil lawsuit. That is, injunctions are enforceable only against gang members who have been served with the order, who are in the target area or safety zone, who are in public view, and who are in violation of one or more of the restrictions as outlined in the injunction. The police cannot use the injunction as the basis of action against someone in the absence of these requirements (but of course they can still take other legal actions against people). To be identified as a gang member, a citizen must be a documented associate of the enjoined gang, and that membership or association must be supported by enough evidence to convince a judge the person served is part of the public nuisance.

Most gang injunction cases have numerous, sometimes hundreds, of declarations from police officers and community members that articulate the nuisance behavior of the gang and its members, including examples of crimes members have engaged in, and why particular members were selected for inclusion into the court order. Even if the individual is not named as a defendant and was added at a later date, the same evidence will need to be made available should the gang member be arrested for violating the order. Further, no one can be arrested or punished for violating a gang injunction unless and until they have knowledge of the court's order by personal service. Community members and citizens living within the target areas are not under any authority of the injunction if they are not named in, or subsequently served with, the order.

Some suggest that gang injunctions may violate the rights of people served with these orders. One community activist interviewed by the media following the Oakdale gang injunction felt it was wrong to sacrifice civil rights for the greater good. Proponents dispute that claim and feel it is the duty of public officials to require gang members to respect the rights of others; if not, they will have their own rights limited within the parameters of the gang injunction or abatement effort. Another resident in the Oakdale mob injunction case felt that if city officials want to make the neighborhood safer, they should help people get jobs and create more programs for kids, claiming injunctions are not the answer to the gang problem, jobs are.

Orange County District Attorney Tony Rackauckas said, in speaking about the Santa Nita gang injunction, "When gangs are active, our quality of life goes down, we will do everything we can to interfere with their activities." According to Los Angeles Assistant City Attorney Marty Vranicar, "The real issue is the civil rights of citizens subjected to gang violence and gang intimidation. When parents and children are unable to play in the parks, whose rights are being violated?

Police officers in most of the cities in Southern California work in areas where police resources are often spread thin and calls for service are typically above national averages. In addition, most police departments in Southern California are reportedly working below normal manpower levels. As such, the attitudes of the police about gang injunctions may vary from jurisdiction to jurisdiction based upon the priorities of each city and jurisdiction.

In some jurisdictions, a gang member may have little chance of getting away with a violation of the local gang injunction due to the police aggressively enforcing the order with a very high-profile proactive presence in the area. In other areas, the police may be mandated to address more serious issues or respond to a backlog of calls for service, and they do not have the time to adequately enforce the current injunctions; as such, the gangs are not impacted by the injunction to the same degree as the area with aggressive enforcement. Because of the expense and because of the importance of aggressive enforcement, it is important to empirically investigate the effectiveness of gang injunctions.

This book contains a synopsis of every gang injuction ever filed in the State of California. Each contains the court case number, target area and other relevant facts.

DEFINITION OF TERMS

A *gang injunction* is an order of a court directing a party to perform a certain act or to refrain from an act or acts. They are civil lawsuits that allege in the complaint that the gang and its members have occupied and used the specified target area in a manner that constitutes a public nuisance under California Civil Code Sections 3479 and 3480. Section 3479 defines a nuisance as anything that is injurious to health, including, but not limited to, the illegal sale of controlled substances; is indecent or offensive to the senses; is an obstruction to the free use of property, so as to interfere with the comfortable enjoyment of life or property; or unlawfully obstructs the free passage or use, in the customary manner, of any navigable lake, river, bay stream, canal, or basin, or any public park, square, street, or highway. In essence, an injunction serves as a protective order to lessen the impact of the criminal gangs for the designated area and the residents that live in the community. The California law is similar to the English Antisocial Behavior Order, which is a civil order made against a person who has been shown to have engaged in conduct that caused or was likely to cause alarm, harassment, or distress to one or more persons not of the same household as himself or herself, and where it is necessary to protect persons from further antisocial acts by the defendant.

Civil gang injunctions can take from a few months to a year or more to obtain permanently. Typically the prosecution asks for temporary relief in the form of a preliminary injunction that is in place while the case goes through the legal system. The process is similar to a situation where your neighbor wants to build an addition to his home that will obstruct your view, and you want him stopped until the potential code violations are addressed. You would file a civil suit and would also ask the court to make him stop building until the issue is resolved.

In this text, California Penal Code has been used. The California Penal Code Section 186.22 defines a *street gang* as the following:

> (a) an ongoing organization, association, of three or more persons whether formal or informal, (b) having as one of its primary activities the commission or attempted commission of one of the designated predicate offenses, (c) which has a common name or common identifying symbol, and (d) whose members individually or collectively engage in a pattern of criminal gang activity.

Gang property abatement is a civil lawsuit initiated by the prosecutor's office in the name of the people of the state that seeks to abate recurring criminal activity at a private property. The property owner who is legally responsible for abating the nuisance at the property and gang members who are using the property to engage in criminal activity are named as defendants. Negligent property managers and tenants who are "friendly" to the gang members may also be named as defendants. A gang property abatement can be apply to any type of privately owned property. This includes single-family dwellings, hotels, motels, apartment buildings, bars, and other commercial locations. The owner and the gang members are sued because they have either directly or indirectly caused or permitted a public nuisance to exist on the property. The gang members do not have to be property owners, managers, or tenants to be named as defendants. In essence, the prosecution files the abatement action to stop, or greatly reduce, the criminal activity at the property. Once a lawsuit is filed, a preliminary injunction against the property owner, gang members, gang associates, or property managers is sought. The injunction against the owner requires that he make comprehensive improvements to the property (such as surveillance systems, gates, lighting) and alter the management practices (such as better tenant screening, new managers, evictions), while the injunction against the gang member defendants includes a stay-away order that prevents them from returning to the property.

Causes of action are typically based on three legal theories, which form the basis of lawsuits and include General Public Nuisance, Civil Code Section 3479; Narcotics Abatement, Health and Safety Code Section 11570, et seq.; and Unfair Competition Law, Business and Professions Code, Section 17200, et seq. Gang injunctions fall under 3479 in most cases.

The *narcotics abatement law* prohibits any property from being used to sell, store, serve, or manufacture narcotics. It authorizes the prosecution on behalf of the state to obtain a broad injunction against the property owner and others engaged in narcotics activity at the property to abate the nuisance. In certain circumstances, the court can order the property owner to live on the property or close down the property for one year. A lawsuit under the narcotics abatement law is given precedence over nearly all other lawsuits on the court's calendar. The statute also expressly allows the nuisance to be proved by the reputation of the property in the community. Further, knowledge of the nuisance is not necessary to establish liability of the property owner. The prosecution may recover attorneys' fees and law enforcement costs of investigation.

Additionally, a penalty of up to $25,000 per defendant may be assessed by the court.

The *general public nuisance statute* defines a nuisance as anything that is injurious to health, indecent, or offensive to the senses, or an obstruction to the free use of property, so as to interfere with the comfortable enjoyment of life or property. The definition also includes the sale of narcotics. The prosecution is authorized to file a public nuisance lawsuit on behalf of the state and obtain injunctive relief. This statute is used by prosecutors to document for the court all criminal activity (not just narcotics) occurring at and directly connected to a gang property that constitutes the nuisance. This may include drive-by and other shootings, fights, gambling, drinking alcoholic beverages in public, loud noise, and any other offensive activity conducted by the gang at or connected to the property. Unlike the narcotics abatement statute, the general public nuisance statute does not authorize recovery of any costs or attorneys' fees. However, like the narcotics abatement statute, an owner's knowledge is not necessary to establish liability.

The *unlawful business practices statute* (commonly referred to as the unfair competition law (UCL)) seeks to enjoin, redress, and punish, among other things, unlawful, unfair, and fraudulent business acts and practices. Unlike the narcotics abatement and general public nuisance causes of action, which are primarily property based, unlawful activity alleged under a UCL cause of action does not have to be connected to the physical property. Virtually any violation of law, including local, state, federal, civil or criminal, statutory, regulatory, or common law, is actionable under the unlawful prong of 17200. Frequently, prosecutors use violations of the narcotics abatement or general public nuisance statute as the basis for the UCL cause of action. In addition to broad injunctive relief and the potential appointment of a receiver to manage the property, civil penalties of up to $2,500 for each act of unlawful competition are available under the UCL. Operating rental housing in a way that violates any laws, including nuisance abatement statutes, is an unlawful business practice that subjects the property owner to liability under the UCL. Unlawful business practices also include using any legitimate business, such as a barbershop or tattoo parlor, for an illegal purpose such as narcotics sales.

A *gang member* is anyone who actively participates in a criminal street gang; has knowledge of, or has engaged in, a pattern of criminal gang activity; and willfully promotes, furthers, or assists in any criminal conduct by members of the gang (California Penal Code Section 186.22). A suspect can be documented as a gang member if he or she meets one or more of the following criteria: (1) admits membership in a specific gang, (2) uses gang hand signs, paraphernalia, tattoos, or clothing associated with a particular gang, (3) is recorded by police as having confirmed close associations with known gang members, (4) is arrested with other known gang members, or (5) is indicated as a gang member by a reliable source. The individual must meet at least two or more of these criteria before he or she is able to be documented as a gang member.

I have identified five stages of gang involvement, all of which can be impacted by gang injunctions in varying degrees. It should be noted that there are no standard lengths of time that individuals remain at any given level, and the gang members themselves do not acknowledge these steps. However, length of exposure to a gang and age at first exposure are contributing categories to an individual's likelihood of advancing within the gang. A gang member can range from someone in the community not known to the police to someone that has a lengthy criminal history; he or she ranges on commitment to the gang and the gang lifestyle, and the level of gang activity he or she engages in. The criteria to document a person as a gang member may also vary from county to county and state to state, making the classification inconsistent between law enforcement agencies.

Stage 1: At Risk or Peripheral

These individuals are not considered gang members by the police but they often know gang members, are related to gang members, and may associate with gang members casually and on a limited basis, mostly watching and imitating the older gang members' behavior. They may like and admire the gang members in the neighborhood and the gang lifestyle, but typically do not participate in the gang's criminal activity. This group is usually between seven and nine years old and is the group in most need of being removed from the presence of gang members to improve their chances of growing up and not joining a gang. These individuals are not typically made targets of gang injunctions because inclusion in a gang injunction requires adequate documentation showing the individual to be an active gang member. However, if such documentation were available, the individual would be classified as an associate or member, rather than a peripheral. These kids desperately need to be the targets of social programs, in-school programs, after-school programs, and other positive and constructive programs that help distance these kids from the gangs they are in danger of joining without some positive form of intervention. One goal of injunctions is to remove the most visible presence of gangs in a particular area, giving these types of programs a better chance of impacting the at-risk kids in the gang communities.

Stage 2: Associates or Affiliates

These individuals associate with gang members on a regular basis and consider gang life normal and acceptable. They find things in common with gang members and are likely to seriously consider joining the gang. Some associates consider themselves members, even if they have not yet been formally initiated. They are commonly called wannabes, peewees, or tiny gangsters. They may dress like gang members and socialize with them, effectively making them part of the gang problem in their neighborhood. The public does not usually know the difference between an associate and a gang member; the difference is oftentimes inconsequential and irrelevant when taking into account the fear and intimidation caused by the presence of a larger group in the community. The fear, intimidation, and nuisance activity still exist, and the problem is only expanded by the presence of gang associates. These associates are sometimes used by older gang members to do menial tasks, such as serving as lookouts, runners for drugs, or for writing graffiti, effectively making them part of, or in some cases the major contributors to, the nuisance problem experienced in the gang injunction areas.

Associates are usually between the ages of 9 and 13. These individuals have potential to be salvaged and may be capable of withdrawing from the gang if they are reached by early-intervention programs and diverted away from the gang. These are the people that benefit from the reduced presence of the gang, maybe more than anyone else, because the bond or hold the gang has on them can be weakened by a properly enforced gang injunction, helping them distance themselves from the gang. Some associates and affiliates are involved in serious criminal conduct in certain cases. At times, documented gang members may pose less of a problem than individuals who are considered merely associates or affiliates. While in associate status, individuals are responsible for a large number of violent acts as they attempt to impress members with their ability to be ruthless and supportive of the group's activities. It is probable that some associates may be looked at when evaluating a gang injunction. However, most gang injunctions name only individuals who can be documented as members, or as having enough contacts in the target area to justify documenting them as a member during the evidence collection phase of the injunction process.

Stage 3: Gang Members

Gang members associate almost exclusively with other gang members, to the exclusion of biological family and former non-gang-affiliated friends. Members may be new to the gang, recently jumped into the gang, or are trying to make a name for themselves. These persons participate in gang crimes and most of the gang's activities. They make up the bulk of a gang's membership and are held responsible for protection of the gang's turf and fellow gang members (Huff, 1998). This individual has typically rejected authority and society in general and is usually aspiring to advance his or her status in the gang. This individual is usually between the ages of 14 and 20 years old and makes up the bulk of every gang injunction target to date.

Stage 4: Hard-Core Gang Members

This gang member has become totally committed to the gang and gang lifestyle, commonly referred to as an OG (or original gangster) or *veterano*. He or she usually rejects any value system other than that of his or her gang, and his or her life revolves around the gang. These members are considered hard core by the authorities, other gang members, and themselves. They have been through the justice system and are often streetwise and influential with their peers. These members value the "code of silence" of the gang; more often than not, they will not talk to the police or snitch on a fellow gang member. These persons will commit any crime or act of violence to further the goals and objectives of the gang. These members are usually between 18 and 25 years old.

Stage 5: Gang Leaders

These members are the upper echelon of the gang's command. This gang member is probably the oldest in the group and likely has an extensive criminal record. He or she has significant respect of the general membership and has the power to direct the gang's activity, whether he or she is involved or not. Leaders have the final say as to who becomes a member, who will die, and what activities the gang is involved in—and may issue punishment within the gang as well. In California, this person is likely a prison gang member calling the shots from within the prison system or is a felon on parole. Often these people distance themselves from the street gang activities and have legitimate businesses that they run as fronts for the gang's drug dealing or other illegal business.

A *gang-related crime* is any crime in which a gang member is the suspect, offender, or victim, regardless of motivation or circumstances. It is recommended by law enforcement that crimes first be classified as gang related, followed by further analysis which may indicate which gang-related crimes are more specifically gang motivated. This method will typically provide a broader picture of gang member criminal activity, allowing law enforcement to conform to whatever gang crime definitions are used in any new or amended anti-gang legislation, and enable the agency to more accurately compare gang crime across jurisdictions.

A *gang-motivated crime* is a crime in which the suspects are identified as gang members, or the person becomes a victim because of his or her specific gang affiliation. The crime is committed for the benefit of or at the direction of the gang. Gang-motivated crimes may involve intergang violence for retaliation or turf protection or other criminal activity affecting the reputation or interests of the gang as a whole. The definition of gang-motivated crime yields significantly fewer gang crimes for statistical purposes than does that for gang-related crime. This is especially true if, under the definition of gang motivated, an agency decides that, to qualify, both suspect and victim must be gang members or the crime must be related to intergang encounters. Depending upon the nature of the gang and the individual members in it, the crimes they commit vary, as does the motivation for the crimes. Drug-oriented gangs commit drug-related crimes; others may specialize in auto theft, shoplifting, or contract killings, or have no specialty and commit a variety of crimes.

Part 1 crimes include reported incidents of murder, robbery, aggravated assault, arson, burglary, rape, motor vehicle theft, and grand theft. Regardless of the FBI index, it is clear that part 1 crimes include the more serious offenses and are the primary concern of the police.

Part 2 crimes include simple assault, curfew offenses, loitering, embezzlement, forgery and counterfeiting, disorderly conduct, driving under the influence, drug offenses, fraud, gambling, liquor offenses, offenses against the family, prostitution, public drunkenness, runaways, minor sex offenses, stolen property, vandalism, vagrancy, and weapons offenses. It is clear that some of the crimes indexed as part 2 by the FBI are the common nuisance offenses committed by the gangs targeted with injunctions.

The primary difference in the index between part 1 and part 2 crimes is that part 1 crimes are derived from crime reports prepared by the police that are submitted to the FBI, as opposed to part 2 crimes, which are based upon actual arrests made for part 2 offenses. An arrest for a gang injunction violation would be considered a part 2 crime.

This distinction exists because part 2 crimes are generally not reported to the FBI but arrest data are. Critics of the UCR note that it only lists reported crimes and is thus, arguably, not useful in learning what the actual crime rates are. One problem with measuring just violent crime rates is that you cannot understand the impact the injunctions have on quality-of-life crimes, the less serious nuisance crimes that have an impact on the community, making an evaluation of part 2 crimes a critical component of this research.

Total calls for service data include all activity in the target areas: everything reported to the police, including part 1 crime, part 2 crime, and all other activity that does not fall into those two categories. Total calls include all calls received by the police, including self-initiated police activity in any given area, such as traffic stops, car accidents, disturbances, suspicious activity, barking dogs, follow-up investigations, etc. By gathering calls for service data, this research went beyond other current studies that did not evaluate total calls. The total calls for service data have provided significant insight into the total draw on police resources that is occurring in the enjoined gang and control gang territories.

NO SINGLE METHOD WILL SOLVE THE PROBLEM

Law enforcement must work together with the business community, schools, religious organizations, and the community as a whole to get involved. However, law enforcement personnel are the ones tasked with the hands-on suppression of gangs; they must be well educated on the processes, procedures, and tactics used to combat the gang problem. In California during the past 25 years, one of those tactics has been the use of civil gang injunctions to suppress gangs in specific areas.

Gang injunctions are not a panacea, they are not the ultimate solution to the gang problem, and their crime-fighting characteristics must be kept in perspective and continually updated and enforced to be effective.

It is acknowledged among members of the law enforcement community that no one method of gang enforcement will solve the gang problem alone; that includes the use of gang injunctions. However, the use of gang injunctions has been perceived as one of the few proactive ways that prosecutors and law enforcement agencies can address the growing gang problem in some of our communities. History has shown us that criminal laws alone are not enough to stop violent gang crime; if they were, we should currently have less crime and fewer gang members because we have more antigang laws today than at any other point in our history.

Dealing with gangs is an evolution; what is done by law enforcement today may be antiquated tomorrow, as gangs are extremely creative and typically have the ability to adapt to the social and economic conditions of the time. Gang injunctions are also an evolution, constantly being shaped by case law and modified to address the ever-changing threat. There may be a day in our future where gang injunctions become obsolete or overturned by the courts and deemed a constitutional violation, or are replaced by local ordinances, laws, or a new progressive policy. For now, however, gang injunctions are still the politically correct tactic that helps politicians show they are tough on crime and on gangs, and the police like the added authority injunctions provide.

The reasons why criminal laws are not enough are discussed throughout this book. These reasons include the complexity of many gang crimes, that gang cases typically involve multiple defendants, making it difficult to find the most culpable member in the group, and that witnesses are intimidated to testify or are criminals in their own right and have little creditability. Unlike criminal laws, civil laws focus on protecting the victims, the law-abiding citizens in the community. The civil injunctions focus on the real victims of gang violence, the community.

A large percentage of the criticisms of gang injunctions have nothing to do with injunctions; they are criticisms of the failure of government to implement long-term social programs to address the root causes of gangs. Gang injunctions are not going to fix broken homes, make parents responsible for their children, reduce the unemployment rate, or solve the problem of poverty in our society, and that is not the purpose or intent of an injunction. However, they may help address some of these issues in a limited supporting role.

Collective efficacy in a community may well improve as the lessened presence of gang members may help the community maintain order in public places and increase use of public facilities. Social capital may also be improved because more involvement in community matters may improve informal networks and interdependence among the community and encourage community involvement.

A community that does not have a visible presence of gangs controlling the streets can only benefit. It is widely accepted that gangs do not benefit their neighborhood; they offer nothing positive, nothing productive; they are by their very nature a burden on society in every way, and the primary goal of every policy maker addressing crime should target these individuals to remove them from the community or encourage them to modify their behavior and obey the law.

Injunctions have the potential to increase community solidarity while at the same time reducing the solidarity of the gang. They can do this by establishing a partnership between the community and the police. The injunction process usually entails the police going out into a community and requesting community members to get involved, at least as far as reporting criminal activity, and at times they ask some in the community to provide declarations for the court to support the need for the injunction. The police typically want the community to report crime and injunction violations and to not accept gangs and gang violence as normal behavior for the neighborhood.

Even if the community members are not consulted or made an integral part of the injunction process, many tend to show support following implementation of the injunction because of the reduced presence of the gangs in the community and improved quality of life.

2

Steps 1 to 5 of the Injunction Process

I have conducted an exhaustive review of hundreds of abatement cases and filed gang injunctions in California, as well as the case law decisions that arose from the filed and attempted cases, and the policies generated during the learning process over the past several decades. In addition to evaluating the theories related to gang injunctions and talking with hundreds of police officers involved in obtaining the injunctions, I have identified 10 recommendations or steps (five of which are covered in this chapter) that may help ensure specific gang injunctions or abatement efforts are effective, fair, and adhere to existing law:

1. Start with a motivated and knowledgeable prosecutor and police officer
2. Accurately identify the nuisance activity and the problem
3. Identify the defendants or gang to be named or targeted by the injunction
4. Identify and describe the target location, target area, or safety zone
5. Collect evidence

STEP 1: START WITH A MOTIVATED AND KNOWLEDGEABLE PROSECUTOR AND POLICE OFFICER

A motivated prosecutor and a police officer or detective who is an expert on the target gang are vital to any project's success. In fact, if you do not have this at the onset, do not proceed; focus on a gang and a jurisdiction where you have the key people needed to do the job. The prosecutor not only must possess knowledge of criminal law and an understanding of gangs, but also must understand the intricacies of civil practice and procedure. There is no substitute for a comprehensive knowledge of the problem. Knowing who the gangs are, where they hang out, what activities they engage in, and when they commit their crimes will all help in the analysis stage of an investigation and help accomplish the ultimate mission of obtaining the order. Every nuisance abatement case should have an investigating officer or gang investigator assigned. The role of the gang investigator is to be the expert about the current status of the criminal activity at the location, and the history or community reputation of the location. An officer who is an expert on the location helps explain to the court the reasons why there is a nuisance there and why certain injunctive terms are being sought and are justified. The gang investigator is really the eyes and ears of the prosecutor in the community. The prosecutor may know much (if not all) of what the gang investigator knows, but he or she certainly does not want to be a witness in his or her own case. When an injunction is sought in the nuisance abatement action, the gang investigator puts all of his or her knowledge about the property into a declaration for the judge. Typically, the gang investigator acquires this information from making arrests at the property, reviewing all crime and arrest reports, meeting with members of the community who are knowledgeable about the location, interviewing gang members and informants about the location, and conducting covert surveillance of the property. In most jurisdictions, an officer or detective is assigned to every felony. It only makes sense that an officer or detective should be assigned to a location where there have been multiple felonies.

Prosecutors assigned to abatement and injunction cases are criminal prosecutors; however, they use civil lawsuits to abate gang activity, requiring them to have knowledge of both criminal and civil laws. There are several benefits to this: (1) by going to civil court, injunctive relief abating the nuisance can be obtained, which can be a highly effective way to deal with the problems; (2) the defendants do not have a right to a jury trial or a court-appointed attorney; and (3) the burden of proof in civil court is a preponderance of the evidence, rather than the heightened beyond a reasonable doubt standard used in criminal proceedings. In addition, the prosecutor must be organized, meticulous, and be able to sort through and make sense out of a potential mountain of evidence in the form of police reports, photographs, and other documents, such as court, probation, and parole data, to name just a few sources. The organizational skills, patience, and ability to prepare the order and follow the gang injunction case to completion are mandatory prerequisites.

If the injunction is to be properly prepared and the complaint filed in a legal and timely manner, this normally requires that the prosecutor be assigned to the injunction project for as long as the case is pending in the system. The police agency investigating the gang injunction must also be dedicated to providing the support and expertise to obtain the injunction, and be committed to enforcing it when it is obtained.

This research has revealed that police willingness to enforce the order is a critical element of an effective gang injunction. There must be an adequate number of police officers in the police department tasked with investigating gang crimes, and jurisdictions that implement gang injunctions must also allocate sufficient resources to adequately address the gang problem and enforce the orders.

The first of eight categories discussed in the literature review evaluated the characteristics of the police and the prosecutor, and how they potentially impact the level of effectiveness of a specific gang injunction. The willingness or ability of the police to enforce an injunction is by many accounts the prevailing category that will or will not dictate if a particular injunction is or is not effective, or if it is ever sought to begin with. Gang injunction efforts are typically labor-intensive and time-consuming, often requiring months of police participation, working together with the prosecution to gather the necessary evidence, draft the declarations, identify the targets and target area, and review hundreds of crime reports, field interviews, calls for service, and gang files and intelligence information. The effort required makes some detectives not want to seek an injunction because they are often expected to maintain their caseload and take on the injunction as a collateral duty, which in some jurisdictions is not always feasible.

As the injunction is prepared to be submitted to the court for review, the role of the police has just started. Once the documents are prepared and filed, the gang members must now be served a copy of the court order, which requires significant police resources to locate and notify the named defendants, or selecting and serving unnamed defendants. After an injunction is served, the injunction goes to court and is granted; there must be a policy and resources available to enforce and maintain it.

An injunction without provisions for enhanced enforcement is merely a hollow threat, especially against hard-core gang members who frequently show disdain for the police and the law and a lack of respect for the rights of those in the community. A reliance on regular police patrols, which are often already stretched to the limits in some urban areas, to stop gangs in these injunction neighborhoods, may result in a poorly implemented response and lower level of effectiveness when compared to areas that have designated police units that specifically target the local gangs and enforce the gang injunctions.

To understand the police perspective, police officers were asked: Why was the injunction sought? Do they feel an injunction was effective? Have they ever made an arrest for an injunction violation? How does it get enforced in their jurisdiction? Does it help make the neighborhood safer in their opinion?

The role envisioned for prosecutors that file civil abatements and injunctions against gangs is to provide a liaison between the field (e.g., police and fire) personnel who target and initiate inspection cases, and prosecutors who carry the cases forward for action and resolution. These prosecutors assist with the case identification, information gathering, and case preparation process, and work with local officials and community groups to promote and explain the process.

STEP 2: ACCURATELY IDENTIFY THE NUISANCE ACTIVITY AND THE PROBLEM

Gang locations targeted with abatement and injunctions frequently have a history of narcotics sales, shootings, and other acts of gang violence. Additionally, gambling, drinking in public, loud parties, and other well-established nuisance activities are typically found at these locations. All criminal activities of the gang are documented and used as part of the abatement process. Applying the public nuisance cause of action to the activities of criminal street gangs may be novel in most states. However, public nuisance law has been used extensively in California and a handful of other states. This is made possible because police officers and the prosecution identify the problem posed by the particular street gang(s) creating the nuisance in the area they feel is the problem. The police are typically tasked with identifying the specific problem, the source of the problem, which gang, the type of gang they are, which specific gang members are creating the nuisance, and the types of crimes they are committing. As soon as all police reports and federal investigative notes are received, they are analyzed to determine whether a nuisance exists at the property. The prosecutor reviewing this evidence is looking for a pattern of criminal activity connected to the property. There is no magic number of criminal incidents that triggers the location being opened for handling. A number of factors are considered together, such as the size of the location, the type of location, the length of time the activity has been occurring, and the type and extent of the activity. Once all of these factors are evaluated and prosecutors determine that they have sufficient evidence to support a lawsuit, a case is initiated. Once initiated, prosecutors start drafting the pleadings (legal paperwork).

It is critical to accurately identify the problem and the source of the problem to justify seeking a gang injunction in a court of law. Proper use of crime analysis units and crime-tracking software can help map gang crime and identify gang hangouts and areas in which gang conflicts are most likely to occur. This is important to justify the borders of the target areas and the selection of specific gang members for inclusion in the order. With a detailed analysis of the problem, police can plan anti-gang operations accordingly, including modification of patrol or special unit schedules to be working when gang crimes are most likely to be occurring. Prosecutors use extensive and varied evidence of the gang's harmful, dangerous, or offensive activities to support their public nuisance complaints.

Abatement of a nuisance "is accomplished by a court of equity by means of an injunction proper and suitable to the facts of each case. Therefore the district attorney or city attorney may bring an action for injunction to abate a public nuisance. For an activity to be actionable as a public nuisance, it must not only meet the elements of public nuisance, but the interference with public rights must be both "substantial and unreasonable."

Courts use an objective test to determine whether the interference is substantial. That is, if normal persons in that locality would not be substantially annoyed or disturbed by the situation, then the invasion is not a significant one. To determine whether the invasion is unreasonable, the court asks if the gravity of the harm outweighs the social utility of the defendant's conduct, taking a number of factors into account. Again the standard is not whether the particular plaintiff found the invasion unreasonable, but whether reasonable persons generally, looking at the whole situation impartially and objectively, would consider it unreasonable.

The characteristics of the gang targeted with the injunction make a difference. Is the gang mobile or territorial? Do they have well-defined borders that they defend? Do they have leaders and were the leaders targeted? How many gangs are in the jurisdiction? How many gang members are there, and what are the names of those gangs, the ethnicity of the gangs, the percentage of the overall gang served or impacted by the injunction, and the gender breakdown of the gang? How many gangs are active within the target area? Why were the targeted gangs chosen over the others? What characteristics of the gang caused the police to believe that an injunction was an appropriate response? The targeted gang(s) should have characteristics that make it susceptible to the restrictions contained in the injunctions.

Where more than one gang is active within a neighborhood, police must decide which gang(s) to target; several injunctions target multiple gangs that operate in the same or overlapping territories. The failure of police to select the appropriate gang may result in the denial of an injunction by the courts or, if granted, short-lived or ineffective relief. Because of the wide variation in gang structure, organization, and activities, injunctive relief may not be an effective intervention for all gangs. Criteria for identifying an appropriate gang for injunctive relief include a gang that is engaged in nuisance-related activity, operates primarily within a limited geographical area with territorial behavior, and falls within the legal definitions of a criminal street gang and an unincorporated association.

The traditional turf-oriented gang is considered an appropriate target because the injunctions are applicable in only the well-defined target area and are limited to the defined geographic area in the court order. Another characteristic of a traditional turf-oriented gang is the existence of a hierarchical structure that may help police identify the leaders of the gang as the primary targets of the injunction. The generational entrenchment of the gang in the neighborhood may play a large role in the effectiveness of the injunction because of the gang's attachment to the target area.

What must be looked at is the type of activity, the types of crimes committed, and whether they are the types that an injunction may be suited to address. Some injunction efforts may be initiated as a result of visible symptoms that have an extremely adverse effect on the targeted neighborhood, and that normal intervention measures, such as law enforcement crackdowns, have been unable to prevent. Visible symptoms range from high-profile events like drive-by shootings involving innocent bystanders, the murder of a police officer or member of the community that may have opposed the gang or testified against the gang, or high levels of physical or social disorder in the neighborhood, such as concentrations of gang graffiti.

Focusing on symptoms may disproportionately bias problem identification, resulting in relief that attacks only the visible signs of the problem, while leaving the underlying and less visible causes of the problem intact. Therefore the survey inquires about the activity or crimes that brought the target gang to the attention of the police.

STEP 3: IDENTIFY THE DEFENDANTS OR GANG TO BE NAMED OR TARGETED BY THE INJUNCTION

Before an attempt is made to obtain a gang injunction, the targeted gang must be evaluated to determine whether it fits the legal definition of a criminal street gang, whether the conduct of its members amounts to a public nuisance, whether sufficient documentation of these facts is likely to exist, and whether the gang and its activities are of the kind that are likely to be abated by the issuance of an injunction. This evaluation includes determining how long the gang has operated in the area and whether it is primarily turf based or transitory. To be effective, this analysis must be the product of a partnership between prosecutor and investigator.

While the pleadings are being drafted, the prosecutors start identifying which people connected to the unlawful activity at the property should be named as defendants. This is a critical step because it can be more difficult to abate the nuisance if the appropriate persons are not named as defendants. The following groups of potential defendants are evaluated:

Property owners: Any and all individuals or entities that currently have an ownership interest in the property are always named as defendants in the lawsuit. The law holds the property owner responsible for the activity on the property; therefore the owner is a necessary party to the lawsuit. It may also be appropriate to name prior owners, if the change in ownership was recent and the nuisance occurred under their ownership.

Gang members: Gang members using the property to facilitate their criminal activity, whether or not they are tenants, are named as defendants. In some instances, in which numerous gang members are using the property for criminal activity, it may not be expedient to name all of them as defendants. In those situations, those who live at the property and those committing the worst offenses at the property are named as defendants.

Gang member associates: Tenants who are not documented gang members in the gang, but who directly or indirectly assist gang members with their criminal activity, are commonly referred to as "friendlies" and may be named as defendants, if their activity can be linked to the property and to the gang.

Property managers: Property managers who are negligent in their duties may be named as defendants.

As the pleadings are being drafted and defendants are being identified, prosecutors determine when the lawsuit will be filed with the court. If there is no federal investigation, then the lawsuit is simply filed when all of the pleadings establishing the nuisance have been drafted. However, abatement projects frequently involve ongoing federal investigations, and in almost all instances, the lawsuits are not filed until federal indictments are issued against the members of the gang. This is necessary when the evidentiary basis of the nuisance lawsuit, in whole or in part, relates to the federal investigation. Filing before the indictments would jeopardize the investigation by prematurely disclosing confidential information. Additionally, by sequencing the filing of the lawsuits with the issuance of indictments and the arrests of the gang members, the abatements and the overall takedown have a much greater impact on the gang.

The evidence submitted in support of the injunction will identify individual members of the gang as the perpetrators of the nuisance activities. The police and prosecutor must document the gang membership of the perpetrators to demonstrate that the conduct is attributable to the gang. But identifying individual members also serves the purpose of designating the individuals who are to be sued or who may be designated to receive service of the summons and complaint on behalf of the gang. Whenever an individual is identified, the documented evidence of the individual's gang membership should be unassailable. It is also advisable that the evidence show that the individual has *personally* engaged in nuisance activities.

This may be especially true where the individual is named personally as a defendant, as there is obviously a stronger argument for enjoining an individual with an extensive criminal history. However, it is important to note that the U.S. Supreme Court has held that an organization and its individual members may properly be enjoined without a showing of specific intent to further unlawful group aims on the part of the individuals, as would be required in a damage section.

The California Supreme Court adopted this rule in *People v. Acuna* (40 Cal. Rptr. 2d 589). Although all but 3 of the 11 defendants who chose to contest entry of the preliminary injunction were shown to have committed acts, primarily drug related, comprising specific elements of the public nuisance, the court held that such individualized proof is not a condition to the entry of preliminary relief based on a showing that it is the gang, acting through its individual members, that is responsible for the conditions prevailing in the area.

Because the focus of a gang injunction case is on the nuisance caused by the gang, the individuals who are identified so that they may be designated for service of the summons and complaint on behalf of the gang need not be the leaders of the gang or the worst perpetrators of gang crime. They simply must be the individuals whose gang membership is most well documented and who preferably have recent ties in the designated area.

What Are DOEs?

Usually, a gang injunction will include people who are not explicitly identified when the injunction first comes into place. That's to make the injunction enduring, and allow law enforcement to apply it to people they identify as gang members without having to get a separate injunction every time a new person pops up on the radar of police. This idea of having DOEs is also controversial. Civil liberties advocates often complain that police officers working under the benefit of gang injunctions are given the discretion to label anyone they encounter in a safe zone as a gang member, which opens these folks to higher penalties and all the restrictions of the gang injunction, without having to be proven to be a gang member in court.

At issue is the ability of the police to serve the injunction on an individual without presenting definitive evidence of gang membership and without court approval. The issue is that while the police could serve hundreds of individuals, they would not have to present any proof to a judge; the people never had their day in court to challenge accusations of gang membership, and weren't provided with a clear way out. It would give the police complete discretion to impose these restrictions without oversight, increasing the potential for misuse by targeting and harassing people.

Opponents argue that the terms of the gang injunctions infringe on one's ability to conduct his or her daily life, causing him or her to risk arrest for participating in family events, working at public establishments, and engaging in other positive and lawful activities. Once a gang injunction is granted, it usually lasts indefinitely and imposes ongoing restrictions against those served with the order. These injunctions effectively function like parole or probation, but with no conviction of any criminal offense and with no definite termination date. In several counties, there are opt-out procedures that provide a way out of the gang injunction for those individuals who demonstrate they are no longer gang members. The American Civil Liberties Union (ACLU) has several ongoing concerns about the use of gang injunctions in recent California court cases.

First, they believe that gang injunctions "affect and infringe the exercise of constitutional rights of those bound by its terms."

Second, gang injunctions target what are considered commonplace and generally perfectly legal and lawful activities. They "thus can have a pervasive impact on the everyday lives of those bound and on their families, especially for those who live and work within the area covered by the injunction."

Third, while they impose "probation-like restrictions" on individuals who stand accused of unlawful activity, they do so without affording individuals the due process protections that they would have under the criminal justice system. There is no right to have council appointed to them by the court. In fact, gang injunctions can impose restraints and sanctions on persons who have not had the opportunity or the means to mount any defense in a civil case. The relative ease and speed with which law enforcement can impose these restraints is undoubtedly a reason for their appeal, but this efficiency should also raise cautionary flags in terms of judicial scrutiny.

Finally, the ACLU argues that while gang injunctions intend to protect the safety of communities, they also may stigmatize broad segments of the community. "This dilemma is underscored by the fact that every gang injunction in this State of which Amicus are aware has been imposed on predominantly persons of color. The potential for racial profiling and racial stereotyping, something that has been a national problem, cannot be ignored in assessing this law enforcement tool."

Specifically, the ACLU often argues that the provisions represent an overly broad attempt to curtail the constitutionally recognized right of freedom of association because they prohibit driving, standing, sitting, walking, gathering, or appearing, anywhere in public view or anyplace accessible to the public, with any known member of the gang.

A trend has been leaning toward using discretion when enforcing injunctions, especially when making arrests for association violations. For example, individuals that are inside a school attending class or on school business, or inside a church, are not arrested typically for injunction violations.

By choosing to seek an injunction for a large geographical area that includes social, community, and commercial centers, one will affect a great number of current associational activities and will inevitably chill future expressive and innocent activities. One concern raised is that if an individual performed basic duties in relation to a public service job, he or she might be in violation of the ordinance if another gang member would patronize that said business. The following amendment to the gang injunction was made to the court:

> Therefore, this Court should amend the association prohibition to allow for other activities essential to daily and productive life, such as presence in the workplace (or while engaging in some lawful business activity), municipal buildings, and counselling or social services offices.
>
> Furthermore, the proposed injunction has no standards, guidelines, or criteria to guide the police's discretion of whom they can serve with the court's order; in fact, the OSC does not even limit the injunction's scope to "active" gang members. And if such an individual cannot afford to retain an attorney to defend him in a civil case, then the only way to effectively challenge the injunction would be to violate its terms and have a public defender challenge the injunction in the resulting prosecution for criminal contempt.

The court ruled previously in *Englebrecht* (88 Cal. App. 4th 1236):

> The need for a standard of proof allowing a greater confidence in the decision reached arises not because the personal activities enjoined are sublime or grand but rather because they are commonplace, and ordinary. While it may be lawful to restrict such activity, it is also extraordinary. The government, in any guise, should not undertake such restrictions without good reason and without firmly establishing the facts making such restrictions necessary.

Moreover, they argue that the court in the Broderick Boys case (West Sacramento) "made clear that this heightened standard of proof applies to the issues of gang membership, reaffirming that a gang injunction may only bind 'active' gang members … that a person is subject to the injunction if the State proves by clear and convincing evidence that the Englebrecht definition is met."

Thus the ACLU argues that the court should limit the gang injunction to those individuals who have had the opportunity to appear in court and have the court determine, based on the evidence before it, that they are indeed active gang members.

I'm not a big fan of the ACLU, which is very selective in whose free speech rights it protects. Too often it appears to be an arm of the Democratic Party, for one.

Who are these 250 people that the ACLU suspects will be served an injunction? How does the ACLU know that they will be served with a gang injunction before service even occurs? Are they just guessing, or do they know? If they know, how do they know? Does the ACLU know of 250 shadowy/hidden gang members that it doesn't want the police to be aware of?

When starting a gang injunction, the gang expert and prosecutor should start by evaluating every known member of the gang they are investigating and evaluate each of them for potential inclusion in an injunction. It is critical that the primary investigator on the case have a comprehensive understanding of the entire gang, then be able to provide justification why select gang members were included, or subsequently served with the injunction.

Gang injunctions have the ability to target the gang's membership at every level. Targeting gang leaders is often viewed as beneficial because they oftentimes direct gang activities. However, unlike Midwest gangs, gangs in Southern California, for example, typically do not have a recognized leader; the leader is often any member that takes control at any particular point in time. Gang injunctions that target members based upon the level of criminal activity they engage in and how the members relate to each other are likely targeting the leaders and the hard-core members responsible for directing much of the violence attributed to the particular gang, which is preferred by police and prosecutors alike.

The police and prosecutor must determine the extent of the gang's involvement in criminal and nuisance activities, and the nature of those activities. It can be argued that each crime that the gang repeatedly perpetrates constitutes a nuisance in itself. For example, shootings endanger the lives of individuals living in the area, and terrify residents who are not even present. Likewise for robberies and other violent and potentially violent crimes. Property crimes create a nuisance by interfering with property.

Graffiti is a special case of property crime that can both damage property and constitute a direct or implied threat from the gang, which typically will engage in graffiti in order to both publicize its dominance of the neighborhood and intimidate residents into fearing the gang. Even the gang's comparatively minor activities may be taken into account in evaluating the nuisance. Many gangs annoy, harass, and intimidate neighborhood residents by publicly congregating in groups while drinking alcohol; blocking streets, sidewalks, and driveways; causing loud disturbances; or trespassing on the property of others. Not only are these activities disturbing in and of themselves, but they collectively create an atmosphere of lawlessness and defiance that contributes to the gang's grip of fear over the neighborhood.

Since the injunction must be necessary to abate the nuisance, the prosecutor must prove that the nuisance is ongoing. A cessation of the gang's activities or a gap between the last documented crime and the hearing on granting an injunction may raise questions regarding the need for the injunction. At the time the lawsuit is filed, prosecutors must be able to establish a pattern of criminal activity amounting to a nuisance at the property. The last documented criminal act at the property should occur within approximately two to three months of filing. This is necessary because the only real defense against a nuisance abatement lawsuit is that the nuisance was abated prior to the time of filing. Accordingly, the closer to the time of filing the criminal activity amounting to a nuisance is established, the easier it is to negate this defense. Depending on the facts of the case and the remedy sought, the time it takes to prepare the abatement lawsuit can vary greatly. A very simple abatement, for example, targeting a single-family dwelling, can be prepared in approximately two weeks. A complicated abatement, for example, concerning a large apartment building, may take up to two months to prepare. Considering that most locations have been problems for years, and that without abatement they will continue to be problems for years to come, the time spent preparing the lawsuit is time well spent. After the lawsuit is filed, the defendants are served with the legal pleadings. At that point, prosecutors seek an injunction from the court to stop the criminal activity from occurring at the property. The terms of the injunction are very fact specific and therefore vary from case to case. Prosecutors consider such factors as the type of criminal activity, the extent of the activity, the duration of the activity, and the physical layout of the property when drafting the injunction. Further, the terms of the injunction do not apply uniformly to each defendant. For example, an injunction against the property owner may require, among other items, hiring a professional on-site property manager; requiring the owner to reside in the building until the nuisance is abated; posting armed security guards on-site; installing high-intensity lighting, fencing, and updated electronic entry systems; evicting problem tenants; and maintaining the property.

Clearly, these terms would be of no use against a gang member defendant. A term that is typically sought against gang member defendants is a stay-away order from the property and the area surrounding the property. If a tenant who is not a gang member but is friendly to the gang is named in the lawsuit, his or her eviction will be sought. If property managers have been named as defendants, the injunction will seek to terminate their employment. Once the preliminary injunction is obtained from the court, the property is monitored for criminal activity for a period ranging from 6 to 18 months. In the vast majority of cases, the implementation of this preliminary injunction will abate the nuisance. If it is clear that the nuisance has been abated, the case is often resolved with the property owner agreeing to a stipulated judgment, including a permanent injunction mirroring the preliminary injunction and a monetary settlement. When the case is completely resolved against the property owner, the court often issues a permanent injunction against all gang member defendants, prohibiting them from being on or near the property.

At times, closure of a gang property may be the only way to effectively abate the nuisance. If the nuisance is not abated during the monitoring period, a trial is held and closure of the property may be sought from the court. Occasionally, in extreme circumstances, prosecutors may seek closure of a property immediately upon the filing of the abatement action. Under any circumstances, in accordance with local and state law, if a closure order is issued by the court, all tenants who are not involved in the criminal activity receive relocation money from the property owner.

STEP 4: IDENTIFY AND DESCRIBE THE TARGET LOCATION, TARGET AREA, OR SAFETY ZONE

The target area or target location characteristics are critical; the geographical or physical area targeted by the injunction is a key element, as the injunction is only applicable in the area that is designated in the order. The same is true of gang abatement; the civil lawsuit applies to the exact location you have described. Physical and social characteristics of the target area are also important to evaluate prior to obtaining an injunction. The economic status of the residents, size of the area, access to the area, and zoning of the area may all play a role when looking at injunction effectiveness. Issues like physical barriers (railroad tracks, airports, rivers, etc.), which may insulate the target area from neighboring areas, and the predominant land use (residential, business, industrial) may also have an impact on the effectiveness of an injunction. In Los Angeles, some of the gangs targeted with injunctions are rigidly tied to certain blocks with well-established territorial lines. In other areas, local gang members and their families often live in rental apartments, and they tend to move frequently; in some of the neighborhoods the community is racially diverse, so territorial boundaries stay relatively porous and the gang is more transient.

Social characteristics, such as whether the area is a multigenerational gang neighborhood or whether a social structure exists that will assist the community in rebuilding a sense of community after the disorder is addressed, are an important category of concern. The survey will seek to evaluate if the target areas in the case studies cover only the target gang's area or if they cover a larger area that may also incorporate rival gangs. The level of effectiveness may be impacted if the gang injunction area is difficult to define, officers have a difficult time understanding the borders, or the area is too small or too large.

To date, gang injunctions have mainly targeted traditional, turf-based gangs by focusing on restraining the activities of gang members within a defined target area. Arguably, the restrictions of a constitutionally viable injunction must be limited to a geographical area. Since the injunction may not be vague in its description or overbroad in the area covered, the injunction must have clearly defined and established boundaries. This means that the gang's nuisance activities must be bounded, as is typically the case for turf-based gangs. The more stable and well established the gang's claimed turf, the more viable the area defined by the injunction. The question of whether or how to pursue a gang injunction against a non-turf-based, or transient or mobile, gang can be difficult if a defined area cannot be articulated.

The locations of the gang's documented crimes and other nuisance activities must be carefully considered. The target area should cover the entire area where the gang creates a nuisance, without unnecessarily covering additional territory. The locations of documented nuisance activities may be mapped, and this can serve as compelling visual evidence of the need for the target area of the requested size and shape.

At a minimum, the target area should include the turf that is openly claimed by the gang, as this is typically where the majority of nuisance activities have occurred or will foreseeably occur. Still, it is persuasive and preferable to provide documented incidents to justify the extent of the target area. Gaps in the target area where there are no documented nuisance activities may present a problem in litigation. On the other hand, the constitutional standard that the injunction be narrowly tailored does not necessarily dictate that the target area be strictly limited to the gang's claimed turf. Under this standard, the extent of the target area is that which is necessary to abate the gang's nuisance.

Several situations have arisen where the evidence has justified expanding the reach of particular gang injunctions. Where a gang travels outside of its claimed turf to commit crimes targeting rivals in other neighborhoods, this may justify having the injunction cover those areas as well. The accompanying map (Figure 2.1) is a good example of this. The large area on the right side of the map is the target area for the Skyline injunction in San Diego. The smaller area on the left side of the map is the territory of the rival Lincoln Park Bloods, which has been added as a target, and is off limits to Skyline because of the potential for violence.

In one case, an injunction covered the defendant gang's turf, and additionally restricted the gang's members from traveling in a vehicle with another member in the claimed turf of a rival located 1½ miles away. In another case, the defendant gang was located in a part of Los Angeles where many rival gangs claimed small pieces of turf separated only by a street, and the gang's members were restrained from being present with any fellow gang member in the turf of any of the rival gangs.

In a similar neighborhood with a high density of gangs, the injunction targeted ten gangs as defendants, and the target area covered the turf of all the gangs, with the restrictions of the gang injunction applying equally anywhere in any of the gangs' turf.

Where the targeted gang occasionally committed crimes outside of its claimed turf and was not closely hemmed in by the turf of another gang, the circumstances justified having the target area cover additional territory to prevent the gang from going just outside the boundaries to gather and commit crimes.

The argument has been successfully made that the defined boundaries of the target area should stretch beyond the gang's claimed turf to the extent necessary to prevent this type of easy circumvention of the injunction's restrictions.

Similarly, geographic features such as roads, highways, rivers, and mountains may play a role in defining the boundaries of the target area. In several cases, the target area has extended to the nearest physical boundary outside of the area where the nuisance

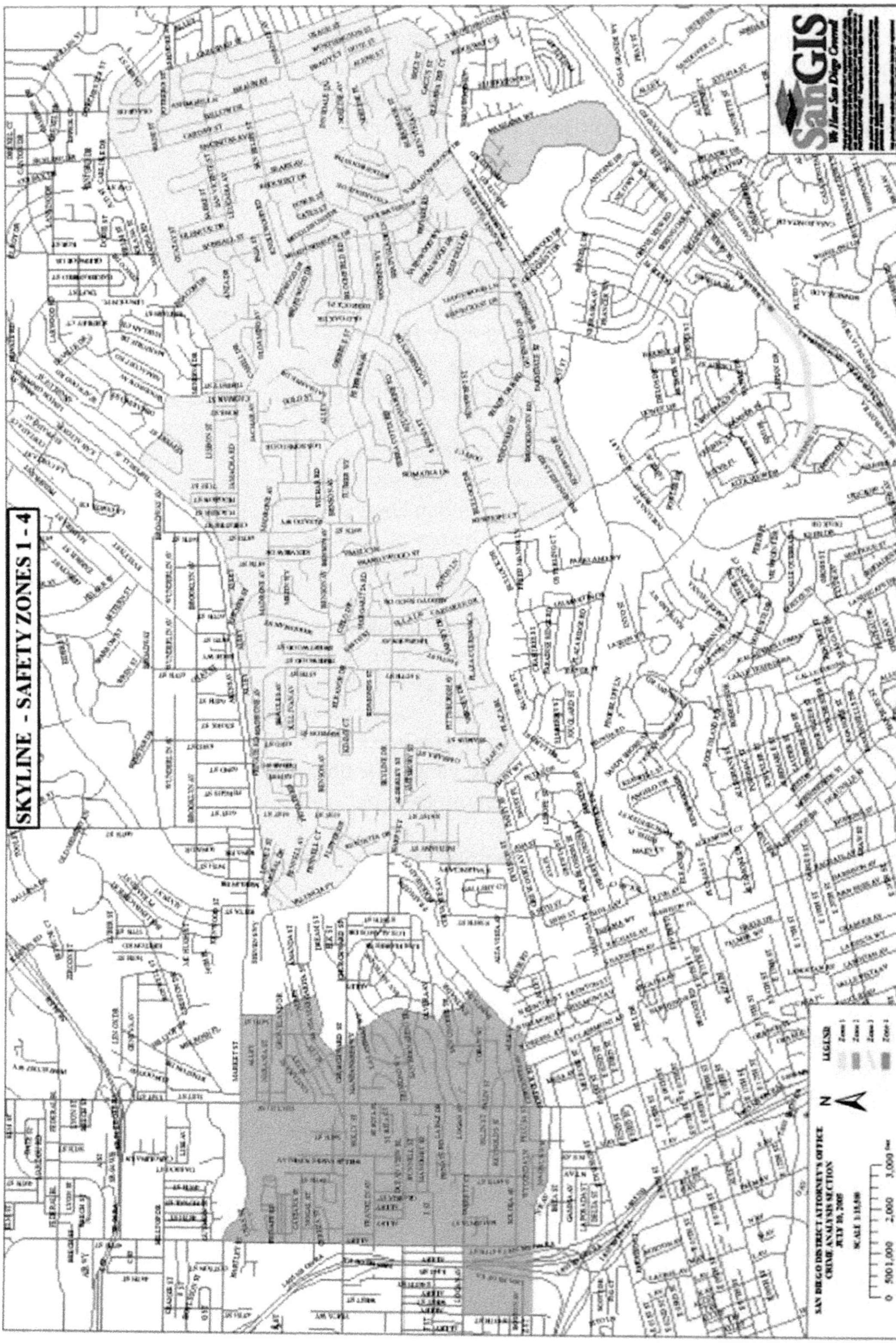

FIGURE 2.1 The Skyline injunction covers the large area on the right. The smaller area, on the left, is the territory of the Lincoln Park Bloods.

was documented because no nearby visible boundary existed, and the need to provide adequate notice of the target area boundary dictated the use of the highway, river, etc.

As a practical matter, prominent boundaries such as highways can serve as physical barriers to the gang moving its activities outside of the target area, so these boundaries should be preferred. The same is true of the claimed turf of neighboring rival gangs. Some gang injunctions obtained consist of target areas that have confusing borders, which may cause apprehension by the police to take action. This researcher recommends picking an area that is clearly delineated and can be mapped clearly. Whenever possible, major streets, freeways, rail lines, and other significant borders should be used to make the identification of the target area easily understood by the police and the gang members.

Many current gang injunction target areas are selected based upon existing police reporting districts. This has the potential to allow for better analysis of the impact of the injunction at a later time. Adequately defining and enjoining the correct turf of the target gang is an important consideration. The boundaries of the area covered by the injunction must be determined based upon the documentary evidence relating to the gang's existence, its activities, and its membership, which can be a monumental task. Organization and a planned approach are necessary to be able to assess the state of the evidence and to avoid needless duplication of effort.

Inclusion of a gang's known turf, when supported by crime statistics, calls for service data, or other reliable sources. The targeted area may be as small as a specific apartment complex, it may be one or two blocks, or it may be the bulk of a particular city. Whatever it is, the area must be justified to the court and supported by the evidence collected.

On the police officer survey conducted for this book, survey question 11 asked officers: What is the size of the gang turf of the gang targeted with the injunction? This question revealed that gang injunctions come in all different sizes and are well distributed in gang area size.

Survey question 12 asked: What percentage of the total gang's turf was made part of the gang injunction target area? Of the respondents, 21.7% of officers said the injunction covered the entire turf of the enjoined gang, whereas 5% said it covered less than the target gang's territory.

Survey question 13 asked officers to describe the general economic status of the gang injunction area. The overwhelming majority of officers described the target areas (81.9%) as being in poverty, followed by 17% that described the area as middle class, and 1.1% of officers described the target area as affluent. Survey question

14 asked officers to describe the zoning in the target area of their injunction. The majority described the injunction areas as residential or mostly residential with some business activity.

Gang Abatement at a Specific Location

The first step is to determine whether the illegal activity at the targeted property constitutes a common or public nuisance as defined in the nuisance abatement statutes. A nuisance abatement action should be considered and an investigation should be initiated if the answer to any of the following questions is yes:

Is the property used for prostitution; gambling; the discharge of a firearm; organized criminal activity; the delivery, possession, manufacture, or use of controlled substances; obscenity; or gang activity?

Is there a history of arrests for one or more of these illegal activities at the property?

Will these illegal activities continue if legal action is not taken?

Does the property have a reputation as a place to frequent for one or more of these illegal activities?

Have the lives or businesses of people in the area surrounding the property suffered or been adversely affected by these illegal activities?

STEP 5: COLLECT EVIDENCE

Most of the evidence needed to support the initiation of a nuisance abatement proceeding is contained in local law enforcement records. The evidence must be fully documented because it may be used in a court of law and discovered by the defendant. The most important evidence is that which shows that the target area or specific property is an area or place to which gang members habitually go for the purpose of those illegal activities addressed by the nuisance abatement statutes in your state, and those restrictions you have outlined and justified in your investigation. This evidence can be obtained from arrest reports, citations, search warrants, incident reports, complaints, calls for police service, and so on. My advice is to make sure that you have all of your information and all the documentation that you're going to need when the case goes to court. You want to make sure that those identified as gang members are actually gang members in those areas or location, and that they are the individuals committing the crimes you are trying to prevent. The process of obtaining a gang injunction includes a period of preparation in which evidence of the gang's criminal and nuisance activities and documentation on the gang's members is gathered and analyzed. This phase of the process is lengthy because targeted gangs typically have a long history of criminal activity, and there is normally a tremendous volume of documentation that must be gathered and reviewed. This process produces the evidence that is submitted to the court in support of the claim that the gang is a public nuisance.

This evidence, which must be in a form admissible in court, includes affidavits testifying to the gang's activities, photographs, and documentary evidence of criminal convictions of the gang's members. This documentation must prove that the conduct is attributable to the gang. In addition to evidence of a pattern of criminal and nuisance conduct, the documentation must identify several of the gang's current members so that the court may order that they be designated to receive service of process on behalf of the gang.

Any documentation that can be compiled indicating illegal activity on the property may be used as evidence. If the investigation shows that an inordinate number of calls for police service have been made and six or more arrests for the same type of illegal activity have occurred in the last six months to a year, the case may be a good nuisance abatement case. Offense reports must establish the habitual use of the property for illegal activities. It is important that the offense reports indicate that the illegal activity occurred, began, or ended on the targeted property or immediately adjacent to it. In other words, the crime must be firmly associated with the target property. The reports must identify the property and be specific in the narrative as to the connection between the crime and the property.

Site visits or surveillance of the property should be conducted to evaluate the physical appearance of the property and to observe the nature of the illegal activities occurring on the property. The site visits will also serve to corroborate (or refute) complaints concerning the property. If code violations of any kind are observed, representatives from any other applicable agency should be contacted and requested to conduct inspections of the property.

Summary of illegal activity. A general summary of the events occurring on the property or in the neighborhood and any pertinent information related to the investigation should be available. Provide a list of all officers who have conducted investigations on the property and those officers who have made arrests on the property. Also, provide a list and give statistical data on calls for police service, general complaint citations, and offense reports generated on the subject property.

General complaint citations. Copies of all general complaint citations that have been issued on the property for the last three years or for whatever period the property has been operating.

Arrest reports. Copies of all arrest reports generated on the property.

Final dispositions. Copies of all final dispositions or pending actions against any person arrested on the property for any of the illegal activities. This may include plea agreements, trial transcripts, probation reports, and other court files that show the official disposition of the case.

Videotapes and photographs. Videotapes and photographs of illegal or disruptive activity on the property make excellent evidence. This evidence will provide demonstrative proof of how the property is maintained and how it is a nuisance to the neighborhood.

Search warrants. Copies of all search warrants served at the property, search warrant returns, and all arrest reports related to the search warrants should be included in this section. The probable cause articulated in the search warrants may contain additional information that will aid in the prosecution of the case.

Correspondence, documents, and notes. Copies are needed of any correspondence, documents, notes, or memos regarding the subject property. Copies of all communications between the property owner, employees, managers, or any other people who have personal knowledge of the property should be included, as well as all registered or certified mail return receipts of correspondence and all documents evidencing an informal meeting with the property owner. This will show the court that your law enforcement agency and the city have attempted to obtain the property owner's cooperation to address the illegal activity before filing suit in the case.

Officer declarations. Officer declarations should be obtained from every officer currently patrolling the neighborhood where the property is located, and from those who have previously patrolled the neighborhood. Officer declarations should also be obtained from every officer who has made an arrest, assisted on calls for police service, or conducted investigations on the property. The declaration should state any observations of illegal activity, the officer's involvement with the property, the property's reputation, and the officer's professional opinion of the property.

Citizen declarations. Citizens living in the vicinity of the property or persons associated with the property can provide helpful information regarding the illegal activities occurring on the property. Written statements in the form of letters, affidavits, or declarations from citizens can be persuasive evidence. If a citizen is threatened by anyone, or if an act of violence has been committed against him or her, you can request that the court order that any personal information obtained remain confidential.

Property and property owner information. The legal owner of the real property must be identified by obtaining a certified copy of the recorded deed (warranty deed or deed of trust) from the county clerk's office or a title agency. The deed will not only provide the name of the owner(s) of the real property, but it will also provide the legal description of the property. The owner(s) of the real property must not be confused with the owner of a business that may be located on the property. The legal owner may be an individual, a group of individuals (joint venture or partnership), or a corporation. This should include the names, addresses, telephone numbers, driver's license numbers, photographs, and criminal histories of owners, managers, employees, agents, or persons who may be directly involved with the ownership or management of the property.

All documents regarding investigations or inspections by regulatory agencies should be included in your case. The governing agency should coordinate its efforts with inspectors and investigators of regulatory agencies—this will not only benefit the case by providing additional evidence, but may also improve the property and help revitalize a deteriorating neighborhood. The property owners may make necessary improvements when they are issued citations for code violations. Since most illegal activities gravitate to neighborhoods that are poorly lit and maintained, such improvements may discourage illegal activity from occurring. Once you have contacted the regulatory agency and citations for code violations have been issued, you must keep communicating with the agency regarding the status and progress of the code violations. Regulatory agencies may differ in each city or county. Below is a list of the types of inspections that may be relevant to your jurisdiction.

- Building (planning and development)
- Fire marshal
- Noise pollution
- Housing code enforcement
- County health department services

- County environmental health services
- Alcoholic beverage commission
- Law enforcement

The focus should first be on gathering all the crime reports relating to the gang and determining if the criminal or nuisance conduct documented therein can be shown to be attributable to the gang's activities. The approach taken depends on the record-keeping system employed by the police agency. Some will classify reports as gang related, which may greatly expedite the process of gathering the bulk of useful reports. Otherwise (and perhaps in addition, if seeking to cast a wider net), a search for reports can be made both by the geographic area and by a gang member's name. The approximate area in which the crime occurs should be known at a near point, and a search for crime reports in this area will return most of the reports desired.

The identities of many of the gang's members should also be determined early on, and a check of their criminal histories will result in many useful reports. Second, a name search of the agency's report database will return more useful information, because oftentimes some of the most compelling evidence comes from those reports wherein the targeted gang member is listed as a victim or witness to a crime. These incidents are often more likely to result in the gang member admitting his gang membership than an incident where the gang member is the suspect. The search by name should be conducted in addition to the geographic search, because it may reveal that the gang is engaging in criminal activity outside of the expected area.

The question of how far back to go while collecting evidence of the gang's activities is a matter of judgment, taking into consideration that the most recent evidence is most salient because of the need to prove the nuisance created by the gang is current and ongoing. In a seriously gang impacted community, the evidence of crime from the past two or three years ought to demonstrate the gang's harmful effect on the community and the pattern of gang activity committed by the gang. Inclusion of older incidents may be deemed useful to increase the bulk of evidence or to demonstrate that the gang has been conducting criminal activities for a long time, and therefore is unlikely to cease unless extraordinary steps are taken.

Document management can quickly become a difficult issue when dealing with large numbers of documents. Some sort of database or spreadsheet that can be used to log each document and describe its contents, the type of document, the gang member or members it relates to, and the officers involved is probably essential. Finally, remember that each document can be used for different purposes, and even unsolved crime reports with no named suspect can be shown to be attributable to the gang through the known circumstances of the crime, the *modus operandi*, or the expert's testimony about the habits of the gang and its rivals.

Most of the evidence presented to the court in gang injunction cases is in the form of written declarations from numerous sources to justify the need for the court order. Virtually every gang injunction includes photographic evidence of gang members posing together displaying hand signs, tattoos, weapons, and showing their affiliation and association with one another. Gang injunctions require having all of the contacts for each gang member included in the primary officer's declaration, which combines all of the evidence into a single document. When collecting evidence in the form of declarations, prepare them in the same style and format to make the documents easily understood by the court. The evidence submitted in support of the injunction must be in the form of properly executed declarations (affidavits) containing admissible evidence that (collectively) establishes each necessary element of public nuisance and justifies the restrictions of the requested injunction, as well as documenting the gang membership of each individual designated either as a defendant or as a person to receive service on behalf of the gang.

Each report that is to be used to support the request for injunction may be converted into a declaration signed by a law enforcement officer who was percipient to the facts contained in the report. As some officers were the authors of several or many of the selected reports, it is not necessary to execute a different declaration for each. Rather, some officer declarations may incorporate the contents of many reports, dealing with many issues and many gang members. Typical gang injunctions are supported by hundreds of separate incidents of gang activity, so it is not necessary to go into great detail for each event.

The goal is to show that the criminal or nuisance activity took place and is attributable to the gang, and the context of the entire evidentiary picture should determine the choice of what to include. All important details, especially the most compelling ones, should be included in the declarations, but no extraneous ones (for example, facts relevant to show probable cause for a traffic stop that resulted in the gang member being arrested for possession of a handgun, while relevant to a criminal case, are unnecessary in the declaration). In addition, the testimony in the declarations must conform to the evidentiary rules for percipient testimony, such as the rules governing hearsay. If statements of people other than the declarant are included, the foundation for the hearsay exception justifying admissibility must be apparent. Civilian declarations are not used in all jurisdictions, because all of the declarations are public record and will in fact be served on the gang members. The temptation to use civilian statements is great because they can provide powerful evidence and prosecutors are conditioned to avoid relying entirely on police officers to make a case. However, the need for civilian declarations should be scrutinized. Endangering civilians by having them testify against the gang is generally unnecessary, as police should have much more evidence in their possession than is necessary to meet the burden of proof that the gang creates a nuisance in the neighborhood. Remember that witness reluctance to testify can itself be compelling evidence of the gang's intimidating control over the neighborhood. Compelling use of other types of evidence, like statistics on reports of shots fired, number of (or lack of) 911 calls in the area, and the infrequency with which willing witnesses come forward, can substitute for civilian testimony. If the decision is made to use civilian declarations, they should be filed under seal for the protection of the witness.

Every injunction has a primary declaration that ties everything together. This is often the declaration by the gang expert that has been working alongside the prosecutor throughout the process. That this officer qualifies under the rules of evidence as an expert on the gang is essential to the success of the case, and the officer should provide detailed testimony describing why each element of public nuisance is satisfied by the gang's activities, explaining the need for each injunctive provision requested. An officer who is experienced in investigating the gang's crimes and who has had many contacts with the gang's members should easily qualify as an expert. Rules of evidence typically require only that, to qualify as an expert, a witness possess specialized knowledge, training, education, or experience that would assist the trier of fact to understand the evidence or determine a fact in issue. The behavior of street gangs being strange and unfamiliar to the average person, this is an appropriate realm for expert testimony. In fact, in those states where the criminal law makes special provisions for gang-related crime, many officers routinely qualify in criminal court as experts on the gang to testify to the gang-related motivation of the crime or the gang membership of the defendant.

Expert testimony is valuable because the expert may testify as to his or her opinion as to any relevant fact, including the ultimate issue to be decided by the trier of fact, and may, in forming the opinion, rely on a wide range of facts or data subject only to the limitation that the facts or data be of a type reasonably relied upon by an expert in the particular field. In addition, the facts and data that constitute the basis for the expert's opinion, even if of a type not normally admissible, may typically be admitted for the purpose of explaining the reasons for the opinion. For this reason, the expert's declaration can be wide ranging, touching on virtually everything he or she knows about the gang. A reading of the expert declaration should convince the judge, or any reader, that the gang is a public nuisance.

The expert's declaration should include issues like the number of years of law enforcement experience, particularly those dealing with the target gang; any non-law enforcement experience with gang members; the number of personal contacts with gang members and members of the target gang; the number of gang crimes investigated or in which the expert assisted in the investigation; any formal or informal training or education on the subject of gangs; and the number of times the expert has testified as an expert on gangs, if at all. For a gang enforcement officer with several years of experience, a statement of expertise can quickly become lengthy.

Virtually everything that is known about the gang may be included as background, both to provide the court with an understanding of the gang and to emphasize the expert's degree of knowledge. Once the expert has given an overview of their experience and how they have developed their expertise, they are able to transition into an educator for the jury as to what the gang issues are. The expert should explain what a gang is, what are the criteria used to document a gang and a gang member, and how the gang the expert is testifying about engages in a pattern of criminal activity. The expert will have an opportunity as the gang expert to list some of the crimes that establish the pattern of criminal activities, murders, assaults, and robberies that the defendants or their criminal street gang commits.

In particular, the expert's testimony should include:

The gang's history. Including its origins and any major events. How familiar is the gang expert, with the particular gang that is on trial? What is the history of the defendant gang? How did the expert learn this history? How many investigations has the expert conducted involving this gang? How many members of the gang have been documented? How does this gang conform to the gang documentation requirements? How big is the gang? What is its territory, alliances, rivalries, structure, hangouts, primary activities, graffiti, symbols, tattoos, monikers, hand signs, etc.?

The gang's names and symbols. Including any alternative names and signs or symbols used by the gang.

The gang's activities. The expert should discuss the purpose of the gang and its primary activities, including what crimes the members commit, and the nature of any other nuisance activities.

Turf: Where do they hang out? How does the expert know?

Rivalries: Who are their rivals? For how long?

Colors: Do they wear any particular kind of clothing?

Graffiti: Do they have characteristic graffiti? Where has the expert seen it?

Hand signs: If the expert has the necessary manual dexterity ask the expert to demonstrate.

Size of the gang: How many members? How many hard-core members? How many members have the expert ever met?

Primary activities: What does this gang do? Do they specialize in a certain type of crime? Do they use a particular method?

The gang's membership. Provide an estimated number of members and known associates that the police department has documented. Determining who is and is not a member of the gang is therefore essential to the success of a gang injunction. This determination involves a process of intelligence gathering, which is the task of police officers assigned to gang enforcement. These officers have, as part of their duties, the job of determining who are the gang members in a particular area, which they do by spending much of their time gathering intelligence by talking to and studying gang members in the area. It is only because these officers are frequently successful in gathering evidence of an individual's gang membership that arrests and prosecutions are able to occur. Such evidence might include gang-related activities and crimes in which the defendant has taken part, the defendant's gang-related tattoos, or the defendant's own admissions of gang membership. All of this evidence may be challenged, impeached, and contradicted by defense counsel (to which the defendant is entitled, regardless of ability to pay) in all criminal contempt prosecutions based on a violation of a gang injunction. Identifying individual members of the gang who actively engage in criminal or nuisance gang activities is necessary not only in building the case that the gang's members create a public nuisance, but also because certain individual gang members must be designated as representatives of the gang to receive notice on behalf of the gang of the legal action against it (see below). The police agency investigating the gang must therefore document the gang's membership and provide evidence of each member's gang membership, which can be used to identify a sufficient number of individual members.

The gang's structure. Explain how the gang is organized, including whether it has any cliques or subgroups, levels of membership, leaders, affiliations with prison gangs or allied street gangs, and how members join and leave the gang. It is also important to describe how and how effectively the gang communicates among its members, as establishing that the gang's members efficiently communicate about issues of importance to the gang is critical to later establishing that the gang was effectively notified of the lawsuit.

The gang's culture. The expert must explain the gang ethos, which is foreign to most outsiders. This includes the scorn for police and disapproval of talking to the police (especially cooperating with police investigations). It also includes the concept of "putting in work" for the gang (or requiring members to engage in criminal activities to further the gang's agenda). How the gang enforces its rules for behavior and the demands on its members should also be discussed.

How the gang commits crimes. Discuss the gang's typical *modus operandi*, including the importance of having multiple gang members assisting in crimes as accomplices or lookouts, and providing support after the fact by maintaining safe houses and engaging in witness intimidation, as examples.

The gang's turf. Describe the boundaries of the gang's turf, as well as the reasons the gang is territorial and the advantages and consequences of claiming turf.

Relationships with other gangs. Any gangs that are rivals should be identified and the nature of the rivalry should be explained.

The gang's criminal activities and nuisance behavior. The crimes the gang regularly commits should be emphasized and discussed in detail. Where the expert has personal knowledge of particular incidents from participating in the investigation, these should be recounted. The distinct nature of the effect that gang-related crime has on the residents of the target area should be explained. The commission of violent crimes (targeting rival gangs as well as non-gang members), the frequency of threats and threatening behavior, the possession and use of weapons, the gang's involvement in narcotics, and the commission of property crimes (everything from robbery to vandalism) should all be covered. Nuisance behavior, though less serious, though should also be documented.

Opinion on the gang membership of individuals identified. The expert should express his or her opinion that each member identified in the supporting documents is a gang member, and explain the reasons he or she holds this belief. He or she should do this for both individual named defendants and identified gang members designated to receive service on behalf of the gang. Linking these individuals to the gang also helps establish that the gang is responsible for the criminal incidents perpetrated by individuals or groups of members recounted in the percipient declarations.

Opine on whether the gang fits any pertinent legal definition of a gang. In California, for example, the penal code defines *criminal street gang*. This definition is helpful in establishing the organization's criminal nature.

Opine on the necessity of a gang injunction and each requested restrictive provision. The expert should explain why each injunction provision is important. He or she can draw on experience as a police officer and the difficulties he or she has encountered in policing gang crime to explain how each requested provision will help abate the gang's activities. The expert should also explain why the target area needs to be of the requested size.

Request for judicial notice. The prosecutor may wish to submit records of gang members' convictions as evidence demonstrating their criminal activities. Having identified numerous gang members elsewhere in the documentation, it should be easy to gather a large number of criminal convictions of members of this group. Court records are a proper subject for judicial notice. Hence, these records will be unimpeachable evidence of the gang's criminal activity.

Ensure documentation of the gang's activities is available. To an extent, the gang's criminal activity is going to be documented in police reports. In seeking an injunction, the prosecutor will rely primarily, indeed almost totally, on these reports. So it is necessary that the gang's criminal and nuisance activities in the target area be documented in some way by the police. In addition, the prosecutor must show that the crimes and nuisance activities were committed by gang members, so the police must have some method for identifying the perpetrators as members of the gang. The documentation may be in the form of crime reports (either initial reports of crime or detectives' investigations), search warrant requests, or nearly any other document the agency produces that may evidence the nuisance caused by the gang and its members. Broad access to police files by the attorney preparing the injunction is critical. In addition to crime reports, police agencies may keep records of field interviews (FIs), typically on FI cards. Where admissions of gang membership are documented on these cards in the absence of a criminal investigation, they can assist in proving the gang membership of individuals, and may also document the frequency with which gang members congregate in the target area and engage in nuisance activities such as loud noise, drinking in public, littering, blocking sidewalks, and other intimidating and antisocial activities for which they were not cited or arrested.

These FI reports are, however, secondary to crime reports, which should largely suffice to prove both the nuisance activities of the gang and the gang membership of the individual suspects. Court records evidencing criminal convictions by members of the gang are strong evidence of the nuisance. These can typically be submitted with a request for judicial notice. Where a gang is problematic enough to merit the consideration of a gang injunction, the sheer volume of criminal activity engaged in by the gang should result in an impressive stack of conviction records that can be identified through normal criminal history checks on the gang members, and documented as such in the other documents filed with the court.

Photos may constitute the most compelling evidence in support of the injunction. Booking photos of gang members should be ordered, particularly where gang-related tattoos are photographed, in order to prove that individuals are members of the gang. Since members of the gang may appear in court dressed not as gang members, these photos will provide the court with an idea of how the gang members present themselves to the community, and will easily defeat claims that the person is not a gang member in most cases. Photos of evidence recovered in searches of gang members, particularly of weapons, narcotics, and other contraband, are highly valuable as well.

The gang's own personal photographs, often seized in searches and kept as evidence by police, can be used to show the gang as it sees itself—party photos typically show gang members posing together, throwing gang hand signs, often holding guns, and engaging in a wide variety of frightening behaviors. Finally, and usually most easy to come by, photos of the gang's graffiti can be submitted to show that the gang defaces property, that it claims turf, the size of the turf that it claims, and that it has a large number of members, that it communicates with its membership and with other gangs using graffiti, and that it uses graffiti to intimidate neighborhood residents and create a sense of lawlessness and feeling of control of the neighborhood by the gang.

Have an expert on the gang available to testify. Testimony from an officer who qualifies under the rules of evidence as an expert with respect to the gang is virtually essential to obtaining the gang injunction. The expert's declaration in support of the injunction is the most important single document in support of the injunction. A suitable officer with the experience, knowledge, training, and particular familiarity with the gang in question must be available to assist in preparing the lawsuit. The requirement that the expert have specialized knowledge that will assist a trier of fact is readily met when the subject is the workings of criminal street gangs about which the average person knows little. Nevertheless, the officer expert should have extensive experience investigating the gang, and should have not just training but percipient knowledge of the gang's activities.

Since the expert should be familiar with all aspects of the evidence in support of the gang injunction, and since the expert's opinion on the various issues concerning the gang will in part dictate the size of the target area, the provisions of the injunction, and other issues, it is preferable that the officer be assigned to work on the project from the beginning and for its duration.

Not Enough Evidence: Consider an Eviction

When there is not enough evidence to bring an abatement lawsuit, prosecutors will evaluate whether gang members or associates can be evicted under existing laws. The law requires landlords to evict tenants arrested for narcotics offenses, gang-related crime, or threats or acts of violence within 1,000 feet of their residences. California Health and Safety Code Section 11571.1 authorizes the prosecution to bring an unlawful detainer action on behalf of a property owner against any tenant arrested for a narcotics offense occurring on the property. Additionally, California Civil Code Section 3485 requires landlords to evict tenants who illegally possess or use a firearm or ammunition. This is true wherever you live and work. The concept is the same: simply apply the same logic to the problem and laws in your areas.

3

Steps 6 to 10 of the Injunction Process

The first five recommendations require a significant collaboration between the prosecutor and the police officers; the second five transition from putting the case together to taking the case to court, the success of which depends on the first five steps being done correctly.

6. Prepare the order, decide which type to obtain.
7. Obtain the order, what activity will you restrict?
8. Notify the defendants.
9. Final disposition: trial or hearing.
10. Enforce and maintain the order, educate the police and community.

STEP 6: PREPARE THE ORDER, DECIDE WHICH TYPE TO OBTAIN

The type of order that was obtained and how the order is drafted impact the issue of effectiveness. Police and prosecutors can typically take one of four actions: sue the gang only, sue the gang and named defendants, sue defendants only and not the gang, or sue the gang with some defendants named in the supporting declarations but not listed as defendants. The complaint may name the gang as the sole defendant, it may name individual defendants in addition to the gang, or it may name only individual defendants. Naming only the gang seems to offer law enforcement flexibility and may lower the costs of bringing the injunction because rather than building a case against each gang member the prosecution intends to bind, the prosecution would only have to build a case against the gang as a whole. Notwithstanding these possible advantages, naming only the gang may present problems if a gang member challenges his or her inclusion or claims that he or she is not a gang member and is not part of the public nuisance.

This injunction approach is sometimes referred to as a discount injunction in the law enforcement community. Rather than build individual cases against each gang member, the prosecution builds a case against the gang as a whole, saving time, money, and resources, at least at the onset. Naming only the gang may present problems if a gang member claims that he or she did not have notice of the injunction or the gang itself was not given proper notice. Due process requires that in order to hold a person accountable to an injunction, he or she must have notice of it. In Los Angeles County, for example, once the injunction against the gang has been granted, gang detectives and the attorneys identify as many members of the gang that they feel are a nuisance as possible and serve them the injunction. This may have advantages in that an injunction can be applied to hundreds of members without involving the labor-intensive research of every defendant for the initial declaration.

Criticism of naming the gang only includes a lack of accountability, who decides who gets served, who tracks who has been served, what criteria are evaluated before the individual is served, and what the status is of those served (in prison, jail, live in the same city, etc.). When federal prosecutors pursue injunctions against large corporations, barring them from violating securities laws or sharing trade secrets, for example, they rarely have trouble finding out who to serve. Every corporation has an "agent for service of process" on file with the secretary of state, and it's that person's job to communicate such information to company officials (California Corporations Code 18220). Filing for an injunction against a street gang is not as easy as filing against a corporation; gangs have no corporate officers, no corporate headquarters, and no agents for service of processes.

However, instead of naming individual gang members, which typically requires considerable paperwork, many injunctions name only the gang as a defendant. In doing so, the gang is treated as an organized association, and a small number of its members are treated as "representatives" of that association. The assumption is that these members will get the word out to the rest of the gang (*People v. Dogtown*, Case C418875). Problems arise of course when too small a number of representatives are served, as the defense may claim that due process procedures were violated.

The premise is that gangs are organized networks, and giving notice to just one or a few members should adequately result in notice to all. Individual members still would need to be served personally with the court orders in order to be prosecuted for violating the injunction. This is why gang-only injunctions are often referred to as the discount method; they do allow for police and prosecutors to process and file more injunctions against more gang members, but they also create concerns about the due process rights of the targeted gang members. This is an area of the law that is under debate at the time of this research and has potential to impact the manner in which gang injunctions are obtained.

The type of order obtained may impact the outcome and overall effectiveness of the injunction. For example, in cases where the police name each defendant in the order, a comprehensive historical overview of the individual gang member is often conducted, and the results incorporated into the court order for the targeted member and his fellow gang members to read. For some gang members this is a validation that the police know who they are, what they have done, and that they are a specific target of the injunction. Sometimes the targeted member is contacted more frequently during the evidence gathering phase to get recent examples of gang activity for the court to review.

This evidence-gathering stage often causes a reidentification of the primary problem gang members, which may result in additions and subtractions from the tentative list of targets. The process of gathering evidence and providing notice to the gang of the impending legal action may have an intervening influence on the gang's activities. Although at times it defies logic that gang members, who openly disregard the criminal law in spite of enhancement statutes that increase penalties for gang-related offenses, would be deterred from antisocial activities by the mere serving of civil court papers, there have been claims by prosecutors and police that the process of acquiring an injunction has an ameliorating effect on the activities of the targeted gang prior to the acquisition of an injunction.

Name the Gang, Name the Individuals, Name Both?

Every gang injunction sought since 1993 has named the gang as a defendant. The California Supreme Court suggested this approach was valid in the landmark case of *People ex rel. Gallo v. Acuna*, 14 Cal. 4th 1090 (1997). Although *Acuna* was a case in which only individual gang members were named as defendants, in upholding the injunction, the court noted that the district attorney could have named the gang itself as a defendant. The approach of suing the gang itself rather than just individual members has come to be the norm in the gang injunction field. In 2007, the California Court of Appeal explicitly validated the idea that a gang is an entity that can be sued.

The *Acuna* court stated the liability of gang members is indistinguishable from time-honored equitable practice applicable to labor unions, abortion protesters, or other identifiable groups. Because such groups can act only through the medium of their membership, it has been a common practice to make the injunction run also to classes of persons through whom the enjoined person may act, such as agents, servants, employees, aiders, and abettors. Though it is now the routine practice to name the gang or the entity as a defendant, agencies that bring gang injunction suits hold different views about whether the lawsuit should also name individual gang members.

Because every gang's membership is fluid, a gang injunction based this holding on the *Acuna* decision as well as an analysis of certain statutes, primarily California Code of Civil Procedure Section 369.5(a), which provides: "A partnership or other unincorporated association, whether organized for profit or not, may sue and be sued in the becomes significantly less useful if the injunction is limited only to those individuals who are named as defendants in the civil lawsuit." Current members recruit new members to join; older members drop out or become inactive because they move away, are incarcerated, or get killed. Where a suit names the gang itself and the injunction runs to its members, the individuals through whom the gang may act, the injunction becomes flexible enough to adapt to changing membership. When an injunction binds the gang as a whole, every new member who receives adequate notice of the injunction is bound by it even if he or she joins the gang long after the final judgment granting the injunction is issued.

To enforce the injunction against any gang member, the prosecutor need only ensure that the documentation is sufficient to prove the individual's gang membership, and that he or she has been served with the judgment granting the injunction. The prosecutor need not take any further action in the issuing court. Because a case must come to a final judgment, going back to court to join new defendants as they become active in the gang may not be possible. Likewise, repeatedly seeking injunctive relief against individual new members as they join the gang may not be practical because of the time and resources required. Still, some agencies prefer to name individual gang members as defendants in addition to the gang itself.

Naming individual members as defendants may ensure that the injunction binds the gang's key members, where there is a concern that the court may balk at issuing an injunction against the gang as an entity. This may be important in jurisdictions in which gang injunctions are new and untested. However, unless the strategy is to keep the lawsuit open indefinitely while new parties are added, or to bring new lawsuits to enjoin new members of the gang as they become known, the court must ultimately be persuaded to issue the injunction against the gang.

Naming individual members may strengthen the argument that the gang has sufficient notice of the lawsuit. While the method for service of summons on an individual is established, the code may not provide for a method of service on an entity such as a gang. Service per the code on a number of individual gang members may strengthen the argument that service of the gang itself was proper. The court must ultimately approve a method of serving the gang entity, however, regardless of individual service requirements.

Naming individuals can preempt defense arguments that due process requires that each individual potentially subject to the injunction be given notice and an opportunity to be heard on whether it should issue. Because naming individual defendants avoids this argument, a later contempt of court prosecution of an individual who was a named defendant in the injunction action is simpler than that of a gang member who was not. However, this argument is in opposition to the idea of suing the gang at all, and must ultimately be confronted and defeated if an injunction against a gang as an entity is to be successfully obtained.

Where an injunction action only names individual defendants, or where only named individuals are prosecuted for violations of the injunction, the injunction will lack the flexibility of one that names the gang as an entity, and which, by its terms, runs against all members of the gang. The gang's membership will change surprisingly quickly, or the gang will soon adapt and only members who were not named will engage in the nuisance activities.

Gangs' ever-changing membership also supports naming the gang as the defendant in another way. Where a judgment granting an injunction is issued against an individual defendant due to his or her gang activities, the judgment is permanent, and will bind the individual permanently regardless of whether he or she later leaves the gang, unless he or she can successfully obtain relief from that judgment in the civil court. Where nonparties to the litigation are prosecuted for contempt of court for violating the injunction as members of the defendant gang, each prosecution requires proof that the individual was a member of the gang at the time of the alleged violation.

This lends credibility to the argument that the gang injunction encourages members to seek to leave the gang. Added to this is the fact that in a criminal prosecution, the defendant is provided counsel and a jury trial, and that proof of gang membership (as with everything) must be beyond a reasonable doubt. It is clear that the procedural protections are greater where nonparties to the civil suit are prosecuted. These considerations of fairness justify themselves, but they also help to quell the controversy that typically surrounds the use of gang injunctions. Where the method chosen to prosecute a gang injunction is shown to have inherent procedural protections, this will assist in convincing the judge that the injunction is appropriate and will help withstand criticism from defense counsel and the public.

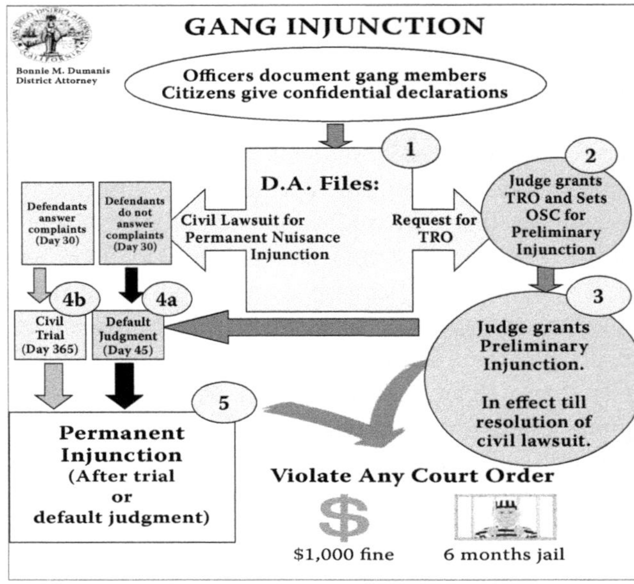

FIGURE 3.1 Injunction Flow Chart (courtesy of San Diego District Attorney Bonnie Dumanis).

Before an injunction may be issued, the complaining party must establish that there are grounds for equitable relief (Figure 3.1); that is, the traditional legal remedy is inadequate. This is easily shown in the case of a criminal street gang's activities because an ordinary damage award will not make a community whole from the harm the gang's activities cause. Physical bodily harm, the loss of the enjoyment of a neighborhood, and other actual and threatened injury constitute unique injury that should not be tolerated and cannot be adequately recompensed, despite the availability of damage actions and the threat of criminal prosecution. Further, injunctive relief is warranted because compensation for these ongoing wrongs would require a multiplicity of suits. Therefore, proof of the gang's dangerous nature and continuous criminal and nuisance activities is again relevant and vital. As an example of the codification of these requirements, California Code of Criminal Procedure Section 526(a) states in part:

> An injunction may be granted in the following cases. When it appears by the complaint or affidavits that the commission or continuance of some act during the litigation would produce waste, or great or irreparable injury, to a party to the action. When pecuniary compensation would not afford adequate relief. When it would be extremely difficult to ascertain the amount of compensation which would afford adequate relief. Where the restraint is necessary to avoid a multiplicity of judicial proceedings. Since an injunction is an exclusively prophylactic measure, the acts sought

to be enjoined must be ongoing or likely to resume. The evidence must show with reasonable certainty that the gang's activities will continue unless restrained.

Requirements for Issuance of Preliminary Injunction

A request for a preliminary injunction (effective only during the pendency of the lawsuit) should typically be made upon filing of the complaint for injunction. There are several good reasons for seeking a preliminary injunction. Most obviously, the preliminary injunction restrains the harm caused by the gang while the case is litigated, a potentially lengthy process. Second, having a court rule on a preliminary injunction at the case's commencement provides a preview of how the court evaluates the strength of the case and the legal issues involved. In considering whether to grant a preliminary injunction, a court must typically consider two factors: the likelihood that the plaintiff will prevail on the merits at trial, and the interim harm that the plaintiff is likely to sustain if the injunction were denied as compared to the harm the defendant is likely to suffer if the preliminary injunction were issued.

The first factor requires the court to evaluate the evidence of public nuisance submitted in support of the preliminary injunction. The second factor requires the court to balance the hardships. Here, the court may consider the quantity and severity of the gang's harmful activities to find that the gang is not unduly burdened by obeying the injunction's restrictions. Since the restrictions imposed in the injunction ought to be relatively easy for a law-abiding person to obey, the community's interest in restraining criminal and nuisance activities should easily outweigh any harm to the defendant gang.

Procedure for Obtaining Preliminary Injunction: Order to Show Cause

A preliminary injunction may be sought through a noticed motion or, more likely, through an order to show cause (OSC). The procedures for a noticed motion are generally straightforward and well known. The OSC is a slightly different procedure that is advantageous because an application for an OSC can be made *ex parte*. Generally a preliminary injunction is sought at the moment the case is filed, in order to immediately impact the gang's activities. Filing an *ex parte* application for an OSC avoids the normal notice requirements for a motion, and the *ex parte* application can be served concurrently with the summons and complaint. In fact, this procedure may be mandated where the preliminary injunction is sought at the commencement of the case. Such is the case in

California. An *ex parte* application for the OSC does require that the defendant be notified. In the typical case, this is done through a phone call to opposing counsel, but where the gang defendant is not represented, this is done by personally delivering a letter detailing the lawsuit, the date, time, and place of the *ex parte* hearing, and the relief requested by the proposed OSC to a sufficient number of the gang's members to provide notice to the gang, and to the individual defendants, if any. The rules relating to proper notice for *ex parte* applications differ from court to court, so consult the rules of the court, any local rules, and the assigned judge's particular rules, for details on the notice requirements.

The OSC orders the defendant(s) to appear to show cause why an injunction should not be issued. The proposed OSC must set forth the terms of the proposed injunction, provide a date for the hearing, and set forth a briefing schedule. The OSC may also provide for the method of service of both the OSC and, importantly, all documents in the action. A party requesting a preliminary injunction may give notice of the request to the opposing or responding party either by serving a noticed motion under Code of Civil Procedure Section 1005 or by obtaining and serving an OSC.

An OSC must be used when a temporary restraining order (TRO) is sought, or if the party against whom the preliminary injunction is sought has not appeared in the action. If the responding party has not appeared, the OSC must be served in the same manner as a summons and complaint. The five steps are:

1. Deliver notice letter to members of the gang and individual defendants, if any (may be done in conjunction with service of the summons and complaint if it has already been filed).
2. File *ex parte* application with proper court, along with (a) proposed OSC, (b) all documents in support (including evidentiary declarations), and (c) declaration(s) detailing notice given to the gang regarding the *ex parte* application.
3. Attend *ex parte* hearing and obtain OSC regarding preliminary injunction.
4. Serve OSC as directed by the court.
5. Obtain preliminary injunction at hearing on OSC.

STEP 7: OBTAIN THE ORDER, WHAT ACTIVITY WILL YOU RESTRICT?

A gang injunction should be tailored to address the specific nuisance activity associated with the specific target gang. A typical gang injunction complaint describes how the gang's activities meet the required legal standard. The court order supports the injunctive relief and often describes specific instances of illegal conduct that form the nuisance. These instances are provided in the declarations accompanying the complaint, often attested to by law enforcement officers in their declarations. The prohibited activities vary from injunction to injunction based upon the evidence that illustrates the need to enjoin a specific activity by the target gang.

The most important and effective provision of a gang injunction is the "do not associate" requirement. A "do not associate" provision restricts gang members' ability to gather in groups and consequently deters concerted actions. The ability to act collectively makes gang crime more dangerous, threatening, and difficult to combat through traditional means, so a restriction on the ability of gang members to associate in public directly addresses this problem. In *Acuna*, the California Supreme Court explicitly upheld the challenged "do not associate" provision. The provision in *Acuna* prohibited "standing, sitting, walking, driving, gathering or appearing anywhere in public view" with any other gang member. California's gang injunctions are generally modeled on this provision. The prosecutor must explain and prove to the court why each injunction provision is necessary. Because gangs' criminal and nuisance activities vary, injunction provisions should be tailored to each gang. The drafter must take care to ensure that each provision is narrowly tailored to the harm caused by the gang, is clear and understandable, and is not overbroad. Provisions that have commonly been included in injunctions obtained by the Los Angeles City Attorney's Office include:

Do Not Associate: Driving, standing, sitting, walking, gathering or appearing, anywhere in public view or anyplace accessible to the public, with any known member of a gang, except when all individuals are inside a school attending class or on school business, and when all individuals are inside a church; provided, however, that this prohibition against associating shall apply to all claims of travel to or from any of those locations.

No Intimidation: Confronting, intimidating, annoying, harassing, threatening, challenging, provoking, assaulting or battering any person known to be a witness to any activity of a gang, known to be a victim of any activity of a gang, or known to be a person who has complained about any activity of a gang.

No Firearms, Imitation Firearms, or Dangerous Weapons: Anywhere in public view or anyplace accessible to the public, possessing any firearm, imitation firearm, ammunition, or illegal weapon as defined in Penal Code section 12020, knowingly remaining in the presence of anyone who is in possession of such firearm, imitation firearm, ammunition or dangerous weapon, or knowingly remaining in the presence of such firearm, imitation firearm, ammunition or dangerous weapon. For purposes of this provision, an imitation firearm means a replica of a firearm that is so substantially similar in physical properties to an existing firearm as to lead a reasonable person to conclude that the replica is a firearm.

Stay Away from Drugs: Without a prescription, selling, possessing, or using any controlled substance or related paraphernalia, including but not limited to rolling papers and pipes used for illegal drug use, knowingly remaining in the presence of anyone selling, possessing, or using any controlled substance or such related paraphernalia, or knowingly remaining in the presence of any controlled substance or such related paraphernalia.

Stay Away from Alcohol: Anywhere in public view or anyplace accessible to the public, except on properly licensed premises, possessing an open container of an alcoholic beverage, knowingly remaining in the presence of anyone possessing an open container of an alcoholic beverage, or knowingly remaining in the presence of an open container of an alcoholic beverage.

No Trespassing: Being present on or in any property not open to the general public, except with the prior written consent of the owner, owner's agent, or the person in lawful possession of the property, or in the presence of and with the voluntary consent of the owner, owner's agent, or the person in lawful possession of the property.

Obey Curfew: Being outside between the hours of 10:00 p.m. on any day and 5:00 a.m. of the following day, unless going to or from a legitimate meeting or entertainment activity, or actively engaged in some business, trade, profession or occupation which requires such presence, or involved in a legitimate emergency situation that requires immediate attention.

No Graffiti or Graffiti Tools: Damaging, defacing, or marking any public property or private property of another, or possessing any spray paint container or felt tip marker.

No Forcible Recruiting: Making any threats or doing anything threatening, including but not limited to striking, battering, destroying or damaging personal property, or disturbing the peace, to cause a person to join a gang.

No Preventing a Member from Leaving the Gang: Making any threats or doing anything threatening, including but not limited to striking, battering, destroying or damaging personal property, or disturbing the peace, (1) to prevent a person from leaving [gang] or (2) to any person known to have left [gang].

Obey All Laws: Failing to obey all laws (1) which prohibit violence and threatened violence including murder, rape, robbery by force or fear, assault and battery, (2) which prohibit

> interference with the property rights of others including trespass, theft, driving or taking a vehicle without the owner's consent, and vandalism, or (3) which prohibit the commission of acts which create a nuisance including the illegal sale of controlled substances and blocking the sidewalk.

These provisions are precisely drafted but also properly restrict activities that could not be prohibited by statute. For example, the Stay Away From Drugs provision places a burden on the enjoined gang member to remove himself or herself from any place where he or she knows drugs are present. This is a sensible rule for a gang member, and also eliminates the obstacle to enforcement created by the need to prove individual possession when narcotics are present among a group of gang members.

Other provisions that courts have approved under appropriate circumstances order gang members to stay away from school grounds or other designated locations, not to act as lookouts for illegal activities or warn of the approach of the police, not to fight with others, and not to use gang gestures or wear or display gang paraphernalia in public. The provisions that may be sought are not limited to this list.

Constitutional challenges to gang injunctions have taken various forms. California courts have addressed challenges based on the right to free association under the First Amendment, vagueness, and overbreadth. The courts have ruled that the challenged provisions of gang injunctions are constitutionally valid, and have articulated the standard for evaluating the provisions under a substantive due process analysis. The approach of the California courts is described below. Prosecutors from other states are encouraged to study these cases in anticipation of challenges to their own gang injunction work.

The Narrowly Tailored Limitation on the Scope of an Injunction

The *Acuna* court identified the proper standard in evaluating whether a provision of an injunction exceeds the limitations imposed by the Constitution. The court must ask "whether the two provisions comply with the constitutional standard announced by the Supreme Court, that is, whether they 'burden no more speech than necessary to serve a significant governmental interest.'" This standard is often referred to as strict scrutiny lite, because it applies the narrowly tailored requirement of traditional strict scrutiny to a significant, though not necessarily compelling, governmental interest. As *Acuna* held that the interest in abating the nuisance created by a criminal street gang is significant, the standard is notable mainly for the requirement that the restrictions imposed by the gang injunction not go beyond what is *required* to abate the nuisance. Thus, all of the provisions in the injunction must be narrowly tailored, so that there is no less restrictive means available to abate the particular aspect of the gang's nuisance targeted by each provision. This requires not just careful drafting, but also thorough evidence gathering and analysis, as each provision must be justified by the examples of the gang's nuisance. Although the U.S. Supreme Court referred only to the burden on speech, the *Acuna* court applied the narrowly tailored requirement to the restriction on social intercourse inherent in the "do not associate" provision.

A gang injunction should be tailored to address the specific nuisance activity associated with the target gang. After setting forth the proper standard for what constitutes a public nuisance, a typical complaint will then paint a portrait of how the gang's activities meet this standard. The points and authorities in support of the injunctive relief may cite specific instances of conduct that form the nuisance. These instances are provided in the declarations accompanying the complaint, often attested to by law enforcement officers in their declarations. The prohibited activities vary from injunction to injunction based upon the evidence that illustrates the need to enjoin a specific activity by the target gang.

STEP 8: NOTIFY THE DEFENDANTS

After the complaint has been filed, the court can issue a summons. Once a summons is prepared it must be personally served on the members of the gang and individual defendants. Once an order is obtained, it is mandatory that the police make a notification to each of the defendants that were impacted and subjected to the terms and rules outlined in the order. Due process requires that in order to hold a person amenable to an injunction, he or she must have notice of it. This includes all of the evidence against him or her, with the exception of anything placed under seal by the court.

Each defendant must be properly served with a summons, before any hearing on the merits of the petition occurs. Rarely in criminal or civil matters is this automatic procedure. It is frequently the case that a police officer, process server, or sheriff's deputy will make more than one trip to a residence to properly serve a defendant. This brings up issues relating to how defendants are served, the manner in which they are served, and the criteria used to determine who is served with the gang injunction. These issues also include who is being served, who keeps track of the service, what criteria are used, how many contacts are required, what type of activity, how recent is the activity in the target area, etc. The unique nature of the gang defendant requires prosecutors to pay special attention to the method by which the gang is served with the documents filed in support of the lawsuit seeking an injunction. This is particularly true of the summons and complaint, which provide the constitutionally required notice to the defendant that a lawsuit against it has commenced.

A gang is an organization that acts as such, and the interests of justice therefore require that it be subject to suit. However, gangs fail to adhere to formalities usually associated with legally recognized organizations, such as the appointment of officers or agents for service of process, designation of a business address, or filing of articles of incorporation. In fact, while gangs take ruthless advantage of their ability to act as entities, they purposely conceal their organizational structure to avoid the legal consequences of their actions. Because there is generally not a statutory method to provide constitutionally adequate service of the summons on a gang, the prosecutor must suggest an appropriate method for service on the entity that would meet this standard. This method should provide for service on the gang by service on a practicable number of the gang's members, as well as any other efforts reasonably calculated to provide the gang's membership with notice. In light of this, is important that the evidence submitted in support of the injunction demonstrate that the gang *is* truly an organization and behaves like one, and that it has methods of efficiently communicating important information to its membership. Examples of how the news of law enforcement actions, like an arrest of a member, spreads through the gang quickly are helpful.

The city attorney then submits documentation to the court for each of the persons to be served on behalf of the gang, establishing their gang membership and allowing the court to be certain that each person is, in fact, a member of the gang, and can accept service on behalf of the gang. It is not until this hearing, of which gang members are notified (this can be in a manner similar to that shown in Figure 3.2), that the court makes the decision to allow the gang to be further notified by service on its members. The issue of whether the court will issue a preliminary injunction against the gang is reserved for another hearing, which occurs only after the service of all the court documents on the court-approved designated gang members has been accomplished. This procedure has been shown to give adequate and effective notice to the targeted gang. Members of the gang frequently show up to the hearings, including the first hearing of which the gang is notified by letter. In one case, members of the targeted gang chartered a bus to provide transportation to the courthouse for all of the members who wished to oppose the issuance of the preliminary injunction. These individuals filled all the available courtroom seats, demonstrating that the gang was clearly aware of the gang injunction proceedings.

FIGURE 3.2 This notice is posted in San Francisco to notify local gang members of the court date for the Eddy Rock injunction case.

In fact, word of the injunction typically travels fast throughout gangs when members are given notice of a possible injunction. Publicity surrounding injunctions, including not just word of mouth but television and other media coverage of the application for injunction, puts the gang on notice. Proof that the gang is on notice is often evidenced by gang graffiti denouncing the injunction, which crops up after the gang members are notified of the injunction proceedings. Police interviews with gang members and their families reveal that news of an injunction spreads throughout the gang and the whole neighborhood. Indeed, before a hearing on one gang injunction, the father of several of the gang's members told police officers that everyone knew about the injunction.

As in any civil case, the summons, complaint, and all other documents filed with the court must be served on the defendant. Because a gang has no fixed address where these can be sent, nor does it have a formal official like a president who can accept service on behalf of the gang, the city attorney requests the court to allow all of these court papers to be served on the gang by serving individual members of the gang. This is the only possible way to ensure that members of the gang are on notice of the lawsuit against the gang. As part of this process, letters are given to gang members advising them that a gang injunction will soon be filed against their gang, and that the city attorney will request at a hearing that this service procedure be approved.

The Yolo County *Broderick Boys* Case

The Yolo DA's office obtained this injunction in 2005. After years of legal battle, the Broderick Boys gang won a reversal of the gang injunction on April 24, 2007. The state appeals court reversed the decision based on the following:

> While evidence reveals a level of street gang criminality plaguing West Sacramento which might well justify injunction relief, the injunction cannot stand because, Yolo County District Attorney Jeff Reisig failed to show that the Broderick Boys is an "unincorporated association for the purpose of service."

The key point to illustrate is that not all injunctions are permanent. The Broderick Boys Gang injunction clearly showed that the DA of Yolo County failed in following the civil service process in order to serve each and every gang member. The office only served one gang member and attempted to argue the service was valid for the entire gang because it fell under the umbrella of the California Corporations Code. Throughout the case, the DA's office relied on the California Corporations Code to try to argue that the Broderick Boys were an unincorporated association capable of being sued as an entity, and that Wolfington (the single gang member served) was the agent for service of process. This case continues to serve as an example of the importance of service to avoid legal challenges.

STEP 9: FINAL DISPOSITION: TRIAL OR HEARING

Every gang injunction has to be presented to a court for a determination to be made if the injunction should be granted. This requires a well-prepared case and enhances the chance of a successful outcome in court. Gang evidence, each named member's history, the size and activity in the target area, and the activity of the target gang as a whole become very important. Some injunctions go through the legal process with virtually no opposition, while others are fought in lengthy trials.

The police and prosecution must assume that a trial is required and that each and every gang member will appear to contest their inclusion in the order. Proceeding on this assumption will increase the likelihood that the case will be successful. One bad inclusion can damage the entire case. That is why target selection is so important. When the active gang members selected have significant nuisance activity attributed to them, and they have recent contacts in the target area, the case presentation is much more persuasive. Preparing civil pleadings requires great care and attention. Small mistakes can have serious consequences, because under the rules of civil procedure, the plaintiff (or the moving party) bears the burden of both prevailing on the substantive issues and complying with the procedural requirements laid out in the state code of civil procedure, the rules of court, the local rules, and the judge's own rules. These rules can be difficult to navigate, particularly for a prosecutor unaccustomed to civil practice. However, the prosecutor must make every effort to comply because overlooking a rule may result in losing an important motion (or the case).

Proposed Preliminary Injunction

The proposed preliminary injunction should mirror the injunction provisions prayed for in the complaint. Each provision of the injunction and the boundaries of the safety zone must be supported by evidence from the supporting declarations. The need for the provisions can be explained in the expert declaration(s), discussed *supra*, and summarized in the supporting memorandum of points and authorities. Each provision must be narrowly tailored to abate the nuisance resulting from the gang's activities.

Ex Parte Application for Order to Show Cause

The *ex parte* application requests that the court issue an OSC why a preliminary injunction should not issued. The application simply sets forth the terms of the requested OSC, in identical language, and briefly states the basis for the application and recites the documents filed in support of the application. An *ex parte* application requires that all parties be notified prior to the *ex parte* appearance. The required nature and content of the notice may be set forth by statute or court rule. The prosecutor should draft a letter detailing the nature of the lawsuit, the relief requested by the proposed OSC, and the date, time, and place of the *ex parte* hearing. The letter should be personally delivered to every party and to a sufficient number of gang members to convince the court that the defendant gang was given notice of the *ex parte* hearing. One or more declarations detailing the notice given and the responses, if any, of the individuals notified should be drafted and filed with the *ex parte* application. The contents of the declaration may be governed by statute, court rule, or the judge's courtroom rules.

Proposed Order to Show Cause

The proposed order to show cause sets a date, time, and place for the hearing on the OSC and sets forth the terms of the proposed preliminary injunction. The OSC should also provide a briefing schedule (see, e.g., Cal. R. Ct. 3.1200 et seq. and Cal. R. Ct. 3.1204).

Memorandum of Points and Authorities in Support of *Ex Parte* Application and Preliminary Injunction

The memorandum of points and authorities summarizes the facts (contained in the declarations and other evidence filed in support) that constitute a public nuisance created by the activities of the gang. Within the page limit allowed, the brief must cite the legal authorities defining public nuisance and explain why the gang's activities constitute a public nuisance, why the gang is an entity or association subject to suit like any other organization, why the proposed method of service on the gang is constitutionally sufficient, how all the requirements for provisional injunctive relief have been satisfied (e.g., the harm to the members of the gang is outweighed by the harm it inflicts on the community), and why the terms of the proposed injunction are necessary to abate the nuisance caused by the gang.

The brief must also cite the relief sought, any response, and whether opposition is expected. It must document: (1) That, within the applicable time under rule 3.1203, the applicant informed the opposing party where and when the application would be made; (2) That the applicant in good faith attempted to inform the opposing party but was unable to do so, specifying the efforts made to inform the opposing party; or (3) that, for reasons specified, the applicant should not be required to inform the opposing party.

Obtaining Judgment Granting Permanent Injunction

Preparing a gang injunction lawsuit requires a great deal of work, and this work all leads up to filing the complaint for injunction and obtaining the preliminary injunction. The ultimate goal, however, is to secure a judgment granting a permanent injunction against the gang. The permanent injunction can be obtained after trial, by default, or by a stipulated judgment between the plaintiff and the opposing parties. There can be no easy template or road map for how to obtain the judgment except in the case of a default. Where a party or parties oppose the injunction, the litigation will proceed differently according to the nature of the opposition's strategy and tactics. The important thing to remember is that civil litigation requires that the plaintiff pay careful attention to deadlines (such as discovery and motion cutoff dates) and file all necessary motions promptly. Unlike in criminal litigation, civil procedural rules are strict and unforgiving, and no rulings can be expected except upon motion of a party.

If the gang or any individual gang member fails to answer the complaint, the plaintiff may file a request for entry of default. Court rules may require that the request be filed soon after the time for answer has elapsed. When default is entered, the plaintiff may seek a default judgment. Local rules may dictate the proper procedure for requesting a default judgment. The proposed permanent injunction should mirror the terms prayed for in the complaint, unless the court requires different terms. In drafting the judgment, take care that the terms are as clear and precise as possible. Not only must they be tailored to the gang's harmful activities, but they must also be clear enough for the gang members who will receive copies of the injunction to understand. When injunction violations are prosecuted, the jury will see the order; jurors must be able to understand it as well. Use plain language wherever possible, and avoid excessive words.

A violation of a gang injunction constitutes contempt and may be brought to the attention of the judge who issued the order to be treated as civil contempt. Preferably, it may be treated as criminal contempt of court, which justifies an arrest by a peace officer based upon probable cause that an individual bound by an injunction has disobeyed it. Section 166 of the California Penal Code, for example, makes contempt of court a misdemeanor punishable by up to six months in jail. Section 166(a)(4) defines this offense as "willful disobedience of the terms as written of any process or court order or out-of-state court order, lawfully issued by any court, including orders pending trial." The ability to enforce gang injunctions by arresting and filing criminal charges against gang members who violate them is distinctly useful and effective, even though the charges are limited to misdemeanors.

Contempt of court penalties may alone serve as a deterrent. But apart from the deterrent effect, the injunction also gives police officers a tool to arrest gang members for conduct that harms the community before it develops into dangerous or violent crime. This preventative enforcement tool is all the more valuable because injunction arrests are generally made based on officers' observations rather than on information from neighborhood residents who may be intimidated by the gang and reluctant to report or testify about gang activities.

Gang members should be personally served with the signed court order or judgment granting the injunction before it is enforced against them, because contempt charges require that the defendant have notice of the terms of the order. Proof of personal service is the most effective way of proving notice. Service should be conducted by officers who will be available to testify at a later date, if needed. Proofs of service should be kept on file to prove that the individual was served and therefore had notice of the injunction. Careful records should be maintained documenting the identity of served gang members, because they may dispute being served when later charged with contempt. Attaching a photo of the person served to the documentation of service or obtaining a signature acknowledging receipt of the injunction may avoid this issue. When individuals who were named as defendants in the civil lawsuit for injunction are later charged with violating the injunction, the fact that the injunction is addressed to that individual is evident from the face of the judgment or order that names the defendant. However, because an injunction that names the gang binds all of its members, a criminal contempt of court prosecution of an unnamed gang member requires proof that the defendant was a gang member at the time of the violation.

Therefore, if prosecutions of gang injunction violations are going to work, ongoing efforts must be made to identify and document the gang's members, and to keep that documentation current. The most common defense to a contempt of court charge for violating the gang injunction is that the defendant recently left the gang. This defense may be defeated with proof of recent gang activity, admissions, or the circumstances of the activity that resulted in the arrest. Because the defendant's gang membership is vital to the prosecution, his or her membership must also be documented by officers in the arrest reports for the gang injunction violation. The prosecution will then require that an officer who is an expert on the gang be called to testify that the defendant was a gang member at the time of the violation. The arresting officer must also know that the individual is currently a gang member before arresting him or her. The court—not the jury—decides whether the injunction is legal. A defendant charged with contempt of court may try to challenge the injunction's legality at his or her contempt of court trial. This is called a collateral attack. Collateral attacks on injunctions are limited to facial defects in the court order. In other words, the defendant may not seek to introduce facts to show that the injunction is invalid and thereby impeach the judgment of the issuing court.

When a member of an enjoined gang violates a gang injunction, that gang member can be prosecuted for contempt of court, which is a misdemeanor. In a contempt prosecution, the defendant has all of the rights due any criminal defendant, including the presumption of innocence, the right to an attorney, the right to a jury trial, the right to call witnesses on his or her behalf, and the right to confront and cross-examine witnesses against him or her and to see the prosecution's evidence. In addition, under California law, the defendant can contest the validity of the underlying injunction in the criminal court in which the prosecution is pending.

To prove that a gang member violated the injunction, the prosecutor must be able to prove all of the following three elements *beyond a reasonable doubt*: (1) that the defendant had notice of the injunction, which is done by proving that he had been personally served a copy of the court order; (2) that the defendant was a gang member at the time of the violation, and was therefore subject to the injunction; and (3) that the defendant did some act that violated the injunction within the defined safety zone. If the defendant was charged, for example, with violating an injunction by associating with another gang member in public within the safety zone, the prosecution would have to convince a jury beyond a reasonable doubt that the defendant was a gang member at the time of the violation, that he or she had been previously served with the injunction, that he or she was in fact associating within the safety zone with another person who was a gang member, and that he or she knew the other person was a gang member.

As noted above, a gang injunction binds the entire gang, including all of the gang's members. All of the injunctions currently in effect in the City of Los Angeles started with a lawsuit that named the gang as a defendant. The resulting injunctions thus bind the gangs themselves, as well as all of the gang's members. It is a person's membership in the gang that places him or her in the category of persons to whom the injunction applies. Whether the individual was a party to the proceedings in which the injunction was sought is not relevant; what is relevant is the issue of the defendant's gang membership.

STEP 10: ENFORCE AND MAINTAIN THE ORDER, EDUCATE THE POLICE AND COMMUNITY

If the gang injunction is implemented and enforced, the gangs have less control over the people and give some other segments of society and public policy higher odds of success. Gang injunctions usually target areas that display characteristics that make the joining of gangs more likely—the neighborhoods that are conducive to gang membership, tolerant of the gangs, and help in the formation of gangs. By focusing on areas that have higher concentrations of gang members and crime, law enforcement may be more productive by being responsive to the needs and concerns of the community. It is important to realize that the success of any injunction lies in the officers working the street and their continuous enforcement efforts throughout the period in which the injunction is in effect.

Once the prosecution makes a successful showing that the gang's activity constitutes a public nuisance, Civil Code Section 3494 authorizes "any public body or officer" to abate the nuisance. Proper enforcement of the order is perhaps the most important step of the ten discussed in this chapter. The enforcement and maintenance of a gang injunction requires time and vigilant attention to ongoing implementation, which can occur over many years. Approached correctly, the injunction can be a long-lasting tool that disrupts the gang's ability to conduct business and create a nuisance in the neighborhoods they once controlled. To increase the potential impact of a gang injunction having a corresponding impact on crime reduction, the order must be enforced and maintained to increase its shelf life or the length of its impact.

Depending upon the jurisdiction, a gang member can be issued a citation or booked in jail. Long Beach Assistant City Prosecutor Daniel Murphy said a "catch-and-release policy" at the county jail lessens the street-level effect of the injunctions, which prohibit assembly by specified gangs. Some prosecutors and police officers have made claims that the deterrent effect is lessened if those getting arrested do not serve a jail sentence. California Senate Bill 1217 treats criminal street gangs as public nuisance and provides for a mandatory minimum term of 10 days' confinement in jail for any person who is in violation of any injunction against the criminal street gang.

The issue of maintenance and enforcement is the key; the fact that gang injunctions aren't enforced uniformly makes evaluating gang injunction effectiveness a difficult task. Police officers use discretion when deciding whether to make arrests for injunction violations. Some gang members on the injunction lists have been caught but charged with more serious crimes, rendering a contempt of court allegation an overlooked lesser offense. Some police say they get more mileage from the gang injunctions by using them as a negotiating tool to gain information on the streets. Such information can help officers connect gang members to each other, find out what battles are heating up, and even solve murders.

Participants in the police survey were asked what is done in their jurisdiction as far as maintenance and enforcement goes. They were also asked to add any information that they believed was relevant to the study that was not addressed in the survey, and to add any comments, suggestions, recommendations, or information relating to injunctions they feel would be important for the law enforcement community to know.

The successful implementation of a gang injunction requires constant vigilance in the target area; no violation should be ignored. To enforce and maintain the order, police must first be aware of the presence and conditions of the order. In San Diego County, the district attorney routinely attends the police training and roll calls to discuss the gang injunction with officers. The Narcotics Information Network prepared a comprehensive brochure for 14 of the San Diego County injunctions in 2007 that includes a map of the target area and photographs of each named defendant to help law enforcement officers enforce the orders. Prosecutors explain how the injunctions are obtained, what the role of the police is, what an injunction violation is, how to make an arrest for an injunction violation, how to write the report, where to file it, and what California Department of Justice outcome the prosecutors are seeking.

The Department of Justice conducts workshops sponsored by the California District Attorneys Association and the State Department of Justice that educate officers about gang injunctions and encourage participation in the enforcement process. They educate officers on the importance of enforcing the order, how to properly document a violation of the order, and how to aggressively enforce the order so the message being sent to the gang is that the police are serious and so is the gang injunction. Again, consistent and aggressive enforcement is critical for evaluating and ensuring effectiveness.

4

Literature and Policy

This chapter reviews the existing research and literature, which potentially provides the theoretical support for using injunctions and gang abatement to combat gangs and reviews the literature that makes specific predictions regarding gang injunction efficacy. In reviewing the literature, it is clear that using civil laws against gangs can be very controversial and brings up issues like racism, community involvement, and constitutional issues. My review has been arranged within eight categories that I feel are the most debated, most controversial, and often most misunderstood. By reviewing the existing work in the field, I also selected the methodological and measurement methods used in Chapters 7–9, including how to measure crime and gang injunction and abatement.

To understand what has been undertaken and formulate policy recommendations to make future injunctions more effective, it is critically important to understand the historical and legal progression of the existing gang injunctions. Discussing where injunctions have been implemented or attempted and identifying major injunction cases that have established precedence and existing case law in the arena of civil gang abatement is important to truly understand gang injunctions.

Although media accounts of injunctions are not empirical evidence that gang injunctions do or do not work, the media has fueled community support or skepticism about specific injunctions, and has provided details relating to many of the injunction efforts statewide. The injunctions to date have had varying degrees of effectiveness, and the results of the individual injunctions may help understand the true benefits or risks associated with gang injunctions. Gang injunctions have a clearly demonstrable positive effect on some neighborhoods; some have even had a remarkable impact.

The historical progression of injunctions highlights early skepticism about the legality of the tactic, current concerns, the denial and dismissal of some injunctions by several courts, the upholding and affirmation of the majority of cases by the courts, the formation of case law, variations in the size of injunction target areas and number of targeted gang members, varying methods of obtaining injunctions, and other relevant events in history that have changed how current injunctions impact the community.

The use of public nuisance law to obtain gang injunctions and fight gang-related problems stemmed from the shortcomings of law enforcement tools available to abate gang violence. To explain these shortcomings and make sense of the progression in a logical fashion, Chapters 11, 12, 13, and 14 were compiled in chronological order by the year in which the injunction was filed. This is important to establish the progression of injunctions and Chapter 17 does from a legal and practical perspective because case law builds upon other cases that came before them. The expanded use of gang injunctions in recent years causes some academics and elected officials concern, as the lack of independent, scholarly evaluation of the effect of injunctions has not been conducted prior to their accelerated use. This overview will also address the studies that have been undertaken to study gang injunction effectiveness. The eight categories of literature may help understand and explain the impact of gang injunction and gang abatement effectiveness. The issues or categories include police response, other enforcement conducted in connection with the injunction, the type of gang, the type of activity that the gang engages in, the type of area or target location, the type of community, the type of order, and the enforcement of the orders.

CATEGORY 1: POLICE RESPONSE

Every known law enforcement technique, policy, or tactic to date is impacted by how the police respond or fail to respond to it. It is believed the more willing the police are to enforce a particular gang injunction, and the more the police are encouraged to exercise their discretion in favor of making an arrest for an injunction violation, the greater the potential impact the injunction will have. Officers that enforce the injunctions in their jurisdictions may make their injunctions more effective in reducing crime, with the opposite being true in areas where little or no enforcement is done.

Police officers have broad discretion in making arrests and selecting which laws and codes they feel are more worthy of police attention. This is especially true when dealing with misdemeanor crimes that typically do not mandate police action. As such, officers can choose a number of possible courses of action in any given situation.

Encouraging enforcement of a particular gang injunction, or assigning officers that feel the gang injunction effort is a worthwhile venture to enforce the orders, may well increase the effectiveness of the injunction against the gang, making it more successful. Most of the failed or ineffective injunctions to date are due to a partial or total lack of enforcement of the injunction by the police responsible for patrolling the area subjected to the injunction.

In essence, the police typically dictate the success, or lack of success, of any gang injunction. The injunction is as effective as the police want it to be in most cases, assuming they selected the correct gang, the correct gang members, served the orders, and aggressively enforced the injunction. A willing police force can make the injunction a useful tool to reduce gang activity by dedicating themselves to identifying, locating, and serving the problem gang members.

The reality is even if the police have the time to respond to a gang injunction violation, have proper staffing, and know of the injunction's existence, if they do not feel that the injunction is worthwhile, they will not be prone to take any enforcement action. For that reason many gang injunctions seek out a motivated prosecutor and motivated police officer at the onset of the injunction that are tasked with ensuring the police are responsive to the injunction and will encourage officers to take action when violations occur. Law enforcement's commitment to the project is likely the key category in the context of whether a gang injunction will or will not be effective.

Akers (1991) proposed that criminality occurs when a criminal act is more reinforcing than punishing. Police that are unwilling or unable to enforce the gang injunction inadvertently or purposefully make injunctions less effective, as the gang members observe the lack of enforcement and are subsequently more likely to choose to violate the gang injunction. The lack of enforcement of a gang injunction violation may also help facilitate material reinforcement for gang members, like money or drugs, or social reinforcement like gang acceptance. If the injunction does not bring about social punishment that outweighs these reinforcements, the injunction will not be effective.

Targeting gangs typically requires a comprehensive understanding of the key players in the local gang, who the leaders are, and how the members are linked and interact with each other. In order to prevent gang crime, you need to understand crime, and the criminal mind. When you think of criminal gang members, think of predators. When you think of predators, you might think of a pack of wild dogs. When the dogs are hungry, they will go out to stalk their prey. The dogs know the watering hole is a good place to find food, because this is where all the animals go to get water. The dogs are skilled hunters; they know the best approach is downwind, so they can track their prey without revealing their location. At just the right moment, the dogs pounce on their victims. They do not run past the injured, the diseased, or slowest ones in favor of the strongest one at the lead of the pack. In fact, it usually is the one that is injured, sick, or simply not paying attention that gets attacked. This is called survival of the fittest or thinning the herd.

The two-legged urban breed of predator, the gang member, works the same way. He or she stalks his or her victims, looking for the easy prey. To be successful against an attack, you do not necessarily have to be the strongest one, but you certainly do not want to be the weakest. One way the police can help is to identify the locations where the gang members, or wild dogs as described above, like to go to find victims, and do what we can to keep the gang members away from those locations to protect the community.

Gang enforcement usually requires significant time, energy, money, and resources to be effective. It is reasonable to believe that gang enforcement operations that are not driven by willing and motivated police officers who conduct proper analysis will not be successful. Unwilling police officers likely do not understand the nature and extent of the gang problem and are probably not as committed to addressing gang crime when compared to motivated officers.

In other areas the police may be willing to enforce the gang injunction, but the prosecution is unwilling or unable to work the case due to their lack of resources. "There's only one deputy district attorney assigned to gang injunctions, and there are four other cities trying to get these things," according to an Oceanside police officer working the Posole injunction. "We try to time it so the district attorney is ready for us." The success or failure of a particular injunction requires a partnership between the police and prosecution to coordinate resources and work together to target the gang effectively.

Some of the unwillingness on the part of the police or prosecution may be due to political or legal concerns. A city's political environment may also affect how the police operate and how successful the level of reform attributed to a gang injunction may be. Both denial of gang problems and overreaction to them can be detrimental to the development and use of gang injunctions. Denial that gang problems exist precludes early intervention efforts and results in gang injunctions not being implemented. On the other hand, some feel that gang injunctions are an overreaction to a local gang problem in the form of excessive police force and are not warranted.

Some feel the gang injunction actually helps the gang by publicizing that the target gang is a problem significant enough to warrant a gang injunction against them, which may inadvertently serve to increase a gang's reputation and cohesion, facilitating the gang's expansion and ultimately leading to more gang crime. Others feel the gangs expand just fine as the result of the police doing nothing, and seeking a gang injunction is better than letting the gang have free rein of the target area.

Other times police agencies are unwilling to seek injunctions because of the controversy relating to the legal and ethical implications of the use of injunctions. Regardless of perceptions, few constitutional rights are absolute. Some police administrators, however, do not agree personally with the concept of an injunction and do not allow injunctions to be sought in their jurisdictions. The compelling state interest in limiting liberties is typically balanced against the right of an individual or a group to engage in certain activity. Gang injunction supporters claim it is a fallacy that somehow we all benefit by protecting the rights of gang members to associate freely and terrorize our communities. Critics of injunctions believe society benefits when the rights of all are protected from being trampled and denied by a few. The legal game is too deadly, the stakes are too high, and the price is too dear to ignore this basic truth. Injunction supporters often feel that a city's unwillingness to take action based upon legal concerns is misguided, and policy makers are doing their citizens an injustice by being more concerned with political concerns or the city's image than targeting the local gang.

To be most effective, police must understand the mechanisms through which their responses to problems can be expected to be effective. Historically, much policing has focused on the principles of deterrence, anticipating that quickly responding to calls for service and follow-up investigations would result in the detection of many offenders and deter would-be offenders from engaging in crime. Of course, research in the 1970s showed that such practices were not very effective in reducing crime. Police have increasingly recognized the limitations of deterrence when applied to gang problems. However, heightened police presence and the increased threat of sanctions—when narrowly focused on particular problems, problem locations, or types of offenders—have achieved reductions in gang-related crime.

Police Response Time

A quick response to a call for service or police officer observation of a potential gang injunction violation may mean less crime than a slow or no response, which may mean more crime for the target area. Due to the number of calls that most police agencies must address on a daily basis, police typically operate on a guarded response policy where police officers respond to the most urgent calls as quickly as possible. Incidents that require the quickest response tend to be in-progress felonies or serious life-threatening emergencies, like serious car accidents or structure fires, and other incidents classified as having an immediate response. From the most extreme level, other incidents are handled based upon what the department feels the appropriate response time should be based upon the available resources in the particular jurisdiction.

Response time may be an indicator of how important the gang injunction is to the police department. A gang injunction violation that is seen as an important call for service or critical self-initiated activity that has an aggressive response may mean greater effectiveness. On the other hand, viewing a gang injunction violation as a low-priority call that may not get dispatched for hours, or if the injunction is not enforced at all, may result in less effective results. Beccaria (1764) asserted that punishment needs to be certain, swift, and severe if it is to be effective, meaning an injunction that is enforced is more effective in theory.

The punishment for violating a gang injunction is often not certain, as police response varies based upon police willingness. The justice system is not always swift due to the high volume of calls for service and limited police resources, and the punishment is not considered severe by most gang members when comparing an injunction violation to other crimes.

Hence, by ensuring that gang injunction violations are swiftly addressed, or mandate a quick priority response, we increase the chance of detection of the gang members in the progress of violating the orders. This allows the police to arrest and the courts to dispense sufficient pain to each offender so that there are both specific (i.e., the particular offender will never choose to break the law again) and general (other potential criminals, observing the punishment of the one offender, are deterred from following in his or her footsteps) deterrences in place.

Combating gangs requires allocation of sufficient time, money, staffing, and other resources to address the problem. Resources do, however, have limits; law enforcement does not have an endless pool of money and resources to draw from. Some of the larger police departments across the country have formed specialized gang units to accomplish the task of gang enforcement, targeting the gangs committing crimes while also attempting to discourage future gang crimes. Gang enforcement, more so than some other types of criminal investigations, requires significant cooperation, collaboration, and coordination among all levels of law enforcement and the community to be successful.

The community in some areas is pleading with law enforcement for help. Yet law enforcement is faced with an increasingly frustrating and demoralizing dilemma. Each time they attempt a creative and innovative approach, whether through new criminal legislation or existing avenues of civil injunctions and other remedies, they find themselves confronted with the accusation that they are acting without regard for the legitimate constitutional rights of gang members.

Extended response times may result in missed opportunities for an arrest as the groups may disband prior to police arrival. Also, community members will see the failure to respond in a timely manner and lose confidence in the police, sending a message to some in the community that the police and prosecution are not concerned about the issues, which may have a corresponding increase in community members' failure to get involved and help the police solve gang crimes committed in the target area. Some feel that police response times are intentionally discriminatory, and that nonenforcement of the law, such as the failure to respond quickly to calls in low-income areas, is an intentional act.

Failure to respond to gang injunction violations can reinforce the community perception that the police do not care and hinder the effectiveness of the gang injunction. To have an increased impact on gang injunction effectiveness, some police jurisdictions shift resources into the gang injunction areas for a period of time to increase the police presence, which typically benefits the injunction area. This reallocation of resources from surrounding communities leaves them less protection, which may result in a reduction of crime in the injunction area and may have a corresponding rise in crime in the surrounding area. Arguably, doing nothing is no better; the risk of potentially empowering the local gang is a lesser evil than letting them operate with impunity as they feel immune from police action.

CATEGORY 2: OTHER ENFORCEMENT THAT IMPACTED RESULTS

Gang injunctions that are part of a larger plan or strategy against the local gang may have more of an impact in the target area. The theory is that the more operations that are simultaneously conducted against the gang, the more effective the injunction may be, resulting in less gang crime. It may not be so much that the injunction is more effective, but it is the effectiveness of the simultaneous program or project that may be benefiting the same target area at the same time, compounding the effectiveness of both the injunction and the other program. Caution is suggested to not expect too much of any one remedy because no single remedy will cure the gang problem; a mix of reforms is typically required for effective results.

Some feel that gang injunctions are or can be a useful police tactic, but because they fail to help break the constant cycle of youths joining gangs they are not effective. Suppression techniques like gang injunctions often fail to address the underlying causes of gangs and gang violence, and some argue that is not their primary purpose. The purpose of an injunction is to lessen or remove the gang from the community, subsequently giving the community the opportunity to improve itself without having to contend with intense gang activity.

Some experts feel that injunctions coupled with other tools for controlling gang activity, such as situational crime prevention, crime prevention through environmental design, crime-free multihousing programs, antiloitering statutes, traffic checkpoints, aggressive truancy and curfew enforcement, and a crackdown on weapons and drug violations, may be more effective. Gang crimes are often more dangerous than other crimes because they are not isolated acts, but links in a chain of events that must be broken. Gang injunctions seek to break the links in the chain by targeting the specific activities of specific members of the targeted gang, making it more difficult for them to commit their crimes within the specified target area.

When evaluating the research, it became apparent that many of the criticisms of gang injunctions are not actually criticisms related to gang injunctions; they are criticisms and concerns about the lack of social programs in the communities targeted with gang injunctions. Gang injunctions do not help people get jobs, and they do not give kids an avenue to engage in productive activities; they don't solve the gang problem. According to San Diego Deputy District Attorney Susan Mazza, there isn't any silver bullet to stop gangs. District Attorney Mazza agrees that to reduce the gang problem, you have to work on all aspects of the problem: it's the poverty, it's the drugs, it's the broken-down family relationships. Gang injunctions may make it more difficult for gang members to sell drugs in the target area, but it is the failure of our society that creates the need for the gang members to sell the drugs in the first place.

Dr. George Tita at the University of California–Irvine analyzes gang violence reduction strategies; Dr. Tita contends that gang injunctions do lower crime. Tita indicates we need both the carrot and the stick to get kids to move away from violence. An injunction is one form of stick that works, at least in the short term. If the injunction is the stick, social programs, job training, and substance abuse counseling are examples of carrots. For example, other sticks or enforcement operations may include undercover narcotics operations, wire taps, street sweeps of gang members, probation and parole operations, and increased zero tolerance patrol.

Many injunctions have been identified as standalone police tactics, not affiliated with any larger program or any organized multiprong effort. This standalone response may potentially make these tactics less effective when compared to those that are part of a larger plan. It can't just be suppression; there's got to be a balanced approach, enforcement alone is a Band-Aid solution. Injunctions are sometimes sought to disperse the heavy presence of gang members in order to pave the way for social programs, and by making the community feel safer to take advantage of some of the existing programs that do not get fully utilized due to the gang activity. Some people feel that gang injunctions can be an effective policing tool for restoring once peaceful neighborhoods, but only when aggressively enforced and when combined with other methods of law enforcement (Cruz, 2006).

A good example of using an injunction in connection with other enforcement operations occurred in October 2009. More than 1,000 police officers and federal agents executed dozens of arrest and search warrants in which members of the Rolling 40's injunction were targeted in an operation called 40 Ounces to Freedom. Seventy-four members of the gang were charged in 23 federal indictments. Forty-five state warrants were executed on the gang that operates within a three-square-mile area of Los Angeles. The Los Angeles Police Department has identified this gang as one of the ten most violent in the city of Los Angeles. The Los Angeles County City Attorney's Office has brought parallel civil actions as part of this investigation. These include five nuisance abatement lawsuits against six separate properties being used by gang members to conduct criminal activity, including drug transactions and illegal weapon storage. For each abatement, the city attorney's office sought an injunction against the owner mandating various improvements, orders to stay away from gang members named as defendants in the lawsuits, civil penalties, and additional fees. The city attorney's office notified property owners that, by law, tenants conducting illegal drug activity must be evicted. A permanent injunction was filed against the gang in 2008.

Some feel that policing that involves only enforcement will solidify the gangs, increasing cohesion among gang members, and making them stronger (Decker, 2000). Some feel that injunctions work best when combined with nonenforcement activities, such as providing economic opportunities to gang members, job training programs, educating parents about gangs, and remedial education and community involvement.

Father Greg Boyle feels that injunctions benefit the gang members themselves, "I mean, eight minutes after one was filed here on the Eastside, I had kids in my office saying, 'Get me a job.' " At its best, Father Boyle says an injunction creates a kind of vigilant heat that moves kids toward the light and away from the gang. To make this possible, some injunctions take great care to not restrict gang members from utilizing services in the gang injunction area if they are included in the gang injunction. For example, in the Harpy's injunction the court order carved out certain times and places when and where the defendants could associate, including the Youth Empowerment Project and facilities of other groups that help young people, without being in violation of the injunction.

The youth project in the Harpy's injunction target area expressed dismay when they heard about the injunction because the order impacted about 20 of its employees and other gang members who used its services. About ten of the Harpy's members named in the injunction were connected to the project according to the project's administrator, Mark Wilson. He said Harpy's members who come into the organization's center indicate they want to change their lives and the facility attempts to help them accomplish that goal. "I'm happy the judge included language which exempts our project from the injunction" (*People v. Harpy's Gang*, 1998).

One stated goal of gang injunctions is to reduce the flagrant gang activity around anti-gang programs like those listed above. By decreasing the visible presence of gang members in close proximity to the anti-gang program facilities, the programs are helped in accomplishing their mission of reducing gang membership without active gang members hindering their efforts. The Mar Vista Family Center on Slauson Avenue, which employs two Culver City Boys members and has helped find jobs for several others, was not included in the injunction, in order to encourage Culver City Boys to take part in the anti-gang programs (*People v. Culver City Boys*, 1999).

Programs to help gang members do exist; sometimes gang members just need to make the choice to participate in the programs and set aside the perception held by many gang members that it is not acceptable for them to use the programs. Some gangs actively discourage their members from attending programs and take it as an insult that someone is trying to learn how to leave the gang. Akers and Burgess (1966) discussed a social learning theory to explain deviancy by combining variables that encouraged delinquency, like social pressure from delinquent peers, with variables that discouraged delinquency, like parental response to discovering delinquency in their children.

Another popular tactic typically used against gangs is gang sweeps of a specific area. These sweeps are intended to provide at least temporary relief to neighborhoods suffering from intense gang and drug activity. These sweeps can neutralize a gang by targeting the gang's leadership, and they are seen as a proactive way to catch the gang off guard by saturating an area that typically sees only an occasional police presence. A sweep can have a psychological impact on the gang, as they see a saturation of police officers in their home territory. The more arrests and contacts conducted in a sweep, the greater impact it will have on the group as a whole.

However, the impact of a successful sweep is usually measured in terms of weeks or months; a gang injunction's impact is typically measured in years. Curfew sweeps and truancy sweeps are also effective against street gangs and have been proven to safeguard the community and lower crime rates during school and evening hours when the gangs are most active. To help ensure that criminal activity does not reassert its dominance after a high-profile sweep, agencies typically maintain an intense patrol presence in the area for several weeks following the sweep to make sure the problem stays at a manageable level.

To help increase young people's economic status and help ensure their success, gang injunctions may help by adding limits and rules for the individual gang members to help keep them law abiding, out of the gang area, and out of prison. Gangs form in response to a lack of legitimate free-time activities for neighborhood youth. For most youths, family, school, and faith institutions offer an array of legitimate activities, enough to keep most children so busy they have no time to hang out. Keeping a potential or current gang member occupied so they have no free time to get involved in criminal activity is a common way to reduce incidents of gang violence. Recreational programs such as sports, music, drama, and community activities help build a sense of self-worth and self-respect in young people.

Failing to respond to areas that are under a heavy burden of gang violence reduces the positive impact social programs in the area may have, because people may be less likely to utilize the programs and services if they do not feel safe doing so. By removing gang members from public view, in theory the police deter lawless residents from committing future crimes and make neighborhoods safer for law-abiding residents.

CATEGORY 3: TYPE OF GANG

The size of the gang selected for an injunction may impact the effectiveness of the gang injunction. Cloward and Ohlin (1960) developed the differential opportunity theory, which identified several types of gangs. Some gangs share similar characteristics, they also differ in some ways, to include their size and territoriality.

Not every gang would make a good candidate for a gang injunction. The structure of gangs in California varies depending primarily on size. The gangs range in size from 5 or 10 to several thousand members, which often causes some of the larger gangs to break up into smaller groups, called cliques or subsets. Smaller gangs are perceived as being better targets of gang injunctions because they are easier to manage, it is easier to identify the problem members, and they typically control a smaller, more controlled target area. The larger the gang, typically the greater the time and labor required to conduct the necessary analysis and prepare the case for court, including selecting the members to be targeted, identifying the target area borders, and collecting the necessary evidence. Others feel that the true size of any gang may be difficult to determine and officers should focus more on the activity committed by the group rather than their numbers.

For example, in August 1994 the Orange Street Locos (OSL) gang was targeted with an injunction. With only 55 active members, according to police databases, OSL was the smallest of Norwalk's five Latino gangs. But despite their size, they gave sheriff's deputies more trouble and committed more violent crimes than gangs twice their size.

Percentage of the Overall Gang Targeted with Injunction

There are reasons to believe that regardless of the overall size of the enjoined gang, whether 50 or 500 members, the percentage of the total gang's membership served with the injunction is a potentially more important category that impacts gang injunction effectiveness than the overall size of the gang. It is logical to assume that serving 50 members of a gang with 75 total members may be more effective than serving 50 members of a gang with 500 total members. This is true because a greater percentage of the gang's membership is restricted by the injunction, making it more difficult for the gang to adapt and respond to the order by having members not included in the injunction do the bidding of the gang in the target area, as opposed to those named or served with the order.

The reason why gang injunctions cause concern for gang members is that they can go to jail simply for being with a fellow gang member; the police do not need to catch them in the act of committing a crime—they simply cannot be with their fellow gang members. Research shows us that gang members are criminals that tend to commit crimes together as groups, and they seem to feel more powerful as a group, as they know that they are more intimidating when they associate together. Reducing the potential size of the total group available to commit crimes in public view in the target area may result in a corresponding drop in crime in the target area.

There may be reasons to believe that adding more members to an injunction simply to increase the numbers may reduce gang injunction effectiveness, and this is the cause of many of the legal challenges against the policy. Gang members that do not have the gang documentation, police contacts, and criminal activity that warrant their inclusion in the order typically make poor candidates for injunctions, and this weakens the overall strength of the case. For example, if only 50 members of a 500-member gang have enough activity to justify being included, then adding more will only weaken the overall case.

Basically a gang injunction is like a chain, it is only as strong as its weakest link. Any gang injunction is only as strong as the activity of the weakest named member will justify. This brings up the issue of selecting the proper gang and members for the injunction. A gang with 75 total members that has 50 very active and violent members may well be a better target of an injunction than a gang with 500 members that do not have significant nuisance activity attributed to the specific members to be targeted.

Targeting Gang Leaders

Targeting gang leaders, making it more difficult for them to enter the target area to direct and control the gang's activity, may have a corresponding impact on the overall membership of the gang. Targeting leaders quickly alerts the entire gang to the presence of the gang injunction, as the communication in gangs is often from the top down, or from the leaders and hard-core members to the general members and associates. It is acknowledged that injunctions cannot address the problems an entire gangs poses in any community; however, attempting to stifle the gang by choosing a select few members may convey more benefit.

The level the targeted gang member holds in the gang needs to be established as part of the evidence collection phase to support the gang injunction, or will need to be explained following an arrest for an injunction violation (Huff, 1998). A gang leader is a gang member that has the power to direct the gang's activity, whether he is involved or not, making him a more important target than a general member. If the leaders have a hard time meeting with the drug dealers and street soldiers that work for them, their ability to lead the gang may be hindered, which may result in increased injunction effectiveness.

Gang leaders often distance themselves from the street gang activities, making it a widely accepted practice to balance the inclusion of leaders along with hard-core and general members of the gang to address the serious and nuisance activity committed by the group.

General members are the most active problem on the streets and typically commit the bulk of gang-related crimes in any community; targeting general members will make the injunction more effective. General members are more likely to be the ones marking buildings with graffiti, stealing cars, committing robberies, and shooting and stabbing rivals to keep their turf. It is the general membership of most gangs that confront the unknown by asking, "Where are you from?"

That is a benign enough statement that most of us would consider a standard question of someone we just met. That same seemingly innocent question in the gang world is probably the single most problematic question a gang member can ask. In most cases, when a group of gang members approach someone and ask, "Where are you from?" they have a fairly good idea that the person is not with them and they are confronting or identifying the unknown person or persons with the intent to cause harm to them on contact. That question is typically followed by a violent act, as the people asking the question do not like the answer or those being asked do not like the question.

Territoriality of the Gang

Each ethnic gang has different degrees of territoriality, which may be a factor in gang injunction effectiveness. Because gangs frequently organize along ethnic lines, that is, by racial, national, linguistic, and cultural background, this researcher classifies gangs primarily by the gangs' ethnicity, primarily Hispanic, African American, Asian, and Caucasian. A territorial gang may be impacted more significantly by a gang injunction than a gang that is not beholden to a geographic area, making territoriality a key prerequisite of an effective gang injunction.

In Southern California, the most territorial gangs tend to be Hispanic and African American ethnic gangs, with some exceptions. The further analysis section of Chapter 8 will evaluate ethnic differences in gang injunctions to evaluate any issues relating to gang injunction effectiveness.

Both Asian and Caucasian gangs do exist and pose tremendous problems for law enforcement; in some jurisdictions they make up the bulk of the gang problem. However, they tend to be more mobile and do not have easily defined territorial boundaries, which makes targeting them with an injunction more difficult. Exceptions exist, and as time goes on some Asian and Caucasian gangs are becoming more territorial and some may be, or may become, viable targets for future injunctions. In some cases Asian and Caucasian concerns for protecting a turf from rivals take a back seat to their primary motivations, such as for-profit crimes or promoting their hate agenda, making them a less viable target of a gang injunction.

Gangs that do not have an identifiable stronghold on any particular community, that are transitory and motivated more by economic gain and less by turf and territorial issues, typically make poor candidates for gang injunctions. Failing to address the issue early in the injunction process will make it difficult for law enforcement to gather evidence and successfully illustrate to the court that the target gang poses a credible threat to the community to a significant enough degree to be considered a public nuisance in the target area. A mobile gang may be better suited for other types of law enforcement action, such as undercover operations or electronic surveillance.

One of the earliest gang injunctions sought attempted to include the entire city of Los Angeles as the target area, which by all accounts is considered too vague and needs to be better defined and supported by evidence of the gang's presence in the area (*People v. Playboy Gangster Crips*, 1987).

CATEGORY 4: TYPE OF ACTIVITY

The more serious the gang crime preinjunction, the greater may be the effectiveness of the injunction when compared to an area without serious gang-related crime. In areas where the gang engages in public acts of violence, gang intimidation, and the public congregation that leads to shootings, stabbings, assaults, and rapes, the injunction may be more effective, as opposed to areas where gangs primarily engage in petty offenses. The type of activity that the target gang engages in is widely accepted as being a category when evaluating gang injunction effectiveness. If a gang is involved in identity theft, for example, an injunction would have little impact because the gang does not need to congregate in public view to conduct that crime and the crime can be conducted in any jurisdiction and is not tied to any geographic area.

Citizens that live in the target area do not care when the shooting starts; if the enjoined gang is doing the shooting or being shot at, the community is no more or no less in danger as a result of the presence of the gang. If the gang members are not allowed to congregate on a street corner, throw gang signs, and wear clothing known to police and gang rivals as being associated with the particular gang, they are significantly less likely to become victims of a serious crime. When any number of the rivals enter the safety zone, seeking out the enjoined gang's members to shoot at, stab, or beat up, and cannot find any, the likelihood of a crime occurring is significantly less. That corresponds to a safer community for the residents as well as for the gang members themselves.

Stopping petty offenses is a key factor, as sometimes the petty crimes lead to violent crimes and should be addressed with the same vigor as petty quality of life offenses. Kenneth Bell, a Crenshaw Mafia gang member, in several police declarations was described as regularly loitering and drinking in public. Bell maintained his only fault is he drinks; when he comes home from work he likes to drink beer in front of his apartment (*People v. Crenshaw Mafia*, 1996).

Kenneth Bell and hundreds of gang members like him argue that much of the activity they engage in is petty and harmless.

However, in situations like Bell standing in front of his apartment drinking a beer, when a rival gang member comes into their territory, it is a sign of serious disrespect that sometimes is dealt with in a violent manner by the local gang.

Even if Bell does not react to the rivals, if the rivals see Bell and recognize him, they may decide to shoot at him, the bullets may or may not hit Bell, or they may hit any number of other people in the apartments. We know gangs enter their rival's neighborhood to deface graffiti by crossing out names, sell dope, recruit new members, disrespect the other gang, or for personal reasons, making the removal of gang members from public view a potentially viable solution to reduce gang violence.

Is the Crime Collective or Individual?

Gangs that have members that primarily commit crimes as individuals may be less effective than gangs that commit crimes primarily as groups. Common suppression strategies against gangs are often believed ineffective because of their reliance on criminal law, which applies equally to all citizens and at all locations, and usually necessitates a showing of individual participation or involvement by each individual person. While there may be variations in the prosecution of criminal laws from one jurisdiction to the other, the individual culpability requirement allows fewer opportunities to attack the group characteristics applicable to street gang activity, in particular the tendency of gangs to act as a group rather than individuals when committing their crimes.

In contrast, because injunctions rely on civil laws that tend to focus more on protecting the community and less on criminal violations, gang injunctions may be well suited to address gang group dynamics and may have better chances of disrupting the entire gang's activity in the designated areas. Gang injunctions attempt to reduce the criminal activity that has its impetus in the group's influence and impact on the individual member. Crimes committed by individual gang members typically benefit the group as a whole, making the group dynamic a primary focus of a gang injunction effort.

The more group crime committed by the target gang, the greater the injunction's impact may be. Akers' differential reinforcement theory integrated differential association and the learning theory of operant conditioning. Operant conditioning argues that behavior is controlled by the consequences of that behavior. If behavior is controlled by consequences, then the gang injunction would tend to be effective if properly enforced, in that it adds additional consequences to violations that would otherwise in most circumstances go unaddressed or may not be a violation of the law to those not included in the civil lawsuit. Edwin Sutherland (1978) proposed a differential association theory that indicates behavior is learned from interactions with other persons. Thus it is hypothesized that individuals will lean toward or away from crime according to the norms and beliefs of their associates.

This hypothesis is substantiated by the literature, indicating that criminal attitudes and associates are two of the most significant correlates of criminal conduct. The single most debated legal issue, and often most controversial provision in any gang injunction, is the no association restriction. Disrupting gang association may well help to prevent future offenses by gang members. Public crimes create an environment that fosters potential violent clashes between the local gang and rivals that innocent passersby might get caught up in.

The gang injunction allows the police to impact several dimensions of the gang's behavior, by potentially impacting the frequency, duration, and intensity of the gang's association. If the gang has less time to spend together in public view, they will have less opportunities to commit crime, due in large part to the increased police presence and added authority granted to the police, allowing them to contact and arrest the gang's members for the injunction violation, as opposed to having to wait for a more serious crime to occur.

CATEGORY 5: TARGET AREA CHARACTERISTICS

Keeping the target areas manageable in size may allow for a greater level of effectiveness than injunctions that encompass larger, more difficult to control areas. The impact of smaller target areas in most cases makes the evidence collection a manageable task. Police use major streets, freeways, rail lines, and other significant borders to make the identification of the target area by both the police and the gang members more easily understood. Some gang injunction target areas are selected based upon existing crime reporting districts to better analyze the impact of the injunction at a later time.

That may make gathering crime statistics a bit easier, but gang territories do not always fall neatly in line with police reporting or jurisdictional lines. Even if it is more work on the front end to gather statistics across several reporting districts or even different police jurisdictions, a more accurate definition of the gang's territory should be a priority in each gang injunction case. It is important to include as much of the gang's turf as possible when supported by crime statistics, calls for service data, or other reliable sources.

On the other hand, not making the area large enough may result in the gang members simply hanging out just beyond the target area, just out of the reach of the police. For example, the Pasadena Denver Lanes gang reportedly shifted from their target area into a nearby housing project, a park, and a strip mall located adjacent to the target area immediately after being served. Unlike other cities, where highly territorial gangs live in very clearly marked neighborhoods, in Pasadena, gang members live throughout the city.

Pasadena police memos noted the gang shifted specifically to avoid the injunction. "Injunctions sound good but gangs have ways of getting around them," according to one 18th Street gang member interviewed by the media. "Gang members laugh at them," according to an 18th Street Pico Union gang member, "and those who are named in the injunctions just move to another place." The reported movement of the gang listed above tends to indicate that the gang took the injunction as a serious enough issue that they modified their turf and activity as a result of the injunction.

Some gangs are not tightly organized and do not control well-established turf, making it more difficult for police to identify gang members, build up a list of the gang's illegal activities, and then go to court for a civil injunction. Santa Maria Police say city gangs are too loosely associated to be affected by a gang injunction, such as the one recently adopted in Lompoc. Santa Maria gangs are less territorial and spread more throughout the city than the typical turf-based gangs, and thus would be largely immune from an injunction. Pasadena and Lompoc, like the other injunction cities, have not studied the issue of gang displacement in any systematic way. But police observations in several jurisdictions suggest how quickly some of the gangs targeted with injunctions have adapted.

No longer do jurisdictional gang maps feature well-defined gang territories outlined in detail. Because the gangs have been moving so much, now police in some jurisdictions track them with pushpins in the map on a wall. Pasadena police reported, "They know we can't do much outside the injunction area. Before the injunctions, they all were hanging out in the same place. Now that they can't hang out there, you don't know where they are. They're all over, and you can't keep track of them." Such frustrations fuel skepticism of the use of gang injunctions. However, having the gang all congregating in one place does not appear to be much better and results in high concentrations of crime as the group is better able to congregate in large numbers without any recourse. This researcher cautions that injunctions typically only work against territorial gangs, whose members won't, or are less likely to, carry on their activities outside their own neighborhoods out of fear of other gangs that control those areas.

The bigger the area the better from a police perspective. The largest gang injunction area to date is approximately 9 square miles (*People v. Avenues*, 2002). The bigger area may make it more difficult for gangs to simply shift their activities within their recognized gang turf. If the gang is not restricted in all areas of their identified turf, they may adapt to the increased enforcement without having to move from the comfort zone that their home turf affords them. The further analysis section of Chapter 8 compared injunction areas of more and less than 1 square mile to evaluate if any difference exists based on area size as the primary variable.

Percentage of Turf Enjoined and Displacement

The percentage of the overall enjoined territory may be a critical issue to evaluate effectiveness. The target area may be as small as a single apartment complex, one or two blocks, or the bulk of a particular city. Whatever the size of the area, incorporating the entire territory of the target gang, so long as it can be justified to the court and supported by the evidence, may increase effectiveness. Gang injunctions have been called ineffective and claims made that they simply move the crime problem from the gang injunction target area to a neighboring community where the restrictions do not apply.

Klein (1995) claimed that injunctions haven't been shown to solve crime but rather to just push it to other areas. The pushing of crime into a different area is commonly referred to as displacement. One's view of displacement likely varies depending upon where you live. If you live in the area where the gang members are displacing or moving from, your view is probably good riddance, as the quality of your life may well be improving. Examples of displacement due to injunction may include the Adelanto's Brown Pride gang (BPG) injunction from December 2009 in San Bernardino, in which police reports tend to show a few BPG members have been displaced, and are appearing in Victorville and San Bernardino.

In the context of gang injunctions, displacement may be a positive or negative result. Sometimes displacement is the desired effect; law enforcement wants the gang members to be put out of place. Gang injunctions target neighborhoods that typically have a well-entrenched gang presence in which typical law enforcement tactics have not proven to be effective in reducing the gang problem. Placing pressure on the local gang to the point where some members may feel committing their crimes elsewhere would give them a better chance of success may well increase the chance of arrest, as the gang member is out of his or her comfort zone and the new area may not be a neighborhood that has history of failing to act or failing to report crimes or suspicious activity. The new areas may not offer the gang member the same support base of friends and family that help him evade justice and cover up his criminal activity that he had in his previous neighborhood.

The reasons why some experts feel displacement is not a significant factor is because the displacement would typically require the gang members to move into rival gang areas. According to Los Angeles District Attorney Gil Garcetti, the injunctions don't simply move crime; faced with a court order, gang members either move their activities inside their homes or even discontinue them in some cases.

Some jurisdictions attempt to enjoin the entire turf of the targeted gang. Deputy District Attorney Steve Lopez stated that some of the Los Angeles injunctions cover the entire territory of the enjoined gang, making it difficult to displace within their own territory in an attempt to avoid the order. For displacement to happen, it would require encroachment into rival gang territory, which is easier said than done. Los Angeles City Attorney Jim McDougal said the injunction he obtained against the Harpy's gang has had a chilling effect on the Harpy's, because unlike other gangs, the Harpy's are locked into a single neighborhood and unable to expand geographically because of adjacent rival turf that is aggressively defended.

Despite the criticism from injunction opponents who say the effort only shifts gang activity from one neighborhood to another, the evidence is to the contrary. In essence, some gang injunctions do not remove or move the target gang from the area. They simply reduce the opportunities for the commission of crimes or target hardening in the target area, making it more difficult to break into houses and steal from shops, and encourage more responsibility and community involvement, which deter potential offenders and specific gang crimes.

On the other hand, there is criticism that better protecting one area will simply increase crime in the now less well-protected adjacent areas due to the shift of police resources, but the evidence is as yet equivocal on whether this occurs. If the injunction simply moves the problem to another area, then some police agencies assess the problem and may, in some cases, file another injunction against the gang in the new area, or modify the current order.

This method does have material value in keeping a single gang from dominating life in an otherwise peaceful neighborhood; however, it does not stop confrontations with rivals. To have an impact on gangs and gang injunction effectiveness, some police jurisdictions shift resources into the gang injunction areas and increase the police presence, which in some cases results in a reduction in crime in those areas. To accomplish this, some police departments pull resources from surrounding communities, leaving them less protected, which may well cause a corresponding rise in crime in one area to accomplish a drop in crime in the gang injunction area that has benefited from the increase in police resources. Arguably, doing nothing is no better. Some feel that targeting the gang with an injunction increases the risk of potentially empowering the local gang. Others feel that by doing nothing, the gang is more empowered by being allowed to operate with impunity, increasing their solidarity and cohesiveness as they feel immune from police action.

Not including an entire gang's turf may result in reduced effectiveness. Some injunctions do not consider the overall size of the gang's turf prior to undertaking the injunction effort; some focus only on that portion of the gang's turf that the crime data support as the most active section of the area. The gang turf may be a small area because the crime data may not support making the area larger when presented to a judge. For example, some injunctions focus on a large housing project as the primary target area, such as the Ramona Gardens housing project in Los Angeles, which is home to the Big Hazard gang; the Jordan Downs housing project in Los Angeles, which is home to the Grape Street Crips; the Nickerson Gardens housing project in Los Angeles, which is home to the Bounty Hunter Bloods in Los Angeles; the Meadowbrook Apartments in San Diego, which is home to the Skyline Piru; and the Bay Vista Apartments in San Diego, which is home to the Lincoln Park Bloods.

Economic Status of the Target Area

Street gang crime is a national problem; no neighborhood, street, sidewalk, or home is completely safe from the mayhem perpetrated by gangs that are trying to protect the turf where they carry out their organized criminal operations (Finn, 1994). In some neighborhoods, however, street gangs are clearly out of control despite the best efforts of traditional law enforcement, and we have reached the point where tough new remedies are needed to combat the problem.

Gang injunctions may or may not be more effective in poverty-stricken areas than in middle-class or affluent areas. Strain theorists believe the strain of living in dilapidated poverty-stricken areas is what causes youth to join gangs and commit crime. Society has defined the means for achieving success through hard work, education, and honesty; the gang subculture has defined the opposite to be true, and their lack of means to attain middle-class goals produces a strain called anomie, which is a social state where controls, limits, and rules are absent or removed from a community. The effects of poverty are more pronounced in the young and most disadvantaged of our society, and it is one of the greatest problems facing our society.

As a result of poverty, gangs form as a mechanism for earning money or obtaining goods and services not available in some cases through legitimate means. As gangs constantly seek to increase their own income, they tend to have the opposite impact on the surrounding community. Gangs in general retard economic growth, reduce property values, and discourage small business by constantly stealing from the corner store, extorting protection money for the privilege of operating a business on the gang's turf, and discouraging customers from coming to the area for fear of becoming a victim of gang crime.

The private possessor rights of private property are often substantially impaired and interfered with, in that owners have to repeatedly expend their own time, labor, material, and money in an attempt to remedy and eradicate the graffiti, collect trash, and repair bullet holes and other damage to their property as a result of local gang activities (*City of San Diego v. West Coast Crips*, 2006). Supporters of injunctions claim that gang injunctions add rules and limits to specific gang members served with the order and help law enforcement address some of the crimes that gang members commit for economic gang; hence gang injunctions may have an impact on gang crime from a strain theorist's point of view.

Gang injunctions implemented in middle-class and affluent neighborhoods may not be as effective as in poverty-stricken areas. The gang subculture is rooted in poverty, and as such the gangs tend to commit the bulk of their crimes in economically deprived areas. Social disorganization refers to the failure of social institutions and social organizations in certain communities to maintain order.

The gang's destruction of the target areas impacts the overall environment in the target area for every citizen living there, not just the gangs, thus allowing and contributing to the gang's ability to control the target area. Gang injunctions reduce the opportunities for the commission of crimes or target hardening in the safety zones, i.e., making it more difficult to break into houses and steal from shops, and encourage more responsibility, which deters potential offenders.

Critics of gang injunctions make claims that gang injunctions are political strategies that city officials use to gain popularity with their constituents to secure elected positions, and to impress the interests of concerned individuals. The use of injunctions, despite political rhetoric, is not the panacea to solve the gang problem. Critics argue the injunction is not about crime or gang abatement but more about protecting special community interests, including but not limited to middle-class communities, public and private institutions, business development, and gentrification or redevelopment projects. Gangs that claim areas with a mainstream interest or middle-class to affluent citizens, may or may not have more money spent on injunctions. This researcher sought to understand what percentage of officers feel the target areas where their injunctions were implemented could be classified as middle-class or affluent communities. Critics claim that special treatment is occurring and some injunctions are being sought and implemented based upon political districts and census bureau income reports rather than gangs that truly need injunctions to stop their flagrant criminal activity. Gang injunctions have been described as stop gap measures; they do not eliminate the local gang in most cases, they do not keep rival gangs out of the target area, and they typically are not going to have a significant impact on business projects and property values on any significant scale.

Zoning in Target Area

The more residential housing units in the target area, the greater the injunction effectiveness may be when compared to an area that consists of industrial and business establishments. Residential housing dwellers are more likely to repair gang-related damage than industrial or business establishments. This is important to gang injunction effectiveness, because according to Wilson and Kelling's broken windows theory (1982), if a window is broken and left unrepaired, all the rest of the windows will soon be broken, because leaving windows broken is an indicator that the community does not have any interest in how the neighborhood looks and lacks a sense of community pride.

Untended physical disorder, antisocial behavior, and nuisance activity all lead to the breakdown of social control and increase crime, including gang-related crime. This would explain the correlation between the amount of residential housing in the gang injunction area and the effectiveness of the gang injunction.

However, injunctions that include substantial business districts may be less effective because gangs tend to focus their activity in residential areas, where it is more difficult to identify the networks in place that support their mission. After studying crime rates in zones around the city of Chicago, Shaw and McKay (1920) discovered significant differences in crime rates in different zones. The area with the highest delinquency rates was the zone in transition, just outside the central business district—what they called the interstitial area. Shaw and McKay theorized that crime rates are higher in areas characterized by urban decay, and a breakdown in the community, family, and neighborhood, which they called social disorganization. Shaw and McKay discovered that the amount of crime increased as one moved toward the center of the city. The crime in this zone is dependent upon structural elements such as poverty, illiteracy, lack of schooling, unemployment, and police presence and enforcement of laws in the target area.

CATEGORY 6: TYPE OF COMMUNITY

Gang injunctions that have community support may be more effective than those in communities that have little or no support (Flynn, 1998). Citizens have varying degrees of concern for the gang problems in their community. A majority of citizens seem to care about the gang problem facing their community but do not know what to do; others do not seem to care and are a big part of the problem rather than the solution. Issues of community involvement in the gang injunction process are not a new problem.

From the very first injunction, *People v. Dogtown*, the district attorney had some trouble getting affidavits to support his contention that gangs were terrorizing neighborhoods by marking their turf with graffiti. The DA said, "We talked to plenty of people who complained, but nobody wanted their names used in court. There was an elderly businessman whose walls were slathered with graffiti, but he was afraid his store would be torched if he covered it; a school principal didn't want to name people he thought were responsible for fear the school would be trashed."

Robert Sampson (1997) defined collective efficacy as a community's ability to maintain order in public places. A community must first have social capital in order to have collective efficacy. Social capital refers to having some informal networks or interdependence, such as relying upon one another within a community. The problem with some of the communities that are deemed in need of an injunction is that community members do not feel they can rely upon one another or have the ability to control their environment. Community support may increase gang injunction effectiveness because the community sees much more gang activity than the police as they live among the gang members. As crime increases so does the fear of the local gang, making community members less likely to report crimes and less likely to provide information to the police.

When the gang feels they will not be reported to the police for their crimes, the community purposefully or inadvertently helps the gangs evade justice for the crimes committed against the community in that area and virtually guarantees that they will again become victims of the gang. The gang injunction has the potential to increase community solidarity while at the same time reducing the solidarity of the gang. Injunctions do this by establishing a partnership between the community and the police.

Community members are not typically consulted or made an integral part of the injunction process; however, some tend to show support following the implementation of the injunction because of the reduced presence of the gangs in the community.

A community that does not get involved may reduce gang injunction effectiveness. In general law enforcement officers are aware of community perceptions about how and why they do what they do to address gang crimes. Law enforcement should be concerned because they want and need the community to support their mission of eradicating gangs from the community. If gangs are as bad as society makes them out to be, why does it seem some people in our communities have more concern for the rights of the gang members than they do the victims of gang crime? Some people feel that if we violate the rights of gang members and get away with it, normal law-abiding people are next. As residents perceive that crime is rising, they react by avoiding public spaces such as parks, and their involvement in neighborhood events is significantly reduced.

The injunction's goal is usually to remove the gang from the local parks so they can be reclaimed for legitimate public activities by law-abiding citizens. The common neighborhood response of not using public spaces for recreation and leisure because of the gang's presence disrupts social balance and community attachment to the target area, which decreases the community's ability to regulate criminal behavior. It also allows the gangs to gain control of the area as they take over public spaces, adding to the level of fear and intimidation in a community.

Police-Initiated Injunctions

Police-initiated injunctions may be more effective than injunctions initiated by any other group. Injunctions initiated by police officers are widely seen as being potentially more advantageous and may have a greater impact than injunctions that are sought as a reaction to a certain event, not properly analyzed, or do not take into account the involved gang and target area. This issue is closely related to police willingness, as people in general tend to be more diligent and work harder on a project that they have an interest in completing as opposed to being directed to undertake a project due to political issues that do not take into account all of the related categories.

The police are the ones typically tasked with identifying the specific problem and its source, which gang is the problem, what type of gang they are, which specific gang members are the problem, and what types of crimes they are committing. In addition, issues like how long it will take to get the injunction, what resources are available to address the problem, and which resources are tasked with doing what, are all the responsibility of the police. Injunctions initiated by other groups may not take into account all of the relevant categories. On the other hand, the involvement of other groups, like significant community involvement, may counter the significance of police initiation.

For example, some injunctions are undertaken because of political motivations. Politicians do not typically help the police when they make grand statements about how the gang injunction they support is going to eliminate and destroy the local gang and that is why they should be reelected for whatever post they seek. For example, Orange County District Attorney Tony Rackauckas, when being interviewed by the press relating to the *Santa Nita* case said, "We consider this a foreclosure notice to these street thugs, we are putting them out of business." Riverside County District Attorney Rod Pacheco told reporters, "The aim of the injunction is to put the gang out of business," following the filing of the Eastside Riva injunction in 2007 (*People v. East Side Riva*, 2007). Politicians do not typically acknowledge limits to the injunctions, at times creating unrealistic expectations of what the injunction can and will accomplish in the community.

CATEGORY 7: TYPE OF ORDER

The type of the order varies significantly from one jurisdiction to the next. Does the naming of individual defendants have a greater psychological impact on the gang member as opposed to an order in which his or her name is not listed? Does the process of serving large numbers of gang members have a more beneficial impact than serving just one or two members of the gang?

A typical gang injunction complaint is usually constructed in one of three ways. The complaint may name the gang as the sole defendant, it may name individual defendants in addition to the gang, or it may name only individual defendants. Naming only the gang seems to offer law enforcement flexibility and may lower the costs of bringing the injunction. Rather than build a case against each gang member the prosecution intends to bind, the prosecution would only have to build a case against the gang as a whole. Notwithstanding these possible advantages, naming only the gang may present problems if a gang member claims that he or she did not have notice of the injunction. Due process requires that in order to hold a person amenable to an injunction, he must have notice of it. If the prosecution names the gang member and serves him with process, the gang member will have a weak notice defense.

In addition, gang injunctions can also vary from jurisdiction to jurisdiction, from one gang to another, and can be drafted to deal with the specific problems associated with the particular gang. As such, gang injunctions may have different restrictions, depending upon the gang they are dealing with, the judicial district they are in, and the discretion of the police and prosecutors involved in each specific case. Also, restrictions may be added or stricken from a specific case after a review by the judge. depending upon the evidence presented in support of the case. If the judge feels the prosecution did not provide enough evidence to support a particular restriction, he or she has judicial discretion to remove specific conditions or dismiss the case all together.

Naming individual gang members in the criminal complaint, where they can see the evidence against them, is widely believed to be more of a deterrent for the individual gang member than being served at a later date as a DOE, or individual to be named later, where no supporting evidence against that member is submitted until a violation of the order has occurred. It is often seen as more fair and ethical to name each member and allow him or her the opportunity to come to court and challenge his or her inclusion in the order, a chance some do not get if not named in the initial complaint and served with the complaint prior to the first court appearance. Some civil rights organizations feel very strongly that, while it may be the law, it is also a discriminatory and unconstitutional infringement of the gang member's rights to not be given the opportunity to protest.

Some opponents feel that because of the illegal actions of a few, some communities have been broadly painted by police and city governments as organized criminal organizations marked for continuous harassment through creative abuses of constitutional powers. Some want to eliminate any erosion of our perceived liberties. Critics claim that subjects named in gang injunctions can have trouble getting jobs because the injunctions show up in employment background checks that will eventually harm neighborhoods and criminalize young people. Claims injunctions make it hard for the gang member to get into the job market are not supported; the overwhelming majority of gang injunction targets have no legitimate job when served, have no desire to get a job, and have no skills to maintain a job should they find one. Critics feel the injunctions simply divide neighborhoods along generational and racial lines.

If the injunction shows up on a background check, so do all of the other crimes the person has been arrested for; it would be difficult to determine what would cause the most harm. While community activists agree that something must be done about the gang problem, they worry that an injunction gives police free rein to harass young Latinos and could permanently stigmatize those listed in the injunction. Despite the fact that most injunctions detail very specific instructions on how the member can get off the order, many have not taken advantage of that option, which does not negate the fact they do have the option.

CATEGORY 8: MAINTENANCE OF THE ORDER

The presence of a local gang coupled with an unhindered ability to congregate may increase the likelihood that major crimes will occur and minor nuisance activity will continue, making enforcement a key category to any injunction's effectiveness. Any violation noticed should be addressed by way of arrest and prosecution to send the message to the individual member, and the group at large, that the order is a serious issue. For that reason, swiftness, certainty, and severity depend heavily on the individual jurisdiction taking the necessary steps to educate officers on the presence of the injunction, who it impacts, and how to enforce it. Enforcement of the orders should be encouraged to send the appropriate message to the gang that the order is a serious issue that demands their attention, whether they like it or not.

To enforce and maintain a gang injunction, the police must first be aware of the presence of the injunction and the conditions of the order. In San Diego County, for example, the district attorney routinely attends area police lineup trainings to discuss the pending gang injunction with officers, how the injunction was obtained, what it means for the police, how to make an arrest for an injunction violation, what an injunction violation is, how to write the report, where to file it, and what outcome the prosecutors are seeking.

If the police are not aware the injunction exists, it stands to reason the gang injunction is completely ineffective and irrelevant. It is a critical function of the lead detectives and prosecution to ensure that the offices that work in the gang injunction areas are made aware of the presence of the injunction, how to enforce it, and how to file the cases.

More Jail Time

Gang injunctions that require a gang member be booked in jail may be more effective than those that cite and release violators. Aggressive enforcement of an injunction enables law enforcement to effectively prevent imminent criminal activity by arresting persons for prohibited patterns of conduct that are known to precede and facilitate the gang crime. Used properly, a gang injunction can help a community take back its streets. However, wielded as a hammer rather than a scalpel, an injunction can do more harm than good—alienating innocent citizens from the officers who are sworn to protect them and eviscerating citizen's civil rights.

The Los Angeles County Sheriff's Department has identified a number of inmates who may be disqualified from the early release program meant to relieve to jail overcrowding. The inmate reception center at the sheriff's department now requires that gang members that violate the conditions of a gang injunction will serve 100% of their sentence in the county jail system. This relates back to Beccaria (1764), adding to the severity of a gang injunction violation.

The Los Angeles Sheriff's Department has taken this vital step to ensure gang injunction violators do not walk the streets after just serving only 10% of their full sentence. Along with the sheriff's department, the superior court will assist in identifying future inmates sentenced under contempt of a court-issued gang injunction and prevent them from being released under the early release program. Injunction violations that use notify warrants or citations to direct the case to court are seen as being less effective than arresting and booking the violators in jail, and are contrary to deterrence theory.

Updated Orders May Be More Effective

The updating of gang injunctions is viewed as a necessary element of every injunction because gangs change over time. The change phenomenon is sometimes referred to as a shelf life, or expiration date. Over time, as older members drop out of the gang, go to prison, or die, the order has less impact on the active membership. Through new recruitment, the cycle of gang activity continues generation to generation. In Los Angeles, some of the injunctions give the gang detectives the opportunity to add new members as they are identified as a problem over time. Failure to update the orders may diminish the power of the injunction.

In San Diego County, where the orders apply only to the named defendants, it has become necessary to revisit the older cases and file new injunctions as they are deemed appropriate to keep the gang under control. This has been done, or is being done, with the Posole gang, Old Town National City gang, Lincoln Park gang, Westside gang, Diablos gang, and Varrio San Marcos gang. Orders obtained six to eight years ago were being updated at the time of this research. The target areas in those cases are being expanded upon, as earlier injunctions tended to have smaller target areas. Also, the status of the members on the first order is being evaluated to see if they should be added to the revised orders, or if the new orders should simply include all members from the newer generation.

Enforcement and maintenance of a gang injunction can occur over many years. If done correctly, the injunction can be a long-lasting tool to disrupt the gang's ability to conduct business in the neighborhoods they once felt they controlled. The successful implementation of a gang injunction requires constant vigilance in the target area; no violation should be ignored, and support by police administration is the key to the overall success of the injunction.

Gang Injunctions and Gang Dynamics

Research indicates that gang members are more likely to commit crimes in groups rather than alone, perhaps because they feel more powerful as part of a group, knowing that the group is more intimidating. Suppression policies like gang injunctions use the full force of both criminal and civil law, generally through a combination of police, prosecution, and incarceration, to deter the criminal activities of entire gangs. The goal of injunctions is to dissolve the gang or reduce their ability to commit crime by removing chronic individual gang members from the community.

Gang injunctions are seen as advantageous by law enforcement officers because they send a message to both the individual gang member and the gang as a whole that their behavior has been identified as a problem and the police will now be taking more serious notice of the gang's activities. In addition, police officers tend to agree that a policy that impacts the entire group's behavior has a better chance of incorporating change for the community, as opposed to a policy that only impacts specific individuals. Law enforcement professionals also embrace cases that limit citizen involvement. Gang injunction violations typically remove citizens from witness lists by making a police officer the primary witness in the case, further protecting the community by shifting the burden of proof to the gang member. As witnesses, local police officers are less susceptible to intimidation than private citizens.

5

Gang Injunction and Gang Abatement Theory

Existing theory on the subject of gangs overwhelmingly suggests that law enforcement can impact the group dynamics of a specific gang and the ability of the gangs to commit crimes by applying pressure on them; it is debatable if this is short or long term in many cases. The research conducted for this book also revealed that gang injunctions have the unique ability to address some of the underlying causes of gang crimes that extend their potential benefit well beyond many other traditional law enforcement suppression tactics. For example, a gang sweep typically provides only temporary relief to a neighborhood under intense pressure from the local gang, as opposed to an injunction that has the potential to have a much more long-lasting benefit—as long as the police want it to be in some cases—assuming proper assessment and maintenance of the injunction is conducted.

Research indicates that gang members are more likely to commit crimes in groups rather than alone, perhaps because they feel more powerful as part of a group, knowing that the group is more intimidating. Suppression policies such as gang injunctions use the full force of both criminal and civil law, generally through a combination of police, prosecution, and incarceration, to deter the criminal activities of entire gangs. The goal of injunctions and abatement is to dissolve the gang, or reduce its ability to commit crime by removing chronic individual gang members from the community.

Various theories explore gang dynamics and gang behavior in greater detail in this book. For example, criminological deterrence theories suggest that increasing punishment may decrease gang-related crime; criminological association theories (Sutherland, 1924) suggest that addressing group processes and negative peer influence may decrease gang-related crime; criminological environmental theories suggest that targeting environmental categories may decrease gang-related crime; and criminological economic theories suggest that addressing economic strain on the gang may decrease gang-related crime. Each of these theoretical models makes specific predictions on what categories may decrease gang-related crime. This book explores the relationship between predictions made from these theories and empirical outcomes associated with gang injunctions.

Criminological theories may help provide the foundation and clarify the rationale as to why gang injunctions and gang abatement efforts are continually sought as a means of suppressing a gang in a particular community. An evaluation of theory or the conceptual support for the implementation and outcome of gang injunctions and abatement may well help determine what it is, if anything, that makes the most common restrictions a potential solution to the gang problem in a designated community. Theory related to gangs may also help with the construction of models that allow for a better understanding of gang behavior, which enhances the development of more effective anti-gang policies and strategies like gang injunctions. Civil gang abatement is based on the conjunction of several theoretical perspectives that lay the foundation for their continued use, such as deterrence theory, association theory, environmental theory, economic theory, and gang dynamics theory.

Common suppression strategies against gangs are often believed ineffective because of their reliance on criminal law, which applies equally to all citizens and at all locations and usually necessitates a showing of individual participation or involvement by each individual person. While there may be variations in the prosecution of criminal laws from one jurisdiction to the other, the individual culpability requirement allows fewer opportunities to attack the group characteristics applicable to street gang activity, in particular the tendency of gangs to act as a group rather than individuals.

In contrast, because injunctions and abatement rely on civil laws that tend to focus more on protecting the community and less on criminal violations, gang injunctions may be better suited to address gang group dynamics and may have better chances of disrupting the entire gang's activity in the designated areas.

Street gangs are commonly viewed as an illness or cancer in their community. Like any illness, the best way to make the community healthy again is with aggressive treatment. Part of that aggressive treatment regimen in some neighborhoods is the implementation of gang injunctions. When evaluating gang injunction effectiveness, we are essentially testing to see if one specific treatment, the gang injunction, was the cause of the improvement, rather than some other change that may have happened during the same time frame, such as significant drug operations targeting the gang's leadership, or significant improvements in the social services in the area.

Almost everyone wants to cure the problem of the cancerous gangs facing our communities; it's just that not everyone can agree if a gang injunction is the best, or even a good treatment option. In addition, some worry that the cure is worse than the disease if civil rights are eroded.

Whether or not an injunction is the best way to rid neighborhoods of gangs, it shouldn't be the only method used. As many who have battled cancer know, there's more to the effort than medicine. Being pro-injunction does not necessarily mean a person is anti-gang intervention or anti-gang prevention. If the purpose of the injunction is to stop or reduce violence and give law-abiding residents the breathing space to rebuild their community, job training and social service programs may speed the effort along. Giving the neighborhood a full course of treatment to include adequate prevention, intervention, and suppression is required to find a long-term solution to the gang problem.

DETERRENCE THEORY: INCREASING RISK AND PUNISHMENT

A basic assumption of the classical school of theory includes the belief that all individuals have free will to make their own decisions. The people who join gangs make free will decisions to join a gang and commit crime based on weighing of advantages vs. the disadvantages of their actions. Akers (1991) expanded on the work of Becerra and Jeremy Bentham (1781) and proposed that overall, human behavior is driven by seeking pleasure while avoiding pain, and that humans learn behaviors by repeating those that are reinforcing and discontinuing those that are punishing. Hedonistic calculus, developed by Jeremy Bentham, proposed that people seek pleasure while at the same time trying to avoid pain. If advantages outweigh disadvantages, the person is less likely to commit crime.

To deter people from committing crime, the punishment or disadvantages need to outweigh the advantages. Critics of injunctions oftentimes argue that a heightened threat of incarceration for gang members isn't a long-term solution to the gang problem. I do not support the position that the gang injunction or a gang abatement effort is the ultimate cure for the gang problem in a specific community, and I, like most other people, recognize the need for long-term solutions to reduce gang membership and gang crime over time. However, I also can see the need to hold current gang members accountable for their actions in accordance with deterrence theory.

If a criminal act brings about material reinforcement like money or jewelry, or social reinforcement like gang acceptance or an enhanced reputation, and does not bring about material and social punishments that outweigh these reinforcements, then the individual will chose to repeat the criminal act. Regardless of the reason or motivations for committing crime, rational choice theory states the decision to do so is a rational choice made after weighing the benefits and consequences of the action.

If people seek pleasure while at the same time trying to avoid pain, law enforcement officers need to make the consequences of committing a crime more painful for the gang member—painful by way of arrest, prosecution, and incarceration. Beccaria (1764) asserted that punishment needs to be certain, swift, and severe if it is to be effective. Much of the frustration of today's criminal justice system is that punishment is often none of those things. In the context of gang injunctions, the punishment is often not certain, the system is not always swift, and the punishment is not considered severe by most gang members when comparing an injunction violation to other crimes.

If Beccaria is correct, public policy makers should strive to implement effective laws and policies to maintain public order. If injunctions are proven to have a positive impact, and are determined to be a viable public policy tool, they would adhere to Beccaria's theory and should be used.

For example, 85% of all injunctions to date contain restrictions that prohibit the served gang members from possessing or consuming alcohol in the target areas and increase penalties. Imagine a gang member that has been served with the local gang injunction is in the target area drinking a beer in the local park when he is subsequently contacted by a police officer. Under normal circumstances where no injunction exists, minus some more severe violation being present, such as a warrant for the subject's arrest, or he is intoxicated to the point he cannot care for himself, the maximum punishment that gang member can expect to receive is a citation and notice to appear in court for a municipal code violation. The infraction may result in a small fine or community service, but will most likely not result in any jail time and will not remove the gang member from the community.

The Varrio Mexicanos Locos gang injunction, for example, contains a provision that restricts gang members from possessing or consuming alcohol in the target areas. Gang injunctions that have provisions addressing alcohol violations in the target area make such an offense more serious. It is unlawful to drink or possess alcoholic beverages, be under the influence of alcohol, or even knowingly remain within 10 feet of an open container of an alcoholic beverage upon being served with a gang injunction that restricts alcohol (*People v. Varrio Mexicanos*, 1994).

If charged with a gang injunction violation in the same case as described above, the gang member can typically expect to be booked in the local jail, rather than be cited and released, in areas where the order is in effect and actively enforced, have a bail set between $5,000 and $25,000 depending upon the jurisdiction, and will need to appear in court within two court days after arrest. If convicted, the gang member in San Diego County, for example, can expect to receive 5 to 10 days in jail for the first violation, 3 years gang probation, and mandatory gang registration conditions per 186.30 of the penal code, all for simply violating the no alcohol restriction. In that example and many like it, the gang injunction significantly enhances the punishment for a minor offense and allows a police officer to book the violator into the local jail rather than simply issuing a citation and releasing the gang member on his or her written promise to appear.

In that sense, gang injunctions can make punishment more severe in many circumstances. The theory is that gang members will feel uncomfortable enjoying their favorite alcoholic beverage in the injunction area, and will take the activity outside public view to avoid contact with the police, further protecting the community by having a less visible gang presence, and improving the quality of life for the community.

The vertical prosecution units make the punishment much more certain because prosecution guidelines are often established, providing more consistent and more severe penalties for specific cases that involve street gangs.

Injunction violations often go to court within days rather than weeks, making them potentially swifter as well. Receiving a citation that has a court date four or six weeks away is not the same as being booked in jail and seeing the judge within a couple of days. An injunction violation must be addressed quickly, as the gang member is in jail or out on bail, requiring a speedy court appearance. The more severe gang injunction violation is addressed more quickly than would be the same basic violation under an alternate municipal or penal code violation.

Some critics argue that a restriction limiting alcohol violations does not help address the problem of gang violence in the community, and it is unfair to the gang members. The judge in the Varrio Lamparas injunction agreed with the critics and felt the gang member's use of alcohol did not pose a crime problem in the target area, and subsequently struck that restriction from the order. Some academics and those in law enforcement disagree with Judge Iwasko and feel that because alcohol usage is such an integral and regular part of socializing within the gang subculture, it should be restricted to help protect the community.

Another interpretation of criminological theory by police is reflected in perceptions that visible problems—such as truancy, hanging out, public drinking, drug dealing, loitering, and intimidation in public places—can lead to more harmful problems such as assaults and shootings. Both police and citizens become concerned when the activities of gang members become more visible, as such behaviors suggest that offenders perceive little risk of detection.

This thinking by police and citizens is consistent with the broken windows premise, suggesting that problem behaviors that are tolerated may increase the prevalence or severity of offending; the environment suggests to offenders that there are opportunities to offend and there is little risk of detection. By responding to low-level problems and public concerns, police signal to community members and gang members that police are available and will address such problems. This resultant attention reduces the anonymity of gang members and increases formal surveillance and guardianship of problem areas. These approaches reflect applications of situational crime prevention described by Clarke (1992) as police increase the risks of detection to gang members, increase the difficulty or effort that must be expended by gang members, reduce the rewards, and remove excuses associated with offending or problem behaviors related to many gangs.

The use of situational crime prevention techniques has significantly expanded the repertoire of police for addressing gang-related problems. Rather than an exclusive focus on criminal sanctions, police can block or limit opportunities for offending by making physical changes in the environment, employing civil techniques to reduce problems, using technology to enhance crime prevention, and limiting access to the means of offending. These concepts are discussed in greater detail in Chapter 20.

Drinking alcohol typically brings the gang closer together to not only maintain the cohesion and social solidarity of the gang, but also affirm masculinity and male togetherness. The restricting of gang members' use of alcohol in the designated target areas is typically recognized as effective because alcohol is a major contributor to gang violence. The increased associated factors with drinking, which include fighting between members, increased tensions, diminished capacity, or lowered inhibitions, may give potential value to limiting access to alcohol in the target areas.

The manner in which the order is enforced may also impact the way the gang members will react to it; the more certain the contact and arrest, the higher the level of injunction effectiveness, in theory. Aggressive, fair, and consistent enforcement is required for gang injunction effectiveness regardless of jurisdiction. Any violation noticed should be addressed by way of arrest and prosecution to send the message to the individual member, and the gang at large, that the order is a serious issue.

For that reason, swiftness, certainty, and severity depend heavily on the individual jurisdiction taking the necessary steps to educate officers on the presence of the injunction, who it impacts, and how to enforce the orders to send the appropriate message to the gang that the order is a serious issue that demands their attention. Aggressive enforcement of an injunction enables law enforcement to effectively prevent imminent criminal activity by arresting persons for prohibited patterns of conduct that are known to precede and facilitate the gang crimes.

Violations of a gang injunction can include criminal or civil sanctions. Typically a criminal filing is preferred in California. Criminal sanctions under Penal Code 166.4(a) can include jail time up to six months, a fine up to $1,000, and gang probation conditions. Putting the gang member on probation, usually gang probation, increases the punishment for future crimes and gives the police a tool to further monitor the gang member for up to three years following their injunction violation arrest. Civil sanctions can include immediate punishment of five days in custody for each violation and a fine up to $1,000. If a defendant violates an injunction, the prosecution has the option of bringing criminal misdemeanor charges under Penal Code Section 372 or Penal Code Section 166.4(a) PC, willful violation of a court order.

The prosecuting agency's choice of whether to pursue contempt charges under Code of Civil Procedure Section 1209 or Penal Code Section 166(a)(4) may be influenced by several factors. The advantages to bringing charges under Section 1209 are (1) the burden of proof against the defendant is only a preponderance of the evidence, (2) attorneys' fees may be recoverable, offsetting the cost of the order, (3) the contemnor possesses no right of appeal review of the contempt charge is only by extraordinary writ, and (4) civil prosecution of juveniles forces parental involvement. The prosecution may also opt for Section 1209 if it would prefer a bench trial in superior court, most often before the judge who issued the original injunction, rather than a jury trial in a court with an unfamiliar judge. A defendant being tried in court under Section 166(a)(4) may collaterally challenge the validity of the original injunctive order he or she is charged with violating.

Advantages to bringing the contempt charge under Section 166(a)(4) include probation terms, a Fourth Amendment waiver, gang registration conditions, and mandating the gang member stay away from the target neighborhood as a condition of probation. The probationary period typically lasts up to 36 months. Other advantages to bringing the contempt charge under Section 166(a)(4) are the longer jail terms and a speedy trial. The length of the jail term may be an important consideration.

Akers' (1991) differential reinforcement theory integrated differential association and the learning theory of operant conditioning. Operant conditioning argues that behavior is controlled by the consequences of that behavior. Similar to Becerra (1998), everyone receives positive reinforcement and negative reinforcement for behavior. If we accept Akers' theory, gang members must learn that their criminal behavior is rewarded negatively in a target area, meaning violations will result in arrest and prosecution in a consistent and aggressive manner. If behavior is controlled by consequences, then the gang injunction would tend to be seen as effective, if properly enforced, in that it adds additional consequences to violations that might otherwise go unaddressed, or may not be a violation of the law to those not included in the civil lawsuit.

Ivan Pavlov conducted research on behavioral conditioning, a psychological principle that holds that the frequency of any behavior can be increased or decreased through reward, punishment, or association with other stimuli. Pavlov worked with dogs that salivated whenever food was presented to them. The dogs were given food only when a bell was rung. After the dogs were conditioned to associate food with the bell, the bell was rung but no food was provided. The dogs continued to salivate each time the bell was rung. Just like dogs, people are conditioned to be criminals over periods of time, and breaking the cycle of gang membership will typically take time and require increased resources in the gang areas to intervene in the gang process. If gang members are conditioned by arrest every time they engage in crime or associate in violation of the court order, they typically will modify their behavior to avoid arrest, which can be made more frequent and certain.

Improved use of deterrence strategies by police has paralleled increased recognition that activities of particular gangs and gang members are highly concentrated in time and space. Drawing upon data collected about gang members through FIs, police increasingly recognize that even the most prolific offenders cannot be everywhere at once. Most chronic offenders spend the majority of their time in or traveling between predictable locations, such as home, school, work, or hangout locations, and are often observed with the same companions. Thus police can increasingly focus their attention on the opportunities for gang-related offenses that occur near these nodes of activity or along the paths from one to the other. This view of offender behavior reflects police understanding of routine activity theory. This understanding of routine activity theory provides police with promising investigative leads when offenses occur. In contrast to offenses that might otherwise have few solvability factors—such as no evidence or witnesses—the careful and repeated documentation by police of gang members, their associates, vehicles, and behaviors provides readily accessible information for follow-up investigations. The documentation thus substantially increases the likelihood of detection, and presumably influences offenders' perceptions about the likelihood of detection.

An understanding of routine activity theory has also assuaged police concerns about displacing gangs and gang members. Contemporary police understand the temporal limitations of tactics such as directed patrols, anticipating only that problems will diminish for a period of time. Police, however, observe diffusion effects associated with directed patrols of gang problems; gang problems do not immediately resume their prior level even after police presence is removed. Instead, problems remain decreased for some period of time, and police can deliver additional doses of police presence at lower levels than the original dosage. These follow-up practices, in which police resources may be pulsed on and off, are a more efficient use of police resources than long-term increases in police presence.

Old Town National City Example: Testing the Resolve of Police

Many gang members are defiant in the face of a gang injunction, and the majority will continue their criminal activities despite being served with the injunction. For example, when the Old Town National City (OTNC) gang injunction was implemented in 1998, one gang member in particular tested the resolve of the police. Upon being served the injunction in Kimball Park, he summarily tore up the injunction and threw it in a trash can next to where he was standing. The following day, he was back in the same park on the same bench wearing a baseball hat with OTNC embroidered on the front; needless to say he was arrested. Nine days later, same park, same defendant, arrested again when he was with a codefendant named in the same injunction. Two months later, he was arrested again for another violation. Following the third arrest, that defendant moved to the San Ysidro area south of the target area. He admitted that the inevitable police contact contributed to him moving from the target area. This member only changed his behavior after being forced to by the pressure applied by the police.

Injunction Violations Help Prove Gang Membership

A gang member that has been named in and served with a gang injunction may be more easily prosecuted at a later date for a gang crime as a result of his or her inclusion in the gang injunction. Inclusion in the gang injunction tends to support and prove the individual's membership in the gang. This is important in California, because crimes committed for the benefit of a street gang have increased punishments associated with them if the street gang allegation can be proven.

California Penal Code Section 186.22(a) defines the street gang allegation, meaning a person actively and currently participated in a criminal street gang, the members of that gang engaged in or have engaged in a pattern of criminal gang activity, that person knew that the gang members engaged in or have engaged in a pattern of criminal gang activity, and that person aided and abetted a member of that gang in committing a crime. When an individual is targeted with an injunction, the same evidence used to include him or her in the injunction can be used to show he or she is a member in the gang and prove the street gang allegation at trial, making the punishment for that member potentially much more severe.

California Penal Code Section 186.22(b) defines the street gang enhancement:

> Any person convicted of a felony committed for the benefit of, at the direction of, or in association with any criminal street gang, with the specific intent to promote, further, or assist in any criminal conduct by gang members, shall, upon conviction of that felony, in addition and consecutive to the punishment prescribed for the felony or attempted felony be punished by an additional term of 2, 3, or 4 years.

In some cases one of the results of a gang injunction violation conviction requires the gang member to formally register as a gang member in the jurisdiction he or she resides. The California Penal Code Section 186.30 requires that a defendant shall register as a gang member if the defendant is found guilty of 186.22(a), active participation in any criminal street gang. This is important in gang injunction cases because gang injunction violation convictions often mean the gang member must register with the local police agency as a gang member.

The registration process typically allows the police to keep better track of that gang member's location and gives them information that may help solve gang crimes should that member be involved at a later date, such as providing fingerprints and photographs that can be used to show to crime victims and compared against evidence left at a crime scene. Section 186.30 states:

> (a) Any person described in subdivision (b) shall register with the chief of police of the city in which he or she resides, or the sheriff of the county if he or she resides in an unincorporated area, within 10 days of release from custody or within 10 days of his or her arrival in any city, county, or city and county to reside there, whichever occurs first. (b) Subdivision (a) shall apply to any person convicted in a criminal court or who has had a petition sustained in a juvenile court in this state for any of the following offenses.

A potential benefit of a gang injunction violation conviction is that police can better hold gang members accountable when they fail to keep the police updated as to their status (Penal Code Section 186.30).

Additional Common Provisions

Thirty-seven percent of all injunctions to date contain a generic provision requiring gang members served with the gang injunction to "obey all laws." This common restriction is closely tied to gang enforcement and is often referred to as the catchall restriction. In a departure from the earlier injunctions that focused on specific crimes tied to the target gang, this restriction simply states that failure to obey all laws that prohibit violence and threatened violence, that prohibit interference with the property rights of others, and that prohibit the commission of acts that create a nuisance are illegal for any of the served members. The advantage to law enforcement is that any violation of any law, including penal code, vehicle code, or municipal code, could constitute a violation of the gang injunction and allow the police to arrest and book the gang member in the local jail.

Eight percent of all injunctions to date contain one or more locations that have been deemed completely off-limits to the served gang members, making them subject to arrest for simply being at the location regardless of the circumstance. For example, the West Coast Crips injunction from San Diego has 20 locations in the two designated target areas that are off-limits to all gang members served with the order. The basis for the off-limit areas is that the defendants use the listed locations as their primary hangouts and conduct the bulk of their nuisance activity at those locations.

The defendants and those acting in concert with them use those locations to hang out, gamble, openly drink alcoholic beverages, use and sell drugs, have sex, plan future crimes, and as safe havens when evading police in the area. The defendants oftentimes block the free passage of people at those locations, litter, and vandalize those locations. In addition, the listed locations are well-known West Coast Crip hangouts by the rivals of the gang, and they are primary locations for rivals to go to seek out West Coast Crips to engage them in crimes of violence.

The 42nd Street injunction makes Gilbert Lindsay Park in Los Angeles completely off-limits to the served gang members (*People v. 42nd St.*, 2004). The Hoovers injunction restricts gang members who do not live in the safety zone from entering or remaining in the safety zone at all hours and all times, unless a health emergency requires their presence there. In order to be considered a resident of the area, the gang member must be a juvenile who lives with a parent or legal guardian, or an adult who owns property or is a signatory to a lease or rental agreement. The Southside Montebello injunction makes Chet Holifield Park off-limits. The Orange Street Locos injunction makes being on the premises of any uninhabited or abandoned building at any time a violation. The Florencia 13 injunction has a restriction for served members to "stay away from Roosevelt Park," making being present at or traveling through Roosevelt Park, located at 7600 Graham Avenue, within the safety zone, including any adjacent sidewalk or parking lot, a violation of the order (*People v. Florencia 13*, 2008).

Twenty percent of all gang injunctions to date contain restrictions that address gang member vehicles in order to reduce their mobility in the area. The most obvious gang status symbol is the gang member's car. In theory, removing the ability of the served gang members from driving a car in the target areas may lessen the ability of the gang to mobilize against rivals, reduce the incidents of hit-and-runs and other traffic accidents, reduce incidents of drunk driving and reckless driving, and most importantly, decrease incidents of drive-by shootings.

Gang members, especially mid-level gang members who engage in drug sales, will typically use a vehicle to conduct their criminal business. It is not uncommon for gang members to have their vehicles registered in the names of family members and friends to keep officials from establishing a paper trail against them. Lower-level gang members often buy cars and fail to register them in their names, or may register the car but tend to not get insurance, and they may not have licenses to drive.

Ten percent of the gang injunctions to date contain restrictions that prohibit the poor driving skills exhibited by some gang members. For example, the Hoovers injunction in Los Angeles impacts several dimensions of vehicle usage. The injunction prohibits unlawful driving of a vehicle, or directing or advising another to drive a vehicle in willful or wanton or reckless disregard for the safety of persons or property, including but not limited to while evading a peace officer as defined in Vehicle Code Sections 2800.1 through 2800.3, or driving a vehicle unless licensed and insured, or in lawful possession thereof.

Unlicensed or uninsured gang members can expect a significant increase in the severity of what may be typically a routine traffic citation for a person not on a gang injunction. A gang member driving without a driver's license or without insurance is not uncommon. Under normal circumstances a citation would be issued and the car may be impounded. Making violation of traffic laws a violation of the gang injunction significantly increases the severity of the violation. This may help reduce incidents of hit-and-run accidents, which typically financially impact residents in the area who are forced to fix damaged property because the gang members frequently do not have insurance.

In every state, including California, drivers are required to demonstrate the ability to pay up to a certain amount to cover their liability if they are involved in a motor vehicle accident. These laws are sometimes called financial responsibility laws. The purpose of the compulsory financial responsibility law is to ensure that all drivers, including gang members and owners of vehicles, are financially responsible for any damage or injury caused by a traffic accident, regardless of fault, and to remove financially irresponsible drivers from the roadways (California Vehicle Code Section 16078, 2004). Drivers must maintain evidence of financial responsibility as specified by law if they drive a motor vehicle, whether they own it or not, or they own a motor vehicle, whether they drive it or not, but allow others to drive it. This is very common with gang members—borrowing family members or friend's cars to go out with fellow gang members to commit crimes, go to gang parties, and cruise rivals areas looking for gang members to confront. The Whittier Varrio Locos injunction has a restriction that requires the gang members to not drive a vehicle in the safety zones unless licensed and insured and in possession thereof.

In addition, the Varrio Hawaiian Gardens injunction restricts riding a bicycle anywhere in public view or a place accessible to the public in an attempt to stop the gang from using bicycles as a means of transporting drugs in the target area and to evade law enforcement officers.

This research has revealed that if gang members are taught that their failure to comply with a gang injunction will more often than not result in enforcement action, crime in the target area can be reduced. Criminological deterrence theories (Akers, 1966; Beccaria, 1764) suggest that increasing punishment decreases gang-related crime, a view that has been supported by this research. The reductions in all classifications of crime reveal that deterrence theory is relevant to gang injunctions and that strict enforcement of injunctions does result in fewer crimes.

Survey question numbers 1–4, 15, 16, 18–20 all address deterrence theory in varying degrees. The reductions in part 1 and part 2 crime revealed that deterrence theory is relevant to gang injunctions and result in fewer crimes being committed. This research has revealed reductions in crime in the areas targeted with gang injunctions compared to control gangs that had no injunction implemented against them. This reduction in crime was statistically significant, proving that there is a relationship between gang injunctions and deterrence.

ASSOCIATION THEORY: GROUP PROCESSES AND NEGATIVE PEER INFLUENCE

All but three gang injunctions filed in California to date contain restrictions that prohibit served gang members from associating together in the designated areas anywhere in public view. The no association restriction is the critical element of gang injunctions according to supporters, and is also one of the most disturbing elements to critics and community advocates and many in the legal and academic community because of perceived constitutional violations.

The no association clause, however, is based in part on the theories of Sutherland (1924), Thrasher (1927), and others who proposed differential association theory, which states criminal behavior is learned from interactions with other persons, and that criminal activity especially is learned within intimate social groups like gangs. Thus, it is hypothesized that when individuals assemble or operate simultaneously as a group, they will lean toward or away from crime according to the norms and beliefs of their associates. This hypothesis has been substantiated with research indicating that criminal attitudes and associates are two of the most significant correlates of criminal gang conduct.

The no association restriction usually contains wording that prohibits the gang members from standing, sitting, walking, driving, bicycling, gathering, or appearing anywhere in public view with any other named defendant, or with any other known gang member. A question this research sought to address is why the restricting of a gang's ability to associate together in the target area has been deemed so important by the police and prosecutors. The no association restriction is the primary restriction in every active gang injunction statewide; is it viable, legal, and necessary? The theory underpinning gang association relies on a dichotomy between two classifications of community members, those who are criminals and those who are law abiding.

By removing gang members and the people who congregate with them from the streets, in theory the police can deter or reduce the chance that gang members will commit future crimes. By placing restrictions or sanctions against them that act as a barrier to their criminal association, the police may make neighborhoods safer for law-abiding residents. In many respects, the police feel that if they can force gang members to spend less time with their fellow gang members, they are actually helping the gang member, not hurting him or her. As far back as biblical times, it has been clear that our associations matter. We are oftentimes judged in society by who we associate with, and our associations can be a benefit or detriment, depending upon the ideology and behavior of our associates.

According to Thrasher (1927), the result of gang association is collective behavior, the development of tradition, camaraderie, esprit de corps, solidarity, group awareness, and close attachment to a local territory. If being together increases the strength of each individual because a group has more power than any one member, then gang injunctions that disrupt the group's ability to be together in designated areas may have a positive impact on gang crime reduction.

Social learning theory supports the position that the no association provision is necessary to stop gang activity, in that people learn how to behave by modeling themselves after others whom they have the opportunity to observe, which is especially true of gangs (Sutherland, 1924). Learning theory suggests that gang members often feel less responsible for their own behavior when acting as part of a group. Therefore limiting gang association may help reduce gang crime in two primary ways. First, it may prevent or reduce the harm created by gang association, or gang members hanging out on the street to support the mission of the gang to claim their territory and antagonize rival gangs who enter it. Second, gang member association in public view makes many law-abiding residents fearful to venture into streets, stores, and parks.

Thus, police officers contend the very presence of gang members on the streets creates a nuisance, independent of any additional criminal activity they might be engaging in. Gang members who congregate in the street are often engaged in crimes. These public crimes often create an environment that fosters potential violent clashes between the local gang and rivals that innocent passersby might get caught up in. Gang members are often encouraged to participate in crimes committed by other members of the group. As such, preventing groups of gang members from congregating in public may limit the chances that an individual gang member will commit a crime because he or she has less backing and support from a larger group.

In areas where the injunction is properly enforced, the gang typically has to meet outside the area or out of public view within their claimed territory to conduct gang-related business. The gang effectively loses some control over the area and must associate inside houses, backyards, or garages, where they cannot be seen in public view, or risk arrest. The removal of the gang from public view has the potential to have a corresponding impact on the violent crime rate in the area because a less visible gang presence on the streets and sidewalks logically limits the opportunity for gang conflicts to occur in the first place.

Frequency, Duration, and Intensity

The gang injunction allows the police to impact several dimensions of the gang's behavior, by potentially impacting the frequency, duration, and intensity of the gang's association. If the gang has less time to spend together in public view, they may have less opportunities to commit crime. This is due in large part to the increased police presence and added authority granted to the police, allowing them to contact and arrest gang members for the injunction violation, as opposed to having to wait for a more serious crime to occur.

The frequency of gang association can be impacted if the gang has to take extra steps to associate, such as leaving the target area or meeting at a location outside public view, making it more difficult for them to congregate without added effort. In general, gang members have a poor work ethic and are generally not willing to put effort into something if an easier way exists. Making it more difficult to congregate in the area may be enough to stop them from associating in some areas completely.

The intensity of the group's association is also lessened when the group is forced outside of public view, making it more difficult for them to remain visible in the area to defend the territory from rivals and intimidate the community. Intensity is also impacted by other common gang injunction restrictions, such as drugs and alcohol.

Perhaps the most immediate proximate cause to many gang-related crimes is criminogenic substances, such as money, guns, and drugs. Money, guns, and drugs can all provide the additional, if not sufficient, cause that helps make a gang crime happen, which also tends to increase the intensity of a gang's interaction. If the gang does not feel comfortable smoking dope and drinking beer in the target area for fear of arrest, the injunction may impact the intensity of the gang's contact with each other. If they have fewer guns, drugs, alcohol, or cash, a reduced level of available criminogenic substances, this may result in less gang crime and a reduced level of group awareness, cohesion, and solidarity, further limiting intensity.

A group of gang members inside a house or in a backyard have less control over the area than when they hang out together in the street or on sidewalks in public view. When the gangs are less visible in the target areas, the community reports that they feel safer and the gang's ability to control the area has been reduced. The intensity of the association may also be reduced because the group is less likely to encounter a rival or potential victim when outside public view, reducing the chance of an altercation or opportunities to commit crimes together.

Eighty-eight percent of all injunctions to date include restrictions prohibiting the possession of a firearm or other designated weapon by the served members of the gang. Intensity of violent crimes is impacted by injunctions that restrict the possession of any firearm, ammunition, knife, baseball bat, screwdriver, or any other weapon.

The Oakland B Street injunction attempted to restrict the possession of any object capable of inflicting serious bodily injury, including metal pipes or rods, glass bottles, rocks, bricks, chains, tire irons, screwdrivers, hammers, crowbars, and razor blades. The B Street injunction was denied by the court in part because some of the provisions were vague and overbroad, as some of the items to be restricted have legitimate uses, making determining the intent of someone possessing a rock or specific tool a difficult task that could invite abuse.

Other injunctions like the Vagos one restrict the possession of replica guns, including BB guns and toys anywhere in public view (*People v. Alcarez*, 1998). The theory behind replicas is that the community often does not know the difference between a real gun and a replica; as such, the gang can terrorize the community and when caught, the only charge would be a low-grade misdemeanor (*People v. 38th St.*, 2004). The restricting of weapons possession is very common and reduces the intensity of gang contacts by reducing the gang's ability to intimidate people, commit crimes, and carry out acts of violence in the community. Intensity is also impacted by restrictions that prohibit fighting in public, making loud noises, and general loitering in public.

Some injunctions target gang intensity by focusing on a gang's ability to socialize and have fun in the target area. These injunctions include restrictions on gambling for money, including playing cards, dominoes, dice, or dog fighting anywhere in public view or any place accessible to the public (*People v. Bounty Hunters*, 2003; *People v. Crenshaw Mafia*, 1996).

Seventy percent of all injunctions to date contain restrictions that prohibit juvenile gang members served with the injunction to be in the designated areas past the designated curfew. The theory is that limiting the potential duration and available hours the gang has to associate may reduce the gang's ability to control their territory.

If under the age of eighteen (18), being in a public place between the hours of 10:00 p.m. and sunrise on any day, or it may indicate 6:00 a.m., of the following day, unless (a) accompanied by a parent or legal guardian, or by a spouse eighteen (18) years of age or older, or (b) performing an errand directed by a parent or legal guardian, or by a spouse eighteen (18) years of age or older, or (c) returning directly home from a public meeting, or a place of public entertainment, such as a movie, play, sporting event, dance or school activity, (d) actively engaged in business, trade, professionalism, or occupation which requires such presence, or (e) involved in a legitimate emergency situation that requires immediate attention.

Some orders also include language that requires the juvenile to have physical evidence of any valid reason for being out of his or her residence at the time he or she deviates from the order (*People v. Rolling Sixty Crips*, 2003).

Section 272 of the penal code proscribes activities that contribute to the delinquency of minors. Some jurisdictions are talking about taking legal action against the parents of minors who associate with gangs to make parents responsible for their children's whereabouts and actions. Law enforcement officers expect parents to know where their minor children are and what they're doing at all times. If parents make a habit of not knowing where their children are, the police may file a case against them for contributing to the delinquency of a minor. The Geer and Schoolyard Crips injunctions make it a violation for any served member to actively and knowingly permit any dependent minor to associate with any member of a criminal street gang, other than members of the minor's family, except while enrolled and attending school or a licensed job training, gang rehabilitation, or drug intervention program (*People v. Geer and Schoolyard Crips*, 2006).

Fifty-five percent of all injunctions to date also contain restrictions that prohibit adult gang members that have been served from being out past the designated curfew in the designated areas. The Orange Street Locos and Blythe Street injunctions were two of the first ones to contain curfews for adults that were held constitutional (*City of Norwalk v. Orange St. Locos*, 1994; *People v. Blythe St.*, 1993). Some of the more recent injunctions simply specify a required curfew that is applicable to both adults and juveniles alike (*People v. Avenues*, 2002).

An adult curfew was denied in the Playboy Gangster Crips injunction (*People v. Playboy Gangster Crips*, 1987) but later deemed valid in subsequent injunctions following the *Acuna* decision (*People v. Big Hazard,* 2005; *People v. Sur Crazy Ones*, 1999). In the Oakdale Mob injunction, the judge denied the 10:00 p.m.

curfew restriction, choosing instead to approve a no loitering provision between midnight and sunrise. The judge in the case stated, "Given the limits on association, the limits on illegal conduct, the limits on loitering and trespassing, what's left to be addressed by the curfew is not really gang activity but the individual's private activity, it seems to me it goes farther than necessary" (*People v. Oakdale Mob*, 2006). The Varrio Whittier Locos injunction contains a no loitering restriction, prohibiting delaying and lingering in any public place for the purpose of engaging in any illegal activity, and also contains a curfew for juveniles and adults (*People v. Whittier Varrio Locos*, 2006). The Florencia 13 injunction has a "do not loiter" restriction that defines loitering as delaying or lingering in or obstructing access to any public place, public view, or anyplace accessible to the public, including streets, sidewalks, and businesses, to benefit the gang, to engage in drug-related activity, or for any unlawful purpose (*People v. Florencia 13*, 2008).

Intimidating Witnesses

Eighty-five percent of all injunctions to date contain restrictions that address gang-related witness intimidation because it is asserted that one of the most difficult problems facing law enforcement is the power of gang members to evade justice by threatening and intimidating the witnesses against them. Gangs that can stand freely in front of private homes and businesses can and do intimidate the community by their mere presence. For that reason, some injunctions prohibit any of the served gang members from "in any manner confronting, intimidating, annoying, harassing, threatening, challenging, provoking, assaulting and/or battering any residents or patrons or visitors to the area, or any other persons who are known to have complained about gang activities" (*People v. Vista Homeboys*, 2005).

Some other cases also include language that restricts gang members from blocking the free passage, ingress or egress, of any person or vehicle on any street, walkway, sidewalk, driveway, alleyway, or other area of public access (*People v. South Vietnam*, 2000; *People v. Venice 13*, 2000). The restrictions listed above are intended to limit the gang's ability to intimidate the community by removing the most visible gang presence in a neighborhood. The net result may positively impact the community's willingness to report crimes and add to the overall perception of safety in the community (Knox, 1999).

This research has revealed that gang injunctions limit the ability of gang members to associate in public view, and that these limitations have resulted in a reduction in crime in the majority of the target areas. Criminological association theories suggest that addressing group processes and negative peer influence decreases gang-related crime, which has been supported by this research. By removing the most visible presence of the most problematic members of the targeted gang in the target areas, this research has revealed statistically significant reductions in crime when compared to baseline and the controls. Criminological association theory addresses the gang's ability to associate, and survey questions 5–8 and 17 address association issues.

ENVIRONMENTAL THEORIES: TARGET AREA ENVIRONMENTAL FACTORS

In the 1920s, the social disorganization theories of crime began to surface. Social disorganization basically refers to the failure of social institutions and organizations in certain communities to maintain order.

Social disorganization theory originated with Thrasher (1927), who believed that gangs originated through the effort of boys to create a society for themselves where one that catered to their needs failed to exist. They sought out the gang to obtain the life satisfaction and rewards that their communities, schools, and families failed to provide. Shaw and McKay (1942) used official police statistics and topographic maps to explain that delinquency, and gang formation occurred in the area around a city center, an area generally in a state of social flux.

Gang injunctions are only applicable in a very well-defined geographical location that is outlined in detail in the supporting declarations included in the civil lawsuit, despite media reports that make it seem to appear that entire cities are subjected to gang injunctions. The target area is usually selected based in large part upon police knowledge of the targeted gang, where they congregate, and what area they claim as their specific territory. The injunctions are typically supported by crime data and crime analysis to highlight the preinjunction level of crime in the area.

Many of the areas selected to be viable targets for gang injunctions exhibit the same social and environmental problems regardless of county.

In 1942, Clifford R. Shaw and Henry D. McKay made one of the first attempts to focus on social conditions that lead to delinquency in a specific area. Shaw and McKay discovered that the amount of crime increased as one moved toward the center of the city. The crime in this zone is dependent upon structural elements such as poverty, illiteracy, lack of schooling, unemployment, and police presence and enforcement of laws in the target area. Robert Sampson

(1997) and colleagues from Harvard University expanded upon the theory in 1997 and added the terms *collective efficacy* and *social capital* to the criminological vocabulary. Collective efficacy refers to a community's ability to maintain order in public places; social capital refers to having some informal networks (interdependence, relying upon one another, ties) within a community. A community must first have social capital in order to have collective efficacy.

After studying crime rates in zones around the city of Chicago, Shaw and McKay (1942) discovered significant differences in crime rates in different zones (Barlow, 1991). The area with the highest delinquency rates was the zone in transition, just outside the central business district, which they called the interstitial area. Shaw and McKay theorized that crime rates are higher in areas characterized by urban decay and a breakdown in the community, family, and neighborhood, which they called social disorganization theory. The theory is based upon crime being a product of decaying and transitional neighborhoods, which are indicative of neighborhoods that are targets of virtually every gang injunction obtained.

The sociological theoretical perspective is based on the idea that the gang subculture is composed of a group of people who participate in a shared system of norms and values that are different from those of the larger culture. These norms and values typically include the gang's destruction of the target areas with graffiti and vandalism, which impacts the overall environment in the target area for every citizen living there, not just the gangs, thus allowing and contributing to the gang's ability to control the target area.

Vandalism and Graffiti

Many restrictions of gang injunctions are designed to help address and protect the physical environment and limit social disorganization in the target areas. Provisions of gang injunctions such as restricting the possession of marker pens, spray paint cans, or other sharp objects capable of defacing private or public property; spray painting, marking with marker pens, scratching, applying stickers, or otherwise applying graffiti on any public or private property, including but not limited to the street, alley, residences, block walls, vehicles, or any other real or personal property, all theoretically help protect the environment.

Gangs use graffiti to identify themselves, identify their territory, and communicate messages such as threats, challenges, descriptions of criminal acts the gang committed, and gang rosters that let the community know who they are and how many members they have. Gang graffiti typically helps the police identify the street gang's territory to justify the injunction to the court, as well as providing other useful information, such as monikers of individual street gang members that may be included in the injunction, indicators of pending gang violence committed by or against the target gang, current rivalries, and the overall size of the gang based upon gang rosters.

The police rely heavily on the presence of graffiti to justify the size of safety zones or target areas, as graffiti is good evidence of the recent and ongoing presence of a gang in a specific neighborhood. For example, when gang detectives start from what is believed to be the center of the gang's territory and follow the graffiti in every direction, it may help define the borders of the gang's territory, or the appropriate territory for the gang injunction. Having recent examples of graffiti around the perimeter of the safety zone is one of the best and most accurate methods to show the gang's recent presence in the area and help prove their claim on the area to a court of law.

Other restrictions address the issue of littering in any public place or place open to public view, and urinating on any public or private property open to public view; all address issues relating to improving the physical environment in the target area and attempt to improve social organization (*People v. Logan Red Steps*, 2002; *People v. White Fence*, 2006).

Some injunctions contain wording that restricts damaging or vandalizing the property of another, both public and private property, including but not limited to any vehicle, light fixture, door, fence, wall, gate, window, building, street sign, utility box, telephone box, trees, or power poles, to help protect the physical environment.

In areas where gangs are allowed to destroy property at will, the physical environment supports the gang subculture and gives the local gang more power and more control over the target area. In 1992, a combined group of police, prosecutors, and neighborhood residents in Los Angeles gathered and determined that the need for other remedies such as trash collection, graffiti cleanup, and building and code enforcement to improve the quality of life in the neighborhood should go hand in hand with each injunction. Thus, civil gang abatement is often viewed as most effective when used as part of a coordinated effort involving law enforcement, community mobilization, and the restoration of municipal services essential to quality of life.

After reviewing every gang injunction obtained in California to date, this study has determined that the majority of the gang injunction areas could be classified as interstitial zones according to Shaw and McKay (1942), areas that are multiuse residential and business districts with high levels of social problems. Shaw and McKay identified three characteristics of interstitial areas, including cultural heterogeneity or residents from different cultures that lack a common value system, mobility or the rapid turnover of residents hindering the development of a common set of neighborhood norms or prescriptions for appropriate behavior, and poverty and low socioeconomic status.

Shaw and McKay found that as people moved away from the interstitial zone into more established zones, delinquency did not continue. Therefore, they argued, environmental factors led to the delinquency and gang crime. If we accept this theory as being true, injunctions that attempt to improve environmental conditions may be deemed as sound public policy.

Broken Windows Theory

According to Wilson and Kelling's broken windows theory, if a window in a building is broken and left unrepaired, all the rest of the windows will soon be broken, as it is an indicator that the community does not have any interest in how the neighborhood looks and they lack a sense of community pride. According to Wilson and Kelling, untended physical disorder, antisocial behavior, and nuisance activity all lead to the breakdown of social control and increase crime.

As residents perceive that crime is rising, they often react by avoiding public spaces such as parks, and their involvement in neighborhood events is significantly reduced. That is why some injunctions revolve around a central community park that gangs tend to use to congregate. The injunction's goal is usually to remove the gang from the local parks so they can be reclaimed for legitimate public activities by law-abiding citizens.

The common neighborhood response of not using public spaces for recreation and leisure because the gang's presence disrupts social balance and community attachment to the target area decreases the community's ability to regulate criminal behavior. It also allows the gangs to gain control of the area as they take over public spaces, adding to the level of fear and intimidation in a community. In speaking about the Old Town National City gang injunction, the mayor of National City stated, "They've taken over our neighborhoods in National City, where their mere presence in our parks is enough to scare innocent people away." As such, many injunctions include neighborhood parks, such as the OTNC gang in Kimball Park, the Vista Homeboys gang in Brengle Terrace Park, the North Side Redondo gang in Perry Park, the Villa Boys gang in Villa Park, the 42nd, 43rd, and 48th Street Gangster Crips in Gilbert Lindsay Park, and Varrio San Marcos in Bradley Park, to name just a few.

As crime in a community increases, so does the fear of the local gang, which often results in those that have the means to leave the area moving from the neighborhood. This leaves behind those that are unable or unwilling to resist the presence of the local gang. The remaining residents become even less likely to report crimes committed by the gang, and less likely to provide information to the police. Residents purposefully or inadvertently help the gangs evade justice for the crimes committed against the community.

Imagine a school bully that hits other children and takes their lunch money; when those children fail to react and do not report the incident or do not fight back, they are guaranteeing that they will again become a victim of the same bully because they have shown they are an easy victim. However, in cases where the child fights the bully and resists losing his or her lunch money, or reports the incident to school officials, the chances of repeat victimization go down. Gang members, like most criminals, are lazy and lack work ethic; if they have to work to commit a crime or they have citizens that are willing to step up and report gang crimes, the gang will often focus their attention on those they know they can get away with victimizing or those they feel they can intimidate. If gang injunctions can show the community that the police care about their safety, and that if the community reports injunction violations and other crimes, the police will work to remove the gang members from the community to help protect the citizens that live there, there may be a corresponding reduction in criminal activity.

In some cases, some members of the community speak out in support of the gang, appearing to be sympathetic to the gang's opposition to the injunction (*People v. Venice Shoreline Crips*, 1999). However, only a small minority of any community is pro-gang members. Most realize the gang offers nothing productive to the neighborhood; this has been shown in community surveys about gang injunctions. However, in some injunction cases the media focuses on the community activist perspective, the perspective that often makes excuses for the gang members, claiming they are being picked on because of age, ethnicity, or social status (*People v. Oxnard Colonia Chiques*, 2004). Speaking on behalf of the gang makes some in the community feel safer, as the gang members may not bother them because they feel as if they are on the same side.

The anti-gang point of view is not always as forthcoming as the critical view in many communities because few members of the community typically want to publicly speak out against the gang for fear of retaliation. For example, the majority of Ramona Garden residents interviewed by the media about the Big Hazard gang injunction in Los Angeles said publicly they are against the bans. However, some residents in the large housing complex, who asked not to be named out of fear of retaliation from their neighbors, approached the media when the gang members were not present and said that violence and crime do exist and they were concerned that having their kids grow up among criminals is a big problem. Many of the citizens living in these areas provide declarations under seal that describe the reality of the situation and provide true insight and evidence as to the gang's nuisance activity in the area.

The problem in some gang injunction neighborhoods is that the long-standing inability of the neighborhood to control the criminal behavior in the area has inspired further social decay to the point where those communities have become so disorganized that they are incapable of reclaiming control of their public space without assistance. The needed assistance is often lead by the police and the prosecution, who are tasked with protecting the public. The police are typically attempting to reverse a trend that has been ongoing in some neighborhoods for three or four generations. It is clear that most of the neighborhoods targeted as gang injunction areas are in desperate need of intervention, and gang injunctions can address some of Wilson and Kelling's concerns. By removing the most visible elements of the gangs seen by all that live and work in the area, the area will typically only improve.

The presence of a local gang coupled with an unhindered ability to congregate increases the likelihood that major crimes will occur and minor nuisance activity will continue. This problem may be addressed in such a manner that encourages the gangs to comply or move from the area by having adequate enforcement of a gang injunction. It may also send a message to some in the community that the police and prosecution are concerned about their issues, which may have a corresponding increase in community member's willingness to get involved and help the police solve gang crimes committed in the target area. Gang injunctions can help areas that are under a heavy burden of gang violence by giving social programs a better chance of success because people may be more likely to utilize the programs and services if they feel safe doing so.

Criminological environmental theories were explored in survey question numbers 11–14, which address criminological environmental theory.

ECONOMIC THEORY: STRAIN THEORISTS

Strain theory perceives delinquency and gang membership as a consequence of the discrepancy between having high economic aspirations and a lack of means by which to achieve them. Karl Marx (1818–1883) assumed that lower classes are always exploited by the "owners" of the means of production. It is the labor of the lower classes that provides for the accumulation of wealth by the upper classes, and the working class suffers under the consequences of a "false class consciousness." This process of being exploited causes some to resort to alternate means of making money, including committing crimes as a means of support.

Strain theory assumes that all youth have similar economic goals (such as wealth, success, and power), but that some youth do not possess legitimate resources with which to attain these goals. Thus, in order to compensate for a lack of means, these youth must resort to illegal activity to achieve their aspirations (Goldstein, 1990). Strain theorists believe that everyone is innately good and would prefer not to deviate from the law. It is the strain of living in dilapidated poverty-stricken areas that causes youth to commit crimes.

Society has defined the means for achieving success through hard work, education, and honesty. The gang subculture has defined the opposite to be true, and their lack of means to attain middle-class goals produces a strain called anomie, which is a social state where controls, limits, and rules are absent or removed from a community. Strain theorists see gang crime as a result of a lack of opportunity, particularly economic opportunity.

Gang injunctions may address this strain by adding rules and limits to specific gang members served with the order to help law enforcement address the crimes that these gang members commit for economic gain. Hence, gang injunctions may have an impact on gang crime from a strain theorist's point of view.

Robert Merton's (1938) anomie theory acknowledged the strain that lower-class youth felt in attempting to achieve middle-class aspirations and outlined ways that they could adapt to this strain. Cloward and Ohlin (1960) expanded upon Merton's strain theory and called it differential opportunity theory. The theory proposed that gang affiliation was the result of lower-class boys lacking access to society-defined goals. They argued that the type of gang that developed would depend on the type of area in which it developed, as even illegitimate means were unevenly distributed.

Cloward and Ohlin (1960) asserted that there are limited opportunities for success in some gang neighborhoods, but there are many illegitimate and illegal structures. Gang injunctions seek to remove some of the more common illegitimate opportunities that often provide the upward mobility, recognition, and success desired within the gang subculture. Cloward and Ohlin also described what they labeled the "retreatist subculture," in which individuals perceive themselves to have limited opportunities for advancement through both legitimate and illegitimate means, and therefore abandon any hope of advancement, frequently turning to drug use.

Economic Opportunity by Selling Drugs

Ninety-two percent of all injunctions to date contain restrictions that prohibit the possession of controlled substances by the served gang members. The theory is that the most significant economic enterprise for the majority of street gangs, which provides individual members and the gang as a whole the upward mobility they desire, is the illegal sale of narcotics. In many communities the bulk of street level distribution of illegal controlled substances is undertaken by the local street gangs.

For that reason, most gang injunctions contain restrictions designed to disrupt the gang's ability to sell drugs and help address the overwhelming problem of drug availability in our society. Some restrictions include: (1) staying away from drugs, including using illegal drugs in public or being under the influence of drugs in public; (2) no drug possession or sales, including participating in the possession or sale of narcotics/drugs, including but not limited to heroin, methamphetamine, cocaine, and marijuana; (3) no possession of related drug paraphernalia, including but not limited to rolling papers or pipes used for illegal drug use; (4) knowingly remaining in the presence of anyone in possession of controlled substances; (5) no acting as lookouts by signaling to, whistling, or acting as a lookout for other persons to warn of the approach of police officers; or (6) no approaching vehicles or interfering with traffic or blocking free passage on a public street (*People v. East Side Piru*, 2004; *People v. Langdon Street*, 1999).

Sixty-five percent of all gang injunctions to date contain restrictions that attempt to hinder a gang's ability to sell narcotics in the designated target areas. Some prohibit gang members served with the order from signaling or warning of approaching police and acting as a lookout during drug sale activities; the language associated with not acting as a drug lookout varies somewhat between existing orders.

For example, the 18th Street Shatto Park injunction specifies, "No acting as a look out, whistling, yelling, or otherwise signaling with a flashlight, walkie talkie, or other means to warn another person of an approaching law enforcement officer, or soliciting, encouraging, or employing another to do so (*People v. 18th Street*, 1998). The Varrio Mexicanos Locos injunction adds: "employing or offering payment for others to do the same" (*People v. Avalos*, 1994). The Venice 13 injunction includes language restricting gang members from "approaching or signaling any other person's motor vehicle, whether stopped or parked, unless a legitimate emergency situation requires such conduct" (*People v. Venice 13*, 2000).

The 18th Street Pico Union injunction contains the wording "no hooks," which is essentially the same as signaling or otherwise attracting another individual for the purpose of drug sales, basically hooking the drug customer and drawing him or her into the location to conduct the drug deal (*People v. 18th Street*, 1997). The Crenshaw Mafia and Lennox 13 injunctions add yelling the terms *five-O* or *one time*, common slang names for the police, when the police are approaching (*People v. Lennox 13*, 1996; *People v. Crenshaw Mafia*, 1996).

Some injunctions restrict drug transactions, such as gang members cannot repeatedly "pass to or receive from a passerby, whether on foot or in a motor vehicle, money or small objects, repeatedly beckoning to, stopping, attempting to stop, engaging in conversation with a passerby, using signals or language indicative of summoning purchasers or sellers of illegal drugs, or transferring small objects or packages for currency in a furtive fashion, or acting as a look out for such activity" (*People v. 18th Street*, 2003).

The Oakdale Mob injunction restricts loitering with the intent to commit a narcotics-related offense as proscribed in Chapter 6 of the Health and Safety Code, Section 11352, which includes loitering in a public place in a manner and under circumstances manifesting the purpose and with the intent to commit a specified offense (*People v. Oakdale Mob*, 2006). The Florencia 13 gang injunction has a "do not toss contraband" restriction, keeping served members from discarding onto any public property or the private property of another, any gun, dangerous weapon, open container of an alcoholic beverage, controlled substance or related paraphernalia, or vandalism tool as defined in Penal Code Sections 594.1 and 594.2, except in the manner in which you are ordered to do so by a law enforcement officer (*People v. Florencia 13*, 2008).

Other injunctions restrict extortion, including collecting taxes or rent for the right to sell drugs in the area; or obtaining property from another with that person's consent induced by invoking the name of the target gang or by other use of force or fear, including threats to injure the person, or his or her property (*People v. Mara Salvatrucha*, 2004). The Varrio Posole injunction added, "owning, possessing, or driving a vehicle found to have any contraband, narcotics, or deadly weapons" (*People v. Varrio Posole*, 1997). Others restrict the use of pagers or cell phones in any public place; however, the *Englebrecht* case ruled the restricting of cell phones and pagers is not allowed (*People v. Englebrecht*, 1998).

The "no cell phones" restriction has since been used with modifications in the wording; for example, the Rolling 40's injunction from Los Angeles in 2007 restricts "possessing or using any cellular or digital phone, walkie-talkie, two-way radio, or communication scanner; except (1) as required for a legal business or occupation and possessed during business hours, or (2) as reasonably required by an actual emergency. Proof of the need for possession or use in a business or occupation or by an emergency as an exception to this provision shall be an affirmative defense to a charge of violation of this provision. The burden of producing evidence of the existence of such need or emergency shall be on the defendant" (*People v. Rolling 40's*, 2007).

The cell phone and pager restrictions are designed to disrupt the gang's ability to communicate with each other during the commission of drug offenses, if the police can articulate that the phone is used for the sole or primary purpose of conducting drug transactions (*People v. Varrio Posole*, 1997). The Eastside Riva gang injunction prohibits the possession of police scanners used to monitor and intercept police communications and two-way radios, unless required for lawful employment, to limit the ability of the gang to evade law enforcement while engaged in criminal activity (*People v. Eastside Riva*, 2007).

Gang injunctions can make it more difficult to sell drugs in the target area because the members that have a propensity to sell drugs can be added to the injunction and restricted by it. In some communities, gang members stand openly in public and act as a drive-thru for customers buying their illegal drugs. When a gang injunction is implemented, police can hinder the gang's ability to sell drugs in the target area by arresting the groups involved in the drug activity. If a gang injunction can make it more difficult for the gang members to distribute their drugs, and increase the risk for potential customers buying the drugs in the injunction target, area customers may be driven out. That may then have a corresponding impact on overall violent crime in the target area and help reduce the profits generated by the gang's drug business in their home territory.

Legal businesses and industries rely on the justice system to enforce contracts and punish those who violate terms of agreements. In the gang world, buyers and sellers rely on their own resources to enforce contracts. Violence is often the only effective preventive measure against unfair trade practices, and gang members have proven that their lack of regard for human life, frequently even their own, contributes to the level of violent crime in their territory. According to the Drug Enforcement Administration (DEA), drug-related violence usually appears in one of three ways: (1) users under the influence of a drug commit a crime, (2) drug users commit violent acts to obtain money or more of the drug, and (3) gang members who sell drugs use violence in the course of conducting business.

The illegal nature of drugs ensures that violence associated with drugs will never go away, but the community level violence may be lessened in specific areas with a gang injunction. If the DEA is correct, gang injunctions that target gang drug operations and limit the gang's ability to openly sell drugs in the target area may have a corresponding reduction in the level of violent crime in the target area. If customers have a hard time finding a dealer in the area, they may find new areas to shop. If rivals cannot find their competitors to rob or kill, less violence may be the result. In addition, many gang members are also drug users and drug addicts who must commit crimes to get money to buy more of the drug they are addicted to, further reducing crime if they are not allowed to be in the target area.

Reducing Property Crimes Like Burglary and Auto Theft

Selling drugs is not the only way gangs make money. Removing the gangs from public view may also have a corresponding impact on economic crimes for the gang, such as theft-related offenses like auto theft, petty theft, shoplifting, burglary, and the more serious offenses like street robberies and carjacking used by gang members to support their drug habits or drug sales or to control their drug turf. Several injunctions attempt to limit the gang's ability to commit specific crimes in the target areas that they are known to have a propensity to commit. Property crimes in some of the target areas are very common.

Some injunctions restrict the possession of burglary tools, including possessing picks, multitool instruments, pliers, wire cutters, slim jims, spark plugs, dent pullers, sling shots, porcelain chips, rocks, bricks, or any other devices capable of breaking into vehicles (*People v. Venice 13*, 2000; *People v. Varrio Posole*, 1997). The variations in tools and orders are indicative of the tools known to be used by the specific gang in each jurisdiction. Others address crimes like identity theft and restrict the possession of fraudulent credit cards, negotiable instruments, checks, identification cards, and other documents used to get money in a fraudulent manner (*People v. 42nd St.*, 2004). Still other orders restrict gang members from congregating in and around specific stores and markets where they are known to engage in shoplifting or other theft-related offenses, making that location off-limits at all times by the named gang member.

Strain Theory's Solution to the Problem

The solution to the gang problem according to strain theorists is increasing young people's economic status to help them avoid strain and become capable of achieving success. To help increase young people's economic status and help ensure their success, gang injunctions may help by adding limits and rules to the individual gang member to help keep him or her law abiding, out of the gang area, and out of prison.

Criminological economic theories (Agnew, 1992; Cloward and Ohlin, 1960) suggest that addressing economic strain on the gang may decrease gang-related crime. When the ability of the gang to sell and distribute narcotics in the target areas was reduced, crime was reduced in the injunction areas when compared to the control areas. Questions 9 and 10 attempt to identify criminological economic type crimes.

PSYCHOLOGICAL GANG DYNAMICS THEORY: GANG CRIME MOTIVATORS

Group dynamics theory attempts to explain gang formation by exploring the process of group development. The theory outlines that gangs in general are characterized by a set of criteria, including social categorization, social reward, interdependence, interaction, and influence. Among some processes characteristic of group development, cohesiveness has been shown to be an especially significant influence on the quality of group interactions, longevity, and success at attaining its goals. If we accept that theory as being true, then the police should seek to disrupt the quality of the gangs' interaction within the target areas, which may have a corresponding impact on the level of crime.

Members of cohesive groups are more likely to be influenced by other group members and place greater value on the group's goals, to be more active and equal participants in discussions, to be less influenced by members leaving the group, to be absent less often, and to remain in the group for a longer period of time. Research has illustrated a positive relationship between group cohesiveness and delinquency, in that gangs are more likely to be engaged in violent activity when the status and solidarity of their gang is threatened, such as in the case where the gang is the target of a gang injunction. Again, if the theory holds true, by impacting the group's ability to control a particular area and conduct gang-related business, the police may be able to reduce gang solidarity.

DISPLACEMENT OR DIFFUSION

It is anticipated that abating gangs and imposing sanctions against property owners at gang hangouts and gang-infested neighborhoods will not only have the intended effect of crime reduction in each particular location or neighborhood, but also have a positive secondary effect of crime reduction in nearby areas.

Many terms have been used to describe this phenomenon, including the "multiplier effect" (Chaiken et al., 1974), the "halo effect" (Scherdin, 1986), "spill over benefits" (Clarke, 1989), and "free rider effects" (Meithe, 1991). Clarke and Weisburd (1994) propose a standard definition of understanding these processes called "diffusion of benefits." They define this term as "the spread of the beneficial influence of an intervention beyond the places which are directly targeted, the individuals who are subject of control, the crimes which are the focus of intervention or the periods in which an intervention is brought."

This is an important concept to discuss because it is often suggested that enjoining or abating a gang at a location simply pushes the problem to another location, a concept known as displacement. Do gang injunctions or gang abatement simply result in a movement of offenders to surrounding communities? Or conversely, can a gang injunction or gang abatement effort lead to improvements in the surrounding communities, a diffusion of crime control benefits?

It has been suggested by critics of injunctions, and other types of gang enforcement actions that focus on a particular area, that gangs simply move just far enough out of the area to avoid the injunction, a phenomenon often referred to as spatial displacement. The limited studies to date tend to support the view that displacement does not seem to be a significant reaction to gang injunctions. Displacement does occur on an individual basis, but mass exoduses from the neighborhoods impacted by gang injunctions have not happened to date based on the existing research. A critical assumption of gang injunctions, however, is that some displacement is an inevitable outcome of focusing law enforcement attention on a specific gang in a specific area. That assumption, however, is seldom total and often inconsequential.

The evaluation of potential displacement or diffusion may, however, be revealed to some degree as a potential by-product of this research by comparing injunction areas to control areas in close proximity to the injunction, and evaluating any changes in crime rates. Of the 25 gang injunctions evaluated in this research, 9 of them share a common border and the others are in close proximity to each other. The gang injunction areas to date have typically resulted in an intense and concentrated law enforcement action against the targeted gang; while the control gang areas had no gang injunctions and no reported significant increased enforcement action. The level of change in the injunction area as well as the control area can be compared, and displacement or diffusion may be revealed if it occurred.

Many gang members and community members feel injunctions do more harm than good because they force gang members to move to a new neighborhood, which creates a void that younger, typically more violent members try to fill. Others feel that if the gang is removed from a particular neighborhood, another gang may identify the weakness and move into and expand their territory. Others, however, feel that if forcing gang members to move outside their comfort zones into a new area occurs, it is a positive because this may increase their chances of being apprehended because they stand out more in their new environment and lack the support structure they may be accustomed to on their home turf.

It should be noted that gang injunctions do not legally require or force gang members to move anywhere; none of the existing gang injunctions reviewed require gang members to move outside the designated target areas. What injunctions do is place restrictions on gang members designed to try to make them stop creating a public nuisance in the area. If the gang members interpret the restrictions as an eviction notice from the neighborhood, that extends beyond the legal authority the injunction provides. Most gang members have no intention of stopping their criminal ways after being served with a gang injunction, and most probably have no intention of modifying their behavior. Many vent to media outlets that the injunction is going to get them killed because they need to move, which is not the case in any of the injunctions filed anywhere in the state of California.

As a result of being served with a gang injunction, some gang members move on to other neighborhoods to avoid the police. Some move to reorganize and continue their criminal activities, while others move to get away from the gang life. If they move to another area to commit their crimes, they will be dealt with by the police; if they move to distance themselves from the gang, the injunction is typically viewed as a success.

There are several potential theoretical and practical benefits of focusing a gang enforcement action at a specific location or neighborhood. Gang crime is out of control in some areas, common in some areas, and virtually nonexistent in other areas. Gang crime tends to cluster at specific locations and certain neighborhoods, resulting in large numbers of gang crime events at specific locations, making a gang injunction a logical and potentially beneficial policy decision. Law enforcement agencies in Southern California do not have endless resources; by focusing on the areas that show a clustering of gang activity, or pockets of gang activity at specific locations, law enforcement appears to be making an appropriate policy decision relating to their allocation of police resources.

COMMON GANG CRIME MOTIVATORS ADDRESSED BY INJUNCTIONS

Street gangs commit crimes for many reasons, such as drug deals gone bad, someone looked at someone wrong, or they wore the wrong color clothing or the wrong symbol in the wrong area. Sometimes valid reasons do not exist; maybe they were just bored and felt like acting out. In most cases, however, a reason exists, and by evaluating the more common gang crime motivators, we may have a better understanding of how gang injunctions can address them and explain why crime rates may be impacted in areas where a gang injunction is implemented.

As part of the literature review, over 200 crimes prosecuted by the San Diego County District Attorney's Gang Prosecution Unit were evaluated and the apparent motives for those crimes were noted. From a review of those cases, five primary or chronic motives were identified, including gang identification, gang turf violations, gang members seeking prestige, gang personal conflicts, and retaliation between gangs. Upon understanding the common motives of gang crimes, a correlation between the gang crime motivators and the common restrictions of gang injunctions was compared to better understand the theoretical benefit of having a gang injunction. In theory, discouraging gang membership by prohibiting behavior that indicates gang membership, including wearing gang colors, flashing gang hand signs, and communicating gang membership or insults to other gangs, may have an impact on the levels of crime in the community.

Limit Gang Identification (Hand Signs and Gang Clothing)

Gang members identify themselves as a gang member and show affiliation with their gang in several ways. Some gang crimes start with one gang confronting another with the question, "Where are you from?" It is typical in the gang world, even when outnumbered, for a gang member to identify himself or herself by gang, despite the virtual guarantee that violence will soon follow. Other times the identification takes the form of a hand sign between two rival gangs as a challenge or sign of disrespect, or wearing a particular article of clothing in a certain area.

All of these gang identification methods often lead to acts of violence, such as fighting, stabbings, drive-by shootings, and murders. Some of the existing gang injunctions address these issues by prohibiting fighting on public streets, alleys, sidewalks, and any other public spaces, including public parks; possessing or discharging a firearm; wearing gang-specific clothing; and displaying gang hand signs (*People v. Mesa Locos*, 1999).

Many injunctions to date contain restrictions against the served members from engaging in various expressions of gang indicia. The Varrio Sureno Town injunction, for example, contains a restriction that prohibits any conscious expression of gang affiliation, support, or allegiance to the gang, including using any words, phrases, physical gestures, or symbols associated with the targeted gang (*People v. Varrio Sureno Town*, 2002). Provisions that restrict specific gang hand signs and the wearing of particular gang clothing are common. These provisions are deemed very important by some police agencies because they address the more visible indicators of a gang's presence that are observable by the citizens who live in the area. They also help by impacting the gang's ability to control the area by making it more difficult for the gang to communicate with each other and intimidate the community via nonverbal communication.

It is common knowledge among law enforcement officers that gangs use nonverbal communication methods, such as physical gestures or symbols, commonly known as hand signs, to communicate with each other and their rivals. As such, some injunctions specifically restrict the uttering or using of any words, phrases, physical gestures, or symbols, commonly known as throwing signs or hand signs, in any way by the target gang or specific clique targeted with the order (*People v. Rolling Sixty Crips*, 2003). It is not sufficient, however, to just say that gang hand signs are not allowed. The declaration of the expert typically describes each known hand sign in a very specific manner, exactly how the hands and fingers are placed to represent whatever name, number, or symbol that gang is trying to communicate.

Gangs identify themselves in the gang community and to fellow and rival gang members by wearing clothing or accessories that show their gang affiliation, including clothing of a specific color, necklaces or belt buckles that bear the gang name, and initials, letters, numbers, or other symbols used by the gang, all of which must be clearly defined in the injunction before that clothing can be restricted.

Injunctions often restrict the wearing of any clothing, jewelry, or other article that has significance to the target gang, whether by color, name, lettering, numbers, or any combination thereof. For example, for the Rolling Sixty Crips, restrictions limit wearing blue, specifically blue shoelaces, blue bandanas, blue headbands, blue head coverings, blue shirts, blue jackets, etc. (*People v. Rolling Sixty Crips*, 2003). The Eastside Riva gang injunction restricts the possession of any item that has any significance to the practices or identification of the gang and includes the displaying of any tattoo or logo in any public place exposed to public view that is known to be a reference to the gang (*People v. Eastside Riva*, 2007).

In Ventura the Colonia Chiques gang has adopted the Dallas Cowboys symbol (*People v. Oxnard Colonia Chiques*, 2004), in National City the gang has adopted the North Carolina college symbol (*City of National City v. OTNC Gang*, 2005), and in San Diego the Sky Line Piru like to wear St. Louis Cardinals and Philadelphia Phillies sports attire because the SL and the P on the hats and clothing can represent their gang name; also, both gangs use the color red to represent bloods (*People v. East Side Piru*, 2004).

The use of sports team attire may be popular among the targeted gang as well as others in the community not affiliated with the gang in any way. This may open doors of doubt and skepticism among community members if used to document gang members solely on the common symbol. The clothing and symbols that are clearly gang related and have no legitimate use are acceptable as a gang documentation criteria, such as specific gang clothing created by the gang members bearing the gang's name, initials, or symbol created by the gang. However, generic sports team attire needs to be supported by other evidence to tie it to the particular gang.

Restricting the ability of gang members to wear sports attire that has been identified as being gang related by the specific injunction has been deemed appropriate because it leads to violence and crime, as rivals who fully understand the true meaning of such clothing can use it to identify fellow gang members. Common clothing has been the cause of some nongang citizens being mistaken as gang members by rivals in specific neighborhoods, which has resulted in violent confrontations and violent crimes. It may be because the rivals do not distinguish between rival gang member and a citizen wearing the clothing, the local gang becomes upset because a citizen is wearing their symbol, or some citizens do not know the meaning or decide the gang will not dictate what clothing they can wear in public.

In Northern California, the Huegla bird symbol has been adopted by several northern Hispanic gangs as a symbol of their allegiance to the northern portion of California (*People v. Oxnard Colonia Chiques*, 2004). The Huegla bird or eagle is a popular symbol, originally adopted by Cesar Chavez and the United Farm Workers during the 1960s. Some non-gang and gang members have these flags hanging in their homes. Critics argue the police have chosen to target this symbol, which is a sign of racism and anti-Hispanic sentiment. Police argue that they do not dictate which symbols the specific gangs use for identification purposes; they are simply responding to what the gangs are doing.

Turf Violations (Keep Rivals Apart to Reduce Confrontations)

Gang injunctions do not stop gang members from going anywhere; they do not physically restrain them from neighborhoods. Many gang injunctions do, however, make attempts to restrict gang members by extending the restrictions from their home turf to the turf of their primary rivals, if the crime statistics support inclusion of a rival's turf as well. When a rival gang member comes into their territory, it is a sign of serious disrespect that sometimes is dealt with in a violent manner by the local gang.

For example, entering a rival gang's neighborhood and defacing graffiti by crossing out names, has cost some gang members their lives. Other times gangs violate a rival's territory to sell dope, recruit new members, disrespect the other gang, or for personal reasons. Sometimes the family of a gang member will move into the area of a rival gang. That member usually has problems when the local gang discovers the rival lives there.

Most gang injunctions address the issues related to gang turf violations by reducing the visible presence of gangs in the area, making it more difficult for rivals to find them; still other injunctions make the primary rivals of the enjoined gangs' territory also part of the gang injunction enforcement zones (*People v. Diablos Gang*, 2001; *People v. Westside Gang*, 2001; *People v. East Side Piru*, 2004). In San Diego, for example, the 86 members of the Eastside Piru gang are restricted in their territory, as well as the territory of their primary rival, the Lincoln Park bloods. The entire target area of the Lincoln Park injunction is a safety zone of the Skyline injunction (*People v. Lincoln Park*, 1998; *People v. Eastside Piru*, 2004).

One advantage of restricting the enjoined gang from the rival's territory is that police can arrest the enjoined members in the areas where their presence is highly likely to result in a crime occurring should their presence be made known to the other gang. Keeping gang members out of their primary rival's territory is a restriction and has been implemented in the Grape Street, Hoovers, and Rolling Sixty Crips injunctions, to name a few.

Elevate Standing or Seeking Prestige

Seeking status and prestige to elevate their standing within the gang and to elevate the status of the gang as a whole is common in the gang subculture. They commit violent crimes to gain the respect of their fellow gang members and to glorify their gang. In today's gang era, the more violent you are, the more respected you are. Most gang injunctions address the issues related to gang members committing crimes to elevate their prestige by targeting the most problematic members and encouraging them to reduce their presence in the area so the younger members have less contact with the older members, less opportunity to show off and demonstrate how violent they are to gain favor with the gang.

It has been contended that a group does not become a gang until it receives recognition as a gang from the community or rival gangs. Once the gang and the individual gang members are recognized by other groups or the community as a whole, the group becomes more cohesive and organized and evolves into a stronger gang. Younger gang members see the violent behavior of their peers being rewarded, so they emulate that behavior and attempt to be more violent than the other. Therefore, based upon different external perceptions of the group's activities, it officially becomes a gang by its reaction to the perceptions of those around the group. By restricting association, for example, a gang injunction may limit the opportunities for the younger members to emulate the older members, reducing incidents of gang violence.

Gang members also enhance their reputations by retaliating against their rivals. When one of their members has been the victim of a battery, assault with a deadly weapon, or murder, a gang must respond and retaliate if they want to be respected. If the gang does not respond to the rival gang's act, this will usually invite more incidents from other gangs. When a gang member is murdered, the retaliation is usually swift if the gangs involved are well established and have a significant number of active members. Sometimes the anniversary date of the death of a dead homeboy/girl will motivate a gang to commit a crime in retaliation (*People v. Oxnard Colonia Chiques*, 2004) for years following a specific crime.

Personal Conflicts (Less Time Together, Less Internal Issues?)

Personal conflicts within the rank and file of gangs when struggles exist for leadership, or when a member violates a rule of the gang, may lead to acts of violence. This violence usually takes the form of a beating, but has resulted in some homicides to keep the gang under control. These conflicts can be over women, drug sales, a member's failure to back up a fellow member, or personal problems between individual members.

The involvement of gangs in the drug business has also resulted in more violence relating to drug sale altercations, laundering of drug money, informing the police, etc. Because most personal conflicts are related to drug usage or sales, gang injunctions may address internal gang problems by limiting public association and the situations that may result in internal issues like failure to back up a fellow member addressing gang drug-related operations (*People v. Rolling Sixty Crips*, 2003).

In some cases, a gang member failing to participate in the crime or back up a fellow member that starts a fight, for example, will suffer potential recourse from his or her own gang. The member's failure to participate or back up fellow members in the commission of gang crimes is seen as an unacceptable act within the gang subculture; it is a sign of weakness and must be dealt with by discipline, usually resulting in a beating by the fellow members of the group.

It can be difficult at times for a gang to conduct gang business as individuals; many times they need to work together as a group to accomplish their goals. Most gangs typically mandate that all members participate in the group's activity or suffer consequences for failing to do so. Gang injunctions may help address the problem because the gang's mere association in public may result in their arrest and draw unwanted attention from police who are often in the area actively looking for violators, resulting in a disruption of the group dynamics. That is another potential reason why a properly implemented and enforced gang injunction has the ability in theory to disrupt the organization of the gang and hinder the gang's ability to conduct business, such as drug dealing, witness intimidation, and turf protection within the designated target area.

Self-Control (Help Them Control Themselves)

Travis Hirschi and Michael Gottfredson (1969) developed social control or social bonding theory. In their work on the causes of delinquency they discuss the bond or relationship an individual gang member has with society. The bond is related to the attachment he has to others, his commitment to appropriate lifestyles, his involvement in conventional values, and his belief in the correctness of the rules of society. Hirschi and Gottfredson argued that the tendency for a gang member to commit crime can be found in his level of self-control, or his ability to control his own behavior. In order for crime and delinquency to occur, individuals with little self-control must be presented with the opportunities to commit delinquent acts.

The injunction's potential to remove that opportunity could lower crime in injunction areas because without sufficient opportunity, crime may be less likely to occur. Individuals with limited self-control are impulsive, physical, and live in the here and now. Most gang members do not think long term; they do not plan for the future, they do not know how long they will live, and they do not expect a long and happy life in most cases. Gang members often have difficulties controlling themselves; as such, the provisions of gang injunctions that impose restrictions on the individual gang members may help them develop some basic level of self-control whether they want it or not.

The West Coast Crips injunction in San Diego contains a restriction never used before, which requires those gang members served with the injunction to seek active employment, education, or employment training, or risk going to jail if contacted in the target area. It specifically states that not retaining and maintaining employment in a lawful occupation or enrolling as a full-time or part-time student in an educational institution or job training program within 90 days of the date of service of the injunction, if not already employed full-time or part-time and attending an educational institution or job training program (*City of San Diego v. West Coast Crips*, 2006).

According to Deputy City Attorney Makini Hammond, the city attorney's office is trying to break up the social organization of this gang; you are not really a gang if you can't hang out with your fellow gang members. The city's mayor and police chief agreed the injunction gives the city another tool in the war against gangs, at least in the short term to reduce the violence and in the long term to eradicate gangs in the city of San Diego (*City of San Diego v. West Coast Crips*, 2006). The City of San Diego has contacted the gang members served with the city injunctions and has given them information on how to participate in several programs to keep them in compliance with the gang injunction, and more importantly on how to become a productive member of society.

Gangs and Schools (Protect Our Youth and Those at Risk)

Some gang injunctions have restrictions directed at protecting schools in the target areas. For example, the Geer Street and Schoolyard Crips gang injunction contains a restriction allowing for "gang-free school zones," which makes it a violation for any served Geer Street or Schoolyard Crip gang member to enter or remain upon any school ground, including four named high schools in the target area, at any time during school hours or at any scheduled school event while not being a student enrolled in the particular school. The served defendants are allowed to drop off and pick up any dependent minor student who is enrolled at the school or attend an event where one of their dependent children is participating in a school event (*People v. Geer and Schoolyard Crips*, 2006).

The Black P Stones injunction contains a gang-free school restriction for a high school, middle school, and elementary school

(*People v. Black P Stones*, 2006). The Crenshaw Mafia injunction makes Morningside High, Monroe Junior High, and Woodworth Elementary Schools off-limits unless the gang member has the written approval and consent from the schools' administrations (*People v. Crenshaw Mafia*, 1996). The Lennox 13 injunction restricts being at Lennox Middle School at any time (*People v. Lennox 13*, 1996). The Barrio Van Nuys injunction has a gang-free school zone restriction that requires served members to refrain from entering or remaining in or on the school grounds of Van Nuys High School, except: (1) during school hours or during a school-sponsored event while a student enrolled at that school, (2) as a parent or guardian while picking up or dropping off a student who is enrolled in that school, or (3) with written permission for entry from the school principal (*People v. Barrio Van Nuys*, May 2009).

These injunctions attempt to go beyond the typical suppression impact and keep kids at the local area schools protected from the local gangs committing crimes in the target areas.

Reduce Gang Recruiting

Gang injunctions have the potential to impact group processes associated with gangs, including limiting the gang's ability to recruit new members. The purpose of a gang injunction is not only to curtail crimes committed by the enjoined gang, but also to play a role in the prevention and intervention of gang activity when possible, including reducing the ability for the gang to attract new members (*People v. Oxnard Colonia Chiques*, 2004). All gangs must have a recruiting process if they want to remain in existence, and as such, some injunctions target gang recruiting and contain language that prohibits "soliciting or recruiting anyone under the age of 18 to join, actively participate in, or associate with the intent to join the target gang" (*People v. 18th Street*, 2004); still others use the same language but add the name of the specific gang involved (*People v. Southside Montebello*, 2004).

The Playboys gang injunction contains a restriction that makes it a violation for any person to force any other person to join the Playboys gang by making threats or doing anything threatening, including without limitation striking, battering, destroying personal property, and disturbing the peace to cause a person to join the gang (*People v. Playboys*, 2006). The Geer/Schoolyard injunction has a restriction entitled "protection of children from gangs," which prohibits any served gang members from soliciting or actively recruiting anyone under the age of 18 to join, actively participate in, or associate with the intent to join a criminal street gang (*People v. Geer and Schoolyard Crips*, 2006). The Chopper City injunction includes making any threats to shoot, stab, strike, hit, batter, injure, assault, disturb the peace, or destroy the personal property of anyone as an incentive to join the gang (*People v. Chopper City*, 2007).

Recruiting is usually conducted by gang members at local schools, on the street, at fast food restaurants and their parking lots, at parties and family get-togethers, in custody, and anywhere else they may find potential members. The need to make it more difficult for a gang to recruit new members is obvious if we in law enforcement hope to have a long-term impact on gangs in the areas they are most active.

A person does not become a gang member overnight; it involves a slow assimilation into the gang that involves older members monitoring the younger member's progress to ensure that the prospective member is able to prove himself or herself. Gang members are almost always required to undergo a gang initiation regardless of ethnicity to prove their worth, courage, and establish a reputation. Usually, this entails the potential member committing specific crimes, or he or she may be required to get "jumped in," which is a fight with several members of his or her gang to show he or she is tough and can take a beating for the gang. Sometimes it requires sex, where females may have to have sex with the male members.

Most gangs recruit from their home territory and expand outward; hence not allowing gang members to hang out openly in public view and at specific locations, such as malls and schools, may impact the recruiting efforts of a gang. Without new recruits, gangs would become isolated and unable to grow in size and power. In California, recruiting gang participation is a felony per Penal Code Section 186.26; however, it is difficult to make and prosecute those cases. If a specific gang injunction can prevent the recruitment of even one child, some would argue the gang injunction was well worth the cost and effort.

How a Gang's Structure Impacts a Gang Injunction (Territorial vs. Mobile)

Structurally there are several categories of street gangs, and understanding individual gang characteristics is necessary before a gang injunction should be considered. According to Thrasher (1927), "The gang is an interstitial group originally formed spontaneously, and then integrated through conflict." It is characterized by the following types of behavior: meeting face to face, milling, movement through space as a unit, conflict, and planning. Gangs vary in level of criminal activity, type of crimes committed, territoriality, and level of violence, overall gang size, and age and gender of the membership. That is why gang injunctions are admittedly not a viable solution to deal with every type of gang that currently exists. It is believed injunctions tend to work better on gangs that are territorial in nature because they are geographical and only applicable in a well-defined area.

Although some gangs share similar characteristics such as selling illegal drugs, committing violent crimes, and intimidating witnesses, they differ in others, such as territoriality, organizational structure, and ethnic background. For that reason not every gang would make a good candidate for a gang injunction. For example, if the gang is very mobile and claims territory all over a particular county, state, or region, it would be difficult to defend restricting the gang members in an entire city or county in most courts. One of the widely accepted prerequisites of an effective gang injunction is that the gang is territorial and creates a public nuisance in the designated target area.

Failing to address these prerequisites early in the process may make it difficult for law enforcement to gather evidence and successfully illustrate to the court that the gang poses a credible threat to the community to a significant enough degree to be considered a public nuisance. Such a gang would be better suited for other types of law enforcement action, such as undercover operations or electronic surveillance. Keeping the target areas manageable in size allows for a greater impact in most cases and makes the evidence collection a manageable task.

Some argue that gang injunctions are supposed to offer long-term effects and remove gangs from the community once implemented. It is important to remember that most gangs targeted by gang injunctions have been around in some cases for three and four generations. The implementation of a gang injunction will most likely not remove a gang problem in the months or years that follow when the problem in most cases has taken several decades to develop. It may, however, alter that gang's behavior and force them to limit their activity in the designated area to provide some relief to the community.

Again, most gangs targeted with an injunction are made up of members that were born and raised in the targeted area. To believe that a law enforcement officer handing the gang member a piece of paper, telling them they cannot engage in certain activities, or risk arrest, will cause them to move out of the area is not typically realistic. Some displacement of individual gang members is a desired effect; if the displacement occurs because the gang member wants to stop associating with his or her gang, it can be called positive displacement. If the moving to a new area reduces the level of crime committed by the gang member, the displacement can be viewed as a positive as opposed to a negative result.

In California, the most territorial gangs tend to be Hispanic and African American ethnic gangs, with some exceptions. Both Asian and Caucasian gangs do exist and pose tremendous problems for law enforcement; however, they tend to be more mobile and tend to not have easily defined territorial boundaries, which makes targeting them with an injunction more difficult. Of course exceptions exist and as time goes on, some Asian and Caucasian gangs are becoming more territorial and some may be, or may become, viable targets for future injunctions. In some cases Asian and Caucasian concerns for protecting a turf from rivals takes a back seat to their primary motivations, such as for-profit crimes or promoting their hate agenda.

A gang that moves freely across an entire city or county would not typically make a viable target for a gang injunction in most cases because a reasonable target area must be defined. One of the earliest gang injunctions sought attempted to include the entire city of Los Angeles as the target area, which by all accounts is considered too vague and needs to be better defined and supported by evidence of the gang's presence in the area (*People v. Playboy Gangster Crips*, 1987). Some gangs do not have an identifiable stronghold on any particular community; they are transitory and motivated by economic gain and less by turf and territorial issues, making them poor candidates for gang injunctions, as target areas need to be well defined.

In April 2005, Los Angeles City Mayor James Hahn announced that the city was seeking to expand upon gang injunctions, and he was considering a citywide gang injunction concept. The plan drew criticism from both sides of the issue. Some legislators have raised questions about whether his proposal can actually be implemented in the County of Los Angeles. Representatives from the American Civil Liberties Union say the plan would be vague and unenforceable. Hahn's plan calls for expanding gang injunctions to cover all of Los Angeles. Hahn said a citywide injunction would prevent gang crime from being pushed from one neighborhood to another. "We want to have a gang-free city in the city of Los Angeles," Hahn said. "We want to put gangs on notice that Los Angeles is off-limits." That may be a nice political sound bite; however, gangs that took generations to form will not likely be pushed out of Los Angeles by way of the gang injunction.

It is difficult to have an understanding of how a particular gang-directed policy will impact gang-related crime without knowing how the groups targeted by the policy are organized, or more specifically, how the group members are connected to one another. Understanding the structure of the gang to be targeted with an injunction is also a critical element of the declaration from the gang expert supporting the request for the injunction. It is acknowledged that not all individuals who display the outward signs of gang membership in a particular neighborhood are actually involved in significant criminal activities; making a comprehensive review of the potential targets a critical step in the injunction process.

It is important to distinguish between the levels of membership in the targeted gang, including the gang leaders, hard-core and violent members, general members, fringe and peripheral members, and the "wannabe" or at-risk population for gang documentation purposes. In the past, an individual's age, physical size, and arrest record were often principal factors in determining where he or she stood in the gang hierarchy; now money derived from narcotic sales and ability to provide resources to the gang also impacts the individual's status within the gang. Understanding the structure and level each potential defendant holds is necessary to support the request for the injunction.

The structure of gangs in California varies depending primarily on size. The gangs range in size from 5 or 10 to several thousand members, which often causes some of the larger gangs to break up into smaller groups, called cliques or subsets. Some gang injunctions target just the smaller cliques or subsets of a larger gang to keep a focus on the most violent groups within the larger gang. Such was the case in San Bernardino, with the injunctions against the 7th Street Gang and the Sur Crazy Ones gang, which are both cliques of the larger Westside Verdugo gang (*People v. Sur Crazy Ones*, 1999; *People v. 7th Street Gang*, 1997); and in San Diego, where the Logan Heights gang consists of Logan 30th Street, Logan 33rd Street, and the Logan Red Steps clique, which was targeted with an injunction (*People v. Logan Red Steps*, 2002).

In February 2007, the Westside 18th Street gang was named as one of the top 10 most wanted gangs in Los Angeles, and plans were formulated to target the gang with the full force of the law, including gang injunctions. The 18th Street gang, more specifically the Westside 18th Street gang, has been the target of seven different gang injunctions to date. Each injunction targets individual cliques of the very large 18th Street gang that operates on an international level, including the Alsace Clique, Pico Union, Highland Gangsters, Shatto Park Locos, Hollywood, Wilshire, and Columbia Little Cycos (*People v. 18th St. Alsace Clique*, 1997; *People v. 18th St. Gang Pico/Union*, 1997; *People v. 18th St. Shatto Park*, 1998; *People v. 18th Street Pico Union #2*, 2002; *People v. 18th Street Hollywood*, 2003; *People v. 18th Street Wilshire*, 2004; *People v. 18th St. CLCS*, 2005).

Gangs like the 18th Street one break up into cliques typically because this brings more territory under the control of the larger gang, making the targeting of cliques vs. the entire gang more appropriate, as injunctions focus on a very specific area, usually under the control of one or a few cliques of the larger group.

6

Legal Criticism of Gang Injunctions and Gang Abatement

The use of gang injunctions is undoubtedly a very controversial policy and legal tool. Groups such as the ACLU have blasted the practice and aggressively fought against it in part because they feel it gives law enforcement officials too much authority, leaving many residents vulnerable to having their constitutional rights violated and being targeted based on impermissible factors such as ethnicity. Under the criminal system, a police officer must have probable cause to make an arrest. By using civil injunctions, some feel the lowered threshold and increase in police discretion takes away that layer of protection that suspected gang members have under a criminal system, and can lead to racially suspect decisions. The debates are evident in the daily media and in specific cases. In addition to legal arguments, there are many debate issues. For example, gang injunctions are not effective, they are racist and unfair, they are not cost-effective, they lack community support, they are unfairly attacked in the media, and when someone gets on an injunction, they can never get off. All of these issues will be discussed in this chapter.

NOT EFFECTIVE DEBATE

Many hold the opinion that gang injunctions are too manpower and man-hour intensive and do not produce the anti-gang results that one good gang wire tap or gang sweep would accomplish. It is very common for academics and critics to overlook the existing research on gang injunctions, especially when the results of the existing research do not conform to their personal beliefs or the research they are conducting at that time. Many critics feel there is little empirical evidence to suggest that gang injunctions are effective in reducing gang activity; this is simply not true.

This book contains the results of two studies conducted to answer the questions: Do gang injunctions reduce crime? And if so, what makes one gang injunction more effective than another? Chapter 8 outlines the results of the largest gang injunction effectiveness study conducted to date, and Chapter 9 contains the results of a police officer survey that identifies the variables or factors that impact injunction effectiveness. In addition, a review of several significant studies on the issue has been discussed throughout the book.

I have heard many critics say that because gang injunctions do not act to deter gang membership or involvement—indicating that when served with a gang injunction, gangs do not view it as a wakeup call to cease gang activity—gang injunctions are not effective in their opinion. It is important to remember that most gangs targeted by gang injunctions have been around for more than one generation, sometimes two, three, or even four generations. The inclusion of a gang member in a gang injunction will most likely not result in them jumping out of the gang, immediately making the decision to become a productive member of society, or eliminate the gang problem in the months or years that immediately follow, when the gang has taken several decades to develop. I think many critics need to keep the expectations of any injunction or abatement effort in perspective and be realistic; it is a rare event that a gang injunction can meet this lofty expectation.

What gang injunctions do, however, in many cases is alter the gang's behavior and, when properly enforced, force them to limit their activity in the designated area and provide some needed relief for the community. Gang injunctions and abatement are all about targeting a gang member's behavior. Again, most gangs targeted with an injunction are made up of members that were raised and grew up in the targeted areas. Believing that a law enforcement officer handing the gang member a piece of paper, or hundreds of pieces of paper in this case, and telling him he cannot engage in certain activities, or risk arrest, will cause the entire gang to disband and the members to stop being criminals is not a realistic expectation of an injunction. It is realistic and proven, however, that injunctions have a positive impact on reducing crime rates in the target areas. Less crime means a safer community and an increased quality of life for the citizens in the community.

A recent example of the police and prosecution's analysis of injunction effectiveness is from San Francisco. Police indicate they have been tracking arrest data since the imposition of each gang injunction filed since 2006, and the San Francisco City Attorney's Office and police have observed a general "cooling off" effect among gang members named in the various injunctions, with markedly fewer arrests citywide following the imposition of injunctions. Since San Francisco's gang injunction program was launched, 46% of identified gang members (43 of 93) have gone without even a single arrest in San Francisco for crimes other than minor violations of the injunction itself. The data also show progressive improvements over time, with only 14% of identified gang members arrested for noninjunction crimes so far in 2010–2011, down from 41% in 2007. In addition, to date no injunction has resulted in an observable migration of gang-related crime or nuisances to adjacent areas or to different neighborhoods, as evidenced by citywide arrest data and observations by experts from the San Francisco Police Department's Gang Task Force. This type of crime reduction is common in gang injunction cases throughout the state.

ILLEGAL DEBATE

Critics argue that gang injunctions are illegal, unconstitutional, and even racist, and therefore their level of effectiveness is irrelevant. Some feel that gang injunctions are bad law, others feel they are good, and still others feel they will eventually produce bad case law and greater legal restrictions against law enforcement, specifically restrictions like the no association and due process arguments will eventually be overturned. Critics view injunctions as an inappropriate use of public funds and as poor public policy. One thing is for sure, the outcome of any case varies greatly based on the jurisdiction, the courts, the appellate courts, and the legal issue at hand in each case.

That is, even when studies show gang injunctions work, they should not be utilized because of legal concerns, according to critics of the policy. For example, we could perhaps reduce crime by implementing a dusk-to-dawn curfew for the entire community and setting up random search checkpoints at all major intersections looking for contraband, but such drastic measures would be unconstitutional. Many police states have little crime, yet they also lack the freedom and privacy that our constitution affords. We do not need a police state to have control of criminals, just common sense and the ability to implement effective laws and policies that will deal with the problem in a real and efficient manner.

The constitutionality of gang injunctions usually requires a legal analysis, taking into account two primary considerations. The first consideration is whether gang activities constitute a public nuisance, and the second is whether it is constitutional to enjoin the activities of a street gang. Analysis to determine if gang activities constitute a public nuisance involves a detailed examination of the common law definitions of public and private nuisances as they have evolved in state courts over the past century. Such analysis must also consider how those principles have been codified in the statutes of California and other states.

California Civil Code Section 3479 defines a public nuisance as anything that is "injurious to health or is indecent or offensive to the senses, or an obstruction to the free use of property, so as to interfere with the comfortable enjoyment of life or property, or unlawfully obstructs the free passage or use, in the customary manner, of any navigable lake, or river, bay, stream, canal, or basin, or any public park, square, street, or highway." As another example, the Varrio Horseshoe gang injunction defines the nuisance area as "any area open to the public, or an alley, plaza, park, driveway, or parking lot, or an automobile, whether moving or not, or a building open to the general public, including one that serves food or drink, or provides entertainment, or the doorways and entrances to a building or dwelling, or the grounds enclosing a building or dwelling" (*People v. Arroyo*, 1998).

The notion of a public nuisance is also addressed in California Penal Code Section 370, which essentially mirrors the civil definition. Penal Code Section 372 makes it a misdemeanor to continue to operate an activity that is a public nuisance. Therefore, California courts have equitable jurisdiction to enjoin a public nuisance and to provide for penalties for a violation of an injunction.

The determination of whether an activity is a nuisance requires the balance of competing interests, the rights of the individual gang member, and the rights of the community. By allowing a cause of action for abatement of a nuisance, the common law courts of England, as well as the subsequent state courts in the United States, recognized a fundamental principle of governance that no liberty is absolute. Like individuals, communities also have rights and the state has a responsibility to govern its citizens by properly balancing individual liberty against the liberties of others.

A basic analysis of public nuisance principles indicates that illicit activities of street gangs are a public nuisance as defined by common law because of a substantial and unreasonable interference with a public right. Residents' property rights at times become subservient to the gang members, who violate or damage residents' property. Such actions are devoid of any public benefit and are an unmitigated interference with the public safety and the welfare rights of the local community.

Accordingly, gang activities are often found to be unreasonable under a public nuisance analysis. Given the totality of the facts, gang activities do substantially interfere with the property rights of the members of the local community. Further, the gang has no social benefit that mitigates its detrimental impact on the community. Thus, street gangs fall within the definition of a public nuisance and can be enjoined upon a showing of proof.

"Public interest in tranquility, security, and protection is invoked only to be blithely dismissed, subordinated to the paramount right of the individual," wrote California Supreme Court Justice Janice Rogers Brown in the *Acuna* case. In *Acuna*, the true nature of the trade-off becomes painfully obvious, according to Brown. She wrote, "Liberty unrestrained is an invitation to anarchy. Freedom and responsibility are joined at the hip."

Some argue against injunctions for fear of a slippery slope; once we accept injunctions against gangs, nothing will prevent the government from seeking injunctions against the PTA or the Boys and Girls Club. Media outlets contribute to and regularly fuel this fear by reporting misleading information about the injunctions, which in some cases creates community apprehension about the policy.

As noted by Justice Brown, who wrote the majority opinion in *Acuna*, "there are few forms of action in the history of law with a history older than suits seeking to halt nuisances, whether public or private." The underlying action for a nuisance is that one must use his own right so as not to infringe on the rights of others, a concept foreign to most gang members. Gang members typically do not have concern for the rights of others, which is why gang injunctions are applicable to them. Gang members rarely make any attempt to avoid infringement on the rights of others and are typically concerned only about themselves, their own interests, and the interests of their gang (*People v. Acuna*, 1995). Reconciliation of the rights of an individual and the rights of society is of particular importance in an action for public nuisance.

A public nuisance is characterized by an unreasonable exercise of an individual right at the expense of a public right. If the public's right is determined to be more important than the exercise of the private right, courts will hold that the exercise of the private right is unreasonable and will enjoin it as a public nuisance. Because gangs have been deemed public nuisances, and because nuisances can be enjoined, gang injunctions are a legal and constitutional method to address gangs in the State of California and elsewhere.

Civil rights groups want to minimize any erosion of our perceived liberties. Critics feel it is not worth damaging our personal liberties to deal with street gangs that represent a very small segment of the total population. Critics feel the temporary safety a gang injunction may or may not provide is not worth the price our liberty is paying. An individual's point of view on this issue typically varies, depending upon where he or she lives and works, raises his or her family, and what role the local gang plays in impacting the quality of his or her life.

Acts of gang violence are not constitutionally protected activities, and the police and prosecution have an obligation to think outside the box and find effective solutions to deal with gangs. In fact, one does not have a constitutional right to be a gang member. To hold otherwise would effectively make the constitution null and void by destroying the ability of the government to protect the citizens. The California Supreme Court has held that gang activities may be enjoined as public nuisances upon demonstration that the gang is such.

According to several civil rights lawyers, the idea of arresting somebody off the front porch violates the First and Fourteenth Amendment rights of the gang members. The ACLU and other critics take the stance that when we as a society give up liberty for the sake of safety, we don't deserve liberty or safety. However, injunction supporters feel that the civil rights espoused by gang members in our society to justify their criminal conduct fail the strict scrutiny test; thus far the state of California and several other states have been able to illustrate a compelling reason to enforce such injunctions to preserve the safety and security of residents at large. Because it is unreasonable to expect the average citizen to constantly be subjected to the inherent intimidation and violence of criminal street gangs, gang injunctions can present an appropriate solution for resolving these conflicting interests.

California Penal Code Section 186.21 declares: "It is the right of every person to be secure and protected from fear, intimidation, and physical harm caused by the activities of violent groups or individuals." Gang members have rights and certainly deserve equal protection and due process under the law. The dilemma is that oftentimes the rights of the community members that have to live in the injunction zones occupied by the neighborhood gang are violated and ignored.

Gang injunctions are intended to help the masses, people in our communities that obey the law, pay their taxes, respect their neighbors, and do not commit crimes, and are targeted at a gang that exists for the sole purpose of committing criminal acts. Offensive and obnoxious exercises of people's rights to free speech or assembly have been the subject of legislative and court action for several centuries, creating the legal category of public nuisances that can legally be abated. Penal Code Section 186.21 embraces the public nuisance doctrine, which is aimed at the protection and redress of community interests and, at least in theory, embodies the kind of collective ideal of civil life that the courts have vindicated by equitable remedies since the beginning of the sixteenth century.

The stated goal of gang injunctions is to return control of specific neighborhoods from the gang members to the law-abiding citizens and improve the quality of life for those in the targeted communities. To accomplish this goal, police and prosecutors argue that the individual rights of gang members, who have been identified as being the cause of the problem in the target areas, need to be restricted. Furthermore, law enforcement contends that the founding fathers of our country never intended the constitution to protect the gang members' rights to sell drugs, terrorize the community, and commit crimes at will.

GANG INJUNCTIONS AND LEGAL ACCUSATIONS OF RACISM

One of the most common specific complaints about injunctions is they are sanctioned racism because ethnic minorities are the most likely targets (Figure 6.1). According to a 2006 survey, 44% of all gang members in the United States are Hispanic, 35% are African American, 14% are Caucasian, 5% are Asian, and 2% are a mix of various ethnic groups. The percentages for Hispanic and African American gangs are slightly higher in California than the national average, where the majority of injunctions have been filed. About 85 to 90% of the gangs that exist in California are either Hispanic or African American in ethnicity.

Based upon the known gang ethnicity, it would be reasonable to assume that roughly 85 to 90% of all injunctions would target either Hispanic or African American gangs by chance alone. However, all but a handful of injunctions in California target ethnic Hispanic or African American gangs. Law enforcement officers and prosecutors explain the ethnic disparity as a by-product of gang territoriality, not racism or ethnicity. Certain ethnic gangs are more territorial than others. African American and Hispanic gangs tend to be more territorial than Asian and Caucasian gangs. Since gang injunctions are enforceable only in very well-defined target areas, injunctions could have a more significant impact on gangs beholden to a territory rather than a gang that moves freely around large areas such as entire counties, or even several states without problem.

FIGURE 6.1 Gang Injunction Protest in Northern California.

FIGURE 6.2 Sign being held by injunction protestor.

Concerns of racial fairness are consistently raised by the critics of gang injunctions and other public order laws or ordinances that target gangs (Figure 6.2). For each person that feels gang injunctions promote public safety, someone else may feel they promote racial tension. Following the *City of Chicago v. Morales* case involving the controversial antiloitering ordinance, the attorney who had argued the case for the winning side called the decision "a victory for young men of color." That comment raised questions about a case in which no claim of racial discrimination was made by the parties or discussed by the court. So why was the issue made a racial rather than public policy one?

It may be due in part to a critical perception that gang injunctions unfairly target ethnic minorities and those that are poor and cannot defend themselves. Race often plays a key role in long-standing constitutional objections to expansive police discretion authorized by new laws and policies, to include gang injunctions and abatement. Some members of ethnic minority groups oppose any police action that targets minority groups, regardless of circumstance or impact.

Justice Mosk, in the dissenting opinion in the *Acuna* case, viewed the injunction as a racially discriminatory deprivation of the rights of Latinos to free association under the First Amendment. The justice and some others in the community characterize gang injunctions as a deprivation of minority rights (*People v. Acuna*, 1995). Gang injunction supporters feel that such arguments may be attempting to divert the true issue and simply seek to scare the community and create racial tension.

Concerns about the enforcement of public order laws will continue to create a debate about potential racial friction and patterns of racial subjugation. Gang injunctions, however, do not implicate race; they target gang-related activities, irrespective of the gang's racial composition. In California, the racial makeup of the majority of gangs is Hispanic, followed by African American, Asian, and Caucasian. The debate over the current ethnicity of gangs in our nation is a social issue well beyond the scope of gang injunctions and is rooted much more in poverty and breakdown of the family unit in our communities.

Many people in the law enforcement community are offended by the suggestion that they seek gang injunctions out of racial hatred. Law enforcement agencies select target gangs based upon several criteria, including the level of criminal activity of the gang, the type of gangs active in the community, the crimes of violence committed by the gang, and the territoriality of the gang. Ethnicity of the gang is immaterial; if the territorial gangs happen to be ethnic minorities, then so be it, according to police.

Others disagree with law enforcement, such as a resident helping to plan the rally against the Broderick Boys injunction. "Racism is the issue; police are targeting the young people to get rid of them, to get them out of town." Many law enforcement jurisdictions have indicated they have been actively searching for qualified Caucasian and Asian gangs to enjoin; however, few have been realistic candidates to be enjoined to date because they are not turf-oriented and they do not have well-defined territories that can be supported by crime data and specific incidents of gang violence in the well-defined area. Asian and Caucasian gangs that are mobile and transitory in nature may make better targets of wire taps, undercover narcotics operations, and other police enforcement tactics that have no correlation to a defined turf or territory. There have been a few cases filed against Asian gang members; for example, in 2000, the *City of San Jose v. S. Vietnam* was filed on July 28 (Santa Clara CV791443), in 2008, the *People v. the Oriental Troop, Mongolian Boys Society, and Lao Pride Gang* was filed on May 12 (Tulare 08-226863), and the *People v. the Oriental Boyz* was filed on September 10 (Los Angeles BC397522). The handful of Caucasian gang members that have been subjected to a gang injunction are typically members of a primarily African American or Hispanic gang that allows for a mixed ethnicity.

The chief of police in Yolo County defended his department's injunction and stated that racism was not a factor; the Broderick gang members were targeted because they were criminals, not due to their ethnic background. The police and prosecution described the injunction as being directed at intervention and prevention as well as suppression, "We won't tolerate activities that jeopardize public safety" (*People v. Broderick Boys*, 2004).

COST DEBATE

Many people in our communities feel money should not be spent on gang injunctions; it should be spent on potentially more beneficial community programs. In the Colonia neighborhood in Ventura County, some in the community feel they would have been better served if the estimated $180,000 price tag to obtain the gang injunction was put back into the local community, such as with park improvements, tutoring programs for kids, library construction, etc.

Not many people would disagree that we need to give these gang members access to alternatives to gang life through employment, job skills training, education, and substance abuse rehabilitation. Most educated academics, police officers, and community members feel we must provide effective social services to families, youth, and young adults involved in or affected by gang violence through mentoring, drug and alcohol abuse counseling, mental health services, prenatal care, and early childhood intervention if a long-term solution to the gang problem is to be reached. The need for social programs does not, however, negate the need for law enforcement and never will.

We have had gangs in this country since the 1800s despite billions being spent on anti-gang programs, to include suppression, intervention, and prevention programs and policies. To think that adding a few social programs will make the gang problem go away is not realistic, just as it is not realistic to think that adding a gang injunction to a community will make the gang problem disappear. There will always be a need to hold criminals accountable for their actions and to control gangs in the more active areas, no matter how many social programs exist.

Some community members have concerns that no public accounting of actual and future anticipated costs of gang injunctions is ever discussed with the community. Gang injunctions are not unlike any other gang enforcement policy. The police do not seek community support to conduct a wire tap investigation of the local gang that may cost much more than a gang injunction, nor do they request community approval to conduct a large-scale gang sweep that may involve police overtime costs. The police have a budget approved by their city council, as do sheriff departments with their county board of supervisors. The police who are trained on how to suppress crime make the decisions on how to spend their budget based upon the needs of their community. In communities where gangs are the primary problem, the department can make a decision to seek an injunction and allocate the funds they feel appropriate to prepare and obtain the injunctions with or without community support.

Some of the neighborhoods targeted with an injunction have lost control of their communities, and drastic measures are needed to help the community and the police gain a basic level of control. While working to gain control, police departments traditionally do not involve the community in the decision-making process when talking about police tactics. According to the chief of police in West Sacramento, referring to police allocation of financial resources, while some may not like this answer, it's simply how they do things (*People v. G-Mobb*, 2004).

COMMUNITY SUPPORT DEBATE

Gang injunctions attempt to create and maintain a safe, healthy, and secure environment for everyone, regardless if they want the help or not. In connection with the philosophies of community-oriented policing, suppression strategies like civil gang injunctions have become more popular despite some critics contentions that gang injunctions sought without sufficient community involvement and with no community review board undermine the partnership between the community and law enforcement. Critics claim that citizens should openly support each injunction before it is implemented, and if the community does not support the injunction, it should not be sought in that community.

In reality the open support of the community is often not necessary, and to expect community support in neighborhoods that tend to not get involved in reporting crimes, do not participate in the political process, and often have a negative and mistrusted view of those in authority, is not always possible. Some critics have requested a community review board to review gang injunction arrests because current policy has inadequate checks and balances, as significant, systematic community input is lacking. The police in every jurisdiction have discretion to make arrests for crimes that occur in their presence when they have probable cause to make the arrest. Critics question the validity of an injunction arrest because all of the evidence used to obtain the injunction and support the arrests is often based solely on police allegations, which they claim are filled with speculation and hearsay.

Some police feel that if it is possible to get an injunction without community involvement, it is better for the community. Police officers do not have a problem testifying against the local gang; that is what they get paid to do. Community members are typically fearful to testify. By having only police officers as your witnesses, the community is protected from potential retaliation as a result of testifying against the gang. Police officers should be the ones to document the evidence and testify in court. If citizens can be left out of that loop, it simply reduces any chance the information gets released, whether purposefully, inadvertently, or by court order, further protecting the community. The police and prosecution have the ability to recognize the problem and have an obligation to take action with or without visible community support.

It is a common law enforcement perception that the honest law-abiding citizens do not speak up as loudly as the problem groups. The gangs and their supporters often complain their constitutional rights are being violated, typically without giving thought to the constitutional rights of the community at large that has to deal with their criminal activity. To say that gang injunctions ignore the communities' needs and concerns is not based on evidence or supported by the existing literature on the subject.

Community members who work, live, or go to school in gang-infested areas often are aware of specific locations, including the private properties in their neighborhoods that are used by gangs to engage in criminal activity. For gang members, these properties are essential to their survival because they provide a safe haven to sell drugs and engage in other criminal activity. Further, the properties help to solidify the gang's control over the neighborhood by becoming the hangout or headquarters for the gang. This is why a large percentage of a police officer's time is spent at these locations, making arrest after arrest, obtaining search warrants, and conducting surveillance or undercover operations in an effort to stop the problems there.

In addition, the collection of citizen declarations requires additional manpower and time to get the case ready for court. Sometimes it is difficult to get citizens to state on the record the scope and nature of the problems. Some citizens do not want the local gang to see the police at their home or business talking to them for an extended period of time for fear the gang will think they are informing to the police.

For example, a total of 100 residents, business owners, and citizens were contacted by officers from the Neighborhood Policing Team during the Old Town National City gang injunction investigation in 1998. A total of 32 citizens decided to make an official statement under penalty of perjury, because they wanted the court to know how they felt about the local gang and how the gang negatively impacted their lives. The other 68 people had concerns and wanted help to suppress the local gang; they just were too fearful to sign their name and describe the gang problem due to concern the gang would somehow find out and retaliate against them.

Some citizens, however, do prepare a declaration about their personal opinions and experiences with the gang problem in the area. Most describe a sense of fear that often prevents them from identifying themselves as witnesses to unlawful activity in the community. They were reluctant to call the police due to fear that they or their family may be hurt as a result of being labeled by the gang as being a snitch. Others expressed concern that the gang would find out that they were talking to the police and that they would be hurt or killed by the retaliatory gang (*City of National City v. OTNC Gang*, 1998).

After police make it clear to citizens that may want to provide information to help obtain the injunction that the information would be protected, some brave citizens do give detailed information. In some cases, the information provided by the citizens is very compelling and helps the city or district attorney justify and prove the existence of the public nuisance. Some judges, especially with the early injunctions, wanted to get a community perspective about how the gang caused a public nuisance. More recent injunctions have tended to not use citizen declarations because the evidence against the gang collected by the police is sufficient to obtain the injunctions without unnecessary citizen involvement that could potentially place the citizens in danger as a result of their assisting law enforcement.

In early March 1998, a business owner in the Old Town National City gang area told how the gang impacted his family and business. He had been operating his store under the daily pressure of the OTNC gang members for some years. He told how groups of OTNC gang members came into his store on a daily basis and shoplifted food, beer, liquor, and other items. He had been robbed over 10 times by gang members in a three-year period before the injunction. His store was routinely covered with gang graffiti, which he had to paint over every week, sometimes more often than that, costing him valuable time and money. He had been the victim of gang intimidation when he testified against two OTNC gang members apprehended after robbing his store. The tires on his vehicle had been slashed following his testimony, and his daughter had her life threatened while she worked behind the counter at the store.

The business owner stated that when the gang members would congregate in front of his store they scared away potential customers. He said that regular customers would not stop at his store when the gang members were out front for fear that they would get robbed or beat up coming or going from the store. The gang members had assaulted him with bricks and other weapons when he had tried to protect his property or stop a theft in progress by OTNC gang members. He admitted that he needed help; he said the store was his life, he could not move, and he barely made enough money to keep the store open and support his family. He said the nearest grocery store was over 2 miles away, and some in the community went to his store to buy milk, bread, diapers, and other essentials because it was convenient.

This business owner is not unlike hundreds of others in gang-enjoined neighborhoods. The injunction had a significant impact on the quality of this man's life, the life of his family, and the welfare of his business. Injunctions were designed to help people like him, and when properly enforced can have a significant positive impact.

The police in virtually every jurisdiction in California do extend their hand to the communities and actively attempt to build partnerships with the community in some regards. The use of gang injunctions may encourage more community involvement and support in solving the gang problem in the target areas, but not always.

MEDIA CAMPAIGN OF MISINFORMATION

Gang members are often aided and abetted by politicians and the media who thrive on sensational reactions that gangs elicit from the community. In some jurisdictions, however, there has been a campaign of misinformation about the proposed injunction being put forth by a small handful of people, typically not representing the will of the masses. It is unclear if this is intentional on their part or simply reflects ignorance about what a gang injunction really does. The media also plays into the campaign of misinformation in some cases by giving the most radical elements of the community a forum to give their views without providing an unbiased discussion of the particular issue. In other cases, the media reports changes in crime rates, up or down, as collected by law enforcement agencies. Many media accounts contain proclamations of the success of gang injunctions. Many jurisdictions have multiple injunctions, and presumably, repetition of their usage follows a positive experience or observable reduction in gang crime, which provides justification for multiple cases.

Some media establishments are more liberal in their views and do not seem to care if their views are biased; their primary concern is the sale of newspapers, not the fair reporting of the news. In addition, some news outlets have conducted studies claiming to have analyzed crime statistics in some injunction areas revealing injunctions do not work. In a dozen cases I have personally requested the data used to support those alleged studies, but the media outlets contacted indicated the data were no longer available and were destroyed, making any verification of the methods used to do the study impossible to recreate or challenge.

The type of community in the target area, how involved they are, whether they openly support or reject the injunction, elected officials' view of the injunctions, media portrayals of the order, activist presence and involvement, etc., all contribute to the critical or supportive views of injunctions.

The police are one small part of the community; they alone will not solve the gang problem. Because problem-oriented interventions call for the collaboration between various law enforcement agencies and non-law enforcement organizations, the participation of nonprosecutorial law enforcement agencies (such as police and probation/parole agencies), social service agencies, and community organizations allows the consideration of response alternatives that are beyond the resources of the prosecutor.

Comparisons can be made between injunction efforts to determine how many and what types of nonprosecutorial organizations have been involved in injunction efforts and whether variations in collaboration have an influence on the acquisition of injunctions. Identities of community organizations will also be used in the community involvement phase of the study. Questions 15 and 16 of the police survey ask the police officers to assess the nature of community involvement by rating the level of involvement and its impact on the injunction decision. By approaching the issue of community involvement from the police perspective, a correlation may be made between the level and impact of community involvement and the injunction's impact on potential crime reduction.

GIVE THEM A WAY OUT OF THE GANG AND OFF THE INJUNCTION: OPTING OUT

The majority of injunctions filed in the past few years are more specific as to how a suspected gang member can request to be removed from an injunction. The gang injunction has the potential to remove a specific member from the group. This provides more potential opportunities for the member to leave the group, giving him or her a viable excuse not to participate in the gang's activity within the target area because he or she is on the gang injunction. However, some suspected gang members feel they were wrongfully added to an injunction, or they are no longer active in the gang and do not feel the evidence against them warrants their inclusion in the specific injunction. For this reason some injunctions contain an opt-out or renunciation or dismissal provision.

Many of the more recent injunctions include provisions that allow members to opt out from the restrictions of the gang injunction. In some aspects this is one restriction that can have a real impact on the life of the gang member that may be thinking of moving on and distancing himself from the gang. It has the potential to give the gang member a way out, not only from the gang injunction but even possibly the gang itself. For example, the Playboys injunction contains a restriction that states, "Don't prevent any person from leaving the Playboys gang," making it a violation for any gang member to prevent a fellow gang member from leaving the gang (*People v. Playboys*, 2006).

According to Los Angeles City Attorney Jule Bishop, her office evaluated numerous gang members served with several different injunctions on a case-by-case basis and have removed dozens of names from service lists when the evidence did not support their inclusion as fair to the gang members. In Los Angeles, no one may have formally opted out in a court of law; however, dozens of gang members have had cases dropped against them because the evidence showing them to be active gang members was not present when the case was filed, or the evidence was not gathered or submitted in time for the first court appearance. According to the Los Angeles city attorney, if a gang member goes five years with no police contact, and can show he or she is no longer part of the problem, he or she can request to the court to be removed from the injunction.

In San Diego County, at least five members have successfully petitioned the courts and have been removed from the injunctions against them. Contrary to media reports, there are very clear instructions that gang members can follow to request they be removed from the orders. Gang members failing to follow the instructions provided does not negate the presence of the instructions. In 2007, the City of San Francisco entered into an agreement between the city attorney's office, the American Civil Liberties Union of Northern California, and the Lawyers' Committee for Civil Rights of the San Francisco Bay Area, establishing an administrative process by which individuals named in civil gang injunctions may petition to opt out from the court-ordered provisions. City Attorney Herrera said the opt-out process "both maximizes civil liberties protections for alleged gang members, and ensures the effectiveness of civil gang injunctions to protect San Francisco neighborhoods from violence and nuisance conduct."

Many gang injunction opponents feel gang members cannot find a way off the injunction list because they can't meet the "high standards" set by the injunctions, including, for example, spending 18 months in school or on a job, signing a document under the penalty of perjury renouncing membership in a gang, and by far the most important, avoiding police contact for 3 to 5 years. Under the terms of the injunction, police contact doesn't necessarily mean an arrest; it can mean simply being questioned. Avoiding the police is viewed as impossible in some of these communities.

Getting Off an Injunction: What Is Required?

As is the case with many of the processes and procedures to obtain an injunction, the same is true with the process to get off one once served. In the interest of fairness, the City of Los Angeles developed a process for those served with a gang injunction and who want the opportunity to demonstrate that they should not be restrained by the gang injunction because they no longer are, or they never were, a gang member.

The Los Angeles City Attorney's Office has put in place a review process for those persons living in the City of Los Angeles who believe they were wrongly served with a gang injunction because they were not then and are not now a gang member, or who were properly served but have since ended their association with the gang. The review process is intended to be informal and does not require the filing of any papers with a court or any appearances before a judge. According to the Los Angeles city attorney, to be eligible for removal from a gang injunction after being personally served, the offender must provide sufficient information for the city attorney's office to positively confirm several key factors (Los Angeles Times, 2007):

1. You no longer are, or you never were, a member of the gang named in the gang injunction.
2. You are not now acting, and you will not in the future act, to promote, further, or assist any of the activities prohibited by the gang injunction on behalf of the gang named in the gang injunction.
3. You are not a member of any other criminal street gang.

The review process is conducted by a senior attorney within the city attorney's office who is not involved in the enforcement of gang injunctions. The attorney will review all of the information in the petition that was submitted, as well as any other available and reliable information concerning the past and present membership or involvement with criminal street gangs. The attorney may contact the individual for additional information and may contact other people who may have information relevant to the review process. If the petition is denied (the individual is not removed from the gang injunction at this time), a new petition may be submitted when significant new information supporting the claim can be provided.

The city attorney's office will keep the information provided in this form confidential to the extent permitted by law. The city attorney's office will not use the information provided in this form to prove any fact essential of any criminal charge the city attorney's office may bring against you in the future. (However, such information may still be used to cross-examine you should you testify at a trial in a case brought by the city attorney's office and should your testimony be inconsistent with the factual information provided in this form.)

Are you currently represented by an attorney (which includes a public defender)in any legal proceeding involving the gang injunction, including (but not limited to) a proceeding in which you are accused of violating the gang injunction (yes or no)? Because of ethical rules applicable to all attorneys, if you answered yes, your petition cannot be considered unless your attorney completes and signs it.

If you do not have a driver's license, please attach a copy of any picture ID, such as a California ID or a student ID card.

The name of the gang(s) appearing on the gang injunction, date (or approximate date) you were served, contact information, address, phone number, other address (if any) you would rather be contacted at, and email address may also be requested.

Have you ever been a member of the gang named in the gang injunction or any other criminal street gang? If you answered yes, please explain below when, how, and why you came to join the gang and when, how, and why you stopped being a member of the gang. Please provide the following information regarding any schools you have attended, including elementary, middle, and high school, a trade school, or college. Please start with your most recent school and work your way backward in time. Please provide the following information regarding any job you currently hold, as well as any other job(s) you held during the past three years. Please start with your current or most recent job and work your way backward in time. Please provide the following contact information for any people who know you and can confirm that you no longer are, or you never were, a member of a criminal street gang. Such people can include family members; neighbors; teachers, principals, and school staff; coaches and former teammates; current and past employers; community leaders and organizers; priests, ministers, reverends, and other religious counselors; social and gang intervention workers; and probation, parole, and police officers. Please use the space below to provide any additional information that you want considered. Such information may include the fact that you recently returned to school, started a new job, or completed a job training or substance abuse program. You can also attach letters and other documents to this form supporting your claim that you no longer are (or never were) a gang member, including letters from the people identified above.

By signing below, you are confirming the accuracy of the following statements:

1. I no longer am, or I never was, a member of the gang named in the gang injunction.
2. I am not now acting, and I will not act in the future, to promote, further, or assist any of the activities prohibited by the gang injunction on behalf of the gang named in the gang injunction.
3. I am not a member of any other criminal street gang.
4. All of the information provided in or with this form is, to the best of my knowledge, true and correct.

Critics claim subjects included in gang injunctions can have trouble getting jobs because the injunctions show up in employment background checks. The truth is that the gang members targeted with gang injunctions typically had no job prior to inclusion in the gang injunction, and most do not seek jobs following inclusion in an injunction. If an employer of a gang member conducts a background check of the applicant, the gang injunction may appear on the record, as do all of the other crimes the person has been arrested for, including all convictions for the individual.

In many cases it would be difficult if not impossible to determine if the injunction was the cause of harm to the gang member applicant, or if it was another crime the applicant previously committed. While community activists agree that something must be done about the gang problem, they worry that an injunction could permanently stigmatize those listed in the injunction. Los Angeles City Attorney Delgadillo announced the implementation of a new screening program in early 2007 to address this issue. The city's First Chance Intervention Program, which allows gang members named in injunctions to be excluded once they enter job training and education programs, was implemented.

The law allows for gang members that stop engaging in criminal activity to be removed from the injunctions, a fact they are all made aware of when served the court orders, including the requirements to do so. The fact that none have taken advantage of that option does not negate that they do have the option. If the gang members did comply with the opt-out provisions, it would mean they have renounced their gang membership, stopped committing crimes, and are no longer part of the problem. That is the ultimate goal of any anti-gang program or policy, including every gang intervention program in the City of Los Angeles and elsewhere.

The permanent order in the Colonia Chiques case, for example, includes an opt-out provision that gives individuals served the opportunity to be eventually dropped from the injunction (*People v. Colonia Chiques*, 2004). The Harpy's injunction specifies that any individual defendant, including those in default, may move the court to be removed from the order, making it unenforceable for them (*People v. Harpy's*, 1998). The requirements to receive this benefit are that the gang member file a proper motion to request dismissal, declare publicly that he or she is now a reformed gang member, is not an active gang member, and has renounced gang life. The defendant must not have been arrested or contacted by the police in a three-year period, not including any time spent in custody. The order also states that no third-party beneficiaries exist, meaning that it is not a defense that a defendant may have been eligible for dismissal in a criminal contempt proceeding.

Other injunctions have added a provision that if any renounced gang member that had been removed commits a new violation, by claiming membership in the gang, associating with known gang members, obtaining new gang-related tattoos, possessing gang-specific paraphernalia, or being arrested with other gang members, he or she may be re-served with the injunction order and the same terms and conditions will again apply to him or her (*People v. 42nd St.*, 2004). In Santa Barbara, the Lompoc gang injunction requires that gang members submit letters to the court renouncing gang membership and must have no arrests for five years before being removed from the injunction, according to Gene Martinez, Santa Barbara County senior deputy district attorney (*People v. Lamparas Primera and Southside*, 2005).

In the *Mesa Locos* case, for example, one defendant removed his gang tattoos, moved from the area, became employed, and had no new police contacts for several years after being served. As a result of the efforts made by the member, the San Diego district attorney dropped the member from the order after he proved he changed his ways (*People v. Varrio Mesa Locos*, 1999). For some gang members, the injunction gives them an out with their gang and can allow them to save face by not being in the target area, giving them an excuse to not participate in the gang's activity, and thus helping them control their own behavior.

San Francisco Policy

The San Francisco city attorney has an opt-out form on its home page and serves every gang member with a copy of the instructions on how to get off the injunction at the same time they are served with the papers informing them they have been added. Any person living in the City of San Francisco who has been served with a gang injunction and who wants the opportunity to demonstrate that they should not be restrained by the gang injunction because they are not active gang members can complete and submit the forms. The instructions inform the person that the gang injunction will be enforced against them if they have been personally served with it. If they are on a gang injunction enforcement list and have been personally served with the injunction, they must provide sufficient information for the city attorney's office to show that (1) they are not an active gang member, and (2) they are not participating in any of the activities prohibited by the gang injunction.

So What is the Review Process?

The review process is intended to provide individuals a fair and accessible way to establish that they are not an active gang member and so should be removed from the gang injunction enforcement list. An individual always has the right to file a motion directly in court seeking removal from a gang injunction. Such a motion can be filed in San Francisco Superior Court to bypass this administrative process.

The steps of the review and removal process are (San Francisco District Attorney, 2009):

1. Filing your petition: You can complete this form, or submit other documentation, as evidence that you are not an active gang member. Instructions on where to file your petition are below.
2. Review of your petition and decision by the city attorney: The city attorney will contact you to schedule an interview to discuss your petition. You have the right to representation at that meeting. The city attorney will also consider any other available and reliable information concerning your past and present membership in or involvement with criminal street gangs.
3. Decision by the city attorney: After the city attorney meets with you and reviews the evidence, he will make a determination as to whether he will support or deny your request for removal. You will be given a written decision, within 30 days, granting or denying your petition to be removed from the gang injunction and stating the reasons for that decision. This decision will be mailed to your home address or, if you prefer for safety or convenience reasons, to another address. If you are denied, you may submit a new petition to the city attorney when you have

new information to report supporting your claim that you are not an active gang member.

4. Petitioning the court for removal: If your request for removal is granted by the city and you have been enjoined by the court in an injunction, you still must file a motion with the San Francisco Superior Court to officially get your name removed from the enforcement list. The city attorney will file papers with the court saying that, after conducting his own investigation, he does not oppose your removal from the gang injunction. If your petition was granted prior to the hearing and you have not been enjoined by the court, the city attorney will simply remove you from the enforcement list. If the city attorney denies your request for removal, you still have the option of going to court and filing papers requesting removal directly from the court. The city attorney may oppose such individuals in court.
5. Opt-out assistance: You may contact Lawyers Committee for Civil Rights at 415-543-9444 with questions regarding the opt-out process and for assistance in identifying relevant community organizations and service providers to support your petition.

Confidentiality

The city attorney's office will keep the information you provide in this petition confidential to the extent required by law and will only use the information you provide to make a decision in this opt-out process, unless the information contained herein is false or misleading at the time it was presented to the city attorney's office or ceases to be true thereafter. The city attorney's office will take into account any privacy concerns raised by you related to the information provided to it.

As a condition of filing this request for opt-out, you must agree not to use the city attorney's response other than in an opt-out motion to the court or to show that you have been removed from the gang injunction enforcement list.

Representation by Counsel

Are you currently represented by an attorney (which includes a public defender) in any legal proceeding involving the gang injunction, including (but not limited to) a proceeding in which you are accused of violating the gang injunction? __ Yes __ No

Because of ethical rules applicable to all attorneys, if you answered yes, your petition cannot be considered unless your attorney completes and signs addendum 1 at the end of this petition. You are not required to have an attorney in order to apply for removal from a gang injunction.

How to Submit Your Petition

Once you have filled out this form, please make a copy of it for your records and submit the original *by mail only* to the San Francisco City Attorney's Office.

Identifying Information

You must complete a detailed personal statement including all of your identifying information: full name (last, first middle), date of birth, the name of the gang(s) appearing on the gang injunction, date you were served, contact information including home address, gang affiliation information, and support for your petition. You need to provide an explanation of why you should no longer be considered an active gang member. You are also asked to provide information regarding any schools you have attended, including middle school, high school, a trade school, or college. You should start with your most recent school and work your way backward in time. The city attorney will use this information only to confirm its factual accuracy. Please provide the following information regarding any job you currently hold, as well as any other job(s) you held during the past three years. Please start with your current or most recent job and work your way backward in time. The city attorney will use this information only to confirm its factual accuracy. Please provide the following contact information for any people who know you and can confirm that you no longer are, or you never were, a member of a criminal street gang. Such people can include family members; neighbors; teachers, principals, and school staff; coaches and former teammates; current and past employers; community leaders and organizers; priests, ministers, reverends, and other religious counselors; social and gang intervention workers; and probation, parole, and police officers. Please use the space below to provide any additional information that you want considered. Such information may include the fact that you recently returned to school, started a new job, or completed a job training or substance abuse program. You can also attach letters and other documents to this form supporting your claim that you no longer are (or never were) a gang member, including letters from the people identified above. By signing below, you will be confirming that all of the information provided in or with this form is, to the best of your knowledge, true and correct. If you are represented by an attorney, you need to provide that information.

7

Research Methodology

There are a lot of studies and research in the world that are not worth the paper they are printed on; they do not follow scientific standards. This is why in any book or research study that is serious and follows the established academic guidelines, the exact methods used to conduct the research must be disclosed and explained in detail. This chapter explains the terminology of this research, including quantitative, retrospective, epidemiological, validity, sampling frame, and sample. This chapter describes the data collection procedures used, the procedures used to analyze the data, the statistical procedures used to verify and explain the data, and compliance of this research with scientific and ethical guidelines.

Based on a practical and theoretical framework, this evaluation used several types of analyses to answer whether an injunction or abatement had its anticipated effect to reduce crime in and around targeted buildings or neighborhoods. The first analysis looks at the impact of the program on targeted buildings or targeted neighborhoods. The next three analyses address whether the program produced a diffusion of benefits by measuring impact beyond targeted places, targeted crimes, and targeted periods of time. Measuring impact at targeted buildings and targeted neighborhoods involved a straightforward process of counting crimes occurring at targeted locations for a specified time interval before the intervention of the injunction or program and comparing it to the number of crimes occurring for a similar time interval after the intervention.

Measuring impact beyond targeted places considers the injunction or program's secondary effect on places not targeted by the intervention. Control areas or catchment areas were evaluated to determine if the injunction or abatement was the cause of the change, and if the desired change resulted in an unwanted consequence of simply moving the crime. Similar to the analysis of targeted buildings described above, crime levels in catchment or control areas were compared before and after the intervention of the injunction or abatement program. Measuring impact beyond targeted crimes was also done; in addition to gang and narcotics activity, the evaluation addresses whether the injunction or abatement program had any potentially positive residual effect on other, more general types of crime. For that purpose, property and index crimes are used as secondary measures in addition to evaluating total calls for service in both injunction and control areas.

Ultimately the decision of which statistical and measurement procedures were selected was based on an understanding of the purpose of this study and the methodology behind it. The data collected were evaluated based upon their relevance, accuracy, timeliness, accessibility, interpretability, and coherence.

Calls for service can be identified by specific injunction and control areas, making it possible to compare Part 1 (violent crime), Part 2 (less serious crime), and total calls (all reported activity in the area) before and after in both the injunction and control areas. The selected methods allowed for evaluation of the overall level of crime activity in both injunction and control areas by evaluating total calls for service in both areas for the same length of time before and after each injunction.

QUANTITATIVE STUDY

I relied on quantitative data analysis to address the research question and evaluate gang injunction effectiveness. This research involved the collection of crime data relating to 25 gang injunctions and 25 matched controls for one year before an injunction was obtained and one year after, to evaluate any reported changes in the level of reported crime in each area, utilizing the same data categories for both enjoined and control gangs. This study is a retrospective study involving a pretest-posttest methodology. Three dependent variables were compiled and categorized in both the injunction and control gang areas at the same relative points in time, including the primary dependent variable Part 1 crime and the secondary dependent variables, Part 2 crime and total calls for police service.

RETROSPECTIVE, QUASI-EXPERIMENTAL STUDY

This research was retrospective, in that it evaluated the data collected after the fact, looking back in retrospect. It is a quasi-experimental design because this study did not randomly assign the groups for treatment. Because no random assignment of groups was done in relationship to the enjoined and control gangs, this study was not a true experiment, and therefore the findings should be interpreted with some caution (Campbell and Stanley, 1963). The formula for this study for the enjoined gangs would be O X

O (observe, treatment, observe), and for the control gang would be O — O (observe, no treatment, observe).

The research consists of a causal comparative design (Campbell and Stanley, 1963), which begins with a noted difference between two or more groups, and then looks for possible causes of this difference. This method focuses on conducting scientific research outside a laboratory to determine which programs work and which do not, and was an excellent model for this research to follow.

I controlled for independent variables because in a causal comparative study in which no manipulation takes place, the groups have already been exposed to the independent variable. The primary quantitative analysis in this study also lacked true randomization, making it a causal comparative study because of the lack of randomization. The groups were already formed in this research, which required simply locating the injunctions and controls to study them.

INITIAL GOAL/QUANTITATIVE ANALYSIS

My initial goal or objective for this was to study every filed gang injunction in Los Angeles, San Diego, San Bernardino, and Ventura Counties. From the total gang injunction population in the counties listed above, data were requested from the law enforcement agencies in each applicable jurisdiction. While making such requests, it became clear that much of the data needed to accomplish this research goal may not be available, or the holders of the information were unable or unwilling to provide the information needed. It is essential in any casual comparative analysis that there are an adequate number of participants used in the study, meaning, in this case, that the study evaluate a sufficient sampling of existing injunctions and that valid, reliable, and sensitive measures are used. It was deemed appropriate to evaluate at least 25 active injunctions based upon the determination of the total number of existing filed gang injunctions (111), which would give the study a significant segment of the current injunction population by existing scientific standards. Only evaluating two or three injunctions, for example, would not have been a large enough sample size to accomplish the goals of this research.

EPIDEMIOLOGICAL STUDY

This is an epidemiological study in which an intervention or treatment is given to a community experiencing problems associated with the presence of a specific street gang. The treatment is the gang injunction; the perceived disease or problem is the local gang targeted with the injunction. Being that it is difficult to have a truly random allocation of injunctions for review due to limitations related to data collection, varying capabilities of the law enforcement jurisdictions, the willingness of the police to provide the requested data, limited police resources to assist in recovering the requested data, and the routine purging of crime data by most police departments, this study consists of an observational design in which a hypothesis was tested. This study included control gangs for use as a comparison to the enjoined gangs, making it more of an analytic study than a descriptive one.

COMPARING TWO POPULATIONS: INJUNCTION AND CONTROL

No two gang neighborhoods can be truly classified as absolutely scientifically identical. Each neighborhood has unique issues, concerns, varying degrees of crime, and varying concentrations of people that are predisposed to committing crime. I took care not to just compare an area adjacent to the gang injunction area as a control, but to attempt to find an area that had similar problems, experiencing the problems associated with a similar gang. Each of the empirical studies to date has compared an area adjacent to or near by the injunction area, without factoring in the gang presence, or lack thereof, in the areas it utilized as a control.

The process of identifying control gangs ultimately was very time-consuming and labor-intensive and required significant cooperation from law enforcement. The process of using control gang areas rather than adjacent areas created limitations in some cases with finding appropriate control gangs. In addition, gang territories do not always fall neatly in line with police reporting districts or jurisdictional lines, and gang activity tends to cluster in certain areas. This made the identification process for locating control gangs different from past studies that compared adjacent areas to the injunctions that take into account adjacent reporting districts, regardless of level of crime, or even if the area has a gang problem or not.

In this study, each gang injunction area was compared to a comparable control gang area for 25 gang injunctions, for one year before and one year after the injunction was implemented. Using statistics and crime data provided by law enforcement responsible for policing the injunction and control areas, I made paired observation comparisons and tested the difference between the two populations. The control gangs, identified and evaluated based upon their similarity to the enjoined gangs, were used for comparison against the enjoined gangs.

Control gang selection relied heavily upon the expert opinion of law enforcement gang experts in areas where injunctions were sought. The experts that provided information about the enjoined gang also assisted in identification of the closest gang to the enjoined gang that did not have an injunction against them, and that had similar characteristics to the enjoined gang to use as a control. With the assistance of the experts, adequate control gangs were identified and data for those areas were made available for 25 gang injunctions in four counties. This process could be repeated by future researchers that evaluate injunctions using the same methodology.

TESTING DEPENDENT VARIABLES: PART 1, PART 2, AND TOTAL CALLS

In this research, the presence or absence of a gang injunction is the independent variable, the treatment or medication that the community needs to treat the cancer of gangs and gang violence in their community. Control areas, matched on important demographic and civic variables, were used as a comparison group. The dependent variable is crime, as inferred by police calls for service, one year before the injunction vs. one year after the injunction.

Once data collection was complete, all of the data relating to each dependent variable were entered into Excel. The same dependent variables for the control gangs were also collected. Data were double-checked for errors and any entry errors were corrected. Both enjoined gang and control gangs had each variable totaled and averaged. For each area, a percentage change was calculated based on the Part 1, Part 2, and total calls for both the year before and the year after the injunction was put into effect.

CONTROL FOR VALIDITY

The primary threat to internal validity was the limitation in finding a suitable control gang within close proximity, the same city or adjoining city, that displayed similar demographics, gang ethnicity, and gang size. It was also determined that it would not be appropriate to compare two similar gangs if it was determined that one had an injunction and the other was the subject of any other significant enforcement effort, such as a large-scale narcotics operation, which may have skewed the findings and prevented reflection on the true impact of the gang injunctions. The gang experts were critical in identifying the presence, or lack of, any other large-scale law enforcement operations or community projects against the control gang that may have made it a poor choice for comparison.

I also sought to compare enjoined and control gang areas that had similar police resources directed to deal with the local gang problem. It was deemed appropriate to rely on the gang officers that are tasked with investigating the enjoined and control gangs to assist in selecting the most appropriate control gangs, as close to the enjoined gangs as possible, based upon the desired characteristics of ethnicity, size, proximity, activity, area demographics, and level of crime. Once the expert identified a potential control gang, the gang was evaluated to confirm its viability as a control.

SAMPLING FRAME AND PROCEDURE

The sampling procedure used in this research consisted of a nonprobability sample, specifically, a convenience sample. Based upon each injunction in the entire population not having an equal chance of being selected, a probability sample was not applicable.

SAMPLE

Data for 25 gang injunctions and 25 matched controls were ultimately obtained and represent a statistically sufficient segment of the total injunction population.

Of the 122 total injunctions known to be in progress or filed at the time of the research, 111 were filed cases and 11 were in progress. Of the 111 filed injunctions, 3 were later denied by the courts, 4 were later dismissed by the prosecution, and 14 were confirmed inactive and no longer enforced according to the law enforcement officers that provided details about each injunction. In addition, court records indicate at least 14 injunctions were more recent than one year, making it impossible to gather the needed statistics for one year postinjunction.

In simple terms, this left 86 potential gang injunctions that were active, and could be potentially evaluated in this research. Of the 86 injunctions, data were requested for 45 where it was believed injunction and suitable control data could be found. After a comprehensive review, only 25 injunctions met the criteria established for this research, meaning a viable control could be found and the necessary data for both injunction and control areas were available from the police and prosecution.

The information provided by police and prosecution in this research indicated that less than 10% of all injunctions were filed in the first 15 years since injunctions became a legal tool (1982–1997), and more than 90% were filed between year 15 and year 25 of their usage (1997–2007). This trend clearly illustrates a surge in gang injunctions in the last decade, despite little scientific review of their effectiveness, and resulted in focusing on injunctions filed more recently.

TREATMENT

The dependent variables or effects (Part 1 crimes, Part 2 crimes, total calls for service) were evaluated against the independent variable (the treatment or gang injunctions) to determine if injunctions impacted one or more of the dependent variables in this study.

INSTRUMENTATION

The gang injunctions selected for review were uploaded into Microsoft Excel and SPSS software to analyze the level of effectiveness of the gang injunctions. The crime statistics data were collected from the Los Angeles Police Department, the Los Angeles city attorney, the San Diego Police Department, the San Diego Sheriff's Department, the San Diego district attorney, the San Bernardino Police Department, the Colton Police Department, and the Oxnard Police Department. The data collected contained raw counts, in Excel format, broken down in varying degrees depending upon the capability of the law enforcement agency providing the data.

The primary quantitative data showed the comparison between the enjoined gang and the control gang, including maps created to illustrate the relationship between injunction and controls that have incorporated into this research. Characteristics of each gang, target area analysis, and tables illustrating the comparisons of the data, broken down by Part 1, Part 2, and calls for service data, have also been included.

DATA ANALYSIS/STATISTICAL PROCEDURES

The findings are presented in tables and figures, including means, standard deviations, percentages, variances, standard errors of the mean, and ranges as appropriate.

Because the design of this study includes pre- and postinjunction data, and because there is a matched control group that also included pre- and postinjunction data, two key comparisons were deemed necessary to properly test both alternate and null hypotheses. To test the hypothesis that gang injunctions are effective in reducing crime, calls for service postinjunction were subtracted from calls for service preinjunction.

This change in calls for service in the injunction areas was compared to similar data from the matched control areas using a paired t-test. If the test demonstrated a statistically significant decrease from preinjunction levels, and if the injunction areas demonstrate significantly fewer calls for service, the interpretation was viewed as empirical support for the effectiveness of gang injunctions. Differences were considered statistically significant at $p < .05$.

In this research, both of the key comparisons must demonstrate statistically significant results at $p < .05$ in the direction of prediction, so there is no need for correction. Being that both comparisons must be statistically significant at $p < .05$, dividing the p value in half is not necessary and would only change the alpha threshold from .05 (1 in 20) to .025 (1 in 40), but in this research the bar has been set much higher. For both comparisons to be statistically significant, the odds by chance alone are $.05 \times .05$, which is 1 in 400; this is 10 times as stringent as the most conservative Bonferroni correction, which divides alpha by the number of comparisons to be made.

Thus the necessary correction is built into this research design and structure. For the exploratory analyses portion of this research, no correction for multiple comparisons was made because I did not want to miss statistically significant findings (type II error) in this new area of research. Every statistical t-test in this research study is composed of paired t-tests, either vs. baseline or vs. matched controls. Because the hypotheses are directional, two-tailed paired t-tests (more conservative) were appropriate for each of the two key comparisons.

The primary dependent variable in this study was Part 1 calls for service, because serious crime is crucial when determining the efficacy of gang injunctions. So the analysis plan was primarily aimed at assessment of Part 1 calls. If Part 1 calls for service in injunction areas significantly decreased from baseline, and the decrease was significantly more than changes from baseline for matched controls, then the analysis of Part 2 calls for service and total calls for service became more important. If Part 1 calls for service did not reveal a significant drop in crime, then the lesser Part 2 calls would not rescue the primary hypothesis because a reduction in lesser crime is not sufficient to deem an injunction successful in this research. However, this may become an interesting question for future researchers, as any statistically significant change would at least tell us what the injunctions are accomplishing.

However, if Part 1 calls dropped significantly in injunction areas, then less total calls becomes more interesting, because any reduction in nonserious crime becomes a potential bonus in evaluating injunction efficacy. Therefore, Part 2 calls for service and total calls for service were tested in parallel to the analysis plan for Part 1 calls for service, but the findings were interpreted using a strict hierarchy, with Part 1 calls remaining the central focus for interpreting the primary hypothesis.

In summary, Part 1 calls for service in injunction areas were compared to baseline, and then compared to the change in matched control areas using a paired t-test, and then the same analyses were conducted in parallel for Part 2 calls and total calls for service. The primary hypothesis was considered supported only if Part 1 crime calls for service significantly dropped in injunction areas while they did not in corresponding control areas.

To determine whether injunctions are effective in reducing crime, a spreadsheet was constructed such that each row represents one injunction and the columns represent calls for service fields, because calls for service comprise the dependent variables in this study. Means were obtained for each injunction and each control to include in the tables, because the mean is the best unbiased estimate of the group.

Similarly, the standard deviations were obtained, using SPSS and Excel software. The data were tabled to include both injunction and control side by side to appreciate the changes in each pair. Tables include what happened in both the 12-month period prior to the injunction and the 12-month period following the injunction. Additionally, these tables include the percentage change that occurred.

To create the primary dependent variable, percentage change in Part 1 calls for service, the percent change from baseline was calculated by subtracting the preinjunction baseline from the postinjunction values, then dividing by the baseline. That is, the change divided by the baseline, expressed as a percentage of baseline. More specifically, [(preinjunction – postinjunction)/preinjunction] × 100 = percent change from baseline. This was done for each dependent variable, Part 1, Part 2, and total calls. Percent change from preinjunction baseline was calculated both for injunctions and for controls.

In addition, further analysis of the same data was conducted to include results by gang ethnicity, gang injunction size, injunctions by county, total gang size, and injunction area size. The data are also shown on a case-by-case basis describing the injunctions and controls, broken down by Part 1 crime, Part 2 crime, and total calls for service in a narrative format.

These paired t-tests provide p values that express whether the change from baseline was significantly different than no change at all. If the change was statistically significant ($p < .05$), and if the change direction indicated a reduction (rather than an increase) in crime, this was considered empirical evidence that injunctions are effective in reducing crime. This was not, however, considered sufficient evidence to make a strong conclusion because this comparison does not take into account what is happening in matched control areas. That is, it is possible that crime dropped in injunction areas, but dropped similarly (or even more) in control areas.

Therefore, the comparison vs. baseline was a crucial first step in determining whether injunctions work, but one additional comparison was needed to reach a strong conclusion. To determine whether the change seen in injunctions was significantly greater than in matched control areas, a paired t-test was used to determine if a difference existed. A nonsignificant p value ($p > .05$) would suggest that injunctions bring no significant benefit over matched control areas. However, if a significant benefit was evident in injunction areas, and if this benefit was significantly greater than any benefit seen on matched controls, this was interpreted as strong evidence that injunctions are effective in reducing crime.

NATURE OF THE SCALES

The scale for the percent change for preinjunction calls and postinjunction calls, including Part 1 calls, Part 2 calls, and total calls for service, is a ratio scale. A ratio scale is one in which intervals between values are meaningful. For example, temperature measured in degrees is a ratio scale because we know a meaningful zero point (absolute zero). In this research we have a meaningful zero to compare to baseline.

COMPARE SAME POINTS IN TIME

The mean change in the crime level was compared within the target areas before and after the gang injunctions were implemented with a contemporaneous mean change in the crime level of the control gangs at the same point in time. This method can produce unbiased estimates of the effects of gang injunctions on crime level by controlling for the factors that drive common crime increases or decreases in both the injunction area and control gang area.

The injunction gang and control gang may or may not share a common border, as long as they are in the same general area. The sharing of a common border would be a critical factor if this research had been focused solely on evaluating potential displacement into adjacent areas or from one area to the other, for example.

It was preferred to select a control gang area rather than just the area nearby the enjoined gang. The control gang used had to have no special enforcement conducted against it other than routine patrol to better understand and evaluate the true impact of the injunction on the enjoined gang. The process of selecting appropriate control gangs required significant input and cooperation from law enforcement officers targeting the enjoined gangs, and that have knowledge of gangs in the surrounding areas of the gang enjoined, including the rivals of the enjoined gang.

Difficulties in finding control gangs included (1) lack of a comparable gang that was not under an injunction, (2) lack of a gang with comparable characteristics, and (3) unavailability of statistics for an otherwise acceptable candidate gang. The use of control gang analysis helped understand the changes in the dependent variables across both neighborhoods at the same points in time.

For example, if crime in general had been increasing or decreasing citywide, both areas would likely have changes indicating that result. However, if the gang injunction had an impact, the analysis should indicate a true measure of the change, taking into account the other potential factors, such as increases or decreases in employment, economic factors, access to social services, etc.

The data was displayed as Part 1 crimes, Part 2 crimes, and calls for service. The use of Part 1 and Part 2 crimes is due to the police department's conformation to the Uniform Crime Reports (UCRs). These UCRs are crime indexes published annually by the Federal Bureau of Investigation (FBI) that summarize the incidences in crime indexes published annually. The UCRs do not use legal definitions of the crimes they index; rather, the definitions are based on an internal FBI classification system.

MEASURING CRIME

A review of the literature regarding the measurement of crime was conducted for this research to summarize and explain, in a nontechnical manner, the various common approaches for measuring crime and to determine which crime measurement method would be best suited to obtain the goals for this research. I addressed the primary question of gang injunction effectiveness: Basically, do gang injunctions reduce crime and achieve their intended outcome by preventing or reducing gang activity in the targeted area, and if so, by how much?

The literature related to the use of differing methodologies to investigate the outcomes of crime reduction initiatives like gang injunctions requires an understanding of the primary crime measurement methods prior to collection and analysis of data. Other issues include determining what offenses should be measured, what unit of analysis should be used, and what the research purpose is in measuring the crime. Crimes have different classifications, but they are all acts committed in violation of a law that prohibits them and authorizes punishment for their commission (Wilson, 1985).

The most widely used measures of crime involve evaluating police records, but records are subject to certain types of error, as crimes may be omitted if not reported. Police records are typically measured in two ways, by observation (gang loitering, drug sales, pimping, and prostitution) and reports from other people (such as victims or witnesses to crimes). It is important to understand that evaluating records is just one method; some research projects measure dollars and cost, some measure conviction rates, some measure arrest rates, and some measure community perception of crime. Each of the methods evaluated has advantages and limitations when compared and based upon the purpose of this research.

Measuring public policy program outcomes is not always easy to understand, and the important outcome measures may not be readily quantifiable. For example, a liquor store owner may hire a private security guard in order to reduce shoplifting and beer dashes, which may also improve the community's overall perception of the store as being a safe place to shop. It is relatively easy to measure the impact of the extra security on shoplifting, for example, by counting the number of attempted and actual incidents of shoplifting before and after the security guard arrived. An evaluation of the liquor store's inventory to sales receipts will show any loss. However, it may be more difficult and costly to assess the local community's overall perception of crime in and around the liquor store.

Certain methods of data collection are resource-intensive; for example, collection of primary data through large-scale audits and public perception surveys can take significant resources to complete, which may still not guarantee any greater accuracy when compared to evaluating crime reports. I had to consider what methods could be successfully implemented with the limited resources available. I also had to evaluate the availability of the data to be collected and if the barriers that prevent access to necessary data could be overcome. Each of the approaches reviewed has advantages and disadvantages in the context of this study, and all were considered before deciding which method(s) to employ and before using and interpreting the data collected.

MEASURING COST

Cost of crime estimates can be a great help to policy makers in ensuring that the maximum benefit is gained from the taxpayer money spent to obtain a gang injunction or gang abatement effort, and to help justify why a particular gang injunction was undertaken when confronted by the media or a concerned public. Economic costs as used in this research include the full impact of a crime on society, encompassing both financial and nonfinancial consequences or social costs, such as trauma, physical injury, and emotional suffering following a gang crime.

It is difficult to calculate the intangible costs of a gang crime. Without accurate estimates of the costs of individual crime types, it would be difficult to make informed decisions about which policy measures are the most cost-effective and desirable. Permitting meaningful comparisons to be made of the costs and benefits of crime reduction measures can help in prioritizing resources, focusing scarce resources on policies that have the biggest impact on the harm caused by crime.

It has been estimated that the cost of one vehicle theft averages $5,600, one burglary averages $2,300, one serious assault averages $19,000, and one murder averages $1,000,000 when calculating the cost of the investigation, arrest, prosecution, and incarceration of the offender(s), and the cost of pain and suffering, health care, loss of income, and emotional issues. If we accept the theory that every crime has a corresponding cost to society, we can to some degree calculate a cost savings or increase associated with a particular gang injunction based upon an identified change in reported crimes. If this research reveals a change in reported crime in the gang injunction areas included in this study, that change will reflect the differences in reported crimes before and after the injunction.

A cost can be attached to each crime resulting in a cost savings or increase for each injunction based upon the reduction or increase in reported crimes. By identifying the financial impact on reported crimes, minus the expense associated with obtaining the injunction, prosecutors can more effectively estimate the true cost-benefit of each injunction. This may be an area where future researchers explore the specific costs associated with future injunctions, to include prosecution, police, and court expenses associated with each new injunction.

Evaluating gang injunctions or any other public policy typically comes down to a cost and benefit analysis to evaluate policy effectiveness based upon the cost of the injunction vs. the perceived or actual benefit. The approach of measuring the relative costs and benefits of crime prevention programs can have an important effect on decisions about implementation of future gang injunctions based upon spending priorities and directions for crime prevention work.

Some cost-related measurements exist, including cost-benefit analysis, cost savings analysis, cost-effectiveness analysis, and cost analysis. The approach that is chosen to evaluate a particular anti-gang initiative will typically depend on just what needs to be learned from the analysis and the funds available to undertake it. These approaches should be used to support a broader decision-making framework, which offers a framework in which to compare programs. Grogger (2002) addressed the issue of cost-effectiveness and highlighted how difficult it is to put an exact price tag on a gang injunction or abatement project.

The police and prosecutors do not typically track the exact number of hours put into the effort; the salaries of those involved vary from one jurisdiction to another; the supplies needed to put the case together vary significantly, and the cost associated with maintaining and prosecuting violations of the order vary from one county to the next. The advantages of gang injunctions may be difficult to quantify in terms of the cost of investigating, arresting, and prosecuting gang case crimes that may have been prevented by the injunction effort. It is also difficult to compare a gang initiative like a gang injunction to a gang intervention program, for example. It is also common sense that there are expenses associated with every gang injunction, and the variations in cost are significantly different based upon the type of injunction sought. Legal challenges to the orders may prolong court costs, and the volume of subjects arrested for violating each injunction may vary. The costs of investigating a particular crime also vary significantly based upon duration of the investigation, duration of the court process, prosecution costs, and costs to the victims and witnesses in personal loss and pain and suffering. I did not focus on the issue of cost, but rather the issue of effectiveness. The cost-to-benefit ratio of gang injunctions was not evaluated in this research.

MEASURING CONVICTIONS

Not every gang crime results in an arrest, and not all gang members who are arrested are convicted. Typically, conviction rates and incarceration ratios coincide with the severity of the offenses the person was convicted of committing. The more severe the offense, the higher the conviction rate and the greater the incarceration rate. Consequently, individuals arrested for murder are more likely to be convicted and sentenced to prison than other types of violent offenses. Gang injunctions address violent crime, as well as nonviolent property crimes and nuisance-related crimes that typically impact the overall quality of life for a community, such as vandalism, loud noise, loitering, and petty theft. For that reason, gang injunctions would not be best evaluated by measuring convictions. Measuring a reduction in reported crimes and measuring community perceptions may be both better suited and more applicable to evaluating well-defined areas targeted with gang injunctions. The conviction rate for injunction violators is, however, typically high.

In Los Angeles, 90 to 94% from July 2001 to December 2006, depending on the court jurisdiction according to the city attorney. Between 6 and 10% of the filed Los Angeles injunction violation cases result in either a not guilty verdict or the case being dismissed by the court or district or city attorney upon review of the evidence. The high conviction rate for those actually brought to court does not take into account the majority of violations that never result in arrest and subsequent conviction.

MEASURING ARRESTS

Not all gang crimes result in a gang member sitting in a jail cell, thus making it an important consideration to distinguish between prevalence and incidence of crime, or the number of people committing crime (known gang offenders) and the number of offenses committed by criminals (known gang offenses). Arrest rates are not necessarily indicative of rates of involvement in illegal gang-related behavior. They can be affected by police bias, police capabilities, lack of police resources, the crime location, and other demographic factors.

Therefore, we know that there are problems in the validity of arrest rates to function as a measure of certain criminal behaviors for certain populations. Some gang members committing crimes in the areas targeted with gang injunctions never get arrested for some or many of the crimes they commit. One reason may be that gangs assert tremendous fear and intimidation in many communities, which makes finding willing witnesses a rare commodity. The net result is that many gang members get away with the crimes they commit because arrests require probable cause and prosecutions require proving the case beyond a reasonable doubt.

Arrest data are typically evaluated during the evidence collection and preparation phase of an injunction and may well support the need for a particular injunction. However, it is cautioned that just looking at arrests will not present a clear picture of the overall crime problem in the gang injunction areas. Gang injunctions may, and many times do, have a tendency to increase the probability of apprehension and arrest for those offenders that have been identified as active problems in the specified target areas. Injunctions can also increase the chance of arrest if offenders continue to engage in criminal activity in the target area.

Clearance statistics measure the proportion of reported crimes that were resolved by an arrest. A single arrest may result in many cases being cleared. For example, one arrest of a serial burglar could clear 50 burglaries if the person was linked to and charged with committing all 50 of these crimes. Other times, multiple arrests may result in a single clearance if the crime was committed by a group of offenders, such as a single gang drive-by shooting that results in five occupants in the car all getting arrested. Measuring arrests appears not to be the preferred method of evaluating gang injunction effectiveness because an arrest is not indicative of the level of crime in the area.

If removing the presence of the active gang members has a corresponding reduction in reported crime, then the injunction may be considered effective regardless of the number of arrests made (National Center for State Courts, 2005).

MEASURING COMMUNITY PERCEPTIONS

National Crime Victimization Surveys

The National Crime Victimization Surveys began in 1972. The results of the surveys in some cases were very different compared to those of the Uniform Crime Reports; for example, cities and towns that the Uniform Crime Reports showed to have little crime turned out, according to the NCVS, to have high rates of crime. As a general rule for most places, NCVS data will most usually show twice as much crime than the UCRs results. NCVS interviewers contact 50,000 households twice each year, and the households are rotated randomly every three years. The NCVS uses the hierarchy rule and records the same Part 1 offenses as the UCRs, but it doesn't ask about offenses that might be too sensitive in an interview situation, like murder and arson.

Not only does the NCVS not measure homicide, but it also doesn't measure commercial crime such as burglaries. This poses an obvious concern for measuring gang injunction effectiveness, because gang members kill other people and also commit thefts from residences and businesses as a means of support, and we do not want to omit these categories of crime.

The NCVS collects information on crimes suffered by individuals and households, whether or not those crimes were reported to law enforcement. It estimates the proportion of each crime type reported to law enforcement, and it summarizes the reasons that victims give for reporting or not reporting the crime. It also provides information about victims (age, sex, race, ethnicity, marital status, income, and educational level), offenders (sex, race, approximate age, and victim-offender relationship), and the crimes (time and place of occurrence, use of weapons, nature of injury, and economic consequences).

Questions typically cover the experiences of victims with the criminal justice system, self-protective measures used by victims, and possible substance abuse by offenders. Supplements are added periodically to obtain detailed information on topics like school-related crime or to gauge theft-related offenses. The problem with this method in the context of evaluating gang injunctions is that it evaluates crime on a national level and it is not possible to isolate the households targeted with the survey by gang injunction area. The scope of these surveys makes them too broad and would not assist in evaluating a specific region, state, city, or gang injunction area within the city. Unlike NCVS, the UCRs data can be broken down to the city and local level, making the evaluation of crimes a viable option when compared to NCVS data.

Localized Community Surveys

Based on the concept of the National Crime Victimization Surveys, Dr. Maxson (2005) and her colleagues conducted a community survey to study if the Verdugo Flats gang injunction in San Bernardino County was effective from a community perspective. Maxson implemented a community survey in three communities, one with the Verdugo Flats civil gang injunction, one adjacent to the injunction area to assess potential displacement issues, and a third comparison area. The goal of the study was to measure the impact of the civil gang injunction on the community residents' perception and experience of crime, to evaluate the neighborhood's quality of life, and to determine whether displacement was a significant result of the injunction.

The study surveyed 797 San Bernardino residents 18 months prior to the injunction, and 1,229 residents 6 months following the implementation of the gang injunction. The study revealed that there was positive evidence of the short-term effects in the injunction area, including less obvious gang presence, fewer reports of gang intimidation, and less fear of confrontation with gang members. This survey method allowed Maxson to focus on the area specifically targeted with the injunction, as well as surrounding areas, by only surveying people in the geographic areas designated by the researchers.

This method appears to have merit for evaluating gang injunction effectiveness, if the researcher has the time and resources to administer the survey and collect and analyze the extensive amount of data obtained from a 30-page detailed survey. In the case of this research, UCRs data may prove to be the more effective and efficient method for evaluating 25 injunctions as opposed to 1, in four counties, involving numerous police jurisdictions, with control gang data used as opposed to adjacent or nearby areas, regardless of gang composition.

Stakeholder Surveys

Edward Allan (2002) conducted a survey of California prosecutors to evaluate the flexibility of gang injunctions and understand how and why injunctions are sought against certain gangs. Gang injunctions are time-consuming and labor-intensive to implement and require significant planning and effort on the part of the prosecutors and police. As such, Allan conducted a categorical data analysis examining all identified gang injunctions filed in the California Superior Court of Los Angeles County between October 26, 1987, and June 30, 2000. Prosecutors that obtained 42 gang injunctions were represented in the study.

Allan found that the gang injunction initiatives were evenly distributed among three categories: high-drug, high-crime, and high-disorder areas. The majority of gang injunction initiatives were determined to be a flexible response to local gang activity. In regards to policy implications, it was one intention of the study to assist local policy makers and participating community entities in deciding whether the strategy of policing by injunction is an appropriate response to gang problems in their community. The study examined whether gang injunction initiatives followed Herman Goldstein's problem-solving methodology consisting of four steps: scanning, analysis, response, and assessment.

The evidence suggested that the problem-solving methodology was widely used in civil gang abatement initiatives, showing gang injunctions involved significant care and evaluation before being implemented. There was evidence of all four steps, indicating that gang injunctions were not simply quick reactions to gang activities. The study also included a comprehensive review of relevant laws and issues unique to the gang injunction process to help understand it (Allan, 2002).

Self-Report Crime Surveys

Self-reporting surveys are good for measuring "victimless" crimes and rarely observed crimes by asking people about crimes they commit. Three types of offenses (usually excluded from victim surveys and police statistics), are measured including prostitution and drug abuse, delinquency, and public order offenses like shoplifting and drunk driving. Most academic researchers and private foundations craft these surveys to address the specific issue they are seeking to evaluate. Much of the information used in recidivism studies is derived from self-report data. A self-report survey is typically administered to high school or college students. Other samples have involved incarcerated prisoners. Regardless of the sample population, the purpose is to get respondents to read the questions and mark down how often they have committed a serious offense and gotten away with it. This of course operates on the assumption that the gang member is telling the truth when he or she answers the questions, which is an assumption many have a difficult time believing, even if the person being surveyed is not identified.

I considered this method and evaluated the potential of interviewing the gang members in the areas subjected to gang injunctions to understand the connection to the local area crime and the gang members targeted with the injunctions. The limitations of this method are problems with the validity and reliability of the responses; many gang members lie or exaggerate on these questionnaires, typically referred to as falsification. Many gang members, especially if interviewed in the presence of fellow gang members, often admit to or take credit for crimes they did not commit to enhance their reputation. In addition, it is easy for researcher bias and measurement error to surface, making self-report surveys a less accurate measurement method than reported crimes.

THE GANG MEMBER'S PERSPECTIVE

I have talked with dozens of gang members that have been served with, and were later arrested for violating, a gang injunction. The general consensus of all the members I have spoken to is that the injunction does hinder their ability to commit crime, but of course these statements are not scientific. A study in 2010 sought to explore this issue. Researchers at the University of Southern California interviewed male youth ages 14 to 21 in areas claimed by gangs that do or do not have a recent gang injunction in place. Their goal was to interview youth who are and are not gang affiliated in three areas in East Los Angeles. These interviews were focused on social identity, perceptual deterrence, and level of involvement with gang activities. The goal of the interviews was to identify two social identities for all respondents, including one clearly or ambiguously anti-social and one conventional or pro-social, which was achieved for 97% of the participants.

The respondent's antisocial identities could be categorized as gang affiliated, other antisocial affiliation (tagger, skater, party posse, or crew), or ambiguous (friends who hang out), or what the police would call gang associates. The questions being asked in this study were: Were any apparent gains in primary gang injunction area offset by losses in smaller gang injunction areas? Do any positive impacts on communities persist? Does a gang injunction strengthen the community in the long run? Does a gang injunction weaken the gangs involved in any way?

The researchers attempted to answer these questions by going door-to-door or engaging youth hanging out in the target areas, offering a $20 incentive to participants. The findings revealed gang identity is weaker than conventional identity, and gang affiliates reported weaker group identity and less trust in the group than affiliates of other antisocial groups. In the end, injunctions may be most useful in terms of the role they may play in more comprehensive approaches to reducing gang crime, intimidation of community residents, and the hold gangs have on our youth.

MEASURING CRIME BY MAPPING

Crime is not spread evenly across police jurisdictions. Crime and gangs tend to clump in some areas and may be absent in others. Most of us tend to use this knowledge in our daily activities by avoiding some places while seeking out others, based upon areas we perceive as being safe. Our choices of neighborhoods, schools, shops, streets, and recreation are governed in part by the understanding that our chances of being a victim of a gang crime are greater in some places than others.

Identifying the areas where gangs are known to commit the majority of their crimes is often the most critical step in the gang injunction process. This mapping analysis requires the use of multiple techniques to understand crime patterns. Crime mapping can most effectively guide police action when production of the maps is guided by crime theories (place, victim, street, or neighborhood). When the analysis indicates significant gang activity, target hardening, increased surveillance, increased offender targeting, and gang injunctions can be implemented by the police to address the problem.

There are different ways of measuring the intensity of gang activity, including the number of anticrime measures installed, the cost of the measures, and the resources spent on project implementation. Crime mapping is often used as a tool in the gang injunction process, but may not be well suited as a stand-alone measurement method to evaluate gang injunction effectiveness. Before and after pictures of crime for large areas make crime mapping more complex and time-consuming, and it may be difficult to compare two different areas that may cross jurisdictional lines.

MEASURING UCRS AND CALLS

Starting in 1929, the FBI's Uniform Crime Reports have been the most widely used source of criminal statistics, or crimes known to police. One criticism of UCRs concerns the reporting practices, as the real amount of crime is never known. Law enforcement practices, or the way the police record data, vary between jurisdictions and from county to county. Methodological problems exist with UCRs data, such as filing a police report not being required and variation in report accuracy and completeness based upon the police jurisdiction. The UCRs collect raw numbers to determine the frequency of crime, and are an ideal method of evaluating the percentage of crime between years. The UCRs break crime down into two categories, Part 1 and Part 2 crimes.

Part 1 crimes are derived from crime reports prepared by the police that are submitted to the FBI. Part 1 crimes include reported incidents of murder, robbery, aggravated assault, arson, burglary, rape, motor vehicle theft, and grand theft. Regardless of the FBI index, it is clear that Part 1 crimes include the more serious offenses and are the primary concern of the police.

Part 2 crimes are based upon actual arrests made for the specified offenses. Part 2 crimes include simple assault, curfew offenses, loitering, embezzlement, vandalism, vagrancy, weapons offenses, and violations of court orders like gang injunctions. A proportion of crime incidents are likely to be unreported due to apathy, tolerance of the behavior, fear of repercussions of reporting, or lack of knowledge of where to report. That is especially true in areas that have a high concentration of gang activity. To bridge the gap between total reported crimes and the real level of activity in any given area, a third category, "total calls for service," was evaluated.

Total calls for service include all activity in the target areas: everything reported to the police, and all calls received by the police, including all self-initiated police activity in any given area, such as traffic stops, car accidents, disturbances, suspicious activity, barking dogs, loud music, reckless driving, follow-up investigations, etc. The objective of understanding the total calls for service is to obtain a more accurate picture of the total level of disorder in the area.

The calls for service data have potential to help the reader understand the total draw on police resources in the enjoined gang and control gang areas, including nuisance activity that does not typically generate a crime report, and may or may not require any citizen to call and report criminal activity. For that reason, the research expanded upon the limited studies to date relating to gang injunction effectiveness, and which have focused solely on evaluating Part 1 crimes or community perception.

How crime rates are calculated typically involves a simple formula to determine the crime rate (number of reported crimes/total population × 100,000). To understand problems with UCRs, one must understand the process by which crimes become known to the police. Problems with UCRs data include the voluntary nature of crime reporting and errors in reporting, definitional variance of crime, accuracy, and transfer accuracy, making the whole crime picture hard to come by. Law enforcement agencies report to the FBI the number of actual offenses known to them regardless of whether anyone was arrested for the crime or if the crime resulted in a conviction.

The UCRs do not include all crimes; they do not include federal crimes. Not all law enforcement agencies submit reports to the FBI. Law enforcement practices hamper accuracy, and if multiple counts occur during a single reported crime, only the most serious offense is recorded. For example, two gang members rob a bank, then flee the scene in their stolen getaway car, and they were both on a gang injunction that prohibited them from being in the area to begin with. In this case only the robbery is reported to the FBI, not the auto theft and the gang injunction violation.

For this reason, this study encountered limitations when it sought to evaluate how many gang members have been arrested for violating gang injunctions. In Appendix B, where the number of arrests for each gang injunction is listed, at least that many have been arrested; it may well be more. However, it is difficult to confirm if the more serious arrests of those gang members on injunctions included additional charges listed for injunction violations.

NATIONAL INCIDENT-BASED REPORTING SYSTEM

Criticisms of UCRs led the FBI to introduce a new crime reporting system entitled the National Incident-Based Reporting System (NIBRS), which was implemented in 1989 and has been slowly phased in. The purpose of NIBRS is to enhance the quantity, quality, and timeliness of crime data, and to improve the methodology used for compiling, analyzing, auditing, and publishing the collected data. NIBRS does away with the original Part 1 and Part 2 designations, and has instead organized offenses into more inclusive group A and group B offenses.

Group A offenses include arson, assault offenses, bribery, burglary, counterfeiting, forgery, vandalism, drug and narcotic offenses, embezzlement, extortion, fraud, gambling, homicide, kidnapping, larceny and theft, motor vehicle theft, pornography, prostitution offenses, robbery, forcible sex offenses, nonviolent sex offenses, possession of stolen property, and weapon-related law offenses.

Group B offenses include writing bad checks, curfew violations, loitering and vagrancy crimes, disorderly conduct in public, driving under the influence, public drunkenness, nonviolent family-related offenses, liquor law violations, voyeurism, runaway offenses, criminal trespassing, and all other offenses not listed.

TWO STUDIES CONDUCTED USING UCRS DATA PRIOR TO THIS THE THIRD

Jeff Grogger Study

In the context of gang injunction-related studies, two major studies to date have looked at gang injunction effectiveness via evaluating Part 1 crimes. One study conducted by Dr. Jeff Grogger (2000) concluded that gang injunctions reduced violent Part 1 crime by 5 to 10% per gang injunction neighborhood. The study evaluated 14 gang injunctions from Los Angeles County in the first year before and after their implementation. Grogger's objective was to evaluate whether gang injunctions reduced crime in the injunction areas or whether they caused spillover or displacement into other areas.

The study used simple before-and-after comparisons of crime rates in the injunction areas for one year before and one year after. The study also used a counterfactual or control area to account for the level of change in crime not caused by the gang injunctions.

For each injunction area, Grogger constructed a comparison area. Grogger measured displacement into the immediate surrounding areas that bordered the injunction areas and found that displacement did not occur into the neighboring reporting districts as originally believed.

Grogger also felt that gang injunctions in some ways provide better constitutional protections as opposed to other law enforcement tactics, as they require significant judicial oversight and involvement as opposed to directed and zero tolerance patrol, for example, which do not require any judicial approval.

Los Angeles Grand Jury Study

In June 2004, the Los Angeles County civil grand jury completed a report that was designed to explain to the public the inner workings of government and discuss what law enforcement should be investigating in Los Angeles (LA Grand Jury, 2004). The grand jury's goal was to evaluate the effectiveness of gang injunctions in the City of Los Angeles. This study also evaluated 14 gang injunctions obtained in the City of Los Angeles (2 of them were the same as the Grogger study and 12 were newer injunctions), including the Bounty Hunters, Rolling Sixty, Avenues, Krazy Ass Mexicans, 18th Street Pico Union, Canoga Park Alabama, Pacoima Project Boys, Culver City Boys, Venice 13, Harbor City Boys and Crips, Venice Shoreline Crips, Langdon Street, Harpy's, and Blythe Street. The study found that crime dropped in the injunction areas that were studied by 10%.

That finding was similar to the findings in the Grogger study, as both studies were conducted in a similar fashion. The potential criticism of both the Grogger and LA grand jury studies is that they used neighboring reporting districts as controls, and not necessarily the territory of a street gang that had similar characteristics to the ones that have been subjected to gang injunctions

For that reason, this study evaluated rival gang territory as opposed to simply an area that is close to the enjoined gang's territory. This makes for a more accurate assessment of the impact of the injunction when comparing two gangs that are as similar in characteristics and area as possible. In addition, this study expanded upon the types of crime committed in the injunction and control areas, providing additional insight into gang injunction effectiveness.

TABLE 7.1

Chapter 8 (25 Injunction Study)	Independent Variable	IV Scale	Scoring Categories
Part 1 crime injunction change from base	Pre- vs. post-	Interval ratio	Pre- vs. post-
Part 1 crime change injunction from control	Injunction vs. control	Interval ratio	Injunction vs. control
Part 2 crime injunction change from base	Pre- vs. post-	Interval ratio	Pre- vs. post-
Part 2 crime change injunction from control	Injunction vs. control	Interval ratio	Injunction vs. Control
Total calls injunction change from base	Pre- vs. post-	Interval ratio	Pre- vs. post-
Total calls change injunction from control	Injunction vs. control	Interval ratio	Injunction vs. control

Chapter 9 (Survey of Police)	Independent Variable	IV Scale	Scoring Categories
1—Worth my time	Y > N	Categorical	Y > N
2—Response time	Q > S or none	Categorical	Q > S or none
3—Other enforcement	Y > N	Categorical	Y > N
4—If yes, what was it	7 categories	Categorical	7 categories
5—Size of the gang	S > L	Ordinal	S > L
6—What % of gang	L > S	Ordinal	L > S
7—Gangs territorial	Y > N	Categorical	Y > N
8—Were leaders targeted	Y > N	Categorical	Y > N
9—Was crime Part 1	Y > N	Categorical	Y > N
10—Collective or individual	Group > individual	Ordinal	Group > individual
11—Gang turf size	S > L	Categorical	S > L
12—What % of turf size enjoined	L > S	Ordinal	L > S
13—Economic status	P > M or higher	Categorical	P > M or higher
14—Zoning in area	R > others	Categorical	R > others
15—How get the injunction	High > low for each	Categorical	High > low for each
16—If aware, who initiated	P > others	Categorical	P > others
17—Type of order	D + G > D or G	Categorical	D + G > D or G
18—Adequately informed	I > NI	Categorical	I > NI
19—Jail or citation	Jail > not jail	Categorical	Jail > not jail
20—New members added	A > NA	Categorical	A > NA

Table 7.1 shows the methods used in both the injunction study (Chapter 8) and the police officer survey (Chapter 9).

8

Results of 25 Injunction Studies

This chapter is organized into four sections to explain the results of the research outlined in the next two chapters. The first section identifies the pairings of injunctions and matched controls, and demonstrates the similarities between them as sufficient to proceed with inferential analyses. The second section addresses the primary and secondary hypotheses of this research, that calls for service would be significantly decreased in injunction areas, both compared to baseline and compared to matched controls. The third section includes further or exploratory analysis of the results, to include results by gang ethnicity, gang injunction size, injunctions by county, total gang size, and injunction area size. The fourth section of this chapter reviews the injunctions on a case-by-case basis describing the injunctions and controls, broken down by Part 1 crime, Part 2 crime, and total calls for service.

To assess the effectiveness of injunctions on calls for service, injunctions were first compared to baseline using a paired t-test. Injunctions and matched controls were then contrasted in percent change from baseline in calls for service using a paired t-test. This schema was followed for Part 1 crime, Part 2 crime, and total calls for service. For each type of call for service, the preinjunction baseline counts, the postinjunction counts, and the percent change from baseline are presented in tables. To aid in understanding key findings, comparisons of injunctions and controls are presented in graphical form for each type of call for service.

SECTION 1: INJUNCTION AND CONTROL PAIRINGS

To truly evaluate if gang injunctions work or not, we need to compare the injunction area to something—have some type of control to make sure the injunction, and not something else, was the cause of any changes. The selection of appropriate control areas for each target area was a critical element of this research; without this component the research would not be viable. Control areas were carefully chosen to match each target injunction, based on four criteria: both gangs were the same ethnicity, both gangs were close in proximity, both gangs' turf was close in terms of square mileage, and both gangs were close in total number of gang members known to be members of the target and control gangs.

The injunctions and the controls were well matched to avoid any statistically significant differences between the injunction group and the control group at baseline. The groups were correlated in square mileage and as well as in number of gang members. If injunction and control groups were not first determined to be similar in square mileage, and in number of gang members, then they would not have been appropriately qualified for statistical analyses. However, this research has revealed that injunction and control groups were well correlated to proceed with investigating the hypotheses.

Descriptive: Injunction versus Control

Injunction areas and matched control areas were close in ethnicity and proximity, similar in square miles of area, and similar in gang membership size. Table 8.1 depicts the pairing of injunctions and matched control areas, the ethnicity of both injunction and control gangs, the distance between the paired areas, and assigns a code number for each pair (n = 25 pairs).

Proximity: Injunctions and matched control areas were close in proximity, averaging 3.4 miles between (SD = 5.3). The furthest distance was 21.2 miles (n = 1, pair number 6 on Table 8.1). Nine of 25 pairs share common borders.

Square miles: Table 8.2 depicts the square miles for injunction and matched control areas. Injunctions averaged 1.5 square miles (SD = 1.8), while control areas averaged 1.6 square miles (SD = 1.4). This difference was not statistically significant, t (24) = 0.4, $p = .66$. Injunctions and controls were similar in square miles.

Number of gang members: Table 8.2 depicts the gang membership size for injunction and matched control areas. Injunctions averaged 215.5 gang members (SD = 188.5), while control areas averaged 195.4 gang members (SD = 140.9) (see Table 8.2). This difference was not statistically significant, t (24) = 1.4, $p = .18$. Although injunction areas had somewhat more gang members than controls, injunction and controls were reasonably similar in number of gang members, which meant that the injunctions and controls were similar enough to proceed with the research.

TABLE 8.1
Injunctions and Matched Controls (Assignment of Pair Numbers)

Pair Number	Injunction	Injunction Ethnicity	Control	Control Ethnicity	Distance Between
1	Varrio Posole Locos	H	Vista Homeboys	H	5.5
2	Varrio San Marcos	H	South Los Gang	H	1.4
3	Old Town National City	H	Shelltown Gamma St.	H	0
4	Varrio Mesa Locos	H	Center Street Gang	H	5.9
5	Linda Vista 13	H	Mission Bay Locos	H	6.1
6	Diablos Gang	H	Fallbrook Locos	H	21.2
7	Westside Gang	H	Encinitas Locos	H	15.2
8	Nestor Gang	H	Imperials Gang	H	0
9	Logan Red Steps	H	Shelltown 38th Street	H	0
10	Center Street Gang	H	South Los Gang	H	11.27
11	Varrio Posole Locos	H	Vista Homeboys	H	5.5
12	Lincoln Park Bloods	B	5/9 Brims	B	0
13	East Side Piru / Skyline	B	West Coast Crips	B	2.1
14	Old Town National City	H	Otay Gang	H	3
15	7th Street Gang	H	Southside Colton	H	3.1
16	Verdugo Flats Gang	H	Northside Colton	H	0.25
17	Project Crips	B	Colton City Crips	B	2.4
18	Canoga Park Alabama	H	Reseda West & South	H	1.6
19	18th Street Pico Union	H	SSK & Drifters	H	0
20	Krazy Ass Mexicans	H	State St & Clarence St.	H	0
21	Rolling Sixty Crips	B	Eight Tray Gangsters	B	0
22	Varrio Nueva Estrada	H	White Fence Evergreen	H	0
23	Grape Street Crips	B	Front Street Crips	B	0.9
24	Bounty Hunter Bloods	B	118th St. East Coast Crips	B	0
25	Colonia Chiques	H	Southside Chiques	H	0
				M	3.4
				SD	5.3

Note: "Pair" refers to the code assigned to each injunction and matched control, which was used throughout. (H) = Hispanic Gang and (B) = Black Gang. Injunctions and controls matched for ethnicity. *M* = Mean Average distance between all 25 pairs. *SD* = Standard Deviation.

Correlation between Injunction and Matched Controls

The injunctions and matched controls were well correlated in square miles and in number of gang members.

Figure 8.1 depicts a scatter plot of square miles for injunction and control, a line of best fit, the equation describing the line of best fit, the correlation (r), and the variance accounted for (r^2) by the relationship. In square miles, injunction and control areas were correlated at $r = +.69$, indicating that the relationship accounted for 48% of the variance in square miles ($r^2 = .48$; see Figure 8.1). This relationship was statistically significant, $p < .0001$.

TABLE 8.2
Square Miles and Number of Gang Members: Injunction v. Control

	Square Miles		Total Gang Members in Each Gang	
Pair	Injunction	Control	Injunction	Control
1	0.6	1.9	146	195
2	0.3	0.5	99	120
3	0.2	0.5	250	150
4	0.1	0.1	98	98
5	0.2	1.6	54	43
6	0.7	3.5	99	80
7	0.5	0.1	94	71
8	3.7	3.5	60	90
9	2.1	1.5	137	116
10	0.1	0.5	98	120
11	0.5	1.9	146	195
12	1.0	1.3	216	219
13	5.2	2.4	527	424
14	4.4	5.0	250	200
15	0.3	2.9	120	165
16	1.3	2.9	260	320
17	0.8	0.4	53	40
18	3.4	2.1	530	340
19	0.7	0.2	200	150
20	0.6	0.5	150	150
21	2.8	1.5	200	200
22	1.3	1.5	200	300
23	0.3	0.2	300	200
24	0.5	0.4	200	200
25	6.7	4.3	900	700
M	1.5	1.6	215.5	195.4
SD	1.8	1.4	188.5	140.9
SEM	0.4	0.3	37.7	28.2

Note: "Pair" refers to the code assigned to each injunction and matched control (see Table 8.1). *M* = Mean Average in sq. miles and gang members. *SD* = Standard Deviation. *SEM* = Standard Error of the Mean.

Figure 8.2 depicts a scatter plot of the number of gang members for injunction and control, a line of best fit, the equation describing the line of best fit, the correlation (r), and the variance accounted for (r^2) by the relationship. For the number of gang members, injunction and control areas were correlated at r = +.94, indicating that the relationship accounted 89% of the variance in number of gang members ($r^2 = .89$; see Figure 8.2). This relationship was statistically significant, $p < .001$.

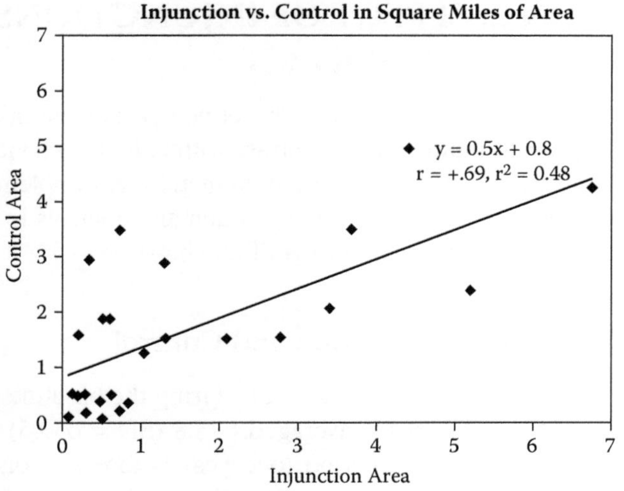

FIGURE 8.1 Scatterplot: Square Miles, Injunction and Control.

Summary of Section 1: Injunction and Control Pairings

Collectively, these findings indicate that the injunction areas and matched control areas were close in proximity, similar in square miles of area, and well correlated in square miles of area. Injunction areas and matched control areas were also similar in gang ethnicity, gang injunction size, and well correlated in total membership size. Therefore it was reasonable to consider the injunction and matched control areas similar enough to proceed with investigating the effect of injunctions on crime calls.

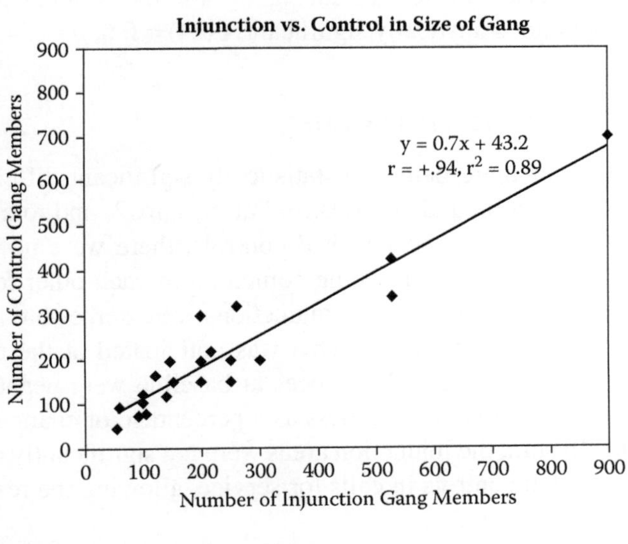

FIGURE 8.2 Scatterplot of number of Gang Members: Injunction and Control.

SECTION 2: EFFECT OF INJUNCTIONS ON CALLS FOR SERVICE

To assess the effect of injunctions, baseline values were taken for one year prior to injunction to contrast with calls for service during the immediate one year after the injunction was implemented. Baseline values were similar for injunction and controls in Part 1 calls, Part 2 calls, and in total calls (Table 8.3).

Baseline Values, Injunction and Control

Injunctions averaged 872.9 Part 1 calls during the baseline period (SD = 1193.5), and controls averaged 648.8 (SD = 630.5) Part 1 calls during the baseline period (one year before and one year after). This difference was not statistically significant, $t\ (24) = 1.1$, $p = .28$.

Baseline Part 2 Calls

Injunctions averaged 2,041.3 Part 2 calls during the baseline period (SD = 3,052.5), and controls averaged 1,628.2 (SD = 1,555.7) Part 2 calls during the baseline period. This difference was not statistically significant, $t\ (24) = 0.8$, $p = .40$.

Baseline Total Calls for Service

Injunctions averaged 6,274.6 total calls for service during the baseline period (SD = 8,421.8), and controls averaged 5,459.2 (SD = 4,222.0) total calls for service during the baseline period. This difference was not statistically significant, $t\ (24) = 0.6$, $p = .54$.

Summary of Baseline Calls

As a result of there being no statistically significant differences between injunction and controls, in Part 1, Part 2, and total calls between injunctions and matched controls, there were no issues that prohibited them from being compared to each other for this research. However, areas with injunctions were somewhat higher in baseline calls for service. This was anticipated at the design stage, and any potential differences at baseline were negated by assessing injunction effectiveness as a percentage of change from baseline. In sum, the injunction areas were not significantly different than match controls in calls for service, allowing the research to proceed.

TABLE 8.3
Baseline Calls for Service: Injunction vs. Control

	Part 1		Part 2		Total Calls	
Pair	Injunction	Control	Injunction	Control	Injunction	Control
1	228	709	304	2615	982	7541
2	126	375	337	400	1727	3035
3	271	651	323	1436	1409	3345
4	352	200	720	500	1650	1000
5	310	1327	435	3574	2243	7856
6	172	519	446	876	1012	6886
7	157	22	168	249	448	1435
8	1008	140	2877	1930	4414	12526
9	2349	1455	2406	1852	26088	12946
10	162	300	703	400	1961	2700
11	263	947	956	2865	2732	8880
12	1544	2710	4841	6354	14748	14520
13	5568	1425	15540	5054	36331	11913
14	600	700	1600	1700	9500	10100
15	306	315	725	931	1926	1833
16	351	404	1050	1058	2875	2904
17	421	89	1065	210	3448	636
18	455	145	2164	425	5278	2425
19	816	126	2440	378	5390	1975
20	165	144	237	325	844	1825
21	765	201	1201	550	3986	2550
22	989	975	2597	2348	5301	4921
23	824	698	2325	1923	5251	3726
24	726	195	2072	553	4821	2553
25	2895	1447	3500	2200	12500	6450
M	872.9	648.8	2041.3	1628.2	6274.6	5459.2
SD	1193.5	630.5	3052.5	1555.7	8421.8	4222.0
SEM	47.7	25.2	122.1	62.2	336.9	168.9

Note: "Pair" refers to the code assigned to each injunction and matched control, see Table 8.1. *M* = Mean Average of baseline calls for all 25 pairs. *SD* = Standard Deviation. *SEM* = Standard Error of the Mean.

Percent Change for Part 1 Crime

Table 8.4 shows that Part 1 calls in gang injunction areas decreased 11.6% compared to baseline (–11.6%), a statistically significant decline, t (24) = 2.8, p = .009. Matched control areas increased 0.8% (+0.8) during the same period. The injunction and control outcomes were in opposite directions: the injunction areas were getting better while the matched control areas were getting worse.

TABLE 8.4
Part 1 Calls: Percent Change From Baseline

	Injunction			Control		
Pair	Before	After	Change	Before	After	Change
1	228	203	–11.0%	709	692	–2.4%
2	126	136	7.9%	375	350	–6.7%
3	271	178	–34.3%	651	438	–32.7%
4	352	288	–18.2%	200	190	–5.0%
5	310	294	–5.2%	1327	1467	10.6%
6	172	226	31.4%	519	1212	133.5%
7	157	181	15.3%	22	16	–27.3%
8	1008	978	–3.0%	140	158	12.9%
9	2349	2355	0.3%	1455	1384	–4.9%
10	162	147	–9.3%	300	290	–3.3%
11	263	143	–45.6%	947	1003	5.9%
12	1544	1435	–7.1%	2710	2513	–7.3%
13	5568	1184	–78.7%	1425	1420	–0.4%
14	600	500	–16.7%	700	600	–14.3%
15	306	279	–8.8%	315	298	–5.4%
16	351	321	–8.5%	404	411	1.7%
17	421	401	–4.8%	89	98	10.1%
18	455	390	–14.3%	145	139	–4.1%
19	816	759	–7.0%	126	115	–8.7%
20	165	123	–25.5%	144	155	7.6%
21	765	745	–2.6%	201	172	–14.4%
22	989	936	–5.4%	975	953	–2.3%
23	824	757	–8.1%	698	672	–3.7%
24	726	693	–4.5%	195	161	–17.4%
25	2895	2120	–26.8%	1447	1400	–3.2%
M	872.9	630.9	–11.6%	648.8	652.3	0.8%
SD	1193.5	602.6		630.5	620.3	
SEM	47.7	24.1		25.2	24.8	

Note: "Pair" refers to the code assigned to each injunction and matched control, see Table 8.1. *M* = Mean Average change in Part 1 calls for all 25 pairs. *SD* = Standard Deviation. *SEM* = Standard Error of the Mean.

The 12.4% net benefit (11.6% + 0.8% = 12.4%) between injunctions and matched controls was statistically significant, t (24) = 2.1, $p = .046$. Overall, these findings suggest that gang injunctions may reduce Part 1 crime (see Table 8.4 and Figure 8.3).

Part 2 Calls for Service

Table 8.5 shows that Part 2 calls in gang injunction areas decreased 15.9% compared to baseline (–15.9%), a statistically significant

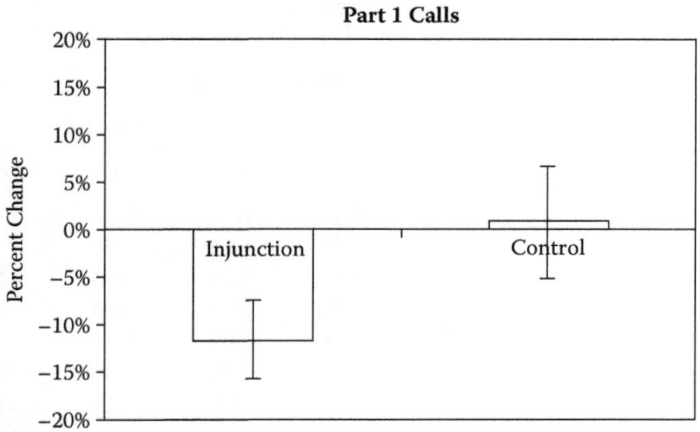

FIGURE 8.3 Part 1 Calls, Percent Change from Baseline.

decline, t (24) = 0.8, p = .40. Matched control areas increased 1.6% (+1.6%) during the same period. The injunction and control outcomes were in opposite directions: the injunction areas were getting better while the matched control areas were getting worse. The 17.5% net benefit (15.9% + 1.6% = 17.5%) between injunctions and matched controls trended toward statistical significance, t (24) = 2.7, p = .01. Overall, these findings suggest that gang injunctions may reduce Part 2 crime (see Table 8.5 and Figure 8.4).

Total Calls for Service

Table 8.6 shows that total calls in gang injunction areas decreased 14.1% compared to baseline (–14.1%), t (24) = 0.6, p = .54. Matched control areas increased 2.3% (+2.3%) during the same period. The injunction and control outcomes were in opposite directions: the injunction areas were getting better while the matched control areas were getting worse. The 16.4% net benefit (14.1% + 2.3% = 16.4%) between injunctions and matched controls trended toward statistical significance, t (24) = 2.9, p = .008. Overall, these findings suggest that gang injunctions may reduce total calls (see Table 8.6 and Figure 8.5).

Summary: Effect of Injunctions on Calls for Service

The primary hypothesis of the present study proffered that Part 1 calls would significantly decrease in injunction areas compared to matched control areas. This hypothesis was supported. Part 1 calls decreased 11.6% compared to baseline, while the matched controls averaged a mild increase of 0.8% in Part 1 calls for service, a net benefit of 12.4% in the injunction area.

TABLE 8.5

Part 2 Calls: Percent Change From Baseline

	Injunction			Control		
Pair	**Before**	**After**	**Change**	**Before**	**After**	**Change**
1	304	279	–8.2%	2615	2817	7.7%
2	337	427	26.7%	400	436	9.0%
3	323	213	–34.1%	1436	853	–40.6%
4	720	600	–16.7%	500	400	–20.0%
5	435	404	–7.1%	3574	3672	2.7%
6	446	287	–35.7%	876	1830	108.9%
7	168	98	–41.7%	249	203	–18.5%
8	2877	2477	–13.9%	1930	2082	7.9%
9	2406	2509	4.3%	1852	1827	–1.3%
10	703	517	–26.5%	400	350	–12.5%
11	956	804	–15.9%	2865	3370	17.6%
12	4841	3652	–24.6%	6354	4908	–22.8%
13	15540	4220	–72.8%	5054	5204	3.0%
14	1600	1500	–6.3%	1700	1600	–5.9%
15	725	637	–12.1%	931	908	–2.5%
16	1050	995	–5.2%	1058	1056	–0.2%
17	1065	1032	–3.1%	210	225	7.1%
18	2164	1230	–43.2%	425	397	–6.6%
19	2440	2080	–14.8%	378	345	–8.7%
20	237	256	8.0%	325	352	8.3%
21	1201	1081	–10.0%	550	567	3.1%
22	2597	2519	–3.0%	2348	2302	–2.0%
23	2325	2134	–8.2%	1923	1956	1.7%
24	2072	2179	5.2%	553	548	–0.9%
25	3500	2100	–40.0%	2200	2300	4.5%
M	2041.3	1369.2	–15.9%	1628.2	1620.3	1.6%
SD	3052.5	1125.2		1555.7	1451.4	
SEM	122.1	45.0		62.2	58.1	

Note: "Pair" refers to the code assigned to each injunction and matched control, see Table 8.1. *M* = Mean Average change in Part 2 calls for all 25 pairs. *SD* = Standard Deviation. *SEM* = Standard Error of the Mean.

The secondary hypotheses of the present study proffered that Part 2 calls and total calls for service would significantly decrease in injunction areas compared to matched control areas. These hypotheses were supported. Part 2 calls decreased 15.9% compared to baseline, while the matched controls averaged a mild increase of 1.6% in Part 2 calls for service, a net benefit of 17.5% in the injunction area. Similarly, total calls for service decreased 14.1% compared to baseline, while the matched controls averaged a mild increase of 2.3% in total calls for service, a net benefit of 16.4% in the injunction area.

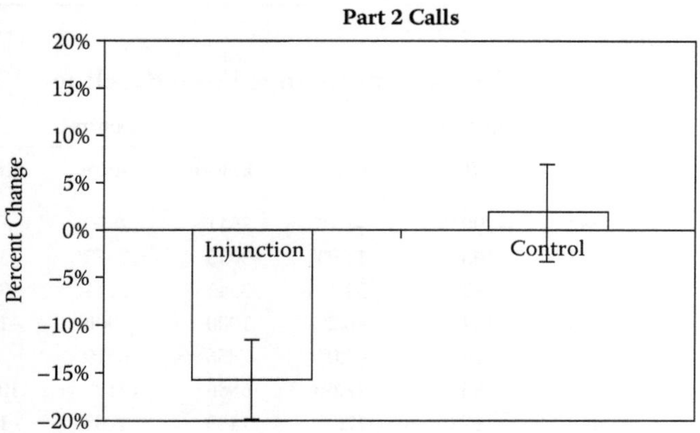

FIGURE 8.4 Part 2 Calls, Percent Change from Baseline.

These findings suggest that injunctions have an effect in that calls for service were significantly reduced compared to baseline and matched controls. The declines in Part 1 calls, Part 2 calls, and total calls for service were statistically significant. The magnitude of the effect was greater than 10% in each case, which is significant for communities. The benefit yielded in the present study was roughly 150 fewer Part 1 calls per injunction per year, 650 fewer Part 2 calls per injunction per year, and 1,750 fewer total calls per injunction per year. These data suggest that injunctions provide a significant benefit to society.

SECTION 3: FURTHER OR EXPLORATORY ANALYSIS

To further describe the data collected and identify other constructs of interest when evaluating gang injunctions, Section 3 evaluates five additional topics. These topics include further analysis of gang injunctions by gang ethnicity, the size of the gang injunction (how many gang members) targeted, the county in which the injunction was implemented, the size of the area in square miles, and the size of the overall gang. This further analysis does not modify or alter the findings of this research; it may, however, help shed some potential light on other variables that may impact gang injunction efficacy and reveal potential research topics for future research.

Variance by Gang Ethnicity

This research sought to identify any differences relating to the impact of gang injunctions based upon the ethnicity of the enjoined gang. This research evaluated 25 gang injunctions from four counties. Of the 25 injunctions evaluated in this research, 19 of them were Hispanic gangs and 6 were African American

TABLE 8.6

Total Calls for Service: Percent Change From Baseline

	Injunction			Control		
Pair	Before	After	Change	Before	After	Change
1	982	902	–8.1%	7541	7850	4.1%
2	1727	1985	14.9%	3035	3375	11.2%
3	1409	929	–34.1%	3345	2214	–33.8%
4	1650	1548	–6.2%	1000	900	–10.0%
5	2243	2198	–2.0%	7856	8519	8.4%
6	1012	834	–17.6%	6886	14197	106.2%
7	448	372	–17.0%	1435	1285	–10.5%
8	4414	4113	–6.8%	12526	12474	–0.4%
9	26088	26213	0.5%	12946	13093	1.1%
10	1961	1615	–17.6%	2700	2500	–7.4%
11	2732	1913	–30.0%	8880	9252	4.2%
12	14748	11108	–24.7%	14520	9862	–32.1%
13	36331	9139	–74.8%	11913	11576	–2.8%
14	9500	8500	–10.5%	10100	9300	–7.9%
15	1926	1821	–5.5%	1833	1921	4.8%
16	2875	2764	–3.9%	2904	2934	1.0%
17	3448	3243	–5.9%	636	664	4.4%
18	5278	3202	–39.3%	2425	2460	1.4%
19	5390	4650	–13.7%	1975	1898	–3.9%
20	844	772	–8.5%	1825	1960	7.4%
21	3986	3841	–3.6%	2550	2610	2.4%
22	5301	5234	–1.3%	4921	5011	1.8%
23	5251	4865	–7.4%	3726	3897	4.6%
24	4821	4959	2.9%	2553	2598	1.8%
25	12500	8600	–31.2%	6450	6500	0.8%
M	6274.6	4612.8	–14.1%	5459.2	5554.0	2.3%
SD	8421.8	5360.0		4222.0	4292.9	
SEM	336.9	214.4		168.9	171.7	

Note: "Pair" refers to the code assigned to each injunction and matched control, see Table 8.1. M = Mean Average change in total calls for all 25 pairs. *SD* = Standard Deviation. *SEM* = Standard Error of the Mean.

gangs. Table 8.7 isolates the same data contained in Table 8.4, but includes only the ethnic Hispanic gangs studied.

Nineteen of the 25 gang injunctions targeted Hispanic gangs. Table 8.7 shows that Part 1 crime in Hispanic gang injunction areas decreased 9.7% compared to baseline (–9.7%), a statistically significant decline, t (18) = 2.4, $p = .02$. Matched control areas increased 2.7% (+2.7%) during the same period. The injunction and control outcomes were in opposite directions: the injunction areas were getting better while the matched control areas were getting worse.

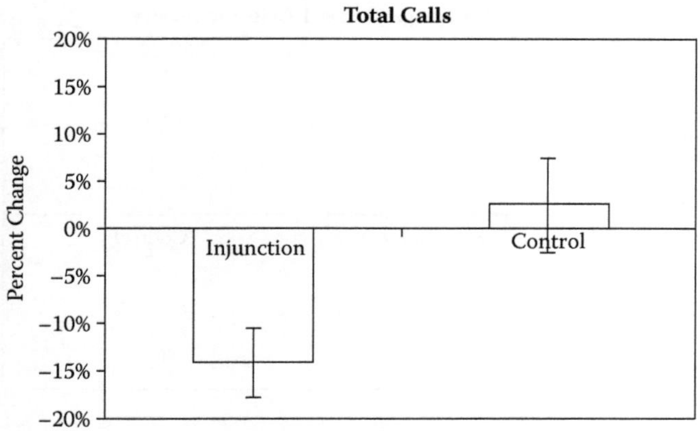

FIGURE 8.5 Total Calls For Service, Percent Change from Baseline.

TABLE 8.7
Part 1 Calls, Percent Change from Baseline for Hispanic Gangs

	Injunction			Control		
Pair	**Before**	**After**	**Change**	**Before**	**After**	**Change**
1	228	203	−11.0%	709	692	−2.4%
2	126	136	7.9%	375	350	-6.7%
3	271	178	−34.3%	651	438	-32.7%
4	352	288	−18.2%	200	190	−5.0%
5	310	294	−5.2%	1327	1467	10.6%
6	172	226	31.4%	519	1212	133.5%
7	157	181	15.3%	22	16	-27.3%
8	1008	978	−3.0%	140	158	12.9%
9	2349	2355	0.3%	1455	1384	−4.9%
10	162	147	−9.3%	300	290	−3.3%
11	263	143	−45.6%	947	1003	5.9%
14	600	500	−16.7%	700	600	−14.3%
15	306	279	−8.8%	315	298	−5.4%
16	351	321	−8.5%	404	411	1.7%
18	455	390	−14.3%	145	139	−4.1%
19	816	759	−7.0%	126	115	−8.7%
20	165	123	−25.5%	144	155	7.6%
22	989	936	−5.4%	975	953	−2.3%
25	2895	2120	−26.8%	1447	1400	−3.2%
M	630.3	555.6	−9.7%	573.7	593.2	2.7%
SD	757.7	648.4		463.2	490.9	
SEM	39.9	34.1		24.4	25.8	

Note: This table includes only the 19 injunctions against ethnic Hispanic gangs for Part 1 crimes. "Pair" refers to the code assigned to each injunction and matched control, see Table 8.1. *M* = Mean Average change for all 19 pairs. *SD* = Standard Deviation. *SEM* = Standard Error of the Mean.

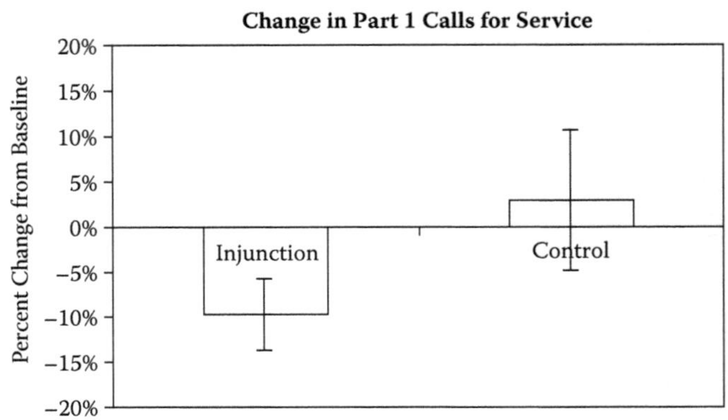

FIGURE 8.6 Hispanic Gangs: Change in Part 1 Calls for Service.

The 12.4% net benefit (9.7% + 2.7% = 12.4%) between injunctions and matched controls trended toward statistical significance, t (18) = 1.9, p = .07. Overall, these findings suggest that gang injunctions may reduce Part 1 calls (see Table 8.7 and Figure 8.6).

Table 8.8 shows that Part 2 crime in Hispanic gang injunction areas decreased 15.0% compared to baseline (–15.0%), a statistically significant decline, t (18) = 3.5, p = .002. Matched control areas increased 2.5% (+2.5%) during the same period. The injunction and control outcomes were in opposite directions: the injunction areas were getting better while the matched control areas were getting worse. The 17.5% net benefit (15.0% + 2.5% = 17.5%) between injunctions and matched controls trended toward statistical significance, t (18) = 2.2, p < .05. Overall, these findings suggest that gang injunctions may reduce Part 2 calls (see Table 8.8 and Figure 8.7).

Table 8.9 shows that total calls in Hispanic gang injunction areas decreased 12.5% compared to baseline (–12.5%), a statistically significant decline, t (18) = 4.0, p < .001. Matched control areas increased 4.1% (+4.1%) during the same period. The injunction and control outcomes were in opposite directions: the injunction areas were getting better while the matched control areas were getting worse. The 16.6% net benefit (12.5% + 4.1% = 16.6%) between injunctions and matched controls trended toward statistical significance, t (18) = 2.5, p < .02. Overall, these findings suggest that gang injunctions may reduce total calls (see Table 8.9 and Figure 8.8).

Summary of Injunctions of Hispanic Gangs

Injunctions reduced crime calls for service while the matched controls experienced rises in crime calls for service. This pattern was evident in Part 1 calls, Part 2 calls, and total calls for service. These findings suggest that, on average, these injunctions against Hispanic gangs were effective.

TABLE 8.8
Part 2 Calls, Percent Change from Baseline for Hispanic Gangs

	Injunction			Control		
Pair	**Before**	**After**	**Change**	**Before**	**After**	**Change**
1	304	279	–8.2%	2615	2817	7.7%
2	337	427	26.7%	400	436	9.0%
3	323	213	–34.1%	1436	853	–40.6%
4	720	600	–16.7%	500	400	–20.0%
5	435	404	–7.1%	3574	3672	2.7%
6	446	287	–35.7%	876	1830	108.9%
7	168	98	–41.7%	249	203	–18.5%
8	2877	2477	–13.9%	1930	2082	7.9%
9	2406	2509	4.3%	1852	1827	–1.3%
10	703	517	–26.5%	400	350	–12.5%
11	956	804	–15.9%	2865	3370	17.6%
14	1600	1500	–6.3%	1700	1600	–5.9%
15	725	637	–12.1%	931	908	–2.5%
16	1050	995	–5.2%	1058	1056	–0.2%
18	2164	1230	–43.2%	425	397	–6.6%
19	2440	2080	–14.8%	378	345	–8.7%
20	237	256	8.0%	325	352	8.3%
22	2597	2519	–3.0%	2348	2302	–2.0%
25	3500	2100	–40.0%	2200	2300	4.5%
M	1262.5	1049.1	–15.0%	1371.7	1426.3	2.5%
SD	1062.2	871.2		1009.6	1102.4	
SEM	55.9	45.9		53.1	58.0	

Note: This table includes only the 19 injunctions against ethnic Hispanic gangs for Part 2 crimes. *M* = Mean Average in sq. miles and gang members. *SD* = Standard Deviation. *SEM* = Standard Error of the Mean.

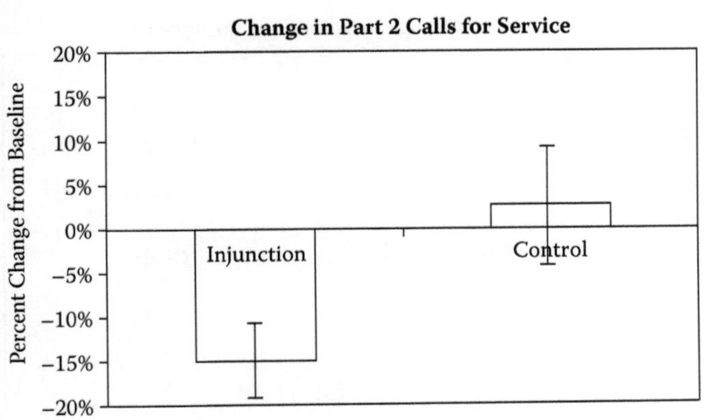

FIGURE 8.7 Hispanic Gangs: Change in Part 2 Calls for Service.

TABLE 8.9
Total Calls, Percent Change from Baseline for Hispanic Gangs

	Injunction			Control		
Pair	**Before**	**After**	**Change**	**Before**	**After**	**Change**
1	982	902	–8.1%	7541	7850	4.1%
2	1727	1985	14.9%	3035	3375	11.2%
3	1409	929	–34.1%	3345	2214	–33.8%
4	1650	1548	–6.2%	1000	900	–10.0%
5	2243	2198	–2.0%	7856	8519	8.4%
6	1012	834	–17.6%	6886	14197	106.2%
7	448	372	–17.0%	1435	1285	–10.5%
8	4414	4113	–6.8%	12526	12474	–0.4%
9	26088	26213	0.5%	12946	13093	1.1%
10	1961	1615	–17.6%	2700	2500	–7.4%
11	2732	1913	–30.0%	8880	9252	4.2%
14	9500	8500	–10.5%	10100	9300	–7.9%
15	1926	1821	–5.5%	1833	1921	4.8%
16	2875	2764	–3.9%	2904	2934	1.0%
18	5278	3202	–39.3%	2425	2460	1.4%
19	5390	4650	–13.7%	1975	1898	–3.9%
20	844	772	–8.5%	1825	1960	7.4%
22	5301	5234	–1.3%	4921	5011	1.8%
25	12500	8600	–31.2%	6450	6500	0.8%
M	4646.3	4113.9	–12.5%	5293.8	5665.4	4.1%
SD	6056.7	5866.3		3803.3	4366.4	
SEM	318.8	308.8		200.2	229.8	

Note: This table includes only the 19 injunctions against ethnic Hispanic gangs for total calls. *M* = Mean Average in sq. miles and gang members. *SD* = Standard Deviation. *SEM* = Standard Error of the Mean.

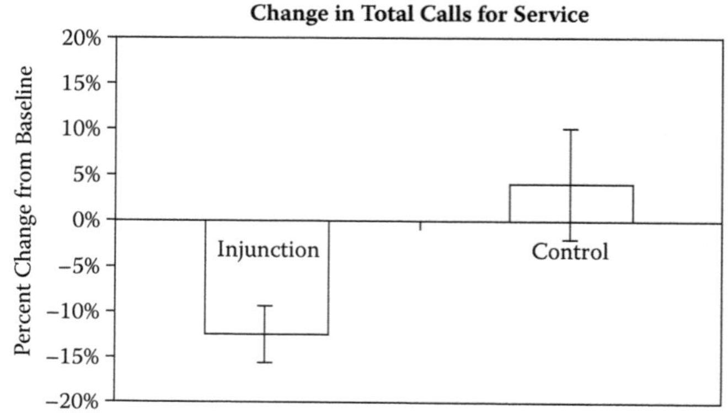

FIGURE 8.8 Hispanic Gangs: Change in Total Calls for Service.

TABLE 8.10
Part 1 Calls, Percent Change from Baseline for African American Gangs

	Injunction			Control		
Pair	**Before**	**After**	**Change**	**Before**	**After**	**Change**
12	1544	1435	–7.1%	2710	2513	–7.3%
13	5568	1184	–78.7%	1425	1420	–0.4%
17	421	401	–4.8%	89	98	10.1%
21	765	745	–2.6%	201	172	–14.4%
23	824	757	–8.1%	698	672	–3.7%
24	726	693	–4.5%	195	161	–17.4%
M	1641.3	869.2	–17.6%	886.3	839.3	–5.5%
SD	1959.1	373.5		1023.2	961.4	
SEM	326.5	62.2		170.5	160.2	

Note: This table includes only the 6 injunctions against ethnic African American gangs for Part 1 crimes. "Pair" refers to the code assigned to each injunction and matched control, see Table 8.1. *M* = Mean Average change for all 6 pairs. *SD* = Standard Deviation. *SEM* = Standard Error of the Mean.

Six of the 25 gang injunctions targeted African American gangs. Table 8.10 shows that Part 1 crime in African American gang injunction areas decreased 17.6% compared to baseline (–17.6%), a statistically significant decline, t (5) = 1.4, $p < 0.21$. Matched control areas decreased 5.5% (–5.5%) during the same period. The injunction and control outcomes were in the same direction: the injunction areas were getting better while the matched control areas were also getting better at a reduced rate. The 12.1% net benefit (17.6% – 5.5% = 12.1%) between injunctions and matched controls trended toward statistical significance, t (5) = 1.1, $p < .33$. Overall, these findings suggest that gang injunctions may reduce Part 1 calls (see Table 8.10 and Figure 8.9).

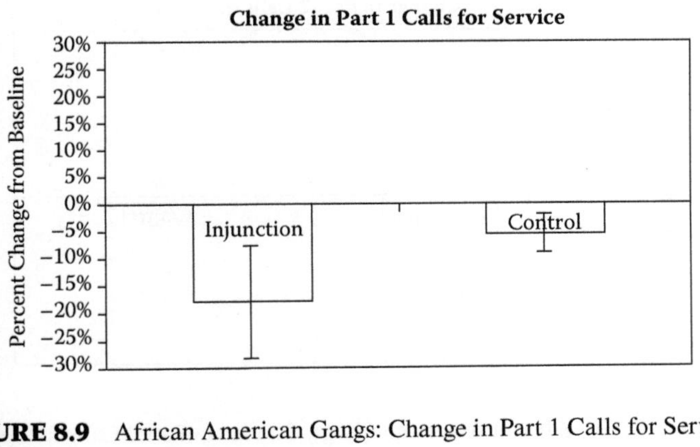

FIGURE 8.9 African American Gangs: Change in Part 1 Calls for Service.

TABLE 8.11
Part 2 Calls, Percent Change from Baseline for African American Gangs

	Injunction			Control		
Pair	**Before**	**After**	**Change**	**Before**	**After**	**Change**
12	4841	3652	–24.6%	6354	4908	–22.8%
13	15540	4220	–72.8%	5054	5204	3.0%
17	1065	1032	–3.1%	210	225	7.1%
21	1201	1081	–10.0%	550	567	3.1%
23	2325	2134	–8.2%	1923	1956	1.7%
24	2072	2179	5.2%	553	548	–0.9%
M	4507.3	2383.0	–18.9%	2440.7	2234.7	–1.5%
SD	5573.3	1312.2		2627.8	2267.4	
SEM	928.9	218.7		438.0	377.9	

Note: This table includes only the 6 injunctions against ethnic African American gangs for Part 2 crimes. *M* = Mean Average in sq. miles and gang members. *SD* = Standard Deviation. *SEM* = Standard Error of the Mean.

Table 8.11 shows that Part 2 crime in African American gang injunction areas decreased 18.9% compared to baseline (–18.9%), a statistically significant decline, t (5) = 1.6, $p < 0.16$. Matched control areas decreased 1.5% (–1.5%) during the same period. The injunction and control outcomes were in the same direction: the injunction areas were getting better while the matched control areas were also getting better at a reduced rate. The 17.4% net benefit (18.9%: 1.5% = 17.4%) between injunctions and matched controls trended toward statistical significance, t (6) = 1.7, $p < .14$. Overall, these findings suggest that gang injunctions may reduce Part 2 calls (see Table 8.11 and Figure 8.10).

Table 8.12 shows that total calls in African American gang injunction areas decreased 18.9% compared to baseline (–18.9%),

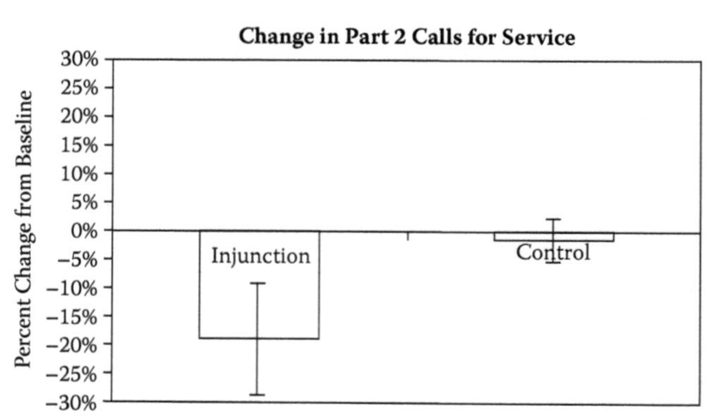

FIGURE 8.10 African American Gangs: Change in Part 2 Calls for Service.

TABLE 8.12
Total Calls, Percent Change from Baseline for African American Gangs

	Injunction			Control		
Pair	Before	After	Change	Before	After	Change
12	14748	11108	–24.7%	14520	9862	–32.1%
13	36331	9139	–74.8%	11913	11576	–2.8%
17	3448	3243	–5.9%	636	664	4.4%
21	3986	3841	–3.6%	2550	2610	2.4%
23	5251	4865	–7.4%	3726	3897	4.6%
24	4821	4959	2.9%	2553	2598	1.8%
M	11430.8	6192.5	–18.9%	5983.0	5201.2	–3.6%
SD	12900.0	3173.5		5749.4	4430.3	
SEM	2150.0	528.9		958.2	738.4	

Note: This table includes only the 6 injunctions against ethnic African American gangs for total calls. *M* = Mean Average in sq. miles and gang members. *SD* = Standard Deviation. *SEM* = Standard Error of the Mean.

a statistically significant decline, t (5) = 1.6, $p < 0.17$. Matched control areas decreased 3.6% (–3.6%) during the same period. The injunction and control outcomes were in the same direction: the injunction areas were getting better while the matched control areas were also getting better at a reduced rate. The 15.3% net benefit (18.9% – 3.6% = 15.3%) between injunctions and matched controls trended toward statistical significance, t (5) = 1.6, $p < 0.17$. Overall, these findings suggest that gang injunctions may reduce total calls (see Table 8.12 and Figure 8.11).

Summary of Ethnicity

The percent change from baseline for Hispanic gangs for Part 1 crimes was 9.7% for injunction and 2.7% for control. The percent

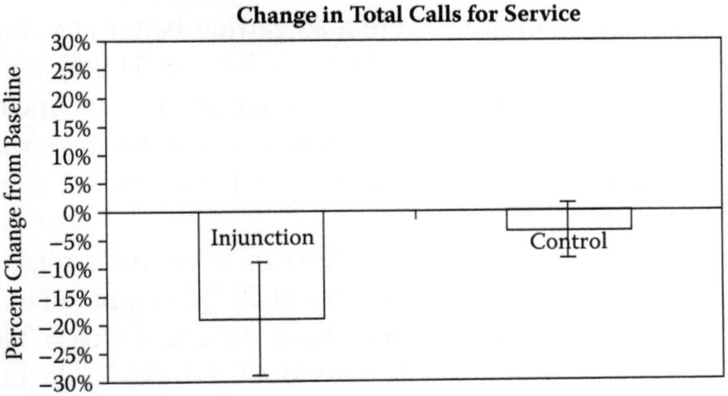

FIGURE 8.11 African American Gangs: Change in Total Calls for Service.

change for African American gangs from baseline for Part 1 crimes was 17.6% for injunction and 5.5% for control. The percent change for Hispanic gangs for Part 2 calls was a 15% reduction for injunctions and a 2.5% increase for control. The percent change for African American gangs for Part 2 calls was 18.9% for injunctions and 1.5% for control.

The percent change for Hispanic gangs for total calls was a 12.5% decrease for injunction and a 4.1% increase for control. The percent change for African American gangs' total calls was 18.9% for injunction and 3.6% for control. In sum, the injunction areas for African American gangs appear to have a more beneficial impact than for Hispanic gangs.

Variance by Gang Injunction Size (More or Less Than 50 Members)

This research sought to identify any differences relating to the impact of gang injunctions based upon the overall size of the gang enjoined. This research evaluated 25 gang injunctions from four counties. Of the 25 injunctions evaluated, 11 of them targeted more than 50 members (named in injunction and served with injunction after being filed combined) and 14 of the injunctions targeted less than 50 members. To evaluate if gang size had any impact on gang injunction effectiveness, this research used 50 gang members as the dividing line to divide the data. The purpose of this further analysis is to evaluate if differences exist between injunctions based upon the number of gang members.

Table 8.13 shows that Part 1 calls in injunctions that target more than 50 members decreased 20.7% compared to baseline (–20.7%), a statistically significant decline, t (10) = 3.1, $p <$ 0.10. Matched control areas decreased 8.8% (–8.8%) during the same period. The injunction and control outcomes were in the same direction: the injunction areas were getting better while the matched control areas were also getting better at a reduced rate. The 11.9% net benefit (20.7% – 8.8% = 11.9%) between injunctions and matched controls trended toward statistical significance, t (10) = 1.6, $p < .15$. Overall, these findings suggest that gang injunctions may reduce Part 1 calls (see Table 8.13 and Figure 8.12).

Table 8.14 shows that Part 2 calls in injunctions that target more than 50 members calls decreased 20.7% compared to baseline (–20.7%), a statistically significant decline, t (10) = 2.8, $p <$ .02. Matched control areas decreased 4.0% (–4.0%) during the same period. The injunction and control outcomes were in the same direction: the injunction areas were getting better while

TABLE 8.13
Part 1 Calls, Percent Change from Baseline for More than 50 Targeted Members

	Injunction			Control		
Pair	**Before**	**After**	**Change**	**Before**	**After**	**Change**
3	271	178	–34.3%	651	438	-32.7%
13	5568	1184	–78.7%	1425	1420	–0.4%
14	600	500	–16.7%	700	600	–14.3%
15	306	279	–8.8%	315	298	–5.4%
18	455	390	–14.3%	145	139	–4.1%
19	816	759	–7.0%	126	115	–8.7%
20	165	123	–25.5%	144	155	7.6%
21	765	745	–2.6%	201	172	–14.4%
23	824	757	–8.1%	698	672	–3.7%
24	726	693	–4.5%	195	161	–17.4%
25	2895	2120	–26.8%	1447	1400	–3.2%
M	1217.4	702.5	–20.7%	549.7	506.4	–8.8%
SD	1621.7	563.8		493.6	485.8	
SEM	147.4	51.3		44.9	44.2	

Note: This table includes only the 11 injunctions that targeted more than 50 members of the enjoined gang, either named defendants or served at a later date for Part 1 crimes. "Pair" refers to the code assigned to each injunction and matched control, see Table 8.1. *M* = Mean Average change for all 11 pairs. *SD* = Standard Deviation. *SEM* = Standard Error of the Mean.

the matched control areas were also getting better at a reduced rate. The 16.7% net benefit (20.7% – 4.0% = 16.7%) between injunctions and matched controls trended toward statistical significance, t (10) = 2.1, $p < .06$. Overall, these findings suggest that gang injunctions may reduce Part 2 calls (see Table 8.14 and Figure 8.13).

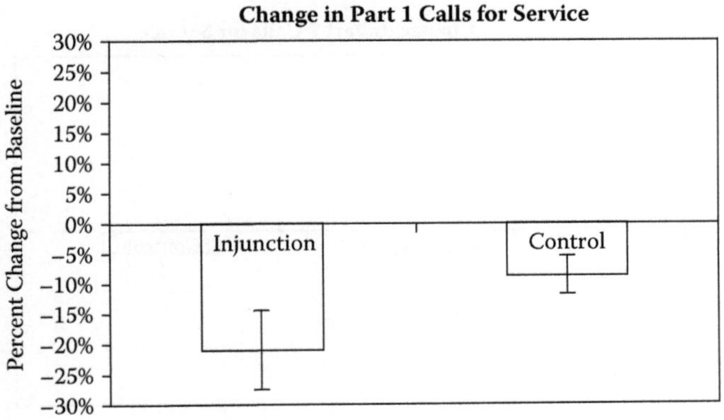

FIGURE 8.12 Part 1 Calls, Percent Change from Baseline More than 50.

TABLE 8.14

Part 2 Calls, Percent Change from Baseline for More than 50 Targeted Members

	Injunction			Control		
Pair	Before	After	Change	Before	After	Change
3	323	213	–34.1%	1436	853	–40.6%
13	15540	4220	–72.8%	5054	5204	3.0%
14	1600	1500	–6.3%	1700	1600	–5.9%
15	725	637	–12.1%	931	908	–2.5%
18	2164	1230	–43.2%	425	397	–6.6%
19	2440	2080	–14.8%	378	345	–8.7%
20	237	256	8.0%	325	352	8.3%
21	1201	1081	–10.0%	550	567	3.1%
23	2325	2134	–8.2%	1923	1956	1.7%
24	2072	2179	5.2%	553	548	–0.9%
25	3500	2100	–40.0%	2200	2300	4.5%
M	2920.6	1602.7	–20.7%	1406.8	1366.4	–4.0%
SD	4300.4	1141.9		1384.4	1442.1	
SEM	390.9	103.8		125.9	131.1	

Note: Figure 14 illustrates the data depicted in Table 8.13 for only the 11 injunctions that targeted more than 50 members of the enjoined gang for Part 1 crime. *M* = Mean Average in sq. miles and gang members. *SD* = Standard Deviation. *SEM* = Standard Error of the Mean.

Table 8.15 shows that total calls in injunctions that target more than 50 members decreased 20.5% compared to baseline (–20.5%), a statistically significant decline, t (10) = 3.0, $p < .01$. Matched control areas decreased 2.3% (–2.3%) during the same period. The injunction and control outcomes were in the same direction: the injunction areas were getting better while the matched control areas were also getting better at a reduced rate. The 18.2% net benefit (20.5% – 2.3% = 18.2%) between injunctions and matched

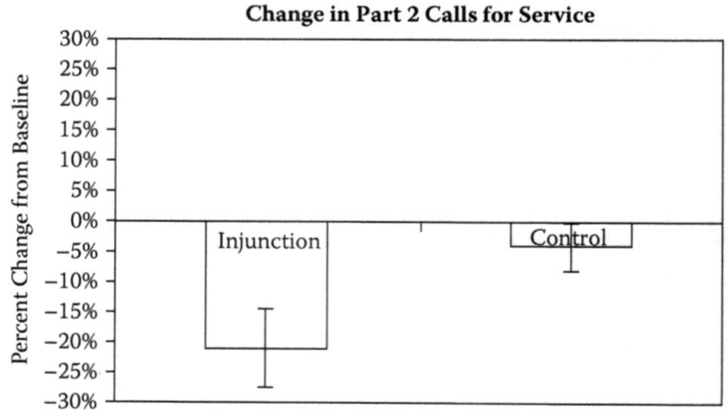

FIGURE 8.13 Part 2 Calls, Percent Change from Baseline More than 50.

TABLE 8.15
Total Calls, Percent Change from Baseline for More than 50 Targeted Members

	Injunction			Control		
Pair	**Before**	**After**	**Change**	**Before**	**After**	**Change**
3	1409	929	–34.1%	3345	2214	–33.8%
13	36331	9139	–74.8%	11913	11576	–2.8%
14	9500	8500	–10.5%	10100	9300	–7.9%
15	1926	1821	–5.5%	1833	1921	4.8%
18	5278	3202	–39.3%	2425	2460	1.4%
19	5390	4650	–13.7%	1975	1898	–3.9%
20	844	772	–8.5%	1825	1960	7.4%
21	3986	3841	–3.6%	2550	2610	2.4%
23	5251	4865	–7.4%	3726	3897	4.6%
24	4821	4959	2.9%	2553	2598	1.8%
25	12500	8600	–31.2%	6450	6500	0.8%
M	7930.5	4661.6	–20.5%	4426.8	4266.7	–2.3%
SD	10023.1	3005.9		3528.9	3366.4	
SEM	911.2	273.3		320.8	306.0	

Note: This table includes only the 11 injunctions that targeted more than 50 members of the enjoined gang, either named defendants or served at a later date for total calls. *M* = Mean Average in sq. miles and gang members. *SD* = Standard Deviation. *SEM* = Standard Error of the Mean.

controls trended toward statistical significance, t (10) = 2.8, $p < .02$. Overall, these findings suggest that gang injunctions may reduce total calls (see Table 8.15 and Figure 8.14).

Table 8.16 shows that Part 1 calls in injunctions that target less than 50 members decreased 4.4% compared to baseline (–4.4%), a statistically significant decline, t (13) = 1.0, $p < 0.34$. Matched control areas increased 9.1% (+9.1%) during the same period. The injunction

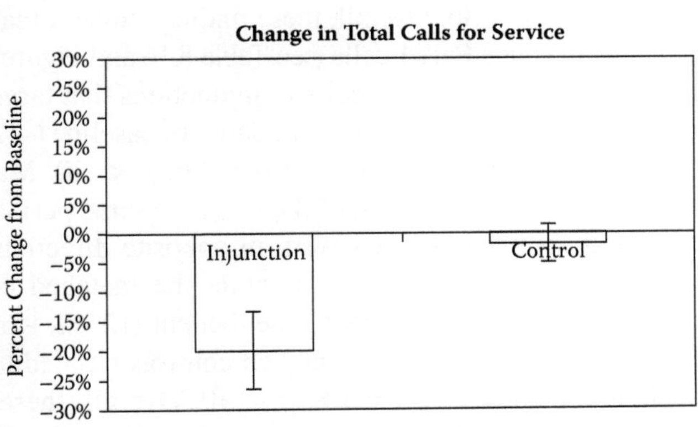

FIGURE 8.14 Total Calls, Percent Change from Baseline More than 50.

TABLE 8.16

Part 1 Calls, Percent Change from Baseline for Less than 50 Targeted Members

	Injunction			Control		
Pair	**Before**	**After**	**Change**	**Before**	**After**	**Change**
1	228	203	–11.0%	709	692	–2.4%
2	126	136	7.9%	375	350	–6.7%
4	352	288	–18.2%	200	190	–5.0%
5	310	294	–5.2%	1327	1467	10.6%
6	172	226	31.4%	519	1212	133.5%
7	157	181	15.3%	22	16	–27.3%
8	1008	978	–3.0%	140	158	12.9%
9	2349	2355	0.3%	1455	1384	–4.9%
10	162	147	–9.3%	300	290	–3.3%
11	263	143	–45.6%	947	1003	5.9%
12	1544	1435	–7.1%	2710	2513	–7.3%
16	351	321	–8.5%	404	411	1.7%
17	421	401	–4.8%	89	98	10.1%
22	989	936	–5.4%	975	953	–2.3%
M	572.5	546.8	–4.4%	707.5	752.6	9.1%
SD	670.5	664.2		755.3	731.4	
SEM	51.6	51.1		58.1	56.3	

Note: This table includes only the 14 injunctions that targeted less than 50 members of the enjoined gang, either named defendants or served at a later date for Part 1 crimes. "Pair" refers to the code assigned to each injunction and matched control, see Table 8.1. *M* = Mean Average for all 14 pairs. *SD* = Standard Deviation. *SEM* = Standard Error of the Mean.

and control outcomes were in opposite directions: the injunction areas were getting better while the matched control areas were getting worse. The 13.5% net benefit (4.4% + 9.1% = 13.5%) between injunctions and matched controls trended toward statistical significance, t (13) = 1.5, $p < .16$. Overall, these findings suggest that gang injunctions may reduce Part 1 calls (see Table 8.16 and Figure 8.15).

Table 8.17 shows that Part 2 calls in injunctions that target less than 50 members decreased 12.9% compared to baseline (–12.9%), a statistically significant decline, t (13) = 2.6, $p < .20$. Matched control areas increased 6.6% (+6.6%) during the same period. The injunction and control outcomes were in opposite directions: the injunction areas were getting better while the matched control areas were getting worse. The 19.5% net benefit (12.9% + 6.6% = 19.5%) between injunctions and matched controls trended toward statistical significance, t (13) = 1.8, $p < .10$. Overall, these findings suggest that gang injunctions may reduce Part 2 calls (see Table 8.17 and Figure 8.16).

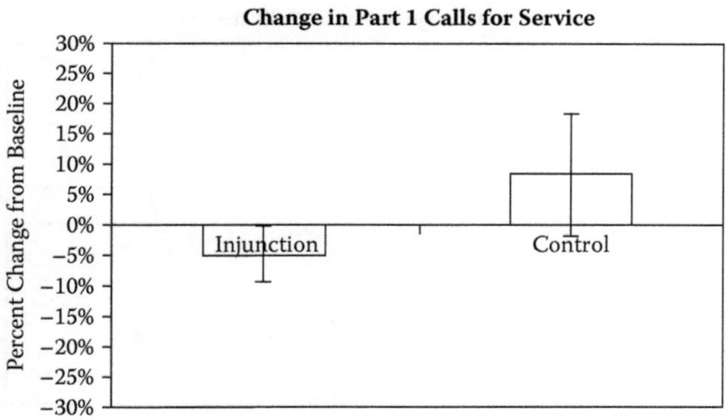

FIGURE 8.15 Part 1 Calls, Percent Change from Baseline Less than 50.

Table 8.18 shows that total calls in injunctions that target less than 50 members decreased 9.6% compared to baseline (–9.6%), a statistically significant decline, t (13) = 2.9, $p < .011$. Matched control areas increased 6.2% (+6.2%) during the same period. The injunction and control outcomes were in opposite directions: the injunction areas

TABLE 8.17

Part 2 Calls, Percent Change from Baseline for Less than 50 Targeted Members

	Injunction			Control		
Pair	Before	After	Change	Before	After	Change
1	304	279	–8.2%	2615	2817	7.7%
2	337	427	26.7%	400	436	9.0%
4	720	600	–16.7%	500	400	–20.0%
5	435	404	–7.1%	3574	3672	2.7%
6	446	287	–35.7%	876	1830	108.9%
7	168	98	–41.7%	249	203	–18.5%
8	2877	2477	–13.9%	1930	2082	7.9%
9	2406	2509	4.3%	1852	1827	–1.3%
10	703	517	–26.5%	400	350	–12.5%
11	956	804	–15.9%	2865	3370	17.6%
12	4841	3652	–24.6%	6354	4908	–22.8%
16	1050	995	–5.2%	1058	1056	–0.2%
17	1065	1032	–3.1%	210	225	7.1%
22	2597	2519	–3.0%	2348	2302	–2.0%
M	1254.5	1083.2	–12.9%	1760.2	1782.8	6.6%
SD	1348.7	1093.9		1770.9	1534.3	
SEM	103.7	84.1		136.2	118.0	

Note: This table includes only the 14 injunctions that targeted less than 50 members of the enjoined gang, either named defendants or served at a later date for Part 2 crimes. *M* = Mean Average in sq. miles and gang members. *SD* = Standard Deviation. *SEM* = Standard Error of the Mean.

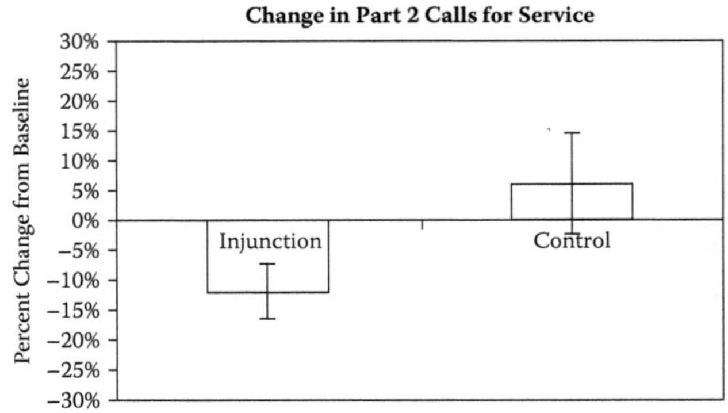

FIGURE 8.16 Part 2 Calls, Percent Change from Baseline Less than 50.

were getting better while the matched control areas were getting worse. The 15.8% net benefit (9.6% + 6.2% = 15.8%) between injunctions and matched controls trended toward statistical significance, t (13) = 1.7, $p < .12$. Overall, these findings suggest that gang injunctions may reduce total calls (see Table 8.18 and Figure 8.17).

TABLE 8.18
Total Calls, Percent Change from Baseline for Less than 50 Targeted Members

	Injunction			Control		
Pair	**Before**	**After**	**Change**	**Before**	**After**	**Change**
1	982	902	–8.1%	7541	7850	4.1%
2	1727	1985	14.9%	3035	3375	11.2%
4	1650	1548	–6.2%	1000	900	–10.0%
5	2243	2198	–2.0%	7856	8519	8.4%
6	1012	834	–17.6%	6886	14197	106.2%
7	448	372	–17.0%	1435	1285	–10.5%
8	4414	4113	–6.8%	12526	12474	–0.4%
9	26088	26213	0.5%	12946	13093	1.1%
10	1961	1615	–17.6%	2700	2500	–7.4%
11	2732	1913	–30.0%	8880	9252	4.2%
12	14748	11108	–24.7%	14520	9862	–32.1%
16	2875	2764	–3.9%	2904	2934	1.0%
17	3448	3243	–5.9%	636	664	4.4%
22	5301	5234	–1.3%	4921	5011	1.8%
M	4948.3	4523.7	–9.6%	6374.2	6685.0	6.2%
SD	7323.7	7063.0		4833.8	4948.3	
SEM	563.4	543.3		371.8	380.6	

Note: This table includes only the 14 injunctions that targeted less than 50 members of the enjoined gang, either named defendants or served at a later date for total calls. *M* = Mean Average in sq. miles and gang members. *SD* = Standard Deviation. *SEM* = Standard Error of the Mean.

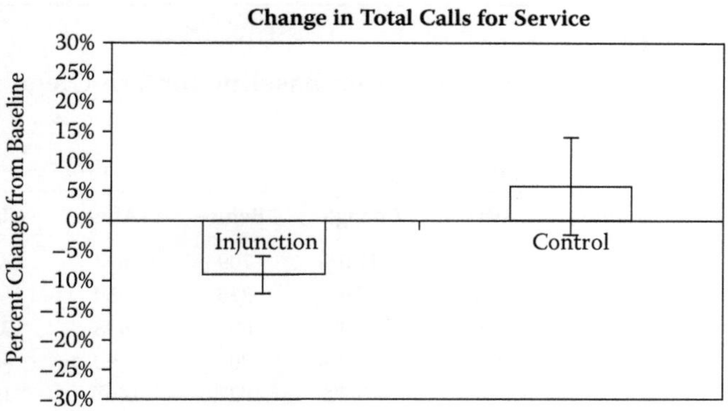

FIGURE 8.17 Total Calls, Percent Change from Baseline Less than 50.

Summary of Gang Injunctions: More versus Less Than 50 Targeted Member Results

The percent change from baseline for injunctions that target more than 50 gang members for Part 1 crimes was a 20.7% reduction for injunction and an 8.8% reduction for control. The percent change from baseline for injunctions that target less than 50 gang members for Part 1 crimes was a 4.4% reduction for injunction and a 9.1% increase for control.

The percent change for more than 50 members for Part 2 calls was a 20.7% reduction for injunctions and a 4.0% reduction for control. The percent change for less than 50 members for Part 2 calls was a 12.9% reduction for injunctions and 6.6% increase for control.

The percent change for more than 50 members for total calls was a 20.5% reduction for injunction and a 2.3% reduction for control. The percent change for less than 50 members for total calls was a 9.6% reduction for injunction and a 6.2% increase for control.

The results tend to indicate that gangs of more than 50 members made potentially better injunction targets than gangs of less than 50 members.

Variance by County

This research sought to identify any differences relating to the impact of gang injunctions based upon the county in which the injunctions were implemented. This research evaluated 25 gang injunctions from four counties. Of the 25 injunctions evaluated, 14 of them targeted gangs from San Diego County, 7 of them targeted gangs from Los Angeles County, 3 of them targeted gangs from San Bernardino, and 1 gang from Ventura County was evaluated.

Table 8.19 shows that Part 1 calls in injunctions that target San Diego County gangs decreased 12.4% compared to baseline

TABLE 8.19
Part 1 Calls, Percent Change from Baseline for San Diego County Gangs

	Injunction			Control		
Pair	**Before**	**After**	**Change**	**Before**	**After**	**Change**
1	228	203	–11.0%	709	692	–2.4%
2	126	136	7.9%	375	350	–6.7%
3	271	178	–34.3%	651	438	–32.7%
4	352	288	–18.2%	200	190	–5.0%
5	310	294	–5.2%	1327	1467	10.6%
6	172	226	31.4%	519	1212	133.5%
7	157	181	15.3%	22	16	–27.3%
8	1008	978	–3.0%	140	158	12.9%
9	2349	2355	0.3%	1455	1384	–4.9%
10	162	147	–9.3%	300	290	–3.3%
11	263	143	–45.6%	947	1003	5.9%
12	1544	1435	–7.1%	2710	2513	–7.3%
13	5568	1184	–78.7%	1425	1420	–0.4%
14	600	500	–16.7%	700	600	–14.3%
M	936.4	589.1	–12.4%	820.0	838.1	4.2%
SD	1481.0	664.5		718.6	698.3	
SEM	105.8	47.5		51.3	49.9	

Note: This table includes only the 14 injunctions that targeted San Diego County gangs for Part 1 crimes. "Pair" refers to the code assigned to each injunction and matched control, see Table 8.1. M = Mean Average for all 14 pairs. *SD* = Standard Deviation. *SEM* = Standard Error of the Mean.

(–12.4%), a statistically significant decline, t (13) = 1.7, $p < 0.11$. Matched control areas increased 4.2% (+4.2%) during the same period. The injunction and control outcomes were in opposite directions: the injunction areas were getting better while the matched control areas were getting worse. The 16.6% net benefit (12.4% + 4.2% = 16.6%) between injunctions and matched controls trended toward statistical significance, t (13) = 1.7, $p < 0.12$. Overall, these findings suggest that gang injunctions may reduce Part 1 calls (see Table 8.19 and Figure 8.18).

Table 8.20 shows that Part 2 calls in injunctions that target San Diego County gangs decreased 19.5% compared to baseline (–19.5%), a statistically significant decline, t (13) = 3.1, $p < .008$. Matched control areas increased 2.5% (+2.5%) during the same period. The injunction and control outcomes were in opposite directions: the injunction areas were getting better while the matched control areas were getting worse. The 22.0% net benefit (19.5% + 2.5% = 22.0%) between injunctions and matched controls trended toward statistical significance, t (13) = 2.0, $p < .07$. Overall, these

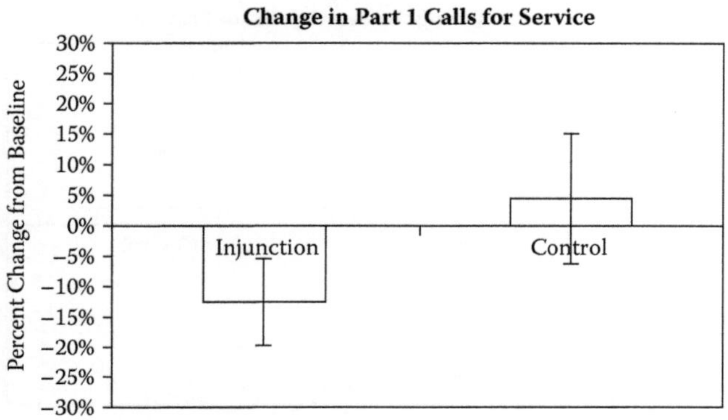

FIGURE 8.18 Part 1 Calls, Percent Change for San Diego County.

findings suggest that gang injunctions may reduce Part 2 calls (see Table 8.20 and Figure 8.19).

Table 8.21 shows that total calls in injunctions that target San Diego County gangs decreased 16.7% compared to baseline (–16.7%), a statistically significant decline, t (13) = 2.9, $p < .011$. Matched control areas increased 2.2% (+2.2%) during the same period. The injunction

TABLE 8.20
Part 2 Calls, Percent Change from Baseline for San Diego County Gangs

	Injunction			Control		
Pair	**Before**	**After**	**Change**	**Before**	**After**	**Change**
1	304	279	–8.2%	2615	2817	7.7%
2	337	427	26.7%	400	436	9.0%
3	323	213	–34.1%	1436	853	–40.6%
4	720	600	–16.7%	500	400	–20.0%
5	435	404	–7.1%	3574	3672	2.7%
6	446	287	–35.7%	876	1830	108.9%
7	168	98	–41.7%	249	203	–18.5%
8	2877	2477	–13.9%	1930	2082	7.9%
9	2406	2509	4.3%	1852	1827	–1.3%
10	703	517	–26.5%	400	350	–12.5%
11	956	804	–15.9%	2865	3370	17.6%
12	4841	3652	–24.6%	6354	4908	–22.8%
13	15540	4220	–72.8%	5054	5204	3.0%
14	1600	1500	–6.3%	1700	1600	–5.9%
M	2261.1	1284.8	–19.5%	2128.9	2110.9	2.5%
SD	4044.2	1374.2		1835.3	1673.1	
SEM	288.9	98.2		131.1	119.5	

Note: This table includes only the 14 injunctions that targeted San Diego County gangs for Part 2 crimes. *M* = Mean Average in sq. miles and gang members. *SD* = Standard Deviation. *SEM* = Standard Error of the Mean.

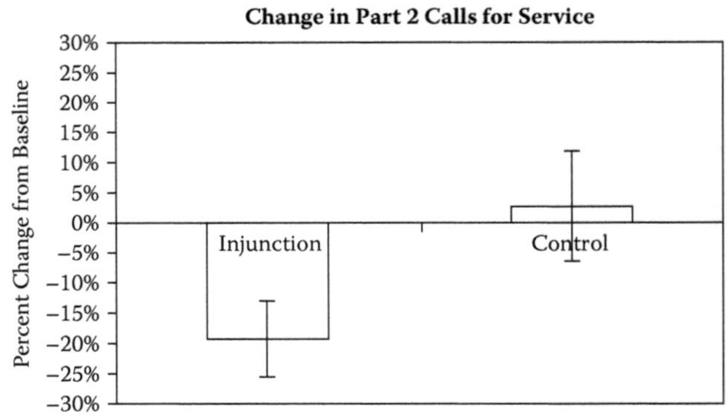

FIGURE 8.19 Part 2 Calls, Percent Change for San Diego County.

and control outcomes were in opposite directions: the injunction areas were getting better while the matched control areas were getting worse. The 18.9% net benefit (16.7% + 2.2% = 18.9%) between injunctions and matched controls trended toward statistical significance, t (13) = 1.9, $p < .07$. Overall, these findings suggest that gang injunctions may reduce total calls (see Table 8.21 and Figure 8.20).

TABLE 8.21
Total Calls, Percent Change from Baseline for San Diego County Gangs

	Injunction			Control		
Pair	**Before**	**After**	**Change**	**Before**	**After**	**Change**
1	982	902	–8.1%	7541	7850	4.1%
2	1727	1985	14.9%	3035	3375	11.2%
3	1409	929	–34.1%	3345	2214	–33.8%
4	1650	1548	–6.2%	1000	900	–10.0%
5	2243	2198	–2.0%	7856	8519	8.4%
6	1012	834	–17.6%	6886	14197	106.2%
7	448	372	–17.0%	1435	1285	–10.5%
8	4414	4113	–6.8%	12526	12474	–0.4%
9	26088	26213	0.5%	12946	13093	1.1%
10	1961	1615	–17.6%	2700	2500	–7.4%
11	2732	1913	–30.0%	8880	9252	4.2%
12	14748	11108	–24.7%	14520	9862	–32.1%
13	36331	9139	–74.8%	11913	11576	–2.8%
14	9500	8500	–10.5%	10100	9300	–7.9%
M	7517.5	5097.8	–16.7%	7477.4	7599.8	2.2%
SD	10964.3	7012.7		4575.1	4662.0	
SEM	783.2	500.9		326.8	333.0	

Note: This table includes only the 14 injunctions that targeted San Diego County gangs for total calls for service. *M* = Mean Average in sq. miles and gang members. *SD* = Standard Deviation. *SEM* = Standard Error of the Mean.

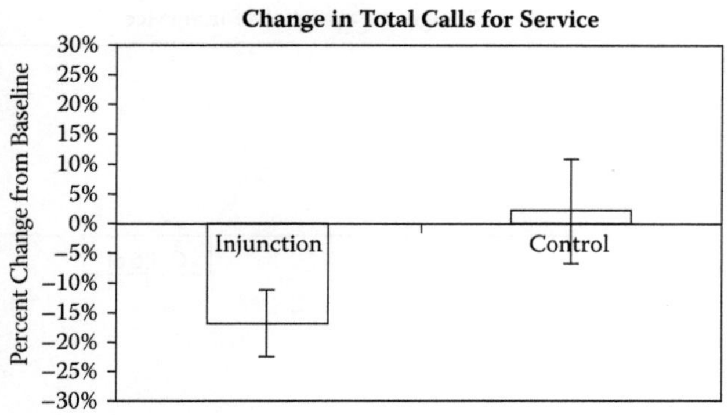

FIGURE 8.20 Total Calls, Percent Change for San Diego County.

Table 8.22 shows that Part 1 calls in injunctions that target Los Angeles County gangs decreased 9.6% compared to baseline (–9.6%), a statistically significant decline, t (6) = 3.2, $p < .018$. Matched control areas decreased 6.2% (–6.2%) during the same period. The injunction and control outcomes were in the same direction: the injunction areas were getting better while the matched control areas were also getting better at a reduced rate. The 3.4% net benefit (9.6% – 6.2% = 3.4%) between injunctions and matched controls trended toward statistical significance, t (6) = 0.6, $p < .55$. Overall, these findings suggest that gang injunctions may reduce Part 1 calls (see Table 8.22 and Figure 8.21).

TABLE 8.22

Part 1 Calls, Percent Change from Baseline for Los Angeles County Gangs

	Injunction			Control		
Pair	**Before**	**After**	**Change**	**Before**	**After**	**Change**
18	455	390	–14.3%	145	139	–4.1%
19	816	759	–7.0%	126	115	–8.7%
20	165	123	–25.5%	144	155	7.6%
21	765	745	–2.6%	201	172	–14.4%
22	989	936	–5.4%	975	953	–2.3%
23	824	757	–8.1%	698	672	–3.7%
24	726	693	–4.5%	195	161	–17.4%
M	677.1	629.0	–9.6%	354.9	338.1	–6.2%
SD	276.8	276.4		339.7	334.5	
SEM	39.5	39.5		48.5	47.8	

Note: This table includes only the 7 injunctions that targeted Los Angeles County gangs for Part 1 crimes. "Pair" refers to the code assigned to each injunction and matched control, see Table 8.1. M = Mean Average for all 7 pairs. SD = Standard Deviation. SEM = Standard Error of the Mean.

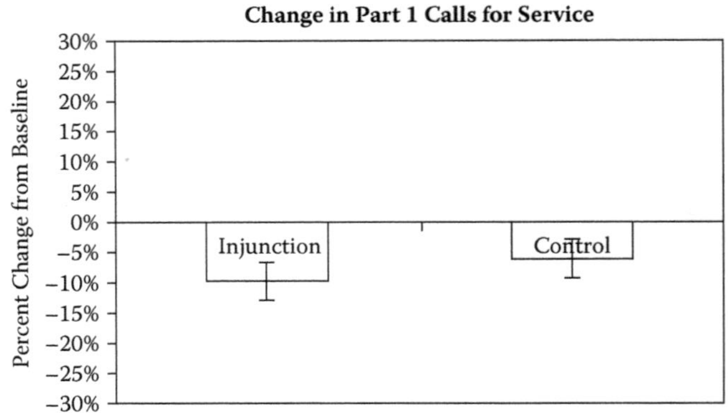

FIGURE 8.21 Part 1 Calls, Percent Change for Los Angeles County.

Table 8.23 shows that Part 2 calls in injunctions that target Los Angeles County gangs decreased 9.4% compared to baseline (–9.4%), a decline, t (6) = 1.5, $p < .192$. Matched control areas decreased 0.7% (–0.7%) during the same period. The injunction and control outcomes were in the same direction: the injunction areas were getting better while the matched control areas were also getting better at a reduced rate. The 8.7% net benefit (9.4% – 0.7% = 8.7%) between injunctions and matched controls trended toward statistical significance, t (6) = 1.7, $p < .15$. Overall, these findings suggest that gang injunctions may reduce Part 2 calls (see Table 8.23 and Figure 8.22).

TABLE 8.23
Part 2 Calls, Percent Change from Baseline for Los Angeles County Gangs

	Injunction			Control		
Pair	**Before**	**After**	**Change**	**Before**	**After**	**Change**
18	2164	1230	–43.2%	425	397	–6.6%
19	2440	2080	–14.8%	378	345	–8.7%
20	237	256	8.0%	325	352	8.3%
21	1201	1081	–10.0%	550	567	3.1%
22	2597	2519	–3.0%	2348	2302	–2.0%
23	2325	2134	–8.2%	1923	1956	1.7%
24	2072	2179	5.2%	553	548	–0.9%
M	1862.3	1639.9	–9.4%	928.9	923.9	–0.7%
SD	846.7	805.9		837.6	834.0	
SEM	121.0	115.1		119.7	119.1	

Note: This table includes only the 7 injunctions that targeted Los Angeles County gangs for Part 2 crimes. *M* = Mean Average in sq. miles and gang members. *SD* = Standard Deviation. *SEM* = Standard Error of the Mean.

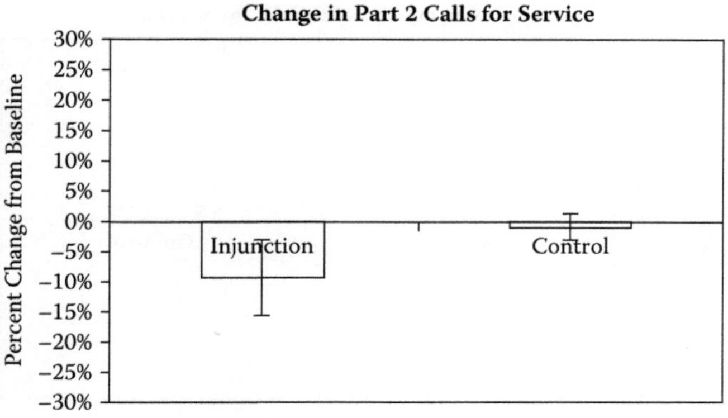

FIGURE 8.22 Part 2 Calls, Percent Change for Los Angeles County.

Table 8.24 shows that total calls in injunctions that target Los Angeles County gangs decreased 10.1% compared to baseline (–10.1%), a decline, t (6) = 1.9, $p < 0.10$. Matched control areas increased 0.7% (+0.7%) during the same period. The injunction and control outcomes were in opposite directions: the injunction areas were getting better while the matched control areas were getting worse. The 7.9% net benefit (10.1%: 2.2% = 7.9%) between injunctions and matched controls trended toward statistical significance, t (6) = 2.4, $p < .05$. Overall, these findings suggest that gang injunctions may reduce total calls (see Table 8.24 and Figure 8.23).

TABLE 8.24
Total Calls, Percent Change from Baseline for Los Angeles County Gangs

	Injunction			Control		
Pair	Before	After	Change	Before	After	Change
18	5278	3202	−39.3%	2425	2460	1.4%
19	5390	4650	−13.7%	1975	1898	−3.9%
20	844	772	−8.5%	1825	1960	7.4%
21	3986	3841	−3.6%	2550	2610	2.4%
22	5301	5234	−1.3%	4921	5011	1.8%
23	5251	4865	−7.4%	3726	3897	4.6%
24	4821	4959	2.9%	2553	2598	1.8%
M	4410.1	3931.9	−10.1%	2853.6	2919.1	2.2%
SD	1647.2	1563.3		1097.8	1133.2	
SEM	235.3	223.3		156.8	161.9	

Note: This table includes only the 7 injunctions that targeted Los Angeles County gangs for total calls for service. *M* = Mean Average in sq. miles and gang members. *SD* = Standard Deviation. *SEM* = Standard Error of the Mean.

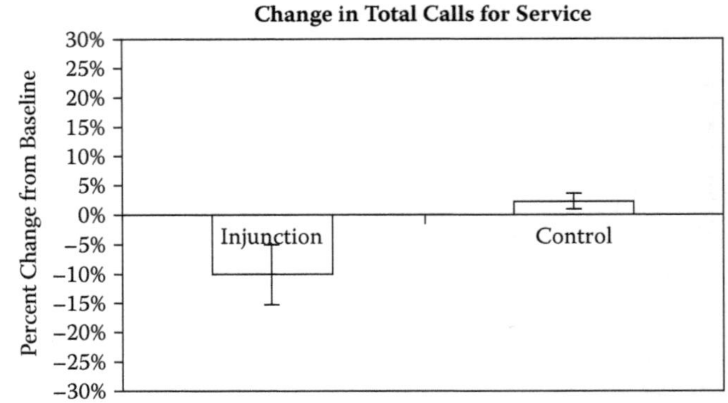

FIGURE 8.23 Total Calls, Percent Change for Los Angeles County.

Table 8.25 shows that Part 1 calls in injunctions that target San Bernardino and Ventura County gangs decreased 12.2% compared to baseline (–12.2%), a decline, t (3) = 2.5, $p < 0.89$. Matched control areas increased 0.8% (+0.8%) during the same period. The injunction and control outcomes were in opposite directions: the injunction areas were getting better while the matched control areas were getting worse. The 11.4% net benefit (12.2% – 0.8% = 11.4%) between injunctions and matched controls trended toward statistical significance, t (3) = 4.4, $p < .01$. Overall, these findings suggest that gang injunctions may reduce Part 1 calls (see Table 8.25 and Figure 8.24).

TABLE 8.25
Part 1 Calls, Percent Change Baseline for San Bernardino & Ventura County

	Injunction			Control		
Pair	**Before**	**After**	**Change**	**Before**	**After**	**Change**
15	306	279	–8.8%	315	298	–5.4%
16	351	321	–8.5%	404	411	1.7%
17	421	401	–4.8%	89	98	10.1%
25	2895	2120	–26.8%	1447	1400	–3.2%
M	993.3	780.3	–12.2%	563.8	551.8	0.8%
SD	1268.7	894.6		603.6	580.1	
SEM	317.2	223.6		150.9	145.0	

Note: This table includes only the 4 injunctions that targeted San Bernardino and Ventura County gangs for Part 1 crimes. "Pair" refers to the code assigned to each injunction and matched control, see Table 8.1. *M* = Mean Average for all 4 pairs. *SD* = Standard Deviation. *SEM* = Standard Error of the Mean.

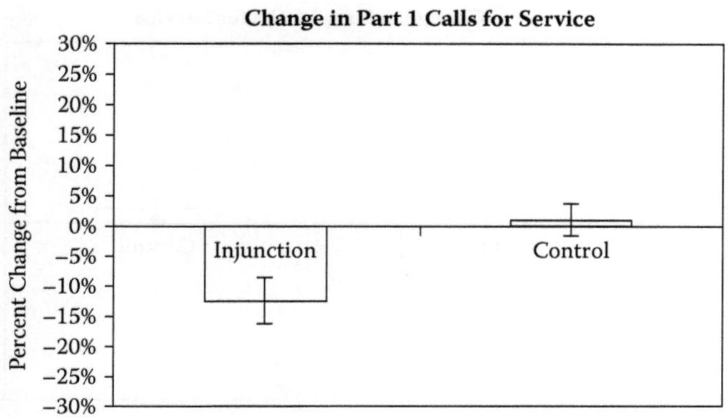

FIGURE 8.24 Part 1 Calls, Percent Change San Bernardino and Ventura.

Table 8.26 shows that Part 2 calls in injunctions that target San Bernardino and Ventura County gangs decreased 15.1% compared to baseline (–15.1%), a decline, t (3) = 1.8, $p < 0.17$. Matched control areas increased 2.3% (+2.3%) during the same period. The injunction and control outcomes were in opposite directions: the injunction areas were getting better while the matched control areas were getting worse. The 17.4% net benefit (15.1% + 2.3% = 17.4%) between injunctions and matched controls trended toward statistical significance, t (3) = 2.4, $p < .08$. Overall, these findings suggest that gang injunctions may reduce Part 2 calls (see Table 8.26 and Figure 8.25).

Table 8.27 shows that total calls in injunctions that target San Bernardino and Ventura County gangs decreased 11.6% compared

TABLE 8.26
Part 2 Calls, Percent Change Baseline for San Bernardino & Ventura County

	Injunction			Control		
Pair	**Before**	**After**	**Change**	**Before**	**After**	**Change**
15	725	637	–12.1%	931	908	–2.5%
16	1050	995	–5.2%	1058	1056	–0.2%
17	1065	1032	–3.1%	210	225	7.1%
25	3500	2100	–40.0%	2200	2300	4.5%
M	1585.0	1191.0	–15.1%	1099.8	1122.3	2.3%
SD	1286.3	631.6		823.1	864.6	
SEM	321.6	157.9		205.8	216.1	

Note: This table includes only the 4 injunctions that targeted San Bernardino and Ventura County gangs for Part 2 crimes. *M* = Mean Average in sq. miles and gang members. *SD* = Standard Deviation. *SEM* = Standard Error of the Mean.

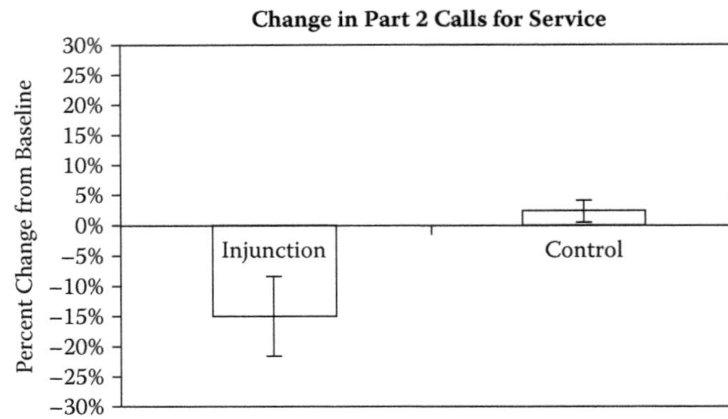

FIGURE 8.25 Part 2 Calls, Percent Change San Bernardino and Ventura.

to baseline (–11.6%), a decline, t (3) = 1.8, $p < 0.17$. Matched control areas increased 2.8% (+2.8%) during the same period. The injunction and control outcomes were in opposite directions: the injunction areas were getting better while the matched control areas were getting worse. The 14.4% net benefit (11.6% + 2.8% = 14.4%) between injunctions and matched controls trended toward statistical significance, t (3) = 3.2, $p < .03$. Overall, these findings suggest that gang injunctions may reduce total calls (see Table 8.27 and Figure 8.26).

Summary of County Analysis

The percent change from baseline for San Diego injunctions for Part 1 crimes was a 12.4% reduction for injunction and a 4.2% increase

TABLE 8.27
Total Calls, Percent Change Baseline for San Bernardino & Ventura County

	Injunction			Control		
Pair	Before	After	Change	Before	After	Change
15	1926	1821	–5.5%	1833	1921	4.8%
16	2875	2764	–3.9%	2904	2934	1.0%
17	3448	3243	–5.9%	636	664	4.4%
25	12500	8600	–31.2%	6450	6500	0.8%
M	5187.3	4107.0	–11.6%	2955.8	3004.8	2.8%
SD	4915.4	3053.0		2506.9	2508.3	
SEM	1228.9	763.3		626.7	627.1	

Note: This table includes only the 4 injunctions that targeted San Bernardino and Ventura County gangs for total calls for service. *M* = Mean Average in sq. miles and gang members. *SD* = Standard Deviation. *SEM* = Standard Error of the Mean.

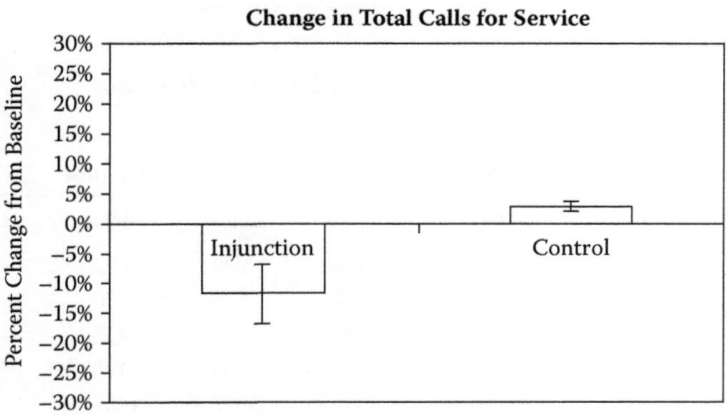

FIGURE 8.26 Total Calls, Percent Change San Bernardino and Ventura.

for control. The percent change from baseline for Los Angeles injunctions for Part 1 crimes was a 9.6% reduction for injunction and a 6.2% reduction for control. The percent change from baseline for San Bernardino and Ventura injunctions for Part 1 crimes was a 12.2% reduction for injunction and an 0.8% increase for control.

The percent change for San Diego Part 2 calls was a 19.5% reduction for injunctions and a 2.5 increase for control. The percent change for Los Angeles Part 2 calls was a 9.4% reduction for injunctions and a 0.7% reduction for control. The percent change for San Bernardino and Ventura Part 2 calls was a 15.1% reduction for injunctions and a 2.3% increase for control.

The percent change for San Diego total calls was a 16.7% reduction for injunction and a 2.2% increase for control. The percent change for Los Angeles total calls was a 10.1% reduction for injunction and a 2.2% increase for control. The percent change for San Bernardino and Ventura total calls was an 11.6% reduction for injunction and a 2.8 increase for control.

In summary, gang injunctions seem to fare better in San Diego County, followed by San Bernardino and Ventura Counties, then Los Angeles County.

Variance by Gang Injunction Area (Square Miles)

This research sought to identify any differences relating to the impact of gang injunctions based upon the size of the overall target area. This research evaluated 25 gang injunctions from four counties. Of the 25 injunctions evaluated, 10 of them targeted gangs in an area of more than 1 square mile and 15 of them targeted gangs in an area of less than 1 square mile. The purpose of this analysis is to evaluate if the size of the target area

TABLE 8.28
Part 1 Calls, Percent Change from Baseline for Less than 1 Square Mile

	Injunction			Control		
Pair	**Before**	**After**	**Change**	**Before**	**After**	**Change**
1	228	203	–11.0%	709	692	–2.4%
2	126	136	7.9%	375	350	–6.7%
3	271	178	–34.3%	651	438	–32.7%
4	352	288	–18.2%	200	190	–5.0%
5	310	294	–5.2%	1327	1467	10.6%
6	172	226	31.4%	519	1212	133.5%
7	157	181	15.3%	22	16	–27.3%
10	162	147	–9.3%	300	290	–3.3%
11	263	143	–45.6%	947	1003	5.9%
15	306	279	–8.8%	315	298	–5.4%
17	421	401	–4.8%	89	98	10.1%
19	816	759	–7.0%	126	115	–8.7%
20	165	123	–25.5%	144	155	7.6%
23	824	757	–8.1%	698	672	–3.7%
24	726	693	–4.5%	195	161	–17.4%
M	353.3	320.5	–8.5%	441.1	477.1	3.7%
SD	240.4	228.1		365.9	442.3	
SEM	16.0	15.2		24.4	29.5	

Note: This table includes only the 15 injunctions that have a target area of less than 1 square mile for Part 1 crimes. "Pair" refers to the code assigned to each injunction and matched control, see Table 8.1. *M* = Mean Average for all 15 pairs. *SD* = Standard Deviation. *SEM* = Standard Error of the Mean.

had any impact on gang injunction effectiveness. This analysis evaluates if differences exist between injunctions based upon target areas.

Table 8.28 shows that Part 1 calls in injunctions that target areas less than 1 square mile decreased 8.5% compared to baseline (–8.5%), a decline, t (14) = 1.8, $p < 0.99$. Matched control areas increased 3.7% (+3.7%) during the same period. The injunction and control outcomes were in opposite directions: the injunction areas were getting better while the matched control areas were getting worse. The 12.2% net benefit (8.5% + 3.7% = 12.2%) between injunctions and matched controls trended toward statistical significance, t (14) = 1.5, $p < .17$. Overall, these findings suggest that gang injunctions may reduce Part 1 calls (see Table 8.28 and Figure 8.27).

Table 8.29 shows that Part 2 calls in injunctions that target areas less than 1 square mile decreased 12.3% compared to baseline

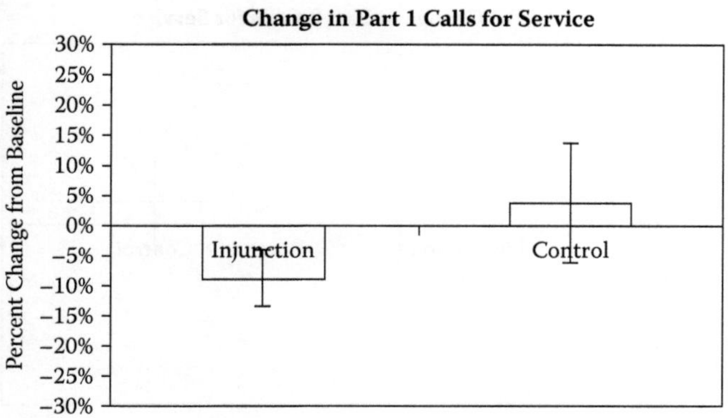

FIGURE 8.27 Part 1 Calls, Percent Change from Baseline Less 1 Sq Mile.

TABLE 8.29
Part 2 Calls, Percent Change from Baseline for Less than 1 Square Mile

	Injunction			Control		
Pair	**Before**	**After**	**Change**	**Before**	**After**	**Change**
1	304	279	−8.2%	2615	2817	7.7%
2	337	427	26.7%	400	436	9.0%
3	323	213	−34.1%	1436	853	−40.6%
4	720	600	−16.7%	500	400	−20.0%
5	435	404	−7.1%	3574	3672	2.7%
6	446	287	−35.7%	876	1830	108.9%
7	168	98	−41.7%	249	203	−18.5%
10	703	517	−26.5%	400	350	−12.5%
11	956	804	−15.9%	2865	3370	17.6%
15	725	637	−12.1%	931	908	−2.5%
17	1065	1032	−3.1%	210	225	7.1%
19	2440	2080	−14.8%	378	345	−8.7%
20	237	256	8.0%	325	352	8.3%
23	2325	2134	−8.2%	1923	1956	1.7%
24	2072	2179	5.2%	553	548	−0.9%
M	883.7	796.5	−12.3%	1149.0	1217.7	4.0%
SD	770.3	731.1		1090.3	1206.2	
SEM	51.4	48.7		72.7	80.4	

Note: This table includes only the 15 injunctions that have a target area of less than 1 square mile for Part 2 crimes. *M* = Mean Average in sq. miles and gang members. *SD* = Standard Deviation. *SEM* = Standard Error of the Mean.

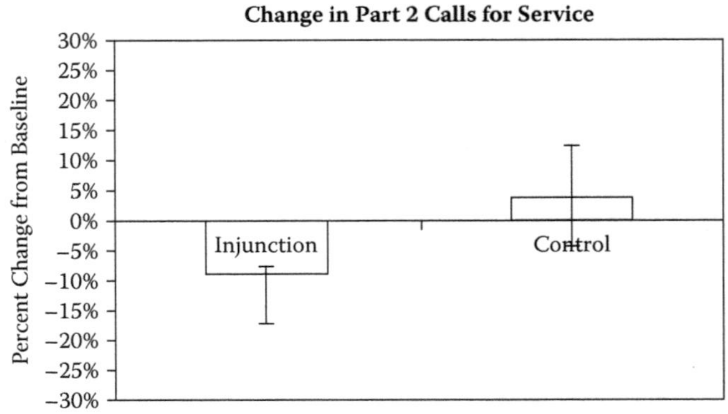

FIGURE 8.28 Part 2 Calls, Percent Change from Baseline Less 1 Sq Mile.

(–12.3%), a decline, t (14) = 2.6, $p < 0.19$. Matched control areas increased 3.7% (+3.7%) during the same period. The injunction and control outcomes were in opposite directions: the injunction areas were getting better while the matched control areas were getting worse. The 16.0% net benefit (12.3% + 3.7% = 16.0%) between injunctions and matched controls trended toward statistical significance, t (14) = 1.7, $p < .12$. Overall, these findings suggest that gang injunctions may reduce Part 2 calls (see Table 8.29 and Figure 8.28).

Table 8.30 shows that total calls in injunctions that target areas less than 1 square mile decreased 10.4% compared to baseline (–10.4%), a decline, t (14) = 3.3, $p < .005$. Matched control areas increased 6.1% (+6.1%) during the same period. The injunction and control outcomes were in opposite directions: the injunction areas were getting better while the matched control areas were getting worse. The 16.4% net benefit (10.4% + 6.1% = 16.4%) between injunctions and matched controls trended toward statistical significance, t (14) = 2.0, $p < .06$. Overall, these findings suggest that gang injunctions may reduce total calls (see Table 8.30 and Figure 8.29).

Table 8.31 shows that Part 1 calls in injunction areas that target an area of more than 1 square mile decreased 16.3% compared to baseline (–16.3%), a decline, t (9) = 2.2, $p < .055$. Matched control areas decreased 3.6% (–3.6%) during the same period. The injunction and control outcomes were in the same direction: the injunction areas were getting better while the matched control areas were also getting better at a reduced rate. The 12.7% net benefit (16.3% – 3.6% = 12.7%) between injunctions and matched controls trended toward statistical significance, t (9) = 1.6, $p < .14$. Overall, these findings suggest that gang injunctions may reduce Part 1 calls (see Table 8.31 and Figure 8.30).

TABLE 8.30
Total Calls, Percent Change from Baseline for Less than 1 Square Mile

	Injunction			Control		
Pair	**Before**	**After**	**Change**	**Before**	**After**	**Change**
1	982	902	−8.1%	7541	7850	4.1%
2	1727	1985	14.9%	3035	3375	11.2%
3	1409	929	−34.1%	3345	2214	−33.8%
4	1650	1548	−6.2%	1000	900	−10.0%
5	2243	2198	−2.0%	7856	8519	8.4%
6	1012	834	−17.6%	6886	14197	106.2%
7	448	372	−17.0%	1435	1285	−10.5%
10	1961	1615	−17.6%	2700	2500	−7.4%
11	2732	1913	−30.0%	8880	9252	4.2%
15	1926	1821	−5.5%	1833	1921	4.8%
17	3448	3243	−5.9%	636	664	4.4%
19	5390	4650	−13.7%	1975	1898	−3.9%
20	844	772	−8.5%	1825	1960	7.4%
23	5251	4865	−7.4%	3726	3897	4.6%
24	4821	4959	2.9%	2553	2598	1.8%
M	2389.6	2173.7	−10.4%	3681.7	4202.0	6.1%
SD	1620.1	1544.1		2721.3	3918.9	
SEM	108.0	102.9		181.4	261.3	

Note: This table includes only the 15 injunctions that have a target area of less than 1 square mile for total calls for service. *M* = Mean Average in sq. miles and gang members. *SD* = Standard Deviation. *SEM* = Standard Error of the Mean.

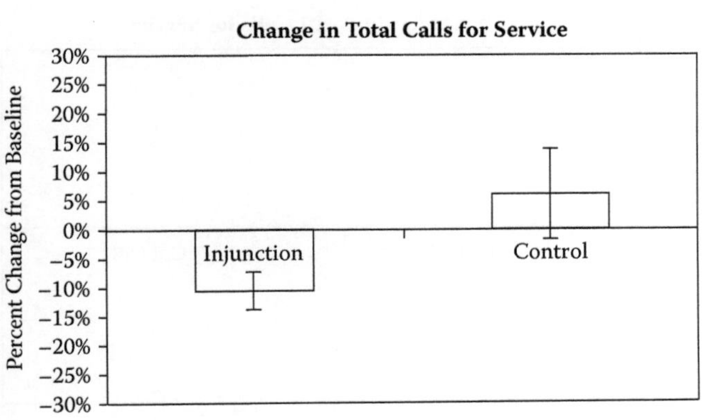

FIGURE 8.29 Total Calls, Percent Change from Baseline Less 1 sq mile.

TABLE 8.31
Part 1 Calls, Percent Change from Baseline for More than 1 Square Mile

	Injunction			Control		
Pair	**Before**	**After**	**Change**	**Before**	**After**	**Change**
8	1008	978	–3.0%	140	158	12.9%
9	2349	2355	0.3%	1455	1384	–4.9%
12	1544	1435	–7.1%	2710	2513	–7.3%
13	5568	1184	–78.7%	1425	1420	–0.4%
14	600	500	–16.7%	700	600	–14.3%
16	351	321	–8.5%	404	411	1.7%
18	455	390	–14.3%	145	139	–4.1%
21	765	745	–2.6%	201	172	–14.4%
22	989	936	–5.4%	975	953	–2.3%
25	2895	2120	–26.8%	1447	1400	–3.2%
M	1652.4	1096.4	–16.3%	960.2	915.0	–3.6%
SD	1607.3	697.1		819.9	770.7	
SEM	160.7	69.7		82.0	77.1	

Note: This table includes only the 10 injunctions that have a target area of more than 1 square mile for Part 1 crimes. "Pair" refers to the code assigned to each injunction and matched control, see Table 8.1. *M* = Mean Average for all 10 pairs. *SD* = Standard Deviation. *SEM* = Standard Error.

Table 8.32 shows that Part 2 calls in injunctions that target an area of more than 1 square mile decreased 21.5% compared to baseline (–21.5%), a decline, t (9) = 2.8, $p < .019$. Matched control areas decreased 2.0% (–2.0%) during the same period. The injunction and control outcomes were in the same direction: the injunction areas were getting better while the matched control

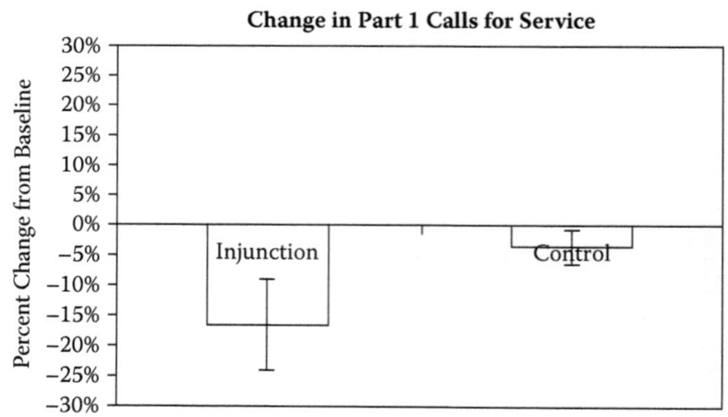

FIGURE 8.30 Part 1 Calls, Percent Change from Baseline More 1 sq mile.

TABLE 8.32
Part 2 Calls, Percent Change from Baseline for More than 1 Square Mile

	Injunction			Control		
Pair	**Before**	**After**	**Change**	**Before**	**After**	**Change**
8	2877	2477	–13.9%	1930	2082	7.9%
9	2406	2509	4.3%	1852	1827	–1.3%
12	4841	3652	–24.6%	6354	4908	–22.8%
13	15540	4220	–72.8%	5054	5204	3.0%
14	1600	1500	–6.3%	1700	1600	–5.9%
16	1050	995	–5.2%	1058	1056	–0.2%
18	2164	1230	–43.2%	425	397	–6.6%
21	1201	1081	–10.0%	550	567	3.1%
22	2597	2519	–3.0%	2348	2302	–2.0%
25	3500	2100	–40.0%	2200	2300	4.5%
M	3777.6	2228.3	–21.5%	2347.1	2224.3	–2.0%
SD	4282.7	1085.2		1909.9	1636.8	
SEM	428.3	108.5		191.0	163.7	

Note: This table includes only the 10 injunctions that have a target area of more than 1 square mile for Part 2 crimes. *M* = Mean Average in sq. miles and gang members. *SD* = Standard Deviation. *SEM* = Standard Error of the Mean.

areas were also getting better at a reduced rate. The 19.5% net benefit (21.5% – 2.0% = 19.5%) between injunctions and matched controls trended toward statistical significance, t (9) = 2.4, $p < .04$. Overall, these findings suggest that gang injunctions may reduce Part 2 calls (see Table 8.32 and Figure 8.31).

Table 8.33 shows that total calls in injunctions that target an area of more than 1 square mile decreased 19.6% compared to baseline (–19.6%), a decline, t (9) = 2.6, $p < .028$. Matched control

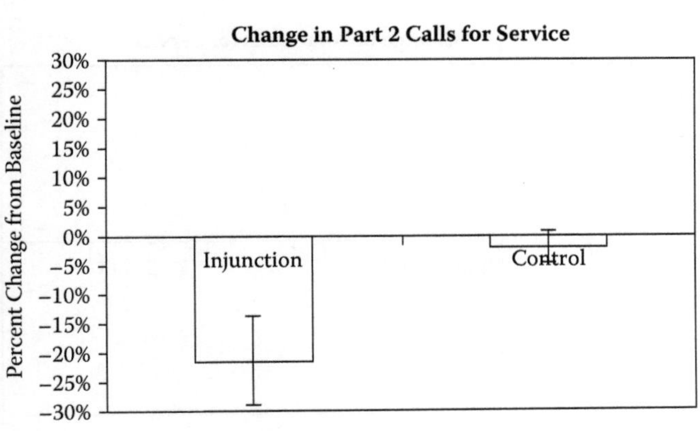

FIGURE 8.31 Part 2 Calls, Percent Change from Baseline More 1 sq mile.

TABLE 8.33
Total Calls, Percent Change from Baseline for More than 1 Square Mile

	Injunction			Control		
Pair	Before	After	Change	Before	After	Change
8	4414	4113	–6.8%	12526	12474	–0.4%
9	26088	26213	0.5%	12946	13093	1.1%
12	14748	11108	–24.7%	14520	9862	–32.1%
13	36331	9139	–74.8%	11913	11576	–2.8%
14	9500	8500	–10.5%	10100	9300	–7.9%
16	2875	2764	–3.9%	2904	2934	1.0%
18	5278	3202	–39.3%	2425	2460	1.4%
21	3986	3841	–3.6%	2550	2610	2.4%
22	5301	5234	–1.3%	4921	5011	1.8%
25	12500	8600	–31.2%	6450	6500	0.8%
M	12102.1	8271.4	–19.6%	8125.5	7582.0	–3.5%
SD	11053.0	6936.5		4780.3	4199.8	
SEM	1105.3	693.7		478.0	420.0	

Note: This table includes only the 10 injunctions that have a target area of more than 1 square mile for total calls for service. *M* = Mean Average in sq. miles and gang members. *SD* = Standard Deviation. *SEM* = Standard Error of the Mean.

areas decreased 3.5% (–3.5%) during the same period. The injunction and control outcomes were in the same direction: the injunction areas were getting better while the matched control areas were also getting better at a reduced rate. The 16.1% net benefit (19.6% – 3.5% = 16.1%) between injunctions and matched controls trended toward statistical significance, t (9) = 2.1, $p < .07$. Overall, these findings suggest that gang injunctions may reduce total calls (see Table 8.33 and Figure 8.32).

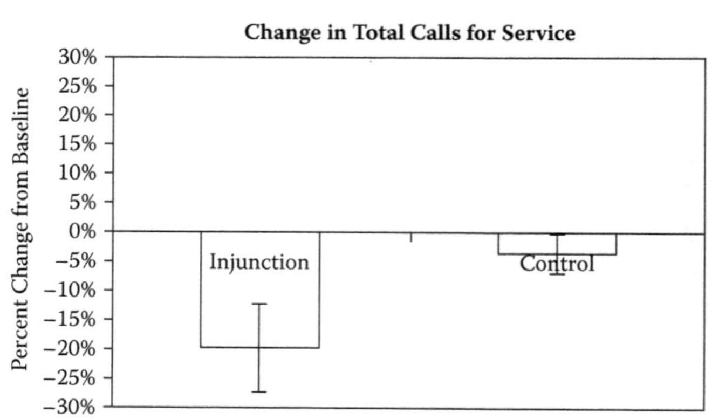

FIGURE 8.32 Total Calls, Percent Change from Baseline More 1 sq mile.

Summary of Square Mileage Analysis

The percent change for less than 1 mile for Part 1 calls was an 8.5% reduction for injunction and 3.7% increase for control. The percent change for more than 1 mile for Part 1 calls was a 16.3% reduction for injunction and a 3.6% reduction for control.

The percent change for less than 1 mile for Part 2 calls was a 12.3% reduction for injunction and a 4.0% increase for control. The percent change for more than 1 mile for Part 2 calls was a 21.5% reduction for injunction and a 2.0% reduction for control. The percent change for less than 1 mile for total calls was a 10.4% reduction for injunction and a 6.1% increase for control. The percent change for more than 1 mile for total calls was a 19.6% reduction for injunction and a 3.5% reduction for control. In summary, gang injunctions less than 1 mile and those more than 1 mile seem to fare about the same.

Variance by Overall Gang Size

This research sought to identify any differences relating to the impact of gang injunctions based upon the size of the overall target gang. This research evaluated 25 gang injunctions from four counties. Of the 25 injunctions evaluated, 17 of them targeted gangs that have more than 100 documented members and 8 of them targeted gangs that have less than 100 documented members. The purpose of this analysis is to evaluate if the size of the target gang had any impact on gang injunction effectiveness. This analysis evaluates if differences exist between injunctions based upon the overall size of the target gang.

Table 8.34 shows that Part 1 calls in injunctions that target gangs having less than 100 total members increased 1.8% compared to baseline (+1.8%), t (7) = 0.31, $p < 0.76$. Matched control areas increased 15.6% (+15.6%) during the same period. The injunction and control outcomes were in the same direction: the injunction areas were getting worse while the matched control areas were also getting worse at an increased rate. The 13.8% net benefit (15.6% – 1.8% = 13.8%) between injunctions and matched controls trended toward statistical significance t (7) = 1.0, $p < .37$. Overall, these findings suggest that gang injunctions may reduce Part 1 calls (see Table 8.34 and Figure 8.33).

Table 8.35 shows that Part 2 calls in injunctions that target gangs having less than 100 total members decreased 14.7% compared to baseline (–14.7%), a decrease, t (7) = 1.9, $p < 0.92$. Matched control areas increased 10.6% (+10.6%) during the same period. The injunction and control outcomes were in opposite directions: the injunction areas were getting better while the matched control

TABLE 8.34
Part 1 Calls, Percent Change from Baseline for Less than 100 Total Members

	Injunction			Control		
Pair	**Before**	**After**	**Change**	**Before**	**After**	**Change**
2	126	136	7.9%	375	350	–6.7%
4	352	288	–18.2%	200	190	–5.0%
5	310	294	–5.2%	1327	1467	10.6%
6	172	226	31.4%	519	1212	133.5%
7	157	181	15.3%	22	16	–27.3%
8	1008	978	–3.0%	140	158	12.9%
10	162	147	–9.3%	300	290	–3.3%
17	421	401	–4.8%	89	98	10.1%
M	338.5	331.4	1.8%	371.5	472.6	15.6%
SD	291.1	275.7		418.3	549.2	
SEM	36.4	34.5		52.3	68.7	

Note: This table includes only the 8 injunctions that target gangs that have less than 100 documented members for Part 1 crimes. "Pair" refers to the code assigned to each injunction and matched control, see Table 8.1. *M* = Mean Average for all 8 pairs. *SD* = Standard Deviation. *SEM* = Standard Error of the Mean.

areas were getting worse. The 25.3% net benefit (14.7% + 10.6% = 25.3%) between injunctions and matched controls trended toward statistical significance, t (7) = 1.4, $p < .20$. Overall, these findings suggest that gang injunctions may reduce Part 2 calls (see Table 8.35 and Figure 8.34).

Table 8.36 shows that total calls in injunctions that target gangs having less than 100 total members decreased 7.3% compared to baseline (–7.3%), a decrease, t (7) = 1.9, $p < 0.10$.

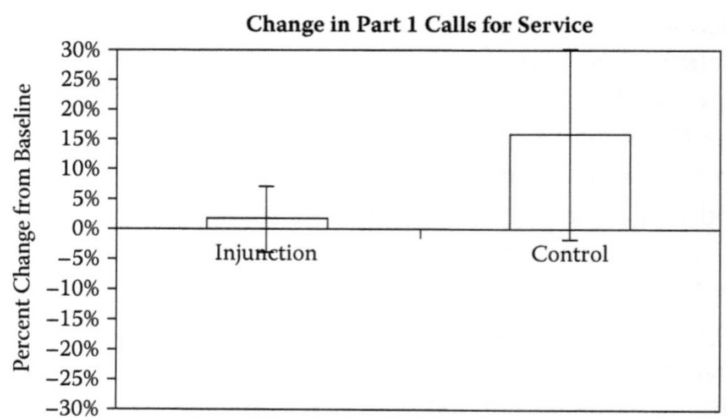

FIGURE 8.33 Part 1 Calls, Percent Change from Baseline Less than 100.

TABLE 8.35
Part 2 Calls, Percent Change from Baseline for Less than 100 Total Members

	Injunction			Control		
Pair	**Before**	**After**	**Change**	**Before**	**After**	**Change**
2	337	427	26.7%	400	436	9.0%
4	720	600	–16.7%	500	400	–20.0%
5	435	404	–7.1%	3574	3672	2.7%
6	446	287	–35.7%	876	1830	108.9%
7	168	98	–41.7%	249	203	–18.5%
8	2877	2477	–13.9%	1930	2082	7.9%
10	703	517	–26.5%	400	350	–12.5%
17	1065	1032	–3.1%	210	225	7.1%
M	843.9	730.3	–14.7%	1017.4	1149.8	10.6%
SD	866.6	755.9		1174.8	1262.4	
SEM	108.3	94.5		146.9	157.8	

Note: This table is only the 8 injunctions that target less than 100 members for Part 2 crimes. *M* = Mean Average in sq. miles and gang members. *SD* = Standard Deviation. *SEM* = Standard Error of the Mean.

Matched control areas increased 12.7% (+12.7%) during the same period. The injunction and control outcomes were in opposite directions: the injunction areas were getting better while the matched control areas were getting worse. The 20.0% net benefit (12.7% + 7.3% = 20.0%) between injunctions and matched controls trended toward statistical significance, t (7) = 1.3, $p < .22$. Overall, these findings suggest that gang injunctions may reduce total calls (see Table 8.36 and Figure 8.35).

Table 8.37 shows that Part 1 calls in injunctions that target gangs having more than 100 total members decreased 17.9% compared

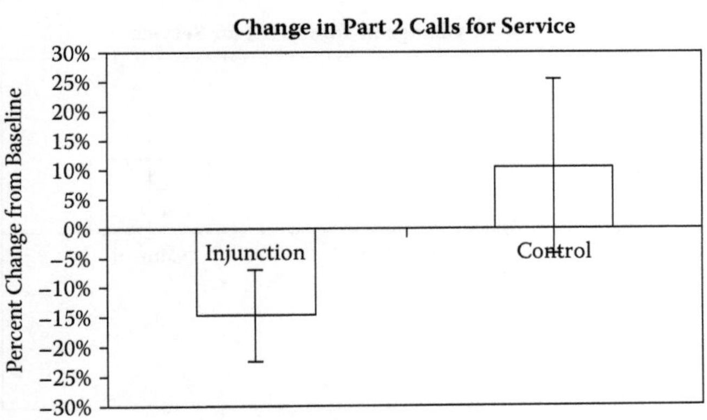

FIGURE 8.34 Part 2 Calls, Percent Change from Baseline Less than 100.

TABLE 8.36
Total Calls, Percent Change from Baseline for Less than 100 Total Members

	Injunction			Control		
Pair	**Before**	**After**	**Change**	**Before**	**After**	**Change**
2	1727	1985	14.9%	3035	3375	11.2%
4	1650	1548	–6.2%	1000	900	–10.0%
5	2243	2198	–2.0%	7856	8519	8.4%
6	1012	834	–17.6%	6886	14197	106.2%
7	448	372	–17.0%	1435	1285	–10.5%
8	4414	4113	–6.8%	12526	12474	–0.4%
10	1961	1615	–17.6%	2700	2500	–7.4%
17	3448	3243	–5.9%	636	664	4.4%
M	2112.9	1988.5	–7.3%	4509.3	5489.3	12.7%
SD	1279.8	1219.5		4197.5	5467.0	
SEM	160.0	152.4		524.7	683.4	

Note: This table includes only the 8 injunctions that target gangs that have less than 100 documented members for total calls for service. *M* = Mean Average in sq. miles and gang members. *SD* = Standard Deviation. *SEM* = Standard Error of the Mean.

to baseline (–17.9%), a decrease, t (16) = 3.7, $p < .002$. Matched control areas decreased 6.2% (–6.2%) during the same period. The injunction and control outcomes were in the same direction: the injunction areas were getting better while the matched control areas were also getting better at a reduced rate. The 11.7% net benefit (17.9% – 6.2% = 11.7%) between injunctions and matched controls trended toward statistical significance, t (16) = 2.1, $p < .05$. Overall, these findings suggest that gang injunctions may reduce Part 1 calls (see Table 8.37 and Figure 8.36).

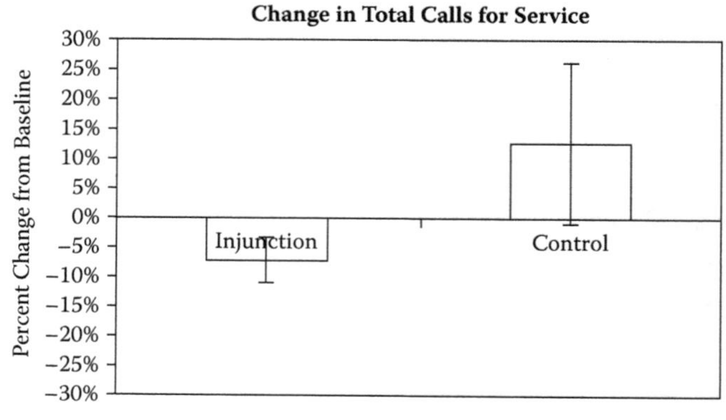

FIGURE 8.35 Total Calls, Percent Change from Baseline Less than 100.

TABLE 8.37
Part 1 Calls, Percent Change from Baseline for More than 100 Total Members

	Injunction			Control		
Pair	**Before**	**After**	**Change**	**Before**	**After**	**Change**
1	228	203	−11.0%	709	692	−2.4%
3	271	178	−34.3%	651	438	−32.7%
9	2349	2355	0.3%	1455	1384	−4.9%
11	263	143	−45.6%	947	1003	5.9%
12	1544	1435	−7.1%	2710	2513	−7.3%
13	5568	1184	−78.7%	1425	1420	−0.4%
14	600	500	−16.7%	700	600	−14.3%
15	306	279	−8.8%	315	298	−5.4%
16	351	321	−8.5%	404	411	1.7%
18	455	390	−14.3%	145	139	−4.1%
19	816	759	−7.0%	126	115	−8.7%
20	165	123	−25.5%	144	155	7.6%
21	765	745	−2.6%	201	172	−14.4%
22	989	936	−5.4%	975	953	−2.3%
23	824	757	−8.1%	698	672	−3.7%
24	726	693	−4.5%	195	161	−17.4%
25	2895	2120	−26.8%	1447	1400	−3.2%
M	1124.4	771.8	−17.9%	779.2	736.8	−6.2%
SD	1374.6	667.4		680.7	649.2	
SEM	80.9	39.3		40.0	38.2	

Note: This table includes only the 17 injunctions that target gangs that have more than 100 documented members for Part 1 crimes. "Pair" refers to the code assigned to each injunction and matched control, see Table 8.1. *M* = Mean Average for all 17 pairs. *SD* = Standard Deviation. *SEM* = Standard Error of the Mean.

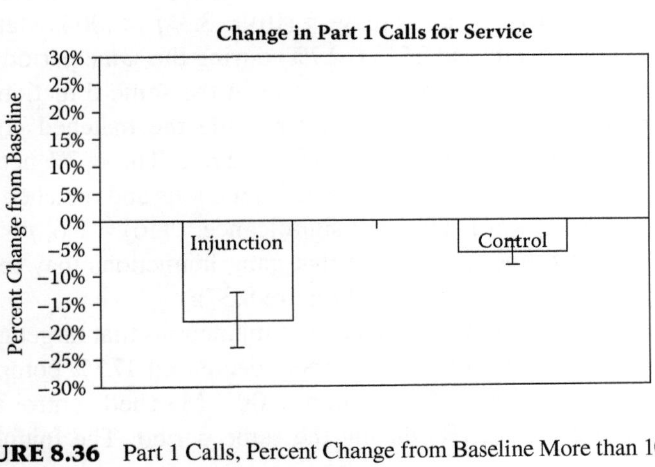

FIGURE 8.36 Part 1 Calls, Percent Change from Baseline More than 100.

TABLE 8.38
Part 2 Calls, Percent Change from Baseline for More than 100 Total Members

	Injunction			Control		
Pair	**Before**	**After**	**Change**	**Before**	**After**	**Change**
1	304	279	−8.2%	2615	2817	7.7%
3	323	213	−34.1%	1436	853	−40.6%
9	2406	2509	4.3%	1852	1827	−1.3%
11	956	804	−15.9%	2865	3370	17.6%
12	4841	3652	−24.6%	6354	4908	−22.8%
13	15540	4220	−72.8%	5054	5204	3.0%
14	1600	1500	−6.3%	1700	1600	−5.9%
15	725	637	−12.1%	931	908	−2.5%
16	1050	995	−5.2%	1058	1056	−0.2%
18	2164	1230	−43.2%	425	397	−6.6%
19	2440	2080	−14.8%	378	345	−8.7%
20	237	256	8.0%	325	352	8.3%
21	1201	1081	−10.0%	550	567	3.1%
22	2597	2519	−3.0%	2348	2302	−2.0%
23	2325	2134	−8.2%	1923	1956	1.7%
24	2072	2179	5.2%	553	548	−0.9%
25	3500	2100	−40.0%	2200	2300	4.5%
M	2604.8	1669.9	−16.5%	1915.7	1841.8	−2.7%
SD	3548.8	1161.4		1658.9	1516.6	
SEM	208.8	68.3		97.6	89.2	

Note: This table includes only the 17 injunctions that target gangs that have more than 100 documented members for Part 2 crimes. *M* = Mean Average in sq. miles and gang members. *SD* = Standard Deviation. *SEM* = Standard Error of the Mean.

Table 8.38 shows that Part 2 calls in injunctions that target gangs having more than 100 total members decreased 16.5% compared to baseline (–16.5%), a decrease, t (16) = 3.3, $p < .004$. Matched control areas decreased 2.7% (–2.7%) during the same period. The injunction and control outcomes were in the same direction: the injunction areas were getting better while the matched control areas were also getting better at a reduced rate. The 11.7% net benefit (17.9% – 6.2% = 11.7%) between injunctions and matched controls trended toward statistical significance, t (16) = 2.6, $p < .02$. Overall, these findings suggest that gang injunctions may reduce Part 2 calls (see Table 8.38 and Figure 8.37).

Table 8.39 shows that total calls in injunctions that target gangs having more than 100 total members decreased 17.3% compared to baseline (–17.3%), t (16) = 3.6, $p < .002$. Matched control areas decreased 2.7% (–2.7%) during the same period. The injunction

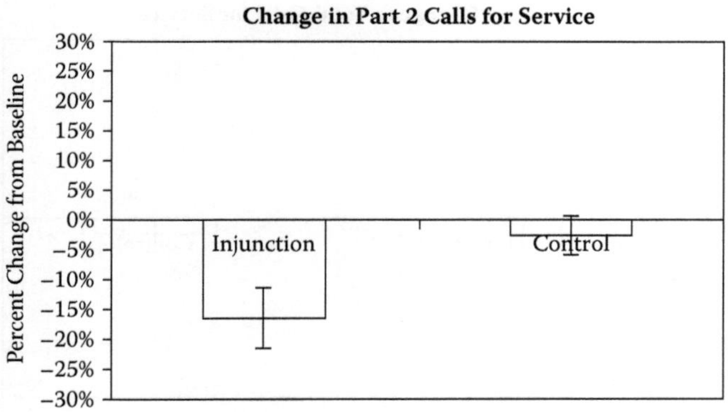

FIGURE 8.37 Part 2 Calls, Percent Change from Baseline More than 100.

TABLE 8.39
Total Calls, Percent Change from Baseline for More than 100 Total Members

	Injunction			Control		
Pair	Before	After	Change	Before	After	Change
1	982	902	−8.1%	7541	7850	4.1%
3	1409	929	−34.1%	3345	2214	−33.8%
9	26088	26213	0.5%	12946	13093	1.1%
11	2732	1913	−30.0%	8880	9252	4.2%
12	14748	11108	−24.7%	14520	9862	−32.1%
13	36331	9139	−74.8%	11913	11576	−2.8%
14	9500	8500	−10.5%	10100	9300	−7.9%
15	1926	1821	−5.5%	1833	1921	4.8%
16	2875	2764	−3.9%	2904	2934	1.0%
18	5278	3202	−39.3%	2425	2460	1.4%
19	5390	4650	−13.7%	1975	1898	−3.9%
20	844	772	−8.5%	1825	1960	7.4%
21	3986	3841	−3.6%	2550	2610	2.4%
22	5301	5234	−1.3%	4921	5011	1.8%
23	5251	4865	−7.4%	3726	3897	4.6%
24	4821	4959	2.9%	2553	2598	1.8%
25	12500	8600	−31.2%	6450	6500	0.8%
M	8233.1	5847.8	−17.3%	5906.3	5584.5	−2.7%
SD	9640.5	6113.9		4285.6	3816.4	
SEM	567.1	359.6		252.1	224.5	

Note: This table includes only the 17 injunctions that target gangs that have more than 100 documented members for total calls for service. *M* = Mean Average in sq. miles and gang members. *SD* = Standard Deviation. *SEM* = Standard Error of the Mean.

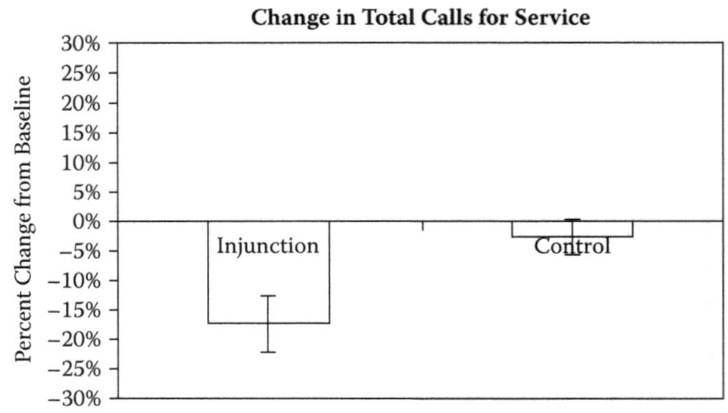

FIGURE 8.38 Gang injunctions may reduce total calls.

and control outcomes were in the same direction: the injunction areas were getting better while the matched control areas were also getting better at a reduced rate. The 14.6% net benefit (17.3% – 2.7% = 14.6%) between injunctions and matched controls trended toward statistical significance, t (16) = 3.1, $p < .01$. Overall, these findings suggest that gang injunctions may reduce total calls (see Table 8.39 and Figure 8.38).

Summary of Overall Gang Size Analysis

The percent change for gangs with less than 100 documented members for Part 1 calls was a 1.8% reduction for injunction and a 15.6% reduction for control. The percent change for gangs with more than 100 documented members for Part 1 calls was a 17.9% reduction for injunction and a 6.2% reduction for control.

The percent change for gangs with less than 100 documented members for Part 2 calls was a 14.7% reduction for injunction and a 10.6% increase for control. The percent change for gangs with more than 100 documented members for Part 2 calls was a 16.5% reduction for injunction and a 2.7% reduction for control.

The percent change for gangs with less than 100 documented members for total calls was a 7.3% reduction for injunction and a 12.7% increase for control. The percent change for gangs with more than 100 documented members for total calls was a 17.3% reduction for injunction and a 2.7% reduction for control. In summary, gang injunctions less than 100 members and those with more than 100 members seemed to fare about the same.

Summary of Further Analysis

The further analysis portion of this research looked at five variables that may or may not impact gang injunction effectiveness.

This section of the research explored several potential dimensions of gang injunctions that future researchers may want to more fully explore, including effectiveness by gang ethnicity, county of origin of the injunction, size of the enjoined gang, size of the gang injunction, and size of the target area. In this research, the sample size was reduced as the data were divided and evaluated to explore possible variables that may help make one injunction more effective.

Limitations with the Injunctions

The majority of gang injunctions obtained statewide were reviewed and evaluated to determine if the case was a potential candidate for inclusion in this research. After a cursory review of the cases based upon the year obtained, jurisdiction, and control gang availability, detailed crime data were requested relating to 45 gang injunction cases from several counties. A total of 45 gang injunctions or approximately half of all active injunctions at the time of this research were sought to gather data and include in this research.

Those 45 injunctions included 18 gang injunctions from Los Angeles County, 16 from San Diego County, 7 from San Bernardino County, 2 from Ventura County, and 2 from Fresno County. Of the 45 injunctions where it was believed data existed for the injunction, attempts were made to identify those injunctions where data could be collected for injunction and controls. Data for 25 injunctions and controls were ultimately collected.

SECTION 4: CASE-BY-CASE ANALYSIS

Section 4 simply takes the data reflected in the tables reviewed thus far and explains them in descriptive form on an injunction-by-injunction basis to help the reader understand the results of any individual injunction reviewed.

Case/Pair 1: Posole and Vista Homeboys: Part 1 Crime

The year before the injunction revealed 228 Part 1 crimes. The year following the injunction revealed 203 Part 1 crimes. The reported difference the year after the injunction was 25 fewer Part 1 crimes, an 11% decrease. The year before for the control revealed 709 Part 1 crimes. The year following for the control revealed 692 Part 1 crimes. The reported difference the year after the injunction was 17 fewer Part 1 crimes, a 2.4% decrease.

Case/Pair 1: Posole and Vista Homeboys: Part 2 Crime

Part 2 before and after for Posole: The year before the injunction revealed 304 Part 2 crimes. The year following the injunction revealed 279 Part 2 crimes. The reported difference the year after the injunction was 25 fewer Part 2 crimes, an 8.2% decrease.

Part 2 before and after for Vista Homeboys: The year before the injunction revealed 2,615 Part 2 crimes. The year following the injunction revealed 2,817 Part 2 crimes. The reported difference the year after the injunction was 202 more Part 2 crimes, a 7.7% increase.

Case/Pair 1: Posole and Vista Homeboys: Total Calls

Calls for service before and after for Posole: The year before the injunction revealed 982 total calls for service. The year following the injunction revealed 902 calls for service. The reported difference the year after the injunction was 80 fewer calls, an 8.1% decrease.

Calls for service for Vista Homeboys: The year before the injunction revealed 7,541 total calls for service. The year following the injunction revealed 7,850 calls for service. The reported difference the year after the injunction was 309 more calls, a 4.1% increase.

Case/Pair 2: San Marcos and South Los: Part 1 Crime

The year before the injunction revealed 126 Part 1 crimes. The year following the injunction revealed 136 Part 1 crimes. The reported difference the year after the injunction was 10 more Part 1 crimes, a 7.9% increase. The year before for the control revealed 375 Part 1 crimes. The year following for the control revealed 350 Part 1 crimes. The reported difference the year after the injunction was 25 fewer Part 1 crimes, a 6.7% decrease.

Case/Pair 2: San Marcos and South Los: Part 2 Crime

Part 2 before and after for San Marcos: The year before the injunction revealed 337 Part 2 crimes. The year following the injunction revealed 427 Part 2 crimes. The reported difference the year after the injunction was 90 more Part 2 crimes, a 26.7% increase.

Part 2 before and after for South Los: The year before the injunction revealed 400 Part 2 crimes. The year following the injunction revealed 436 Part 2 crimes. The reported difference the year after the injunction was 36 more Part 2 crimes, a 9% increase.

Case/Pair 2: San Marcos and South Los: Total Calls

Calls for service before and after for San Marcos: The year before the injunction revealed 1,727 total calls for service. The year following the injunction revealed 1,985 calls for service. The reported difference the year after the injunction was 258 more calls, a 14.9% increase.

Calls for service for South Los: The year before the injunction revealed 3,035 total calls for service. The year following the injunction revealed 3,375 calls for service. The reported difference the year after the injunction was 340 more calls, an 11.2% increase.

Case/Pair 3: Old Town National City and Shelltown Gamma: Part 1 Crime

The year before the injunction revealed 271 Part 1 crimes. The year following the injunction revealed 178 Part 1 crimes. The reported difference the year after the injunction was 93 fewer Part 1 crimes, a 34.3% decrease. The year before for the control revealed 651 Part 1 crimes. The year following for the control revealed 438 Part 1 crimes. The reported difference the year after the injunction was 213 fewer Part 1 crimes, a 32.7% decrease.

Case/Pair 3: Old Town National City and Shelltown Gamma: Part 2 Crime

Part 2 before and after for OTNC: The year before the injunction revealed 323 Part 2 crimes. The year following the injunction revealed 213 Part 2 crimes. The reported difference the year after the injunction was 110 fewer Part 2 crimes, a 34.1% decrease.

Part 2 before and after for Shelltown Gamma: The year before the injunction revealed 1,436 Part 2 crimes. The year following the injunction revealed 853 Part 2 crimes. The reported difference the year after the injunction was 583 fewer Part 2 crimes, a 40.6% decrease.

Case/Pair 3: Old Town National City and Shelltown Gamma: Total Calls

Calls for service before and after for OTNC: The year before the injunction revealed 1,409 total calls for service. The year following the injunction revealed 929 calls for service. The reported difference the year after the injunction was 480 fewer calls, a 34.1% decrease.

Calls for service for Shelltown Gamma: The year before the injunction revealed 3,345 total calls for service. The year following the injunction revealed 2,214 calls for service. The reported difference the year after the injunction was 1,131 more calls, a 33.8% decrease.

Case/Pair 4: Mesa Locos and Center Street: Part 1 Crime

The year before the injunction revealed 352 Part 1 crimes. The year following the injunction revealed 288 Part 1 crimes. The reported difference the year after the injunction was 64 fewer Part 1 crimes, an 18.2% decrease. The year before for the control revealed 200 Part 1 crimes. The year following for the control revealed 190 Part 1 crimes. The reported difference the year after the injunction was 10 fewer Part 1 crimes, a 5% decrease.

Case/Pair 4: Mesa Locos and Center Street: Part 2 Crime

Part 2 before and after for Center Street: The year before the injunction revealed 500 Part 2 crimes. The year following the injunction revealed 400 Part 2 crimes. The reported difference the year after the injunction was 100 fewer Part 2 crimes, a 20% decrease.

Part 2 before and after for Mesa: The year before the injunction revealed 720 Part 2 crimes. The year following the injunction revealed 600 Part 2 crimes. The reported difference the year after the injunction was 120 fewer Part 2 crimes, a 16.7% decrease.

Case/Pair 4: Mesa Locos and Center Street: Total Calls

Calls for service before and after for Mesa: The year before the injunction revealed 1,650 total calls for service. The year following the injunction revealed 1,548 calls for service.

The reported difference the year after the injunction was 102 fewer calls, a 6.2% decrease.

Calls for service for Center Street: The year before the injunction revealed 1,000 total calls for service. The year following the injunction revealed 900 calls for service. The reported difference the year after the injunction was 100 fewer calls, a 10% decrease.

Case/Pair 5: Linda Vista and Mission Bay: Part 1 Crime

The year before the injunction revealed 310 Part 1 crimes. The year following the injunction revealed 294 Part 1 crimes. The reported difference the year after the injunction was 16 fewer Part 1 crimes, a 5.2% decrease. The year before for the control revealed 1,327 Part 1 crimes. The year following for the control revealed 1,467 Part 1 crimes. The reported difference the year after the injunction was 140 more Part 1 crimes, a 10.6% increase.

Case/Pair 5: Linda Vista and Mission Bay: Part 2 Crime

Part 2 before and after for Linda Vista: The year before the injunction revealed 435 Part 2 crimes. The year following the injunction revealed 404 Part 2 crimes. The reported difference the year after the injunction was 31 fewer Part 2 crimes, a 7.2% decrease.

Part 2 before and after for Mission Bay: The year before the injunction revealed 3,574 Part 2 crimes. The year following the injunction revealed 3,672 Part 2 crimes. The reported difference the year after the injunction was 98 more Part 2 crimes, a 2.7% increase.

Case/Pair 5: Linda Vista and Mission Bay: Total Calls

Calls for service before and after for Linda Vista: The year before the injunction revealed 2,243 total calls for service. The year following the injunction revealed 2,198 calls for service. The reported difference the year after the injunction was 45 fewer calls, a 2% decrease.

Calls for service for Mission Bay: The year before the injunction revealed 7,856 total calls for service. The year following the injunction revealed 8,519 calls for service. The reported difference the year after the injunction was 663 more calls, an 8.4% increase.

Case/Pair 6: Diablos and Fallbrook Locos: Part 1 Crime

The year before the injunction revealed 172 Part 1 crimes. The year following the injunction revealed 226 Part 1 crimes. The reported difference the year after the injunction was 54 more Part 1 crimes, a 31.4% increase. The year before for the control revealed 519 Part 1 crimes. The year following for the control revealed 1,212 Part 1 crimes. The reported difference the year after the injunction was 693 more Part 1 crimes, a 133.5% increase.

Case/Pair 6: Diablos and Fallbrook Locos: Part 2 Crime

Part 2 before and after for Diablos: The year before the injunction revealed 446 Part 2 crimes. The year following the injunction revealed 287 Part 2 crimes. The reported difference the year after the injunction was 159 fewer Part 2 crimes, a 35.7% decrease.

Part 2 before and after for Fallbrook Locos: The year before the injunction revealed 876 Part 2 crimes. The year following the injunction revealed 1,830 Part 2 crimes. The reported difference the year after the injunction was 954 more Part 2 crimes, a 108.9% increase.

Case/Pair 6: Diablos and Fallbrook Locos: Total Calls

Calls for service before and after for Diablos: The year before the injunction revealed 1,012 total calls for service. The year following the injunction revealed 834 calls for service. The reported difference the year after the injunction was 178 fewer calls, a 17.6% decrease.

Calls for service for Fallbrook Locos: The year before the injunction revealed 6,886 total calls for service. The year following the injunction revealed 14,197 calls for service. The reported difference the year after the injunction was 7,311 more calls, a 106.2% increase.

Case/Pair 7: Westside and Encinitas Locos: Part 1 Crime

The year before the injunction revealed 157 Part 1 crimes. The year following the injunction revealed 181 Part 1 crimes. The reported difference the year after the injunction was 24 more Part 1 crimes, a 15.3% increase. The year before for the control revealed 22 Part 1 crimes. The year following for the control revealed 16 Part 1 crimes.

The reported difference the year after the injunction was 6 fewer Part 1 crimes, a 27.3% decrease.

Case/Pair 7: Westside and Encinitas Locos: Part 2 Crime

Part 2 before and after for Westside: The year before the injunction revealed 168 Part 2 crimes. The year following the injunction revealed 98 Part 2 crimes. The reported difference the year after the injunction was 70 fewer Part 2 crimes, a 41.7% decrease.

Part 2 before and after for Encinitas Locos: The year before the injunction revealed 249 Part 2 crimes. The year following the injunction revealed 203 Part 2 crimes. The reported difference the year after the injunction was 46 fewer Part 2 crimes, an 18.5% decrease.

Case/Pair 7: Westside and Encinitas Locos: Total Calls

Calls for service before and after for Westside: The year before the injunction revealed 448 total calls for service. The year following the injunction revealed 372 calls for service. The reported difference the year after the injunction was 76 fewer calls, a 17% decrease.

Calls for service for Encinitas Locos: The year before the injunction revealed 1,435 total calls for service. The year following the injunction revealed 1,285 calls for service. The reported difference the year after the injunction was 150 fewer calls, a 10.5% decrease.

Case/Pair 8: Nestor and Imperials: Part 1 Crime

The year before the injunction revealed 1,008 Part 1 crimes. The year following the injunction revealed 978 Part 1 crimes. The reported difference the year after the injunction was 30 fewer Part 1 crimes, a 3% decrease. The year before for the control revealed 140 Part 1 crimes. The year following for the control revealed 158 Part 1 crimes. The reported difference the year after the injunction was 18 more Part 1 crimes, a 12.9% increase.

Case/Pair 8: Nestor and Imperials: Part 2 Crime

Part 2 before and after for Nestor: The year before the injunction revealed 2,877 Part 2 crimes. The year following the injunction revealed 2,477 Part 2 crimes. The reported difference the year after the injunction was 400 fewer Part 2 crimes, a 13.9% decrease.

Part 2 before and after for Imperials: The year before the injunction revealed 1,930 Part 2 crimes. The year following the injunction revealed 2,082 Part 2 crimes. The reported difference the year after the injunction was 152 more Part 2 crimes, a 7.9% increase.

Case/Pair 8: Nestor and Imperials: Total Calls

Calls for service before and after for Nestor: The year before the injunction revealed 4,414 total calls for service. The year following the injunction revealed 4,113 calls for service. The reported difference the year after the injunction was 301 fewer calls, a 6.8% decrease.

Calls for service for Imperials: The year before the injunction revealed 12,526 total calls for service. The year following the injunction revealed 12,474 calls for service. The reported difference the year after the injunction was 52 fewer calls, a 0.4% decrease.

Case/Pair 9: Logan Red Steps and Shelltown 38th Street: Part 1 Crime

The year before the injunction revealed 2,349 Part 1 crimes. The year following the injunction revealed 2,355 Part 1 crimes. The reported difference the year after the injunction was 6 more Part 1 crimes, a 0.3% increase. The year before for the control revealed 1,455 Part 1 crimes. The year following for the control revealed 1,384 Part 1 crimes. The reported difference the year after the injunction was 71 fewer Part 1 crimes, a 4.9% decrease.

Case/Pair 9: Logan Red Steps and Shelltown: Part 2 Crime

Part 2 before and after for Logan Red Steps: The year before the injunction revealed 2,406 Part 2 crimes. The year following the injunction revealed 2,509 Part 2 crimes. The reported difference the year after the injunction was 103 more Part 2 crimes, a 4.3% increase.

Part 2 before and after for Shelltown 38th Street: The year before the injunction revealed 1,852 Part 2 crimes. The year following the injunction revealed 1,827 Part 2 crimes. The reported difference the year after the injunction was 25 fewer Part 2 crimes, a 1.3% decrease.

Case/Pair 9: Logan Red Steps and Shelltown 38th Street: Total Calls

Calls for service before and after for Logan Red Steps: The year before the injunction revealed 26,088 total calls for service. The year following the injunction revealed 26,213 calls for service. The reported difference the year after the injunction was 125 more calls, a 0.5% increase.

Calls for service for Shelltown 38th Street: The year before the injunction revealed 12,946 total calls for service. The year following the injunction revealed 13,093 calls for service. The reported difference the year after the injunction was 147 more calls, a 1.1% increase.

Case/Pair 10: Center Street and South Los: Part 1 Crime

The year before the injunction revealed 162 Part 1 crimes. The year following the injunction revealed 147 Part 1 crimes. The reported difference the year after the injunction was 15 fewer Part 1 crimes, a 9.3% decrease. The year before for the control revealed 300 Part 1 crimes. The year following for the control revealed 290 Part 1 crimes. The reported difference the year after the injunction was 10 fewer Part 1 crimes, a 3.3% decrease.

Case/Pair 10: Center Street and South Los: Part 2 Crime

Part 2 before and after for Center Street: The year before the injunction revealed 703 Part 2 crimes. The year following the injunction revealed 517 Part 2 crimes. The reported difference the year after the injunction was 186 fewer Part 2 crimes, a 26.5% decrease.

Part 2 before and after for South Los: The year before the injunction revealed 400 Part 2 crimes. The year following the injunction revealed 350 Part 2 crimes. The reported difference the year after the injunction was 50 fewer Part 2 crimes, a 12.5% decrease.

Case/Pair 10: Center Street and South Los: Total Calls

Calls for service before and after for Center Street: The year before the injunction revealed 1,961 total calls for service.

The year following the injunction revealed 1,615 calls for service. The reported difference the year after the injunction was 346 fewer calls, a 17.6% decrease.

Calls for service for South Los: The year before the injunction revealed 2,700 total calls for service. The year following the injunction revealed 2,500 calls for service. The reported difference the year after the injunction was 200 fewer calls, a 7.4% decrease.

Case/Pair 11: Posole and Vista Homeboys: Part 1 Crime

The year before the injunction revealed 263 Part 1 crimes. The year following the injunction revealed 143 Part 1 crimes. The reported difference the year after the injunction was 120 fewer Part 1 crimes, a 45.6% decrease. The year before for the control revealed 947 Part 1 crimes. The year following for the control revealed 1,003 Part 1 crimes. The reported difference the year after the injunction was 56 more Part 1 crimes, a 5.9% increase.

Case/Pair 11: Posole and Vista Homeboys: Part 2 Crime

Part 2 before and after for Posole: The year before the injunction revealed 956 Part 2 crimes. The year following the injunction revealed 804 Part 2 crimes. The reported difference the year after the injunction was 152 fewer Part 2 crimes, a 15.9% decrease.

Part 2 before and after for Vista Homeboys: The year before the injunction revealed 2,865 Part 2 crimes. The year following the injunction revealed 3,370 Part 2 crimes. The reported difference the year after the injunction was 505 more Part 2 crimes, a 17.6% increase.

Case/Pair 11: Posole and Vista Homeboys: Total Calls

Calls for service before and after for Posole: The year before the injunction revealed 2,732 total calls for service. The year following the injunction revealed 1,913 calls for service. The reported difference the year after the injunction was 819 fewer calls, a 30% decrease.

Calls for service for Vista Homeboys: The year before the injunction revealed 8,880 total calls for service. The year following the injunction revealed 9,252 calls for service. The reported difference the year after the injunction was 372 more calls, a 4.2% increase.

Case/Pair 12: Lincoln Park and 5/9 Brims: Part 1 Crime

The year before the injunction revealed 1,544 Part 1 crimes. The year following the injunction revealed 1,435 Part 1 crimes. The reported difference the year after the injunction was 109 fewer Part 1 crimes, a 7.1% decrease. The year before for the control revealed 2,710 Part 1 crimes. The year following for the control revealed 2,513 Part 1 crimes. The reported difference the year after the injunction was 197 fewer Part 1 crimes, a 7.3% decrease.

Case/Pair 12: Lincoln Park and 5/9 Brims: Part 2 Crime

Part 2 before and after for Lincoln Park: The year before the injunction revealed 4,841 Part 2 crimes. The year following the injunction revealed 3,652 Part 2 crimes. The reported difference the year after the injunction was 1,189 fewer Part 2 crimes, a 24.6% decrease.

Part 2 before and after for 5/9 Brims: The year before the injunction revealed 6,354 Part 2 crimes. The year following the injunction revealed 4,908 Part 2 crimes. The reported difference the year after the injunction was 1,446 fewer Part 2 crimes, a 22.8% decrease.

Case/Pair 12: Lincoln Park and 5/9 Brims: Total Calls

Calls for service before and after for Lincoln Park: The year before the injunction revealed 14,748 total calls for service. The year following the injunction revealed 11,108 calls for service. The reported difference the year after the injunction was 3,640 fewer calls, a 24.7% decrease.

Calls for service for 5/9 Brims: The year before the injunction revealed 14,250 total calls for service. The year following the injunction revealed 9,862 calls for service. The reported difference the year after the injunction was 4,658 fewer calls, a 32.1% decrease.

Case/Pair 13: Skyline Piru and West Coast Crips: Part 1 Crime

The year before the injunction revealed 5,568 Part 1 crimes. The year following the injunction revealed 1,184 Part 1 crimes. The reported difference the year after the injunction was 4,384 fewer Part 1 crimes, a 78.7% decrease. The year before for the control revealed 1,425 Part 1 crimes. The year following for the control revealed 1,420 Part 1 crimes. The reported difference the year after the injunction was 5 fewer Part 1 crimes, a 0.4% decrease.

Case/Pair 13: Skyline Piru and West Coast Crips: Part 2 Crime

Part 2 before and after for Skyline Piru: The year before the injunction revealed 15,540 Part 2 crimes. The year following the injunction revealed 4,220 Part 2 crimes. The reported difference the year after the injunction was 11,320 fewer Part 2 crimes, a 72.8% decrease.

Part 2 before and after for West Coast Crips: The year before the injunction revealed 5,054 Part 2 crimes. The year following the injunction revealed 5,204 Part 2 crimes. The reported difference the year after the injunction was 150 more Part 2 crimes, a 3.0% increase.

Case/Pair 13: Skyline Piru and West Coast Crips: Total Calls

Calls for service before and after for Skyline Piru: The year before the injunction revealed 36,331 total calls for service. The year following the injunction revealed 9,139 calls for service. The reported difference the year after the injunction was 27,192 fewer calls, a 74.8% decrease.

Calls for service for West Coast Crips: The year before the injunction revealed 11,913 total calls for service. The year following the injunction revealed 11,576 calls for service. The reported difference the year after the injunction was 337 fewer calls, a 2.8% decrease.

Case/Pair 14: Old Town National City and Otay: Part 1 Crime

The year before the injunction revealed 600 Part 1 crimes. The year following the injunction revealed 500 Part 1 crimes. The reported difference the year after the injunction was 100 fewer Part 1 crimes, a 16.7% decrease. The year before for the control revealed 700 Part 1 crimes. The year following for the control revealed 600 Part 1 crimes. The reported difference the year after the injunction was 100 fewer Part 1 crimes, a 14.3% decrease.

Case/Pair 14: Old Town National City and Otay: Part 2 Crimes

Part 2 before and after for OTNC: The year before the injunction revealed 1,600 Part 2 crimes. The year following the injunction revealed 1,500 Part 2 crimes. The reported difference the year after the injunction was 100 fewer Part 2 crimes, a 6.3% decrease.

Part 2 before and after for Otay: The year before the injunction revealed 1,700 Part 2 crimes. The year following the injunction revealed 1,600 Part 2 crimes. The reported difference the year after the injunction was 100 fewer Part 2 crimes, a 5.9% decrease.

Case/Pair 14: Old Town National City and Otay: Total Calls

Calls for service before and after for OTNC: The year before the injunction revealed 9,500 total calls for service. The year following the injunction revealed 8,500 calls for service. The reported difference the year after the injunction was 1,000 fewer calls, a 10.5% decrease.

Calls for service for Otay: The year before the injunction revealed 10,100 total calls for service. The year following the injunction revealed 9,300 calls for service. The reported difference the year after the injunction was 800 fewer calls, a 7.9% decrease.

Case/Pair 15: 7th Street and Southside Colton: Part 1 Crime

The year before the injunction revealed 306 Part 1 crimes. The year following the injunction revealed 279 Part 1 crimes. The reported difference the year after the injunction was 27 fewer Part 1 crimes, an 8.8% decrease. The year before for the control revealed 315 Part 1 crimes. The year following for the control revealed 298 Part 1 crimes. The reported difference the year after the injunction was 17 fewer Part 1 crimes, a 5.4% decrease.

Case/Pair 15: 7th Street and Southside Colton: Part 2 Crime

Part 2 before and after for 7th Street: The year before the injunction revealed 725 Part 2 crimes. The year following the injunction revealed 637 Part 2 crimes. The reported difference the year after the injunction was 88 fewer Part 2 crimes, a 12.1% decrease.

Part 2 before and after for Southside Colton: The year before the injunction revealed 931 Part 2 crimes. The year following the injunction revealed 908 Part 2 crimes.

The reported difference the year after the injunction was 23 fewer Part 2 crimes, a 4.5% decrease.

Case/Pair 15: 7th Street and Southside Colton: Total Calls

Calls for service before and after for 7th Street: The year before the injunction revealed 1,926 total calls for service. The year following the injunction revealed 1,821 calls for service. The reported difference the year after the injunction was 105 fewer calls, a 5.5% decrease.

Calls for service for Southside Colton: The year before the injunction revealed 1,833 total calls for service. The year following the injunction revealed 1,921 calls for service. The reported difference the year after the injunction was 88 more calls, a 4.8% increase.

Case/Pair 16: Verdugo Flats and Northside Colton: Part 1 Crime

The year before the injunction revealed 351 Part 1 crimes. The year following the injunction revealed 321 Part 1 crimes. The reported difference the year after the injunction was 30 fewer Part 1 crimes, an 8.5% decrease. The year before for the control revealed 404 Part 1 crimes. The year following for the control revealed 411 Part 1 crimes. The reported difference the year after the injunction was 7 more Part 1 crimes, a 1.7% increase.

Case/Pair 16: Verdugo Flats and Northside Colton: Part 2 Crime

Part 2 before and after for Verdugo Flats: The year before the injunction revealed 1,050 Part 2 crimes. The year following the injunction revealed 995 Part 2 crimes. The reported difference the year after the injunction was 55 fewer Part 2 crimes, a 5.2% decrease.

Part 2 before and after for Northside Colton: The year before the injunction revealed 1,058 Part 2 crimes. The year following the injunction revealed 1,056 Part 2 crimes. The reported difference the year after the injunction was 2 fewer Part 2 crimes, a 0.2% decrease.

Case/Pair 16: Verdugo Flats and Northside Colton: Total Calls

Calls for service before and after for Verdugo Flats: The year before the injunction revealed 2,875 total calls for service.

The year following the injunction revealed 2,764 calls for service. The reported difference the year after the injunction was 111 fewer calls, a 3.9% decrease.

Calls for service for Northside Colton: The year before the injunction revealed 2,904 total calls for service. The year following the injunction revealed 2,934 calls for service. The reported difference the year after the injunction was 30 more calls, a 1.0% increase.

Case/Pair 17: Project Crips and Colton City Crips: Part 1 Crime

The year before the injunction revealed 421 Part 1 crimes. The year following the injunction revealed 401 Part 1 crimes. The reported difference the year after the injunction was 20 fewer Part 1 crimes, a 4.8% decrease. The year before for the control revealed 89 Part 1 crimes. The year following for the control revealed 98 Part 1 crimes. The reported difference the year after the injunction was 9 more Part 1 crimes, a 10.1% increase.

Case/Pair 17: Project Crips and Colton City Crips: Part 2 Crime

Part 2 before and after for Project Crips: The year before the injunction revealed 1,065 Part 2 crimes. The year following the injunction revealed 1,032 Part 2 crimes. The reported difference the year after the injunction was 33 fewer Part 2 crimes, a 3.1% decrease.

Part 2 before and after for Colton City Crips: The year before the injunction revealed 210 Part 2 crimes. The year following the injunction revealed 225 Part 2 crimes. The reported difference the year after the injunction was 15 more Part 2 crimes, a 7.1% increase.

Case/Pair 17: Project Crips and Colton City Crips: Total Calls

Calls for service before and after for Project Crips: The year before the injunction revealed 3,448 total calls for service. The year following the injunction revealed 3,243 calls for service. The reported difference the year after the injunction was 205 fewer calls, a 5.9% decrease.

Calls for service for Colton City Crips: The year before the injunction revealed 636 total calls for service. The year following the injunction revealed 664 calls for service.

The reported difference the year after the injunction was 28 more calls, a 4.4% increase.

Case/Pair 18: Canoga Park and Reseda South/Westside: Part 1 Crime

The year before the injunction revealed 455 Part 1 crimes. The year following the injunction revealed 390 Part 1 crimes. The reported difference the year after the injunction was 65 fewer Part 1 crimes, a 14.3% decrease. The year before for the control revealed 145 Part 1 crimes. The year following for the control revealed 139 Part 1 crimes. The reported difference the year after the injunction was 6 fewer Part 1 crimes, a 4.1% decrease.

Case/Pair 18: Canoga Park and Reseda South/Westside: Part 2 Crime

Part 2 before and after for Canoga Park Alabama: The year before the injunction revealed 2,164 Part 2 crimes. The year following the injunction revealed 1,230 Part 2 crimes. The reported difference the year after the injunction was 934 fewer Part 2 crimes, a 43.2% decrease.

Part 2 before and after for Reseda South and Westside: The year before the injunction revealed 425 Part 2 crimes. The year following the injunction revealed 397 Part 2 crimes. The reported difference the year after the injunction was 28 fewer Part 2 crimes, a 6.6% decrease.

Case/Pair 18: Canoga Park Alabama and Reseda South/Westside: Total Calls

Calls for service before and after for Canoga Park Alabama: The year before the injunction revealed 5,278 total calls for service. The year following the injunction revealed 3,202 calls for service. The reported difference the year after the injunction was 2,076 fewer calls, a 39.3% decrease.

Calls for service for Reseda South and Westside: The year before the injunction revealed 2,425 total calls for service. The year following the injunction revealed 2,460 calls for service. The reported difference the year after the injunction was 35 more calls, a 1.4% increase.

Case/Pair 19: 18th Street Pico Union and SSK/Drifters Gang: Part 1 Crime

The year before the injunction revealed 816 Part 1 crimes. The year following the injunction revealed 759 Part 1 crimes. The reported difference the year after the injunction was 57 fewer Part 1 crimes, a 7% decrease. The year before for the control revealed 126 Part 1 crimes. The year following for the control revealed 115 Part 1 crimes. The reported difference the year after the injunction was 11 fewer Part 1 crimes, an 8.7 decrease.

Case/Pair 19: 18th Street Pico and SSK/Drifters Gang: Part 2 Crime

Part 2 before and after for 18th Street Pico Union: The year before the injunction revealed 2,440 Part 2 crimes. The year following the injunction revealed 2,080 Part 2 crimes. The reported difference the year after the injunction was 360 fewer Part 2 crimes, a 14.8% decrease.

Part 2 before and after for SSK and Drifters: The year before the injunction revealed 378 Part 2 crimes. The year following the injunction revealed 345 Part 2 crimes. The reported difference the year after the injunction was 33 fewer Part 2 crimes, an 8.7% decrease.

Case/Pair 19: 18th Street Pico Union and SSK/Drifters Gang: Total Calls

Calls for service before and after for 18th Street Pico Union: The year before the injunction revealed 5,390 total calls for service. The year following the injunction revealed 4,650 calls for service. The reported difference the year after the injunction was 740 fewer calls, a 13.7% decrease.

Calls for service for SSK and Drifters: The year before the injunction revealed 1,975 total calls for service. The year following the injunction revealed 1,898 calls for service. The reported difference the year after the injunction was 77 fewer calls, a 3.9% decrease.

Case/Pair 20: Krazy Ass Mexicans and State/Clarence Street: Part 1 Crime

The year before the injunction revealed 165 Part 1 crimes. The year following the injunction revealed 123 Part 1 crimes. The reported difference the year after the injunction was 42 fewer Part 1 crimes, a 25.5% decrease. The year before for the control revealed 144 Part 1 crimes. The year following for the control revealed 155 Part 1 crimes. The reported difference the year after the injunction was 11 more Part 1 crimes, a 7.6% increase.

Case/Pair 20: Krazy Ass Mexicans and State/ Clarence Street: Part 2 Crime

Part 2 before and after for Krazy Ass Mexicans: The year before the injunction revealed 237 Part 2 crimes. The year following the injunction revealed 256 Part 2 crimes. The reported difference the year after the injunction was 19 more Part 2 crimes, an 8% increase.

Part 2 before and after for State and Clarence Street: The year before the injunction revealed 325 Part 2 crimes. The year following the injunction revealed 352 Part 2 crimes. The reported difference the year after the injunction was 27 more Part 2 crimes, an 8.3% increase.

Case/Pair 20: Krazy Ass Mexicans and State/Clarence Street: Total Calls

Calls for service before and after for Krazy Ass Mexicans: The year before the injunction revealed 844 total calls for service. The year following the injunction revealed 772 calls for service. The reported difference the year after the injunction was 72 fewer calls, an 8.5% decrease.

Calls for service for State and Clarence Street: The year before the injunction revealed 1,825 total calls for service. The year following the injunction revealed 1,960 calls for service. The reported difference the year after the injunction was 135 more calls, a 7.4% increase.

Case/Pair 21: Rolling Sixty Crips and Eight Tray Gangsters: Part 1 Crime

The year before the injunction revealed 765 Part 1 crimes. The year following the injunction revealed 745 Part 1 crimes. The reported difference the year after the injunction was 24 fewer Part 1 crimes, a 2.6% decrease. The year before for the control revealed 201 Part 1 crimes. The year following for the control revealed 172 Part 1 crimes. The reported difference the year after the injunction was 29 fewer Part 1 crimes, a 14.4% decrease.

Case/Pair 21: Rolling Sixty Crips and Eight Tray Gangsters: Part 2 Crime

Part 2 before and after for Rolling Sixty Crips: The year before the injunction revealed 1,201 Part 2 crimes. The year following the injunction revealed 1,081 Part 2 crimes. The reported difference the year after the injunction was 120 fewer Part 2 crimes, a 10% decrease.

Part 2 before and after for Eight Tray Gangsters: The year before the injunction revealed 550 Part 2 crimes. The year following the injunction revealed 567 Part 2 crimes. The reported difference the year after the injunction was 17 more Part 2 crimes, a 3.1% increase.

Case/Pair 21: Rolling Sixty Crips and Eight Tray Gangsters: Total Calls

Calls for service before and after for Rolling Sixty Crips: The year before the injunction revealed 3,986 total calls for service. The year following the injunction revealed 3,841 calls for service. The reported difference the year after the injunction was 145 fewer calls, a 3.6% decrease.

Calls for service for Eight Tray Gangsters: The year before the injunction revealed 2,550 total calls for service. The year following the injunction revealed 2,610 calls for service. The reported difference the year after the injunction was 60 more calls, a 2.4% increase.

Case/Pair 22: Varrio Nueva Estrada and White Fence: Part 1 Crime

The year before the injunction revealed 989 Part 1 crimes. The year following the injunction revealed 936 Part 1 crimes. The reported difference the year after the injunction was 53 fewer Part 1 crimes, a 5.4% decrease. The year before for the control revealed 975 Part 1 crimes. The year following for the control revealed 953 Part 1 crimes. The reported difference the year after the injunction was 22 fewer Part 1 crimes, a 2.3% decrease.

Case/Pair 22: Varrio Nueva Estrada and White Fence: Part 2 Crime

Part 2 before and after for Varrio Nueva Estrada: The year before the injunction revealed 2,597 Part 2 crimes. The year following the injunction revealed 2,519 Part 2 crimes. The reported difference the year after the injunction was 78 fewer Part 2 crimes, a 3% decrease.

Part 2 before and after for White Fence: The year before the injunction revealed 2,348 Part 2 crimes. The year following the injunction revealed 2,302 Part 2 crimes. The reported difference the year after the injunction was 46 fewer Part 2 crimes, a 2% decrease.

Case/Pair 22: Varrio Nueva Estrada and White Fence: Total Calls

Calls for service before and after for Varrio Nueva Estrada: The year before the injunction revealed 5,301 total calls for service. The year following the injunction revealed 5,234 calls for service. The reported difference the year after the injunction was 67 fewer calls, a 1.3% decrease.

Calls for service for White Fence: The year before the injunction revealed 4,921 total calls for service. The year following the injunction revealed 5,011 calls for service. The reported difference the year after the injunction was 90 more calls, a 1.8% increase.

Case/Pair 23: Grape Street Crips and 97th Street Crips: Part 1 Crime

The year before the injunction revealed 824 Part 1 crimes. The year following the injunction revealed 757 Part 1 crimes. The reported difference the year after the injunction was 67 fewer Part 1 crimes, an 8.1% decrease. The year before for the control revealed 698 Part 1 crimes. The year following for the control revealed 672 Part 1 crimes. The reported difference the year after the injunction was 26 fewer Part 1 crimes, a 3.7% decrease.

Case/Pair 23: Grape Street Crips and 97th Street Crips: Part 2 Crime

Part 2 before and after for Grape Street Crips: The year before the injunction revealed 2,325 Part 2 crimes. The year following the injunction revealed 2,134 Part 2 crimes. The reported difference the year after the injunction was 191 fewer Part 2 crimes, an 8.2% decrease.

Part 2 before and after for the 97th Street Crips: The year before the injunction revealed 1,923 Part 2 crimes. The year following the injunction revealed 1,956 Part 2 crimes. The reported difference the year after the injunction was 33 more Part 2 crimes, a 1.7% increase.

Case/Pair 23: Grape Street Crips and 97th Street Crips: Total Calls

Calls for service before and after for Grape Street Crips: The year before the injunction revealed 5,251 total calls for service. The year following the injunction revealed 4,865 calls for service. The reported difference the year after the injunction was 386 fewer calls, a 7.4% decrease.

Calls for service for the 97th Street Crips: The year before the injunction revealed 3,726 total calls for service. The year following the injunction revealed 3,897 calls for service. The reported difference the year after the injunction was 171 more calls, a 4.6% increase.

Case/Pair 24: Bounty Hunter Bloods and Front/Back Street Crips: Part 1 Crime

The year before the injunction revealed 726 Part 1 crimes. The year following the injunction revealed 693 Part 1 crimes. The reported difference the year after the injunction was 33 fewer Part 1 crimes, a 4.5% decrease. The year before for the control revealed 195 Part 1 crimes. The year following for the control revealed 161 Part 1 crimes. The reported difference the year after the injunction was 34 fewer Part 1 crimes, a 17.4% decrease.

Case/Pair 24: Bounty Hunter Bloods and Front/Back Street Crips: Part 2 Crime

Part 2 before and after for Bounty Hunter Bloods: The year before the injunction revealed 2,072 Part 2 crimes. The year following the injunction revealed 2,179 Part 2 crimes. The reported difference the year after the injunction was 107 more Part 2 crimes, a 5.2% increase.

Part 2 before and after for Front and Back Street Crips: The year before the injunction revealed 553 Part 2 crimes. The year following the injunction revealed 548 Part 2 crimes. The reported difference the year after the injunction was 5 fewer Part 2 crimes, a 0.9% decrease.

Case/Pair 24: Bounty Hunter Bloods and Front/Back Street Crips: Total Calls

Calls for service before and after for Bounty Hunter Bloods: The year before the injunction revealed 4,821 total calls for service. The year following the injunction revealed 4,959 calls for service. The reported difference the year after the injunction was 138 more calls, a 2.9% increase.

Calls for service for the Front and Back Street Crips: The year before the injunction revealed 2,553 total calls for service.

The year following the injunction revealed 2,598 calls for service. The reported difference the year after the injunction was 45 more calls, a 1.8% increase.

Case/Pair 25: Colonia Chiques and Southside Chiques: Part 1 Crime

The year before the injunction revealed 2,895 Part 1 crimes. The year following the injunction revealed 2,120 Part 1 crimes. The reported difference the year after the injunction was 775 fewer Part 1 crimes, a 26.8% decrease. The year before for the control revealed 1,447 Part 1 crimes. The year following for the control revealed 1,400 Part 1 crimes. The reported difference the year after the injunction was 47 fewer Part 1 crimes, a 3.2% decrease.

Case/Pair 25: Colonia Chiques and Southside Chiques: Part 2 Crime

Part 2 before and after for Colonia Chiques: The year before the injunction revealed 3,500 Part 2 crimes. The year following the injunction revealed 2,100 Part 2 crimes. The reported difference the year after the injunction was 1,400 fewer Part 2 crimes, a 40% decrease.

Part 2 before and after for Southside Chiques: The year before the injunction revealed 2,200 Part 2 crimes. The year following the injunction revealed 2,300 Part 2 crimes. The reported difference the year after the injunction was 100 more Part 2 crimes, a 4.5% increase.

Case/Pair 25: Colonia Chiques and Southside Chiques: Total Calls

Calls for service before and after for Colonia Chiques: The year before the injunction revealed 12,500 total calls for service. The year following the injunction revealed 8,600 calls for service. The reported difference the year after the injunction was 3,900 fewer calls, a 31.2% decrease.

Calls for service for Southside Chiques: The year before the injunction revealed 6,450 total calls for service. The year following the injunction revealed 6,500 calls for service. The reported difference the year after the injunction was 50 more calls, a 0.8% increase.

Compare Injunction and Control for Part 1 Crime

The average number of Part 1 crimes for the injunction areas preinjunction was 788.7. The average number of Part 1 crimes postinjunction was 568.8. The average difference was 219.8 fewer Part 1 calls or a 27.9% decrease in Part 1 crime. The average number of Part 1 crimes for the control areas preinjunction was 615.5. The average number of Part 1 crimes postinjunction was 621.1. The average difference was 5.6 more Part 1 calls or a 0.9% increase.

Summary of Part 1 Crime

Part 1 crime was reduced in the injunction areas and increased slightly in the control areas. The findings indicate that Part 1 crime for both the injunction area and the control areas combined averaged 1,404.2 the year before and 1,190 the year after the injunctions.

Compare Injunction and Control for Part 2 Crime

The average number of Part 2 crimes for the injunction areas preinjunction was 1,980.5. The average number of Part 2 crimes postinjunction was 1,338.8. The average difference was 641.8 fewer Part 2 calls or a 32.4% decrease. The average number of Part 2 crimes for the control areas preinjunction was 1,604.4. The average number of Part 2 crimes postinjunction was 1,592. The average difference was 12.4 fewer Part 2 calls or a 0.8% decrease.

Summary of Part 2 Crime

Total Part 2 crime was reduced in both the injunction and control areas, with the decrease being much more significant in the injunction areas than in the control areas. The findings indicate that Part 2 crime for both the injunction area and the control areas combined averaged 3,584.9 the year before and 2,930.8 the year after the injunctions.

Compare Injunction and Control for Total Calls

The average number of total calls for the injunction areas preinjunction was 6,015.2. The average number of total calls postinjunction was 4,446.7. The average difference was 1,568.5 fewer calls or a 26.1% decrease. The average number of total calls for the control areas preinjunction was 5,418. The average number of total calls postinjunction was 5,514.6. The average difference was 96.6 more calls or a 1.8% increase.

Summary of Total Calls

Total calls for police service decreased in the injunction areas and increased slightly in the control areas. The findings indicate that the total number of calls for both the injunction area and the control areas combined averaged 11,433.2 preinjunction and 9,961.3 postinjunction, a difference of 1,471.9 calls or a 12.9% decrease.

Policy or Political Differences That May Have Impacted the Results

Policy and political differences may play a role in gang injunction efficacy, especially when looking at the county breakdown analysis. For example, in San Diego County, where gang injunctions include only named defendants, the injunctions seem to have a higher level of efficacy when compared to Los Angeles, for example, where the gang is oftentimes the only named defendants with members added at a subsequent date. In addition, variations in gang ethnicity and gang size also have political implications that may impact results.

9

Police Officers from 25 Gang Injunction Areas Surveyed

Why an injunction is more or less effective when compared to another is an interesting question. This police officer survey sought to expand upon the research study in Chapter 8, in which 25 injunctions were evaluated and compared against control gangs to further understand why, or why not, the injunctions were effective. This survey questioned police officers who work gangs in the 25 gang injunction area jurisdictions evaluated in the multicounty analysis in Chapter 8 during the same time period. This survey explored what the police officers tasked with enforcement of a specific injunction believe helps or does not help make gang injunctions more effective, and more importantly, what variables impacted the specific injunctions evaluated.

SURVEY METHODS

A 20-question survey of gang unit police officers (n = 93) further explored dimensions of the 25 gang injunctions evaluated, including gang size, proportion of gang covered, whether leaders were named targets covered by the injunction, turf size, turf zoning, economic status of the area, gang mobility, type of injunction, and enforcement issues, such as average police response time. The survey was given to attempt to further explain what makes a particular gang injunction more or less effective, in the opinion of the police officers that work in each of the 25 gang injunction areas.

The survey items were viewed independently, with the p-value threshold modified using the strict Bonferroni correction. Given that this portion of the research was purely exploratory and not inferential (like with pretest–posttest with matched controls to determine whether injunctions work), treating items independently and then correcting for multiple comparisons seemed to be an appropriate approach for this survey.

I also choose to approach the outcomes or differences among survey responses to some of the questions in other ways. One approach was to categorize injunctions as successful or unsuccessful based on the primary quantitative analysis of gang injunctions. This made the outcome binary, successful or unsuccessful, and a table of frequencies was created using categorical statistics to determine whether certain survey responses were associated with successful outcomes. This approach used the cross tabs feature of SPSS to generate the necessary statistics. The advantage of cross tabs helped determine if there was any disproportionality in how the frequencies were spread across cells in the table. The method used is chi-square analysis. If the chi is significant, then the correlation becomes interesting, because a significant correlation in cross tabs identifies if any disproportionality was systematic. That allowed for evaluation of the tables and the relationship between survey responses and outcome. Survey item findings are categorical, so they were expressed as frequencies and percentages for each response item.

To determine whether these survey item responses were related to injunction outcomes, these data were split into response categories, then contrasted vs. whether the injunction was successful or unsuccessful. For these purposes, success was operationally defined as a net drop in Part 1 calls. If an injunction did not demonstrate a net drop in Part 1 calls, either because there was no change from preinjunction levels or because crime increased in that injunction area, this was categorized as less Part 1 crime (21 of 25 cases).

Once injunction success outcome was been determined, these data were entered into cross tabs in SPSS. Cross tabs provided both the table of frequencies per response split by injunction success or nonsuccess, and provided the necessary statistical output to make specific determinations. To determine whether the split of response × outcome was significantly different than expected chance proportions, the chi-square statistics were calculated. A statistically significant chi-square ($p < .05$) was interpreted as evidence that the data were not distributed equally (proportionately).

If data were disproportionately distributed, as indicated by a significant chi-square, the Pearson correlation indicated whether this pattern was systematic. In other words, the chi-square tells us the unevenness and the correlation and tells us if the unevenness is systematic. A statistically significant Pearson correlation, in conjunction with viewing the frequencies and proportions in the cross tabs table, was used to demonstrate any significant relationships between survey items and injunction outcomes. The use of cross tabs allowed for an exploratory analysis of the specific hypothesis for each survey question to evaluate if any significant relationship exists between each survey hypothesis and injunction success or a percent change in Part 1 crime.

INJUNCTION EFFECTIVENESS

When discussing gang injunction effectiveness, or the effectiveness of any enforcement-driven policy, it is widely acknowledged that the primary category impacting the level of effectiveness between injunction efforts is the ability or willingness of the police to enforce the orders. A gang injunction is a worthless piece of paper if the law enforcement jurisdictions involved do not enforce the order. To identify law enforcement attitudes and perceptions of gang injunction initiatives, stage 3 of this research, a survey of police officers, was conducted to identify potential categories that may impact gang injunction effectiveness.

Police officers are the ones on the street tasked with enforcing the orders, and as such, they are often in the best position to identify the potential factors that can aid or hinder a gang injunction's impact on a particular community. The police officer survey was designed to evaluate eight primary categories that may impact changes in the levels of effectiveness from one injunction effort to the other. The following is a brief overview of the eight categories addressed by the police survey to evaluate gang injunction effectiveness.

One goal of this book was to identify other potential enforcement operations or community programs that may have impacted the effectiveness of the 25 injunctions evaluated. If the injunction is a component of a broader program, gang injunction effectiveness may be influenced by the goals of the broader program. An injunction implemented as a standalone program provides one form of intervention that may only address the symptoms of the gang problem, and any impact is likely to be relatively short in duration. As part of a broader program designed to give defendants some alternatives to gang membership, injunctions may work in concert with other interventions to address the causes of gang activity.

It is hoped that these insights will lead to a greater understanding of which dimensions predict gang injunction effectiveness and optimize future injunctions. These insights are exploratory in nature and may lead to a greater understanding of gang injunction effectiveness. It is hoped that the findings will serve to formulate cogent recommendations to be considered for future injunctions.

At the time of the survey, the officers revealed the presence of at least 122 gang injunctions (filed, attempted, denied, dismissed, or pending) against at least 146 different gangs. All California injunctions to date combined targeted at least 7,394 gang members and resulted in at least 2,294 arrests. The total geographical area of all the filed gang injunctions covers at least 170 square miles of the state's 155,959 total square miles. That equates to about 0.01% of the state's total area being impacted by a gang injunction.

SURVEY DESIGN

The survey was a cross-sectional random effects study because it represented only one slice of the total gang injunction population, and it did not control any aspects of the population. This research did not assign officers to groups or to the treatment, and did not assign gang injunctions to particular gangs.

SURVEY TARGET POPULATION/PARTICIPANTS

The population from which the sample was drawn for the police officer survey required that each participant was a police officer, as defined by California Penal Code Section 830.1. Each officer worked in a full-time capacity as a law enforcement officer in one of the gang injunction areas evaluated in this research, including those studied in San Diego, San Bernardino, Los Angeles, and Ventura counties.

Those police officers were asked to provide information as to how some gangs, gang members, and gang injunctions exist in their respective jurisdictions. The California Commission on Peace Officer Standards of Training (POST) has compiled a listing of all California law enforcement agencies and the total number of sworn police officers who work for each agency. Those data were used to identify the agencies in order to request that their officers complete the survey, as well as to determine the ratio of gang members to police officers.

The procedure used in this research consisted of a nonprobability sample, specifically a convenience sample. Based upon each member of the sample population not having an equal chance of being selected, a probability sample would not be applicable. The sampling frame or list of names was requested from each agency to be surveyed. A contact person at each agency was selected and asked to help identify those officers tasked with investigating gangs. They were requested to help facilitate getting the surveys distributed to their officers and allow them the time to complete surveys. The Los Angeles Police Department, for example, requires command level approval before allowing its officers to complete surveys. The contact person from each agency was asked to collect the completed surveys if distributed in paper form, and facilitate their return so they could be included in the study, or direct their officers to the Internet link to complete the survey online.

The goal of this research was to survey all of the officers working in the injunction areas that have some nexus to gang enforcement. For example, the survey did not request input from traffic accident investigators or child abuse investigators if they did not have frequent contacts with the gangs within their jurisdictions.

SAMPLE

Ninety-three (n = 93) police officers in the areas covered by the 25 injunctions included in the foundational research were selected from the jurisdictions of the cases that this research evaluated to establish a one-to-one correspondence between the primary quantitative analysis and the survey.

The police officer survey was created for this research to further explain the results of the primary quantitative analysis. The survey instrument consisted of 20 questions and was formatted and administered in two ways: by utilizing an Internet survey service, and in person. It was deemed very important to keep the survey short, as most police agencies require the survey be manageable to allow the officers to take the survey before or after a police officer's shift or during a preshift briefing.

This research primarily used surveymonkey.com to deliver a reliable survey that could be administered in a consistent manner. Survey Monkey was selected as the best method because it allows the researcher to administer a blinded study, making it impossible to know the name of the police officer who provided the information. It uses codes to make sure the experimenter cannot match up the data with the survey participant. The blinded survey is important so law enforcement officers can express their true feelings without fear that any negative or unpopular opinions would have any impact on them. The survey addressed the eight categories or concepts outlined in Chapter 1, including police response, other enforcement or programs, type of gang, type of gang members, type of activity, type of area, type of order, and maintenance of the order. To further ensure the survey was a valid measure, it was distributed to select university faculty members and the research committee for their review. This allowed the researcher to make sure that the questions asked address the categories being measured and could be easily understood.

SURVEY WAS PILOTED

To further ensure reliability of the survey it was piloted or administered to a group of 10 police officers in two cities where several injunctions have been obtained (San Diego and National City).

This research allowed one week to pass, and then administered the same survey to the same officers to see if the results were reliable over time. The officers used in the reliability survey were not part of the later study and were utilized solely to test the survey instrument created for this study. Any confusing or unreliable questions were modified to make the results more reliable before being distributed to the identified participants.

SURVEY DATA COLLECTION PROCEDURES

The data for this research were gathered using the survey questionnaire that was administered to each police department that has had exposure to one of the gang injunctions evaluated in the primary quantitative portion of this study. The officers had the option to complete the survey online via an Internet survey service, have the survey mailed to a predetermined point of contact at each respective agency, or to complte it in person. Return postage was provided for those agencies in areas not conducive for surveys being personally collected. The bulk of the officers surveyed via paper were from San Diego County. San Bernardino, Los Angeles, and Ventura Counties completed the online survey or the survey was administered via mail. The results of the survey were collected and the data are represented in this chapter.

The survey items are mostly categorical, but some are ordinal scales. Issues like whether the injunction is a good use of time, or who initiated the injunction, can be made into a list of survey items that are categorical in nature. The area in square city blocks is an ordinal scale, because the lower categories represent smaller injunctions and the highest categories represent large injunctions. Ordinal means that each successive category is larger, for example, like lining up kids from tallest to shortest.

CONNECTING THE SURVEY TO THE CASE STUDIES

In order to make absolutely sure the police officers taking the survey would feel confident that their responses would be confidential if they chose to keep them that way, to encourage honest responses, the survey could be taken online and the officer could choose not to give his or her name. This was critical in the research because a police officer may feel that his responses may get back to his supervisor, and could be used against him if his opinion

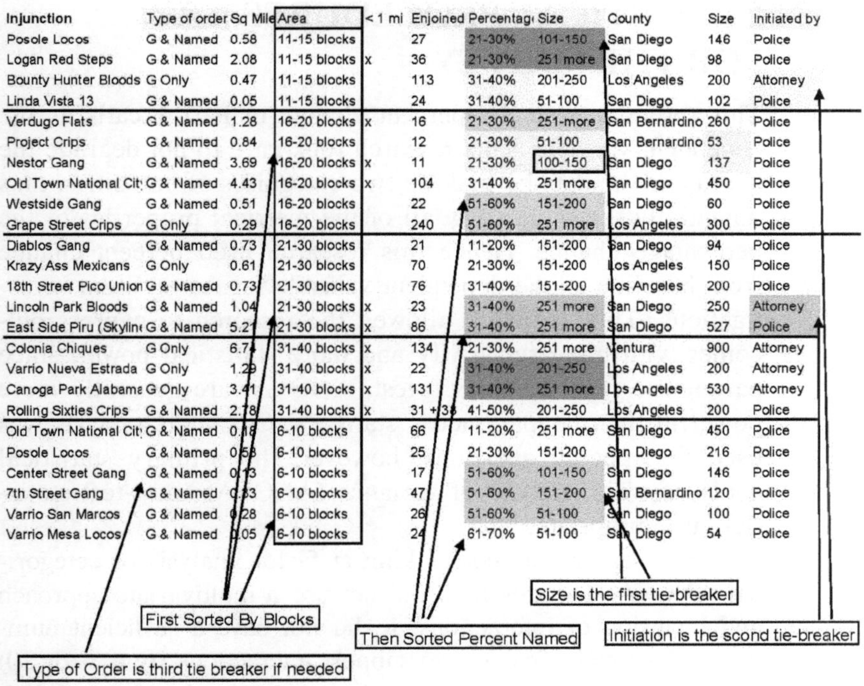

Injunction	Type of order	Sq Mile	Area	< 1 mi	Enjoined	Percentage	Size	County	Size	Initiated by
Posole Locos	G & Named	0.58	11-15 blocks		27	21-30%	101-150	San Diego	146	Police
Logan Red Steps	G & Named	2.08	11-15 blocks	x	36	21-30%	251 more	San Diego	98	Police
Bounty Hunter Bloods	G Only	0.47	11-15 blocks		113	31-40%	201-250	Los Angeles	200	Attorney
Linda Vista 13	G & Named	0.05	11-15 blocks		24	31-40%	51-100	San Diego	102	Police
Verdugo Flats	G & Named	1.28	16-20 blocks	x	16	21-30%	251-more	San Bernardino	260	Police
Project Crips	G & Named	0.84	16-20 blocks		12	21-30%	51-100	San Bernardino	53	Police
Nestor Gang	G & Named	3.69	16-20 blocks	x	11	21-30%	100-150	San Diego	137	Police
Old Town National Cit	G & Named	4.43	16-20 blocks	x	104	31-40%	251 more	San Diego	450	Police
Westside Gang	G & Named	0.51	16-20 blocks		22	51-60%	151-200	San Diego	60	Police
Grape Street Crips	G Only	0.29	16-20 blocks		240	51-60%	251 more	Los Angeles	300	Police
Diablos Gang	G & Named	0.73	21-30 blocks		21	11-20%	151-200	San Diego	94	Police
Krazy Ass Mexicans	G Only	0.61	21-30 blocks		70	21-30%	151-200	Los Angeles	150	Police
18th Street Pico Union	G & Named	0.73	21-30 blocks		76	31-40%	151-200	Los Angeles	200	Police
Lincoln Park Bloods	G & Named	1.04	21-30 blocks	x	23	31-40%	251 more	San Diego	250	Attorney
East Side Piru (Skylin	G & Named	5.21	21-30 blocks	x	86	31-40%	251 more	San Diego	527	Police
Colonia Chiques	G Only	6.74	31-40 blocks	x	134	21-30%	251 more	Ventura	900	Attorney
Varrio Nueva Estrada	G Only	1.29	31-40 blocks	x	22	31-40%	201-250	Los Angeles	200	Attorney
Canoga Park Alabama	G Only	3.41	31-40 blocks	x	131	31-40%	251 more	Los Angeles	530	Attorney
Rolling Sixties Crips	G & Named	2.78	31-40 blocks	x	31 + 38	41-50%	201-250	Los Angeles	200	Police
Old Town National Cit	G & Named	0.18	6-10 blocks		66	11-20%	251 more	San Diego	450	Police
Posole Locos	G & Named	0.58	6-10 blocks		25	21-30%	151-200	San Diego	216	Police
Center Street Gang	G & Named	0.13	6-10 blocks		17	51-60%	101-150	San Diego	146	Police
7th Street Gang	G & Named	0.33	6-10 blocks		47	51-60%	151-200	San Bernardino	120	Police
Varrio San Marcos	G & Named	0.28	6-10 blocks		26	51-60%	51-100	San Diego	100	Police
Varrio Mesa Locos	G & Named	0.05	6-10 blocks		24	61-70%	51-100	San Diego	54	Police

FIGURE 9.1 Researchers can use survey data to link survey participants to their injunction.

differed from the view of his supervisor or department. For this reason, some of the 93 officers did opt to not identify themselves, and they were matched to the specific injunction via other means to make sure they were free to be as honest as possible. Upon completion of the police officer surveys, the surveys were matched to corresponding injunctions. This was done by evaluating the survey items relating to the demography of each injunction, including the size of the injunction in blocks of area, the percentage of blocks named in the injunction, the type of order, the number of gang members in the gang, and who initiated the injunction. This allowed the researcher to uniquely identify the survey participants to their injunctions without compromising the identity of the survey participant (Figure 9.1).

Any survey that was ambiguous regarding injunction identification, if any, was compared to the time stamp provided by Survey Monkey for each participant, and compared to the date of mailings to specific police stations participating in this proposed study. The data provided within the survey output was sufficient for identifying with some certainty which surveys came from which injunctions. If the survey participant could not be connected to a specific gang injunction, the survey was removed from the study and the process and procedures were explained in the results chapter.

STATISTICAL PROCEDURES FOR THE SURVEY

This research used the percent change in Part 1 calls as the dependent variable. This research took care to not degrade the quality of the data by making two categories of outcomes, thus potentially throwing away all of the metrical properties of the percentage change. Hence this research used percent change from baseline as the dependent variable for survey item investigations. This approach allowed the research to express outcomes with more sensitivity and more statistical power, since parametric type statistics (t-test, ANOVA) are generally more powerful than nonparametric statistics. Cross tab analysis was used for specific questions; however, the primary statistical analyses were analysis of variance (ANOVA) and t-test statistics, as appropriate.

This research was not looking at factor analysis or categorical ANOVA. This research did not use a multivariate approach and inclusion of interactions. It did not have a sufficient number of degrees of freedom to support interactions from 8 (or 20) categories. If this research found statistically significant differences between responses on a particular item, that difference was described in tables, and provided the p-value for the rarity of that difference vs. pure chance.

This research took into account that making so many independent tests may inflate the overall false alarm error rate (type 1 error), so the solution to this problem was to correct for making multiple comparisons. The survey analysis made 20 comparisons; thus a Bonferroni alpha-splitting correction shifts the alpha threshold for statistical significance from .05 to .0025 (.05 split by 20). In these comparisons, the calculated p-value stays the same but the threshold is shifted. To avoid unnecessary confusion, this research will report the outcome versus both thresholds.

DATA ANALYSIS

The findings are presented in tables and graphs, including frequencies, percentages, means, standard deviations, analysis of variance, and ranges, as appropriate. To test the hypothesis that gang injunctions "work" in reducing crime, calls for service postinjunction were subtracted from the calls for service preinjunction. This change in calls for service in the injunction areas was compared to data from the matched control areas using ANOVA. If the injunction areas demonstrate a statistically significant decrease from preinjunction levels, and if the injunction areas demonstrate significantly fewer calls for service, this was interpreted as empirical support for the effectiveness of gang injunctions.

Lastly, because of the possible impact of important variables in determining the effectiveness of injunctions, each of the ANOVA statistics was repeated, including economic, social, and other demographic variables. This step was taken to ensure that any positive effects of gang injunctions cannot be argued to be due exclusively to these extraneous categories. Differences were considered statistically significant at $p < .05$. The terms *successful* and *unsuccessful* were used to relate the first part of the study, the analysis of 25 injunctions, to the second part, the police officer survey, to further explain the results.

Of the 25 injunctions reviewed, 4 did not have a direct reduction in Part 1 crime from baseline; they include pairs 2, 6, 7, and 9, respectively. That is not to say these injunctions have not been a benefit for the communities in which they were implemented, but to say they were less effective than the other 21 that had reductions at baseline for Part 1 crime only. These injunctions did have direct benefits when looking at Part 2 crimes and total calls to varying degrees.

LIMITATIONS

Any good study identifies the potential weaknesses of the study and the bounds of the study. This research evaluated the effectiveness of gang injunctions as a method of reducing crime and improving the quality of life for residents in a limited area. One limitation of this study is that the attitudes and perceptions about gang injunctions from the point of view of the community and gang members were not the primary focus. This research focused on the point of view from a law enforcement perspective because that is one area of the total existing research that is weak, as no studies have been done to evaluate law enforcement perceptions relating to gang injunctions.

POLICE OFFICER SURVEY RESULTS

Each of the 20 questions was evaluated to determine which factors may or may not impact gang injunction success. Each of the 20 questions addresses an aspect of one of the eight primary categories evaluated and discussed throughout this research. Being that this research has revealed that gang injunctions do in fact reduce crime in the areas they are implemented, the police officer survey compares and contrasts some of the different categories or factors that may be related to the research question and gang injunction effectiveness.

Description of Participant Demography

A total of 93 (n = 93) police officers completed the survey. Utilizing www.surveymonkey.com as a link to the participants as well as face-to-face meetings with officers, this research was able to reach officers working in each of the gang injunction areas evaluated in the primary quantitative analysis portion of this research.

Results Survey Question 1: Making an Arrest for a Gang Injunction Violation Is an Effective Use of My Time?

92.4% of all officers surveyed feel that making an arrest for a gang injunction violation is a worthwhile use of their time, 4.8% feel that it is not worth their time, 1.9% said they did not know, and 1% said yes and no, depends on circumstances—good leverage tool, but felt it could be bad because it relocates them to areas where you can no longer find them. The hypothesis for this question is that an answer of yes will result in more effective injunctions than an answer of no (Y > N).

Results Survey Question 2: Gang Injunction Violations Are Responded to in Which Manner in My Jurisdiction?

Of 93 participants who completed the survey, 86 reported knowing the response speed to the injunction within their jurisdiction; 70 were from jurisdictions that respond quickly to injunction violation (81.4%), 12 were from jurisdictions that respond slowly to injunction violation (14.0%), and 4 were from jurisdictions that do not respond to injunction violations (4.7%). Seven either didn't respond or reported that they did not know. Comparing fast vs. slow response, participants reported fast response (70 of 82, 85.6%) significantly more than slow response ($p < .0000000001$, sign test), suggesting that most injunction violations are responded to quickly rather than slowly.

Cross tabs of response speed and injunction success are displayed in Tables 9.1 and 9.2. Of 15 participants from the four unsuccessful injunctions evaluated in this research, 13 (86.7%) reported quick response and 2 (13.3%) reported slow response. Of 71 participants from successful injunctions, 57 (80.3%) reported quick response, 10 (14.1%) reported slow response, and 4 (5.6%) reported no response to injunction violations. This proportionality was not statistically significant by chi-square, χ^2 (degrees of freedom = 2) = 0.9, $p = .63$, or by Pearson correlation, $r = .09$, $p = .42$. These findings suggest that response speed frequencies were not represented disproportionately across injunction success, and that there was no systematic relationship between response speed and injunction success.

Because chi-square assumes an expected minimum frequency of five per cell, the analysis of violation response speed and

TABLE 9.1

Survey Question 2: Cross Tabs of Enforcement Speed and Injunction Success

Speed of Enforcement	Successful Injunction	Not Successful	Total
Not enforced	4		4
Slow	10	2	12
Quick	57	13	70
Total	71	15	86

Note: Three cells have expected counts less than 5, which may render chi-square unstable.

injunction success was repeated, including "not enforced" (n = 4) with slow response to create a new category of "slow response or not enforced" (n = 16). Quick response remained n = 70. This reduction transformed the data into a 2 × 2 arrangement.

Similar to the primary analysis, successful injunctions were associated with an 80.3% quick response to violations, and unsuccessful injunctions were associated with an 86.7% quick response. This proportionality was not statistically significant, (degrees of freedom = 1) = 0.3, $p = .56$, and these data showed no statistically significant correlation, r = .06, $p = .57$.

Summary of Response Speed and Injunction Success

Most participants (~80%) reported quick response to injunction violations, but these data provide no statistically significant evidence that supports a relationship between response speed and injunction success. The hypothesis for this question was that a quick response to a gang injunction violation would result in greater effectiveness than a slow response, which would have a greater level of effectiveness than no response (Q > S > N). Using cross tabs as the statistical method, no statistically significant evidence of a relationship between response speed and injunction success was identified.

TABLE 9.2

Survey Question 2: Reduced Cross Tabs of Speed and Injunction Success

	Successful Injunction	Not Successful	Total
Slow or not enforced	14	2	16
Quick	57	13	70
Total	71	15	86

Results Survey Question 3: If Aware of the Presence of an Injunction, Was the Injunction Part of a Larger Intervention or Enforcement Program?

Of 93 participants who completed the survey, 80 reported knowing whether their injunction was part of a larger intervention; 47 were from injunctions that were part of a larger intervention (58.8%), and 33 were from injunctions that were not part of a larger intervention (41.3%). This difference was not statistically significant (sign test, $p = .15$).

Part of a Larger Intervention and Injunction Success

Cross tabs of part of a larger intervention and injunction success are displayed in Table 9.3. Of 13 participants from unsuccessful injunctions, 6 (46.2%) were part of a larger intervention and 7 (53.8%) were not part of a larger intervention. Of 67 participants from successful injunctions, 41 (61.2%) were part of a larger intervention and 26 (38.8%) were not part of a larger intervention. This proportionality in frequencies was not statistically significant, (degrees of freedom = 1) = 1.0, $p = .31$, and there was no statistically significant correlation between variables ($r = .11$, $p = .32$). These findings suggest no significant relationship between injunction success and being part of a larger intervention or enforcement program. The hypothesis for this question is that a yes response, indicating the presence of a larger intervention program, will have more effectiveness than a no response (Y > N).

Results Survey Question 4: If Yes to Question 3, What Were the Goals of the Larger Program?

35.1% of all officers surveyed stated that gang sweeps were done in connection with the injunction, 17.5% said increased uniformed patrol, 8.8% said task force involvement, 1.8% said wire taps, 22.8% said gang intervention programs, 1.8% said gang education programs, 3.5% said community redevelopment. 8.8% provided other information, including the goal of reducing violence in the city; assisting in gang members' identification, gang tracking, and

TABLE 9.3
Cross Tabs: Part of a Larger Intervention and Injunction Success

Part of a Larger Intervention?	Successful Injunction	Not Successful	Total
No	26	7	33
Yes	41	6	47
Total	67	13	80

enforcement, and the implementation of a gang unit; and lower crime rates at specific locations, or that they did not know the overall goals. Forty-eight officers skipped this question. The hypothesis for this question is that a yes response, indicating the presence of a larger intervention program, will have more than a no response (Y > N).

Results Survey Question 5: What Is the Size of the Gang You Targeted with the Injunction?

Of 93 participants who completed the survey, 88 reported knowing the size of the gang within their injunction, 11 reported the gang size to be less than 50 members (12.5%), 22 reported the gang size as 51–100 members (25%), 16 reported the gang size as 101–150 members (18.2%), 11 reported the gang size as 151–200 members (12.5%), 6 reported the gang size as 201–250 members, and 22 reported a gang size of over 250 members (31.8%).

Gang Size and Injunction Success

Gang sizes by injunction success frequencies are displayed in Table 9.4. To foster the assumptions of chi-square statistics, the data analyzed were split into larger gang membership and smaller gang membership groups. Four splits were made: over 250 members vs. 250 or fewer members, over 200 members vs. 200 or fewer members, over 150 members vs. 150 or fewer members, and over 100 members vs. 100 or fewer members. For each split, the cross tabs are presented, along with chi-square and correlation statistics, including p-values.

TABLE 9.4
Cross Tabs: Gang Size and Injunction Success

Gang Size	Successful Injunction	Not Successful	Total
Less than 50	8	3	11
51–100	21	1	22
101–150	14	2	16
151–200	9	2	11
201–250	6		6
Over 250	16	6	22
Total	74	14	88

Note: Six cells have expected counts less than 5, which may render chi-square unstable.

TABLE 9.5

Cross Tabs: Gang Size of 250 or More and Injunction Success

	Successful Injunction	Not Successful	Total
250 or fewer	58	8	66
More than 250	16	6	22
Total	74	14	88

Gangs of 250 or More and Injunction Success

Cross tabs of gang size (split at 250 members) and injunction success are displayed in Table 9.5. Of 14 participants from unsuccessful injunctions, 6 (42.9%) were gang size of over 250 members, compared to 16 of 74 participants (21.6%) from successful injunctions. This difference was not statistically significant, but it trended toward statistical significance, (degrees of freedom = 1) = 2.8, $p = .09$. Similarly, Pearson correlation (.17, p = .09) and Spearman rho correlation (.17, $p = .09$) each trended toward statistical significance.

Gangs of 200 or More and Injunction Success

Cross tabs of gang size (split at 200 members) and injunction success are displayed in Table 9.6. Of 14 participants from unsuccessful injunctions, 6 (42.9%) were gang size of over 250 members, compared to 22 of 74 participants (29.7%) from successful injunctions. This difference was not statistically significant, (degrees of freedom = 1) = 0.9, $p = .33$. Pearson correlation (.10, $p = .34$) and Spearman rho correlation (.10, $p = .34$) were not statistically significant.

Gangs of 150 or More and Injunction Success

Cross tabs of gang size (split at 150 members) and injunction success are displayed in Table 9.7. Of 14 participants from unsuccessful injunctions, 8 (57.1%) were gang size of over 250 members, compared to 31 of 74 participants (41.8%) from successful injunctions.

TABLE 9.6

Cross Tabs: Gang Size of 200 or More and Injunction Success

	Successful Injunction	Not Successful	Total
200 or fewer	52	8	60
More than 200	22	6	28
Total	74	14	88

TABLE 9.7
Cross Tabs: Gang Size of 150 or More and Injunction Success

	Successful Injunction	Not Successful	Total
150 or fewer	43	6	49
More than 150	31	8	39
Total	74	14	88

This difference was not statistically significant, (degrees of freedom = 1) = 1.1, $p = .29$. Pearson correlation (.11, $p = .30$) and Spearman rho correlation (.11, $p = .30$) were not statistically significant.

Gangs of 100 or More and Injunction Success

Cross tabs of gang size (split at 100 members) and injunction success are displayed in Table 9.8. Of 14 participants from unsuccessful injunctions, 10 (71.4%) were gang size of over 250 members, compared to 45 of 74 participants (60.1%) from successful injunctions. This difference was not statistically significant, (degrees of freedom = 1) = 0.5, $p = .45$. Pearson correlation (.08, $p = .46$) and Spearman rho correlation (.08, $p = .46$) were not statistically significant.

Summary of Gang Size and Injunction Success

Gangs were well spread in size, with gangs as small as 50 or fewer members (12.5%) up to gangs of over 250 members (31.8%) within the participant's injunction. There was no statistically significant relationship between gang size and injunction success, but splitting gangs at 250 members provided a statistical trend (p = .09), indicating more injunction success with smaller gang size. The hypothesis for this question is that a smaller gang size was more effective than a large gang size (S > L).

TABLE 9.8
Cross Tabs: Gang Size of 100 or More and Injunction Success

	Successful Injunction	Not Successful	Total
100 or fewer	29	4	33
More than 100	45	10	55
Total	74	14	88

TABLE 9.9
Cross Tabs: Percent Named in the Injunction vs. Injunction Success

Percent Named	Successful Injunction	Not Successful	Total
Unsure	5	1	6
1–10%	7	1	8
11–20%	11	1	12
21–30%	12	3	15
31–40%	13	4	17
41–50%	11		11
51–60%	8	2	10
61–70%	4		4
71–80%	3		3
81–90%	4		4
91–100%	3	3	
Total	78	15	93

Results Survey Question 6: What Percentage of the Overall Gang Size Was Actually Named in the Injunction or Later Served with the Injunction?

All 93 participants who completed the survey provided a percentage of gang members named in the injunction. These percentages along with injunction success frequencies are displayed in Table 9.9. Data were well spread across percentage of gang members named in the injunction, ranging from 91–100% (3 of 93) to 10% or less (8 of 93). The most common intervals were 31–40% (17 of 93) and 21–30% (15 of 93). Each decile interval was represented by at least three respondents. Six of 93 respondents were not sure of the percentage of gang members named in their injunction.

To foster the assumptions of chi-square statistics, these data were split into two groups: over 50% named in the injunction vs. 50% or fewer named in the injunction. Sixty-three of 87 responses were from injunctions with less than 50%, and 24 of 87 were from injunctions with more than 50% of the gang named in the injunction (see Table 9.10). This difference was statistically significant ($p < .0001$, sign test). This finding suggests that most of the respondents were from injunctions with less than 50% of the gang members named in the injunction.

Summary of Percentage of Gang Served and Success

Of 14 participants from unsuccessful injunctions, 9 (63.4%) were from injunctions with less than 50% of the gang named in the injunction, compared to 54 of 73 participants (74.0%) from

TABLE 9.10
Reduced Cross Tabs: Percent Named in the Injunction vs. Injunction Success

Percent of Gang Named	Successful Injunction	Not Successful	Total
Less than 50%	54	9	63
More than 50%	19	5	24
Total	73	14	87

successful injunctions. This difference was not statistically significant, (degrees of freedom = 1) = 0.6, p =.46. Pearson correlation (.08, p = .46) and Spearman rho correlation (.08, p = .46) were not statistically significant. The finding provides no clear evidence of a relationship between the percentage of the gang named in the injunction and injunction success. The hypothesis for this question is that the larger the percentage of the gang that is targeted, the more effective the gang injunction will be (L > S).

Results Survey Question 7: Were the Gang Leaders Targeted with the Injunction?

Of 93 participants who completed the survey, 88 reported knowing whether their injunction targeted the leaders of the gang, 80 were from injunctions that did target the gang's leadership (90.9%), and 8 were from injunctions that did not target the leadership (9.1%). This difference was statistically significant (sign test, p < .0000000000000001). Most injunctions targeted leaders.

Summary of Leaders Targeted and Injunction Success

Of 14 participants from the four unsuccessful injunctions, 13 (92.9%) were from injunctions with the leaders named in them, compared to 67 of 74 participants (90.5%) from successful

TABLE 9.11
Cross Tabs: Leader Targeted in the Injunction and Injunction Success

Leader Targeted?	Successful Injunction	Not Successful	Total
No	7	1	8
Yes	67	13	80
Total	74	14	88

injunctions. This difference was not statistically significant, (degrees of freedom = 1) = 0.1, $p = .79$. Pearson correlation (.03, $p = .79$) and Spearman rho correlation (.03, $p = .79$) were not statistically significant. The finding provides no clear evidence of a relationship between naming the gang leader in the injunction and injunction success. The hypothesis for this question is that a yes response, indicating the leaders of the gang were targeted, will have more effectiveness than a no response (Y > N).

Results Survey Question 8: The Gangs in My Jurisdiction Are Territorial and Have Well-Defined Borders That They Actively Defend Against Rivals

87.5% of all officers said yes, 8.3% of all officers said no, and 2.1% of officers said they did not know. Nine officers failed to answer this question. The hypothesis for this question is that a yes response, indicating the gang is territorial, will have more effectiveness than a no response (Y > N).

Results Survey Question 9: Was the Activity That Originally Brought the Gang Problems in the Injunction Part 1 Crime?

81.2% said yes, 4.2% said no, and 14.6% said they do not know. Nine officers skipped this question. The hypothesis for this question is that a yes response, indicating the gang engages in Part 1 crime, will have more effectiveness than a no response (P1 > P2).

Results Survey Question 10: Gang Crime in My Jurisdiction Is Committed by Gang Members Working as Individuals Rather Than Working Together as a Group

8.4% of officers said always, 58.9% said sometimes, 29.5% said almost never, and 3.2% said never. Ten officers did not answer the question. The hypothesis for this question is that a yes response, indicating the gang commits crime as a collective group, will have more effectiveness than a no response (Y > N).

Results Survey Question 11: What Is the Size of the Gang Turf of the Gang You Targeted with the Injunction?

3.3% of officers said 1 to 5 square city blocks, 17.4% said 6 to 10 square city blocks, 15.2% said 11 to 15 square city blocks, 27.2% said 16 to 20 square city blocks, 15.2% said 21 to 30 square city blocks, 14.1% said 31 to 40 square city blocks, and 7.6% added comments that included they were not sure or did not know, the injunction covered a couple of specific beats, or the injunction covered the entire city area. The hypothesis for this question is that a smaller area will be more effective than a larger area (S > L).

Results Survey Question 12: What Percentage of the Total Gang's Turf Was Made Part of the Gang Injunction Target Area?

21.7% of officers said the injunction covered the entire turf of the enjoined gang, 31.5% said ¾ or more of the entire gang turf, 23.9% said over ½ of the gang's turf, 18.5% said ¼ of the gang's turf, 1.1% less than 5% of the gang's turf, and 3.3% said they were unsure or did not know. Thirteen officers skipped this question. The hypothesis for this question is that the larger the percentage of the gang's turf that is enjoined, the greater the effectiveness of the injunction (L > S).

Results Survey Question 13: What Is the General Economic Status of the Gang Injunction Area?

81.9% of officers described the area as being in poverty, 17% described the area as middle class, and 1.1% of officers described the target area as affluent. Eleven officers skipped this question. The hypothesis for this question is that a gang injunction will be more effective in a poverty-stricken area than in a middle-class area, and a middle-class area will be more effective than an affluent area (P > M > A).

Results Survey Question 14: What Best Describes the Zoning in the Target Area?

24.5% of all officers said the gang injunction area was all residential, 4.3% said all business or industrial, 67% said mostly residential with some businesses, 3.2% said mostly business with some residential, and 1.1% said the two were probably equal with low-income housing units. The hypothesis for this question is that an injunction implemented in a residential area will have a greater impact than an injunction implemented in business district areas (R > B).

Results Survey Question 15: How Was the Injunction Obtained? Rate the Following Groups' Level of Participation in the Decision to Obtain the Injunction

The Community

9% of officers described the community as very involved, 52% said somewhat involved, 34% said not involved, and 5% of officers said the community opposed the injunction.

Elected Officials

10% of officers described local elected officials as very involved, 43% said somewhat involved, 45% said not involved, and 1% of officers said the elected officials opposed the injunction.

TABLE 9.12
Cross Tabs: Who Requested the Injunction?

Who Requested the Injunction?	Frequency	Percent
Other or don't know	5	5.4
Elected officials	2	2.2
Police	78	83.9
The district or city attorneys	8	8.6
Total	93	100

The Police

86% of officers described their involvement as being very involved, 17% said somewhat involved, 2% said not involved, and 1% of officers said they opposed the injunction.

The District or City Attorney

80% of officers who answered described the district or city attorney as very involved, 17% said somewhat involved, 2% said not involved, and 1% of officers said the prosecutors opposed the injunction. Fourteen officers skipped the question.

The hypothesis for this question is that an injunction with significant police participation will be more effective when compared to other groups' participation (P > O).

Results Survey Question 16: If Aware of an Injunction, Who Initially Requested the Injunction?

Of 93 participants who completed the survey, 80 were from injunctions that were requested or initiated by the police (83.9%), 8 were requested by the city or district attorney, (8.6%), and 2 were requested by elected officials (2.2%). Most injunctions were requested or initiated by the police.

Requestor of the Injunction and Injunction Success

Because most injunctions were requested by police, these data were reduced to two groups: injunction requested by police (n = 78) vs. injunction not requested by police (n = 15) (Table 9.13).

Results Survey Question 17: Which of the Following Below Best Describes the Injunction in Your Area?

21.5% of all officers said their gang injunction names the gang as the only defendant, 57% said the injunction names individual members as well as the gang as defendants, 11.8% said the injunction named only individual defendants and not the gang, and 9.7% of officers said they did not know. Twelve officers skipped this question.

TABLE 9.13
Cross Tabs: Who Requested the Injunction and Injunction Success?

Who Requested the Injunction?	Successful Injunction	Not Successful	Total
Not police	12	3	15
Police	66	12	78
Total	78	15	93

The hypothesis for this question is that an injunction that names the defendants plus the gang will be more effective than injunctions that name just the gang (D + G > G).

Results Survey Question 18: Does Your Department Keep You Adequately Informed as to the Status of the Injunction?

Of 93 participants who completed the survey, 91 reported how their department kept them informed of the injunctions status; 69 were from injunctions that did keep officers informed (75.8%) (Table 9.14), 22 were from injunctions that did not keep officers informed (24.2%), and 2 participants did not know or did not answer the question. This difference was statistically significant (sign test, $p < .000001$). Most participants, roughly three of four, reported that they were kept adequately informed on the status of the injunction.

Keeping Informed and Injunction Success

Of 14 participants from the four unsuccessful injunctions, 9 (63.4%) were kept informed on the injunction, compared to 60 of 77 participants (77.9%) from successful injunctions. This difference was not statistically significant, (degrees of freedom = 1) = 1.2, p =.27. Pearson correlation (.11, p = .28) and Spearman rho correlation (.11, p = .28) were not statistically significant. The finding provides no clear evidence of a relationship between keeping informed of the injunction and injunction success.

TABLE 9.14
Cross Tabs: Keeping Informed and Injunction Success

Keep You Informed?	Successful Injunction	Not Successful	Total
No	17	5	22
Yes	60	9	69
Total	77	14	91

The hypothesis for this question is that an injunction where the police are informed will be more effective than injunctions where the police are not informed (I > NI).

Results Survey Question 19: If an Arrest Is Made for a Gang Injunction Violation, What Is the Typical Response in Your Jurisdiction?

92.5% of officers said those arrested for an injunction violation were booked in the local jail, and 7.5% said they did not know. None of the officers surveyed said those arrested were issued a citation or notice to appear, and none indicated they released the gang members with the case being submitted for a prosecution review and issuance of an arrest warrant. The hypothesis for this question is that an injunction where violators are booked in jail will be more effective than those where violators are cited and released (J > C).

Results Survey Question 20: In My Jurisdiction We Constantly Evaluate the Injunction and Add or Remove Members as It Becomes Necessary to Keep the Injunction Current

46.2% of officers said yes, 23.7% said no, 30.1% said they did not know. Twelve officers skipped this question. The hypothesis for this question is that an injunction that adds new members as they are identified as becoming a problem will be more effective than an injunction that does not add new members (A > NA).

THE POLICE OFFICER SURVEY

Thank you for taking the 8 to 10 minutes necessary to complete this survey of law enforcement professionals regarding gang injunctions. Your participation in this survey is voluntary and at your own discretion. Your identity will not be made known to the researcher.

1. Making an arrest for a gang injunction violation is an effective use of my time?
   Yes
   No
   Don't know
   Other (please specify) _____________

2. Gang injunction violations are responded to in which manner in my jurisdiction?
   Quickly (aggressive)
   Slowly (nonaggressive)
   Not enforced
   Don't know

3. If aware of the presence of an injunction, was the injunction part of a larger intervention or enforcement program?
   Yes
   No
   Don't know
   Other (please specify) ____________

4. If the answer to question 3 was yes (if not skip question), what were the goals of the larger program?
   Gang sweeps
   Increased uniformed patrol
   Task force enforcement
   Wire taps
   Gang intervention programs
   Gang education programs
   Community redevelopment
   Other (please specify) ____________

5. What is the size of the gang targeted with the injunction?
   50 or less
   51–100 members
   101–150 members
   151–200 members
   201–250 members
   251 or more members
   Other (please specify) __________

6. What percentage of the overall gang size was actually named in the injunction or later served with the injunction?
   1–10%
   11–20%
   21–30%
   31–40%
   41–50%
   51–60%
   61–70%
   71–80%
   81–90%
   91–100%

7. Were the gang leaders targeted with the injunction?
   Yes
   No
   Don't know

8. The gangs in my jurisdiction are territorial and have well-defined borders that they actively defend against rivals?
   Yes
   No
   Don't know

9. Was the activity that originally brought the gang problems in the injunction area Part 1 crime?
   Yes
   No
   Don't know

10. Gang crime in my jurisdiction is committed by gang members working as individuals rather than working together as a group.
    Always
    Sometimes
    Almost never
    Never

11. What is the size of the gang turf of the gang targeted with the injunction?
    1–5 square city blocks
    6–10 square city blocks
    11–15 square city blocks
    16–20 square city blocks
    21–30 square city blocks
    31–40 square city blocks
    Other (please specify) _______________

12. What percentage of the total gang's turf was made part of the gang injunction target area?
    The entire gang's territory
    ¾ or more of the entire turf
    ½ or more of the entire turf
    ¼ or more of the entire turf
    Less than 5% of turf
    Other (please specify) __________

13. What is the general economic status of the gang injunction area targeted?
    Affluent
    Middle class
    Poverty
    Don't know

14. What best describes the zoning in the target area?
    All residential
    All business
    Mostly residential with some business
    Mostly business with some residential
    Other (please specify) ____________

15. How was the injunction obtained? Rate the following groups' (community, elected officials, police, district/city attorney) level of participation in the decision to obtain the injunction.
    Very involved
    Somewhat involved
    Not involved
    Opposed the injunction
    Don't know

16. If aware of an injunction in your jurisdiction, who initially requested the injunction?
    Police
    District or city attorney
    Community
    Elected officials
    Other (please specify) _________

17. Which of the following below best describes the injunction in your area?
    It names the gang as the sole defendant
    It names only individual defendants and *not* the gang
    It names individual defendants and the gang
    Don't know

18. Does your department keep you adequately informed as to the status of the injunction?
    Yes
    No
    Don't know

19. If an arrest is made for a gang injunction violation, what is the typical response in your jurisdiction?
    Arrested and booked in jail
    Arrested and issued citation or notice to appear
    Released with case being submitted to DA/CA for review
    Don't know

20. In my jurisdiction we constantly evaluate the injunction and add or remove members as it becomes necessary to keep the injunction current.
    Yes
    No
    Don't know

10

Research and Conclusions about Effectiveness

Do gang injunctions reduce crime? This question was the basis for the 25-gang injunction study outlined in Chapter 8 and the police officer survey outlined in Chapter 9. The key findings of this research revealed that gang injunctions are effective and that crime goes down in the areas where gang injunctions are implemented.

The bottom line is that less crime benefits society as a whole. A decrease in calls means less gang violence and an improved quality of life in the areas in which gang injunctions are implemented.

Part 1 calls decreased 11.6% compared to baseline, while the matched controls averaged a mild increase of 0.8% in Part 1 calls for service, a net benefit of 12.4% in the injunction area. Part 2 calls decreased 15.9% compared to baseline, while the matched controls averaged a mild increase of 1.6% in Part 2 calls for service, a net benefit of 17.5% in the injunction area. Total calls for service decreased 14.1% compared to baseline, while the matched controls averaged a mild increase of 2.3% in total calls for service, a net benefit of 16.4% in the injunction area.

Not only were declines in Part 1 calls, Part 2 calls, and total calls for service statistically significant, but the magnitude of the effect was greater than 10% in each case, which is significant in real world terms. The benefit in the present study was roughly 150 fewer Part 1 calls per injunction per year, 650 fewer Part 2 calls per injunction per year, and 1,750 fewer total calls per injunction per year. These data suggest that injunctions confer significant benefit to society.

The studies conducted to date indicate that gang injunctions may help reduce crime with varying degrees of effectiveness (Allan, 2002; Grogger, 2000; Los Angeles Grand Jury, 2004; Maxson, 2003, O'Deane, 2007). Gang crime and gang violence are increasing in many communities, growing exponentially, imbuing the citizenry with well-founded fear. If the research provides empirical evidence that gang injunctions do not work, policy makers may need to shift resources, thereby saving time and money. If the research provides empirical evidence that gang injunctions do work, thereby fostering a more civil, less fearful society, injunctions may be considered more frequently.

GROGGER STUDY: FIRST SCIENTIFIC LOOK AT EFFECTIVENESS

In July 2000, Professor Jeff Grogger from the University of California–Los Angeles conducted a study of the effects of Los Angeles county gang injunctions on reported crime. The study conducted by Grogger concluded that gang injunctions reduced violent crime by 5 to 10% per neighborhood. The report, published in the *Journal of Law and Economics*, looked at eight years of data from various injunction zones in the Los Angeles County area. The study evaluated 14 gang injunctions from Los Angeles County in the first year after their implementation.

Grogger's objective was to evaluate whether gang injunctions reduce crime in an injunction area and whether they cause spillover or displacement. The study used simple before and after comparisons of crime rates in the injunction areas for one year before and one year after. The study also used a counterfactual or control area to account for the level of change in crime not caused by the gang injunctions. The Grogger study evaluated the reporting districts included in the gang injunctions and control areas that were as similar to the injunction reporting districts as possible, with the exception of no gang injunction being in place. The Grogger study made an effort to filter out any potential impact that other factors may have on injunctions, such as the economy and the unemployment rate.

For each injunction area, Grogger constructed a comparison area. Grogger found that displacement did not occur in the neighboring reporting districts as originally believed. Grogger measured displacement into the immediate surrounding areas that bordered the injunction areas. Grogger also felt that gang injunctions in many ways provide better constitutional protections as opposed to other law enforcement tactics, as they require significant judicial oversight and involvement, as opposed to directed and zero tolerance patrol, for example, that do not.

Grogger also addressed the issue of cost-effectiveness and highlighted how difficult it is to put an exact price tag on a gang injunction. The police and prosecutors do not track the number of hours put into the effort, the salaries and supplies needed to put the case together, and the cost associated with maintaining and prosecuting violations of the order.

If one murder is prevented in the target area, for example, the cost savings could be significant. Estimates are in the hundreds of thousands of dollars for a typical gang murder case, from the investigation, arrest, prosecution, and incarceration of the gang members responsible. In addition, the social costs to address health care for other shooting and stabbings in the injunctions zones are difficult to calculate. In the Posole gang injunction case from San Diego, for example, 10 murders occurred in a two-year period before the injunction was implemented. No murders occurred for four years following the implementation. No other suppression was noted except the injunction. If we assumed that the injunction broke a cycle of violence and prevented even one murder because the gang's presence was reduced, the injunction was extremely cost-effective. The estimated $20,000 price tag pales in comparison to the price tag of just one typical murder investigation.

EDWARD ALLAN STUDY (SURVEY OF PROSECUTORS)

In 2002, Edward L. Allan conducted research that he entitled *Policing by Injunction: Problem Oriented Dimensions of Civil Gang Abatement in the State of California*. This study explored the scope of flexibility, community involvement, and problem-solving processes utilized in the acquisition stage of the civil injunction process in the State of California. The study defined and explored the concept of flexibility in the gang injunction implementation process. The study suggested that the provisions of requested restrictions and situational characteristics varied across the injunction initiatives he studied in his research. The study also evaluated the impact of community involvement in the decision-making process and concluded that citizen involvement allowed for greater visibility for the procedures used to address the specific problems. Results regarding community involvement also suggested that the assumption that community organizations can serve as a proxy for the community was incorrect, at least in the highly disorganized neighborhoods commonly targeted by gang injunctions. The study also examined whether gang injunction initiatives followed Herman Goldstein's problem-solving methodology consisting of four steps: scanning, analysis, response, and assessment. The evidence suggested that the problem-solving methodology was widely used in civil gang abatement initiatives. There was evidence of all four steps, indicating that gang injunctions were not simply quick reactions to gang activities. Gang injunctions are time-consuming and labor-intensive and require significant planning and effort.

A categorical data analysis was conducted examining all identified gang injunction cases filed with the California Superior Court from October 26, 1987, through June 30, 2000. Forty-two gang injunctions were represented in the study. The initiatives were evenly distributed among three categories: high-drug, high-crime, and high-disorder initiatives. The strongest and most straightforward evidence of flexibility was the categorization of injunction initiatives requested by the prosecutor, which displayed a high level of variation. The majority of gang injunction initiatives were a flexible response to local gang activity. In regards to policy implications, it was the intent of the study to assist local policy makers and participating community entities in deciding whether the strategy of policing by injunction is an appropriate response to gang problems in their community. The study also included a comprehensive review of relevant laws and issues unique to the gang injunction process.

LOS ANGELES GRAND JURY STUDY, JUNE 2004

In June 2004, the Los Angeles County civil grand jury completed a report that was designed to explain to the public the inner workings of government and discuss what law enforcement should be investigating (LA Grand Jury, 2004). The Los Angeles grand jury report was entitled *A Management Review of the Effectiveness of Civil Gang Injunctions*. The civil grand jury is divided into several committees that investigate certain departments of city or county government or special districts and what activities they are involved in, including the implementation of gang injunctions. The report was a management audit of gang injunctions within Los Angeles County and the City of Los Angeles.

In Los Angeles County most gang injunctions are obtained as a joint effort between the district attorney and the city attorney. The agencies collaborate to abate gang activities that constitute a public nuisance. The grand jury's goal was to evaluate the effectiveness of gang injunctions in the City of Los Angeles. The study evaluated 14 gang injunctions obtained in the City of Los Angeles, including the Bounty Hunters, Rolling Sixty, Avenues, Krazy Ass Mexicans, 18th Street Pico Union, Canoga Park Alabama, Pacoima Project Boys, Culver City Boys, Venice 13, Harbor City Boys and Crips, Venice Shoreline Crips, Langdon Street, Harpy's, and Blythe Street. The study found that crime dropped in the injunction areas that were studied by 10%. That finding was similar to the findings in the Grogger study, as both studies were conducted in a similar fashion. The potential criticism of both the Grogger and LA grand jury studies is that both studied neighboring reporting districts, not necessarily the territory of a street gang that has similar characteristics to the ones that have been subjected to a gang injunction. For that reason, I have focused my research on evaluating rival gang territory as opposed to an area that is close to the enjoined gang's territory. I feel that would be a more accurate assessment of the impact of the injunction when comparing two gangs that are as similar in characteristics and area as possible.

MAXSON COMMUNITY STUDY OF VERDUGO FLATS

In 2005, Dr. Cheryl Maxson of the University of California–Irvine conducted a community survey of citizens in San Bernardino County to evaluate and assess the community impact and perceptions of the Verdugo Flats gang injunction (*People v. Verdugo Flats Gang*, 2003) implemented on March 10, 2003. The project was an assessment of the effects of the gang injunction on the targeted and surrounding communities. Maxson and her colleagues conducted a survey over an 18-month period to evaluate the gang injunction. They combined a community survey and observational data in three communities, one with the Verdugo Flats civil gang injunction, one to assess potential displacement issues, and a third comparison area. The goal of the study was to measure the impact of the civil gang injunction on the community residents' perception and experience of crime and neighborhood quality of life. The study also wanted to determine whether programmatic effects or displacement is the result of the injunctions, simply displacing gang activity to surrounding areas.

The study surveyed 797 San Bernardino residents in 5 neighborhoods 18 months prior to and 1,229 residents 6 months following the implementation of the Verdugo Flats gang injunction. The research hypothesis was tested before and after using a nonequivalent comparison group design with multiple comparisons being made. Two similarly disordered areas were compared. The study revealed that there was positive evidence of the short-term effects in an injunction area, including less gang presence, fewer reports of gang intimidation, and less fear of confrontation with gang members. The study showed no significant changes in the long-term outcomes with the exception of less fear of crime in the injunction areas.

The study suggests that slight improvements are made for the immediate future following the implementation of gang injunctions. The study also determined that the effects of gang injunctions might be substantially improved if other efforts to improve social programs and gang intervention programs are implemented in conjunction with the gang injunctions. Few in the field of gang enforcement would argue with that apparently obvious finding. The study does not address steps that law enforcement can take to make injunctions more effective. The most critical category in gang injunction effectiveness is the police and their willingness and ability to enforce the order. That is why the orders must be treated like a car, each requiring regular maintenance to ensure they operate properly. Regular maintenance for a gang injunction may include adding new members as they become a problem, modification of target areas as they may change over time, educating officers in injunction areas to keep new officers up to date on the injunctions, etc.

The study reinforces the importance of maintaining and updating the orders so they remain current and control the behavior of the gang members that are actively creating a nuisance. It has been said that gang injunctions have a shelf life, meaning that over time they tend to have a diminishing impact because older gang members die, go to prison, or fade away from the gangs, leaving the next generation of gang members to take over the criminal activities. That is why the gathering of gang intelligence information is a constantly ongoing process, and so too is the gang injunction process. The Verdugo Flats injunction studied by Maxson is also one of the cases included in this research. The Verdugo Flats injunction area was compared against the North Side Colton gang in the neighboring City of Colton to evaluate any reported changes in crimes reported to the police. This research sought to evaluate the injunction to compare the corresponding change in level of crime and contrast the results of the case in this study against those of the case as reviewed in Maxson's study.

FRESNO GRAND JURY MAKES GANG INJUNCTION RECOMMENDATIONS

In December 2005, the Fresno County grand jury met to discuss the implementation of gang injunctions in their county. The grand jury felt it was important to review the status of the Multiagency Gang Enforcement Consortium (MAGEC), which is responsible for obtaining and enforcing gang injunctions. The grand jury found that temporary and permanent civil injunctions were helpful in prohibiting gang members from associating with other gang members, intimidating people, and using guns and other weapons, based upon interviews with concerned citizens and police officials. Fresno County has 223 active gangs with approximately 11,000 members according to the grand jury. At the time of this research, four of those gangs were targeted with an injunction.

O'DEANE GANG INJUNCTION STUDY—SEPTEMBER 2007

In September 2007, the research study in this book was concluded. The purpose of this study was to determine whether gang injunctions reduce crime, when compared to baseline and matched control areas. Twenty-five gang injunctions from four California counties were evaluated by extracting crime data from court records and police agencies. The control areas (communities with a similar gang problem but no gang injunctions) were matched for similar gang ethnicity, gang size, proximity, and gang activity. Calls for service were evaluated for one year preinjunction and one year postinjunction using paired t-tests, which revealed that gang injunctions reduce crime. Calls for service were significantly reduced compared to baseline and matched controls.

Part 1 (violent crime) calls decreased 11.6% compared to baseline, while controls averaged an increase of 0.8%, a net benefit of 12.4%. Part 2 (less serious) calls decreased 15.9% compared to baseline, while controls averaged a mild increase of 1.6%, a net benefit of 17.5%. Total calls for service decreased 14.1% compared to baseline, while controls averaged an increase of 2.3%, a net benefit of 16.4%. This research promotes positive social change by identifying gang injunctions as an effective means to reduce crime, an important goal for public policy makers.

O'DEANE GANG INJUNCTION STUDY—NOVEMBER 2007

The police survey component of this research has revealed that the majority of the survey participants reported a fast response (70 of 82, or 85.6%) to a gang injunction violation significantly more than a slow response, suggesting that most injunction violations are responded to quickly rather than slowly. These data provided no statistically significant evidence that supports a relationship between response speed and injunction success. Even if not scientifically significant, it does seem supported in that, of the 25 injunctions evaluated in this study, 21 of them resulted in a reduction in crime without taking into account the controls, indicating that police response is a contributing factor to injunction success. This research supports deterrence theory in that police agencies that allocate sufficient resources to enforce the gang injunction have a more positive impact.

In addition, police agencies that implement other enforcement operations that coexist with the injunction, such as narcotics operations, wire taps, street sweeps, probation and parole operations, and increased zero tolerance patrol, will enhance the effectiveness of the gang injunction. The findings of this research suggest no scientifically significant relationship between injunction success and being part of a larger intervention or enforcement program. Despite the lack of scientific significance, however, having multiple initiatives against the target gang has not revealed any negative impact, making multiple interventions more beneficial than an injunction effort as an independent tactic.

To gauge police attitudes, question 1 asked officers if making an arrest for a gang injunction violation is an effective use of their time. The majority of officers felt that an injunction arrest was a beneficial use of time, and the majority of officers supported arrests over no action being taken. If the police felt it is worthwhile to make an arrest for violating an injunction, the injunction was more effective.

Survey question 15 asked officers to rate the community, elected officials, the police, and the prosecution's level of participation in the decision to obtain the injunction in their jurisdiction. The majority of officers described their involvement as being very involved, 17% said somewhat involved, 2% said not involved, and 1% of officers said they opposed the injunction. Survey question 16 asked officers, if they were aware of an injunction, who initially requested it. The majority of officers identified the police as the ones who initiated the gang injunction. Deterrence theory suggests that officers that do not know about the injunction will not be able to take action, which will reduce injunction effectiveness. Survey question 18 asked if officers felt their department kept them adequately informed as to the status of the injunction. The majority of officers felt their department did keep them informed of the injunction's status.

Survey question 19 asked if an arrest is made for an injunction violation, what the typical response in their jurisdiction is. The majority of officers (92.5%) said injunction violators were booked in the local jail subsequent to a gang injunction violation arrest. Survey question 20 asked officers if their jurisdiction evaluated the injunction over time and added or removed members as it became necessary to keep the injunction current. Slightly less than half of the officers felt their jurisdiction adequately updates their injunctions.

Police officers, in collaboration with the prosecution, are responsible for identifying the problem posed by the particular street gang creating the nuisance in the target area, in violation of 3479 and 3480 of the California Civil Code. The police are the ones typically tasked with identifying the specific problem, the source of the problem, which gang, what type of gang, which specific gang members, and what types of crimes they are committing.

It is critical to accurately identify the problem and the source of the problem to justify the need for the gang injunction in a court of law. With a detailed analysis of the problem, police can plan anti-gang operations accordingly, including modification of patrol or special unit schedules to be working when gang crimes are most likely to be occurring. Proper use of crime analysis units and crime-tracking software can help map gang crime and identify gang hangouts and areas that gang conflicts are most likely to occur. This is important to justify the borders of the target areas, as well as the selection of specific gang members for inclusion in the order.

The gang to be targeted by the injunction needs to be explained. Question 5 on the police survey revealed the gang injunctions evaluated in this research were well spread in gang size. There was no statistically significant relationship between gang size and injunction success, but splitting gangs at 250 members provided a statistical trend indicating more injunction success with a smaller gang size. Smaller gangs are easier to control and typically claim a smaller, more manageable territory. The findings of this research tend to support targeting gangs with less than 250 members to increase success; however, gang size is just one of many variables and can be overcome by allocating more resources to address larger gang problems, or by breaking larger gangs down into cliques or subsets, then targeting the cliques as independent entities.

Related to gang size, survey question 6 revealed that there was no clear evidence of a relationship between the percentage of the gang named in the injunction and injunction success. This may be explained by the ability of the gang injunction to target those members that have been identified as creating the particular problem in the target area. Percentage of the gang may not be a factor if those individuals targeted are the correct people responsible for committing the crime in the area. By comparison with control gangs, crime went down on average in a very significant manner for enjoined gangs. The percentage of the total gang's membership varied between injunction efforts, indicating that the percentage of members enjoined should be significant enough to enjoin all those members that have been identified as being part of the problem.

Survey question 8 asked if officers feel the gangs in their jurisdiction are territorial and have well-defined borders that they actively defend against rivals. This question revealed that the majority of gangs are considered territorial by the officers surveyed, which is a desired gang characteristic for an effective gang injunction, as gang injunctions are only applicable to the area defined in the court order.

COMPARING THE EMPIRICAL FINDINGS

I support the findings of each of the four significant existing empirical studies conducted relating to gang injunctions prior to the research undertaken for this book. This research revealed gang injunctions had a net benefit of a 12.4% reduction in Part 1 crimes in the injunction areas, a slightly higher percentage when compared to existing studies, which estimate the benefit at approximately a 10% reduction in Part 1 crime (Grogger, 2000; Los Angeles Grand Jury, 2004). This variation is likely due to several factors, including sample size and categories of crime collected. This study expanded upon the sample size in both the Grogger and Los Angeles grand jury studies from 14 to 25 gang injunctions. This researcher also expanded upon the categories of data collected, increasing the crimes to be evaluated from just four types of Part 1 crime to include all Part 1 crimes and all Part 2 crimes. In addition, the total calls for service in the injunction and control areas were measured.

This study also used control gang areas as opposed to areas that were merely adjacent to the injunction, as was done in each of the previous studies (Grogger, 2000; Los Angeles Grand Jury, 2004; Maxson, 2003). This was deemed by this researcher to be a more appropriate and accurate comparison due to the common clustering of gang activity in certain areas. Other studies (Grogger, 2000; Los Angeles Grand Jury, 2004) compare injunction areas to adjacent areas, regardless of the gang composition of the adjacent areas used as the control. By comparing two similar areas, under the control of two similar gangs, this study took an additional step to ensure that a more accurate comparison was made.

The existing studies of effectiveness from Grogger and the Los Angeles grand jury focused solely on Los Angeles County injunctions; the Maxson study focused on San Bernardino County, but only evaluated one gang injunction. This researcher expanded significantly upon the scope of the existing research that focused solely on Los Angeles County, to include the Counties of Los Angeles, Ventura, San Bernardino, and San Diego. This allowed for a better understanding of gang injunction effectiveness throughout Southern California, as opposed to just a few portions of Los Angeles County.

This multicounty approach allowed for comparisons to be made between counties, evaluating the potential impact between varying types of orders, different sized gangs, different ethnic gangs, and different police agency responses to gang injunctions.

Grogger (2000) found that gang injunctions reduce violent crime by 5–10%, dependent upon the injunction. This researcher supports the findings of Grogger that gang injunctions are effective in reducing violent crime. This researcher expanded the scope of the Grogger study. This likely contributed to the variation in results. Grogger focused on limited categories of Part 1 violent crime. In this research, by evaluating every category of Part 1 crime, including crimes like auto theft and burglary, the number of reported Part 1 crimes increased significantly between the Grogger study and this study. This researcher supported Grogger's findings that Part 1 crime was reduced following the implementation of the 25 gang injunctions evaluated from baseline and on average.

The Los Angeles grand jury (2004) found that gang injunctions reduce violent crime by 10% in the target areas. This study supports the findings of the Los Angeles grand jury that gang injunctions work in reducing violent crime. The Los Angeles grand jury and the Grogger study had two gang injunctions in common: the Blythe Street and the Harpy's injunction were evaluated in both studies. The Los Angeles grand jury evaluated 12 additional recent injunctions that followed the work of Grogger. Similar to Grogger, the Los Angles study followed the same methodological format, and basic procedures were used.

This study evaluated six injunctions in common with the Los Angeles grand jury study; all of the Los Angeles cases evaluated in this research with the exception of the Grape Street injunction were also part of the Los Angeles grand jury study. However, this research went beyond the data collected and expanded the evaluation to include all Part 1 crime, Part 2 crime, and total calls for service.

Maxson (2005) found that the community of people living in the Verdugo Flats neighborhood in San Bernardino had less fear of crime following the implementation of the Verdugo Flats gang injunction. This research included the Verdugo Flats injunction as one of the 25 cases that was evaluated. By evaluating the Verdugo Flats injunction, this researcher concluded that the injunction did have a beneficial impact on reducing crime. When evaluating the injunction, this researcher compared the Verdugo Flats gang against the Northside Colton gang as a control group. More importantly, this researcher used objective measures (crime calls) rather than subjective ones (reported community perceptions).

This researcher supports Maxson's view that the community members in the Verdugo Fats neighborhood would feel safer and see a less visible presence of gang members. The area did experience an 8.5% reduction in Part 1 crime, a 5.2% decrease in Part 2 crimes, and a 3.9% reduction in total calls for service, which supports the position that the community may feel safer. When comparing the Verdugo Flats area to the Northside Colton control gang area, it was clear that the presence of the gang injunction was the decisive factor. The Northside Colton gang area experienced overall slight increases in crime, while the Verdugo Flats area experienced a crime reduction.

The Maxson study (2005), although scientifically sound, was limited in scope to reviewing one gang injunction. In the Maxson study, assumptions were made about the entire universe of injunctions and the potential long-term impact of gang injunctions based upon the one injunction evaluated, which may not allow a significant enough sample. It is not known if more enforcement the year following the injunction may have led to a longer-lasting benefit or increased feeling of safety in the community. The Maxson study evaluated community perceptions for 18 months following the injunction; a longer view may be required to evaluate the true impact of injunctions and make assessments as to their long-term effectiveness.

To further understand the potential long-term impact of gang injunctions discussed in the Maxson study, this researcher evaluated six gang injunctions from San Diego County that were updated and redone approximately five to eight years between the first and second injunctions, to evaluate if the long-term impact of gang injunctions could be further explained beyond the scope of community perceptions in the one injunction area evaluated in the Maxson study. By reviewing a grouping of six injunctions, as opposed to one, and by reviewing the status of the targeted gang members five to eight years later, long-term impact may be further explained.

Allan (2002) conducted a study in which California prosecutors were surveyed to evaluate why certain gangs and neighborhoods were selected to be targets of gang injunctions, and if gang injunctions are an effective policy to address gangs. Allan concluded that gang injunctions are a productive way for the police and the prosecution to work together to help the community address serious crime as well as less serious nuisance activity. This study supported Allan's study and concurred that gang injunctions are a proactive tool that offers a flexible and responsible use of public resources based upon the scientifically significant reduction in crime in injunction areas when compared to baseline and the controls.

LONG-TERM IMPACT OF SIX GANG INJUNCTIONS EVALUATED

In response to the Maxson study (2005) and numerous media accounts of problems associated with not knowing the long-term impact of gang injunctions, this researcher took the opportunity to evaluate the six gangs in San Diego County that have had two gang injunctions implemented against them. The method used to update San Diego County gang injunctions requires the filing of a new injunction as the gang evolves over time, to keep it up to date and relevant.

San Diego County gang injunctions name each defendant in the case; members are not added at a later date in the same manner as is commonly done in Los Angeles County. The refiling of injunctions is necessary to keep the injunction relevant and effective. Over time gang members die, go to prison, move out of the area, or simply stop being active. As older members distance themselves from the gang, younger members are typically created, and many become part of the problem over time, creating the need for continued analysis and updating of the gang injunctions.

This researcher did not collect crime statistics for the entire period between the first and second injunctions against each gang, as that timeframe was between five and seven years. This researcher did evaluate the status of the gang members named in the first injunction to determine what happened to them between the first and second injunctions against their gang.

In each of the six gang injunctions cases reviewed, the police officers that obtained the first injunction and those that obtained the second injunction provided updated data on each named member. They evaluated every member named in the first injunction as part of their investigation to determine if they were still active gang members that were still part of the public nuisance in the target area, potentially requiring their inclusion in the second injunction. In addition, all six San Diego injunctions that were redone had the size of the target area modified in the second injunction, all made larger to some degree.

The Posole, Old Town National City, Lincoln Park Bloods, Westside, Diablos, and Varrio San Marcos gangs are the six in San Diego County that have been the subject of two injunctions each or have had their injunctions modified or updated.

The long-term evaluation of the six injunctions updated in San Diego reveals that many gang members included in injunctions do not stop their criminal activity after being served with the first injunction. This does not come as a surprise to many law enforcement officers, as the gang members selected to be included in injunctions are typically the most active and most problematic members of the gang.

If the majority of the named gang members commit future crimes, how can it be argued that injunctions have a scientifically significant impact on crime reduction? Perhaps the threat of being served with an injunction somehow dissuades the less involved individuals (not named) from getting involved, thereby reducing crime. Perhaps the enjoined gang members become more visible targets of the police as a result of their inclusion in an injunction, which enhances their chance of rearrest due to the additional police presence of officers searching for violations of the injunctions. Perhaps those that do not reoffend leave the area, which reduces crime in the target areas. Or perhaps, those that do reoffend do so less often as a result of the injunction due to fear of being apprehended, reducing the volume of crimes committed in the target areas.

In San Diego County, the targeted members are named in the orders and all evidence against the gang and its members is to be provided at the onset of the case. All evidence in the possession of the police must be presented to the court and taken into consideration when deciding to add or not add a specific individual to a gang injunction. It also helps the police prove a pattern of criminal activity by the gang and the individual members by tracking all contact with law enforcement in a chronological manner.

Critics of gang injunctions often interpret arrests of gang members named as defendants in the injunctions as a failure of the injunction to curtail criminal activity (Russell, 2004). If that is the case, they should also seek to identify how many gang members stopped being criminals upon being served with injunctions and view those members as an injunction success.

By reviewing the six San Diego injunctions, 185 gang members were named in the six original San Diego injunctions. Of those 185 gang members, 49 of them (27%) were added to the second injunction against their gang, between five and seven years later, because they were still active and still part of the nuisance in the target areas according to police records.

The 136 gang members (73%) that were not included in the second injunction were not included for several reasons. Of the 136 members not included, 4 were murder victims and 80 were serving lengthy prison sentences for committing new violent offenses. The San Diego County District Attorney's Office does not include gang members as named defendants in an injunction if they are in custody and are not due to be released within the first year the injunction is filed. However, 52 members appeared to be nonactive and had no recent contacts with law enforcement in their gang's territory, and most had no contacts anywhere in San Diego County.

It appears that 62% of the gang members served with an injunction against their gangs did not make an effort to change their criminal ways; however, 38% did to some degree and had no or very little activity that would be sufficient to support them remaining on the second injunction against their gang.

The second injunction against each gang increased the number of named gang members now impacted by the two injunctions; the combined defendants totaled 486 gang members on all six of the second injunctions combined.

A total of 301 new gang members were added to the second injunctions (535 gang members named in the 12 injunctions; however, 49 individuals were included in both the first and second injunctions against their gang, 486 total individuals). It is apparent that the injunctions against the six gangs did not cause the gangs to cease to exist, and about two-thirds of the members named in the first injunction continued to be criminals, as evidenced by their arrests and convictions for new crimes after being enjoined.

The findings of this six-injunction review also suggest that the police did not reduce their enforcement efforts against the enjoined gang members, as the majority of the members named in the first injunctions were rearrested and in prison for new felony offenses. This finding supports the position that gang members are typically defiant and tend to continue their criminal activity until being stopped by arrest and incarceration. The majority of gang members in the first injunctions continued to be criminals; however, they did not all continue to commit crimes. This fact indicates some positive benefit for some of the members named in the six gang injunctions on a long-term basis.

LIMITATIONS

This researcher was restricted by several limitations as the research progressed. One significant limitation was the level of cooperation from the police agencies that maintained the required crime data. This researcher was limited to the injunctions where requested data could be located, primarily those injunctions in the Southern California region. Southern California was the primary region targeted for this research due in part to its having the majority of statewide injunctions (105 out of 122 total), the accessibility to the data, and the proximity of the researcher to the data and the agencies holding the data.

This study did not evaluate any injunctions from the northern counties in California and did not evaluate any injunctions implemented in states other than California. Some of the limitations related to data collection were circumvented by getting the information from the prosecutors rather than the police, if the prosecutors were in possession of the statistical data gathered at the time of the injunction. This was true especially in some of the earlier injunction cases where data were printed out before being purged from the electronic files of the police and maintained in the city attorney's or district attorney's files.

This researcher only evaluated crime statistics for one year before and one year after each injunction and control included in the study. This researcher did not evaluate multiple years before and after in order to keep the comparisons the same based upon the varying degrees of data being made available. It is not known what, if any, variation may have existed by evaluating longer periods of time. This was due in large part to the extensive amount of data involved in this research, making it too labor-intensive to extend the pre-post injunction analysis.

This researcher did not evaluate the perceptions of the community, the police, or even the gang members. This researcher focused on quantitative methods to evaluate gang injunction efficacy and not long-term qualitative analysis.

SUGGESTIONS FOR FUTURE RESEARCH

Future scholars should consider replicating the present study with a wider sample of injunctions, including the California injunctions that were not included in the present study, or gang injunctions implemented in other states. At least eight other states have implemented gang injunctions at the time of this research.

Future scholars should consider longer-term follow-up than the one-year period used in the present study. Ultimately, society needs to determine the long-term impact of gang injunctions. A longitudinal study may reveal variations in the level of gang injunction effectiveness if the pre- and post-time periods are increased to cover multiple years before and after the gang injunction's implementation.

Future scholars should consider conducting a careful cost-benefit analysis of injunctions that would reveal the net benefit injunctions bring to society by calculating the costs associated with obtaining the injunction vs. the benefits derived from the injunction. Future scholars may want to track the expenses associated with implementing an injunction, including prosecution and police salaries, court costs, deposition and copying expenses, etc., to determine the specific cost of each injunction.

Future scholars should consider measuring arrests and crime convictions in addition to calls for service, so that the impact of injunctions can be understood more clearly.

Future scholars should consider investigating ways to make smaller injunctions (targeting less than 1 square mile, gangs with fewer than 100 members, or fewer than 50 members), as they work better in reducing crime. Further, future scholars should consider investigating ways to make injunctions in Los Angeles County work better than those of the other counties in the Southern California region.

Future scholars should consider investigating potential interactions between court-mandated gang injunctions and community safety organizations, like Neighborhood Watch. Future scholars may want to explore the relationship between gang injunctions and community and social services to determine if injunctions have any potential impact on those organizations.

WHAT ARE THE POLICY RECOMMENDATIONS?

The present findings support policies that increase the usage of gang injunctions toward reducing crime calls for service, especially violent crime. Further, the present findings suggest that for best results, naming more gang members in the injunction may confer greater benefit than naming fewer gang members.

Policy decisions should include the allocation of resources and expertise to evaluate interventions like gang injunctions. Without feedback in the form of carefully constructed empirical research, society will never know if a policy suits its needs. If injunctions work, policy makers need to know. If injunctions don't work, policy makers need to know. Part of policy feedback is tracking costs. Without cost-benefit analysis, the benefit of a gang injunction cannot be fully appreciated as a policy tool in reducing crime. The present investigation provides empirical evidence that gang injunctions can work in reducing violent crime, less serious crime, and total calls for service compared to matched controls. Policy makers should finance impartial empirical investigations of future interventions for the good of society.

RESEARCH CONCLUSION

After conducting this research the take-home message is that injunctions clearly have a significant impact on Part 1 crimes in the first year following the gang injunction. That one fact alone is likely enough to justify the time and expense that is required of a typical gang injunction case. Part 1 crimes are the most serious, and oftentimes the most costly to investigate and prosecute. In addition, Part 2 crimes also decreased in gang injunction areas, as did overall calls for service. Overall, the results showed that injunctions had a positive impact on the communities involved, which clearly indicates positive social change and improved living conditions in the areas in which gang injunctions are implemented.

An evaluation of the usefulness of gang injunctions as a tool created to enhance law enforcement's ability to protect the community, especially in terms of their applicability to specific community problems and current case law, was necessary for public policy makers and law enforcement to make well-informed decisions whether or not to implement a gang injunction in their jurisdictions. To accomplish this, relevant theories, laws, legal decisions, and case law had to be evaluated to assess the feasibility, practicality, legality, and need for a gang injunction in a given community.

Based upon the analysis and research conducted, the final finding of this researcher is that gang injunctions should be used on a continuing basis and more resources should be directed into the enforcement and maintenance of gang injunctions across the state. The results indicate that despite concerns, despite all gang injunctions not being flawless examples of perfection, it is clear the time, energy, and resources directed toward gang injunctions can greatly improve the quality of life in the communities in which they are implemented.

It is also clear that the 36,132,147 people living in the State of California at the time of this research deserve that their public policy makers and law enforcement officers do what they can to help address the very serious gang problem facing our society. Even the 266,470 individuals that have chosen the gang life by joining one of the 3,880 different street gangs in the State of California deserve the assistance of their public policy makers to help them break free from their gangs and become productive members of society. For those members that fail to respond or participate in social and health programs, injunctions should continue to be used to hold them accountable for the daily criminal and nuisance activity they create.

To date, all injunctions in California targeted at least 7,394 gang members and resulted in at least 2,327 of those gang members getting arrested. As evidenced by the long-term impact of six San Diego injunctions, it is clear that some of those targeted with injunctions do break free from their gang after being served with the court orders. This illustrates the potential power of a gang injunction to extend past being a traditional gang suppression tool, making it a tool that can also have a positive impact on gang intervention, by giving some gang members an excuse to distance themselves from their gang.

The total geographical area of every gang injunction to date covers about 250 square miles; the state consists of 155,959 total square miles. Gang injunctions are an effective policy for reducing gang crime in the 0.01% of the state's total area. Based on the findings of this research, law enforcement should evaluate more gang territory to potentially be placed under the restrictions of gang injunctions and continually seek to improve gang injunction policy.

11

The Birth of Gang Injunctions

Between 1980 and 1981, the Los Angeles County District Attorney's Office and the Los Angeles City Attorney's Office conducted hundreds of civil actions against street gangs, mostly in the form of single *situs* abatements that targeted private residences and single locations where gang members were hanging out and engaging in drug dealing.

During the years 1981–1982, the city attorney's office alone filed over 300 abatements. These gang abatements are believed to be the early precursors to gang injunctions as we know them today. These abatements targeted specific houses or businesses that were used as gang hangouts, targeting the gangs by suing the owners of the properties that facilitated the use of the property by the gangs to conduct business. Some examples of single *situs* cases are cited as contributing to the concept of the modern-day gang injunction.

On September 9, 1980, the Orange County District Attorney's Office sought an injunction against a group of gang members that were congregating around a local house in Santa Ana (*People v. Rubacava*). The injunction focused on a house on West Henderson Place. A temporary injunction was granted, the preliminary injunction was denied. The proposed injunction did not name the gang; it targeted individual gang members identified as creating a nuisance. The temporary injunction did reportedly disperse the gang members and eliminate the problem at that specific house, despite the preliminary injunction not being granted.

In June 1981, the Pomona City Attorney obtained an injunction against the Northside Pomona gang. The injunction, widely viewed as a precursor to the current-day injunction, named 12 gang members, but did not name the gang as a defendant. In this case, a preliminary injunction was granted against the owner of the house that was the cause of the problem on July 8, 1981. The court did not include any of the 12 gang members as defendants; however, the problem was solved by placing pressure on the home owner to address the problem or risk losing the property (*People v. Garcia*).

On August 21, 1981, the Los Angeles District Attorney's Office sought an injunction against the Alwood Street Lodies gang. The injunction named five people as defendants and did not name the gang. The five members of the gang were targeted at a specific house located in West Covina. The preliminary injunction was granted on September 3, 1981. The Alwood Street Lodies, Northside Pomona, and the hundreds of other gang members targeted either directly or indirectly in the single *situs* injunctions in the early 1980s inspired the concept of the gang injunction as used today.

YEAR 1982

People v. Dogtown, Primera and 62nd Street East Coast Crips Gangs (Los Angeles Case C418875), July 22, 1982

On July 22, 1982, the Los Angeles City Attorney and the Los Angeles Police Department obtained a temporary restraining order against three named gangs: the Dogtown, Primera Flats, and 62nd Street East Coast Crips gangs (*People v. Dogtown*, 1982). Seventy-two members of the three gangs were targeted by a temporary restraining order (TRO) and civil gang injunction. This was the first gang injunction to sue a gang as an unincorporated association (Allan, 2002). The injunction also named individual gang members as defendants. The injunction only had four restrictions aimed at reducing graffiti, including prohibiting graffiti on private and public property, trespassing on private property with the intent to place graffiti, and an order for the gangs to clean up the graffiti that displayed the name of their gangs. The injunction also requested that the 72 named defendants be required to do five hours of community service to clean graffiti.

The theory behind the graffiti cleanup was based in part on the theories of Thrasher (1927) that indicated the result of the collective gang behavior is solidarity, group awareness, and attachment to a local territory. The graffiti attributed to the gangs, covering storefronts, billboards, houses, and fences (*New York Times*, 1983), allowed the gangs to control their territory. The Dogtown, Primera Flats, and 62nd Street East Coast Crips gangs were ordered to clean their own turf. In December, Judge John H. Cole of superior court inspired the effort by ordering five days in jail for the 72 named members unless they cooperated with the drive led by the city attorney, Ira Reiner. The civil action argued that the gangs should be held collectively responsible for their members' vandalism.

California Corporations Code Used against Gangs

The *People v. Dogtown* injunction was the first to use California Corporations Code 18035 in a unique way at the time. The code defines an "unincorporated association" as an unincorporated group of two or more persons joined by mutual consent for a common purpose, whether organized for profit or not. Members and officers of an unincorporated association are often unsure of how to address fundamental matters of governance, which is especially true when talking about a gang as an unincorporated association. An unincorporated association may be a social club, charitable group, mutual aid society, homeowner's association, political group, religious society, or other similar group. Although some unincorporated associations are legally sophisticated, others are small, informal groups, and operate without legal counsel, such as street gangs.

California Corporations Code 18220 defines the rules for how an unincorporated association is sued and how service is made. In gang injunction cases, a member of the group or several members are designated as an agent of the gang for the purpose of service of the process. Section 415.20 of the Code of Civil Procedure indicates the court or judge may make an order that service be made upon the unincorporated association by delivery of a copy of the process to one or more of the association's members designated in the order, and by mailing a copy of the process to the association at its last known address. Service in this manner constitutes personal service upon the unincorporated association. Once the gang is served, the gang can be taken to court and sued and an injunction can be obtained against them.

However, unlike a street gang, when injunctions are filed against corporations barring them from violating securities laws, it is not difficult to find out who needs to be served. Every corporation has an agent for service of process on file with the secretary of state. But filing for an injunction against a street gang is not that simple. Gangs have no CEOs, corporate headquarters, or agents for service of process. Cheryl Maxson stated that treating a few gang members as official representatives of the gang involves a "somewhat dubious presumption" that these representatives will give adequate notice to the rest of the gang.

Long Beach City Prosecutor Dan Murphy said the assumption is based on the gang expert's knowledge of the gang and police observations of how information is circulated in the gang. Of course issues of due process arise when too few gang members are served as representatives, especially when those served as representatives do not live in the area or they are in custody at the time they are served, creating legal debates of how those members could realistically notify the entire gang about the action against them.

The power of courts to control corporations and unions by way of injunctions was established by the Federal Anti-Injunction (Norris–LaGuardia) Act of 1932, the 1947 Taft–Hartley Labor Act, and the 1959 Labor Management Reporting and Disclosure Act. These acts have restricted and granted power to use labor injunctions, which have been used as the basis for gang injunctions.

YEAR 1987

People v. Playboy Gangster Crips (Los Angeles Case WEC118860), October 26, 1987

On October 26, 1987, the Los Angeles City Attorney and the Los Angeles Police filed an injunction against the Playboy Gangster Crips gang (*People v. Playboy Gangster Crips*, 1987). The injunction was the first of its kind in that it contained a wide array of provisions never attempted before aimed at restricting the ability of the gang to operate and commit gang-related crimes. The preliminary injunction named 23 defendants and was granted on December 11, 1987. The injunction was ultimately limited in scope, as the judge only allowed restrictions that were listed in the penal code and struck down the primary law enforcement goal: the no association provision, which the court deemed was not appropriate.

The injunction was also the first to name DOEs, or any other members of the gang not yet identified, to be added at a later date if deemed appropriate by the police. The injunction initially had no borders other than to name the entire city of Los Angeles as the target area. The injunction was ultimately granted for only a 26-square-block area and granted to include only activities that were illegal by existing statute. The judge found that the injunction was vague and overbroad and did not provide sufficient evidence to restrict the gang members.

A staff lawyer for the American Civil Liberties Union Foundation of Southern California was granted permission to enter the case in opposition to the city attorney's office. The ACLU termed the proposed restrictions "an attempt to enforce criminal laws without abiding by basic criminal justice protections." Later, she told reporters that the ACLU "is completely appalled at violent crime but that authorities should step up lawful law enforcement rather than undertake civil action containing a laundry list of constitutional problems." The police responded by stating, "We're not talking about fraternal organizations, we're talking about criminal cartels." The police justified the request for an injunction by saying they made 517 arrests in the 26-square-block Cadillac-Corning neighborhood the year following the injunction, 323 of them for drug-related offenses.

On November 6, 1987, the *Los Angeles Times* wrote an article describing the injunction, and the results of the temporary restraining order hearing that was one of the first attempts to obtain an injunction against a gang. Judge Deering ruled the city attorney's request for a temporary restraining order against the Playboy Gangster Crips was too broad to grant. The ACLU viewed the proposed restrictions as "an attempt to enforce criminal laws without abiding by basic criminal justice protections." The ACLU went on to say, "This is the first time that they would characterize anything going on in the City of Los Angeles as coming close to a police state." City Attorney Hahn responded to the criticism that elements of his lawsuit against a street gang might be unconstitutional and modified his proposal, no longer asking to bar members from associating with each other, from leaving their homes between 7 p.m. and 7 a.m., and from wearing gang attire. The new order was watered down from the original version to address legal issues not experienced or addressed at the time. At the time of the *Playboy Gangster Crips* case, no case law existed to guide the courts and the idea had not been tested prior to that case.

The *Playboy Gangster Crips* case also started a precedent of naming DOEs, or people to be identified and served at a later date, which has since become the norm for many of the injunctions obtained in California. The order named 23 defendants and then added 52 more members at later dates. Critics argued that naming DOEs gave the police broad powers to arrest individuals that were not gang members but just lived in the community and grew up in the community alongside other gang members. Filing a suit against the gang, and then adding DOEs as they become a problem, has since proven to be an effective technique to keep injunctions relevant. This practice helps to keep the injunction current by identifying and adding qualifying members as they become known to law enforcement. Nuisance abatement suits had previously been used to enjoin houses of ill repute from peddling their wares and to stop noise and pollution associated with activities such as urban oil drilling. It didn't take a rocket scientist to deduce that a street gang exhibited all the characteristics of a public nuisance, defined by California law as anything that is "injurious to health, … or is indecent or offensive to the senses, or an obstruction to the free use of property, so as to interfere with the comfortable enjoyment of life or property" (Cal. Civ. Code § 3479). Bullets from drive-by shootings, murals of profane graffiti, and daily shakedowns from gang "tax collectors" certainly fit the bill as nuisances.

The judge who considered the 1987 lawsuit agreed that the gang's activities amounted to a public nuisance, yet he refused to give prosecutors the full injunction they sought. The judge merely enjoined the Playboy Gangster Crips from committing *illegal* acts that amounted to a nuisance—ordering the gang to desist from trespassing, damaging others' property, urinating on the street, and littering. The judge denied the prosecutors' request to prohibit the Playboys from wearing gang clothing, associating with one another, and being out after curfew, finding that these prohibitions were overbroad in content.

This was a hollow victory. The reason an injunction is so desirable for law enforcement is that the police do not have the resources to pursue gang members when they commit bona fide crimes. If *innocent* activity is enjoined, police have a much easier time detecting such conduct. The police can then arrest the gang members for violating the injunction, and the prosecutor can charge the members with contempt of court—a misdemeanor carrying up to six months in jail and a fine of up to $1,000 under California Penal Code Section 166.

Another tremendous advantage of an injunction on innocent activity is that it gives officers added reasons to detain individuals to investigate serious crimes. If an officer stops and searches a person without reasonable suspicion that he or she has committed a crime, evidence seized from the person, such as a gun or drugs, must be suppressed under the Fourth Amendment (see *In re Tony C.*, 21 Cal. 3d 888, 893 (1978)). So long as an officer has reason to believe that the person committed some crime, it is irrelevant that the offense is used as a pretext to detain and search the person to uncover a greater or different crime (*Whren v. U.S.*, 517 U.S. 806 (1996)). Stops for gang clothing thus justify uncovering possession for sale of cocaine—and being out during curfew may yield sawed-off shotguns.

If what is enjoined is already illegal, law enforcement's two purposes are not substantially advanced—at least not enough to make it worth the time and expense needed to get an injunction.

12

Gang Injunctions 1990–1999

YEAR 1992

Fairview Property Associates v. Westside Playboys (Los Angeles Case EC009117), July 1, 1992

On June 17, 1992, the Burbank Police Department worked with a private law firm to assist a private community association in obtaining a gang injunction against the Westside Playboy gang in the City of Burbank. The injunction named the gang and 43 individual members. The defendants were ordered to remain 2,500 yards away from the 2300 block of North Fairview Street. The injunction restricted intimidating witnesses and blocking free passage, including private driveways and public thoroughfares. The preliminary injunction was granted on July 1, 1992.

People v. Acosta (Los Angeles Case EC010205), October 7, 1992

On October 7, 1992, the Burbank city attorney and the Burbank Police Department sought an injunction against the Barrio Elmwood Rifa gang. (*People v. Acosta*, 1992). The target area consisted of an entire city block that the gang called home. The injunction did not name the gang as a defendant; it did, however, name 34 members of the gang. This was the first injunction to include the "no association" clause prohibiting gathering, or appearing anywhere in public view, with any other defendant anywhere in the target area. The no association restriction usually contains wording that prohibits the gang members from standing, sitting, walking, driving, bicycling, gathering, or appearing anywhere in public view with any other defendant therein, or with any other known gang member. This injunction was also part of a larger gang project, which included mentoring programs, tutoring, and improving recreational facilities. On November 2, 1992, the preliminary injunction was granted. On May 5, 1993, the injunction against the Barrio Elmwood Rifa gang was made permanent. The injunction had been served to 84 additional members of the gang as of June 22, 2005.

YEAR 1993

People v. Blythe Street Gang (Los Angeles Case LC020525), February 22, 1993

On February 22, 1993, the Los Angeles city attorney and the Los Angeles police sought an injunction against the Blythe Street gang (*People v. Blythe Street Gang*, 1993). The Blythe injunction was one of the more contested injunctions at that time. The Blythe injunction initially listed 57 defendants that claimed a territory in the Van Nuys and Devonshire areas of Los Angeles, covering six LAPD reporting districts, specifically Chase Street to the north, Van Nuys Boulevard to the east, Valerio Street to the south, and Sepulveda Boulevard to the west. The Blythe Street gang had approximately 700 members when implemented. Between 2000 and 2005, 205 Blythe Street gang members were served with the injunction and 119 were arrested for gang injunction violations. This injunction was not a part of any larger project or concurrent initiatives operating in the target areas according to police. The Blythe street gang started out as a car club that had rivalries with car clubs from San Fernando and Panorama City, which resulted in violent confrontations. Blythe converted from a car club into one of the largest gangs in the San Fernando Valley, with approximately 700 members in 1993. Due to the significant violence attributed to the gang, they became the first San Fernando Valley gang to be targeted with an injunction. According to Los Angeles City Attorney Jule Bishop, the injunction resulted in a tremendous reduction in crime, despite the findings of the ACLU study done following the case. The preliminary injunction was granted on April 27, 1993.

People v. Acuna (Santa Clara Case 729322), February 26, 1993

On February 26, 1993, the San Jose city attorney and the San Jose police in Santa Clara County sought an injunction against the Varrio Surenos Locos and Treces gang (*People v. Acuna*, 1993). The City of San Jose named 38 members of the gang that were congregating in the Rocksprings area and requested an injunction against the gang based on public nuisance law. The injunction would impose up to six months in jail or a $1,000 fine for engaging in such activities as being seen in public with another known gang member, wearing certain clothing, or carrying screwdrivers, pens, pagers, and spark plugs. Because the injunction came via a civil suit, those declared gang members were not allowed protections ensured in criminal proceedings, such as the right to an appointed attorney, a jury trial, or criminal justice standards of proof.

The case was the first by the City of San Jose to address the gang problems by using a civil gang injunction. The city submitted over 1,000 pages of evidence in support of the case, including police and citizen declarations, which outlined how the gang met the criteria established to define a gang, as well as the activity committed by the gang and the named defendants. The court granted the request for a temporary restraining order and issued an order to show cause as to why the preliminary injunction should not be granted. On June 28, 1993, following the hearing, the court issued the preliminary injunction against the 33 nonappearing defendants and continued the hearing as to the five remaining defendants that opposed the order. At the next hearing, the original five that opposed the order were joined by six additional defendants who sought to have the preliminary injunction vacated. After the court was briefed and heard the matter, the court issued the order against all of the defendants, the 11 in opposition included.

Blythe Injunction (False Promises), ACLU Study and City Attorney Response

On May 28, 1993, the American Civil Liberties Union released a report evaluating the effectiveness of the Blythe Street gang injunction. In a memo to Los Angeles District Attorney Gil Garcetti and Los Angeles City Attorney James K. Hahn accompanying the report, representatives from the ACLU wrote, "Our report reaches what we believe may be surprising conclusions. Not only did the injunction not lead to a reduction in violent crime and drug trafficking as a whole, but crime increased enormously." The letter continued, "We believe that these conditions were influenced greatly and exacerbated by patterns of crime and drug trafficking that evolved after the Blythe Street injunction." The case study by the ACLU examined trend data and found that the net effect of the Blythe Street injunction was an increase in violent crime and drug trafficking. Being that this research is designed to evaluate gang injunction effectiveness, the ACLU study was evaluated in detail to study the methods used to reach their conclusions.

The report examined crime data for 19 LAPD reporting districts that included the area covered under the injunction. The neighborhood under injunction is Reporting District 925 in the Van Nuys Division. RD 925 is bordered by Woodman Avenue to the east, the

405 Freeway to the west, Osborne Street to the north, and Victory Boulevard to the south. The report examined LAPD information on criminal activity in the area in question from late 1992, before the injunction was issued, through late 1994 or early 1995, more than 18 months following the court order. Three kinds of data were analyzed: numbers of reported violent crime (aggravated assault, rape, robbery, and homicide), calls for service, and felony drug arrests. These data were examined from four perspectives: Reporting District 925 alone (which includes the entire injunction area), the RDs located immediately north of the injunction area (where violent crime significantly increased following the injunction), the 19 RDs in the valley, and the City of Los Angeles as a whole.

The four reporting districts immediately north of the injunction area saw an increase in the number of violent crimes, calls for police service, and felony drug arrests. This pattern was consistent with the view that the Blythe injunction did not solve, but simply moved, the criminal activity outside the area. In the 19 reporting district areas, violent crime reportedly increased 52.1% between February 1993 and June 1993, and 27.1% between April 1993 and August 1994. Between February 1993 and August 1994 total violent crime in the City of Los Angeles rose only 16.5%; from April 1993 through July 1993, total violent crime increased 8.6%. The ACLU report claimed that instead of reducing criminal activity in the area covered by the injunction, violent crime and drug trafficking actually increased in this area. Further, crime increased considerably in the adjacent areas and crime statistics were higher in the 19 reporting district zones surrounding and including the injunction area than for Los Angeles as a whole.

Los Angeles prosecutors attacked the report as flawed. Assistant City Attorney Jule Bishop claimed, "The report isn't worth the paper it's printed on." In 1997, the Los Angeles City Attorney's Office conducted an evaluation of the Blythe injunction and the ACLU Blythe report. The city attorney called the report statistical mumbo jumbo of the worst kind because it connected disconnected facts and drew grandiose conclusions not supported by the data (*People v. Blythe Street*, 1993). One problem with measuring just violent crime rates is that you cannot understand the impact the injunctions have on quality of life crimes, the less serious nuisance crimes that have an impact on the community. Malcolm Klein noted that the ACLU study was "fairly minimal" in scope, relying entirely on aggregated crime statistics.

Issues of crime displacement and a cost-benefit analysis were allegedly evaluated, but the findings of the ACLU did not use scientific methods. Also, the LAPD did not reveal the same findings as the ACLU. The ACLU report studied statistics from all over the Van Nuys Division, which had 27 active gangs in the area, including the Blythe Street gang at that time. The study compared the Blythe Street gang territory to neighborhoods outside the division, and the ACLU appeared to be selecting those districts in the surrounding areas that had lower crime rates and ignored those divisions with higher rates in an attempt to skew the results to make crime appear to be going up in Van Nuys, according to Los Angeles City Attorney Jule Bishop. Despite the ACLU's claim that the injunctions had no benefit and increased crime, on May 23, 1996, the gang unit of the city attorney's office received a letter from the ACLU withdrawing from the Blythe Street injunction case. They ultimately never represented any client in the case, despite their claims that the injunction actually had a negative impact on crime rates.

This gang injunction was also one of those studied in the Los Angeles grand jury report in June 2004. According to the grand jury, this injunction resulted in a reduction in total reported crimes and Part 1 crimes in the target area. Preinjunction there were 155 total crimes, postinjunction (six months) there were 117 total crimes. Part 1 crimes preinjunction were 92, postinjunction they fell to 66 crimes (LA Grand Jury, 2004). According to the Grogger study, the net result of this injunction immediately following implementation was 38 less total crimes and 26 less serious Part 1 crimes (Grogger, 2000). Both the Grogger study and the Los Angeles grand jury study conflict with the findings of the ACLU in the Blythe study report.

People v. Amaya (Orange County Case 713223), June 30, 1993 (Attempt)

On June 30, 1993, the Orange County district attorney and the Westminster police sought an injunction against 59 members of the West Trece gang (*People v. Amaya*, 1993). The proposed injunction named individual defendants only and did not name the gang. On July 1, 1993, a temporary restraining order was issued against the gang. On August 30, 1993, the request for an injunction was denied by a superior court judge on the grounds that one of the provisions violated the constitutional rights of the gang members, the right to association, and all of the other provisions were already violations of the penal code. There was little case law at the time that decided the issue, as the Varrio Sureno Trece case had only been filed four months earlier and had not been adjudicated. Orange County District Attorney Investigator Al Valdez, who worked on the case, stated that the bad publicity the case generated created community opposition that caused the case to fail because it lacked support in the media and parts of the community sympathetic to the gang members; thus the judge failed to grant the order.

Strategies against Gang Environments Forms in LA to Help Get Gang Injunctions

In December 1993, the Los Angeles District Attorney's Office established a special unit to implement gang injunctions and assist the various cities within Los Angeles County to obtain gang injunctions. The Strategy Against Gang Environments (SAGE) program started in the City of Norwalk in December 1993 (Office of the District Attorney SAGE Handbook, 1996). The SAGE program stresses thinking outside the box, flexibility, collaboration with other agencies, and community outreach in seeking alternatives for dealing with gang activity that causes the fear and intimidation that cripples some of our communities. SAGE relies heavily on the use of gang injunctions, in conjunction with other interventions, to abate gang activity that tends to have a long-term negative impact on the community. The SAGE program attempts to remove or lessen the impact the gang has on the community by addressing the environmental impact of the target gang.

Other prosecuting agencies around the State of California have been exposed to the SAGE guidelines through training provided by the Los Angeles District Attorney's Office. SAGE attorneys have instructed prosecutors and have collaborated with the Los Angeles City Attorney's Office in numerous gang injunction initiatives. As a result, the problem-oriented approach implicit in the SAGE program is well represented in the education of the gang injunction process for agencies throughout the state. Declaring the ultimate goal of gang injunctions as the coordination of various community-based policing efforts to improve the quality of life in neighborhoods, the strategy is described as a coordinated effort between law enforcement agencies and local residents to reduce illegal gang activity. This approach is employed with other strategies to address neighborhood problems.

The objective of the program is to make the criminal justice system more responsive to the needs of the community, with the ultimate goal of increasing the quality of community life for all community members, including the offenders. Victimology is the study of why certain people are victims of crime and how lifestyles affect the chances that a certain person will fall victim to a crime. The field of victimology can cover a wide number of disciplines, including sociology, psychology, criminal justice, law, and advocacy. The SAGE program attempts to stress enforcement to allow the opposing disciplines to take hold and impact the quality of life for those in the community.

The agents of criminal justice should tailor their work so that its main purpose is to enhance community living, especially through reducing the paralysis of fear, the indignities of disorder, and the agony of criminal victimization. Civil gang abatement falls squarely within the ideal of community justice. Flexibility in tailoring responses to the local circumstances of the public nuisance and collaborating with the community to identify problems and formulate the appropriate response, are hallmarks of the problem-oriented perspective, community prosecution, and civil gang abatement. The improvement of the quality of life in gang-plagued neighborhoods is the goal advanced by the sparse literature on civil gang abatement.

YEAR 1994

People v. Avalos (Santa Clara Case CV739089), March 16, 1994

On March 16, 1994, the city attorney for the City of San Jose in Santa Clara County sought an injunction against the Varrio Mexicanos Locos gang. The injunction did not name the gang as a defendant; it did, however, name 24 individual members (*People v. Avalos*, 1994). The target was a small area known as Appian Lane, a four-block area that contained an elementary school and several multiunit apartment complexes, specifically Melbourne Avenue to the south, the railroad tracks to the north and west, and McLaughlin Avenue to the east.

People v. B Street Boys (Alameda Case 735405-4), May 18, 1994 (Attempt)

On May 18, 1994, the Alameda County district attorney and the Oakland police sought an injunction against the B Street Boys gang (*People v. B Street Boys*, 1994). On June 17, 1994, the ACLU represented the gang and was successful in preventing the injunction from being implemented. The injunction named the gang and 17 individual members as defendants, and targeted the area between A Street to the north, C Street to the south, 92nd Avenue to the west, and 98th Avenue to the east. The injunction sought to restrict any of the members of the gang from coming within 1,000 feet of the target area unless they could articulate a legitimate reason for being in the enjoined area, such as employment or residency. Judge James R. Lambden ruled that the injunction was overbroad and vague, and that the court should not further enjoin criminal activity that had existing remedy of law.

According to an ACLU staff attorney who litigated *Oakland v. B Street Boys*, the perceived success of gang abatement injunctions is not the pivotal issue. Whether they work in reducing crime or not, they flagrantly violate the rights of groups targeted specifically because of their age, ethnicity, and relationships. According to the ACLU, "Illegal searches may also work, but our Constitution doesn't permit them, lest we were to allow the government to impose a complete police state." The Oakland DA did not pursue the issue any further (ACLU News, 1997), as they decided to wait for more supporting case law and constitutional analysis by the higher courts.

City of Norwalk v. Orange Street Locos (Los Angeles Case VC016746), July 21, 1994

On July 21, 1994, the Los Angeles County district attorney, Norwalk city attorney, and Los Angeles Sheriff's Department sought an injunction against the Orange Street Locos gang (*City of Norwalk v. Orange Street Locos*, 1994). The injunction targeted 22 defendants that claimed a 20-square-block territory in the central portion of the City of Norwalk. The target area for the injunction was San Antonio Drive to the north, Foster Road to the northeast, Rosecrans Avenue to the south, Norwalk Boulevard to the east, and Orange Street to the southwest. The attorneys that worked the case were Deanne Castorena from the LA district attorney and Kevin Gano from the City of Norwalk. This injunction was hailed a success by the police following its implementation and resulted in at least 15 arrests for violations; according to police, the gang simply stopped congregating in the streets and alleyways following implementation.

On August 25, 1994, the preliminary injunction against the Orange Street Locos gang was granted. On September 8, 1995, the permanent injunction against the Orange Street Locos gang (*City of Norwalk v. Orange Street Locos*, 1994) was granted. After the injunction, the change in the neighborhood once overwhelmed by a local gang has been dramatic according to area residents. Their turf was covered with graffiti. Gang members were responsible for dozens of crimes, from car theft and drug possession to assault and armed robbery. Today, the graffiti is gone; children play basketball after school, rollerblade, and swing on the swing sets. The neighborhood's metamorphosis occurred almost immediately after the court order enjoined the activities of 22 OSL members.

The local sheriff's station documented the injunction's progress in weekly memos. The number of calls to the sheriff's department went down by nearly a third, and very few of the calls were in any way related to gangs. The memos report just a few crimes committed by gang members not listed in the injunction. Only five injunction defendants were prosecuted for violating the court order. The gang injunction was one of the cases studied by Grogger in the April 2002 *Journal of Law and Economics*. As of March 2010, the Los Angeles District Attorney's Office reported that this injunction is not enforced because the gang is defunct.

YEAR 1995

City of Long Beach v. Westside Longos (Los Angeles Case NC17601), October 6, 1995

On October 6, 1995, the Los Angeles County district attorney, the Long Beach city attorney, and Long Beach police sought an injunction against the Westside Longos gang (*City of Long Beach v. Westside Longos*, 1995). The injunction sued the gang and 30 named defendants and targeted the southwest portion of the City of Long Beach, from 20th Street to the north, Pacific Coast Highway to the south, the 710 Freeway to the east, and Santa Fe to the west. The attorneys that worked the case were Cynthia Zuniga from the LA district attorney and Bob Hight from the Long Beach city attorney. In the year following the implementation of the injunction, the police department made 27 arrests for violations of it. According to police, the citizens in the area claimed that the injunctions was "the greatest thing that ever happened" to the target area. On October 23, 1995, the preliminary injunction against the Westside Longos was granted. This gang injunction was one of the cases studied by Grogger in the April 2002 *Journal of Law and Economics*. On July 14, 1997, the permanent injunction against the Westside Longos was granted. As of June 2010, the Westside Longos gang injunction was not being enforced because the gang was no longer active in the safety zone.

City of Pasadena v. Pasadena Denver Lanes (Los Angeles Case GC015651), October 25, 1995

On October 25, 1995, the Los Angeles County District Attorney's Office, the City of Pasadena city attorney, and the Pasadena police sought an injunction against the Pasadena Denver Lanes gang, a large blood gang active in northwest Pasadena (*City of Pasadena v. Pasadena Denver Lanes*, 1995). This injunction named 35 defendants and targeted the area from Washington Boulevard to the north, Orange Grove Boulevard to the south, Marengo Avenue to the east, and Fair Oaks Avenue to the west. The attorneys that worked the case were Deanne Castorena from the District Attorney's Office and Yvette McDowell from the Pasadena City Attorney's Office.

A police study revealed that in the first three months after the injunction calls for service in the target area decreased by 26%, as opposed to a 2% decrease citywide. The injunction sparked the formation of the neighborhood association, which focused on tutoring and mentoring youth in the target area so they did not join the gang. The injunction was credited with the formation of the association, because prior to it being implemented, the neighborhood would not meet for fear of retaliation from the gang members.

A side benefit attributed to the Pasadena injunction was the Injunction Conjunction project. The program was designed to find and implement long-term gang prevention strategies in the City of Pasadena. The Pasadena coalition for a nonviolent city hosted a series of eight meetings between the community, police, and prosecutors, which further discussed how the gangs in the area could be reduced. A program that provided job and life skills training to the gang members was established. At the end of the first 15-week program, seven of the gang members were employed as a result of the project and the skills they learned. On December 6, 1995, the preliminary injunction against the Pasadena Denver Lanes gang was granted (*City of Pasadena v. Pasadena Denver Lanes*, 1995). This gang injunction was one of those studied in the Grogger study. On December 6, 1995, the preliminary injunction was granted. On December 24, 1996, the permanent injunction against the Pasadena Denver Lanes gang was granted. As of June 2010, the Pasadena Denver Lanes injunction was no longer being enforced because the chief of the Pasadena PD opposed enforcement.

YEAR 1996

City of Redondo Beach v. North Side Redondo 13 (Los Angeles Case YC026580), April 30, 1996

On April 30, 1996, the Redondo Beach city attorney and Redondo Beach Police Department sought an injunction against 27 members of the North Side Redondo 13 gang (*City of Redondo Beach v. North Side Redondo 13*, 1996). Members of the North Side Redondo (NSR) gang, a particularly violent gang, had been using Perry Park as an informal headquarters for NSR activity; in the judgment of the police and their declarations in support of the case, the park had become the single most significant factor in the growing strength of the gang. The injunction targeted Perry Park and the surrounding 24-block area. For five months the police department's Gang Enforcement Team collected evidence to prove the case in court and illustrated the activities conducted by specific gang members to be included in the injunction (Skipper, 1997). On June 28, 1996, the injunction against the North Side Redondo

13 gang was made permanent (*City of Redondo Beach v. North Side Redondo 13*, 1996).

The transformation of Perry Park began in 1996 when neighborhood residents and the city council succeeded in getting an injunction against gang-related activities placed on the park. The city could see that some in the community were avoiding public spaces such as Perry Park due to the local gang and took action to correct the problem. After more than $1 million spent on renovations from state and federal government funds, the park now boasts a teen center, new playground equipment, and a renovated senior center. The injunction prohibited drinking alcoholic beverages or even being within 10 feet of an open, and partially or wholly full, container of alcohol in public or a place in public view; and making, causing, or encouraging others to make loud noise of any kind that would be deemed loud by a reasonable person, including but not limited to playing loud music, participating in boisterous parties, and engaging in exhibitions of speed in vehicles with the attendant noise, roaring of engines, and screeching of tires. The injunction restricted gang association or congregating, but unlike other injunctions, this order specified the association to be in groups of three or more, and only in Perry Park or within 10 yards of the outside fence surrounding Perry Park.

City of Pasadena v. Villa Boys and Krazy Boys (Los Angeles Case GC016746/GC017109), June 13, 1996

On June 13, 1996, the Los Angeles County District Attorney's Office, the City of Pasadena city attorney, and the Pasadena police sought an injunction against two gangs, the Villa Boyz and the Krazy Boyz (*City of Pasadena v. Villa Boys and Krazy Boys*, 1996). The injunction named 26 defendants and targeted the northwest portion of the City of Pasadena, from Orange Grove Boulevard to the north, the Foothill Freeway to the south, El Molino Avenue to the east, and Summit Avenue to the west. According to police, just prior to the injunction being implemented the gangs were at war, which resulted in four murders in a five-week period. As a result of the injunction and increased police patrols, the war seemed to end immediately, with no more murders occurring for the next year. In addition, park and recreation officials for the Villa Park stated that park usage by parents bringing their children there increased significantly following the injunction being implemented.

Residents along the streets of northwest Pasadena described a transformation of gang activities in the 12-square-block zone. "Things are beautiful," said resident Rudy Partida. "The night crawlers are gone and the whole neighborhood is on an up."

Pasadena Police Sergeant Jim Shear wrote a memo describing an unprecedented change in the community: "The last week has netted no arrests and no calls for service." Only a handful of people were ever prosecuted for violations of the injunction; none has been prosecuted since September 1996. One reason for the change is that the injunctions energized the community. Residents started getting involved, suing landlords who were renting to troublemakers; since then, the neighborhood association has organized numerous block cleanups, a tutoring program, and an absentee landlord group. Another factor is that the injunctions actually scared off gang members. "It never ceases to amaze me," says Attorney Webb. "We prosecute these guys for drive-bys, murders, rape, and they're seemingly unfazed. As soon as we hit 'em with a lot of paperwork, they disappear."

Bernard Melekian, who became Pasadena's police chief about the same time the city was seeking its second court order, called the injunctions "an intellectual substitute for responsible public policy" and preferred a combination of hard police work and community services to combat gangs. The Special Enforcement Section targeted the hardest gang members with vigorous enforcement of probation and parole violations, and the department started an early intervention program with first-time juvenile offenders. "There are aggressive enforcement ways to deal with known gang members," Melekian says. "All we've done is move their hangout, which is fine if you live in the injunction area so why don't we enjoin the entire city?" According to the chief, the net result of the Pasadena injunction was to move the gang into another area, indicating that the injunction did have an impact on the gang in the target area. Unlike random aggressive enforcement of gangs, aggressive enforcement of an injunction enables law enforcement to effectively prevent imminent criminal activity by arresting persons for prohibited patterns of conduct that are known to precede and facilitate the gang crimes. The case utilized a temporary restraining order issued on July 13, 1996. On July 12, 1996, the preliminary injunction against the Villa Boyz and Krazy Boyz was granted (*City of Pasadena v. Villa Boys and Krazy Boys*, 1996). On May 6, 1997, the permanent injunction against the Villa Boyz and Krazy Boyz was granted (*City of Pasadena v. Villa Boys and Krazy Boys*, 1996). As of June 2010, the Villa Boys/Krazy Boys injunction was not being enforced because the chief of police in Pasadena opposes enforcement.

People v. Headhunters (SB Case SCV30441), June 20, 1996 (Attempt)

On June 20, 1996, the Fontana city attorney and the Fontana police sought an injunction against 39 members of the Headhunters gang

(*People v. Headhunters*, 1996). The City of Fontana utilized a private law firm to obtain the gang injunction for the city. The law firm of Best, Best, and Krieger filed the order against the gang and 39 individuals. The injunction covered a territory in the City of Fontana, specifically Jurupa Avenue to the north, Live Oak Avenue to the east, the San Bernardino/Riverside County line to the south, and the Fontana/Ontario City limits to the west. On July 3, 1996, the injunction was denied as the city only filed six declarations in support of the injunction. The court denied the request because of a perceived lack of specific evidence to show the gang created a nuisance in the target area and that the target gang posed a credible threat to the community to a significant enough degree to be considered a public nuisance. The evidence must be clear and convincing and show the gang is a public nuisance and the targeted gang members are responsible for the problem.

People v. Lennox-13 (Los Angeles Case YC027006), July 30, 1996

On July 30, 1996, the Los Angeles County District Attorney's Office and Los Angeles County sheriff sought an injunction against the Lennox-13 gang (*People v. Lennox-13*, 1996). The injunction named 37 defendants and targeted two areas in the west Lennox area of Los Angeles: Area 1 was from Century Boulevard to the north, 104th Street to the south, Dalerose Avenue to the east, and Felton Avenue to the west. Area 2 was from Lennox Boulevard to the north, 112th Street to the south, Dalerose Avenue to the east, and Redfern Avenue to the west. The attorney that worked the case was Jonlyn Callahan from the district attorney. This gang injunction was one of the cases studied by Grogger in the April 2002 *Journal of Law and Economics* (Grogger, 2002). On September 11, 1996, the preliminary injunction against the Lennox-13 gang was granted (*People v. Lennox-13*, 1996). On February 3, 1999, the permanent injunction against the Lennox-13 gang was granted (*People v. Lennox-13*, 1996).

City of Commerce v. Chopper 12 (Los Angeles Case BC155927), August 20, 1996

On August 20, 1996, the City of Commerce and the Los Angeles Sheriff's Department sought an injunction against the Chopper 12 gang (*City of Commerce v. Chopper 12*, 1996). The injunction named 39 defendants that claimed a territory in the City of Commerce. This gang injunction was one of the cases studied in the April 2002 *Journal of Law and Economics* (Grogger, 2002). On November 14, 1996, the preliminary injunction was granted.

On April 15, 1998, the permanent injunction against the Chopper 12 gang was granted (*City of Commerce v. Chopper 12 Gang*, 1996). Arnoldo Beltran and Agustìn Medina were the attorneys involved in drafting the injunction that enjoined members of the Chopper 12 gang, essentially prohibiting them from congregating around city-owned facilities, harassing innocent bystanders, and engaging in criminal activity of any sort. According to Medina, the city saw a decrease in crime around the park. "Gang injunctions can be very effective in thwarting gang activity," Medina believes.

City of Inglewood v. Crenshaw Mafia (Los Angeles Case YC028318), December 17, 1996

On December 17, 1996, the Los Angeles County District Attorney's Office and Los Angeles Sheriff's Office sought an injunction against the Crenshaw Mafia gang, a very active blood gang in the Darby and Dixon area of the City of Inglewood, an area often called the deadliest neighborhood in the south bay at that time (*City of Inglewood v. Crenshaw Mafia*, 1996). The injunction named 41 defendants and targeted the area from Century Boulevard to the north, 104th Street to the south, Crenshaw Boulevard to the east, and Yukon Avenue to the west. The attorney that worked the case was Henry Kerner from the district attorney's office. In the four years preceding the injunction, the gang had been involved in 19 murders in the target area. In the two years following the implementation of the injunction no murders were attributed to the gang and at least 14 arrests were made for violations of the injunction. On January 29, 1997, the preliminary injunction was granted against the Crenshaw Mafia gang (*City of Inglewood v. Crenshaw Mafia*, 1996). On May 13, 1998, the permanent injunction was granted against the Crenshaw Mafia gang.

Twelve of the defendants appeared in court. The defendants asked Judge Robert Mallano for a public defender, but the judge said no. This was a civil court, he explained. There was no guarantee of representation. Travon Donte Adkins, whose nickname is Lil Lunchmeat, told the judge he wanted all the police officers who made statements about him to submit to lie detector tests. But Mallano said he would be basing his decision exclusively on the written record. If the gang members had objections, he said, they should have hired a lawyer and filed written briefs before the court hearing. By the time the judge finally granted the injunction, the defendants were stunned and angry. "None of us knew what an injunction was," said defendant Kenneth Bell. "We thought we were going to have some public assistance. I don't know civil cases. I've never been sued in my life. We got no legal aid, period. Nobody's backing us." Said Adkins, about the suggestion that he hire a lawyer, "That's the whole point. They know we don't got any money." He asked to be excused and left the courtroom shouting, "They know niggas ain't got no money." As of June 2010, according to the Los Angeles district attorney, the Crenshaw Mafia gang injunction was not enforced due to lack of resources by the Inglewood city attorney.

YEAR 1997

People v. 18th Street Gang Alsace Clique (Los Angeles Case BC167915), March 21, 1997

On March 21, 1997, the Los Angles County District Attorney's Office, the Los Angeles city attorney, and the Los Angeles Police Department filed the first of some injunctions against the 18th Street gang Alsace Jefferson clique (*People v. 18th Street Gang Alsace Clique*, 1997). The injunction sued the gang as the only defendant in the case and listed 18 gang members in the supporting declarations, restricting them from standing, sitting, walking, gathering, or appearing in groups of two or more in a 1-square-mile area (Figure 12.1), specifically the area from Westhaven Street to the north, Jefferson Boulevard to the south, Alsace Avenue to the east, and Hauser Boulevard to the west. This injunction was evaluated by the city attorney's office following the injunction. According to the city attorney, by comparing the year before the injunction and the year after the injunction, a 47.2% reduction in crime was reported in the target area.

One of the gang members, Gusatvo Guzman, was stopped and interviewed by the media as he left the courthouse. Guzman, who's nickname is Bullet, said, "That man trying to set his own rules, ya know what I mean, but it ain't going down like that, not in the neighborhood" (City News Service, 1997c). In issuing his order the judge said there is sufficient evidence to show the 18 defendants named in the injunction were involved in gang and criminal activity, including robbery, drug sales, blocking sidewalks, and urinating in public.

People v. Brown Nation (Los Angeles Case VC 24170), March 27, 1997 (Attempt)

On March 27, 1997, the Los Angeles County District Attorney's Office and the Los Angeles police filed an injunction against the Brown Nation gang (*People v. Brown Nation*, 1997). This injunction named 16 defendants that claimed areas in two separate

FIGURE 12.1 Map of *People v. Brown Nation.*

incorporated cities, the southwest Bellflower area and northeast Long Beach area, specifically from the Artesia Freeway to the north, South Street to the south, Lakewood Boulevard to the east, and Paramount Boulevard to the west. This injunction was a solo project of the Los Angeles County District Attorney's Office. The attorney that worked the case was Deanne Castorena. On November 14, 1997, the injunction against the Brown Nation was dismissed. This injunction never made it past the complaint stage and the preliminary injunction was never filed after it had been determined that the existing gang was virtually defunct and the criminal activity associated with the gang was nonexistent. After a review of the case and the gang's activity, the case was dismissed at the request of the district attorney (*People v. Brown Nation*, 1997).

City of Long Beach v. West Coast Crips (Los Angeles Case NC021240), May 5, 1997

On May 5, 1997, the Los Angeles County District Attorney's Office, the Long Beach city attorney, and the Long Beach police filed an injunction against the West Coast Crips gang in Long Beach (*City of Long Beach v. West Coast Crips*, 1997). The injunction named 46 defendants that claimed a territory in the west portion of the City of Long Beach from 34th Street to the north, Canton Avenue to the south, Delta to the east, and the Union Pacific Railroad tracks to the west (CBS News, 1997). In the 50-block area targeted in North Long Beach, Deputy District Attorney Cynthia Zuniga said gang members were selling drugs and committing drive-by shootings, burglaries, car thefts, and robberies. The injunction was the second sought in North Long Beach. "Some residents have left the area, because of intolerable living conditions caused by the gang," Zuniga said.

The gang injunction was seen as a catalyst for the community to begin to address crime associated with two large apartment complexes used by the gang as hangouts. The community improved security and put gates and other physical barriers in the complexes that greatly reduced reported crimes following the injunction. This gang injunction was one of the cases studied in by Grogger the April 2002 *Journal of Law and Economics*. On June 10, 1997, the preliminary injunction was issued against the West Coast Crips (*City of Long Beach v. West Coast Crips*, 1997). On May 21, 1998, the permanent injunction was issued against the West Coast Crips (*City of Long Beach v. West Coast Crips*, 1997). As of June 2010, the Los Angeles district attorney indicated that the West Coast Crips gang injunction was not being enforced because the gang was defunct in the target area.

People v. 18th Street Gang Pico/Union (Los Angeles Case BC175684), August 1, 1997

On August 1, 1997, the Los Angeles district attorney and the Los Angeles police filed an injunction against the 18th Street Gang Pico Union clique (*People v. 18th Street Gang Pico/Union*, 1997). The injunction named 50 defendants and sued the entire gang as an entity. The target area for the injunction (Figure 12.2) is the Harbor Freeway to the east, Hoover Street to the west, Washington Boulevard to the south, and 9th Street to the north, and the entire target area included a 100-yard buffer in every direction outside of it. The preliminary injunction was issued on August 29, 1997. The injunction was one of the largest to date and actually impacted three 18th Street gang cliques. The LAPD reported a 62% decrease in Part 1 crimes in the target area in the six months following the injunction. This gang injunction was one of the cases studied by Grogger in the April 2002 *Journal of Law and Economics* (Grogger, 2002). On November 10, 1998, the injunction against the 18th Street Pico Union was made permanent (*People v. 18th Street Gang Pico/Union*, 1997).

Following implementation of the injunction, patrol officers called the target area a ghost town. There was visibly less gang clustering, and reported incidents of gang violence went down 50%. Cliff Akiyama, a University of Virginia graduate student who worked with the LAPD on the project, confirmed that crime was reduced in the target areas. Akiyama credited the injunction strategy that targeted quality of life crimes in the area as being the source of the positive change (Levy, 1997). On September 21, 1999, the district attorney appeared *ex parte* before Judge James Bascue and advised the judge of concerns regarding the credibility of some of the declarations filed in support of the 18th Street Pico Union injunction (*People v. 18th Street Gang Pico/Union*, 1997). The district attorney requested a temporary stay of the permanent injunction and it was granted. The injunction was stayed several times after that, including June 20, 2000, and December 20, 2000. The problem with the injunction was that three of the six gang investigators used to support the gang injunction have subsequently been terminated by the LAPD or identified as targets in the Rampart investigation.

Unfortunately, the testimony of the three remaining experts related to the history and operation of the gang, rather than to individual contacts of gang members and direct observations of nuisance activity (Lopez, 1999). A substantial number of other

FIGURE 12.2 Map of *People v. 18th Street Pico Union.*

officers that provided declarations in support of the injunction were similarly under investigation. Redaction of all of the questionable officer's declarations would have amounted to the injunction not having enough probable cause to support its existence. To compound the problem even further, the LAPD SEU (formerly known as CRASH) was not fully staffed and did not have enough qualified experts to provide new declarations at that time (Los Angeles City Attorney Gang Prosecution, 1995). The dramatic statements from some of the police officers were used by the Los Angeles County district attorney and the city attorney to obtain the injunction against dozens of 18th Street members in the Rampart Division. When the truth of some of the declarations had been questioned, it undermined two court injunctions against 18th Street gang members.

The ACLU applauded the swift decision by the district attorney's office to halt implementation of the 18th Street gang injunction. The injunction, clearly based on some false affidavits by members of the now infamous Rampart CRASH unit, could not possibly have withstood a court challenge in light of recent evidence of perjury and corruption in the unit. Allegations of police abuse in enforcing gang injunctions are not limited to 18th Street. All affidavits underlying gang injunctions citywide were carefully reviewed (Schroeder, 1999).

People v. 7th Street Gang (San Bernardino Case SCVSS42552), October 24, 1997

On October 24, 1997, the San Bernardino city attorney and the San Bernardino Police Department sought an injunction against the 7th Street gang (*People v. 7th Street Gang*, 1997). The 7th Street gang is a subset of the Westside Verdugo gang. The injunction named 47 defendants and targeted the territory of the 7th Street gang in the City of San Bernardino, specifically the area bordered by 16th Street to the north, 5th Street to the south, Mount Vernon to the west, and the Interstate 215 to the east. The attorney that worked the case was Deputy City Attorney Paula Coleman. On November 12, 1997, the preliminary injunction against the 7th Street gang was granted (*People v. 7th Street Gang*, 1997). On November 13, 1997, the city attorney also filed a court order requiring the court to set the bail of any arrested defendants at $20,000 (Penal Code Section 1275). That required a consistent bail for any of the defendants arrested for an injunction violation. That started a trend in which some police departments began requesting bail increases to keep injunction violators in custody. On November 30, 1998, the injunction against the 7th Street gang (subset of the Westside Verdugo gang) was made permanent by Judge John P. Wade (*People v. 7th Street Gang*, 1997).

San Bernardino police filed the city's first gang injunction in 1995 against 67 members of the 7th Street gang after a series of increased patrols failed to curb violence, said San Bernardino police Lt. R.C. Garcia. The city has since seen a 95% decrease in the targeted area, Garcia said. "Nothing else has worked long term," Garcia said. "We've seen lots of short-term solutions work temporarily, but it seems they were always waiting in the wings to take over." San Bernardino has filed seven injunctions against different gangs in other parts of the city and has reduced crime in selected neighborhoods, San Bernardino Deputy City Attorney Jolena Grider said. She added that 90% of the targeted suspects usually abide by the injunction. San Bernardino is now struggling with some gangs that migrate to different parts of the city, outside the injunction area. The city can counter by filing multiple injunctions against the same gang as it migrates. "In another way, we can follow them and let them know, 'We're watching you,'" Grider said. "In some neighborhoods, children couldn't play outside and this stopped gang members from taking over." Gang injunctions can be effective by creating a chilling effect on gang members facing possible parole or probation violations, said San Bernardino Deputy District Attorney Mark Vos. He added that they only work in situations in which a gang is loyal to its own turf in the problem areas. "There are added benefits of a court ordering gangsters not to congregate," Vos said. "For most gang injunction programs in Southern California, the places find a benefit and decline of crime to make it worthwhile."

People v. Varrio Posole Locos (San Diego Case N76652), November 26, 1997

On November 26, 1997, the San Diego County district attorney and the Oceanside Police Department sought an injunction against the Varrio Posole Locos gang (*People v. Varrio Posole Locos*, 1997). The injunction named 28 members of the gang and targeted an area in the City of Oceanside, specifically the area from Interstate 5 to the west, Mission Avenue to the south, Carey Road to the east, and State Route 76 to the north. On December 11, 1997, the Varrio Posole preliminary gang injunction was granted by Judge John S. Einhorn against 28 individual defendants. On February 17, 1999, the Varrio Posole gang injunction was made permanent (*People v. Varrio Posole Locos*, 1997). The order was officially filed with the court on March 30, 1999. According to Deputy District Attorney Susan Mazza, in the two years before the gang was served with the injunction, 10 suspected gang-related murders were committed in the city; in the year following the gang injunction, no murders occurred.

YEAR 1998

People v. Mara Salvatrucha (Los Angeles Case BC187039), March 4, 1998

On March 4, 1998, the Los Angeles County District Attorney's Office, the Los Angeles City Attorney's Office, and the Los Angeles police sought an injunction against the Mara Salvatrucha gang (*People v. Mara Salvatrucha*, 1998). The injunction named 40 defendants that claimed a territory in the East Hollywood area of Los Angeles, specifically the area from Sunset Boulevard to the north, Melrose Avenue to the south, Normandie Avenue to the east, and Van Ness Avenue to the west (The Associated Press, 1997). This gang injunction was one of the cases studied by Grogger in the April 2002 *Journal of Law and Economics* (Grogger, 2002). On April 13, 1998, the preliminary injunction against the Mara Salvatrucha gang was issued (*People v. Mara Salvatrucha*, 1998). Judge Patricia Collins issued the preliminary injunction against 30 of the defendants, none of which responded to the complaint for injunctive relief. On September 18, 2003, the injunction obtained against the Mara Salvatrucha gang in April 1998 was dismissed. The preliminary injunction in this case was in place for over five years before the district attorney decided to dismiss it due to allegations that officer declarations were tainted by officers that were implicated in the Rampart corruption investigation in Los Angeles at that time.

People v. 18th Street Shatto Park (Los Angeles Case BC190334), May 1, 1998

On May 1, 1998, the Los Angeles County district attorney and the Los Angeles Police Department sought an injunction against 90 members of the 18th Street Shatto Park and Columbia Little Cycos cliques of the 18th Street gang (*People v. 18th Street Gang Shatto Park*, 1998). This injunction sued the gang and 90 named members that claimed a territory in the LAPD Rampart area, specifically two safety zones. Safety zone 1 is Normandie to the west, Beverly Boulevard to the north, Westmorland Avenue to the east, and 7th Street to the south. Safety zone 2 is Alvarado Street to the west, Beverly Boulevard to the north, Beaudry Avenue to the east, and Wilshire Boulevard to the south. This gang injunction was one of the cases studied by Grogger in the April 2002 *Journal of Law and Economics*. On June 30, 1998, the preliminary injunction was issued against the seven additional defendants who were represented by private counsel (*People v. 18th*

Street Gang Shatto Park, 1998). On July 9, 1998, Judge Fumiko Wasserman issued a preliminary injunction against 74 defendants who defaulted after failing to answer the complaint in the 18th Street Shatto Park case (*People v. 18th Street Gang Shatto Park*, 1998).

On September 22, 1999, the LA district attorney appeared *ex parte* before Judge Wasserman and advised her that they had concerns with the credibility of some of the declarations filed in support of the request for injunctive relief. The court issued a temporary stay of the preliminary injunction and postponed the default prove-up hearing as to the 74 defendants. Judge Wasserman granted several requests for continuances. As in the case of the Pico Union injunction, a substantial number of officers who submitted declarations in support of the Shatto Park injunction were under investigation at that time, including five experts used in that case. If the declarations of those officers were removed from the probable cause used to support the injunction, the injunction would not be supported by enough probable cause to pass the legal burden. At around the same time the injunction was dismissed, the U.S. Attorney's Office conducted a large-scale operation against the Shatto Park clique of the 18th Street gang, and 26 defendants were indicted on federal charges related to that investigation.

On March 2, 2001, the injunction against the 18th Street Shatto Park gang was dismissed. Later evaluation of the gang and the target area revealed that pursuing an injunction against the Shatto Park clique was not warranted as the prior injunction, along with the federal investigation, severely limited the gang's activity to the point that a new injunction was not deemed necessary by the district attorney. The injunction against the Pico Union clique of 18th Street was redone and a new injunction was obtained (*People v. 18th Street Gang Shatto Park*, 1998).

People v. Arroyo—Varrio Horseshoe, Westside Mob, Sur Santos Pride, and Eastside Clanton Gangs (Santa Clara Case CV775225), July 10, 1998

On July 10, 1998, the Santa Clara district attorney sought an injunction against four gangs in a 9-square-block area of the county known as the Almaden/Vine area (*People v. Arroyo*, 1998). The injunction named 4 gangs and 47 individuals as defendants and targeted the area from Duane Street to the north, Oak Street to the east, 1st Street to the south, and Willow Avenue to the west. The permanent order was granted on September 4, 1998, and was filed under seal.

People v. Harpy's Gang (Los Angeles Case BC192678), July 16, 1998

On June 16, 1998, the Los Angeles County city attorney and the Los Angeles police sought an injunction against the Harpy's gang (*People v. Harpy's Gang*, 1998). The injunction sued the gang and named 33 individual defendants and targeted an area in the Rampart, Southwest, and Newton Divisions of the LAPD and covered 12 reporting districts, specifically Washington Boulevard to the north, Figueroa Street to the east, Jefferson Boulevard to the south, and Normandie Avenue to the west. A superior court judge ordered the Harpy's members to stop terrorizing the neighborhood near USC and to stop publicly associating with each other on their turf. In approving the fifth injunction leveled against a Los Angeles gang by the city attorney's office since 1997, Judge Reginald Dunn called the Harpy's a "criminal street gang that creates a significant public nuisance" (Becerra, 1998). The Harpy's gang had 350 total members.

Between 1998 and 2005, 58 additional members had been served and were now enjoined by the injunction and 31 arrests were made for violating the gang injunction. This injunction was not a part of any larger project or concurrent initiatives operating in the target areas. The injunction was sought because of the significant narcotic sales attributed to the gang. The office of the city attorney conducted an analysis of this case the year following the injunction. During the first full quarter that the Harpy's injunction was implemented, the local community enjoyed a 29% reduction in serious crime, including a 44% reduction in street robberies (LA City Attorney, 1999).

This gang injunction was one of the cases studied by Grogger in the April 2002 *Journal of Law and Economics* (Grogger, 2002). This gang injunction was also one of those studied in the Los Angeles grand jury report in June 2004 (LA Grand Jury, 2004). This injunction resulted in a reduction in total reported crimes and Part 1 crimes in the target area. Preinjunction there were 59 total crimes, postinjunction (six months) there were 53 total crimes. Part 1 crimes preinjunction were 42, postinjunction they fell to 35 crimes (LA Grand Jury, 2004). The net result of this injunction immediately following implementation was six less total crimes and seven less serious Part 1 crimes. On August 4, 1998, the preliminary injunction against the Harpy's gang was granted (*People v. Harpy's Gang*, 1998). On July 17, 2000, the permanent gang injunction was granted against the Harpy's gang.

People v. Original Bloods (San Joaquin Case CV05505), July 28, 1998

On July 28, 1998, the San Joaquin district attorney and the Stockton police sought an injunction against the Original Bloods gang in Stockton (*People v. Original Bloods*, 1998). The local jurisdiction was unable to provide a copy of this case for any further details.

People v. Alcarez—Vagos Gang (Monterey Case 115095), July 30, 1998

On July 30, 1998, the Salinas City Attorney's Office filed an injunction against the Vagos, or Vagos Sureno gang (*People v. Alcarez*, 1998). The injunction enjoined 14 named defendants in a five-block area in the City of Salinas in Monterey County, specifically Garner Avenue to the east, Del Monte Boulevard to the west, Pacific Avenue to the north, and Green Street to the south. It also included the 1000 to 1100 blocks of Elkington Street. The no association clause in this case provided a couple of exceptions to the no association rule and allowed any two defendants to be together if in their lawful place of employment, if inside a private residence, if with an immediate family member, or if commuting directly to and from their place of employment. This injunction provided detailed instructions to the defendants on how they can opt out and be removed from the order. The injunction allows any defendants to petition to be removed from the order if they remain arrest-free for a period of two years following being served.

It also allows defendants to get their name removed if they complete the local second chance youth program and provide proof of certification. The second chance youth program requires that the defendants serve 100 hours of community service with a qualified nonprofit organization. The defendants, all of whom were male, also have to complete a men's alternative to violence program, need to enroll in a legitimate educational institution, vocational, or job training program, or be employed for a minimum of 30 hours per week (Jones, 1998). They must also complete a minimum of 40 hours of drug and alcohol, violence, or other counseling as recommended by the program. Some feel that injunctions make it hard for the gang member to get into the job market; this injunction sought to help gang members by providing them motivation to distance themselves from the gang and seek out skills to help them stay away from the gang on a long-term basis (National Institute of Justice, 2002). Some gang members have no legitimate job, have no desire to get a job, and have no skills to maintain a job should they find one; this injunction is an example of the trend to help gang members in the injunction process (Thompson and Jason, 1998). The order was made permanent on July 9, 1999.

People v. Varrio San Marcos (San Diego Case N078777), August 3, 1998

On August 3, 1998, the San Diego County District Attorney's Office and the San Diego County Sheriff's Office sought an injunction against the Varrio San Marcos gang (*People v. Varrio San Marcos*, 1998). The injunction named 26 members of the Varrio San Marcos gang and covered a territory in San Marcos, specifically from Grandon Avenue between Beverly Place and Via Bella Maria, Via Bella Maria between Grandon Avenue and 1st Street, 1st Street between Via Bella Maria and South Las Flores Drive, South Las Flores Drive between 1st Street and Grand Avenue and Linda Vista Drive, Linda Vista Drive between South Rancho Santa Fe Road and Pacific Street, Pacific Street between Linda Vista Drive and Bradley Park, and Bradley Park. This is one of the injunctions studied in this research. The control gang is South Los. The City of San Marcos essentially has two gangs, the enjoined Varrio San Marcos (west side of the city) and the control gang South Los (east side of the city). The South Los gang in San Marcos originated in Los Angeles and started in 1998 in San Marcos. In 1996, both gangs had almost the same membership, just over 100 members per gang. The City of San Marcos had a population of about 60,000 people. On September 28, 1998, the preliminary injunction against the Varrio San Marcos gang was granted by Judge John S. Einhorn. On November 1, 1999, the Varrio San Marcos gang injunction was made permanent (*People v. Varrio San Marcos*, 1998).

City of Compton v. Compton Varrio Flats, Aka Tortilla Flats Gang (Los Angeles Case TC011598), August 20, 1998

On August 20, 1998, the Los Angeles District Attorney's Office and the Compton Police Department sought an injunction against the Varrio Tortilla Flats gang in Compton (*City of Compton v. Compton Varrio Tortilla Flats Gang*, 1998). The injunction listed 48 defendants and targeted the area of central Compton, specifically Rosecrans Avenue to the north, Magnolia Street to the south, Magnolia Street to the east, and Mathisen Avenue to the west, including the 100 block of East Elm Street, East Cedar Street, East Maple Street, and East Spruce Street. The injunction was a solo project of the Los Angeles County District Attorney's Office;

the attorney that worked the case is Jonlyn Callahan. On October 8, 1998, the preliminary injunction was issued against the Varrio Tortilla Flats gang (*City of Compton v. Compton Varrio Tortilla Flats Gang*, 1998). On June 23, 2000, the permanent injunction was issued against the Varrio Tortilla Flats gang (*City of Compton v. Compton Varrio Tortilla Flats Gang*, 1998). On June 23, 2000, Judge James Kaddo issued the permanent injunction against the Compton Tortilla Flats gang. According to the Los Angeles district attorney, the Compton Varrio Flats injunction was not enforced as of June 2010 due to a shift from Compton PD to LASD.

City of San Diego v. Lincoln Park (San Diego Case 725795), November 19, 1998 (Updated in 2004)

On November 19, 1998, the San Diego City Attorney's Office and the San Diego Police Department sought an injunction against the Lincoln Park Bloods gang (*People v. Lincoln Park*, 1998). The injunction named 23 members of the Lincoln Park gang and targeted the area of southeast San Diego, specifically the area from 45th Street to the west, Magnus Way to the south, Euclid Avenue to the east, and Imperial Avenue to the north. The Lincoln Park Bloods target area is about 0.64 miles in size. The Lincoln Park gang has 216 members; the control gang, 5/9 Brims, has 219 members. The 5/9 Brims claim an area southwest of Lincoln Park. There are several theories of how the gang got its name; one is it had 5 OGs and 9 soldiers at the time of its inception, another is all of the original founding members were born in 1959, and another is the gang was an offshoot of the 59th Street gang in Los Angeles. The 5/9 Brims as known today started in 1973 and is considered the first blood gang in San Diego. The Lincoln Park Bloods began in the early 1980s and were originally known as the School Yard Piru. In March 2004, this order was updated and amended under the same case number; see 2004 section for update. The modified injunction adds 21 gang members who are barred from a variety of activities within a roughly 2-square-mile section of southeastern San Diego, including gathering or appearing in public with any member of the gang they claim.

In March 2004, the San Diego City Attorney's Office and the San Diego Police Department amended the 1998 injunction against the Lincoln Park Bloods gang (*People v. Lincoln Park*, 1998). The amended injunction updated the 21 originally named defendants in the 1998 injunction and added 23 new defendants that targeted the area of southeast San Diego, specifically the area from 45th Street to the west, Magnus Way to the south, Euclid Avenue to the east, and Imperial Avenue to the north. This is an example of the process used to update gang injunctions in San Diego County, where it is typically a more formal and time-intensive process for adding new defendants to an order.

City of National City v. Old Town National City Gang (San Diego Case SB007194), December 15, 1998

On December 15, 1998, the National City attorney and the National City police sought an injunction against the Old Town National City gang (*People v. Alcala—Old Town National City Gang*, 1998). The injunction named 62 defendants and targeted the area on the west side of National City, specifically the area from National City Boulevard to the east, Wilson Avenue to the west, Civic Center Drive to the north, and 18th Street to the south. The injunction also covers the area of the 1100 to 1200 blocks of East Avenue and Kimball Park (entire park area). Thirty-two arrests were made for violations of the OTNC gang injunction. This is one of the injunctions researched in this study; the control gang is the Shelltown gang, which borders the OTNC gang to the north of Division Street, 43rd Street to the east, the 15 Freeway to the west, and Market Street to the north. The Shelltown gang had about 200 members in 1991 and was established in the 1950s. On June 25, 1999, the Old Town National City gang injunction was made permanent (*People v. Alcala—Old Town National City Gang*, 1998).

YEAR 1999

People v. Langdon Street Gang (Los Angeles Case LC048292), March 26, 1999

On March 26, 1999, the Los Angeles city attorney and the Los Angeles police sought an injunction against the Langdon Street gang (*People v. Langdon Street Gang*, 1999). The injunction sued the gang and named 31 individual defendants and targeted an area in the Devonshire Division, specifically two target areas (Figure 12.3). Area 1 is from Nordhoff to the north, Roscoe Boulevard to the south, Sepulveda Boulevard to the east, and the 405 Freeway to the west. Area 2 is Gloria Avenue to the west, the 405 Freeway to the east, Tupper Street to the north, and Nordhoff to the south. The Langdon Street gang had 205 total members. Between 2000 and 2005, 95 additional Langdon Street members were enjoined by the injunction and 27 were arrested for violating the gang injunction. This injunction was not a part of any larger project or concurrent initiatives operating in the target areas. The injunction was sought because of the significant narcotic sales and violent crimes attributed to the gang.

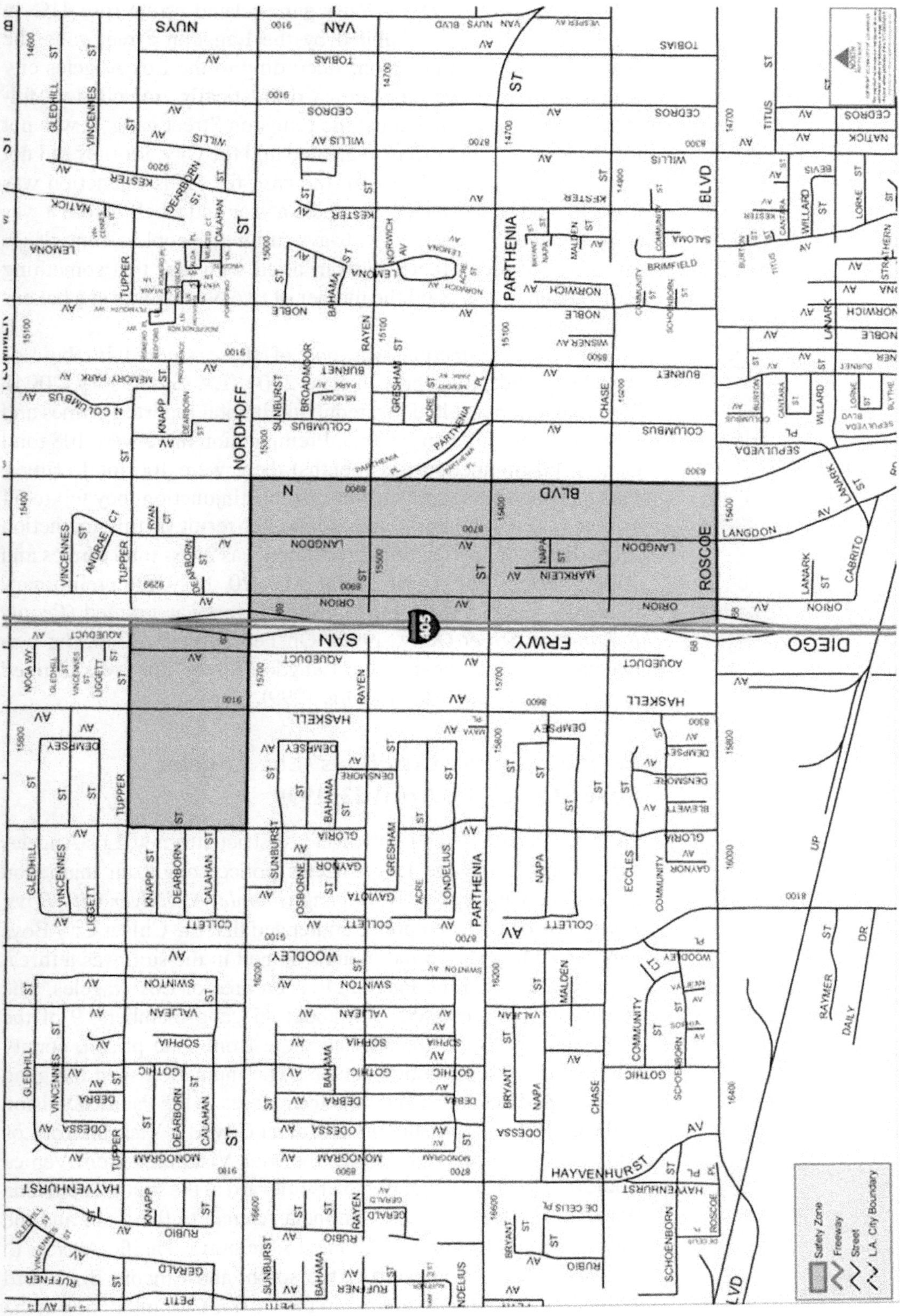

FIGURE 12.3 Map of *People v. Langdon Street Gang.*

According to *LA Daily News* gang-related crime rose 11% in the North Hills area inhabited by the Langdon Street gang the year following the injunction. According to the Los Angeles city attorney, gang crime went down dramatically immediately following the injunction against the Langdon Street gang. It was not made clear what data were evaluated and the City attorney did not have any supporting data with the case file. This injunction was opposed and supported in the media a year and a half before it was implemented. "The street is always full with people selling drugs and I pass through there, but I'm filled with fear that something will happen to me," said the mother of two, who works at a bakery until 2:30 a.m.

This gang injunction was one of those studied in the Los Angeles grand jury report in June 2004 (LA Grand Jury, 2004). This injunction resulted in a reduction in total reported crimes and Part 1 crimes in the target area. Preinjunction there were 108 total crimes, postinjunction (six months) there were 106 total crimes. Part 1 crimes preinjunction were 64, postinjunction they fell to 54 crimes (LA Grand Jury, 2004). The net result of this injunction immediately following implementation was 2 less total crimes and 10 less serious Part 1 crimes. On May 20, 1999, the preliminary injunction against the Langdon Street gang was granted (*People v. Langdon Street Gang*, 1999). On February 17, 2000, the permanent injunction against the Langdon Street gang was granted (*People v. Langdon Street Gang*, 1999).

People v. Culver City Boys (Los Angeles Case SC056980), April 23, 1999

On April 23, 1999, the Los Angeles district attorney, Los Angeles city attorney, and the Los Angeles police sought an injunction against the Culver City Boys gang (*People vs. Culver City Boys*, 1999). Prosecutors and police contended that the Culver City Boys gang, including the 76 individuals named in the suit, was a threat to public safety in the Pacific Division area of Los Angeles. The courtroom was crowded with about 45 gang members; 9 of the gang members were transported there from state prison, county jail, and juvenile detention centers. The injunction sued the gang and named defendants, and targeted an area in the Pacific Division of the LAPD covering the City of Culver City Mar Vista area of Los Angeles, specifically two areas, the Mar Vista area from Venice Boulevard to the north, Jefferson Boulevard to the south, Sepulveda Boulevard to the east, and Centinela Avenue to the west; and the Oakwood area from Rose Avenue to the north, Pacific Avenue to the west, Venice Boulevard to the south, and Lincoln Boulevard to the east. The Oakwood area in the Culver City injunction is the same as the target area in the Venice Shoreline Crips injunction. The injunction area covered seven LAPD reporting districts. The attorney that worked on the project was Jonlyn Callahan.

The Culver City Boys gang had 318 total members. This injunction was not a part of any larger project or concurrent initiatives operating in the target areas. The injunction was sought because of the significant violent activity, including several murders attributed to the gang. This gang injunction was one those studied in the Los Angeles grand jury report in June 2004 (LA Grand Jury, 2004). This injunction resulted in a reduction in total reported crimes and Part 1 crimes in the target area. Preinjunction there were 48 total crimes, postinjunction (6 months) there were 42 total crimes. Part 1 crimes preinjunction were 28, postinjunction they fell to 22 crimes (LA Grand Jury, 2004). The net result of this injunction immediately following implementation was six less total crimes and six less serious Part 1 crimes. On June 3, 1999, the preliminary injunction was issued against the Culver City Boys (*People v. Culver City Boys*, 1999). On March 27, 2001, the permanent injunction was issued against the Culver City Boys (*People v. Culver City Boys*, 1999; Los Angeles City Attorney Gang Prosecution Section, 1995). As of January 2010, the Culver City Boys gang injunction (issued March 27, 2001, against gangs with over 300 members) had been served to 131 members and resulted in at least 107 arrests for violating the order.

People v. Venice Shoreline Crips (Los Angeles Case SC057282), May 21, 1999

On May 21, 1999, the Los Angeles city attorney, the Los Angeles district attorney, and the Los Angles police sought an injunction against the Venice Shoreline Crips street gang that claimed a territory of the Pacific Division of the LAPD, in the Oakwood area of Venice, California (*People v. Venice Shoreline Crips*, 1999). The injunction named 38 defendants and targeted the area from Rose Avenue to the north, Venice Boulevard to the south, Lincoln Boulevard to the east, and Pacific Avenue to the west (Figure 12.4). The attorney that worked on the project was Allan Nadir (LA city attorney). The Venice Shoreline gang had 269 total members. Between 1999 and 2005, 73 additional members had been served and were now enjoined by the injunction. Twenty-two Venice Shoreline members were arrested in the target area for violating the gang injunction. This injunction was not a part of any larger project or concurrent initiatives operating in the target areas. The injunction was sought because of the significant narcotic sales attributed to the gang. The injunction covered five LAPD reporting districts.

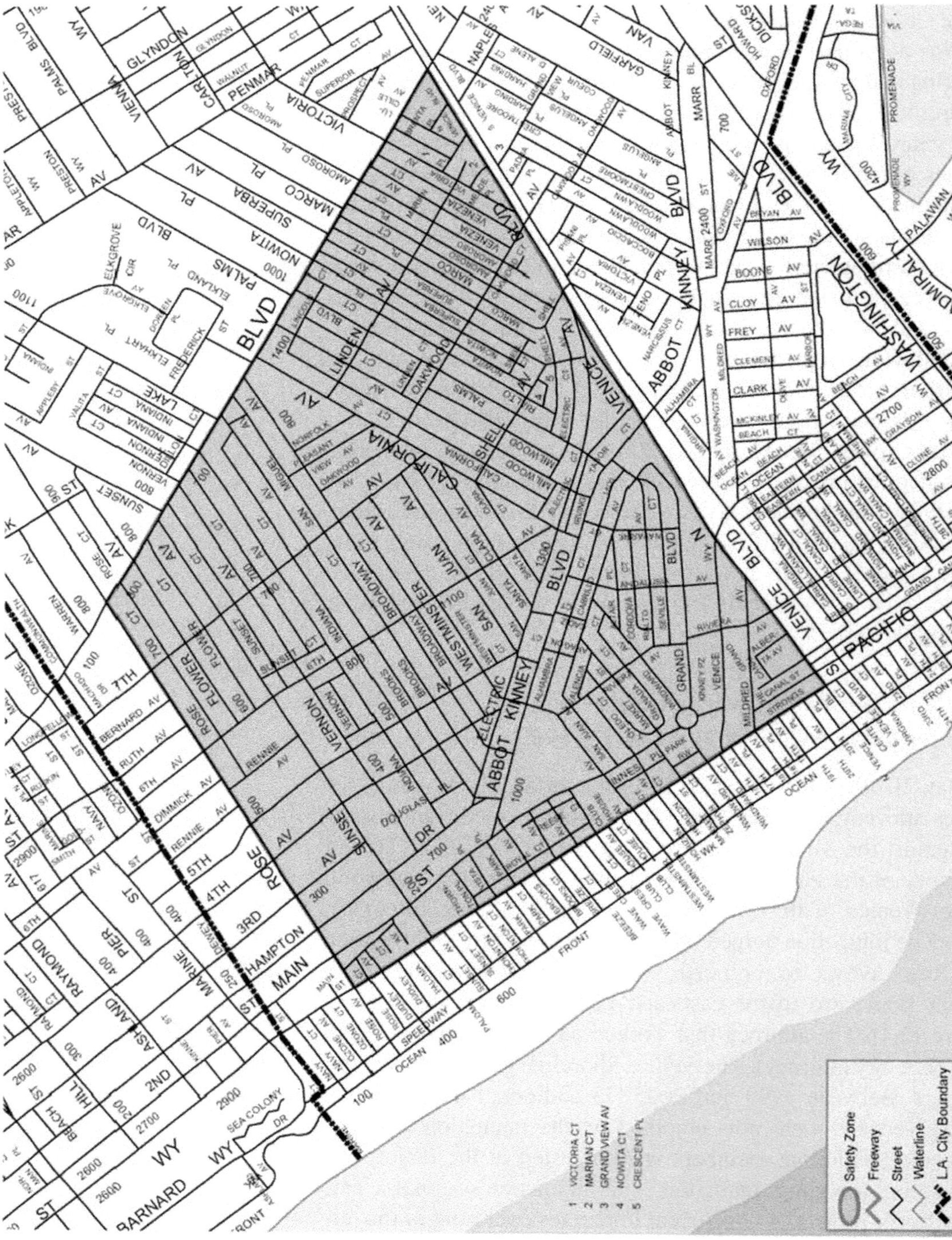

FIGURE 12.4 Map of *People v. Venice Shoreline Crips.*

This injunction was vigorously opposed. The Nation of Islam has even rallied to support the gang. Twenty-seven of the members retained private council in the case. A motion for summary judgment was granted against 25 defendants. This gang injunction was one of those studied in the Los Angeles grand jury report in June 2004 (LA Grand Jury, 2004). This injunction resulted in a reduction in total reported crimes and Part 1 crimes in the target area. Preinjunction there were 93 total crimes, postinjunction (six months) there were 81 total crimes. Part 1 crimes preinjunction were 55, postinjunction they fell to 49 (LA Grand Jury, 2004). The net result of this injunction immediately following implementation was 12 less total crimes and 6 less serious Part 1 crimes. On July 21, 1999, the preliminary injunction was issued against the Venice Shoreline Crips by Judge David Perez (*People v. Venice Shoreline Crips*, 1999). On October 18, 2000, the permanent injunction was issued against the Venice Shoreline Crips by Judge David Perez (*People v. Venice Shoreline Crips*, 1999). As of January 2010, the Venice Shoreline Crips gang injunction (issued October 8, 2000, against gangs with over 250 members) had been served to 130 members and resulted in at least 100 arrests for violating the order.

People v. Sur Crazy Ones (San Bernardino Case SCVSS58315), June 24, 1999

On June 24, 1999, the San Bernardino district/city attorney and the San Bernardino police sought an injunction against the Sur Crazy Ones gang (*People v. Sur Crazy Ones*, 1999). The injunction named 12 defendants and covers the territory of the Sur Crazy Ones street gang in the City of San Bernardino, specifically 16th Street to the north, Baseline Street to the south, Mount Vernon to the west, and the Interstate 215 to the east. On June 29, 1999, San Bernardino filed an order requiring bail to be set at $20,000 for any violations of the Sur Crazy Ones gang injunction (*People v. Sur Crazy Ones*, 1999). On March 23, 2000, the injunction against the Sur Crazy Ones (subset of the Westside Verdugo gang) was made permanent (*People v. Sur Crazy Ones*, 1999).

People v. Varrio Mesa Locos (San Diego Case N82223), August 20, 1999

On August 20, 1999, the San Diego District Attorney's Office and the Oceanside Police Department sought an injunction against the Varrio Mesa Locos gang (*People v. Varrio Mesa Locos*, 1999). The injunction named 24 members of the Mesa gang and targeted the area of Oceanside, specifically Libby Lake to the north, North River Road to the south, Calle Vallecitos to the east, and Calle

Montecito to the west. On August 24, 1999, an amended order to show cause was filed in the Mesa Locos gang injunction. The gang members were served notice that they were to appear on September 1, 1999, to show cause as to why they should not be enjoined by the injunction being sought against them (*People v. Varrio Mesa Locos*, 1999). On September 1, 1999, the preliminary injunction against the Varrio Mesa Locos was granted. On June 1, 2000, the injunction against 24 members of the Varrio Mesa Locos gang was made permanent (*People v. Varrio Mesa Locos*, 1999).

People v. Harbor City Gang and the Harbor City Crips (Los Angeles Case NC026769), November 12, 1999

On November 12, 1999, the Los Angeles city attorney and the Los Angeles police sought an injunction against the Harbor City gang and the Harbor City Crips (*People v. Harbor City Gang and Harbor City Crips*, 1999). The injunction sued both of the gangs as named defendants and named 24 individual defendants, 16 from the Harbor City gang and 8 from the Harbor City Crips. The injunction targeted the area between Western Avenue to the west, Pacific Coast Highway to the south, Vermont Avenue to the east, and Lomita Boulevard to the north. The Harbor City Boys had 115 total members, the Harbor City Crips 80. Between 2000 and 2005, 46 additional Harbor City Boys and 27 additional Harbor City Crips were enjoined by the injunction. Thirty-one Harbor City Boys and 24 Harbor City Crips were arrested for violations. This injunction was not a part of any larger project or concurrent initiatives operating in the target areas. The injunction was sought because of the significant narcotic sales attributed to both groups that coexist in the same geographical areas.

This gang injunction was one of those studied in the Los Angeles grand jury report in June 2004 (LA Grand Jury, 2004). This injunction resulted in an increase in total reported crimes and an increase in Part 1 crimes in the target area. Preinjunction there were 95 total crimes, postinjunction (six months) there were 100 total crimes. Part 1 crimes preinjunction were 57, postinjunction they increased to 60 crimes (LA Grand Jury, 2004). The net result of this injunction immediately following implementation was five additional total crimes and three more serious Part 1 crimes. On January 12, 2000, the preliminary injunction against the Harbor City gang and the Harbor City Crips was granted (*People v. Harbor City Gang and Harbor City Crips*, 1999). On January 27, 2000, the permanent injunction against the Harbor City gang and the Harbor City Crips was granted (*People v. Harbor City Gang and Harbor City Crips,* 1999).

13

Gang Injunctions 2000–2009

YEARS 2000–2009

People v. Venice 13 Gang (Los Angeles Case SC060375), February 4, 2000

On February 4, 2000, the Los Angeles City Attorney sought an injunction against the Venice 13 gang that claimed a territory in the Venice Oakwood area of Los Angeles, specifically Rose Avenue to the north, Venice Boulevard to the south, Pacific Avenue to the west, and Walgrove Avenue to the east; a second area encompassed Venice Boulevard to the north, Washington Boulevard to the south, Lincoln Boulevard to the west, and Centinela Avenue to the east (Figure 13.1). The injunction sued the gang as an association and named 29 defendants as well. The Venice 13 gang had 293 total members.

Between 2000 and 2005, 48 additional members had been served and were now enjoined by the injunction. Thirteen members were arrested in the target area for violating the gang injunction. This injunction was not a part of any larger project or concurrent initiatives operating in the target areas. The injunction was sought because of the significant violent crime and witness intimidation in the target area. This gang injunction was one of the injunctions studied in the Los Angeles grand jury report in June 2004 (LA Grand Jury, 2004). This injunction resulted in a slight increase in total reported crimes and an increase in Part 1 crimes in the target area. Preinjunction there were 74 total crimes, postinjunction (six months) there were 75 total crimes. Part 1 crimes preinjunction were 44, postinjunction they increased to 47 crimes. The net result of this injunction immediately following implementation was one additional total crime and three more serious Part 1 crimes. On March 17, 2000, the preliminary injunction against the Venice 13 gang

FIGURE 13.1 Map of *People v. Venice 13.*

was granted. On January 12, 2001, the permanent injunction against the Venice 13 gang was granted. On October 19, 2001, the revised permanent injunction against the Venice 13 gang was granted.

People v. Linda Vista 13 Gang (San Diego Case GIC745162), March 24, 2000

On March 24, 2000, the San Diego District Attorney's Office and the San Diego Police Department sought an injunction against the Linda Vista 13 gang. The injunction named 24 defendants and targeted an area in the Linda Vista area of San Diego, specifically the 6800 to 7200 block of Linda Vista Road, the 2100 to 2500 blocks of Ulric Street, the 2100 to 2200 blocks of Comstock Street, the 6500 to 6700 blocks of Kelly Street, the 2200 to 2400 blocks of Morley Street, the 6500 to 6800 blocks of Tait Street, Kelly Street Park (2170 Jacobs Way), the 6900 to 7000 blocks of Fulton Street, the 2200 to 2300 blocks of Burroughs Street, and the 6900 to 7000 blocks of Eastman Street. On April 12, 2000, the preliminary injunction was granted against the Linda Vista 13 gang by Judge Thomas LaVoy. On March 23, 2001, the permanent injunction against the Linda Vista 13 gang was granted. On July 25, 2002, one of the defendants in the Linda Vista 13 gang injunction requested to have his name removed from the order because he stated he was no longer a member of the gang. The San Diego County district attorney agreed that if the defendant could go a year without any new contact with police or in the presence of gang members he would be removed. On January 22, 2003, the San Diego County district attorney and the judge agreed to have defendant Christian Leyva removed from the injunction after he had gone a year without a police contact.

City of San Jose v. South Vietnam (Santa Clara Case CV791443), July 28, 2000

On July 28, 2000, the city attorney for the City of San Jose in Santa Clara County sought an injunction against the South Vietnam gang. The injunction named the gang and six individual members. The target area for this injunction is a shopping center known as the Caribbee Shopping Center that contains multiple retail establishments, restaurants, and other types of business, including a pool hall where the Vietnamese gang congregated and conducted a large part of the gang's business.

YEAR 2001

People v. Five Time Hometown Crips (San Bernardino SCVSS080319), January 13, 2001

On January 13, 2001, the San Bernardino district attorney filed a complaint against the Five Time Hometown Crips gang and 29 members of the gang. The San Bernardino district attorney also filed an order with the court requesting bail to be set at $25,000 for any violation of the Five Time Hometown Crips gang injunction pursuant to Penal Code Section 1275. This action brings up an interesting point when considering the effectiveness of gang injunctions. When gang members are arrested and booked in jail for a violation of the injunction, it is often considered more effective than if they were issued a citation and released. It is also beneficial to the success of a gang injunction if gang members remain in custody while awaiting their first court appearance. It tends to cause more cases to plead out at the first court hearing. On January 13, 2003, the permanent injunction against the Five Time Hometown Crips Gang was granted. The injunction covers the territory of the Five Time Hometown Crips street gang in the City of San Bernardino, specifically the area from Etiwanda Avenue to the north, Rialto Avenue to the south, Pepper Avenue to the west, and Terrace Street to the east.

People v. Pacoima Project Boys (Los Angeles Case PC027254Y), March 20, 2001

On March 20, 2001, the Los Angeles city attorney and the Los Angeles Police sought an injunction against the 300-member Pacoima Project Boys gang. The injunction sued the gang as an entity and named 15 members of the gang. The injunction forbids any of the served members of the order to associate in a zone contained in the Foothill Division of the LAPD, specifically Paxton Street on the north, Glen Oaks Boulevard on the east, Pierce Street on the south, and San Fernando Road on the west. The boundaries of the targeted zone also include the San Fernando Housing project, which runs from Pierce Street to Van Nuys Boulevard, and David Gonzalez Park in Pacoima. The target area covers two LAPD reporting districts. Between 2001 and 2005, 130 additional members had been served and were now enjoined by the injunction. Ninety-eight Pacoima members were arrested for violating the gang injunction during that time.

This injunction was a part of a CLEAR program effort to target the gangs in that area at the time. The injunction was sought because of the significant narcotic sales attributed to the gang.

On August 22, 2001, the permanent gang injunction against the Pacoima Project Boys was granted. An *LA Daily News* article claimed that the number of crimes committed in the Pacoima area, which the Project Boys gang considers its turf, had climbed 37% since a permanent injunction was imposed in October 2001. Like most news media articles, it did not make reference to how the statistics were gathered and analyzed and did not use a control gang in the research and analysis. This gang injunction was one of the cases studied in the Los Angeles grand jury report in June 2004 (LA Grand Jury, 2004). This injunction resulted in an increase in total reported crimes and an increase in Part 1 crimes in the target area. Preinjunction there were 78 total crimes, postinjunction (six months) there were 97 total crimes. Part 1 crimes preinjunction were 44, postinjunction they increased to 54 crimes. The net result of this injunction immediately following implementation was 19 additional total crimes and 10 more serious Part 1 crimes.

People v. Eastside and Westside Wilmas (Los Angeles Case NC030080), May 23, 2001

On May 23, 2001, the Los Angeles City Attorney's Office and the Los Angeles Police Department sought an injunction against the Eastside Wilmas and Westside Wilmas street gangs. This injunction targeted two rival gangs that have an estimated 1,000 members combined in one order, focusing on 37 members from the two gangs. The Eastside Wilmas gang was a named defendant along with 17 members; the Westside Wilmas was a named defendant along with 20 members. The injunction targeted the Wilmington area of Los Angeles, specifically Lomita Boulevard to the north, Alameda Street on the east, Harry Bridges Boulevard to the south, and the 110 Harbor Freeway on the west.

The Eastside gang had 564 members and the Westside gang had 599 members. Between 2001 and 2005, 116 additional Westside members and 107 additional Eastside members had been served and were now enjoined by the injunction. Forty-eight Westside and 29 Eastside members were arrested for violating the gang injunction. This injunction was not a part of any larger project or concurrent initiatives operating in the target areas. The injunction was sought because of the significant narcotic sales attributed to the gang. On March 9, 2004, the permanent injunction against the Eastside and Westside Wilmas gangs was granted.

People v. Diablos Gang (San Diego Case GIN013906), July 13, 2001

On July 13, 2001, the San Diego County District Attorney's Office and the Escondido Police Department sought an injunction against the Diablos gang. The injunction named 21 members of the Diablos gang and covered a territory in Escondido, specifically N. Broadway to the west, E. Mission Avenue to the north, N. Rose Street to the east, and E. Valley Parkway to the south. On July 27, 2001, the preliminary injunction against the Diablos gang was granted. On January 11, 2002, the permanent injunction against 21 members of the Diablos gang was made permanent by Judge Joan P. Weber.

People v. Westside Gang (San Diego Case GIN013907), July 13, 2001

On July 13, 2001, the San Diego County district attorney and the Escondido police sought an injunction against the Westside gang in Escondido. The injunction targeted 22 members of the Westside gang. The target area was from West 4th Avenue between Upas and Escondido Blvd. to the north, West 15th to the south, Escondido Boulevard to the east, Upas Street to the west, and Westside Park located at 333 S. Spruce Street. On September 7, 2001, the preliminary injunction against the Westside gang was granted. On July 11, 2002, the permanent injunction against the Westside gang was granted (*People v. Westside Gang*, 2001) by Judge Joan P. Weber. In the year following the injunction, the Escondido police arrested 13 alleged gang members on suspicion of violating the injunction. The city was initially home to the Santos gang, which eventually evolved into the Diablos, police said. Friction in the Diablos gang during the mid-1980s resulted in a faction of its members splitting away to form the Westside gang, creating the problems that lead to the injunction.

People v. Eastside Longos (Los Angeles Case NC030660), August 31, 2001

On August 31, 2001, the Los Angeles city attorney and the Long Beach Police Department sought an injunction against 27 members of the Eastside Longos gang. The injunction target area has two safety zones. The first is from the Pacific Coast Highway to the north, Locust Avenue to the east, Anaheim Street to the south, and Daisy Avenue to the west. The second target area is from Atlantic and Martin Luther King Avenues to the north, Pacific Coast Highway to the east, Junipero Avenue to the south, and

4th Street to the west. On November 24, 2002, the Los Angeles County Superior Court granted the request for a permanent injunction against the Eastside Longos street gang and 23 of its most active members.

YEAR 2002

People v. Canoga Park Alabama (Los Angeles Case BC267153), January 29, 2002

On January 29, 2002, the Los Angeles city attorney, Los Angeles district attorney, and the Los Angeles police sought an injunction against the Canoga Park Alabama gang. The target area is contained in the Devonshire and West Valley Divisions of the LAPD and covers 17 LAPD reporting districts, or about 3.41 square miles, specifically Nordhoff and Roscoe to the north, Topanga Canyon Boulevard to the west, Winnetka Avenue to the east, and Vanowen Street to the south. The injunction sued the gang as an association and did not name any individual defendants, but listed information on 23 individuals in the supporting declarations. The Canoga Park gang had 340 total members. Between 2002 and 2005, 131 total members had been served and were now enjoined by the injunction. Sixty-three Canoga Park members were arrested in the target area for violating the gang injunction. This injunction was not a part of any larger project or concurrent initiatives operating in the target areas. The injunction was sought because of the significant narcotic sales attributed to the gang.

According to a *LA Daily News* study, gang crime in an area of Canoga Park had fallen 18% from April 2002 to April 2004, following the injunction imposed against the Canoga Park Alabama gang. The article did not reference if crime in surrounding areas increased or decreased and did not use a control gang in the research and analysis. It is assumed that the injunction was the cause of the reduction in crime; it is unknown if any other enforcement was ongoing that may have had an impact on the results. This gang injunction was one of those studied in the Los Angeles grand jury report in June 2004 (LA Grand Jury, 2004). This injunction resulted in an increase in total reported crimes and a reduction in Part 1 crimes in the target area. Preinjunction there were 83 total crimes, postinjunction (six months) there were 84 total crimes. Part 1 crimes preinjunction were 51, postinjunction they fell to 47 crimes (LA Grand Jury, 2004). The net result of this injunction immediately following implementation was one additional total crime and four less serious Part 1 crimes. On April 24, 2002, the permanent injunction against the Canoga Park Alabama gang was granted.

People v. Nestor Gang (San Diego Case GIS9068), February 27, 2002

On February 27, 2002, the San Diego County district attorney and the San Diego Police Department sought an injunction against the Nestor street gang that claims a territory in south San Diego. The injunction against 11 members of the Nestor gang was made permanent on July 15, 2002. The injunction targets the area from Palm Avenue to the north, 15th Street to the west, Interstate 5, Oro Vista, and International Roads to the east, and Monument Road to the south. This case is evaluated in this research. The Imperials gang was selected as the control gang for this case. The Imperials congregate between Palm Avenue to the north, Satellite Boulevard to the south, Interstate 5 to the east, and Imperial Beach to the west. The Imperials gang had 57 members at the time of the injunction; Nestor had 20 members. The Imperials gang was originally part of the Sidro Boys until the late 1960s, when the area was divided by the interstate. The Nestor gang was started in 1989. On April 4, 2002, the preliminary injunction against the Nestor gang was granted, and on July 15, 2002, the permanent injunction against the Nestor gang was granted.

People v. 18th Street Pico Union (Los Angeles Case BC272030), April 16, 2002 (Redoing the 18th Street Pico Union That Was Previously Dismissed)

On April 16, 2002, the Los Angeles city attorney, the Los Angeles district attorney, and the Los Angles Police Department sought a second injunction against the 18th Street gang in the Pico Union area; the first was dismissed after allegations of police misconduct in that case. The new injunction named 29 defendants and also sued the entire gang. The 18th Street Pico Union gang had 1,778 total members. Between 2002 and 2005, 76 additional members had been served and were now enjoined by the injunction. Sixty-nine 18th Street members were arrested in the target area for violating the gang injunction. This injunction was not a part of any larger project or concurrent initiatives operating in the target areas. The injunction was sought because of the significant narcotic sales attributed to the gang.

The target area for the injunction is contained in the Rampart Division of the LAPD, specifically James Wood Boulevard to the north, Interstate 10 to the south, the 110 Freeway to the east, and Hoover Street to the west. The attorneys that worked on the project were Jonlyn Callahan (LADA) and Kelly Huynh. The injunction covers six reporting districts of the LAPD. This gang injunction was one of the 14 studied in the Los Angeles grand jury report in June 2004. This injunction resulted in a reduction in total reported crimes and Part 1 crimes in the target area. Preinjunction there were 74 total crimes, postinjunction (six months) there were 63 total crimes. Part 1 crimes preinjunction were 50, postinjunction they fell to 42 crimes (LA grand jury, 2004). The net result of this injunction immediately following implementation was 11 less total crimes and 8 less serious Part 1 crimes. On October 18, 2002, the permanent injunction against the 18th Street Pico Union gang was granted, no preliminary injunction was sought. Since June 2010, 166 gang members have been served and 118 of them have been arrested, some for violating the order on more than one occasion.

People v. Varrio Sureno Town (Santa Clara Case CV811217), September 19, 2002

On September 19, 2002, the city attorney for the City of San Jose in Santa Clara County sought a second injunction against the VST gang. The injunction named the gang and 29 individual members in two target areas. One area is known as Richmond Menker, specifically from Highway 280 to the north, Menker Avenue to the east, Kingman Avenue to the south, and Leigh Avenue to the west. The second area is known as the Winchester Cadillac zone, specifically Loma Verde Drive to the north, Winchester Boulevard to the east, Impala Drive to the south, and Eden Avenue to the west (*People v. Varrio Surreno Town*, 2002).

People v. Krazy Ass Mexicans (Los Angeles Case BC282629), October 3, 2002

On October 3, 2002, the Los Angeles city attorney, Los Angeles district attorney, and the Los Angeles police sought an injunction against the Krazy Ass Mexicans gang. The injunction targets an area in the Hollenbeck Division of the LAPD, specifically the area from Soto Street to the west, Cesar Chavez Avenue to the south, Indiana Street to the east, and Interstate 10 to the north. The injunction covers three LAPD reporting districts.

In the complaint, which mentions 16 gang members by name and 200 others as John Does, the city alleges that KAM creates a threatening atmosphere in the neighborhood by selling and using drugs on the street, having gang shootouts, robbing and harassing passersby, and retaliating violently against residents who report crimes, in addition to some lesser offenses.

The injunction, like some others, sues the gang as the sole defendant, naming some members in the supporting declarations, but not as defendants. The KAM gang had 192 total members. Between 2002 and 2005, 70 members had been served and were now enjoined by the injunction. Forty-seven KAM members were arrested in the target area for violating the gang injunction. This injunction was not a part of any larger project or concurrent initiatives operating in the target areas. The injunction was sought because of the significant violent crimes attributed to the group, including 62 separate incidents and 5 murders leading up to the injunction.

This gang injunction was one of those studied in the Los Angeles grand jury report in June 2004. This injunction resulted in a reduction in total reported crimes and Part 1 crimes in the target area. Preinjunction there were 71 total crimes, postinjunction (six months) there were 63 total crimes. Part 1 crimes preinjunction were 42, postinjunction they fell to 39 crimes (LA Grand Jury, 2004). The net result of this injunction immediately following implementation was eight less total crimes and three less serious Part 1 crimes. On October 25, 2002, the preliminary injunction against the Krazy Ass Mexicans gang was granted. On January 16, 2003, the permanent injunction against the Krazy Ass Mexicans gang was granted. The lawsuit alleged that KAM was an unincorporated association and that the conduct and activities of the gang and its members constitute a public nuisance. Filed with the lawsuit to substantiate the allegations against the gang were over 80 declarations documenting over 168 incidents, and 35 records of criminal convictions, including 12 convictions for predicate felonies, which qualify KAM as a criminal street gang.

People v. Logan Heights Red Steps Gang (San Diego Case GIC798708), November 1, 2002

On November 1, 2002, the San Diego County District Attorney's Office and the San Diego Police Department sought an injunction against the Logan Heights Red Steps Gang (*People v. Logan Heights Red Steps Gang*, 2002). The injunction targeted 36 members of the Logan Red Steps that claim a territory in the Logan Heights section of San Diego, specifically the area from 1200 Imperial Avenue and Interstate 15 to the north, Wabash and 32nd Street to the east, 12th Street to the west, and Harbor Drive to the south. At the time of the injunction the Red Steps had 137 members. The subset of Logan started in 1975 and gained their name because of the red painted steps in front of 2100 Newton Avenue. The actual red steps are gone but the gang is not. The Logan gang is believed to have started in the early 1940s as a car club called the Los Lobos, but did not evolve into a significant gang until the 1960s. On November 22, 2002, the preliminary injunction against the Logan Heights Red Steps gang was granted by Judge John S. Einhorn. On April 10, 2003, the permanent injunction against the Logan Heights Red Steps gang was granted.

People v. Avenues Gang (Los Angeles Case BC287137), December 17, 2002

On December 17, 2002, the Los Angeles city attorney, Los Angeles district attorney, and Los Angeles police sought an injunction against the Avenues gang. The injunction sues the gang as an association and does not name individual defendants but does discuss 25 members in the declarations. It targets an area in the Northeast Division of the LAPD, specifically a zone covering 9.7 square miles, which includes Glassell Park, Cypress Park, Highland Park, and part of Montecito Heights. The Avenues injunction covers 15 reporting districts of the LAPD. The Avenues gang had 446 total members. Between 2002 and 2005, 97 members had been served and were now enjoined by the injunction. Fifty-one Avenues members were arrested in the target area for violating the gang injunction. This injunction was not a part of any larger project or concurrent initiatives operating in the target areas. The injunction was sought because of the significant narcotic sales attributed to the gang.

This gang injunction was one of those studied in the Los Angeles grand jury report in June 2004 (LA Grand Jury, 2004). This injunction resulted in a reduction in total reported crimes and Part 1 crimes in the target area. Preinjunction there were 82 total crimes, postinjunction (six months) there were 77 total crimes. Part 1 crimes preinjunction were 47, postinjunction they fell to 42 crimes. The net result of this injunction immediately following implementation was five less total crimes and five less serious Part 1 crimes. On January 29, 2003, the preliminary injunction against the Avenues gang was granted. On April 7, 2003, the permanent injunction against the Avenues gang was granted.

YEAR 2003

People v. Verdugo Flats (San Bernardino Case SCVSS092975), March 10, 2003

On March 10, 2003, the San Bernardino district attorney and the San Bernardino Police Department sought an injunction against the Verdugo Flats Southside gang. The injunction covers the territory of the Verdugo Flats street gang in the City of San Bernardino, specifically Third Street to the north, Grant Avenue to the south, Muscott to the west, and the Interstate 215 to the east. On March 10, 2003, the injunction against the Verdugo Flats Southside gang was made permanent. On April 4, 2003, the San Bernardino district attorney filed an order with the court requiring that bail be set at $25,000 for any violations of the Verdugo Flats gang injunction.

People v. Insane Crip (Los Angeles Case NC033946), April 16, 2003

On April 16, 2003, the Long Beach city attorney and the Long Beach police sought an injunction against 11 members of the Insane Crip gang. The injunction named the gang and 11 named defendants and targeted the area from Burnett Street to the north, Orange Avenue to the east, East Pacific Coast Highway to the south, and Magnolia Avenue to the west. The injunction was made permanent on May 27, 2004.

People v. Rolling Sixty Crips (Los Angeles Case BC298646), July 8, 2003

On July 8, 2003, the Los Angeles city attorney, Los Angeles district attorney, and the Los Angeles police sought an injunction against the Rolling Sixty Crips. The injunction targets an area in the 77th Street Division of the Los Angeles Police, specifically the Hyde Park area of Los Angeles (Figure 13.2). The injunction that named 31 defendants covers nine LAPD reporting districts. The South Los Angeles gang had allegedly been responsible for more than 30 murders between 2001 and 2002; the injunction was the city's 17th to date. The Rolling Sixty Crips gang had 837 total members. Between 2003 and 2005, 38 additional members had been served and were now enjoined by the injunction. Eighteen Rolling Sixty members were arrested in the target area for violating the gang injunction. This injunction was not a part of any larger project or concurrent initiatives operating in the target areas. The injunction was sought because of the significant narcotic sales attributed to the gang and prohibited two or more gang members in one vehicle from entering a neighborhood claimed by any of five named rivals, the Van Ness Gangsters, the Eight Trey Gangsters, the Crenshaw Mafia, the Inglewood Family, and the 62 Brims.

This gang injunction was one of those studied in the Los Angeles grand jury report in June 2004. This injunction resulted in a reduction in total reported crimes and Part 1 crimes in the target area. Preinjunction there were 124 total crimes, postinjunction (six months) there were 110 total crimes. Part 1 crimes preinjunction were 74, postinjunction they fell to 69 crimes. The net result of this injunction immediately following implementation was 13

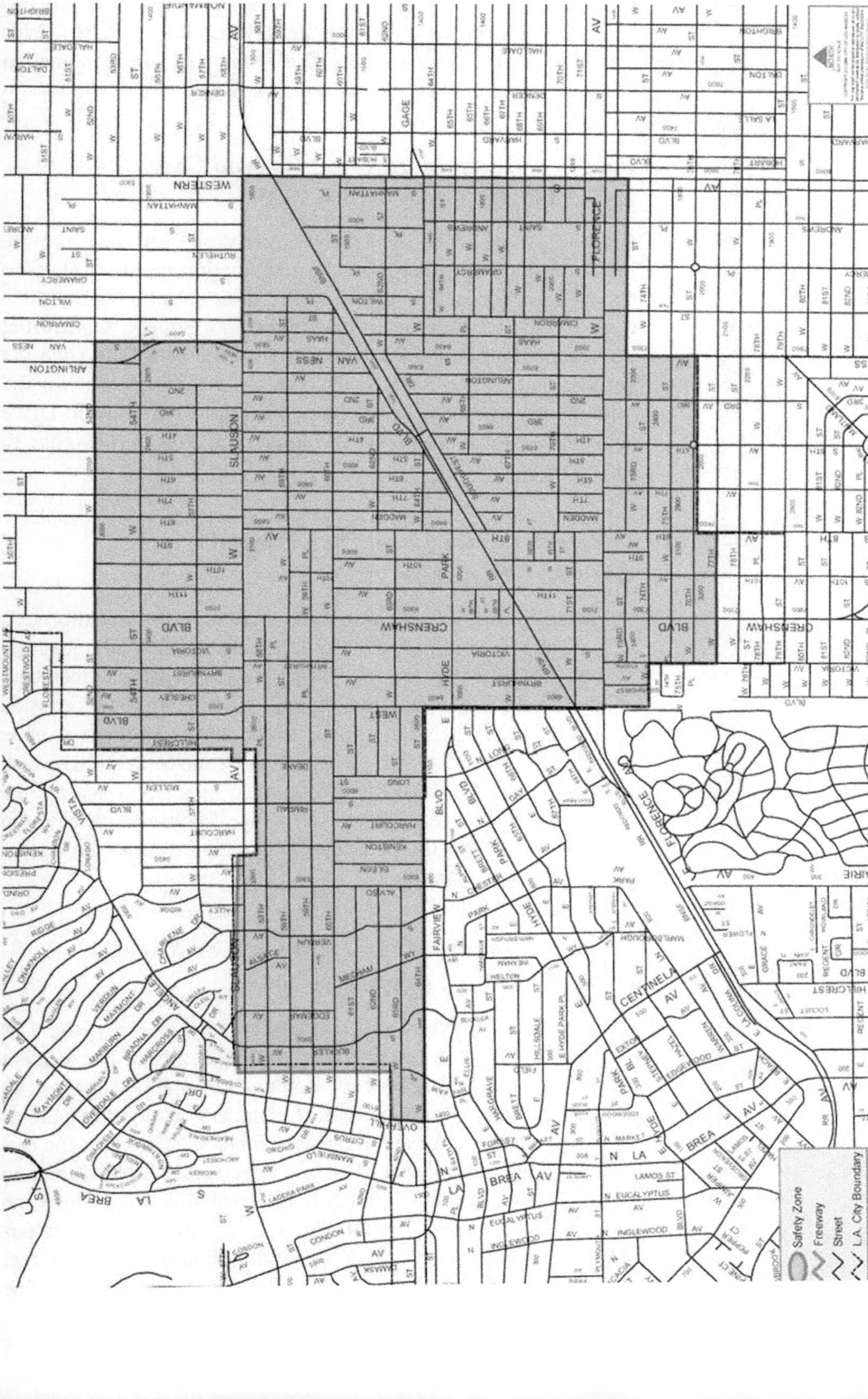

FIGURE 13.2 Map of *People v. Rolling Sixty Crips.*

less total crimes and 4 less serious Part 1 crimes. On October 1, 2003, the preliminary injunction against the Rolling Sixty Crips was granted. On November 24, 2003, the permanent injunction against the Rolling Sixty Crips was granted.

People v. Chankla Bulldogs (Fresno Case 03CECG02881), August 15, 2003

On August 15, 2003, the Fresno County city attorney and the Fresno Police Department sought an injunction against the Fresno Chankla Bulldogs. The Chankla Bulldogs street gang claims a territory in the City of Sanger in Fresno County, California. The injunction named 22 members in some detail but sued the gang as an entity and not as individuals. The target area for the injunction was Annadale Avenue to the north, Millwood Drive to the east, North Avenue to the south, and Academy Avenue to the west.

People v. Center Street (San Diego Case GIN032007), August 22, 2003

On August 22, 2003, the San Diego County District Attorney's Office and the Oceanside Police Department sought an injunction against the Center Street gang. The injunction targeted 17 members of the Center Street gang that claim a territory in the Oceanside area, specifically Mission Avenue to the north, Missouri Avenue to the south, Interstate 5 to the east, and Horne Street to the west. On September 12, 2003, the preliminary injunction against the Center Street gang was granted by Judge Michael Kirkman. On December 3, 2003, the permanent injunction against the Center Street gang was granted.

People v. Bounty Hunter Bloods (Los Angeles Case BC301433), August 26, 2003

On August 26, 2003, the Los Angeles city attorney, the Los Angeles district attorney, and the Los Angles Police Department sought an injunction against the Bounty Hunter Bloods gang. The injunction did not name individual members; it sued the gang as an entity. The order covers a 20-square-block territory in the Los Angeles Police Southeast Division, specifically 108th Street to the north, the Imperial Highway to the south, the MTA Blue Line tracks to the east, and Central Avenue to the west. The entire target area includes 100 yards in every direction outside the target area and covers an area contained in three reporting districts. The

Bounty Hunters gang had 800 total members. Between 2003 and 2005, 113 members had been served and were now enjoined by the injunction, and 51 Bounty members were arrested in the target area for violating the gang injunction. This injunction was not a part of any larger project or concurrent initiatives operating in the target areas.

This gang injunction was one of those studied in the Los Angeles grand jury report in June 2004. This injunction resulted in a reduction in total reported crimes and Part 1 crimes in the target area. Preinjunction there were 147 total crimes, postinjunction (six months) there were 100 total crimes. Part 1 crimes preinjunction were 97, postinjunction they fell to 63 crimes. The net result of this injunction immediately following implementation was 47 less total crimes and 33 less serious Part 1 crimes. On October 1, 2003, the preliminary injunction against the Bounty Hunters gang was granted. On December 2, 2003, the permanent injunction against the Bounty Hunters gang was granted. Since June 2010, at least 424 gang members had been served and at least 232 arrested for violating this order according to the LAPD Southeast Station.

People v. Delman Heights Bloods (San Bernardino Case SCVSS107068), October 9, 2003

On October 9, 2003, the San Bernardino district attorney and the San Bernardino Police Department sought an injunction against the Delman Heights Bloods gang. The injunction covers the territory of the Delman Heights street gang in the City of San Bernardino, specifically Cajon Boulevard to the north, Highland Avenue to the south, California Street to the west, and Medical Center Drive to the east.

People v. Varrio Posole Locos (San Diego Case GIN033214), October 17, 2003

On October 17, 2003, the San Diego District Attorney's Office and the Oceanside Police Department sought a second injunction against the Varrio Posole Locos gang. The injunction named 25 members and targeted an area in the City of Oceanside, specifically Interstate 5 to the west, Mission Avenue to the south, Carey Road to the east, and State Route 76 to the north. On November 10, 2003, the preliminary injunction against the Posole gang was granted by Judge Michael Kirkman. On March 2, 2004, the permanent injunction against the Posole gang was granted.

People v. Project Crips (San Bernardino Case SCVSS109373), November 4, 2003

On November 4, 2003, the San Bernardino district attorney and the San Bernardino Police Department sought an injunction against the Project Crips gang. The injunction covers the territory of the Project Crips street gang in the City of San Bernardino, specifically Baseline Street to the north, Seventh Street to the south, State Street to the west, and Western Avenue to the east. On December 10, 2003, the preliminary injunction against the Project Crips street gang was granted.

People v. 18th Street Hollywood (Los Angeles Case BC305434), November 4, 2003

On November 4, 2003, the Los Angeles city attorney, the Los Angeles district attorney, and the Los Angles Police Department sought an injunction against the 18th Street Hollywood gang. The injunction sued the gang as an association and did not name any individual defendants. It targeted an area in Hollywood, specifically Santa Monica Boulevard to the south, Sierra Bonita Avenue to the west, Franklin Avenue and the Hollywood Freeway to the north, and Robinson Avenue to the east. The 18th Street gang had 1,000 total members. Between 2003 and 2005, 27 members had been served and were now enjoined by the injunction. Ten members were arrested for violating the gang injunction. This injunction was not a part of any larger project or concurrent initiatives operating in the target areas. The injunction was sought because of the significant narcotic sales attributed to the gang. In Hollywood, an injunction against the 18th Street Gang has resulted in a 50% decrease in Part 1 crimes.

YEAR 2004

People v. Westside Longos (Los Angeles Case NC035222), January 12, 2004

On January 12, 2004, the City of Long Beach sought a second injunction against the Westside Longos gang, the first being completed in October 1995. The injunction named the gang as the sole defendant and subsequently resulted in 84 members of the gang being served as of August 2005. The injunction targeted the area from Pacific Coast Highway to the south, Long Beach Freeway to the east, Hill Street to the north, and Terminal Island Highway on the west. In December 2004, the Westside Longos gang injunction from Long Beach became permanent.

People v. Mara Salvatrucha Hollywood (Los Angeles Case BC311766), March 9, 2004

On March 9, 2004, the Los Angeles city attorney, Los Angeles district attorney, and Los Angeles police sought an injunction against the Mara Salvatrucha Hollywood gang. The injunction named the gang as the sole defendant and targeted two areas, the first from Sunset Boulevard to the north, Vermont Avenue to the east, Beverly Boulevard to the south, and Gower Street to the west; the second from 3rd Street to the north, Olympic Boulevard to the south, Western Avenue to the west, and Alvarado to the east. The Mara Salvatrucha gang had 923 total members. Between 2004 and 2005, 95 members had been served and were now enjoined by the injunction. During this time, 36 Mara Salvatrucha members were arrested in the target area for violating the gang injunction. This injunction was not a part of any larger project or concurrent initiatives operating in the target areas. The injunction was sought because of the significant narcotic sales attributed to the gang.

People v. Oxnard Colonia Chiques (Ventura Case CIV226032), April 2, 2004

On April 2, 2004, the district attorney for the County of Ventura sought a gang injunction against the Colonia Chiques gang. The injunction named the gang as the sole defendant. This injunction received potentially more media attention than any others to date, much of it negative, claiming that the injunction was flawed and was an abuse of the authority of the district attorney. The injunction resulted in the longest trial in injunction history to this point to prove the necessity of the injunction to the courts. Ultimately, the prosecution prevailed and the injunction was granted. The injunction named the gang as the sole defendant and named some of the members in the supporting declarations. On June 1, 2004, the preliminary injunction against the Colonia Chiques gang was granted.

The Colonia Chiques gang injunction in Oxnard has been active in one incarnation or another since about the 1950s. Since 2001, members of the gang have committed 300 robberies. Chiques have also committed 400+ gang assaults, and during a 15-month period there were 14 homicides believed to have been committed by Chiques members. In all, Chiques were involved in more than 2,000 crimes, from graffiti to homicide, from 2000 to 2004. The injunction declares a public nuisance, and the 1,400-page document has more than 130 declarations of the same.

Under the injunction terms, alleged Colonia Chiques gang members who are served cannot associate with other members, wear Dallas Cowboys attire, stay out past 10 p.m., or engage in other gang-related activities in the safety zone. Those who are arrested for violating the injunction could face up to six months in jail and a $1,000 fine. The injunction covers a 6.6-square-mile safety zone around Oxnard's La Colonia. Deputy District Attorney Karen Wold applauded Bysshe's inclusion of an opt-out process, which would allow "recovering" Colonia Chiques gang members to join a program for 24 months. The 12-step type program would provide education and job assistance, support groups, and free removal of tattoos.

People v. 18th Street Wilshire (Los Angeles Case BC313309), April 6, 2004

On April 6, 2004, the Los Angeles city attorney, Los Angeles district attorney, and the Los Angles police sought an injunction against the 18th Street Wilshire gang. The injunction sued the gang as an association and did not name any individual defendants. It targets several areas in the Wilshire and Shatto Park areas, including the area from Beverly Boulevard to the north, Normandie Avenue to the east, Wilshire Boulevard to the south, and Western Avenue to the west. The 18th Street gang had 1,000 total members. Between 2004 and 2005, 15 members had been served and were now enjoined by the injunction. On June 29, 2004, the permanent injunction against the 18th Street Wilshire gang was granted.

People v. East Side Piru, aka Skyline (San Diego Case GIC827117), April 16, 2004

On April 16, 2004, the San Diego County District Attorney's Office and the San Diego Police Department sought an injunction against the Skyline East Side Piru gang. The injunction originally targeted 90 members of the Skyline street gang. This was later modified to include 86 members after four were removed following further review by the district attorney's office during the court process. The target area for the injunction consisted of the Skyline community in Southeast San Diego (Figure 13.3). This is one of the injunctions evaluated in this research. The Eastside Piru or Skyline gang was selected for an injunction because it was the most significant problem gang in San Diego County at the time. The ESP gang had 527 members; the only suitable control gang was the West Coast Crips gang, which had 474 members at the same point in time.

The ESP gang started in the 1970s as a Crip gang. The change from Crip to Blood took place around 1975 when Interstate 805 divided the area between southeast San Diego and downtown.

FIGURE 13.3 Map of *People v. Eastside Piru.*

Geographically in San Diego, Crips are on the west side and Bloods are on the east side. As the gang was moved east and transformed to a blood faction, the gang grew in numbers and became much more violent in the 1980s. Like other gangs, the gang has some cliques: 69th Street, O'Farrell Park, Gangster Pimp Mafia, Meadowbrook Assassins, Niggas Banging Alderely, and Parkside. The control gang is the West Coast Crips. On May 14, 2004, an amended preliminary injunction was filed in the Skyline gang injunction. On April 15, 2005, the Skyline injunction was made permanent.

Evaluation of the Analysis Typically Needed to Obtain an Injunction: The Skyline Example

The Skyline gang injunction ultimately named 86 defendants; however, a review of the entire gang was conducted to identify those 86 members. Every great general from the Civil War to the present has stressed the importance of knowing your enemy, his or her strengths and weaknesses, as well as your own capabilities. As such, if law enforcement treats the gang problem like they were fighting a war, they would want to know as much about the enemy as possible. Where are their strongholds? Where do they store weapons and drugs to support their operations? How many troops do they have? What is the level of training each of those troops or members has?

Proper analysis of the gang to be targeted by an injunction allows the police to understand the mind-set and common methods of the "enemy," the areas in which they conduct their criminal activity, and the times of day, and the days of the week they are most active. Understanding the gang allows for more effective gang suppression operations and helps select the best method to target the particular gang.

Prior to seeking an injunction against the Skyline gang, also known as the Eastside Piru in San Diego County, extensive analysis of the gang was conducted. When evaluating a gang injunction, it is important to first know the status of all identified members of the gang to help establish the list of the most problematic members; this is especially true if you are going to name the members in the court documents. The analysis of the Skyline gang included a review of police department files, California Department of Corrections records, California Youth Authority records, Gang Suppression Unit records from the probation department, San Diego Police Department records division searches, and a review of court files on current and past cases. After a comprehensive review of the gang, 627 total members were identified. The level of criminal activity attributed to those members varied significantly from member to member, making further analysis necessary.

It should be noted, however, that the true number of Skyline members was estimated to be closer to 1,000 members based in part upon the identification of hundreds (approximately 400) of associates listed on field interview reports and arrest reports of known members that have been contacted or arrested by the police, but that were not documented at that time. A large number of gang members also admit gang membership when being classified by correctional facilities at the state and local levels and in parole and probation files and databases. Most of those undocumented associates or companions have been contacted on numerous occasions with documented members and meet one or more of the other required criteria to be documented as members, but have not been documented for various reasons. Based upon the review of the gang, conversations with police officers, and interviews with known members of the Skyline gang, it was estimated that only between 60 and 65% of the gang's total membership was actually known to law enforcement.

An interesting fact was uncovered during the analysis showing that only 18 of the 627 known members of the gang were juveniles. That accounted for only 2.8% of the gang's known membership. After discussing the issue with several police agencies in the area, and after comparing Skyline to other gangs in the area, that number was deemed extremely low. The majority of the juveniles suspected of being members of the gang (conservatively estimated to be 200) were not getting documented as members for some reason. Having those members properly documented would help police in the future with gang prosecutions and gang investigations.

As of February 26, 2004, the analysis into the Skyline gang indicated that there were 627 Skyline members, 544 of them documented with the San Diego Police Department according to the lead detective on the case. In addition, the California Youth Authority had identified 41 members of the gang not documented by the San Diego Police, who admitted they were Skyline gang members during their classification interviews. Likewise, the Gang Suppression Unit of the probation department identified 31 Skyline members not documented by the San Diego Police. And finally, the gang detectives assigned to the Skyline gang had 11 members ready to be documented that were in the final gang documentation approval phase. This is not an uncommon phenomenon in the realm of gang documentation. It is not realistic to think that every member of every gang is properly documented. Many times individual gang members are active in the gang for long periods of time before being seen on the radar of police on the streets. As such, a comprehensive analysis of the gang prior to seeking an injunction gives the investigators a much clearer picture of the true size of the gang they are dealing with.

Further review of the 627 Skyline members revealed that 22.5% of the gang's total membership was in custody at the time the injunction was being prepared, 113 (18%) of them were currently in the custody of the California Department of Corrections, 11 (1.5%) of them were in the custody of the California Youth Authority, and 22 (3.0%) of them were in the custody of the San Diego County Jail. In addition, 7.5% of the gang's total membership was identified as being on parole, 31 (5.5%) of them were on parole from the CDC, and 13 (2%) of them were on parole from the CYA. Another 7.5% of the gang's total membership was on probation, 9 (1%) of them were on standard probation, and 41 (6.5%) of them were on probation with the Gang Suppression Unit.

This analysis helped to better understand the history of the gang's individual members to make a better-informed decision as to which members to target with the injunction. A review of the list of the entire gang was narrowed down to 112 potential targets based upon the level of recent activity in the target area attributed to each individual member. Of the 112 potential target members, 17.5% of them were in custody. More importantly, they were scheduled to be released from custody within the first year of the injunction. In addition, 15% of the injunction targets were on parole and 7% were on probation. As a result of further analysis conducted, the list of 112 gang members was scaled down to 90 potential names.

The scaling down was the result of final review of the intelligence data, revealing that some of the gang's members had moved out of the area, some had jobs, and the prosecution had some concerns about managing such a large case. At the time, it was the largest injunction ever attempted in San Diego County. The preliminary injunction that was later submitted to the court had 90 members on it, containing a mixture of violent offenders, drug dealers, and petty vandals and thieves. The preliminary order ended up with 86 named defendants. Four of the gang members argued to the court that they were trying to get out of the gang and were not intending on remaining active in the gang. From April 16, 2004, until April 16, 2005, when the order was made permanent, none of the four members that contested the order had been contacted in the target areas or anywhere else by any law enforcement agency. As such, the district attorney did not pursue adding them to the final order in the interest of fairness. The analysis gave the police and prosecution a comprehensive understanding of the street gang to be targeted, allowing for an easy justification to the court of the gang's danger to the community, and the nuisance and criminal activity that could be attributed to the gang.

People v. G-Mobb (Sacramento County Case 04AS02821), July 13, 2004

On July 13, 2004, the Sacramento city attorney in the County of Sacramento sought an injunction against the G-Mobb gang operating in the West Sacramento Police jurisdiction. The injunction named the gang as a defendant, as well as six members of the gang. The injunction covered an area in West Sacramento, specifically Doss Way to the north, Brookfield Drive to the south, Franklin Boulevard to the east, and Morrison Creek to the west. The injunction essentially covered an entire apartment complex called the Franklin Villa complex. The attorney that handled the case was Dennis Beck. On October 29, 2004, the injunction against the G-Mobb gang in the City of West Sacramento was made preliminary. On May 2, 2005, the injunction against the G-Mobb gang in the City of West Sacramento was made permanent.

People v. 38th Street (Los Angeles Case BC319166), July 28, 2004

On July 28, 2004, the Los Angeles city attorney, Los Angeles district attorney, and Los Angeles police sought an injunction against the 38th Street Newton gang. The injunction did not name any individual defendants from the estimated 350-member gang that has existed since the 1920s, but sued the gang as the sole defendant. The injunction targeted a 3.87-square-mile area from Washington Boulevard to the north, Alameda Street to the east, Slauson Avenue to the south, and San Pedro Street to the west. The 38th Street gang had 334 total members. Between 2004 and 2005, 28 members had been served and were now enjoined by the injunction. Two 38th Street members were arrested in the target area for violating the gang injunction. This injunction was not a part of any larger project or concurrent initiatives operating in the target areas. The injunction was sought because of the significant narcotic sales attributed to the gang. On November 22, 2004, the injunction against the 38th Street Newton gang was made permanent.

People v. Varrio Nueva Estrada Hollenbeck (Los Angeles Case BC319981), August 12, 2004

On August 12, 2004, the Los Angeles city attorney, Los Angeles district attorney, and Los Angeles police sought an injunction against the Varrio Nueva Estrada Hollenbeck gang (*People v.*

Varrio Nueva Estrada Hollenbeck, 2004). The gang was named as the sole defendant and no individual members were named. The injunction targeted the area from the Interstate 5 freeway to the north, Soto Street to the west, and the Los Angeles city limit to the south and east. The VNE gang had 597 total members. Between 2004 and 2005, 22 members had been served and were now enjoined by the injunction. Two VNE members were arrested for violating the gang injunction. This injunction was a part of a CLEAR program targeting the area. The injunction was sought because of the significant narcotic sales attributed to the gang. On September 21, 2004, the preliminary injunction against the Varrio Nueva Estrada Hollenbeck gang was granted.

People v. Parkside Bulldogs (Fresno Case 04CECG02777), September 27, 2004

On September 27, 2004, the Fresno County district attorney sought an injunction against the Parkside Bulldogs gang. The injunction named 19 members in some detail but sued the gang as an entity and not as individuals. The injunction targeted the area between Olive Avenue to the north, Hughes Avenue to the west, Nielsen Avenue to the south, and Palm Avenue to the east. The complaint was filed and 30 members of the gang were served with the notice of the complaint. The district attorney worked with the Fresno Police to obtain the injunction against the gang. Sixty members of the gang were served with the order following its implementation, and there have been about 100 arrests for violations of the injunction. On October 7, 2004, the court issued the preliminary injunction against the Parkside Bulldogs gang.

People v. Southside Montebello (Los Angeles Case BC324344), November 10, 2004

On November 10, 2004, the city attorney for the City of Montebello filed an injunction against the Southside Montebello gang. The city attorney for the city is the law firm of Alvarez-Glassman & Colvin, which obtained the court order on behalf of Montebello. The private law firm is the contract city attorney for Montebello, Pomona, Pico Rivera, Bell Gardens, La Puente, West Covina, and Walnut. The attorney that handled the case was Sean Beehler. The injunction targeted an area in Montebello, specifically the area between Beverley Boulevard and Poplar Avenue, Garfield Avenue, Allston Street to the south, and the city limits to the east. The injunction sued the gang as the sole defendant but did name 28 of the gang's members in detail in the supporting declarations. On December 15, 2004, the city attorney for the

City of Montebello obtained the preliminary injunction against the Southside Montebello gang (*People v. Southside Montebello*, 2004). On January 31, 2005, the city attorney for the City of Montebello obtained a permanent injunction against the Southside Montebello gang.

People v. California Garden Crips (San Bernardino Case SCVSS119636), November 23, 2004

On November 23, 2004, the San Bernardino district attorney and the San Bernardino Police Department sought an injunction against the California Garden Crips. The injunction covers the territory of the California Garden Crips gang in the City of San Bernardino, specifically Macy Street to the west, Pennsylvania Street to the east, Baseline Street to the south, and Eighteenth Street to the north. The injunction sued the gang as well as 20 individually named defendants. On April 29, 2005, the injunction against the California Garden Crips street gang was made permanent.

People v. 42nd, 43rd, 48th Street Gangster Crips (Los Angeles Case BC326016), December 16, 2004

On December 16, 2004, the Los Angeles city attorney, Los Angeles district attorney, and Los Angeles police sought an injunction against the 42nd, 43rd, and 48th Street Gangster Crips. The target area is approximately 7.5 square miles. The 42nd, 43rd, and 48th Street Gangster Crips are the only named defendants, all unincorporated associations. The safety zone can more specifically be defined as the area between Washington Boulevard on the north, Florence Avenue on the south, Alameda Street on the east, and the 110 Harbor Freeway on the west. On January 18, 2005, the preliminary injunction against the 42nd Street Gangster Crips was granted by Los Angeles Superior Court Judge David Yaffe. On April 7, 2005, the injunction against the 42nd Street Gangster Crips was made permanent.

People v. Broderick Boys (Yolo County Case CV04-2085), December 30, 2004

On December 30, 2004, the Sacramento city attorney filed an injunction against the Broderick Boys gang in the City of West Sacramento (*People v. Broderick Boys*, 2004). This case, like some before it, listed the gang as the sole defendant; it did not name any individual defendants. The injunction sought to abate a public nuisance through the use of what is commonly known as a gang injunction against defendant Broderick Boys aka BRK aka BSK aka Norteno aka Norte aka XIV, an unincorporated association alleged to be a criminal street gang. The target area is approximately 3 square miles in an area located in the City of West Sacramento, bounded by Harbor Boulevard to the west, the West Sacramento River to the north and to the east, and by Highway 50/Business Loop 80 and State Route 275 to the south.

On January 24, 2005, the court issued the preliminary injunction against the Broderick Boys gang. On February 3, 2005, the permanent injunction against the Broderick Boys was granted. On February 9, 2005, the service of the injunction began. Over the course of the next couple of weeks, over 80 members had been served the order. On July 28, 2005, the American Civil Liberties Union filed a memorandum of points and authorities in support of a motion to set aside default judgment granting the permanent injunction against the Broderick Boys gang. Since authorities obtained the court order targeting the 350-member West Sacramento street gang known as the Broderick Boys, the police had made 10 arrests of members on a variety of charges and say the injunction is working to reduce crime. On September 27, 2005, the motion against the Broderick Boys gang injunction went to court. The court sided with the prosecution; the case was appealed by the ACLU and is pending litigation. As a result of the ACLU analysis of the *Broderick Boys* case, the ACLU formed the opinion that the default judgment and injunction violated fundamental due process principles that ensure that persons whose property and liberty interests are affected receive notice and a fair opportunity to be heard. The fact that gang members do not show up does not reduce their due process. That is true when given notice and they fail to appear. But some argue they never even had the chance to appear, and were never given a court date to stand before a judge and argue their side.

YEAR 2005

People v. Grape Street Crips (Los Angeles Case BC330087), March 10, 2005

On March 10, 2005, the Los Angeles city attorney, Los Angeles district attorney, and Los Angeles police sought an injunction against the Grape Street Crips. The injunction named the gang as the sole defendant and discussed 16 individuals in the order. The injunction targeted the area from Santa Ana Boulevard to the south, Compton Avenue to the west, 92nd Street to the north, and Alameda to the east. On May 25, 2005, the Grape Street Crip injunction was made permanent. The original Grape Street injunction applied to 16 gang members, listed by name, and granted police permission to add others who met at least two of the LAPD's nine "gang membership criteria," which include tattoos, nicknames, and style of dress.

More than 240 names were added to the court order in the nine months following its implementation, and 175 arrests were made for injunction violations. "There is no conspiracy to get everybody you can on this gang injunction," said LAPD Sgt. Timothy Pearce, who heads the gang detail in Jordan Downs. "The people that are on there are gang members. They may not have a record, but they're with the wrong people in the wrong places. We look at the totality of circumstances." Totality of circumstances, however, can convey different meanings to those inside and outside of Jordan Downs, a bleak collection of aging barracks style apartments where school failure and joblessness leave hundreds of young men aimless and idle. Some residents concede the project seems quieter since the injunction went into effect.

People v. Hoovers and Troubles (Los Angeles Case BC330272), March 15, 2005

On March 15, 2005, the Los Angeles city attorney, Los Angeles district attorney, and Los Angeles police sought an injunction against the Hoovers gang and the Trouble gang. The injunction named both gangs as defendants, as well as 56 individual defendants. Seventy-four members were identified in the declarations in support of the order. On May 24, 2005, the preliminary injunction against the Hoovers gang was granted. On June 29, 2005, the permanent injunction against the Hoovers gang was granted.

People v. 18th St. CLCS and Nine Other Gangs (Los Angeles Case BC332713), May 2, 2005

On May 2, 2005, the Los Angeles city attorney, Los Angeles district attorney, and Los Angeles police sought an injunction against the 18th Street and nine other gangs. This case is actually an injunction against 10 different gangs, including some gangs and tagger crews. In addition to the 18th Street gang, the Crazy Riders, DIA (Down in Action), Krazy Town (KTO), La Raza Loca, Orphans, Rockwood Street Locos, Varrio Vista Rifa, Wanderers, and Whitmer Street Locos are all enjoined in the case. This injunction was in some ways a renewal of an earlier injunction from 1998 (*People v. 18th St. Gang Shatto Park*, 1998). The target area where all 10 gangs congregate is roughly 2.9 square miles, specifically the 110 Harbor Freeway to the east, James M. Wood Boulevard to the south, Normandie Avenue to the west, and Beverly Boulevard to the north (Figure 13.4). On June 3, 2005, the preliminary injunction against

FIGURE 13.4 Map of *People v. 18th St.* and nine other gangs.

the 18th Street and nine other gangs was granted. On September 11, 2005, the permanent injunction against the 18th Street gang and nine additional gangs was granted.

People v. Vista Homeboys (San Diego Case GIN044867), May 27, 2005

On May 27, 2005, the San Diego County District Attorney's Office and the San Diego County Sheriff's Department sought an injunction against the Vista Homeboys gang. The injunction targeted 89 members of the Vista-based gang, specifically the area from Vista Village Drive to the north, Goodwin Drive to the east, Eucalyptus Avenue to the south, and Santa Fe Avenue to the west. The VHB injunction has two smaller safety zones as well.

Example of Serving a Large Number of Defendants at One Time

In many cases, the manner in which the defendants are notified may impact the overall success of the injunction. Gang members that have been included in gang injunctions tend to avoid the personal service of the applicable orders when they know the police are looking for them. With a few exceptions, most gang members are not eager to receive the injunction papers and willfully avoid service by staying with friends, having family members lie for them as to where they are; some stop going to school and leave their jobs, if they have one, to avoid being located. Many have indicated that if they cannot be found in a short period of time, the police will discontinue looking for them and take them off of the list or simply move on and focus on someone else. For this primary reason, this research recommends well-organized operations be conducted to ensure the service of the required court documents.

In San Diego County, for example, the gang injunctions (like the Vista Homeboys injunction) tend to list a greater number of named defendants when compared to other California counties. The more defendants named, typically the longer it will take to find and legally serve each named defendant. Planning a service operation requires significant preparation. The Vista Homeboys injunction required the assigning of officers to teams, and giving the teams of officers packets containing all relevant forms, proof of service forms, and other necessary information relating to the status of the individual gang member they will look for. This serves several purposes; primarily it sends a message to the community and the gang that the police are serious about the injunction based upon the show of force and dedication of resources to the project. In addition, the serving of all of the documents in a short period of time makes it less likely that gang members will have opportunities to avoid service by temporarily moving away from the area or having friends and family hinder police efforts to find them.

The use of a large number of officers also allows for enforcement to be taken against the gang during the service operation. For example, if a gang member has an active warrant or is on probation or parole at the time of the service operation, it may impact the contact when the officers serve the named gang member. If the gang member is in violation of the law at the time of service, this research recommends making any applicable arrest to further send the message to the gang that the injunction has come and things are going to be different within the target area.

People v. Lamparas Primera and Southside (Santa Barbara 1148758), June 1, 2005

The Santa Barbara injunction against the Lampara gang was granted; however, the superior court judge limited the order well beyond that experienced by most jurisdictions. The judge did not restrict alcohol usage and did not restrict lookout activity, despite the case law that has articulated the restrictions have been held constitutional. The district attorney in Santa Barbara decided not to appeal the judge's modifications to the order and has enforced the version that was implemented. Members of the rival Southside and Westside gangs can be arrested, fined, and jailed if they're caught associating with other known gang members, fighting, possessing weapons, wearing gang clothing, flashing gang symbols, blocking passage of other persons on the street, and participating in numerous other activities. Proponents of the injunction have said it helps police keep the peace in an area prone to gang violence. Opponents had expressed concern that gang members could get arrested for innocent daily activities.

People v. Big Hazard (Los Angeles Case BC335749), June 28, 2005

On June 28, 2005, the Los Angeles city attorney sought an injunction against the Hazard Grande gang. The injunction sued the gang as the sole defendant and did not name individual defendants. The target area was specifically Cornwell and San Pablo Street to the west, Valley Boulevard to the north, India Street to the east, and Marengo Street to the south (*People v. Big Hazard*, 2005). Hazard Grande, which originated in the 1940s, uses the Ramona Gardens housing project as a base of operations for an array of criminal activities. The injunction safety zone is bounded by Cornwell, San Pablo, Marengo, North Indiana Streets, and Valley Boulevard.

People v. Old Town National City (San Diego Case GIS22336), October 7, 2005

The Old Town National City was targeted in San Diego in 2005 in an effort to expand the 1998 effort of the city attorney. On October 7, 2005, the San Diego County District Attorney's Office and the National City Police Department sought an injunction against the Old Town National City gang. The injunction targeted 104 members of the OTNC street gang and greatly expanded the first injunction against the same gang obtained by the city attorney in 1998. The Old Town National City injunction was made preliminary on October 8, 2005. The target area, which was on the Westside of National City in 1998, expanded to include over three-quarters of the city in 2005, specifically from Euclid Avenue to the east (Figure 13.5).

People v. Hoovers Gang (Los Angeles Case BC341872), October 24, 2005

On October 24, 2005, the Los Angeles sheriff and the Los Angeles County district attorney targeted the Hoover Crips, aka the Hoover Criminals street gang in the Lennox and Inglewood areas of Los Angeles (*People v. Hoovers*, 2005). The injunction names the gang as the sole defendant and is directed at any member of any Hoover clique. The court order applies equally to members of the Hoover sets or cliques known as Five-Deuce (52nd Street), Five-Nine (59th Street), Seven-Four (74th Street), Eight-Trey (83rd Street), Nine-Deuce (92nd Street), Nine-Four (94th Street), One-O-Seven (107th Street), and Eleven-Deuce (112th Street). Additionally, this court order applies to any gang member who only identifies himself as a Hoover, Hoover Criminal, or Hoover Crip and declines to identify his set or clique or claims that he is not part of a set or clique. The safety zone is bounded by Century Boulevard to the north, Normandie Avenue to the west, Imperial Highway to the south, and Vermont Avenue to the east, and extends 100 yards to the outside of each of these four boundaries.

The Los Angeles Sheriff's Department has encouraged its deputies to enforce this order and made recommendations on how to deal with violations of the order. All deputies have been directed to check to see if the gang member is on probation or parole at the time they have violated the injunction. The bail on probation

FIGURE 13.5 Map of *People v. Old Town National City.*

and parole violations is higher than the violation of a court order. Oficers are instructed to always book for the felony of misdemeanor probation violation (PC 1203.2) or juvenile probation violation (WIC 777) rather than the PC 166(a)(4). The bail on the PC 166(a)(4) is $5,000; on PC 1203.2 it is $10,000, and on WIC 777, there is no bail. Again, the theory is to keep the gang members in jail and off the streets, making the punishment for a gang injunction violation as severe as possible. On December 14, 2005, the preliminary injunction was granted. On February 8, 2006, the permanent injunction was granted.

People v. Modoc Boys (Fresno Case 05CECG03696), November 28, 2005

On November 28, 2005, the Fresno Police and the Fresno District Attorney's Office filed an injunction against the Modoc Boys gang in Fresno. The injunction names the gang as the only defendant but lists 22 members in the supporting declarations. The target area is East Whites Bridge Avenue to the north, B Street to the east, East Kearney Boulevard to the south, and South Thorne Street to the west. In the injunction, District Attorney Greg Anderson defined terrorism as the unlawful use or threatened use of force or violence to intimidate or coerce societies or governments. He goes on to say that society is well aware of the unspeakable violence that foreign terrorists can inflict on this country and its citizens. Anderson goes on to say that violent robberies, beatings, shootings, and murders occur on a daily basis by local terrorist groups known as criminal street gangs.

San Francisco County Takes a Look at the Gang Injunction Policy

In December 2005, San Francisco City Attorney Dennis Herrera began a municipal–federal partnership to pursue civil injunctions against gangs in San Francisco in an effort to stem the rising tide of gang-related violence plaguing the city. The city attorney's civil gang injunction program was established between the U.S. Attorney's Office for the northern district of California in San Francisco, and resulted in close collaboration with the San Francisco Police Department and the San Francisco District Attorney's Office. As part of the civil gang injunction partnership with the U.S. attorney, deputy city attorneys were cross-designated as special assistant U.S. attorneys and coordinated efforts in both offices. Within Herrera's office, the Civil Gang Injunction Team works alongside the Code Enforcement and Resident Protection Team under a newly created Neighborhood and Resident Safety Division with the goal of reducing gang related public nuisances in the City of San Francisco.

Not Every Injunction Considered Is Implemented: PPHG (Pimps, Playboys, Hustlers, and Gangsters) Example

In December 2005, San Bernardino police officials announced plans to start the injunction process against the PPHG gang. The city attorney announced it would take several months before the evidence was submitted and the paperwork filed in court. A majority of the PPHG members live in Rialto, but the gang was responsible for crime in the City of San Bernardino.

After the police conducted their investigation, it was determined that the PPHG gang would not make a good candidate for a gang injunction. The analysis revealed that the gang was less territorial than originally anticipated, and while conducting operations against the gang, the gang reacted by spreading out over a wide area. Another interesting point about this proposed injunction that was never filed is that the media was notified before the injunction was filed. In San Diego County, for example, it is a guarded secret that a particular gang is the subject of an injunction until it is filed in court. This is an informal policy to protect the investigation and not provide advanced notice to the gang, to reduce opportunities for the gang to circumvent the order.

YEAR 2006

People v. Olive Street Pomona (Los Angeles Case KC047752), February 1, 2006

On February 1, 2006, the Pomona Police Department targeted the Olive Street gang with an injunction. The injunction named the gang as the sole defendant but did list 64 members in the description of known members that cannot associate together in the target areas. The Olive Street gang, also known as Pomona Sur, is restricted in the City of Pomona, specifically E. Lexington Avenue to the north, S. Towne Avenue to the east, the 60 Freeway to the south, and S. Garvey Avenue to the west.

People v. Geer Street and Schoolyard Crips (Los Angeles Case BC349468), March 23, 2006

On March 23, 2006, the Los Angeles city attorney targeted two Crip gang sets in the City of Los Angeles. The injunction named only the two gangs as defendants; it did not name individual members. The target area for the injunction is referred to as the mid-city safety zone, specifically Olympic Boulevard to the north, Crenshaw Boulevard to the east, Jefferson Boulevard to the south, and Fairfax Boulevard to the west.

City of San Diego v. West Coast Crips (San Diego Case GIC864852), April 25, 2006

On April 25, 2006, the San Diego city attorney and the San Diego Police Department filed an injunction against the West Coast Crips gang. The injunction named the gang and 50 individual members as defendants. This injunction was the second filed by the city attorney and the first targeting a Crips gang in San Diego. The injunction has two target areas; target area 1 is bordered by Highway 94 to the north, Highway 15 to the east, and Interstate 5 to the south and west. Target area 2 is bordered by Highway 94 to the north, Euclid Avenue to the east, Imperial Avenue to the south, and Highway 15 to the west. This injunction contains some of the same restrictions of the injunctions before it, with a couple of exceptions.

In February 2007, a West Coast Crip gang member was released from prison following a three-year sentence for selling marijuana. Upon his release, fresh out of prison, he was eager to return to the places he missed. Upon his release, he now had to face the reality that he had to modify his criminal behavior in the gang injunction area, and if unwilling to do so, he would have to consider moving to avoid violating the terms of his parole and the gang injunction. What this gang member and the media consistently fail to understand is that the West Coast Crip injunction does not require that he move anywhere. He and his fellow gang members are free and encouraged to be productive members of society and stop being gang members. The gang injunction restricts him from associating with West Coast Crip gang members, hanging out at locations identified as West Coast Crip strongholds, and identifying himself as a West Coast Crip. By most accounts he and other gang members like him will likely benefit from the injunction in the long run.

People v. Playboys (Los Angeles Case BC351990), May 8, 2006

On May 11, 2006, the Los Angeles city attorney sought an injunction against the Playboys gang. The injunction named the gang as the sole defendant. The injunction covers two areas. The first is called the south park area, from Vernon Avenue to the north, Central Avenue to the east, Slauson Avenue to the south, and the 110 Freeway to the west. The second area, known as Pico Fedora, is Olympic Boulevard to the north, Vermont Avenue to the east, Venice Boulevard to the south, and Ardmore Avenue to the west.

People v. Black P Stones (Los Angeles Case BC352951), May 25, 2006

On May 25, 2006, the Los Angeles city attorney sought an injunction against the Black P Stones. According to City Attorney Rocky Delgadillo, the Black P Stones street gang had been terrorizing the Baldwin Village area of Los Angeles (Figure 13.6) for some years leading up to the injunction. The injunction names the gang as the sole defendant. The complaint names 55 members of the gang in the supporting documents and restricts them in two areas. The first area is from Crenshaw Boulevard to the west, Country Club and Pico Boulevard to the north, Western, Normandie, and Arlington to the east, and 30th and 29th Streets to the south. The second area is from Rodeo and Coliseum to the north, Crenshaw to the east, Santo Tomas Drive to the south, and Brea Avenue to the west. On July 25, 2006, the preliminary injunction was granted. On September 21, 2006, the permanent injunction was granted.

People v. White Fence (Los Angeles Case BC353596), June 8, 2006

On June 8, 2006, the Los Angeles city attorney sought an injunction against the White Fence gang in the City of Los Angeles. The injunction named the gang as the sole defendant and targeted two zones, specifically zone A from 4th Street to the north, Indiana Street to the east, and the Interstate 5 freeway to the south and west; and zone B from Franklin Avenue to the north, Vermont Avenue to the east, Santa Monica Boulevard to the south, and Gower Street to the west.

People v. Santa Nita (Orange County Case 06CC06903), June 8, 2006

On June 8, 2006, the Orange County district attorney and the Santa Ana police sought an injunction against the Santa Nita gang in the City of Santa Ana. The preliminary injunction signed by Orange County Superior Court Judge Daniel Didier marked the first time this legal tool had been successfully used in Orange County. The injunction named 155 members of the Santa Nita gang and the parents of 21 juveniles. Only about 50 people named in the injunction and issued summonses to the hearing showed up, a few wearing ties, others wearing dress shirts and slacks or jeans. Some were accompanied by their parents. The target area encompasses about 2 square miles, roughly from McFadden Avenue north to Trask Avenue, bordered on the west by Harbor Boulevard and on the east by the Santa Ana River.

FIGURE 13.6 Map of *People v. Black P Stones.*

Operation Safe Neighborhood began in November 2005 when Santa Ana City Attorney Joseph Fletcher, Santa Ana Police Chief Paul Walters, Garden Grove Police Chief Joe Polisar, and other Orange County law enforcement decided it was time to make Orange County even more inhospitable to gangs. They began looking into getting injunctions on street gang members to prevent them from building their criminal networks. On June 14, these 15 agencies helped serve 134 of the 155 named defendants with the gang injunction. The police had the help of 225 officers from Anaheim, Cal State Fullerton, Costa Mesa, Parole, Probation, Fullerton, Garden Grove, Irvine, Newport Beach, Orange, OCDA Bureau of Investigation, Orange County Sheriff, Santa Ana, Tustin, and Westminster. Crime in the area dropped 46% in the five months following the injunction being implemented. On November 3, 2006, the first Orange County gang injunction was made permanent against a Santa Ana criminal street gang. Gang-related crime in the safety zone has decreased by 55%.

People v. Southside Chiques (Ventura Case CIV242491), July 27, 2006

On July 27, 2006, the Ventura County district attorney and the Oxnard Police Department sought an injunction against the Southside Chiques gang in the City of Oxnard. The injunction names the gang as the sole defendant and names 18 members in the supporting complaint. The target area is from Woodley Road to the north, Rose Avenue to the east, E. Hueneme to the south, and the City of Port Hueneme to the west. The injunction covers a 4.26-square-mile safety zone, some of which overlaps the existing 6.6-square-mile Colonia Chiques safety zone. Since the injunction became permanent, police have made 45 arrests for safety zone violations, and all of them have been successfully prosecuted, according to Neail Holland, a detective with the Oxnard Police Department specializing in gang investigations. According to Karen Wold, "People don't want to have these restrictions in their life. They say they'd rather just do something else. It makes gangs less attractive."

People v. East Side Victoria (San Bernardino VCVVS042664), August 2, 2006

On August 2, 2006, the San Bernardino district attorney and the San Bernardino Sheriff's Department sought an injunction against the Eastside Victoria gang. The safety zone covers the majority of Old Town, with areas on both sides of Seventh Street, north to D Street, including Forest Park. It extends to Pebble Beach Drive on the south, La Paz Drive on the west, and a portion of Hesperia Road on the east. For the first time in the history of the San Bernardino County Sheriff's Department, authorities were granted a gang injunction in an effort to reduce crime and relieve area residents of the intimidation of living within a gang territory. The injunction took the better part of a year to plan and execute, as officials had to establish the terms and have the document approved by a judge. By late August, officials began serving the gang members. Forty-nine gang members were served with the injunction, and only three gang members appeared in court to protest its terms. On September 11, 2006, the preliminary injunction was granted.

People v. Orange Cove Rifa Bulldogs and Orange Cove Sur (Fresno County Case 06CECG02815), August 23, 2006

The Fresno County district attorney sought an injunction against the Orange Cove Rifa Bulldogs and the Orange Cove Sur. The injunction names the two gangs as defendants, as well as 22 Orange Cove Bulldogs and 16 Orange Cove Sur members named in the complaint. The target area is Monson Avenue to the east, Adams and Jacobs Avenue to the north, Hills Valley Road to the west, and South and Parlier Avenues to the south.

People v. Clover, Eastlake, and Lincoln Heights (Los Angeles County Case BC358881), September 20, 2006

The Los Angeles city attorney and the Los Angeles police sought an injunction against three gangs that claim a common turf. The injunction named all three gangs as defendants and named 10 members of each gang in the complaint. The targeted area is from the Pasadena Freeway to the north, Soto to the east, Valley and Mission to the south, and Main to the west.

People v. Oakdale Mob (San Francisco Case CGC06456517), September 27, 2006

The San Francisco city attorney and the San Francisco Police Department sought the county's first civil injunction against the Oakdale Mob street gang in September 2006. The injunction named the gang as the sole defendant. The target area is bounded by Navy Road to the north, Palou to the south, Griffith to the east, and Ingalls to the west. It includes, among other residences, the 133-unit Oakdale public housing development. Machaela Hoctor, a deputy city attorney, said that the city had notified three Oakdale gang members and that, although the Oakdale Mob and its members were aware of the action, none appeared in court. Superior Court Judge Peter Busch, however, rejected the city's argument that a 10 p.m. curfew was also needed, choosing instead to approve a no loitering provision between midnight and sunrise. Given the limits on association, the limits on illegal conduct, and the limits on loitering and trespassing, what's left to be addressed by the curfew is not really gang activity but the individual's private activity.

According to the San Francisco Superior Court's March 15, 2007 judgment granting permanent injunction against the Oakdale Mob, the court ordered the safety zone to be located in the City and County of San Francisco, bounded by Griffith Street to the east, Palou Avenue to the south, Ingalls Street to the west, and Navy Road to the north, continuing straight beyond the end of Navy Road to where it would intersect with Ingalls Street, and including both sides of those four boundaries streets.

People v. Dogtown (Los Angeles BC359945), October 6, 2006

The Los Angeles city attorney and the Los Angeles police sought an injunction against the Dogtown gang on October 6, 2006. The injunction named the gang as the sole defendant but did list 17 individual members in the complaint. The injunction covers two areas; the first is the William Mead housing, north Main Street, east Elmyra Street, Bolero Lane, and Leroy Street; the second area is from Figueroa Street to the north, Granada Street to the east, Holland Avenue to the south, and Aldama Street to the west. According to the LAPD, the Dogtown gang that used to reign over the William Mead housing project is no longer in the area.

People v. Highland Park (Los Angeles County Case BC359944), October 6, 2006

On October 6, 2006, the Los Angeles city attorney and the Los Angeles Police Department sought an injunction against the Highland Park crew, a 300-member gang that claims a territory in northeast Los Angeles. "Gangs in the Highland Park area are terrorizing residents and should be declared a public nuisance with an injunction to prevent members from associating with each other," a lawsuit filed by the City Attorney's Office said. The lawsuits described safety zones in which the city sought to enforce injunctions against the gang. The Highland Park gang safety zone includes the area near the intersection of Eagle Rock and Colorado Boulevards, plus York Boulevard and Avenues 40 and 50. The injunction names the gang as the sole defendant. The preliminary injunction was granted on November 13, 2006.

People v. Junior Mafia Gang (Los Angeles County VC047440), October 6, 2006

On October 6, 2006, the City of Bell Gardens sought an injunction against the Junior Mafia gang. The injunction names the gang as the only defendant and covers the area between Gange Avenue, Chalet Drive, Hannon Street, and Ira Avenue. A total of 92 individual members of the gang are mentioned in the complaint as not being able to associate with each other. The defendants were served by the Bell Gardens Police Department.

People v. Boys from the Hood (Orange County 06CC10916), October 12, 2006

On November 20, 2006, the Orange County District Attorney's Office and the Anaheim police obtained an injunction against the Boys from the Hood gang in the City of Anaheim. The injunction named the gang and 77 individuals in the target area, specifically the area bounded by: to the north, 1-5 Freeway from Harbor Boulevard to Gene Autry Way and Gene Autry Way from the 1-5 Freeway to State College Boulevard; to the west, Harbor Boulevard between the 1-5 Freeway and Chapman Avenue; to the east, State College Boulevard between Gene Autry Way and Chapman Avenue; to the south, Chapman Avenue between State College Boulevard and Harbor Boulevard. Judge Daniel J. Didier marked the second time in five months that this legal tool had been used in the county. Similar injunctions had been imposed in Los Angeles, San Diego, and Santa Clara Counties. The judge's order established a 1.6-square-mile zone in Anaheim and portions of Orange and Garden Grove, near Ponderosa Park in the Wakefield neighborhood, in which gang members must obey a 10 p.m. curfew, not drink in public, not wear gang attire, and not associate in public with members of the group. In Anaheim, an injunction against the Boys from the Hood gang has seen a 50% decrease in assaults and a 75% decrease in shots fired. On February 9, 2007, this injunction was made permanent. Serious and violent felonies have decreased by up to 40% in the safety zone.

People v. Whittier Varrio Locos (Los Angeles County BC363464), December 15, 2006

The city attorney for the City of Whittier and the Whittier Police Department sought an injunction against the Whittier Varrio Locos gang on December 15, 2006. The injunction named the gang and 46 individual members as defendants in the case. Superior Court Judge David Yaffe issued the preliminary injunction against the gang on February 5, 2007.

People v. Westside Gang (San Diego Case GIN057995), December 26, 2006

On December 26, 2006, the San Diego County District Attorney's Office and the Escondido police sought an injunction against the Westside gang. The gang injunction names the gang and 58 individual members and covers the target area between Grand to the north, Juniper to the east, Felicita to the south, and Upas to the west. This is the second gang injunction filed against the Westside gang, the first was filed on July 13, 2001. The Westside gang injunction went to court on January 18, 2007, where the preliminary injunction was granted.

People v. Diablos Gang (San Diego Case GIN057995), December 26, 2006

On December 26, 2006, the San Diego County District Attorney's Office and the Escondido police sought an injunction against the Diablos gang. The gang injunction names the gang and 50 individual members of the gang. It covers the target area between Lincoln to the north, Midway to the east, Grand and Flower to the south, and Escondido Boulevard to the west. This is the second gang injunction filed against the Diablos gang; the first was filed on July 13, 2001 (*People v. Diablos Gang*, 2006). The Diablos injunction went to court on January 16, 2007, where the preliminary injunction was granted.

YEAR 2007

Stay-Away Orders Used in Connection with Gang Injunctions

In January 2007, several counties began to expand the scope of their gang injunctions by identifying gang members on probation or parole who are members of a gang that has an injunction against them, and appling a stay-away order against those members as long as they are on probation or parole. Such orders are included in the terms of offenders' probation and forbid them from being in the gang injunction target areas and apply the same restrictions to them as long as they are under the jurisdiction of the probation department or state parole. Officials hope these orders will make gang injunctions more effective than current injunctions. Stay-away orders, which were employed against drug users on skid row, can be easier to enforce, because they are a condition of probation and a violation can immediately put the offender back in jail. Under a new early release policy set to be implemented soon, the Los Angeles County sheriff will no longer hold inmates sentenced to county jail under gang injunctions for their entire sentences.

San Bernardino District Attorney Forms Gang Injunction Unit

On February 15, 2007, with the support of the board of supervisors and the Police Chiefs and Sheriff's Association, District Attorney Michael A. Ramos implemented a Gang Injunction Unit, which allowed two deputy district attorneys to civilly abate gangs in target areas. This was the first time gang injunctions were used in unincorporated areas of the county.

Canoga Park Alabama, March 21, 2007

Canoga Park Alabama is active in 4.65 square miles of the Valley floor, roughly bounded by Topanga Canyon Boulevard east to Winnetka Avenue and from Roscoe Boulevard south to Vanowen Street. Block after block of aging, high-density apartments line the residential streets in this overlooked part of the West Valley, mere miles from the upscale Topanga mall.

Los Angeles City Attorney Establishes Gang Injunction Guidelines

Los Angeles city officials unveiled new anti-gang injunction guidelines in April 2007. These new guidelines were adopted after an extensive review to strengthen, formalize, and codify the city's gang injunction protocols and to govern obtaining and enforcing the orders. "Our gang injunctions are a critical tool in my new comprehensive anti-gang program, and my effort to protect our neighborhoods and safeguard the civil liberties of all city residents," said Los Angeles City Attorney Rocky Delgadillo. Some of the protocol changes were made in response to the criticism that the system makes it nearly impossible for people who turn their lives around or are mistakenly placed on a list to get out from under a court order. Complaints that not one of the people named in or served with gang injunctions in the last two decades has been able to get off the list have fueled the formation of a formal system under which someone can have his or her name removed from an injunction through a hearing with top administrators from Delgadillo's office. The city attorney dropped a requirement that anyone who wants to be delisted publicly renounce membership in the gang in which he or she allegedly was involved. None has, partly in fear of retaliation by gang members.

The guidelines also include the adoption of a stringent definition of a criminal street gang, formalizing a long-standing city attorney policy that injunction service requires a city attorney give prior approval before a suspected gang member may be served with a gang injunction, requiring that service of the injunction be based on documented evidence establishing gang membership beyond a reasonable doubt, and be based on a showing of active participation in the gang within the past five years. The new guidelines also require a periodic review process for new injunctions to determine if individual gang members who were served with gang injunctions should remain subject to the injunction's enforcement. The guidelines established creation of a reviewing authority and review process for existing injunctions to afford those served with injunctions a flexible and reliable process to be taken off injunctions.

Los Angeles Police Form "Top 10" Gang List

The Los Angeles Police publicly named 11 gangs as priority targets of the full force of the law. The gangs are the Black P-Stones, Mara Salvatrucha (MS-13), Rolling 30's, 40's, and Sixty Crips, Westside 18th Street, 204th Street, Avenues, Canoga Park Alabama, Grape Street Crips, and La Miranda Locos. Of the 11 gangs named, 8 currently have gang injunctions against them. The Rolling 30's, 204th Street, and La Miranda gangs have been publicly warned that an injunction is on the way; the other 8 top gangs have at least one injunction against them. Los Angeles officials want to go after members of the city's most dangerous gangs, and have committed more than 200 LAPD officers to a force that will also include FBI agents, prosecutors, and probation officers. According to the LAPD, the 11 gangs on this list accounted for 6% of the city's violent crimes last year.

People v. Norteños (San Francisco Case CGC-07-464492), June 21, 2007

On June 21, 2007, the San Francisco County District Attorney's Office and the San Francisco police sought an injunction against the Norteños gang. The gang injunction names the gang as the sole defendant and covers the 60-square-block target area of the Mission District from Cesar Chavez Street to the south, Valencia Street to the west, Potrero Avenue to the east, and 21st and 23rd Streets to the north. The Norteños street gang is a component of the Nuestra Familia prison gang that has warred since the 1960s with the Sureños, who are known in prison as the Mexican Mafia. There are roughly 300 Norteños in San Francisco that may become targets of this injunction if their level of criminal activity warrants their inclusion. According to the San Francisco Superior Court's order of October 12, 2007 granting preliminary injunctions, the safety zone enjoining members of the Norteño gang "is defined as an 'L' shaped area generally bordered by 23rd Street to the north (but extending to 21st Street at Alabama Street), Valencia to the west, Cesar Chavez to the south, Potrero Avenue to the east, and extending to encompass La Raza Parl, also known as Potrero Del Sol Park."

People v. Chopper City, Knock Out Posse, Norteños, and Eddy Rock (San Francisco Case CGC-07-464493), June 21, 2007

On June 21, 2007, the San Francisco County District Attorney's Office and the San Francisco police sought an injunction against three western addition gangs, including the Chopper City gang, Knock Out Possee, and Eddy Rock gang (*People v. Eddy Rock*, 2007). The gang injunction names the gangs as the sole defendants and covers the six-square-block target area bordered by Ellis Street on the north, Divisadero Street on the west, Turk Street on the south, and Steiner Street on the east. The Knock Out Posse and Chopper City gangs have about 45 active members that were likely targets of the injunction. The Eddy Rock gang has about 20 members that were likely targets based around the Yerba Buena Plaza East public housing project. Their activities would be limited in a second target area bordered by Ellis Street on the north, Gough Street on the east, Turk Street on the south, and Webster Street on the west.

AB 104 Signed

In July 2007 a bill was passed that gives city attorneys the tools they need to pursue gang injunctions in order to protect their communities. The governor signed a bill that allows city attorneys to crack down on gang activities. "Ensuring that Californians are protected in our communities and safe in their own homes is my number one priority. We need to give our cities, prosecutors, and law enforcement officials the tools they need to keep our citizens safe," said Governor Arnold Schwarzenegger. AB 104 ensures that city attorneys are able to access state and local criminal history information to support their petitions in pursuing civil gang injunctions or drug abatement actions. A gang injunction strikes at the criminal organization and is an important tool in keeping communities safe. This bill clarifies a provision that is vital in helping cities move forward to obtain them. After signing the bill, Schwarzenegger issued a statement calling the use of gang injunctions "an important component in our efforts to curb gang activity, because it gives cities greater access to the crucial information they need in order to stop these criminal organizations from terrorizing our neighborhoods."

People v. Hawaiian Gardens (Los Angeles Case BC375773), September 21, 2007

The Los Angeles County District Attorney's Office and the City of Cypress filed an injunction against the Varrio Hawaiian Gardens gang. The injunction named the gang as the sole defendant; however, it did name, but was not limited to, 30 individual members. The safety zone covered areas in the Cities of Hawaiian Gardens, Cypress, and Lakewood, from Del Amo Boulevard to the north, Grand Circle to the east, East Wardlow to the south, and Interstate 605 to the west. In Hawaiian Gardens, an injunction against members of the Varrio Hawaiian Gardens Gang has resulted in a 24% decrease in crime and a 43% decrease in assaults. In Hawaiian Gardens, Part 1 crime dropped 55% from 2006 to 2009. The preliminary injunction was issued September 21, 2007 and the permanent injunction on March 7, 2008. Most residents attribute the crime rate decrease to the gang injunction order and the proactive enforcement efforts of the sheriff's department. As of June 2010, the gang has more than 1,000 active members, of which 283 were served and 460 have been arrested according to the LASD Lakewood Station and the Long Beach PD.

People v. East Side Riva (Riverside Case RIC478810), August 22, 2007

The Riverside County District Attorney's Office and the Riverside police filed the county's first-ever gang injunction against the East Side Riva criminal street gang on August 22, 2007. The injunction named the gang as the sole defendant; however, it did name, but was not limited to, 114 individuals in the complaint. The injunction prohibited members from certain activities or behaviors in public spaces within a roughly 3-square-mile section of western Riverside County they claim as their turf. Authorities named 114 of the suspected 700 members of the gang, considered the county's largest, in the injunction. District Attorney Pacheco said those named had a combined 333 convictions, ranging from murder to assault, and 46 more cases pending.

DDA Pacheco said at a news conference about the criminal justice system: "We tend to be reactive." The gang commits crime and the police respond, he said. "Injunctions are proactive." Pacheco said another benefit of the injunction is that it "will literally last forever." "When you're dealing with people of this mindset, they become more brazen and dangerous," said Deputy District Attorney Jack Lucky, who drafted the suit. "Just like any court order, once someone violates it, you can charge them with a crime."

People v. Varrio Viejo (Orange County 07CC19689), October 11, 2007

The Varrio Viejo gang restrictions apply to a 1½-square-mile area in San Juan Capistrano and Mission Viejo. An Orange County Superior Court judge approved a preliminary injunction against more than 220 alleged members of two rival gangs, including one in the historic mission town of San Juan Capistrano. The injunction approved by Judge Daniel J. Didier indicated that alleged members of the Varrio Viejo and Varrio Chico gangs would be arrested if they were seen associating with one another, wearing gang clothing, or making gang hand signs.

The safety zone is defined as follows: the Varrio Viejo criminal street gang claims three general areas in the cities of San Juan Capistrano and Mission Viejo. The first area consists of the campus of Capistrano Valley High School located at 26301 Via Escolar, Mission Viejo. The second area is bounded to the north by Via Escolar, continuing southeast along the Mission Viejo city line to Trabuco Creek Road, continuing southwest to the 1-5 freeway, continuing north to Via Escolar. The third area is bounded to the north by Junipero Serra Road, continuing west to Camino Capistrano, continuing south to Oso Road, continuing west from Oso Road to the west side of the Trabuco Creek river bed, continuing south down the river bed to Alipaz Street, continuing south to Calle Lucana, continuing westbound to Via Belardes, continuing south to the east side fence line of the Capistrano Valley Church located at 32032 Del Obispo Street, continuing south to the south fence line of the church, continuing west along the south fence line to the cement wall that encloses the Carolinas condominium complex, continuing south to the south wall of the Carolinas condominium complex, continuing east along the south wall and continuing along the fence line that runs south of the Casitas de Alipaz housing complex to Alipaz Street, continuing north to Del Obispo Street, continuing northeast to Ortega Highway, continuing east to the 1-5 freeway, continuing north to Junipero Serra Road. The safety zone is approximately 1.5 square miles.

On January 25, 2008, the two injunctions were made permanent against rival criminal street gangs in San Clemente and San Juan Capistrano. This has resulted in a 13.5% reduction of gang-related crimes in the San Clemente safety zone and a reduction of 28.5% in the San Juan Capistrano safety zone.

People v. Varrio Chico (Orange County 07CC19690), October 11, 2007

Varrio Chico restrictions apply to a 2.2-square-mile area in San Clemente. The injunctions affect 226 alleged members of the San Juan Capistrano-based Varrio Viejo and San Clemente-based Varrio Chico street gangs. Under the terms of the injunctions, alleged gang members can be arrested if they are seen hanging out together, wearing gang type clothes, or breaking an assigned curfew of 10 p.m. The terms of the injunctions apply only to those named in the injunction when they are in a 1.3-square-mile portion of San Juan Capistrano and a 2.2-square-mile section of San Clemente outlined in the injunctions. For some who live in the designated gang zones, the decision to make the injunctions permanent was not a surprise. "I believe it's a little unfair, and it's a shame they went through with it," said Diana Pina-Mendoza. "You can't do anything about it. We're just going to have to learn to live with it." Others in the community are still actively protesting the injunctions, with more than 30 people showing up to a candlelight vigil and rally. Organizers have promised a larger protest against the injunctions in the near future. But authorities argue the injunctions are an effective way to fight crime in the area, which has been affected by drugs, thefts, vandalism, and assaults. Since the temporary injunction was approved by Judge Daniel J. Didier in November, 20 alleged members of Varrio Chico have been arrested for injunction violations. Two alleged members of Varrio Viejo have been arrested for similar infractions. According to court documents, deputies patrolling the area have seen a drop in gang-related calls since the temporary injunction was approved. According to the Orange County District Attorney's Office, 11 people named in the Varrio Viejo injunction and two named in the Varrio Chico injunction have filed a response to the injunctions, challenging their inclusion in the court order. The cases of those people will be sent to court to be determined. Those who are not active participants in the gangs can be removed from the injunction by petitioning the district attorney's office, or through the trial process. This has resulted in a 13.5% reduction of gang-related crimes in the San Clemente safety zone.

On January 25, 2008, two injunctions were made permanent against rival criminal street gangs in San Clemente and San Juan Capistrano. This has resulted in a 13.5% reduction of gang-related crimes in the San Clemente safety zone and a reduction of 28.5% in the San Juan Capistrano safety zone.

People v. Varrio San Marcos (San Diego 07-00057284), October 19, 2007

On October 19, 2007, the San Diego County District Attorney's Office obtained an injunction against the Varrio San Marcos gang. The injunction named the gang and 93 individual gang members as defendants. The preliminary injunction was granted on November 28, 2007, and the injunction was made permanent on September 16, 2008. The injunction covers three safety zones and expands upon an existing injunction against the gang (Figure 13.7).

One of the safety zones is bounded roughly by South Las Flores Road to the west, South Rancho Santa Fe Road to the east, La Casita Drive to the south, and South Santa Fe Avenue to the north, with some additional areas on the eastern and western sides of the zone. Another zone is bounded generally by Highway 78 to the south, Knoll Road to the west, North Twin Oaks Valley Road to the east, and Richmar Road to the north, with some additional areas beyond those roads. The third zone is bounded generally by Mulberry Drive to the west, East Mission Road diagonally southeast to Woodland Parkway, a northeast diagonal on Woodland Parkway to Rock Springs Road, east to Douglas Avenue, north to Quiet Hills Drive and Fulton Road, and from the intersection of Fulton Road and Woodland Parkway southwest to Woodland Parkway and Rock Springs Road. The three safety zones represent 1.89 square miles, or 7.8% of the entire city of San Marcos, which is 24.28 square miles. Gang members had taken over several public parks, including Bradley Park and Woodland Park, through graffiti and violence, leaving children without a safe place to play or practice sports, said District Attorney Bonnie M. Dumanis.

People v. Rolling 40's Crips, 46 Top Dollar Hustler Crips, and 46 Neighborhood Crips (Los Angeles Case BC380229), November 5, 2007

On November 5, 2007, the Los Angeles City Attorney's Office filed an injunction against the Rolling 40's Crips, 46 Top Dollar Hustler Crips, and 46 Neighborhood Crips. The permanent injunction was granted on March 8, 2008. The Vernon Corridor safety

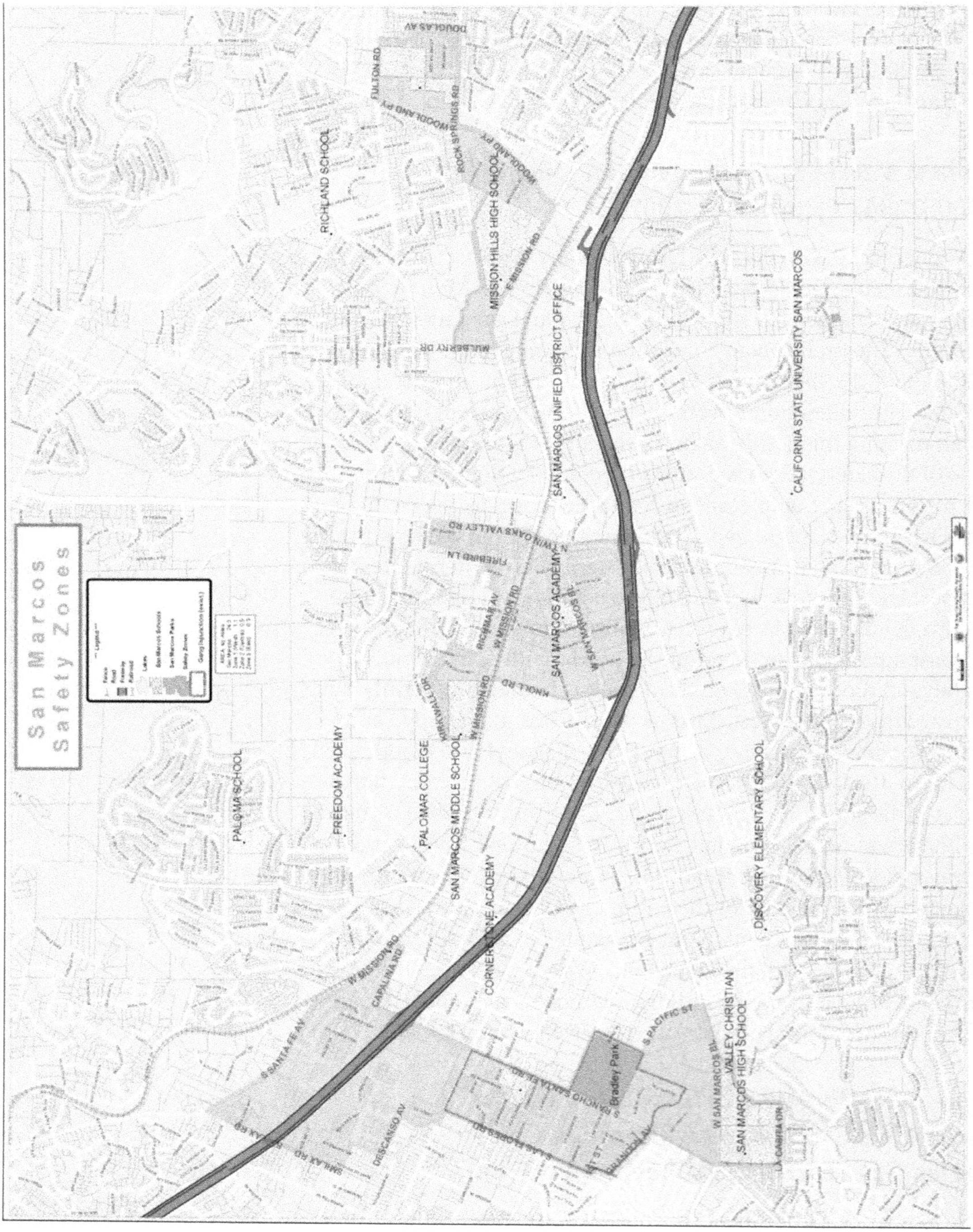

FIGURE 13.7 Map of *People v. Varrio San Marcos*.

zone, located in South Los Angeles, had boundaries as follows: Crenshaw Boulevard in the west, the Harbor Freeway (SR110) in the east, Martin Luther King Boulevard in the north, 52nd Street in the south, and extending 100 yards beyond each of these boundary streets.

The injunction includes a no cell phones restriction: Possessing or using any cellular or digital phone, walkie-talkie, two-way radio, or communication scanner; except (1) as required for a legal business or occupation and possessed during business hours, or (2) as reasonably required by an actual emergency. Proof of the need for possession or use in a business or occupation or by an emergency as an exception to this provision shall be an affirmative defense to a charge of violation of this provision. The burden of producing evidence of the existence of such need or emergency shall be on the defendant (*People v. Rolling 40's*, 2007). Preliminary issued on January 29, 2008, permanent on March 3, 2008.

Dog Pound Gangsters (Fresno County Case 07GI05), November 29, 2007

The Fresno County district attorney sought an injunction against the Dog Pound Gangsters. The safety zone, located in the City of Fresno, has been occupied by defendants who were accused of causing a public nuisance with their actions—threatening the freedom, health, safety, senses, and right to free use and enjoyment of property of the people who live, work, visit, and pass through the safety zone.

In seeking the injunction, the district attorney said:

> Defendants collectively, individually, and in concert, have brought and bring violence into the safety zone, creating a threatening atmosphere in which residents must live and work. Defendants repeatedly arm themselves with guns and other dangerous weapons and engage in violent, aggressive, and destructive behavior, which is injurious to the health and safety of the community in the safety zone. Residents are prisoners and victims of the defendants' wars against rival gangs, and the foreseeable retaliation by rival gangs against defendants.
>
> Defendants demonstrate a blatant disregard for the lives and safety of innocent victims, including children, who get caught in the crossfire of these activities. Bullets, shell casings, and loaded firearms have been found throughout the safety zone. Residents live in constant fear of shootings, stabbings, and random violence breaking out at any moment on the streets, sidewalks, and public areas in the

safety zone. The violent acts of these gang members have endangered residents' lives and shattered their sense of peace and security.

Defendants terrorize and intimidate the community in the safety zone by gathering in groups, flaunting their gang tattoos, and brandishing the name of Dog Pound Gangsters as a sword to strike fear into the community. This fear allows defendants to commit their crimes unchecked. After committing their crimes, defendants again invoke Dog Pound Gangsters as a shield behind which to hide and avoid accountability for their actions. If any defendant believes that a victim or witness has reported a crime, the gang invokes the name Dog Pound Gangsters and retaliates against the person, home, car, business, and other property of the witness or victim.

Defendants often threaten victims and witnesses to their crimes, thus avoiding prosecution for their criminal conduct and ensuring that the nuisance will continue unabated. Because of these actions, the good people in the safety zone rightly believe they are at risk if they report crime. Law enforcement is not able to function as it should when victims and witnesses, including those witnesses who themselves are committing crimes, are too afraid of retaliation from defendants to speak to the police and prosecutors. This intimidation causes a nuisance by depriving the community of their comfortable enjoyment of life and property, and by creating an atmosphere that is injurious to the community's health, and indecent and offensive to the senses.

Defendants believe and act as if they own the safety zone, treating the homes and yards of residents, public grounds, businesses, churches, and schools as if they were the personal property of the defendants. Residences, businesses, churches, and schools are vandalized by graffiti of the Dog Pound Gangsters. Residents have their yards used as escape routes when gang members flee from pursuing law enforcement officers. Residents have their rights in their private property substantially impaired and interfered with by defendants. Defendants' behavior obstructs the free use of property by the owners and their tenants in the safety zone.

Throughout the safety zone, defendants loiter in large numbers, using drugs, occasionally selling drugs, drinking, littering, threatening, assaulting, and robbing residents and other innocents in streets and public places, open to public view and in front of children. They also commit these acts at apartment complexes and on private property that they have forcefully usurped from lawful residents. Defendants hang out on sidewalks, in the streets, and in residents' yards in the safety zone, thereby obstructing the free use of property by the visitors and residents of the safety zone. Law-abiding people are forced to stay indoors at night to avoid being harassed by gang members and to avoid becoming a victim of, or a witness to, defendants' criminal and nuisance activities. These criminal and nuisance activities and subsequent victimization of the residents by defendants is injurious to the health, offensive to the senses, and interferes with the comfortable enjoyment of life and property in the safety zone.

Defendants confront residents and those passing through the safety zone with the classic turf-based street gang challenge: "Where you from?" or "What you bang?" and by flashing their gang signs and tattoos. The victims are then harassed if they fail to respond with the "right" answer. The only right answer to these gang challenges would be if the victim were from the challenger's gang or from an allied gang. Defendants will not tolerate a rival gang member being in turf they claim as their own. A gang member being in a rival gang turf is considered to be disrespect to that rival gang, which is punishable by violence by these Defendants. Defendants' turf-based conduct, challenging and aggressively confronting others, is at best injurious and offensive to the senses, a deprivation of the comfortable enjoyment of life and property, and all too often, injurious or fatal to the health of the people challenged.

Defendants use the sidewalks, streets, private walkways, and residents' yards to congregate, drink alcohol, take and sell illegal narcotics, conduct illegal activities, and harass pedestrians. As defendants continue to drink and use and sell drugs, they become disorderly and dangerous. Fortified by alcohol and the support of their fellow gang members, defendants target and harass innocent members of the community in the safety zone. This behavior constitutes a nuisance in that it is indecent and offensive to the senses, and interferes with the comfortable enjoyment of life and property in the safety zone.

Defendants seek to proclaim their ownership of the safety zone, to bolster the notoriety of their gang, and to physically degrade the safety zone by the repeated painting of their gang graffiti on walls of businesses and residences, and other public and private property within the safety zone. Defendants commit their graffiti vandalism by using spray paint cans and felt-tip markers, as well as other techniques and devices. This visual blight acts as a constant reminder to the community, rival gang members, and anyone venturing into the safety zone that this neighborhood is claimed by Dog Pound Gangsters. "Cross-outs" and "187" (referring to Penal Code Section 187, murder) send a stark message of threatened violence. The writings and etchings are meant to intimidate and dissuade people from complaining to the police department or other city officials, and to notify rival gangs and others that the marked area is the turf of Dog Pound Gangsters and that they should keep out. The property rights of the owners and their tenants are substantially impaired and interfered with because they are forced to repeatedly expend time, labor, and money in a vain attempt to eradicate defendants' gang graffiti. Moreover, it is injurious to the health of the residents, and their comfortable enjoyment of life and property are harmed, when the Dog Pound Gangsters' gang graffiti attracts foreseeable and violent retaliation from rival street gangs.

Defendants, collectively, individually, and in concert, commit even more of their criminal, nuisance, and gang activity under the cover of darkness. Nuisance activity ranging from illegal drug use and loud parties, reckless driving and driving under the influence, and drinking in public, to drug sales, robberies, beatings, arson, shootings and assaults is more likely to occur in the late evening and early morning hours.

As a result of the behavior of the defendants, many community members in the safety zone have suffered and suffer great emotional distress. Their days are filled with fear, intimidation, anxiety, and quite often an invasion of privacy. Residents are forced to stay inside their homes, especially at night. Windows are covered with large iron gratings. When they do venture outside, they have to take alternative routes to avoid constant harassment, intimidation, and gang warfare. Parents are afraid to allow their children to play outdoors because of the criminal and nuisance activities of defendants. Unless restrained by this court, defendants will continue to maintain the nuisance, by participating in and encouraging the criminal and nuisance activities alleged herein.

Plaintiff has no plain, speedy, or adequate remedy at law and will continue to suffer irreparable damage, injury, and harm unless equitable relief is granted. Criminal prosecution has not stopped defendants' criminal and nuisance activities. Defendants, collectively and individually, and in concert, threaten the victims and witnesses to their crimes, serving to reinforce the Dog Pound Gangsters' menacing reputation, avoid prosecution for their criminal conduct, and ensure that the nuisance will continue unabated. The conduct of defendants will continue to cause great and irreparable injury to the people who live and work in the safety zone. Residents and visitors to the safety zone are victimized by defendants' murders, shootings, robberies, assaults, witness intimidation, narcotics sales, gang graffiti, vandalism, vehicle theft, and other gang-related activities.

Unless restrained by this court, defendants will continue to maintain the nuisance and continue the acts complained of, and each act has been, and will be, without the consent, against the will, and in violation of the rights of plaintiff. Unless restrained by this court, defendants will continue to confront and intimidate their victims. They will dissuade victims and witnesses from reporting crimes and nuisance behavior to the police, and from testifying after reports are made, thereby evading responsibility for their criminal conduct. The public interest in tranquility and security, and basic public order, is threatened by defendants' oppressive and widespread witness intimidation. The activities and conduct of defendants, as alleged in this complaint, constitute an interference with the rights of the community at large in the safety zone, and as a result, constitute a public nuisance. Defendant is a cause of the public nuisance that exists in the safety zone.

California Code of Civil Procedure Section 731 authorizes the District Attorney of Fresno County to enjoin public nuisances in the name of the people of the State of California. In addition, under these facts, injunctive relief is appropriate under Code of Civil Procedure Section 526. The peace, safety, and quiet enjoyment of the lives and property of the residents and other members of the community in the safety zone are being, and will continue to be, disturbed and threatened unless equitable relief in the form of an injunction as prayed for against defendants is granted."

The injunction was granted in July 2007.

People v. 204th Street and Eastside Torrance (Los Angeles BC381942), December 7, 2007

On December 7, 2007, the Los Angeles City Attorney's Office filed an injunction against the 204th Street gang and the Eastside

Torrance gang. Twenty-two members of the 204th Street gang and 23 members of the Eastside Torrance gang were cited in the injunction; however, only the two gangs were named as defendants. The safety zone established by the injunction is bounded by Del Amo Boulevard to the north, Western Avenue on the west, Lomita Boulevard on the south, and Normandie Avenue on the east. It extends 100 yards to the outside of each boundary.

East Side Torrance formed in the 1970s, getting its name from its location. Although the area it calls home has a Torrance mailing address, it is east of the city's boundary in the Harbor Gateway area of Los Angeles. Its territory is bounded by Western, Sepulveda Boulevard, Normandie, and Carson Street, according to an affidavit filed by Los Angeles Police Detective Dan Robbins in support of the gang injunction. East Side Torrance feuded with Torrance's La Rana gang, which helped create the 204th Street gang in the 1980s. East Side Torrance's rivals include 204th Street to the north, Harbor City Boys and Harbor City Crips to the south, and Tortilla Flats in the unincorporated area to the east. The preliminary injunction was issued on March 4, 2008, and made permanent on July 7, 2008.

YEAR 2008

People v. Mob Piru Gang Compton (Los Angeles TC021658), January 24, 2008

City officials asked a judge to ban members of the Mob Piru street gang from being able to congregate in a neighborhood of Compton and asked that the order include Marion "Suge" Knight. Knight, the cofounder of Death Row Records, was 1 of 200 people the officials said were members of Mob Piru. The injunction would have banned them from congregating, carrying guns, drinking alcohol in public, or staying out past 10 p.m. Knight called the injunction "a publicity stunt. This is crazy," he told the *Los Angeles Times*. "I'm a 42-year-old businessman, not a gang member. I don't even live in Compton anymore."

Authorities contended that the Mob Piru gang had terrorized the neighborhood for years, with buying and selling of drugs, discharging firearms, robbing and assaulting residents, and creating an atmosphere of fear and intimidation. A Los Angeles County Sheriff's Department gang task force had worked for the previous two years to get gang members off the streets with aggressive enforcement of immigration, housing, and parole violations. The injunction would have created a huge safety zone in the neighborhood bounded by Bullis Road on the west, Pine Street on the north, Thorson Avenue on the east, and Rosecrans Avenue on the south. The injunction was ultimately not granted by the court and is not in effect.

People v. San Fer Gang (Case No. BC388726), April 10, 2008

On August 11, 2008, a permanent gang injunction prohibited criminal conduct by hundreds of documented members of the San Fer gang. Judge Gregory W. Alarcon signed the injunction that designated a San Fer Gang safety zone (Figure 13.8)—enclosed by Interstate 5 to the west, Interstate 210 to the north and east, and State Highway 118 to the south. As of June 2010, at least 139 members of the gang had been served and more than 50 had been arrested for violating this injunction according to the San Fernando Police. The gang injunction against the San Fer gang has been imposed by the courts on a 9.5-square-mile area of the Northeast San Fernando Valley, encompassing most of Sylmar, a northwest portion of Pacoima, and all of San Fernando City (most of the rest of Pacoima had already been under a gang injunction for years against the Pacoima Flats, Projects Boys, and other Pacoima gangs). The Preliminary injunction was issued on June 24, 2008, and made permanent on August 11, 2008.

People v. South Side Kings (Tulare County Case 08-226862), April 28, 2008

The district attorney in Tulare County filed an injunction against the South Side Kings, aka the SSK gang. Judge Lloyd Hicks ordered the injunction against the South Side Kings street gang in Ivanhoe, beginning at the intersection of road 160 and Jasmine Avenue, north to road 156, east to road 161, west to road 160—basically anywhere in Ivanhoe. Visalia police officers knocked on doors across Visalia Friday looking for suspected members of four street gangs. Friday's temporary injunction was the second Hicks has issued in a week. The first was against more than 250 members of the South Side Kings gang in Ivanhoe. The Tulare County District Attorney's Office sought the orders against both gangs based on claims that their criminal activities, including murders, shootings, robberies, drug sales, and a laundry list of other crimes, constitute a "public nuisance" on Visalia's north side. Prosecutors sought the creation of safety zones, where they would be barred from certain activities or risk being arrested.

FIGURE 13.8 Map of *People v. San Fer Gang.*

People v. Northside Visalia/Mexican Gangster Boys/Encina Street Riders/Northside Birdland (Tulare County 0-226863), May 6, 2008

Tulare County sought an order for permanent gang injunction barring Norteño gang members from gathering publicly or engaging in other activities in part of north Visalia. The injunction affects members of four gangs: North Side Visalia, Mexican Gangster Boys, Encina Street Riders, and North Side Birdland. None showed up to challenge the injunction according to the district attorney for Tulare County. The injunction creates a safe zone in the neighborhoods between Houston Avenue and Ferguson Street and by Dinuba Boulevard and Burke Street. Prosecutors sought the creation of safety zones where gang members would be barred from certain activities or risk being arrested, including a large swath of northern Visalia from just south of Lincoln Oval Park to north of Birdland.

People v. Oriental Troop/Mongolian Boys Society/Lao Pride Gangsters (Tulare County 08-226863), May 12, 2008

The Oriental Troop street gang injunction covers the same north Visalia safe zone targeted by the Norteños' injunction. Visalia police served members of several street gangs with the gang injunction, including the Oriental Troop, or OT; the Mongolian Boys Society, also known as MBS; and Lao Pride or Lao Pride Crips, or LPC. The safe zone established by the injunction amounts to about 1 square mile, reaching from Race Avenue on the south to Riggin Avenue and St. Johns Parkway on the north, and from Dinuba Boulevard on the west to Burke and Santa Fe streets on the east.

People v. Southside Rialto (San Bernardino CIVSS808850), July 1, 2008

The San Bernardino DA's Office obtained an injunction against the Southside Rialto gang from Superior Court Judge Christopher J. Warner after he found that the Rialto gang met the requirements to be deemed a public nuisance. The police served 30 members with the gang injunction, barring them from congregating, displaying gang tattoos, and flashing hand signs within a 2-mile safety zone between Rialto and San Bernardino Avenues on the north and south and Pepper and Lilac Avenues on the east and west. Although many have publicly protested their inclusion, saying they have left the gang life behind, none made formal arguments through an attorney.

The preliminary injunction against South Side Rialto was the fourth to be granted in the inland region since the summer of 2007.

The SSR gang is a Hispanic gang established in the 1970s. It has approximately 75 active members that operate in the approximate 1.5-square-mile safety zone. According to the district attorney, the injunction has been drastically reduced loitering by gang members. The injunction drove gang activity underground. Rialto police say the injunction has had great psychological effect. The preliminary injunction was granted on September 25, 2008, and the permanent injunction was granted on November 17, 2008.

People v. Colton City Crips (San Bernardino CIVSS811223), August 18, 2008

The San Bernardino DA's Office and the Colton police sought an injunction against the Colton City Crips. Authorities sought to banish the 55 or so members of the Colton City Crips from the Arbor Terrace apartment complex on Rancho Avenue. Not only does the injunction ban gang members from flashing gang signs and gathering together, they are also not allowed to set foot in the safety zone. Police say the injunction resulted in a decline in drug dealing and a disappearance of gang members. Residents report the apartment complex is "a great place to live because they feel safer there now and it's much more like home."

This was the first gang injunction filed by the San Bernardino County District Attorney's Office where banishment had been requested. A gang injunction banishing Colton City Crips from the Arbor Terrace apartment complex located at the northeast corner of Rancho and Mill Streets makes gang members subject to arrest just for being on the premises. Nonresident gang members are no longer allowed on the property. The Colton City Crips is a criminal street gang that first appeared in the City of Colton in the mid to late 1980s. Its oldest members are now in their 40s. The youngest members are in their teens, with even younger children waiting to join the gang. Crimes committed by the gang range from homicide to burglary, with drug dealing as the predominant criminal activity. The preliminary injunction was granted on September 24, 2008, On October 5, 2010, the permanent injunction was granted.

People v. All for Crime, Barrio Mojados, Blood Stone Villans, Florencia 13, Oriental Boyz, and Pueblo Bishops (LA Case BC397522), September 5, 2008

The safety zone is located in the City of Los Angeles within a boundary that begins at the intersection of San Pedro Street and Washington Boulevard, continues east along Washington

Boulevard until Alameda Street, continues south along Alameda Street until Slauson Avenue, continues west along Slauson Avenue until Central Avenue, continues south along Central Avenue until Manchester Avenue, continues west along Manchester Avenue until Van Ness Avenue, continues north along Van Ness Avenue until Vernon Avenue, continues east along Vernon Avenue until San Pedro Street, at which point it continues north along San Pedro Street until it reaches the intersection of San Pedro Street and Washington Boulevard, and including both sides of the boundary streets, but not including the roadbed of the Harbor (I-110) Freeway. The preliminary injunction was granted on October 3, 2008, and made permanent on January 14, 2009.

People v. Orange County Criminals (Orange Co. Case 30-2008-00107172), June 4, 2008

On September 26, 2008, the fifth injunction in Orange County was made permanent against the first City of Orange criminal street gang. There was an 18% reduction in violent crime in the Orange safety zone in the year following the implementation of the injunction. The preliminary injunction was signed by Judge Daniel Didier and was served individually to 68 named gang members, as well as to the parents of juveniles, on June 4, 2008, by more than 80 officers representing eight agencies throughout Orange County. The injunction was a cooperative effort between the Cities of Anaheim, Garden Grove, Orange, Placentia, and Tustin, the Orange Police Department, Orange County district attorney, Orange County Sheriff's Department, Orange County Probation Department, and California Department of Corrections and Rehabilitation. The Orange criminal street gang is a violent, traditional turf-oriented gang with approximately 150 documented members that has been active since 1990.

The 1.4-square-mile safety zone consists of residential and commercial areas located primarily west of the 55 State Route Freeway and throughout Eisenhower Park, two small unattached areas (Parker-La Veta and Hoover Wilson), and Highland Street between Lincoln Avenue and Palmyara Avenue. Between January 2005 and December 2007, criminal activity within the safety zone resulted in the documentation of 5 gang murder participants, 4 attempted murder participants, 57 firearm or dangerous weapons violations, 8 blockings of free passage, 34 fights, 4 stolen vehicles, 20 drug or paraphernalia-related incidents, 11 trespasses, 55 graffiti crimes, 11 burglaries or burglar tools, 305 loitering calls, 46 intimidations, 55 curfew violations, 62 gang clothing, and 524 associations with the street gang.

People v. Barrio Dream Home Gang (Riverside INC077903), June 10, 2008

On June 10, 2008, the Riverside County District Attorney's Office went to court, seeking an injunction against the Barrio Dream Homes gang. Authorities said about 100 documented members of the gang had committed more than 700 crimes, ranging from graffiti to murder, between 2001 and 2008.

"These criminal activities have established Barrio Dream Homes as a public nusiance and reinforced the need for a gang injunction to help law enforcement suppress their crimes," the Riverside County District Attorney's Office said in a press release.

This injunction has four safety zones: the first begins at the westerly line of Ramon Road and the northerly line of San Luis Rey Drive, west to Mission Drive, north to San Joaquin Drive, and then defines the target area via various city parcels.

A preliminary injunction was granted a month later, prohibiting gang members from "associating with each other, loitering, or staying out past curfew and enforces several other restrictions within the designated safety zone," the office said in a separate press release.

"Gangs achieve their power from their associations and their territory. If we can remove their ability to associate within the territory we render them powerless," said Rod Pacheco, the district attorney.

People v. East Side Pain, aka Ghost Town Bloods (LA Case BC 399741), October 10, 2008

The safety zone is a 0.88-square-mile area in Wilmington covering territory from Avalon on the west, Deloras Drive on the north over to Wilmington Avenue on the east, Lomita Boulevard on the north, Drumm on the east, and Pacific Coast Highway on the southern border (Figure 13.9). The injunction sought to establish a gang-free zone through stay-away orders from Watson Park, an East Wilmington vest pocket park near Watson Avenue and O Street, a location known for gang congregation and other illegal activities, as well as Banning Senior High School, a source for gang recruitment. The East Side Pain gang was the target of a July 2007 multiagency takedown involving more than 500 law enforcement officers, which included 55 warrants executed simultaneously leading to multiple federal indictments, 5 federal forfeitures, and more than 15 state violation arrests, as well as 5 property nuisance abatement actions taken by the city attorney's Safe Neighborhoods Division. The gang had also been linked to two homicides since July 2007, as well as 635 narcotics-related arrests. The preliminary injunction was granted on December 17, 2008, and made permanent on June 11, 2009.

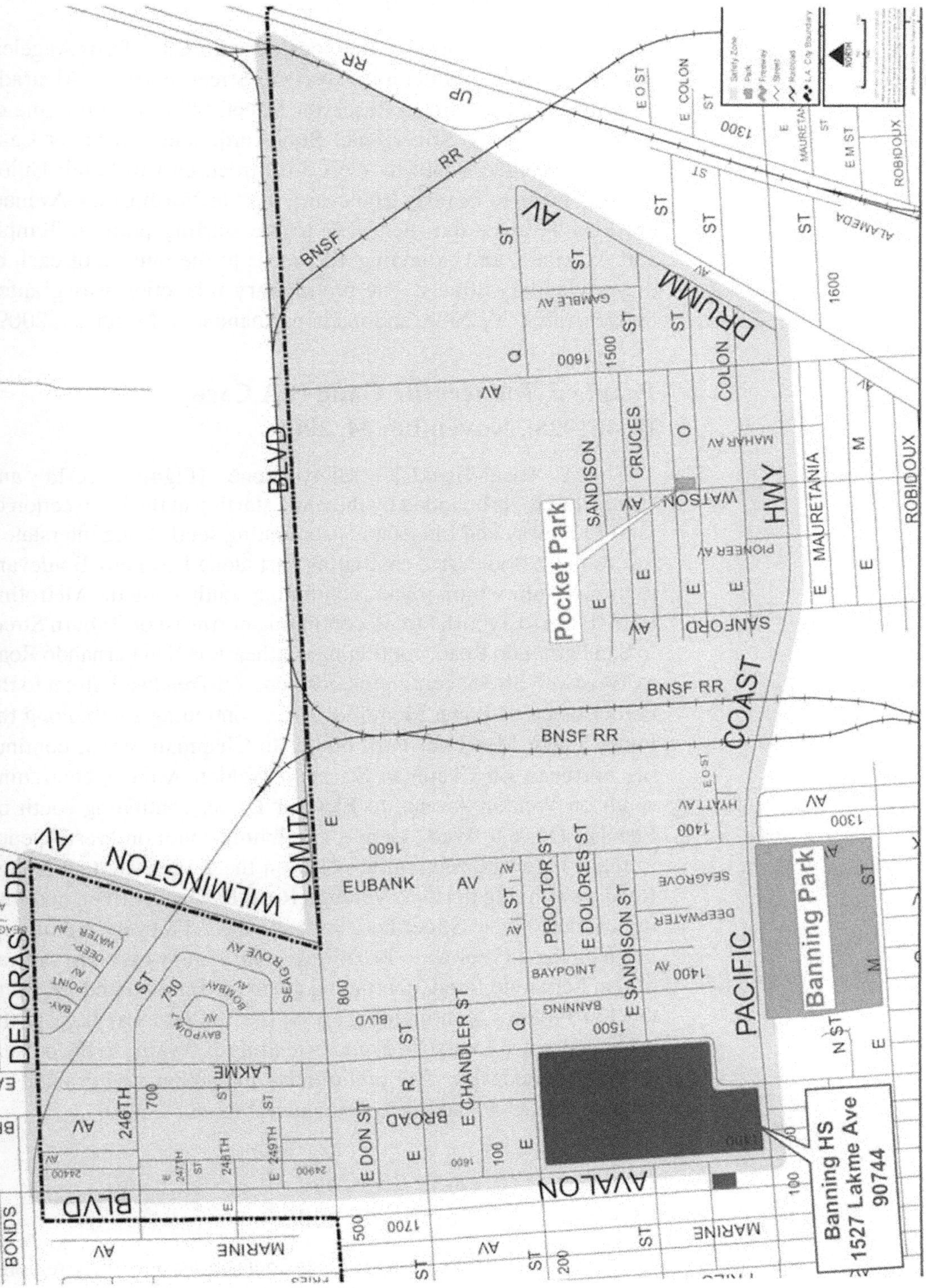

FIGURE 13.9 Map of *People v. Eastside Pain*.

People v. Temple Street (LA Case BC401190), November 3, 2008

The safety zone (Figure 13.10) is located in the City of Los Angeles, starting at Temple Street and Alvarado Street, north on Alvarado past Sunset Boulevard to Reservoir Street, west along the line of Reservoir Street to Silver Lake Boulevard, south on Silver Lake to Virgil Avenue, south to West 3rd Street, east to South Union Avenue, north to Beverly Boulevard, west to North Union Avenue, north to Temple, and then west to the starting point at Temple and Alvarado, and extending 100 yards to the outside of each of those boundary streets. The preliminary injunction was granted on December 30, 2008, and made permanent on March 27, 2009.

People v. Toonerville Gang (LA Case BC401928), November 14, 2008

The LA River-Glendale safety zone (Figure 13.11a and Figure 13.11b) is bounded by the route starting at the intersection of the 13 Freeway and Interstate 5, continuing south along Interstate 5 to Los Feliz Boulevard, continuing east along Los Feliz Boulevard to the Metrolink train tracks, continuing south along the Metrolink train tracks to Tyburn Street, continuing northeast on Tyburn Street to San Fernando Road, continuing southeast on San Fernando Road to Treadwell Street, continuing northeast on Treadwell Street to the border of Fores Lawn Memorial Park, continuing south along the Forest Lawn Memorial Park border to Chapman Street, continuing northeast on Chapman Street to Weldon Avenue, continuing south on Weldon Avenue to Fletcher Drive, continuing south on Fletcher Drive to West Avenue, continuing south on West Avenue to the 2 Freeway, continuing north on the 2 Freeway to Verdugo Road, continuing north to Verdugo Road to Maple Street, continuing east on Maple Street until it meets the 2 Freeway, continuing north on the 2 Freeway to Broadway, continuing west on Broadway to San Fernando Road, continuing north on San Fernando Road to the 134 Freeway, continuing west on the 134 Freeway back to the starting point at Interstate 5, and extending 100 yards to the outside of these boundaries. The preliminary injunction was granted on January 28, 2009 and made permanent March 18, 2009.

People v. Florencia 13 (Case BC403340), December 8, 2008

The safety zone in the County of Los Angeles consists of three regions: A, B, and C. Region A is a four-sided area of approximately 6.5

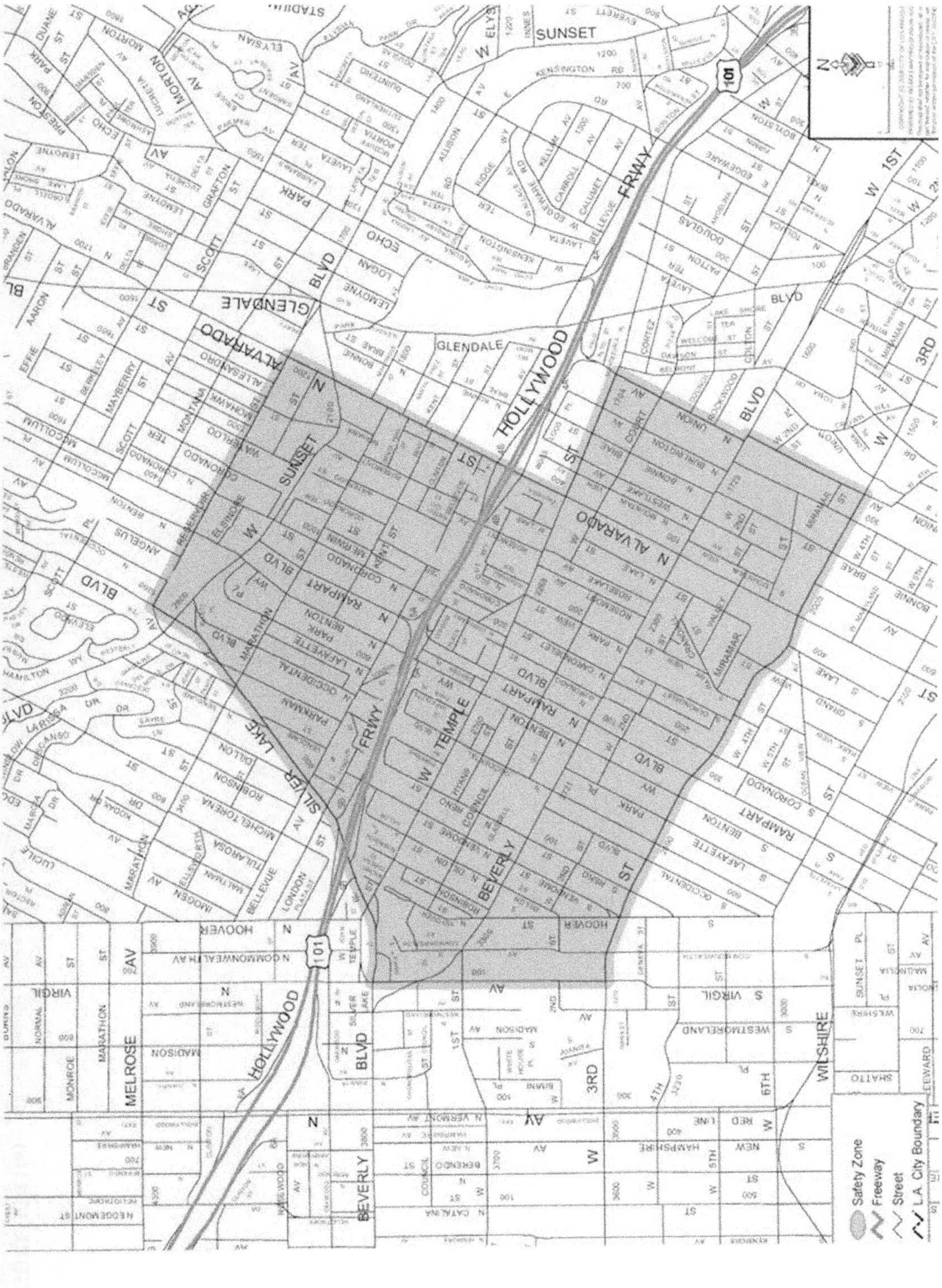

FIGURE 13.10 Map of *People v. Temple Street.*

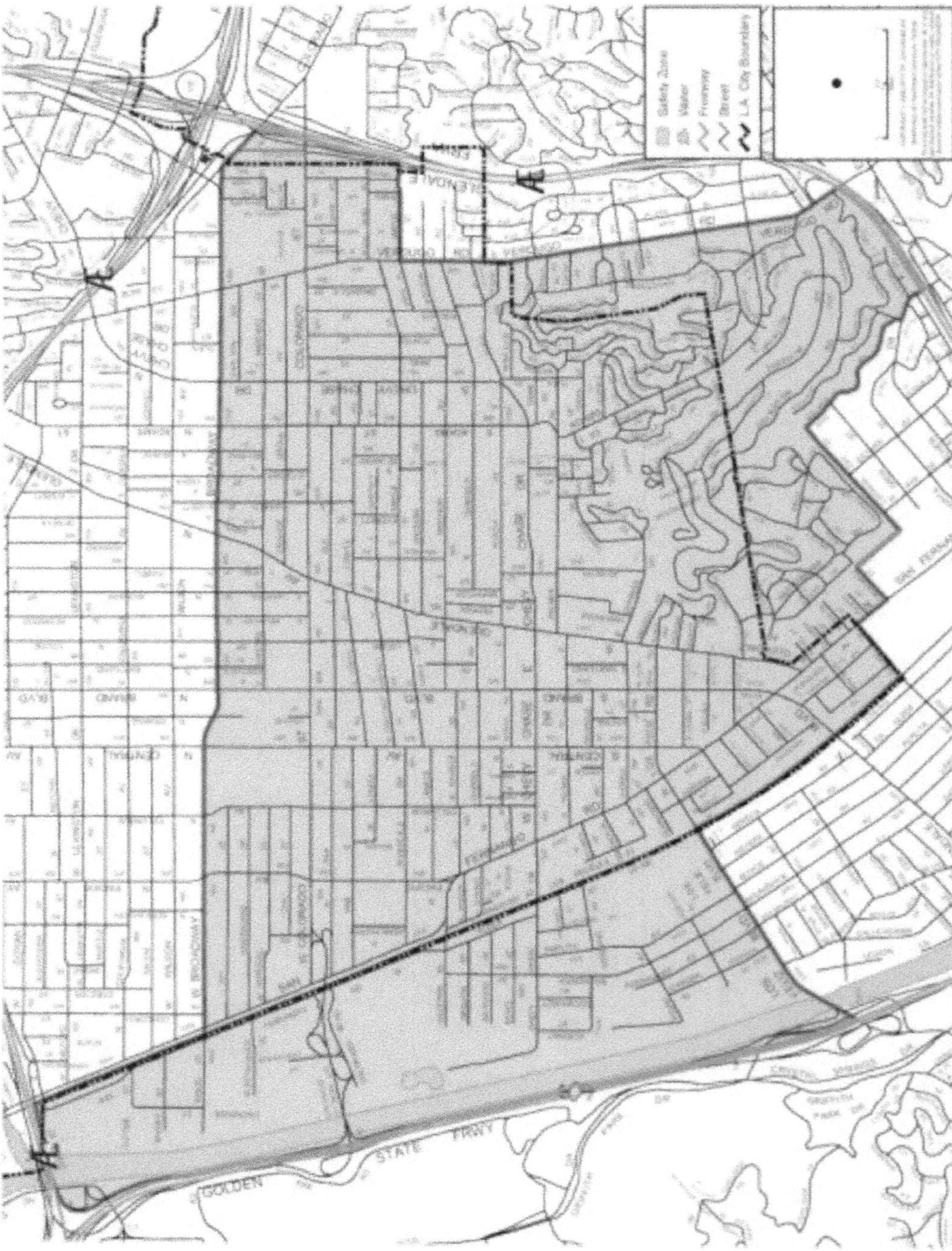

(a)

FIGURE 13.11(a) Map of *People v. Toonerville Gang.*

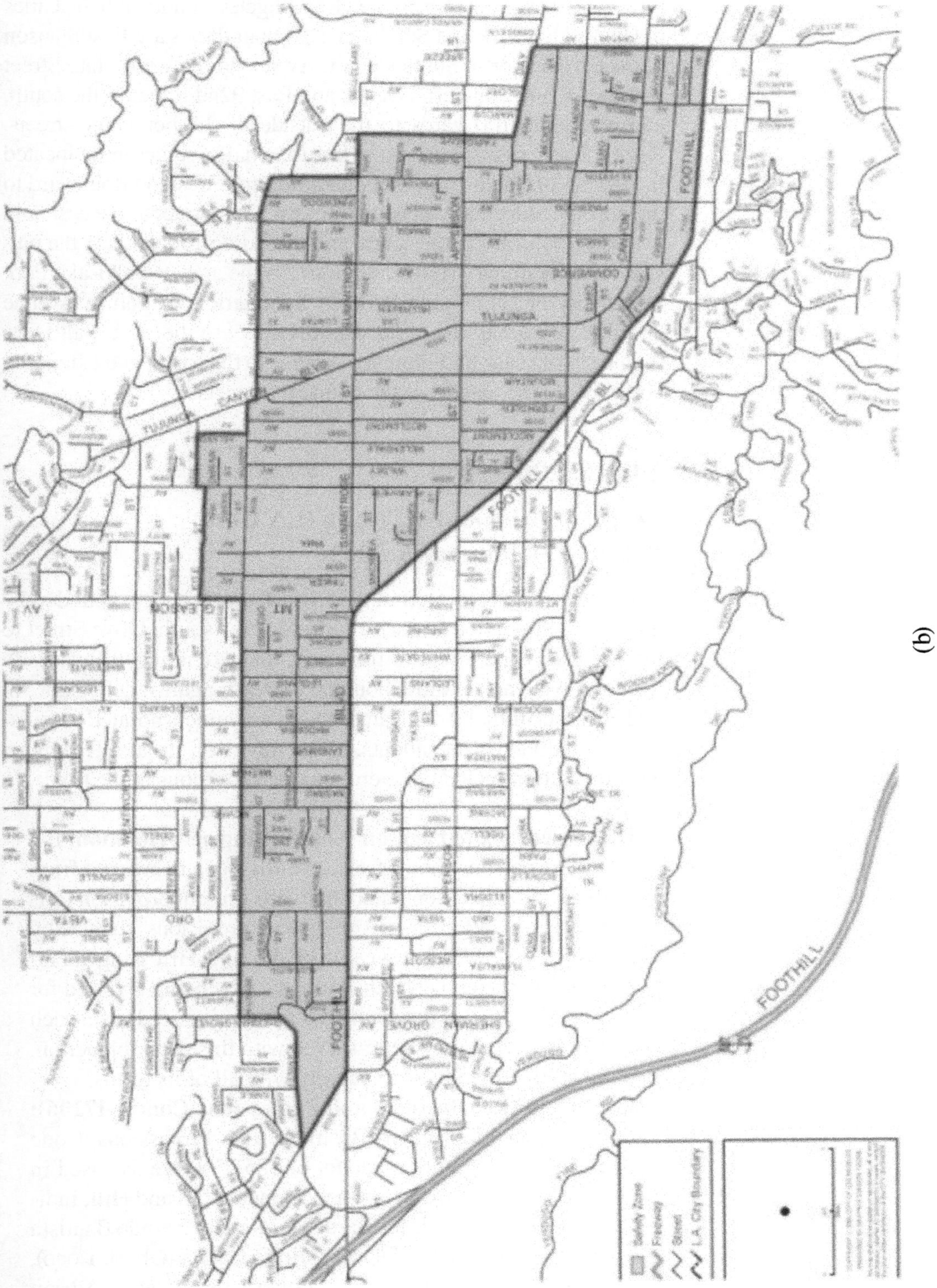

FIGURE 13.11(b) (Continued)

square miles in Los Angeles County and is located in the Florence-Firestone area of unincorporated Los Angeles County and the Cities of Huntington Park and South Gate. Its boundaries are East Slauson Avenue to the north, South Central Avenue to the west, State Street to the east, and Southern Avenue and East 92nd Street to the south, and extending 100 yards to the outside of the boundary streets. Region B is a four-sided area of less than half a square mile located in the City of South Gate. Its boundaries are Firestone Boulevard to the north, California Avenue to the west, Otis Street to the east, and Tweedy Boulevard to the south, and extending 100 yards to the outside of the boundary streets. Region C is the area of Salt Lake Park in the City of Huntington Park. Its boundaries are Saturn Avenue and Bell Avenue to the north, Newell Street to the west, Salt Lake Avenue to the east, and Florence Avenue to the south, and extending 100 yards to the outside of the boundary streets.

YEAR 2009

People v. 5th and Hill Gang (LA Case BC380877), January 6, 2009

The safety zone is located in the City of Los Angeles, bounded by San Pedro Street to the east, 9th Street to the south, Olive Street to the west, and 2nd Street to the north, and extending 100 yards to the outside of each of those boundary streets, against defendant 5th and Hill, a criminal street gang sued as an unincorporated association, 13 individual defendants, all members of 5th and Hill gang. This injunction included several unique provisions at the time.

Dismissed "served person" committing new violation: If a served person who has successfully been dismissed from this gang injunction pursuant to this opt-out provision fails to abide by all of the above opt-out provisions, such as by associating with known active 5th and Hill gang members, by getting new gang tattoos, or by being arrested for any crime that is determined to be gang related, then such served person may be re-served with this gang injunction, and will be required to comply with all of its terms.

Civil penalties (Business and Professions Code § 17206): Civil penalties under Business and Professions Code Section 17206 in the amount of $857,500 are assessed in favor of plaintiff, and against defendant 5th and Hill, individual defendants Jesus Barcenas (Nene), Everado Bautista aka Everado Osorio (Flash), Adolfo Catala (Ghost, Loco), Alex/Alejandro Delatorre (Looney, Toro), Jesus Adrian

Gonzalez (Face, Chuy), Carlos Edgar Hernandez (Scrappy, Tiny), Juan Bautista Osorio (Flame), Carlos Quiroz (Charlie), Marco David Rivera (Huero, Miclo), Gustavo Roman, Jr. (Perikin), and Cesar Tovar (Bam Bam), and each of them, jointly and severally, for their violations of Business and Professions Code Section 17200.

Damages under Penal Code § 186.22a(c): Damages in the amount of $4,200,000 are awarded in favor of plaintiff, and against defendant 5th and Hill, and the individual defendants.

The preliminary injunction was granted on February 5, 2008, and the permanent injunction on January 6, 2009.

True Crime Boys (Riverside Case INC085113), March 30, 2009

Two gangs, the West Drive Locos and True Crime Boys, were served with notification of a pending civil lawsuit against their criminal street gangs. The lawsuit notification gave official notice of the district attorney's intent to seek a judge's approval of a preliminary injunction in Indio court. The eight-month investigation also uncovered problems with illegal immigrant gang members and partnered resources with Immigration and Customs Enforcement (ICE). As part of an ongoing program, the Riverside County District Attorney's Office works with the U.S. attorney to federally prosecute gang members who have entered the country illegally. On March 30, 2009, ICE served search warrants and executed arrest warrants for every known illegal immigrant gang member in the Desert Hot Springs region.

West Drive Locos (Riverside Case INC085116), March 30, 2009

The West Drive Locos and True Crime Boys have been served with notification of a pending civil lawsuit against their criminal street gangs. The lawsuit notification gives official notice of the district attorney's intent to seek a judge's approval of a preliminary injunction in Indio court. The eight-month investigation also uncovered problems with illegal immigrant gang members and partnered resources with Immigration and Customs Enforcement (ICE). As part of an ongoing program, the Riverside County District Attorney's Office works with the U.S. attorney to federally prosecute gang members who have entered the country illegally. On March 30, 2009, ICE served search warrants and executed arrest warrants for every known illegal immigrant gang member in the Desert Hot Springs region.

Varrio East Side Reedley (VESR) (Fresno DA Case 09GI06), March 20, 2009

The Varrio East Side Reedley (VESR) gang was targeted with an injunction requesting injunctive relief enjoining and restraining the Varrio East Side Reedley (VESR) criminal street gang, all of its members, and all persons acting under, in concert with, for the benefit of, at the direction of, or in association with Varrio East Side Reedley (VESR), from engaging in or performing directly or indirectly, any of the following activities in the safety zone. The preliminary injunction was granted in July, 2009.

The "Safety Zone," a key element of the injunction, starts at the intersection of Buttonwillow and Dinuba Avenue, north along Buttonwillow to Springfield Avenue, west to East Avenue and South to Dinuba Avenue.

People v. Barrio Van Nuys (LA Case BC413147), May 6, 2009

Van Nuys authorities pursued an injunction against the Barrio Van Nuys gang, including Van Nuys High School and the Van Nuys government center in the safety zone.

The goals of the injunction, Los Angeles Superior Court Judge James C. Chalfant said in a press release, were to make the government center safer for employees and those doing business there, and to stop gang recruitment at the high school.

"The gang's members proclaim and control this part of town as their own territory or turf," Chalfant said.

While it is not unusual for a high school to be included in a gang injunction, it is to include the government center, said Bruce Riordan, director of the anti-gang operations for the Los Angeles City Attorney's Office.

"We believe that this is the first injunction safety zone to include a 'civic center' and 'courthouse,'" said Riordan.

"This gang morphed into a criminal street gang in the '70s, so for 40 years the Van Nuys community has really been under the thumb of this gang," said Deputy City Attorney Travis Austin, who argued the case in court.

The injunction covers a 4.7-square-mile area bordered by Sherman Way to the north, Woodman Avenue to the east, Burbank Boulevard to the south and the 405 (San Diego) Freeway to the west.

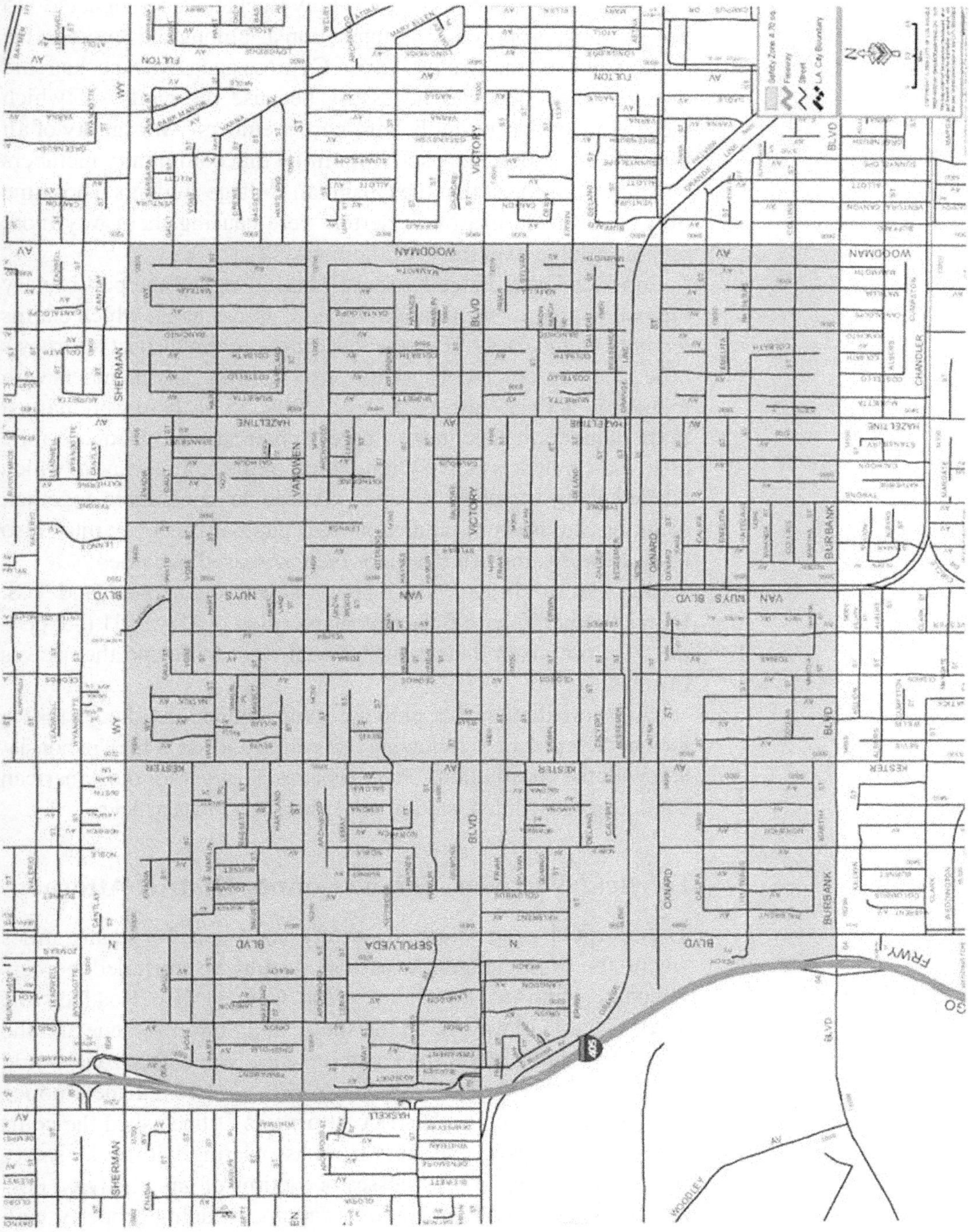

FIGURE 13.12 Map of *People v. Barrio Van Nuys.*

Orange Varrio Cypress Gang (Orange Case 30-2009-00118739), May 14, 2009

Orange County District Attorney Tony Rackauckas designated 115 people in his proposed gang injunction as among the "most active participants in" the Orange Varrio Cypress gang. Rackauckas said that the injunction was necessary because the gang—of which these 115 were purportedly hard-core members—was guilty of all manner of heinous crimes. (Never mind that community members continued to protest that the Chapman College students who came over drunk from nearby Fullerton were causing them way more regular trouble than the OVC homeboys.)

Superior Court Judge Kazharu Makino signed the preliminary injunction against the Orange Varrio Cypress gang, which claims territory in the City of Orange, according to the district attorney's office. Law enforcement authorities served 108 gang members with injunction notices starting in April 2009; 55 of them were named in the injunction. The judge's order demarcates a 3.8-square-mile area, mostly in downtown Orange west of the 55 Freeway, in which alleged gang members are not allowed to congregate together, drink or use drugs in public, or wear gang attire. They must also obey a curfew and other laws or face increased penalties.

But the validity of the injunction was challenged and U.S. District Judge Valerie Baker Fairbank ruled in May 2011 that people were not given their constitutional right to defend themselves in court.

"Any jurisdiction that employs gang injunctions should take a look at their practices following this ruling and see if they're consistent with the constitution," Peter Bibring, a lawyer for the American Civil Liberties Union, said in an Associated Press article.

Fairfield Norteños, Solano County District Attorney

The Fairfield gang injunction safety zone is a 4.2 square miles where the Norteño gang's activity would be curtailed borders Interstate Highway 80 on the west, Cement Hill Road on the north, State Highway 12 on the south, and Sunset Avenue and the Union Pacific Railroad tracks on the east. The safety zone would also extend 100 yards beyond the zone's borders. Fairfield police and the Solano County District Attorney's Office asked the court to prohibit the gang members from associating within the safety zone, intimidating any witnesses or victims of gang activity, possessing firearms and dangerous weapons, defacing property with graffiti, selling or using illegal drugs, possessing open containers of alcohol, committing a host of crimes, and trespassing on property not open to the public.

Swan Bloods, Florencia 13, Main Street Crips, and 7-Trey Hustlers Gangster Crips (Los Angeles Case BC415694), June 12, 2009

The safety zone is located in the City of Los Angeles bounded by Florence Avenue to the north, Central Avenue to the east, Manchester Avenue to the south, and the 110 Freeway to the west (but not including the roadbed of the freeway), and extending 100 yards to the outside of each of these boundaries. As of June 2010, at least 261 gang members had been served with this injunction and at least 30 had been arrested according to the Huntington Park Police Department, South Gate Police Department, and LASD Century Station. The F-13 injunction covers almost 7 square miles of territory, including portions of Florence-Firestone, Huntington Park, and South Gate. Preliminary injunction was granted on August 24, 2009, and made permanent on December 15, 2009.

People v. Deep South Side Nortenos (Case 642033 (South Modesto) Stanislaus County), July 1, 2010

The district attorney's office sought an injunction that encompasses multiple rival gangs and gang groups in one neighborhood. Modesto Police Captain Mike Harris said west Modesto would top his list, but the airport neighborhood could use the gang injunction as well. Harris said west Modesto and the airport neighborhood each have many hardworking residents who live in fear of gangs (Figure 13.13a and Figure 13.13b). "I wish we could do (gang injunctions) everywhere," Harris said. "It has to go where the biggest problem is. We can't just arbitrarily pick an area." Harris said a new injunction zone in west Modesto could include the area bordered by Highway 99, Carpenter Road, Maze Boulevard, and the Tuolumne River. But he said creating boundaries would be up to the district attorney's office, which would spearhead the effort for a new gang injunction. The permanent injunction was issued on September 10, 2009.

People v. Monrovia Nuevo Varrio and Duroc Crips (Case BC423490 Los Angeles County), October 9, 2009

Judge David Yaffee of Los Angeles Superior Court granted the injunction against 21 members of the Duroc Crips gang and 17 members of the Monrovia Nuevo Varrio gang. Monrovia's injunction specifies that the identified members of the two gangs cannot congregate in public, drink alcohol, unlawfully possess weapons, or cause graffiti inside of or within 100 yards of a safety zone. The

(a)

(b)

FIGURE 13.13 Photos of anti-gang injunction graffiti.

injunction was sought jointly by the City of Monrovia and the Los Angeles County District Attorney's Office. Gang members who congregate or engage in gang-related activities within the 6-square-mile safety zone face arrest and prosecution. The zone's boundaries are Foothill Boulevard to the north, Fifth Avenue to the west, and Mountain Avenue to the east. The southern boundary, which traverses through Monrovia and an unincorporated area of Los Angeles County, runs along Duarte Road, South Peck Road, and South Live

Oak Avenue. As of June 2010, at least 10 members had been served with the injunction and no reported arrests were made according to the LASD Temple Station and the Monrovia Police Department. The injunction was made permanent on June 10, 2010.

Inland Empire Black Rag Mafia: Not Sought

This gang was evaluated for an injunction, and after analysis was not sought by the police attorneys working the case. This gang may be a viable target in the future in the areas between Seventh Street to Base Line and from Western Avenue to State Street.

Hard Times Gang (OC Case 30-2009-00325327 Garden Grove Gang Injunction), December 3, 2009

On January 28, 2010, Orange County Superior Court Judge Kazharu Makino issued an injunction against the Hard Times street gang, the first time Orange County named a gang as the sole defendant.

Garden City police served the injunction to 49 gang members, preventing them from terrorizing their community and acting as a public nuisance, a department press release said.

The safety zone is 4.46 square miles, from east of Newhope Street, west of the Santa Ana Flood Control Channel, south of Chapman Avenue, and north of West 1st Street.

The Hard Times gang has been active since the 1970s. Between December 2005 and May 2009, four of the gang's members participated in three murders, according to the press release. Police also documented or arrested 12 Hard Times members for attempted murder, 17 for assault, 50 for firearms or dangerous weapons violations, 7 for burglary or possession of burglary tools, 5 for vehicle theft, 73 for drug violations, 21 for fighting, 1 for robbery, 389 for graffiti or vandalism tools, 42 for disturbing the peace, 29 for intimidation, 88 for alcohol in public, 20 for trespassing, 25 for blocking free passage, 5 for displaying gang hand signs, 18 for wearing gang clothing, 213 for loitering, 139 for curfew, 390 for associating with other members of the same criminal street gang, and for 166 violations of other laws. Additional crimes were committed but not documented because many citizens who live and work in these neighborhoods are reluctant to cooperate with police for fear of retaliation from the gang.

On February 9, 2007, an injunction was made permanent against an Anaheim criminal street gang. Serious and violent felonies have decreased by up to 40% in the safety zone, which is specifically the Palma Vista territory: Palma Vista Avenue in Garden Grove extending from the centerline of Palma Vista Avenue north and south until reaching the cinder block wall that surrounds the properties. Palma Vista Avenue in Garden Grove extending from the west curb line of Euclid Street west until the west property line of the alley that parallels Steele Street. These properties include the structures, driveways, carports, and alleys located between the 10700 block of Palma Vista Street east until the 11000 block of Palma Vista Avenue. Buena-Clinton Territory: 300 feet north of the north curb line of Chapman Avenue between the 12500 and 13500 blocks, extending south 300 feet west of the west curb line of Harbor Boulevard between the 12000 and 13000 blocks, extending west 300 feet north of the north curb line of Garden Grove Boulevard between the 12500 block and the 11600 block, extending south 300 feet west of the west curb line of Newhope Street from the 13000–14000 blocks in Garden Grove and continuing into the City of Santa Ana from 1600 North Newhope Street until the 100 North Newhope Street block, extending east 300 feet south of the north curb line between the 4500 West First Street block in Santa Ana and the east property line of the Santa Ana River flood control channel, extending north along the east property line of the Santa Ana River flood control channel where it intersects the 2900 block of West First Street until ending where it intersects the north curb line near 1400 West Memory Lane in the City of Santa Ana, extending west 300 feet north of the north curb line from 1400 West Memory Lane and continuing 300 feet north of the north curb line where Memory Lane changes names to Garden Grove Boulevard from the 3500–4000 West Garden Grove Boulevard block in the City of Orange, extending north 300 feet east of the east curb line of Lewis Street between the 13000 and 12000 blocks, extending north to 300 feet north of the north curb line of Chapman Avenue between the 12500 and 13500 25 blocks.

Adelanto's Brown Pride Gang (CIVVS908103 San Bernardino County), December 17, 2009

The safety zone is bordered roughly on the south by Joshua Avenue, east of Perimeter Road to the east, Avalon Avenue to the north, and Otter Avenue on the west. It includes several schools and Richardson Park. The Adelanto Brown Pride gang (BPG) has about 100 members and has been in existence for 20 years. The permanent gang injunction was granted by the Victorville Superior Court against the Brown Pride gang.

BPG is a Hispanic gang that was established in 1989 as a tagging crew, but morphed into a full-fledged criminal street gang doing all manner of crime, including murder. Approximately 80–100 members have been identified. The preliminary injunction was granted on February 11, 2010, and the permanent injunction was granted on April 1, 2010.

14

Gang Injunctions 2010 and Beyond

YEAR 2010

People v. North Side Oakland Gang (Alameda Case), February 2010

The safety zones in this injunction include roughly 100 blocks of North Oakland between I-580, Emeryville, Berkeley, and Telegraph Avenue. It will also limit the presence of the gangs on the streets by setting a curfew for the 19 people named in the injunction between the hours of 10 p.m. and 5 a.m. If any of the 19 members of the gang are caught engaging in prohibited activities like associating with other gang members, selling drugs, or possessing firearms, they can be found in contempt of court.

In January 2007, Alameda County Superior Court Judge Robert Freedman held a hearing on a motion to bar the Oakland law firm Siegel & Yee from representing Norteños gang members who are named in the city's suit. The DA alleged that the law firm has a conflict of interest because City Councilwoman Jane Brunner is a member of the firm, and it also represents Oakland Mayor Jean Quan. Attorneys Michael Siegel and Jose Luis Fuentes, who are members of the Siegel & Yee firm, said the firm has dropped out of the case and Norteños members are now represented by a newly formed nonprofit group called Communities United for Restorative Youth Justice (CURYJ). Siegel and Fuentes both belong to the new group but are still in the law firm. Fuentes said the firm has set up "fire walls" to prevent any confidential information from getting to other members, such as Brunner. But Freedman ruled that there's no evidence that CURYJ "is an organization recognized by the State Bar or serves any purpose other than as a vehicle for Siegel and Fuentes to accomplish an 'end run'" around conflict of interest rules. Freedman said that he doesn't think it's a conflict of interest for the law firm to represent Quan, but he said Brunner's involvement as both a member of the law firm and a member of the city council is "problematic." A hearing on the merits of the city attorney's bid to get an injunction against alleged Norteños members was still scheduled, but Freedman said the hearing may be postponed if all the preliminary procedural issues in the case aren't resolved before.

In February 2010, the court ruled the firm could represent accused gang members. However, Judge Freedman denied the defense motion to have the state appoint attorneys to the defendants, saying there is no existing case or law that gives him the authority to make such an order. One of the chief complaints made by injunction opponents has been that the lawsuit can result in jail time, but doesn't offer the same protection of a court-ordered attorney that a criminal case would offer.

People v. Jeffrey Street Gang (Orange Co. Case 30-2010-00363220), April 15, 2010

The safety zone is in Anaheim and is defined as the area from the south curb line of Katella Avenue on the south, to the east curb line of CasaVista Street, to the north curb line of Casa Grande Street continuing to the cinder block wall at the dead end of Casa Grande Street on the east, continuing along of the cinder block wall to the east and then on the south of the apartment complex located at 1128 W. Casa Grande Street, continuing along the cinder block wall located on the south and on the west of the apartments located at 1847 and 1837 S. Jacalene Lane, continuing along the cinder block wall bordering the west side of the property located at 1176 W. Katella Avenue, continuing along the cinder block wall and fence on the west border of the property located at 1198 W. Katella Avenue, to the south curb line of Katella Avenue, to the east curb line of Ninth Street, to the light pole located between the addresses of 1916 and 1922 S. Ninth Street, continuing directly west to the cinder block wall bordering the south side of Stoddard Park, continuing along the cinder block wall surrounding Stoddard Park to the south and on the west, continuing to the chain link fence located on the west of Stoddard Park, to the south curb line of Katella Avenue, to the west curb line of Euclid Street on the west, to the south curb line of Cris Avenue, to the east curb line of Nutwood Street on the west, to the north curb line of Ball Road on the north, to the west curb line of Loara Street, to the north curb line of Beacon Avenue on the north, continuing to the east curb line of Disneyland Drive on the east, continuing to the south curb line of Katella Avenue on the south.

People v. Westside Gang (San Diego Case 37-2009-00061924), May 22, 2010

The border of the safety zone begins at the intersection of W. Grand Avenue and N. Escondido Boulevard. The border extends north to the intersection with W. El Norte Parkway and includes the 100 through 1200 blocks of N. Escondido Boulevard. From N. Escondido Boulevard and W. EI Norte Parkway, the border extends east to the intersection with N. Broadway and includes the 200 through 100 blocks of W. El Norte Parkway. From W. El Norte Parkway and N. Broadway, the border extends south to the intersection with E. Lincoln Avenue and includes the 1200 through 1000 blocks of N. Broadway. From N. Broadway and E. Lincoln Avenue, the border extends east to the intersection with N. Midway Drive and includes the 100 through 1900 blocks of E. Lincoln Avenue. From E. Lincoln Avenue and N. Midway Drive, the border extends south to the intersection with E. Grand Avenue and includes the 900 through 100 blocks of N. Midway Drive. From N. Midway Drive and E. Grand Avenue, the border extends west to the intersection of N. Ash Street and includes the 1900 through 1200 blocks of E. Grand. Zone 2 from the eastern boundary is the 100 block of south Juniper Street from Grand Avenue to the 1600 block of south Juniper Street to Felicita Avenue. The southern boundary will be the 200 block of east Felicita Avenue from Juniper Street to the 600 block of west Felicita Avenue at Redwood Street. The boundary then turns north on Redwood Street from the 1600 block of south Redwood Street. The boundary then turns west on 15th Avenue at the 700 block of west 15th Avenue and continues to the 900 block of west 15th Avenue. The border then turns north at the lS00 block of south Upas Street and runs north to Valley Parkway at what would be the intersection of Upas Street (Upas Street ends in the 100 block of S. Upas Street at Murray Court, and would continue in a straight line to Valley Parkway). At Valley Parkway, the zone turns east in the 900 block of west Valley Parkway and runs east (where Valley Parkway turns into Grand Avenue at the 800 block) to Juniper Street at the 200 block of east Grand Avenue and extends 100 yards to the outside of each of the boundary streets listed herein.

People v. Diablos Gang (San Diego Case 37-2009-00061923), May 22, 2010

The border of the safety zone begins at the intersection of W. Grand Avenue and N. Escondido Boulevard. The border extends north to the intersection with W. El Norte Parkway and includes the 100 through 1200 blocks of N. Escondido Boulevard. From N. Escondido

Boulevard and W. El Norte Parkway, the border extends east to the intersection with N. Broadway and includes the 200 through 100 blocks of W. El Norte Parkway. From W. El Norte Parkway and N. Broadway, the border extends south to the intersection with E. Lincoln Avenue and includes the 1200 through 1000 blocks of N. Broadway. From N. Broadway and E. Lincoln Avenue, the border extends east to the intersection with N. Midway Drive and includes the 100 through 1900 blocks of E. Lincoln Avenue. From E. Lincoln Avenue and N. Midway Drive, the border extends south to the intersection with E. Grand Avenue and includes the 900 through 100 blocks of N. Midway Drive. From N. Midway Drive and E. Grand Avenue, the border extends west to the intersection of N. Ash Street and includes the 1900 through 1200 blocks of E. Grand Avenue. From E. Grand Avenue and N. Ash Street, the border extends south to the intersection with E. 3rd Avenue and includes the 100 through 200 blocks of S. Ash Street. From S. Ash Street and E. 3rd Avenue, the border extends west to the intersection with S. Fig Street and includes the 1100 through 700 blocks of E. 3rd Avenue. From E. 3rd Avenue and S. Fig Street, the border extends north to the intersection with E. Grand Avenue and includes the 200 through 100 blocks of S. Fig Street. From S. Fig Street and E. Grand Avenue, the border extends west to the intersection of N. Escondido Boulevard and includes the 600 block of E. Grand Avenue through the 200 block of W. Grand Avenue and extends 100 yards to the outside of each of the boundary streets listed herein.

Zone 2 is from the eastern boundary is the 100 block of south Juniper Street from Grand Avenue to the 1600 block of south Juniper Street to Felicita Avenue. The southern boundary will be the 200 block of east Felicita Avenue from Juniper Street to the 600 block of west Felicita Avenue at Redwood Street. The boundary then turns north on Redwood Street from the 1600 block of south Redwood Street to the 1500 block of south Redwood Street at 15th Avenue. The boundary then turns west on 15th Avenue at the 700 block of west 15th Avenue and continues to the 900 block of west 15th Avenue. The border then turns north at the 1500 block of south Upas Street and runs north to Valley Parkway at what would be the intersection of Upas Street (Upas Street ends in the 100 block of S. Upas Street at Murray Court, and would continue in a straight line to Valley Parkway). At Valley Parkway, the safety zone turns east in the 900 block of west Valley.

People v. Center Street Gang (San Diego Case 37-2010-00051319), May 24, 2010

The border of the safety zone begins at the territory bounded to the north by Mission Avenue from Home Street to Interstate 5, to the south by Missouri Avenue, to the east by Interstate 5, and extending along Division Street across Interstate 5 to the east curb line of Country Club Lane. It continues north on Country Club Lane to Maxson Street, including the apartment complex at 201 Country Club Lane; to the west by Horne Street, and extending 100 yards to the outside of each of those boundary streets. The border of zone 2 starts at State Route 76 from Interstate 5 to a perpendicular line through an undeveloped area from the 800 block of Carey Road (north boundary). From the perpendicular line through an undeveloped area from Highway 76 to the 800 block of Carey Road southbound to the 100 block of Carey Road at the intersection of Canyon Drive (east boundary). From the intersection of Carey Road and Canyon Drive north to the intersection of Canyon Drive and the 2000 block of Mission Avenue. West from the 2000 block of Mission Avenue to the 1000 block of Mission Avenue to the intersection of Mission Avenue and Home Street (south boundary). North from the 200 block of Home Street to the 1000 block of Civic Center (west boundary). From the 1000 block of Civic Center east to the freeway overpass at Interstate 5. From the freeway overpass at Interstate 5 and Civic Center north to Highway 76 and extending 100 yards to the outside of each of those boundary streets.

April 22, 2010, Santa Barbara Considering Injunctions

In April of 2010, the City of Santa Barbara started to consider the idea of a gang injunction. Police Chief Cam Sanchez confirmed that he was studying the feasibility of implementing a gang injunction within city limits, something he has vigorously opposed in the past. While Sanchez cautioned that no decision would be made for several months, he said changing circumstances including several high-profile gang-related homicides involving juvenile perpetrators have softened his opposition. "I've been attending a lot of community meetings, and I'm hearing, even in Latino neighborhoods, that I'm not tough enough on gangs," he said, according to Giana Magnoli, a reporter at Noozhawk in Santa Barbara. "People are tired of being intimidated in their own neighborhoods; they're tired of having their children jumped in."

Even the most successful gang injunctions, Sanchez said, can't eliminate gangs; some work better than others. He said his department has studied the experience Lompoc and Oxnard have had with their injunctions, as well as other data that might illuminate whether such an injunction would be appropriate for Santa Barbara. That work, being conducted in concert with the city attorney's and district attorney's offices, will take months to complete.

Typically, gang injunctions are labor-intensive operations, in which specific individuals with suspected or known gang affiliations are barred from congregating in or around specific locations, such as Bohnett Park on the westside or the Pennywise Market on the eastside, Sanchez said. He noted that merely serving suspected gang members with injunction notices could exceed the available officer power of his department. The city eventually obtained its first gang injunction in March of 2011 against two gangs in the city.

People v. Central City Skid Row Gangs (Grape St. and Others) (Los Angeles Case BC435316), April 7, 2010

The site of this announcement is Gladys Park, at East Sixth and Gladys Streets, a postage-stamp-sized recreation area that has been plagued with drug dealing despite a 2006 Safer Cities Initiative that brought a swarm of police to Center City East (and a successful lawsuit by the ACLU that prevents cops from arresting homeless people for sleeping on sidewalks).

People v. Metro Transit Assassins Gang (Ls Angeles Case BC44003), June 21, 2010

Los Angeles City Attorney Carmen Trutanich pursued an injunction against the tagging crew known as the Metro Transit Assassins in 2010, claiming the gang had done 500 pieces of graffiti on property belonging to the Metro Transportation Authority.

The gang used spray cans to paint freeways, trains, trucks, and venues to spread its name. It even rented a helicopter to scout a sight along the Los Angeles River Bank, and deposited a quarter-mile long tag on a concrete wall that cost $4 million to remove.

A civil lawsuit against the gang sought $1.25 million in fines and $3.7 million in damages for the graffiti.

The gang challenged the request for an injunction, arguing that the graffiti was artwork which was protected by the First Amendment. Los Angeles Superior Court Judge Deirdre Hall rejected that argument in May 2011.

People v. Down Below Gangsters and Towerside Gang (San Francisco Case CG-C-10-502262), August 5, 2010

This injunction was filed against two feuding cliques in the Visitacion Valley neighborhood. The civil action names 41 adult members of the Down Below Gangsters and the Towerside Gang as having engaged in "gang-related criminal and nuisance activity." According to the complaint, the two sets have a bitter rivalry that accounted for 10 murders over the previous three years. The gangs are also accused of drug sales, aggravated assaults, robberies, vandalism, and threatening residents who "snitch," or cooperate with law enforcement. The Down Below Gangsters are based near the Sunnydale housing projects, while the Towerside Gang claims territory around the Heritage Homes and Britton Courts housing projects. The proposed safety zone covers less than 2/10 of a square mile. The proposed safety zone is an approximately 0.18-square-mile L-shaped area bordered by Schwerin Avenue, Visitacion Avenue, and Hahn Street, and the Sunnydale Public Housing Development's northern, western, and southern borders, the latter of which then proceeds along Velasco Avenue. The safety zone encompasses both known gang turfs and an adjoining buffer zone between and near the two turf areas.

People v. South Side Indio Gang (Riverside Case INC10010946), November 2010

A judge in Indio has ruled that prosecutors can begin serving 125 people named in a gang injunction lawsuit designed to establish a 13.8-mile "safety zone" perimeter within the city. The 1,200-page gang injunction names 126 people and documents their ties to the South Side Indio gang. However, Deputy District Attorney Kristi Daw emphasized that the injunction doesn't apply to only those named in it. The injunction only applies to a limited safety zone within the heart of Indio. The zone contains 17 schools and 6 public parks. The district attorney's office determined that area because of the high number of chases, drug busts, and graffiti there. The injunction says the gang has created an "atmosphere of fear" in that area.

15

Gang Injunctions Outside California

TEXAS

Outside of California, the next state in line in which gang injunctions have become a tool to target gangs is Texas. In 1995, a Texas law was enacted that allowed a court to enjoin a gang member from engaging in the organized criminal activities of a criminal combination or criminal street gang.

In 1998, the City of Austin, through the Travis County District Attorney's Office, became the first Texas city to utilize this law when it sought a temporary injunction against members of a local street gang dealing drugs in an apartment complex. The case was dismissed without seeking a permanent injunction, but the goal of decreasing criminal activity was achieved.

Chapter 125 of the Texas Civil Practice and Remedies Code and Section 101.70 of the Texas Alcoholic Beverage Code are considered the Texas nuisance abatement statutes. These statutes permit law enforcement agencies to close any piece of property involved in illegal activities, including violations of the Texas Penal Code, the Texas Alcoholic Beverage Code, and the Texas Controlled Substances Act.

Austin, Texas

In July 1998, eight gang members were targeted with an injunction in a 0.5-square-mile area in a northeast Austin neighborhood. The Travis County District Attorney's Office filed its petition for an injunction, claiming that the eight were gang members who sell drugs, recruit customers, run from the police, and intimidate people in the neighborhood. The petition sought to prevent them from congregating in groups of two or more in an area bordered on the west by Cameron Road, on the north by Cloverleaf Drive, on the east by Belfast Drive, and on the south by East 51st Street.

The proposed injunction came with a list of 17 prohibited activities in the target area, including:

- Standing, sitting, walking, driving, gathering, or appearing in public with another one of the eight or with any other known member of the gang in which they allegedly belong
- Possessing, using, or delivering narcotics or drug paraphernalia, and possessing pagers or beepers in public
- Communicating with anyone in a vehicle, obstructing traffic, using gang hand signs, wearing gang colors, or acting as a lookout
- Using abusive language, threatening, harassing, or intimidating people either in retaliation or to prevent them from complaining to police

The injunction would also make two convenience stores on Cameron Road near Broadmoor Drive off-limits to any of the eight. The punishment for violations would be up to 10 days in jail for contempt of court. Besides being together, those activities include loitering around pay phones; using pay phones and pagers in the neighborhood to facilitate a crime; using abusive, harassing, or threatening language; and hanging around several businesses and apartment complexes.

San Antonio, Texas—Lincoln Court Gangsters and Lincoln Court Kings

In 1999, the City of San Antonio through the Bexar County District Attorney's Office filed a successful civil gang injunction against 38 defendants of two rival street gangs. On September 9, 1999, 32 gang members were targeted with a two-year injunction prohibiting alleged members of the groups from associating, spraying graffiti paint, or recruiting new members. The safety zone is bordered on the north by Waverly Avenue, on the west by Wilson, which then becomes N.W. 24th Street, on the south by W. Martin Street, and on the east by N. Sabinas Street. The petition alleges that the 25 named defendants, ranging in age from 13 to 30 years old, are members of the Lincoln Court Gangsters or the Lincoln Court Kings, and have regularly associated to commit crimes, ranging from violent offenses to weapons and narcotics offenses, thus creating a public nuisance. The Lincoln Court Gangsters are affiliated with the Bloods gang, with origins in Los Angeles, California. The Lincoln Court Kings are a subset of the Kings gang, with origins in Chicago, Illinois, and New York, New York.

El Paso, Texas—Barrio Azteca

In 2003, the El Paso Police Department, in partnership with the El Paso County Attorney's Office, implemented a new strategy for dealing with criminal gangs. In this case, the gang injunction covered the area known in El Paso as the Segundo Barrio, or as it was referred to in the injunction, the Safe Community Zone. "The Aztecas have long sent out a message to other gangs in the city that the Segundo Barrio is their hood and their barrio," said Sgt. Marylou Carrillo, who headed the Community Response Against Street Hoodlums (CRASH) Unit at the time. The gang injunction applied to 32 of the 35 initial defendants. The remaining three Barrio Azteca members requested a jury trial and as a result, the injunction was extended an additional year for them.

Among those restrictions, gang members listed in the injunction could not associate with each other, had a 10:00 p.m. curfew, were prohibited from using cell phones and pagers in public, and were not allowed inside many of the area restaurants and bars that were frequented by the gang and used to facilitate the distribution of narcotics. The Barrio Azteca gang, the largest and most active prison gang in the El Paso area, was founded in the mid-1980s. The gang was created primarily to serve as a protective organization and to unite all Hispanic inmates from the El Paso area. Most of the original members were from the Second Ward (Segundo Barrio) area of El Paso, which is located in the south central region of the city. As the Aztecas grew in numbers, they became involved in the now-standard activities of prison gangs: narcotics, extortion, assaults, murders, theft, and intimidation. The Aztecas recruit directly from the pool of street gang members who have been arrested or imprisoned; however, they also form alliances and intimidate various street level gangs who have not progressed to the prison system.

El Paso's gang injunction was unique for Texas and the nation in that it was considered the first-ever attempt to curb the illegal activities of a *confirmed prison-based gang* whose illicit criminal operations extended out into the streets. If a defendant violates one of the restrictions listed in a civil gang injunction, they are charged under TX. PC. 71.021, "Violation of a Court Order Enjoining Organized Crime," which is a Class A misdemeanor punishable by up to a year in jail or a $4,000 fine or both. Under the Civil Practice and Remedies Code, defendants are also subject to a civil contempt charge resulting in up to 30 days in jail or a maximum fine of $10,000 or both. Additionally, if a defendant violates any other offense under another section, he or she may be prosecuted for that offense as well.

The following are a sample of just a few of the 35 restrictions that were used in the first injunction initiated in El Paso:

- Associating, standing, sitting, walking, driving, bicycling, gathering, or appearing anywhere in public with any other defendants named in the injunction
- Signaling to, or acting as a lookout for, other persons to warn of the approach of police officers
- Remaining in any one public place under circumstances that would warrant a reasonable person to believe that the purpose of that behavior is to control identifiable areas, intimidate others from entering those areas, or conceal or engage in illegal activities
- Remaining in a public place between the hours of 10:00 p.m. and 6:00 a.m.
- Using or making words, phrases, physical gestures, or symbols commonly known as gang hand signs
- Engaging in any conduct that violates the laws of the State of Texas or ordinances of the City of El Paso
- Being banned from entering various business establishments known to be frequented by Barrio Azteca gang members for the purpose of trafficking narcotics

Since many of the Barrio Azteca members are drug users and are continuously involved in criminal activity in order to maintain their habit, the implementation of this injunction attributed to a 33% drop in burglary of business, 20% drop in robbery, and 15% drop in burglary of autos. Overall crime since the gang injunction was granted decreased approximately 12% within the Safe Community Zone. Most importantly, during that period members of the Barrio Azteca gang seemed to be continually turning against each other upon their arrest. Their organization, although still active throughout El Paso, was altered and created distrust among their membership, and many of the initial defendants listed on the injunction have relocated, are incarcerated, or don't know whom to trust anymore.

Wichita Falls, Texas—Varrio Carnales

On August 31, 2006, the Varrio Carnales (VC), Spanish for neighborhood brothers, was targeted with an injunction by the Wichita Falls Police Department. The injunction was in response to gang activity between the VCs and their rival gang, the Puro Li'l Mafia (PLM).

After years of arrests and analysis by law enforcement, police determined that most of the gang activity occurred in a

1.5-square-mile area in central Wichita Falls. Police called this hot zone VC Safety Zone No. 1. In the middle of the hot zone is Wichita Falls High School, with 1,300 students. The petition was filed and a temporary restraining order issued by the 89th District Court. The court issued an order authorizing the police to give personal service of the restraining order. That same evening, some 25 officers set out to locate and serve each and every defendant with a copy of the restraining order.

On September 18, 2006, the temporary gang injunction was ordered into effect by the district court. The injunction named 21 members of the VC street gang. Violations of the injunctions are common (police have made more than 50 arrests since the injunctions went into effect), but so are additional crimes while gang members are out on bond. The VC gang injunction revolves around certain prohibitions in a set safety zone. The VC Safety Zone No. 1 was created because it is where the VC tended to commit the majority of its criminal activity and where many of the gang members lived and went to school. Within the safety zone, the trial court prohibited named defendants from engaging in 29 specific activities, including associating with other gang members, possessing alcohol, wearing gang colors, and violating curfew. Although these activities are not generally illegal, because a judge has determined that the prohibitions are reasonably related to stopping gang activity, they were included in the injunction.

It should be noted that a defendant in a civil gang injunction case receives due process prior to being placed on a gang injunction. Such defendants have the right to retain legal counsel and the right to a jury trial. The 29 VC gang prohibitions apply only to defendants who have been afforded said due process of law. Gang injunction violations constitute a Class A misdemeanor.

The DA's office has been very successful in obtaining convictions for these violators, and there are generally multiple injunction violations per arrest. Convictions typically result in 10 months' incarceration per incident, but unfortunately, gang members habitually violate injunction prohibitions while released on bond for their initial offenses. The lack of severe and immediate consequences emboldens the gangs and frustrates the law enforcement officers tasked with gang suppression. When a gang member repeatedly violates a gang injunction, the community suffers and individuals are put in harm's way.

Section 125.066 of the Civil Practice and Remedies Code authorizes violators of gang injunctions to be held in civil contempt of court. Punishment for contempt was set by statute at 10 to 30 days in jail and $1,000 to $10,000 per violation. A contempt of court proceeding can be completed quickly, and a conviction places the gang member behind bars without possibility of bonding out.

Gang injunctions and related litigation and contempt proceedings have been successful. Gang activity has been reduced by approximately 18%, and gang members are not the brazen band of thugs that once terrorized the community. They are more timid in public and are forced to operate much more in the shadows because they can no longer gather openly or travel together in the safety zone. This disruption greatly affects their ability to utilize the gang's main asset: intimidation through numbers. An unforeseen benefit has recently materialized in that the local gangs are finding it more difficult to recruit new members—law enforcement's actions seem to be adversely affecting the gang's coolness factor.

On November 9, 2010, Harris County sought an injunction against the Bloods and Crips gangs who have menaced a northeast Houston apartment complex, helping label it the region's most dangerous. The county filed its first anti-gang civil injunction, a lawsuit that will target 33 documented gang members who are suspected of selling drugs in the 700-unit Haverstock Hills complex and the surrounding community in the northwest corner of Aldine Bender and the Eastex Freeway. More than 2,400 people live at the complex, 800 of whom are children, but the number of people milling about in Haverstock can grow to nearly 4,000 at night, police said. In August, prosecutors said they were trying to set up a 3-square-mile "gang safety zone" targeting gang memberswho have habitually engaged in at least five instances of organized criminal activity in a year's span, but would not identify the area.

Suing gang members in civil court means prosecutors can bar suspects from associating with each other. Similar lawsuits in other Texas cities have prohibited gang members from going out in public after 9 p.m. or possessing a cell phone in a car. Prosecutors also can prohibit gang clothing, gang hand signs, and possession of spray paint, for up to 10 years. In 2009, police responded to more than 3,000 calls at the complex. On October 7, 2010, the Court of Criminal Appeals of Texas has affirmed Wichita Falls' gang injunction and the conviction of a defendant under the Varrio Carnales gang injunction. Mario Rico Martinez, now 21, was named in the city's first gang injunction and pleaded guilty to five offenses related to injunction violations that occurred in December 2006 and January, February, April and September 2007. He was sentenced to 305 days in jail and was fined $4,000 for each counts. In early 2009, the Second Court of Appeals in Fort Worth upheld the constitutionality of elements of the injunction that were brought up on appeal in Martinez's case. The Wichita County Public Defenders' Office appealed that court's decision to the Court of Criminal Appeals. The office argued Martinez was prohibited from wearing gang clothing or making gang signs, but the information did not specify what those were; their case claimed the injunction is too vague and grants police officers too much power in determining the type of suspected conduct that violates the law. The Court of Criminal Appeals unanimous stated in part, "We hold that the Fort Worth Court of Appeals did not err" in holding that the applicable section of the Texas Civil Practice and Remedies Code does not violate the separation of powers doctrine, the opinion reads. Section 125.065(a)(2) "permits a judge to impose reasonable requirements when enjoining criminal street activity..." and a violation is punishable under Penal Code Section 72.021. "We also conclude that the court of appeals correctly determined that the provision of the injunction prohibiting Mario Rico Martinez from making gang hand signs and wearing gang clothing did not violate the First Amendment and was not unconstitutionally vague."

UTAH

On September 9, 2010, the Weber County district attorney sought an unprecedented gang injunction that would prohibit the Ogden Trece gang and any of its members from associating or otherwise engaging in numerous lawful activities anywhere within the City of Ogden. In its lawsuit, Weber County asked the court to label Ogden Trece, and all of its members, a "public nuisance," and to issue a permanent injunction that would prohibit those alleged members from, among other things, associating with other alleged members of the group from possessing legal firearms, drinking alcohol (on both public and private property), and engaging in numerous other kinds of constitutionally protected expressive speech and activities. These prohibitions would apply to anyone identified by law enforcement, in its own discretion and with no judicial oversight, to be a member of Ogden Trece.

Defense attorneys have filed motions seeking dismissal of the injunction as they argue the injunction violates the First, Second, and Fourteenth Amendment rights of, respectively, free speech and assembly, to bear arms, and equal protection under the U.S. Constitution and corresponding sections of the Utah Constitution. The Utah Supreme Court has denied a petition for emergency relief that would have halted the enforcement of Ogden's controversial gang injunction. The injunction was entered September 28 by 2nd District Judge Ernie Jones after he declared the 485-member Ogden Trece gang a public nuisance. Attorneys for the American Civil Liberties Union asked the Supreme Court to review the injunction almost immediately after it went into effect, arguing that it was too broad and violated the constitutional rights of all citizens suspected of being in and associated with the gang.

MINNESOTA

On May 1, 2009, Ramsey County Judge Gregg Johnson issued what is believed to be Minnesota's first civil gang injunction. The temporary injunction applies to 10 members of the Sureño 13 street gang, and prohibits them from undertaking a variety of activities during St. Paul's Cinco de Mayo celebration. City officials sought the injunction in response to a shooting incident that occurred at the end of the 2008 Cinco event. During the celebration's waning hours, two teenagers were wounded in a drive-by shooting that police suspect was linked to Sureño gang members. In order to stave off such violence at the 2009 gathering, the St. Paul City Attorney's Office turned to a 2007 Minnesota law that allows a temporary injunction to be enforced against criminal gangs. Such an injunction can restrict interactions between gang members for a set period of time, or can prohibit them from entering certain physical areas. In a press release issued after Judge Johnson's order was signed, City Attorney John Choi said, "We are really pleased with the order because it recognizes that criminal gangs are a public nuisance. The public has a right to be free from criminal gang violence and intimidation."

Minnesota's gang injunction law allows a judge to issue an order to prevent members of a criminal gang from "engaging in gang activities." The injunction can include specific requirements meant to prevent future gang-related actions. For instance, Judge Johnson's order in the Sureño matter prohibits members from "associating, standing, sitting, walking, driving, bicycling, gathering, or appearing anywhere in public view" with other named gang members at the Cinco de Mayo event. The order contains exceptions related to school or church attendance by these members. It also prohibits members from wearing clothing that includes references to the gang, or from using "words, phrases, physical gestures" or other forms of communication to identify or refer to the gang. According to Minnesota law, the court must balance "state interests in public safety against constitutional freedoms" when it considers imposing such requirements.

Violations of the injunction—such as meeting with gang members within a prohibited area—are criminal offenses. The gang injunction applies to criminal gangs, defined by law as associations of three or more people who engage in patterns of criminal activity. Specific gang members are also frequently named in such orders. A governmental entity may apply to a district court judge to obtain a gang injunction. Subsequently, the judge has to find that the gang is a public nuisance. To obtain an injunction, the government has to meet the civil law threshold of a "preponderance of the evidence," which is lower than the threshold needed to obtain a criminal conviction.

The Minnesota gang injunction law is relatively new, and has yet to be tested by Minnesota's higher courts. Elsewhere, the California Supreme Court upheld that state's gang injunction law. In a related matter, the Illinois Supreme Court struck down a Chicago loitering ordinance that had been applied to gang members. The court found the ordinance to be impermissibly vague. The U.S. Supreme Court affirmed the Illinois high court's decision in the 1999 case *Chicago v. Morales*. This decision led other cities to narrowly craft civil gang injunctions, in order to avoid due process concerns. For instance, while Chicago police officers had used their own discretion to apply the loitering ordinance, subsequent civil gang injunctions relied on evidentiary hearings, named individual defendants, and set out specific, prohibited.

TENNESSEE

In 2009, the State of Tennessee enacted a nuisance law that would allow police to file civil suits against gang members. Those suits would ban known gang members from hanging out in certain areas, patronizing certain businesses, or associating with certain people. Violating those civil orders could then become a criminal charge.

16

How Many Gangs, Gang Members, and Gang Injunctions Are There?

This information is critical because existing data relating to the true scope and magnitude depicting the number of gangs, gang members, and gang injunctions are unclear. Depending on the source, some researchers feel the gang problem is getting better; others feel it is getting worse. By contacting law enforcement directly to collect information for this book, the number of injunction cases, gang members, gangs, and things like percentage of gang members by county enjoined or arrested could be calculated.

This book contains a synopsis of every gang injunction ever filed in the State of California. Each synopsis contains the court case number, target area and other relevant facts.

The following is a breakdown of the results for each of the 58 counties in California, including reported gangs, gang members, and gang injunctions by individual city based on the expert opinion of some of the police that work in those jurisdictions (Figure 16.1). The counties that reported gang injunctions have their injunction cases listed by case name, case number, date filed, primary police agency involved, number of defendants named in or served with each injunction, and number of confirmed arrests for a violation of that injunction. Jurisdictions that have obtained or attempted an injunction are listed with the name of the city in bold font to distinguish it from jurisdictions with no injunction activity.

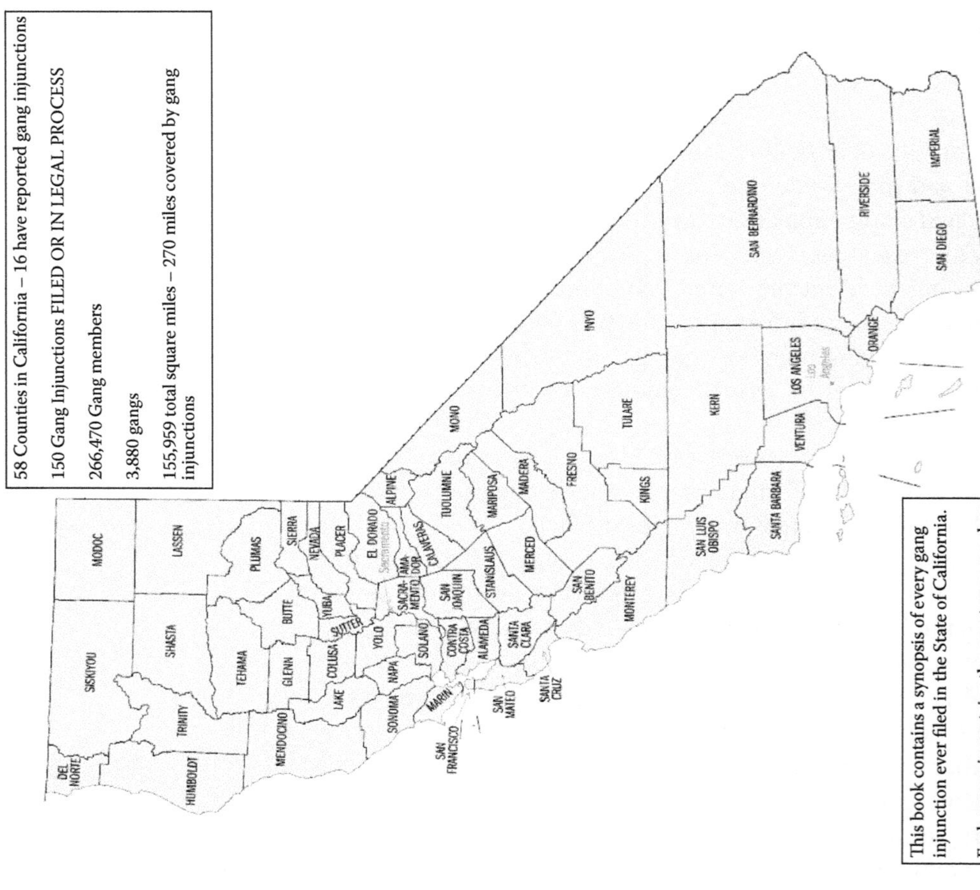

FIGURE 16.1 Map of California.

Alameda County—1 Injunction and 1 Gang Attempt

	Opinion 2006		Estimated True		Projected 2011–2012	
City	Members	Gangs	Members	Gangs	Members	Gangs
Alameda Sheriff/ Fremont	1,600	35	1,600	35	1,600	35
Hayward PD	100	5	100	5	100	5
Oakland PD	960	3	960	3	960	3
Total	2,660	43	2,660	43	2,660	43

1) *People v. B Street Boys* 735405-4 *May 18, 1994* *OPD* *17/0*
2) *People v. Northside Oakland* *February 2010*

Alpine County—0 Gang Injunctions

	Opinion 2006		Estimated True		Projected 2011–2012	
City	Members	Gangs	Members	Gangs	Members	Gangs
Alpine County	0	0	0	0	0	0
Total	0	0	0	0	0	0

Amador County—0 Gang Injunctions

	Opinion 2006		Estimated True		Projected 2011–2012	
City	Members	Gangs	Members	Gangs	Members	Gangs
Amador County	0	0	0	0	0	0
Total	0	0	0	0	0	0

Butte County—0 Gang Injunctions

	Opinion 2006		Estimated True		Projected 2011–2012	
City	Members	Gangs	Members	Gangs	Members	Gangs
Butte Sheriff	17	5	17	5	17	5
Chico PD	10	1	10	1	10	1
Oroville PD	30	2	30	2	30	2
Palermo	10	1	10	1	10	1
Total	67	9	67	9	67	9

Calaveras County—0 Gang Injunctions

	Opinion 2006		Estimated True		Projected 2011–2012	
City	Members	Gangs	Members	Gangs	Members	Gangs
Calaveras Sheriff	12	1	12	1	12	1
Valley Springs	30	1	35	1	40	1
Total	42	2	47	2	52	2

Colusa County—0 Gang Injunctions

	Opinion 2006		Estimated True		Projected 2011–2012	
City	Members	Gangs	Members	Gangs	Members	Gangs
Colusa PD	15	1	15	1	15	1
Total	15	1	15	1	15	1

Contra Costa County—0 Gang Injunctions

	Opinion 2006		Estimated True		Projected 2011–2012	
City	Members	Gangs	Members	Gangs	Members	Gangs
Bethel Island	20	1	20	1	20	1
Brentwood PD	40	2	40	2	40	2
Concord PD	780	19	780	19	780	19
Contra Costa Sheriff	50	6	50	6	50	6
Pleasant Hill	—	—	—	—	—	—
Walnut Creek	—	—	—	—	—	—
Contra Costa SO (East)	450	14	450	14	450	14
Antioch	—	—	—	—	—	—
Bay Point	—	—	—	—	—	—
Byron	—	—	—	—	—	—
Knightsen	—	—	—	—	—	—
Oakley City	—	—	—	—	—	—
Contra Costa SO (West)	450	9	450	9	450	9
Crockett	—	—	—	—	—	—
El Cerrito	—	—	—	—	—	—
Hercules	—	—	—	—	—	—
Pinole	—	—	—	—	—	—
Pittsburg PD	100	7	100	7	100	7
Richmond PD	502	7	502	8	502	8
San Pablo PD	455	4	455	4	455	4
Vine Hill	10	1	10	1	10	1
Total	2,855	70	2,855	70	2,855	70

Del Norte County—0 Gang Injunctions

	Opinion 2006		Estimated True		Projected 2011–2012	
City	Members	Gangs	Members	Gangs	Members	Gangs
Crescent City PD	4	1	4	1	4	1
Total	4	1	4	1	4	1

El Dorado County—0 Gang Injunctions

	Opinion 2006		Estimated True		Projected 2011–2012	
City	Members	Gangs	Members	Gangs	Members	Gangs
Placerville PD	12	4	12	4	12	4
Total	12	4	12	4	12	4

Fresno County—6 Gang Injunctions

	Opinion 2006		Estimated True		Projected 2011–2012	
City	Members	Gangs	Members	Gangs	Members	Gangs
Clovis PD	20	2	20	2	20	2
Coalinga PD	120	9	150	10	150	10
Easton	10	1	10	1	10	1
Firebaugh PD	31	2	35	2	40	2
Fowler PD	14	1	14	1	14	1
Fresno PD	910	21	920	21	1,000	21
Fresno CO Sheriff	8,323	273	8,647	274	9,082	274
Huron PD	106	4	120	4	130	4
Kerman PD	57	3	57	3	63	3
Kingsburg PD	7	1	7	1	7	1
Laton	36	1	36	1	36	1
Mendota	124	2	130	2	130	2
Orange Cove	268	2	268	2	268	2
Parlier PD	97	3	100	3	120	3
Reedley PD	114	2	116	2	125	2
Riverdale	13	2	15	2	15	2
San Joaquin City	66	2	70	2	70	2
Sanger PD	356	2	360	2	370	2
Selma PD	312	4	330	4	350	4
Total	10,954	337	11,405	338	12,000	337

Fresno County—6 Gang Injunctions (Continued)

1) *People v. Chankla Bulldogs*	03CECG02881	August 15, 2003	SPD	22/15
2) *People v. Parkside Bulldogs*	04CECG027777	September 27, 2004	FPD	30/15
3) *People v. Modoc Boys*	05CECG03696	November 28, 2005	FPD	22/15
4) *People v. OC Bulldogs and Sur*	06CECG02815	August 23, 2006	FSO	40/10
5) *People v. Dog Pound Gangsters*	07GI105	November 29, 2007	FPD	0/0
6) *People v. Varrio East Side Reedley*	09GI106	March 20, 2009	FPD	0/0

Glenn County—0 Gang Injunctions

	Opinion 2006		Estimated True		Projected 2011–2012	
City	**Members**	**Gangs**	**Members**	**Gangs**	**Members**	**Gangs**
Glenn County Sheriff	17	2	17	2	17	2
Total	17	2	17	2	17	2

Humbolt County—0 Gang Injunctions

	Opinion 2006		Estimated True		Projected 2011–2012	
City	**Members**	**Gangs**	**Members**	**Gangs**	**Members**	**Gangs**
Eureka PD	75	4	80	4	80	4
Humbolt Sheriff	55	2	60	2	60	2
Total	130	6	140	6	140	6

Imperial County—0 Gang Injunctions

	Opinion 2006		Estimated True		Projected 2011–2012	
City	**Members**	**Gangs**	**Members**	**Gangs**	**Members**	**Gangs**
Brawley PD	290	2	300	2	333	2
Calexico PD	200	5	200	5	210	6
Calipatria PD	30	1	30	1	33	1
El Centro PD	310	3	320	3	330	3
Holtville PD	20	1	20	1	22	1
Imperial PD	100	2	100	2	110	2
Sheriff/ unincorporated	150	15	150	15	165	16
Bombay Beach	—	—	—	—	—	—
Heber	—	—	—	—	—	—
Niland	—	—	—	—	—	—
Ocotillo	—	—	—	—	—	—

Imperial County—0 Gang Injunctions (Continued)

	Opinion 2006		Estimated True		Projected 2011–2012	
City	Members	Gangs	Members	Gangs	Members	Gangs
Salton City	—	—	—	—	—	—
Seelly	—	—	—	—	—	—
Winterhaven	—	—	—	—	—	—
Westmorland PD	30	1	30	1	33	1
Total	1,130	30	1,150	30	1,236	32

Inyo County—0 Gang Injunctions

	Opinion 2006		Estimated True		Projected 2011–2012	
City	Members	Gangs	Members	Gangs	Members	Gangs
Inyo County Sheriff	0	0	0	0	0	0
Total	0	0	0	0	0	0

Kern County—0 Gang Injunctions

	Opinion 2006		Estimated True		Projected 2011–2012	
City	Members	Gangs	Members	Gangs	Members	Gangs
Arvin PD	75	1	100	1	100	1
Bakersfield PD	3,463	32	4,189	38	4,200	38
Bear Valley PD	10	1	10	1	10	1
Boron	15	1	15	1	17	1
Buttonwillow	18	1	18	1	20	1
China Lake	16	1	16	1	20	1
Delano PD	60	6	64	6	70	6
Frazier Sheriff	10	1	10	1	12	1
Frazier Park	—	—	—	—	—	—
Pine Mountain	—	—	—	—	—	—
Glennvile Sheriff	19	1	22	1	25	1
Woody	—	—	—	—	—	—
Kern Valley Sheriff	36	3	40	3	50	3
Kernville	—	—	—	—	—	—
Wofford Heights	—	—	—	—	—	—
Lake Isabella	—	—	—	—	—	—
Lamont Sheriff	181	2	190	2	200	2
McFarland Sheriff	198	2	200	2	220	2
Mojave Sheriff	10	1	10	1	10	1
Oildale Sheriff	17	1	17	1	20	1

Kern County—0 Gang Injunctions (Continued)

	Opinion 2006		Estimated True		Projected 2011–2012	
City	Members	Gangs	Members	Gangs	Members	Gangs
Ridgecrest PD	13	1	15	1	15	1
Rosamond Sheriff	17	1	17	1	17	1
Shafter PD	59	1	70	1	70	1
Stallion Springs PD	14	1	15	1	20	1
Taft PD	0	0	0	0	0	0
Tehachapi Sheriff	29	1	30	1	35	1
Wasco Sheriff	93	1	95	1	100	1
Total	4,371	62	5,147	66	5,231	66

Kings County—0 Gang Injunctions

	Opinion 2006		Estimated True		Projected 2011–2012	
City	Members	Gangs	Members	Gangs	Members	Gangs
King County Sheriff	50	2	50	2	50	2
Total	50	2	50	2	50	2

Lake County—0 Gang Injunctions

	Opinion 2006		Estimated True		Projected 2011–2012	
City	Members	Gangs	Members	Gangs	Members	Gangs
Lake County Sheriff	0	0	0	0	0	0
Total	0	0	0	0	0	0

Lassen County—0 Gang Injunctions

	Opinion 2006		Estimated True		Projected 2011–2012	
City	Members	Gangs	Members	Gangs	Members	Gangs
Susanville PD	49	2	55	2	60	2
Total	49	2	55	2	60	2

Los Angeles County—74 Filed Gang Injunctions and 6 Pending

	Opinion 2006		Estimated True		Projected 2011–2012	
City	**Members**	**Gangs**	**Members**	**Gangs**	**Members**	**Gangs**
Alhambra PD	580	38	600	80	620	80
Arcadia PD						
Antelope Valley Sheriff	150	3	200	3	210	3
Lancaster	—	—	—	—	—	—
Avalon Sheriff	15	1	15	1	17	1
Catalina Island	—	—	—	—	—	—
Azusa PD	75	1	75	1	80	1
Baldwin Park PD	1,276	2	1,300	2	1,340	2
Bell PD	190	9	230	9	253	9
Bell Gardens PD	420	40	500	40	525	40
Burbank PD	174	8	174	10	180	10
Carson Sheriff	3,560	44	4,500	44	3,900	44
Larson	—	—	—	—	—	—
Lomita	—	—	—	—	—	—
Rancho Dominguez	—	—	—	—	—	—
Unincorp. Gardena	—	—	—	—	—	—
Unincorp. Torrance	—	—	—	—	—	—
Century Sheriff	9,739	61	9,739	61	10,000	61
Firestone	—	—	—	—	—	—
Lynnwood	—	—	—	—	—	—
Unincorp. Compton	—	—	—	—	—	—
Watts	—	—	—	—	—	—
Claremont PD	10	1	10	1	13	1
Compton	6,250	43	6,250	43	6,300	43
Covina PD	250	25	250	25	275	25
Crescenta Sheriff	140	1	140	1	150	1
Flintridge	—	—	—	—	—	—
Altadena	—	—	—	—	—	—
Culver City PD	350	3	350	3	365	3
Downey PD	400	5	400	10	420	10
East LA Sheriff	4,110	29	4,200	29	4,220	29
Cudahy	—	—	—	—	—	—
Commerce	—	—	—	—	—	—
El Monte PD	1,400	6	1,400	6	1,425	6
Gardena PD	150	6	150	6	160	6
Glendale PD	475	3	475	3	500	3
Hawthorne PD	4,850	83	5,000	83	5,000	83
Huntington Park PD	510	16	520	16	540	16
Industry Sheriff	500	18	500	20	525	20
Bassett	—	—	—	—	—	—
La Habra Heights	—	—	—	—	—	—
La Puente	—	—	—	—	—	—
Inglewood PD	7,096	29	9,000	29	9,050	29

Los Angeles County—74 Filed Gang Injunctions and 6 Pending (Continued)

	Opinion 2006		Estimated True		Projected 2011–2012	
City	**Members**	**Gangs**	**Members**	**Gangs**	**Members**	**Gangs**
Irwindale PD	8	1	8	1	10	1
La Verne PD	75	4	75	4	80	4
Lakewood Sheriff	1,050	30	1,050	30	1,070	30
Artesia	—	—	—	—	—	—
Bellflower	—	—	—	—	—	—
Cerritos	—	—	—	—	—	—
Hawaiian Gardens	—	—	—	—	—	—
Paramount	—	—	—	—	—	—
Lennox Sheriff	8,275	37	8,300	37	8,325	37
Gardina	—	—	—	—	—	—
Lawndale	—	—	—	—	—	—
Unincorp. Hawthorne	—	—	—	—	—	—
Unincorp. Inglewood	—	—	—	—	—	—
Lomita Sheriff	350	8	400	8	410	8
Rancho Palos Verdes	—	—	—	—	—	—
Rolling Hills	—	—	—	—	—	—
Long Beach	9,110	53	10,000	66	10,300	66
Los Angeles Police	58,160	407	64,429	407	70,000	420
Lost Hills Sheriff	20	1	50	1	50	1
Agoura Hills	—	—	—	—	—	—
Calabasas	—	—	—	—	—	—
Hidden Hills	—	—	—	—	—	—
Malibu	—	—	—	—	—	—
Westlake Village	—	—	—	—	—	—
Maywood PD	3,550	18	3,600	18	3,625	18
Monrovia PD	200	1	200	1	210	1
Montebello PD	250	5	350	5	370	5
Monterey Park PD	250	9	250	9	260	9
Norwalk Sheriff	4,112	29	4,300	29	4,350	29
La Miranda	—	—	—	—	—	—
Unincorp. Whittier	—	—	—	—	—	—
Palmdale Sheriff	635	31	650	31	675	31
Pasadena PD	1,120	24	1,150	24	1,170	24
Pico Rivera Sheriff	1,225	28	1,808	28	1,810	28
Pomona PD	3,050	25	3,100	25	3,100	25
Redondo Beach PD	100	1	100	1	110	1
San Fernando PD	861	1	861	1	900	1
San Gabriel PD	300	6	300	6	315	6
Santa Clarita Sheriff	1,320	25	1,320	25	1,350	25
Santa Monica PD	250	10	250	10	260	10
Signal Hill PD	15	2	15	2	17	2

Los Angeles County—74 Filed Gang Injunctions and 6 Pending (Continued)

	Opinion 2006		Estimated True		Projected 2011–2012	
City	Members	Gangs	Members	Gangs	Members	Gangs
South Gate PD	510	24	510	24	520	24
South Pasadena PD	200	3	200	3	220	3
Temple Sheriff	2,556	23	2,556	23	2,600	23
Bradbury	—	—	—	—	—	—
Duarte	—	—	—	—	—	—
Rosemeade	—	—	—	—	—	—
South El Monte	—	—	—	—	—	—
Temple City	—	—	—	—	—	—
Torrance PD	60	1	60	1	63	1
Walnut Sheriff	2,510	15	2,510	15	2,520	15
Diamond Bar	—	—	—	—	—	—
Rowland Height	—	—	—	—	—	—
San Dimas	—	—	—	—	—	—
West Covina PD	2,020	9	2,050	9	2,075	9
West Hollywood	30	1	30	1	32	1
Whittier PD	350	5	350	5	360	5
Total	145,192	1,337	154,860	1,367	163,245	1,369

1) *People v. Dogtown Primera Flats, 62nd St.*	C418875	July 22, 1982	LAPD	72/25
2) *People v. Playboy Gangster Crips*	WEC118860	October 26, 1987	LAPD	48/15
3) *Fairview Properties v. Westside Playboys*	EC009117	June 17, 1992	BPD	43/8
4) *People v. Barrio Elmwood Rifa*	EC 010205	October 7, 1992	BPD	117/5
5) *People v. Blythe St. Gang*	LC020525	February 22, 1993	LAPD	319/119
6) *City of Norwalk v. Orange St. Locos*	VC016746	July 21, 1994	LASO	22/15
7) *City of Long Beach v. Westside Longos*	NC17601	October 6, 1995	LBPD	57/5
8) *City of Pasadena v. Denver Lanes*	GC015651	October 25, 1995	PPD	65/5
9) *City of Redondo Beach v. NSR 13*	YC026580	April 30, 1996	RPD	28/20
10) *City of Pasadena v. Villa and Krazy Boys*	GC017109	June 13, 1996	PPD	26/5
11) *People v. Lennox-13*	YC027006	July 30, 1996	LASO	37/5
12) *City of Commerce v. Chopper-12*	BC155927	August 20, 1996	LASO	39/5
13) *City of Inglewood v. Crenshaw Mafia*	YC028318	December 17, 1996	LASO	82/14
14) *People v. 18th St. Gang* (Alsace clique)	BC167915	March 21, 1997	LAPD	58/28
15) *People v. Brown Nation*	VC024170	March 27, 1997	LAPD	16/00
16) *City of Long Beach v. Westcoast Crips*	NC021240	May 5, 1997	LBPD	66/5
17) *People v. 18th St. Gang* (Pico/Union clique)	BC175684	August 1, 1997	LAPD	50/00
18) *People v. Mara Salvatrucha*	BC187039	March 4, 1998	LAPD	40/11
19) *People v. 18th St. Gang* (Shatto Park clique)	BC190334	May 1, 1998	LAPD	140/40
20) *People v. Harpy's Gang*	BC192678	July 16, 1998	LAPD	91/31
21) *City of Compton v. Tortilla Flats Gang*	TC011598	August 25, 1998	LASO	68/12
22) *People v. Langdon Street Gang*	LC048292	March 26, 1999	LAPD	131/27
23) *People v. Culver City Boys*	SC056980	April 23, 1999	LAPD	186/17
24) *People v. Venice Shoreline Crips*	SC057282	May 21, 1999	LAPD	111/22
25) *People v. Harbor City/HC Crips*	NC026769	November 12, 1999	LAPD	97/57
26) *People v. Venice 13*	SC060375	February 4, 2000	LAPD	77/13
27) *People v. Pacoima Project Boys*	PC027254	March 20, 2001	LAPD	145/98
28) *People v. East and Westside Wilmas*	NC030080	May 23, 2001	LAPD	260/78
29) *People v. Eastside Longos*	NC030660	August 31, 2001	LBPD	60/15
30) *People v. Canoga Park Alabama*	BC267153	January 29, 2002	LAPD	131/63
31) *People v. 18th Street* (Pico Union 2)	BC272030	April 16, 2002	LAPD	105/69
32) *People v. Krazy Ass Mexicans*	BC282629	October 3, 2002	LAPD	70/49
33) *People v. Avenues Gang*	BC287137	December 17, 2002	LAPD	197/51

Los Angeles County—74 Filed Gang Injunctions and 6 Pending (Continued)

34) *People v. Insane Crip Gang*	NC033946	April 16, 2003	LBPD	26/10
35) *People v. Rolling Sixty Crips*	BC298846	July 8, 2003	LAPD	69/18
36) *People v. Bounty Hunter Bloods*	BC301433	August 26, 2003	LAPD	113/51
37) *People v. 18th Street Hollywood*	BC305434	November 4, 2003	LAPD	127/10
38) *People v. Mara Salvatrucha Hollywood*	BC311766	March 9, 2004	LAPD	95/36
39) *People v. Westside Longos*	NC035222	January 12, 2004	LBPD	84/15
40) *People v. 18th Street* (Wilshire clique)	BC313309	April 6, 2004	LAPD	15/12
41) *People v. 38th Street Newton*	BC319166	July 28, 2004	LAPD	28/12
42) *People v. Varrio Nueva Estrada Hollenbeck*	BC319981	August 12, 2004	LAPD	22/10
43) *People v. Southside Montebello*	BC324344	November 10, 2004	MPD	28/8
44) *People v. 42nd St. Gangster Crips*	BC326016	December 16, 2004	LAPD	20/8
45) *People v. Grape Street Crips*	BC330087	March 10, 2005	LAPD	240/168
46) *People v. Hoover Crips*	BC330272	March 15, 2005	LAPD	74/5
47) *People v. 18th Street*	BC332713	May 2, 2005	LAPD	31/5
48) *People v. Big Hazard*	BC335749	June 28, 2005	LAPD	120/5
49) *People v. Hoover Crips Gang*	BC341872	October 24, 2005	LAPD	28/20
50) *People v. Olive Street Pomona*	KC047752	February 1, 2006	PPD	64/5
51) *People v. Geer and Schoolyard Crips*	BC349468	March 23, 2006	LAPD	77/13
52) *People v. Playboys*	BC351990	May 8, 2006	LAPD	20/12
53) *People v. Black P Stones*	BC352951	May 25, 2006	LAPD	55/10
54) *People v. White Fence*	BC353596	June 8, 2006	LAPD	30/20
55) *People v. Clover, Eastlake and Lincoln Hts.*	BC358881	September 20, 2006	LAPD	120/10
56) *People v. Dogtown*	BC359945	October 6, 2006	LAPD	120/10
57) *People v. Highland Park*	BC359944	October 6, 2006	LAPD	20/10
58) *People v. Junior Mafia Gang*	VC047440	October 6, 2006	BGPD	20/10
59) *People v. Whittier Varrio Locos*	BC363464	December 15, 2006	WPD	46/5
60) *People v. Hawaiian Gardens*	BC375573	August 13, 2007	LASO	30/4
61) *People v. Rolling 40, 46 TD's, 46 NHC*	BC380229	November 5, 2007	LAPD	0/0
62) *People v. 5th and Hill Gang*	BC380877	November 16, 2007	LAPD	0/0
63) *People v. 204th and ES Torrance*	BC381942	December 7, 2007	LAPD	0/0
64) *People v. Mob Piru*	TC021658	January 24, 2008	CPD	0/0
65) *People v. San Fer Gang*	BC388726	April 17, 2008	LAPD	0/0
66) *People v. AOC, BM, F13, PB, BV, OBZ*	BC397522	September 10, 2008	LAPD	0/0
67) *People v. Eastside Pain*	BC399741	October 10, 2008	LAPD	0/0
68) *People v. Temple Street*	BC401190	November 3, 2008	LAPD	0/0
69) *People v. Toonerville*	BC401928	November 14, 2008	LAPD	0/0
70) *People v. Florencia 13*	BC403340	December 8, 2008	LAPD	0/0
71) *People v. Barrio Van Nuys*	BC413147	May 14, 2009	LAPD	0/0
72) *People v. Swans, F-13, 7-Trey, Main St.*	BC415694	June 12, 2009	LAPD	0/0
73) *People v. Monrovia Nuevo Varrio/Duroc*	BC423490	October 9, 2009	MPD	0/0
74) *People v. Central City (Skid Row) and Grape*	BC435316	April 7, 2010	LAPD	0/0
75) *People v. Metro Transit Assassins*	BC440034	June 21, 2010	LAPD	0/0

Madera County—0 Gang Injunctions

	Opinion 2006		Estimated True		Projected 2011–2012	
City	Members	Gangs	Members	Gangs	Members	Gangs
Chowchilla PD						
Madera PD	548	20	600	20	650	20
Madera Sheriff	620	23	640	23	700	23
Total	1,168	43	1,240	43	1,350	43

Marin County—0 Gang Injunctions

	Opinion 2006		Estimated True		Projected 2011–2012	
City	Members	Gangs	Members	Gangs	Members	Gangs
Novato PD	45	4	45	4	45	4
San Rafael PD	200	2	200	2	200	2
Total	245	6	245	6	245	6

Mariposa County—0 Gang Injunctions

	Opinion 2006		Estimated True		Projected 2011–2012	
City	Members	Gangs	Members	Gangs	Members	Gangs
Mariposa Sheriff	0	0	0	0	0	0
Total	0	0	0	0	0	0

Mendocino County—0 Gang Injunctions

	Opinion 2006		Estimated True		Projected 2011–2012	
City	Members	Gangs	Members	Gangs	Members	Gangs
Mendocino Sheriff	0	0	0	0	0	0
Total	0	0	0	0	0	0

Merced County—0 Gang Injunctions

	Opinion 2006		Estimated True		Projected 2011–2012	
City	Members	Gangs	Members	Gangs	Members	Gangs
Atwater PD	325	7	381	7	400	7
Dos Palos PD	25	1	25	1	25	1
Gustine PD						
Livingston PD	47	1	47	1	47	1
Los Banos PD	148	8	160	8	170	8
Merced PD	456	10	460	10	460	10
Merced Sheriff	243	4	245	4	250	4
Winton	13	1	13	1	15	1
Total	1,257	32	1,331	32	1,367	32

Modoc County—0 Gang Injunctions

	Opinion 2006		Estimated True		Projected 2011–2012	
City	Members	Gangs	Members	Gangs	Members	Gangs
Modoc Sheriff	0	0	0	0	0	0
Total	0	0	0	0	0	0

Mono County—0 Gang Injunctions

	Opinion 2006		Estimated True		Projected 2011–2012	
City	Members	Gangs	Members	Gangs	Members	Gangs
Mono County Sheriff	0	0	0	0	0	0
Mammoth Lakes PD	0	0	0	0	0	0
Total	0	0	0	0	0	0

Monterey County—1 Gang Injunction

	Opinion 2006		Estimated True		Projected 2011–2012	
City	Members	Gangs	Members	Gangs	Members	Gangs
Monterey Sheriff	1,250	6	1,250	6	1,250	6
Salinas PD	3,173	31	3,173	31	3,173	31
Total	4,423	37	4,423	37	4,423	37

1) *People v. Vagos Sureno Gang* 115095 July 30, 1998 SPD 14/5

Napa County—0 Gang Injunctions

	Opinion 2006		Estimated True		Projected 2011–2012	
City	Members	Gangs	Members	Gangs	Members	Gangs
Callistoga PD	17	2	17	2	17	2
Napa PD						
Napa County Sheriff	200	5	250	5	250	5
Total	217	7	267	7	267	7

Nevada County—0 Gang Injunctions

	Opinion 2006		Estimated True		Projected 2011–2012	
City	Members	Gangs	Members	Gangs	Members	Gangs
Nevada County Sheriff	0	0	0	0	0	0
Total	0	0	0	0	0	0

Orange County—8 Gang Injunctions and 1 Attempt

	Opinion 2006		Estimated True		Projected 2011–2012	
City	Members	Gangs	Members	Gangs	Members	Gangs
Anaheim PD	4,894	63	5,053	64	5,153	65
Brea PD	**500**	**3**	**550**	**4**	**575**	**4**
Yorba Linda	—	—	—	—	—	—
Buena Park PD	705	3	1,000	3	1,050	3
Costa Mesa PD	150	5	150	5	160	5
Cypress PD	50	1	50	1	52	1
Fountain Valley PD	34	1	34	1	36	1
Fullerton PD	915	4	1,100	4	1,110	4
Garden Grove PD	2,467	74	2,500	80	2,550	82
Huntington Beach PD	315	2	350	2	355	2
Irvine PD	300	20	300	20	310	20
La Habra PD	700	5	700	5	720	5
Los Alamitos PD	20	1	20	1	25	1
Midway City Sheriff	72	1	72	1	75	1
Mission Viejo Sheriff	56	3	56	3	60	3
Newport Beach	10	1	10	1	12	1
Orange PD	400	20	400	20	420	20
Orange County Sheriff	1,735	16	1,800	18	1,900	20
All other cities	—	—	—	—	—	—
Placentia PD	525	3	525	3	535	3
San Clemente Sheriff	252	4	252	4	265	4
San Juan Capistrano	251	1	251	1	275	1
Santa Ana PD	6,400	82	7,000	82	7,200	140

Orange County—8 Gang Injunctions and 1 Attempt (Continued)

	Opinion 2006		Estimated True		Projected 2011–2012	
City	Members	Gangs	Members	Gangs	Members	Gangs
Tustin PD	750	13	750	15	760	15
Westminster PD	2,995	37	3,200	37	3,300	40
Total	24,496	363	26,223	375	26,908	385

1) *People v. West Trece Gang*	713223	June 30, 1993	WPD	59/00
2) *People v. Santa Nita* (Santa Ana)	06CC06903	July 7, 2006	SAPD	301/50
3) *People v. Boys from the Hood* (Anaheim)	06CC10916	October 16, 2006	APD	88/20
4) *People v. Varrio Chico* (San Clemente)	07CC19690	October 11, 2007		
5) *People v. Varrio Viejo* (San Juan Capistrano)	07CC19689	October 11, 2007		
6) *People v. Orange County Criminals*	08-00107172	June 4, 2008		
7) Orange Varrio Cypress gang (Orange)	09-00118739	May 14, 2009		
8) Hard Times gang (Garden Grove)	09-00325327	December 3, 2009		
9) *People v. Jeffrey Street Gang* (Anaheim)	10-00363220	April 15, 2010		

Placer County—0 Gang Injunctions

	Opinion 2006		Estimated True		Projected 2011–2012	
City	Members	Gangs	Members	Gangs	Members	Gangs
Placer County Sheriff	62	8	70	8	100	8
Total	62	8	70	8	100	8

The following areas reported no gangs, no gang members, and no gang injunctions in their jurisdictions: Auburn PD, Colfax, Dollar Point, Forest Hill, Granite Bay, Kings Beach, Lincoln PD, Loomis Town, Meadow Vista, North Auburn, Rocklin PD, Roseville PD, Sunnyside, and Tahoe Vista.

Plumas County—0 Gang Injunctions

	Opinion 2006		Estimated True		Projected 2011–2012	
City	Members	Gangs	Members	Gangs	Members	Gangs
Plumas County Sheriff	0	0	0	0	0	0
Total	0	0	0	0	0	0

Riverside County—3 Gang Injunctions

	Opinion 2006		Estimated True		Projected 2011–2012	
City	Members	Gangs	Members	Gangs	Members	Gangs
Banning PD	120	7	120	7	125	7
Beaumont PD	30	1	30	1	32	1
Blythe PD	110	2	120	2	130	2
Cathederal City PD	91	3	100	3	105	3
Coachella	276	16	400	7	400	7
Corona PD	322	13	322	13	322	13
Desert Hot Springs PD	60	2	60	2	65	2
Hemet PD	61	3	61	3	68	3
Aguanga	—	—	—	—	—	—
Indio PD	361	8	500	10	500	10
100 Palms	—	—	—	—	—	—
Jurupa Valley	181	5	181	5	190	5
Glen Avon	—	—	—	—	—	—
Mira Loma	—	—	—	—	—	—
Rubidoux	—	—	—	—	—	—
Sunnyslope	—	—	—	—	—	—
Lake Elsinore Sheriff	174	5	200	5	200	5
La Quinta Sheriff	36	2	36	2	40	2
Moreno Valley Sheriff	368	7	400	7	405	7
Meade Valley	—	—	—	—	—	—
Murrieta PD	20	2	20	2	22	2
Norco Sheriff	89	2	100	2	105	2
Palm Springs PD	150	2	150	2	160	2
Perris Sheriff	325	7	330	7	335	7
Riverside PD	2,620	86	2,800	86	2,850	88
San Jacinto	102	1	102	1	105	1
Temecula Sheriff	61	3	61	3	65	3
Total	5,557	177	6,088	179	6,213	181

1) *People v. Eastside Riva* 112/3 RIC478810 August 22, 2007 RPD
2) *People v. Barrio Dream Home* INC077903 July 10, 2008
3) *West Drive Locos and True Crime Boys* March 27, 2009

The following areas reported no gangs, no gang members, and no gang injunctions in their jurisdictions: Canyon Lake, Indian Wells, Palm Desert, and Rancho Mirage. Riverside has obtained one gang injunction.

Sacramento County—1 Gang Injunction

	Opinion 2006		Estimated True		Projected 2011–2012	
City	**Members**	**Gangs**	**Members**	**Gangs**	**Members**	**Gangs**
Sacramento Sheriff	3,423	107	3,500	107	3,423	107
Sacramento PD	500	10	500	10	500	10
Total	3,923	117	3,923	117	3,923	117

1) *People v. G-Mobb* 04AS02821 July 13, 2004 SPD 6/5

San Benito County—0 Gang Injunctions

	Opinion 2006		Estimated True		Projected 2011–2012	
City	**Members**	**Gangs**	**Members**	**Gangs**	**Members**	**Gangs**
San Benito Sheriff	0	0	0	0	0	0
Total	0	0	0	0	0	0

San Bernardino County—10 Filed Gang Injunctions and 1 Attempt

	Opinion 2006		Estimated True		Projected 2011–2012	
City	**Members**	**Gangs**	**Members**	**Gangs**	**Members**	**Gangs**
Adelanto	5	1	5	1	5	1
Apple Valley Sheriff	250	20	250	20	250	20
Barstow PD	500	4	500	4	500	4
Big Bear Lake Sheriff	2	1	2	1	2	1
Central Sheriff Station	2,853	14	2,900	14	2,900	14
Grand Terrace	—	—	—	—	—	—
Loma Linda	—	—	—	—	—	—
Unincorp. Colton	—	—	—	—	—	—
Chino PD	1,110	10	1,150	10	1,150	10
Chino Hills	1,975	13	1,975	13	1,975	13
Colton PD	980	9	1,000	9	1,000	9
Fontana PD	861	16	900	16	900	16

San Bernardino County—10 Filed Gang Injunctions and 1 Attempt (Continued)

	Opinion 2006		Estimated True		Projected 2011–2012	
City	Members	Gangs	Members	Gangs	Members	Gangs
Fontana Sheriff	1,179	17	1,200	17	1,200	17
Bloomington	—	—	—	—	—	—
Rancho Cucamonga	—	—	—	—	—	—
Hesperia Sheriff	100	5	100	5	100	5
Highland Sheriff	183	10	200	10	200	10
Montclair	400	8	400	8	400	8
Needles	40	2	40	2	40	2
Ontario	3,209	20	3,409	20	3,409	20
Redlands PD	470	2	470	2	470	2
Rialto PD						
San Bernardino PD	3,057	83	3,057	83	3,057	83
Twenty Nine Palms	116	1	200	2	200	2
Upland PD	2,036	10	2,036	10	2,036	10
Victor Valley Sheriff	100	10	100	10	100	10
Wrightwood	—	—	—	—	—	—
Unincorp. Victorville	—	—	—	—	—	—
Victorville Sheriff	300	15	300	15	300	15
Yucaipa Sheriff	195	3	195	3	195	3
Yuca Valley	25	1	25	1	25	1
Total	19,996	265	20,282	265	20,282	265

1) *People v. Fontana Headhunters*	SCVSS30441	June 20, 1996	FPD	39/00
2) *People v. 7th Street Gang*	SCVSS42552	October 24, 1997	SBPD	47/20
3) *People v. Sur Crazy Ones*	SCVSS58315	June 24, 1999	SBPD	12/10
4) *People v. Verdugo Flats Gang*	SCVSS092975	March 10, 2003	SBPD	16/25
5) *People v. Delman Heights Bloods*	SCVSS107068	October 9, 2003	SBPD	12/10
6) *People v. Project Crips*	SCVSS109373	November 3, 2003	SBPD	12/10
7) *People v. 5 Time Hometown Crips*	SCVSS080319	January 13, 2003	SBPD	29/5
8) *People v. California Garden Crips*	SCVSS119636	November 23, 2004	SBPD	12/5
9) *People v. East Side Victoria*	VCVVS042664	August 2, 2006	SBSO	137/20
10) *People v. Southside Rialto*	CIVSS808850	July 1, 2008		
11) *People v. Colton City Crips*	CIVSS811223	August 18, 2008		
12) Adelanto's Brown Pride Gang	CIVVS908103	December 17, 2009		

Hustla Squad Clicc, February 6, 2009

San Diego County—22 Filed Gang Injunctions and 1 Pending

City	Opinion 2006 Members	Opinion 2006 Gangs	Estimated True Members	Estimated True Gangs	Projected 2011–2012 Members	Projected 2011–2012 Gangs
Carlsbad PD	73	1	85	1	90	1
Chula Vista PD	490	3	766	6	770	8
Del Mar/Encinitas Sheriff	85	1	85	1	90	1
El Cajon PD	165	7	400	7	410	8
Escondido PD	512	6	600	6	640	6
Escondido Sheriff	157	2	160	2	160	2
Fallbrook Sheriff	150	1	190	2	195	2
Imperial Beach Sheriff	235	8	235	8	235	8
Lakeside Sheriff	25	2	50	2	50	2
Lemon Grove Sheriff	275	2	300	2	300	2
Leucadia Sheriff	15	1	15	1	17	1
National City PD	615	7	700	7	720	7
Oceanside PD	1,650	13	1,700	13	1,700	13
Poway Sheriff	65	1	70	2	70	2
San Diego PD	5,290	72	6,300	72	7,000	72
San Marcos Sheriff	368	2	370	2	375	2
Santee Sheriff	9	1	9	1	10	1
Solana Beach Sheriff	35	1	35	1	38	1
Spring Valley Sheriff	283	4	300	6	320	6
Vista Sheriff	395	1	495	2	510	3
Total	10,892	137	12,865	140	13,700	143

1) *People v. Varrio Posole Locos*	N76652	November 26, 1997	OPD	27/14
2) *People v. Varrio San Marcos*	N078777	August 3, 1998	SDSO	26/11
3) *City of San Diego v. Lincoln Park Bloods*	725795	November 19, 1998	SDPD	23/8
Update case	725795	March 2004	SDPD	21/5
4) *City of National City v. OTNC Gang*	SB007194	December 15, 1998	NCPD	66/32
5) *People v. Varrio Mesa Locos*	N82223	August 20, 1999	OPD	24/7
6) *People v. Linda Vista 13 Gang*	GIC745162	Mar. 24, 2000	SDPD	24/7
7) *People v. Diablos Gang*	GIN013906	January 13, 2001	EPD	21/8
8) *People v. Westside Gang*	GIN013907	January 13, 2001	EPD	22/13
9) *People v. Nestor Gang*	GIS9068	February 27, 2002	SDPD	11/5
10) *People v. Logan Red Steps*	GIC798708	November 1, 2002	SDPD	36/11
11) *People v. Center Street Gang*	GIN032007	August 22, 2003	OPD	17/7
12) *People v. Varrio Posole Locos 2*	GIN033214	October 17, 2003	OPD	25/17
13) *People v. East Side Piru/Skyline*	GIC827117	April 16, 2004	SDPD	86/16
14) *People v. Vista Homeboys*	GIN044867	May 27, 2005	SDSO	89/7
15) *People v. Old Town National City*	GIS22336	October 7, 2005	NCPD	104/13
16) *City of San Diego v. West Coast Crips*	GIC864852	April 25, 2006	SDPD	50/2
17) *People v. Diablos Gang 2*	GIN057995	December 26, 2006	EPD	50/10
18) *People v. Westside Gang 2*	GIN057994	December 26, 2006	EPD	58/10
19) *People v. Varrio San Marcos*	370757284	October 19, 2007	SDSO	93/0
20) *People v. Diablos 3*	370961923	March 22, 2010	EPD	
21) *People v. Westside 3*	370961924	May 22, 2010	EPD	
22) *People v. Center Street 2*	371051319	May 24, 2010	OPD	

San Francisco County—4 Gang Injunctions

	Opinion 2006		Estimated True		Projected 2011–2012	
City	**Members**	**Gangs**	**Members**	**Gangs**	**Members**	**Gangs**
San Francisco PD	1,200	18	1,300	18	1,300	18
Total	1,200	18	1,300	18	1,300	18

1) *People v. Oakdale Mob*	CGC06456517	September 27, 2006	SFPD	22/10
2) *People v. Nortenos*	CGC-07-464492	June 21, 2007	SFPD	30/5
3) *People v. Chopper City, Knock Out Posse, and Eddy Rock*	CGC-07-464493	June 21, 2007	SFPD	65/5

4) *People v. Down Below Gangsters and Towerside Gang* (San Francisco case CG-C-10-502262) August 2010

San Joaquin County—1 Gang Injunction

	Opinion 2006		Estimated True		Projected 2011–2012	
City	**Members**	**Gangs**	**Members**	**Gangs**	**Members**	**Gangs**
Eacalon PD						
Lodi PD	400	12	450	12	500	12
Manteca PD	105	4	126	4	130	4
Ripon PD	0	0	0	0	0	0
San Joaquin Sheriff	481	25	552	25	600	25
Stockton PD	2,739	85	3,000	85	3,200	85
Tracy PD	111	5	114	5	120	5
Total	3,886	131	4,242	131	4,350	131

1) *People v. Original Bloods*	CV 05505	July 28, 1998	SPD	10/5

San Luis Obispo County—0 Gang Injunctions

	Opinion 2006		Estimated True		Projected 2011–2012	
City	**Members**	**Gangs**	**Members**	**Gangs**	**Members**	**Gangs**
Arroyo Grande PD	50	1	55	1	55	1
Atascadero PD	26	1	30	1	30	1
Avila Beach	5	1	10	1	10	1
California Valley	7	1	10	1	10	1
Cambria	5	1	5	1	5	1
Cayucos	10	1	10	1	10	1
Creston	5	1	8	1	8	1
Grover Beach PD	48	1	50	1	50	1
Los Osos Sheriff	27	1	30	1	30	1
Morro Bay PD	24	1	25	1	25	1

San Luis Obispo County—0 Gang Injunctions (Continued)

City	Opinion 2006		Estimated True		Projected 2011–2012	
	Members	Gangs	Members	Gangs	Members	Gangs
Nipomo Sheriff	155	1	160	1	160	1
Oceano Sheriff	149	1	150	1	155	1
Paso Robles PD	164	1	170	1	175	1
Pismo Beach PD	7	1	10	1	15	1
San Luis Obispo PD	29	1	30	2	30	2
San Miguel Sheriff	18	1	20	1	20	1
San Simeon	10	1	10	1	15	1
Santa Margarita	7	1	10	1	10	1
Shadon Sheriff	7	1	10	1	10	1
Templeton Sheriff	26	1	30	1	30	1
Total	779	20	833	21	853	21

San Mateo County—0 Gang Injunctions

City	Opinion 2006		Estimated True		Projected 2011–2012	
	Members	Gangs	Members	Gangs	Members	Gangs
Broadmoor PD	20	2	20	2	20	2
Daly City PD	140	4	140	4	140	4
East Palo Alto	564	14	565	19	565	19
Menlo Park PD	155	5	155	5	155	5
Pacifica PD	40	2	40	2	40	2
Redwood City PD	240	10	240	10	240	10
San Bruno PD	60	3	60	3	60	3
San Mateo PD	150	4	150	4	150	4
San Mateo Sheriff	0	0	0	0	0	0
South San Francisco PD	100	4	100	4	100	4
Total	1,469	48	1,470	53	1,470	53

Santa Barbara County—1 Gang Injunction

City	Opinion 2006		Estimated True		Projected 2011–2012	
	Members	Gangs	Members	Gangs	Members	Gangs
Carpinteria	50	1	55	1	55	1
Goleta Sheriff	260	3	320	3	330	3
Guadalupe PD	25	1	50	1	50	1
Lompoc PD	424	4	450	4	500	5
Santa Barbara City	426	15	450	15	500	15

Santa Barbara County—1 Gang Injunction (Continued)

	Opinion 2006		Estimated True		Projected 2011–2012	
City	Members	Gangs	Members	Gangs	Members	Gangs
Santa Barbara Sheriff	310	10	320	10	320	10
Unincorp. Lompoc	—	—	—	—	—	—
All other unincorp.	—	—	—	—	—	—
Santa Maria PD	1,640	7	1,650	7	1,660	7
Santa Maria Sheriff	25	1	25	1	25	1
Total	3,160	42	3,320	42	3,440	43

1) *People v. Varrio's Lampara's Primera and Southside* 1148758 July 1, 2005 LPD 10/5

Santa Clara County—5 Gang Injunctions

	Opinion 2006		Estimated True		Projected 2011–2012	
City	Members	Gangs	Members	Gangs	Members	Gangs
Gilroy PD	400	8	400	8	400	8
San Jose PD	4,202	310	4,202	310	4,202	310
Total	4,602	318	4,602	318	4,602	318

1) *People v. Varrio Sureno Treces/Locos*	CV729322	February 26, 1993	SJPD	38/34
2) *People v. Varrio Mexicanos Locos*	CV739089	March 16, 1994	SJPD	24/10
3) *People v. VHS, WSM, SSP and ESC Gangs*	CV775225	July 10, 1998	SJPD	47/25
4) *People v. SVN* (South Vietnam)	CV791443	July 28, 2000	SJPD	6/3
5) *People v. Varrio Sureno Treces*	CV811217	September 19, 2002	SJPD	29/10

Santa Cruz County—0 Gang Injunctions

	Opinion 2006		Estimated True		Projected 2011–2012	
City	Members	Gangs	Members	Gangs	Members	Gangs
Santa Cruz PD	200	9	200	9	200	9
Total	200	9	200	9	200	9

Shasta County—0 Gang Injunctions

	Opinion 2006		Estimated True		Projected 2011–2012	
City	Members	Gangs	Members	Gangs	Members	Gangs
Redding PD	81	7	81	7	81	7
Shasta County Sheriff	28	7	28	7	18	7
Total	109	14	109	14	109	14

Sierra County—0 Gang Injunctions

	Opinion 2006		Estimated True		Projected 2011–2012	
City	Members	Gangs	Members	Gangs	Members	Gangs
Sierra County Sheriff	0	0	0	0	0	0
Total	0	0	0	0	0	0

Siskiyou County—0 Gang Injunctions

	Opinion 2006		Estimated True		Projected 2011–2012	
City	Members	Gangs	Members	Gangs	Members	Gangs
Siskiyou Sheriff	100	15	100	15	100	15
Total	100	15	100	15	100	15

Solano County—1 Gang Injunction

	Opinion 2006		Estimated True		Projected 2011–2012	
City	Members	Gangs	Members	Gangs	Members	Gangs
Vacaville PD	180	7	190	7	200	7
Vallejo PD	250	20	250	25	250	25
Total	430	27	440	32	450	32

Fairfield Norteños, Solano County District Attorney, July 1, 2010

Sonoma County—0 Gang Injunction

	Opinion 2006		Estimated True		Projected 2011–2012	
City	Members	Gangs	Members	Gangs	Members	Gangs
Petaluma PD	50	2	50	2	50	2
Santa Rosa PD	100	6	200	6	200	6
Sonoma Sheriff	2,350	10	2,350	10	2,350	10
Total	2,500	18	2,500	18	2,500	18

Stanislaus County—1 Gang Injunction

	Opinion 2006		Estimated True		Projected 2011–2012	
City	Members	Gangs	Members	Gangs	Members	Gangs
Modesto PD	6	1	7	1	7	1
Stanislaus Sheriff	200	4	200	4	200	4
Total	206	5	207	5	207	5

People V. Deep South Side Norteños, case 642033 (South Modesto)

Sutter County—0 Gang Injunctions

	Opinion 2006		Estimated True		Projected 2011–2012	
City	Members	Gangs	Members	Gangs	Members	Gangs
Sutter County Sheriff	0	0	0	0	0	0
Total	0	0	0	0	0	0

Tehama County—0 Gang Injunctions

	Opinion 2006		Estimated True		Projected 2011–2012	
City	Members	Gangs	Members	Gangs	Members	Gangs
Tehama County Sheriff	150	5	150	5	150	5
Total	150	5	150	5	150	5

Trinity County—0 Gang Injunctions

	Opinion 2006		Estimated True		Projected 2011–2012	
City	Members	Gangs	Members	Gangs	Members	Gangs
Trinity County Sheriff	0	0	0	0	0	0
Total	0	0	0	0	0	0

Tulare County—0 Gang Injunctions

City	Opinion 2006		Estimated True		Projected 2011–2012	
	Members	Gangs	Members	Gangs	Members	Gangs
Dinuba PD	24	1	25	1	30	1
Earlimart	50	1	50	1	50	1
Farmersville PD	53	1	55	1	60	1
Lindsay PD	101	2	108	2	110	2
Orosi	93	2	93	2	93	2
Porterville PD	129	3	134	3	140	3
Strathmore	50	1	50	1	50	1
Tulare PD	350	18	500	20	500	20
Tulare Sheriff	0	0	0	0	0	0
Visalia PD	300	10	300	10	300	10
Woodlake PD	50	1	50	1	50	1
Total	1,200	40	1,365	42	1,383	42

Tuolumne County—0 Gang Injunctions

City	Opinion 2006		Estimated True		Projected 2011–2012	
	Members	Gangs	Members	Gangs	Members	Gangs
Tuolumne Sheriff	0	0	0	0	0	0
Total	0	0	0	0	0	0

Ventura County—2 Filed Gang Injunctions and 1 Pending

City	Opinion 2006		Estimated True		Projected 2011–2012	
	Members	Gangs	Members	Gangs	Members	Gangs
Camarillo	60	2	60	2	60	2
Fillmore	45	2	50	2	55	2
Moorpark Sheriff	140	1	140	1	140	1
Thousand Oaks Sheriff	160	5	170	5	180	5
Ojai Sheriff	50	2	50	2	50	2
Oxnard PD	3,300	12	3,350	12	3,375	12
Port Hueneme PD	20	1	20	1	20	1
Santa Clara Sheriff	120	1	130	1	130	1
Santa Paula PD	300	5	300	5	350	6
Simi Valley PD	70	2	80	2	80	2
Ventura PD	800	9	800	9	800	9
West Ventura County	280	4	280	4	300	4
Total	5,345	46	5,430	46	5,540	47

Ventura County—2 Filed Gang Injunctions and 1 Pending (Continued)

1) *People v. Oxnard Colonia Chiques*	CIV226032	April 2, 2004	OPD	134/150
2) *People v. Oxnard Southside Chiques*	CIV242491	July 27, 2006	OPD	143/112
3) *People v. Port Hueneme Gang*	Pending			

Yolo County—1 Gang Injunction (Dismissed)

	Opinion 2006		Estimated True		Projected 2011–2012	
City	**Members**	**Gangs**	**Members**	**Gangs**	**Members**	**Gangs**
West Sacramento PD	800	8	800	8	800	8
Winters PD	100	2	100	2	100	2
Woodland PD	150	5	150	5	150	5
Total	1,050	13	1,050	13	1,050	13

1) *People v. Broderick Boys*	CV04-2085	December 30, 2004	WSPD	85/5

Yuba County—0 Gang Injunctions

	Opinion 2006		Estimated True		Projected 2011–2012	
City	**Members**	**Gangs**	**Members**	**Gangs**	**Members**	**Gangs**
Marysville PD	300	20	300	20	300	20
Yuba County Sheriff						
Total	300	20	300	20	300	20

SYNOPSIS OF COUNTY ANALYSIS

By making personal contact with each law enforcement jurisdiction in the State of California, it is believed the list of gangs, gang members, and gang injunctions is complete at the time of this research. However, the survey relied on each jurisdiction providing information about each case to verify the presence of an injunction and details about the injunction, as no central database exists that tracks gang injunctions. This list may not be all-inclusive and the results should not be viewed with caution as the police could have missed or not included injunctions in the legal process that have not been filed.

Santa Barbara County—1 Gang Injunction

1) *People v. Varrio's Lampara's Primera and Southside*	1148758	July 1, 2005	LPD	10/5

April 22, 2010, **Santa Barbara** City Police Chief Cam Sanchez confirmed

Santa Clara County—5 Gang Injunctions

1) *People v. Varrio Sureno Treces/Locos*	CV729322	February 26, 1993	SJPD	38/34
2) *People v. Varrio Mexicanos Locos*	CV739089	March 16, 1994	SJPD	24/10
3) *People v. VHS, WSM, SSP and ESC Gangs*	CV775225	July 10, 1998	SJPD	47/25
4) *People v. SVN* (South Vietnam)	CV791443	July 28, 2000	SJPD	6/3
5) *People v. Varrio Sureno Treces*	CV811217	Sep. 19, 2002	SJPD	29/10

Tulare County—3 Gang Injunctions

1) *People v. South Side Kings*	08-226862	April 28, 2008	IPD	0/0
2) *People v. NS Visalia/MGB/ESR/NSB*	08-226863	May 6, 2008	VPD	0/0
3) *People v. Oriental Troop/MBS/LPG*	08-226863	May 12, 2008	VPD	0/0

Ventura County—2 Filed Gang Injunctions and 1 Pending

1) *People v. Oxnard Colonia Chiques*	CIV226032	April 2, 2004	OPD	134/150
2) *People v. Oxnard Southside Chiques*	CIV242491	July 27, 2006	OPD	143/112
3) *People v. Port Hueneme Gang*	Pending			

Yolo County—1 Gang Injunction (Dismissed)

1) *People v. Broderick Boys*	CV04-2085	December 30, 2004	WSPD	85/5

17

Gang Injunctions, Gang Abatement, and the Law

Prosecutors obtain gang injunctions by applying the law of public nuisance to the particular harms criminal street gangs cause. We normally associate nuisance with trifling annoyances, and indeed nuisance law originally developed out of the need to address minor offenses. However, the nuisance doctrine applies equally to the activities of criminal street gangs, and is an effective tool for tackling serious gang violence. Since gang injunctions started to be used as a tool more than 25 years ago, several cases have shaped how they are drafted and implemented. These cases all stem from common law public nuisances that involve some interference with the interests of the community at large, interests that were recognized as rights of the general public entitled to protection.

Applying constitutional principles to gang injunctions requires a clear understanding of the injunctions. Gang injunctions usually contain similar prohibitions that address various aspects of a gang's control over an area. Gang injunctions normally include restrictions on local movement, e.g., being outdoors after dark, fleeing from police, or illegally entering the home of another. These restrictions have been attacked on numerous constitutional grounds, specifically on the doctrines of vagueness and overbreadth, the First Amendment right to free association, the First Amendment right to freedom of expression, and procedural due process. The cases discussed in this chapter explore these issues in detail.

CASE LAW: *CITY OF CHICAGO V. MORALES*, 119 S.CT. 1849. (CHICAGO ANTILOITERING ORDINANCE)

In 1992, the Chicago City Council enacted the Gang Congregation Ordinance, which provided that whenever a police officer observes a person whom he or she reasonably believes to be a criminal street gang member loitering in any public place with one or more other persons, he or she shall order all such persons to disperse and remove themselves from the area. Any person who did not promptly obey such an order was in violation of the ordinance. This ordinance was later determined to be unconstitutional, and some compare this case to the use of gang injunctions still today. The big difference here is that the comparison is between a civil lawsuit and a city ordinance, which are two very different things. The Illinois Supreme Court concluded that the ordinance violated due process of law because it was unconstitutionally vague and lent itself to arbitrary enforcement (*Chicago v. Morales*, 1997). Because the ordinance failed to give the ordinary citizen adequate notice of what is forbidden and what is permitted, it is impermissibly vague. The term *loiter* may have a common and accepted meaning, but the ordinance's definition of that term "to remain in any one place with no apparent purpose" did not. This vagueness about what loitering is covered and what is not eliminated the ordinance. The Illinois Supreme Court correctly concluded that the ordinance did not provide sufficiently specific limits on the enforcement discretion of the police to meet constitutional standards for definiteness and clarity.

CASE LAW: *PEOPLE V. GONZALES*, 910 P.2D 1366 (CAL. 1996).

One Blythe Street gang member, defendant Jessie Gonzales, also known as "Speedy," fought his case to the California Supreme Court. Gonzales was arrested after he tossed a bottle of beer, ran from police, and forced his way inside a house to evade police without the permission of the homeowner. Gonzalez claimed that because the injunction violation case against him was filed in a municipal court, and the injunction was obtained in superior court, the defendant did not have an opportunity for proper relief (*People v. Gonzalez*, 1996). In this case Jessie was found guilty of violating the injunction. The conviction was used as a test case to challenge the validity of the controversial gang injunctions. Gonzalez denied he was a gang member, and he felt that a municipal court judge did not have proper jurisdiction to review an order issued by a superior court judge.

The court of appeals held that all criminal cases filed for violations of 166.4(a) PC must be filed directly in superior court. The state supreme court overruled the appeal court's decision and held that a municipal court judge does have "some limited right of review" over an order issued by a superior court judge. Since the ruling in the *Gonzales* case, virtually all gang injunction violation cases have been filed in superior court as criminal misdemeanor violations. It is the preferred method when compared to civil contempt violations that have a maximum penalty of five days in custody. A criminal violation allows the prosecutor to seek probation and jail time for repeat offenders, which increases the severity of the violations.

CASE LAW: *PEOPLE V. ACUNA* (CAL. APP. 1995), APRIL 24, 1995

On April 24, 2005, the Court of Appeals for the Sixth District upheld the issuance of the Sur Trece injunction, but struck down every provision in the order that was not already a violation of statutory law (*People v. Acuna*, 1995). The decision invalidated 15 of the 24 provisions in the preliminary injunction sought by the Santa Clara district attorney in February 1993. The California Court of Appeals also ruled that the "harassing, intimidating, and annoying" language of the injunction was unconstitutionally vague and overbroad, and that the prohibition of the gang members congregating in Rocksprings violated their First Amendment right to free association.

The San Jose City Council authorized an appeal of that decision to the California Supreme Court, resulting in the opinion reported in *People ex rel. Gallo vs. Acuna* (1997), 14 Cal. 4th 1090. The appellate court upheld only those provisions that enjoined criminal conduct, as in the case of the Playboy Gangster Crips from 1987 in Los Angeles. The California Court of Appeals found that the injunction against the Varrio Sureno Treces gang was overbroad and did not sufficiently define the prohibited activities or provide a definite standard for police enforcement and ascertainment of guilt (*People v. Acuna*, 1997). The City of San Jose appealed to the state supreme court arguing to reinstate 2 of the 15 provisions that were struck down, which included the no association clause and the no confronting, intimidating, harassing, and threatening clause. The appeal to the state supreme court was filed.

CASE LAW: *PEOPLE EX REL. GALLO VS. ACUNA* (1997), 14 CAL. 4TH 1090

On January 30, 1997, the constitutionality of gang injunctions as we know them today was established. The California Supreme Court ruled that the City of San Jose may implement a civil gang injunction that restricts noncriminal behavior if committed by alleged gang members in a particular neighborhood. The court overturned the April 1995 appellate court decision in the case

(*People v. Acuna*, 1997). The ACLU and others in opposition to gang injunctions were forced to acknowledge that the decision by the state's highest court would add momentum and increase usage of the increasingly popular technique. What the ACLU missed but the courts did not is that the liberty of the peaceful, law-abiding residents of the community must be preserved, and the freedom for those whose ill conduct is detrimental to the community does not take precedence.

The 4–3 ruling, overturning the court of appeals decision, upheld a San Jose injunction that barred the gang members from "standing, sitting, walking, driving, gathering or appearing anywhere in public view" with each other in a four-block neighborhood. "Liberty unrestrained is an invitation to anarchy," Justice Janice Rogers Brown wrote for the court. "Freedom and responsibility are joined at the hip." The decision removes a legal cloud over such gang abatement injunctions, which have been growing in popularity in California as a tool to combat gangs (Dolan, 1997).

This case gave law enforcement the framework for what is needed to seek and obtain gang injunctions. But civil libertarians argue that these injunctions go too far, violating such basic constitutional rights as freedom of speech and freedom of association. Justice Ming W. Chin agreed that courts can prohibit behavior even if it is legal but objected that the injunction was necessary. The judge stated, "I do not discount the serious threat to community values that criminal street gangs pose, nevertheless, we cannot turn a blind eye to the necessities of proof. Individuals should not be named as gang members without corroborating evidence that they substantially contributed to the nuisance or intended to do so in the future."

The ACLU argued the case before the high court, stating that San Jose's gang injunction was unconstitutionally vague and overbroad and targeted Latino youths without sufficient proof that they have committed any crimes or harassed residents. The ACLU stance was because the defendants are suspected gang members, they are stripped of a variety of constitutional freedoms; the rights to associate, to assemble, and the right to due process. The ACLU felt the ruling effectively placed lawmaking power in the hands of judges instead of the legislature, making it unconstitutional. The case submitted contained substantial evidence that the gang was responsible for significant crimes and the named defendants were responsible for some of them.

The California Supreme Court held that the gang injunction was neither vague nor overbroad because its terms were reasonably clear in the context of the Varrio Sureno Treces gang. The court also held that the anti-gang injunction did not violate the free association rights of the Varrio Sur Treces members because there is no cognizable First Amendment right to free association implicated by membership in a criminal street gang. Although the Varrio Sur Treces members sought certiorari by the U.S. Supreme Court, the writ was denied. Thus, in California, anti-gang injunctions have become an established law enforcement tool.

ISSUE OF PROCEDURAL DUE PROCESS

Due process is a legal concept that ensures the government will not deprive a person of life, liberty, or property without following the due process of the law. The Fourteenth Amendment outlines the due process right. In the context of gang injunctions, due process is often related to procedural fairness. At a minimum, it includes an individual's right to be adequately notified of the charges or proceedings involving him or her, and the opportunity to be heard at these hearings. In criminal cases, fair procedures protect the accused from cruel and unusual punishment, which is the result of an innocent person being wrongly convicted.

The unique nature of the anti-gang injunction raises concerns that gang injunctions violate the procedural due process rights of gang members. The U.S. Supreme Court set forth a three-part balancing test to determine the appropriate level of process required where there has been a deprivation of a right in a civil proceeding. This test requires the court to weigh (1) the nature of the individual right at stake, (2) the risk of an erroneous deprivation of the right, and (3) the state's interest in expedience. The frequent failure of gang members to attend their hearings after being served and the nonappointment of counsel for indigent gang members do not violate the procedural due process of the accused gang member. Each gang member may attend the hearing, or file the proper response to inclusion in the order to the court, to explain why the proposed injunction would not be applicable to him or her, assuming he or she follows the proper legal and procedural guidelines.

The lack of court-appointed counsel at a gang injunction proceeding also complies with procedural due process requirements. Courts are typically unwilling to recognize a right to counsel for any gang injunctive hearings because associations of gang members simply are not fundamental rights and losing at the hearing will not result in the loss of liberty, and the gang member will not risk going to jail, just for being included in the injunction; it requires that he or she violate the order. Loss of liberty is not a potential recourse until a future violation of the order occurs, which is a criminal offense that may result in the gang member going to jail.

As a result, no due process rights are violated by these injunctions where named defendants were served and provided the opportunity to come to court to be heard. What is not as clear are the ongoing cases in which gang defendants are added to gang injunctions after they have been implemented. In some cases no members are named and the gang is the only named defendant; then as many as several hundred gang members are added at a later date as DOEs. These members are not afforded the opportunity to come to court to present an argument against their inclusion in the order at the time of filing. The first time the gang members get the opportunity to come to court is if or when they are arrested for a violation of the order. San Diego's approach, for example, has differed from Los Angeles' in that it has more steps to screen gang members at the beginning, and it has a greater role for judges rather than relying on the discretion of prosecutors and police.

The inclusion of DOEs and the service of a small number, in some cases just one representative, of the gang highlights the due process issue and brings it to the forefront of the legal debate regarding the use of gang injunctions. To prevent rulings against injunctions in the context of due process, district and city attorneys are more apt to individually name every gang member and enumerate the exact activities that the gang member has engaged in and what the gang members are prohibited from doing, or serve a greater number of members of the gang as representatives.

California law permits designating unknown defendants by a fictitious name in order to allow defendants who might be discovered in the future to be added to the lawsuit (Code of Civil Procedure Section 474). Under this procedure, lawyers practicing in California routinely allege, in addition to the named defendant(s), a certain number of defendants who are usually designated as DOEs. DOE defendants represent a legal shortcut for additional parties to be made defendants after a lawsuit is filed, if such a need arises. Although these DOEs appear on the face of the complaints for gang injunctions, they are not the procedure used to add defendants to make them subject to a gang injunction, as all members of the gang are subject to the injunction once it is issued. When the court issues a judgment granting an injunction, the DOE defendants are routinely dismissed, and all future prosecutions of gang members for violating the gang injunction proceed by proving in each case that the defendant is a gang member.

The Yolo County gang injunction against the Broderick Boys gang was challenged based upon a due process violation (*People v. Broderick Boys*, 2004). Critics of injunctions challenge the inclusion of DOEs based in part on the method of service, which they feel violates the fundamental due process right by failure to provide notice and an opportunity to be heard to persons who were known to the police when the case was filed. Due process requires that notice be reasonably executed to properly inform those whose interests are directly affected by the pending gang injunction.

Critics argue that when police and prosecutors only serve a small number of the gang when they have full knowledge of hundreds of members in some cases, it is a flagrant attempt to circumvent the rights of the gang members. Prosecutors argue that service to a few core members of the gang is sufficient, as the gangs have complex communication networks and word quickly spreads throughout the gang upon service to a small number. The ACLU and others argue that the prosecution ignores its own records and willfully chooses to avoid opposition to the orders, which may be legal but lacks ethical considerations.

Critics argue that this method of service prohibits binding unnamed parties by a judgment entered against a representative gang if the representative party fails to provide an adequate defense in the proceeding. As a result of the ACLU analysis of the *Broderick Boys* case, the ACLU formed the opinion that the default judgment and injunction violated fundamental due process principles that ensure that persons whose property and liberty interests are affected receive notice and a fair opportunity to be heard. According the ACLU, the district attorney deprived the future defendants of the right to be heard, despite the fact that they had a list of 350 members of the gang that they could have provided notice to, or at least attempted to provide notice to. As a result of the lack of notification, the district attorney did not have an objection or opposition to its case; the court effectively only heard one side of the argument. The ACLU feels due process of law requires more and the case is currently on appeal.

In March 2010, the Third District Court of Appeals in Sacramento partially upheld a preliminary injunction against the Broderick Boys. In a 44-page opinion issued by the appellate court, it supports Yolo County Superior Court Judge Kathleen M. White's preliminary injunction that would restrict the activities of alleged gang members in a defined area of West Sacramento. "We conclude sufficient, credible evidence supports the trial court's conclusion the Broderick Boys is a criminal street gang whose activities have created a public nuisance in the designated area," the opinion read. However, it found provisions dealing with controlled substances and the consumption of alcohol too vague to be enforced. But the Yolo County District Attorney's Office can request the lower court to amend these provisions so they can be enforced, according to the ruling.

ISSUE OF VAGUENESS

The *Acuna* court identified two types of constitutional vagueness challenges: (1) where the meaning of the statute (or order) is insufficiently clear and concrete, so as to provide inadequate notice as to what conduct is proscribed, and (2) where it provides insufficient guidelines to law enforcement so as to reduce the potential for arbitrary and discriminatory enforcement. The wording of the challenged provisions in *Acuna* was sufficiently clear, although the court resorted to reading a knowledge *mens rea* requirement into both provisions. For example, the prohibition on associating with "any other known" gang member was interpreted to mean any person *known by the defendant* to be a gang member. This illustrates the level of care required when drafting the injunction's provisions, which should be as precise and unambiguous as possible.

The doctrine of vagueness or void-for-vagueness doctrine holds that a law is facially invalid if persons of common intelligence cannot necessarily guess its meaning and differ as to its application. The court has indicated that a higher degree of clarity is demanded when the law in question threatens fundamental First Amendment rights. As an overbreadth concern might be cured by a narrowing interpretation by a state court, so too a vagueness problem that appears on the face of the statute might be cured by means of a clarifying judicial interpretation (a "saving construction") by a state court. Under the void-for-vagueness doctrine, a vague law is a violation of due process because the law does not provide fair warning of a prohibition and fails to set standards for enforcement that would govern the exercise of the police power.

Arguments that gang injunctions are unconstitutional and vague were fueled by the 1999 U.S. Supreme Court decision in *City of Chicago v. Morales* (1997). The *Morales* decision does not impact gang injunctions because that case deals with a gang loitering ordinance. In *Morales*, the Supreme Court determined the constitutionality of a gang loitering ordinance, not a gang injunction. The Chicago ordinance (Chicago Police General Order 92-4) prohibited individuals from loitering with gang members. The ordinance defined *gang member* as any individual a police officer reasonably believes to be in a gang. Unlike the gang loitering ordinance at issue in *Morales*, gang injunctions clearly define the term *gang member* as well as specific types of prohibited conduct. The *Morales* court recognized the narrow scope of its holding, stating expressly that the decision was limited to the specific ambiguities in the Chicago ordinance.

In reviewing the potential vagueness of the *Acuna* injunction, the California Court of Appeals held paragraph (a) unduly vague because it prohibited association with any other known gang member. The court of appeals found that such language was vague because a defendant could potentially be punished for associating with a person known to be a gang member by the police but not by the defendant. The California Supreme Court, however, believed that the element of knowledge "is fairly implied in the decree," and that to the extent that it was not, the trial court would impose a knowledge requirement when and if paragraph (a) of the injunction was enforced. Despite the supreme court's view, most agencies do require some degree of knowledge when enforcing these violations. A gang injunction defendant's companion must reveal some evidence that the defendant knew his companion was a gang member, such as prior contacts together, visible tattoos, similar dress, admissions, or statements.

Additionally, the terms *confront*, *annoy*, *provoke*, *challenge*, and *harass* were held by the court of appeals to not be reasonably certain so as to provide a clear and understandable standard of conduct. Upon its own analysis, the *Acuna* court held terms such as "intimidating, harassing, touching, pushing, shoving, crowding or assaulting persons" to not be unduly vague in the context of an injunction. The California Supreme Court believed there to be no difference between the terms used in the other types of civil injunctions. Since the terms were ruled constitutional in other cases, the *Acuna* court held them to be constitutional in the *Acuna* injunction.

When the terms *confront*, *annoy*, *provoke*, *challenge*, and *harass* are read with the knowledge of the gang's activity toward neighborhood residents in mind, it is clear that any conduct by the gang that is intended as retaliation against residents is prohibited. Any conduct that reasonably resembles a confrontation, an annoyance, a provocation, a challenge, or harassment is unlawful (McClellan, 1998). Therefore, the court held that gang injunctions and the primary terminology are not unduly vague. Under vagueness principles, a regulation must be sufficiently clear in defining the conduct that is prohibited. Thus a regulation is unconstitutionally void for vagueness if it will not be understood by individuals of ordinary intelligence (*Kolender v. Lawson*, 461 U.S. 352, 357–61 1983).

Some opponents argue that restrictions on gang member associations are void for vagueness because a *gang member* cannot be defined objectively. These arguments are totally without merit because a *gang member* is a well-defined term in the California Street Terrorism Enforcement and Prevention Act, which provides the definition of a gang member (California Penal Code Section 186.22). A gang member is anyone who actively participates in a criminal street gang; has knowledge in, or has engaged in, a pattern of criminal gang activity; and willfully promotes, furthers, or assists in any criminal conduct by members of the gang.

A witness representing the gang members' interests in the *Ventura Colonia Chiques* trial argued that "characterizing any street gang as a criminal organization is an inaccurate depiction that draws upon a minority of the actions committed by a gang and its members." Some critics have gone so far as to classify street gangs as noncriminal organizations, calling them loosely knit groups of youths that grew up together in the same community that simply share similar ethnic and racial characteristics (Klein, 1995). The arguments of some of those that actively defend the groups targeted by injunctions do not understand the definition of a gang; they are typically inaccurate and misguided. Of course one could argue that the degree and level of criminal sophistication among different gangs may vary, but every documented gang in the State of California is a criminal organization. That is not open for debate, as the documented gangs must comply with the Department of Justice guidelines or they will not be considered a gang by law enforcement. If the gang is not involved in criminal activity, it would not be called a gang, would not be classified as a street gang per 186.22 PC, and would not be sought as a target of a gang injunction.

Every gang injunction obtained in California meets the penal code definition of a gang; none of the gang injunctions in California have targeted a group that was not first defined as a gang. Opponents also argue that gang injunctions are overly vague because gang injunctions target entire gangs. Injunctions only apply to those members named as defendants or that have been selected and served with the orders. Not every member of a particular gang was sought out and served the injunction in most cases. Not every member will qualify for inclusion in the injunction. The gang injunction does not target affiliates and mere friends of affiliates, as suggested by some in opposition, unless they have supporting criminal activity that can be attributed to their gang membership. The subjects served with gang injunctions are gang members that have proven they are either violent members of the gang or are involved in the less serious nuisance-related criminal activity that adds to the neighborhood's deterioration. Simply put, they have been identified as the most active or most problematic gang members within the designated safety zone for each injunction.

ISSUE OF OVERBREADTH

The *Acuna* court addressed an overbreadth challenge to the terms of the injunction. A finding of overbreadth requires showing that there is a danger that First Amendment protections of parties not before the court may be significantly compromised. *Acuna* denied the overbreadth challenge, finding that such a danger is not as present in a judicial order arising from a proceeding prompted by particular events as it would be in an abstract statute (*Acuna*, 14 Cal. 4th at 1114). Although the injunction in *Acuna* did not bind the gang itself or its nonnamed members, later decisions expressly upholding the application of gang injunctions to nonparty members of the targeted gang lend support to the conclusion that an overbreadth challenge would fail in that context as well.

Caution must be exercised in obtaining gang injunctions to ensure that they are not overbroad. The *Acuna* court indicated that the gang injunction was not overbroad because it was solely directed at the 38 named defendants. No persons other than the named defendants were subject to the prohibitions of the injunction, thereby preventing the injunction from infringing upon other persons' First Amendment rights. The state high court also determined that an individual's rights cannot be protected at the expense of a community's right to security and protection. The injunction placed no restrictions on gang members outside of the enjoined gang's area, and members were free to associate with one another outside that area. The court therefore concluded, given the factual showing made by the city in support of preliminary relief, the carnival-like atmosphere of collective mayhem, we cannot say that the ban on any association between gang members within the neighborhood goes beyond what is required to abate the nuisance.

The *Acuna* court therefore held that the provision was not overbroad as implemented against gang members. A regulation is unconstitutionally overbroad only if it burdens a substantial amount of constitutionally protected activity while purporting to restrict only unprotected activity [*Broadrick v. Oklahoma*, 413 U.S. 601, 615 (1973)], which was not the case in *Acuna*. In plain English, select your target area well, be able to justify the size of the area, the members to be included, and keep it as focused as you can to avoid overbroad issues and legal challenges.

ISSUE OF RIGHT TO FREE ASSOCIATION

Provisions preventing members of the enjoined gang from associating with each other in public may be challenged as a violation of the First Amendment right to free association. In *Acuna*, the California Supreme Court explained that "the United States Supreme Court has made it clear that, although the Constitution recognizes and shields from government intrusion a *limited* right of association, it does not recognize a generalized right of "social association"' [*Acuna*, 14 Cal. 4th at 1110; quoting *Dallas v. Stanglin*, 490 U.S. 19, 25 (1989)]. To be protected, the claimed right of association must fall into certain categories—those with an intrinsic or intimate value, or those that are instrumental to forms of religious or political expression or activity (Id.). The *Acuna* court held that the right of gang members to associate did not fall into either of these categories.

Quoting the U.S. Supreme Court, *Acuna* states that "freedom of association, in the sense protected by the First Amendment, 'does not extend to joining with others for the purpose of depriving third parties of their lawful rights'" [Id. at 1112; quoting *Madsen v. Women's Health Ctr.*, Inc., 512 U.S. 753, 776 (1994)]. Prosecutors must be aware of the possibility that the constitutions of other states may be interpreted by courts in those states to provide a broader right to free association than the U.S. or California Constitutions.

The fact that some of the gang's members live in the area covered by the injunction or have relatives who live in the area or who are also in the gang does not render the restriction on associating unconstitutional. The California Court of Appeals in *In Re Englebrecht*, 67 Cal. App. 4th 486 (1998) held that these distinctions do not transform gang activities into intrinsic or intimate associational activities. Whenever gang members are associating in public, whether going to or from home and regardless of the familial relationship between the gang members, their activities remain nonintimate gang activities [Id. at 496; "The familial nexus is not carte blanche for creating a public nuisance"; see also *People v. Englebrecht*, 88 Cal. App. 4th 1236, 1263 (2001)]. ("While the injunction may place some burden on family contact in the target area, it by no means has, in our view, a fundamental impact on general family association. Any liberalization of the injunction to try to allow greater familial contact in the target area would limit the effectiveness of the injunction.") Because many gangs include several generations of people in the same family as well as numerous extended family members, an injunction would not be effective if it exempted family members from the prohibition on associating.

The First Amendment does not specifically mention the right of association. The concept can be understood to have grown out of the First Amendment's guarantee of a right to peaceably assemble and petition the government. To petition the government effectively one might join others who have the same grievances. This liberty, then, was conceived to protect an association of people to achieve some lawful political end, not the congregation of a criminal street gang. The freedom of association protects one's membership in any organization that is not involved in criminal activity. The Constitution does not expressly provide for a right of association. Gradually the First Amendment and the liberty interest secured by the Fourteenth Amendment have been interpreted to protect a person's right to associate with others who share similar ideas, interests, and goals, even if those groups exist for the purpose of committing crime, such as street gangs.

The California legislature has found and declared that "it is the right of every person, regardless of race, color, creed, religion, national origin, sex, age, sexual orientation, or handicap, to be secure and protected from fear, intimidation, and physical harm caused by the activities of violent groups and individuals." "The freedom to leave one's house and move about at will, and to have a measure of personal security is implicit in the concept of ordered liberty enshrined in the history and basic constitutional documents of English-speaking peoples," wrote Califonia Supreme Court Justice Janice Rogers. The penal code further explains, "It is not the intent of this chapter to interfere with the exercise of the constitutionally protected rights of freedom of expression and association. The legislature hereby recognizes the constitutional right of every citizen to harbor and express beliefs on any lawful subject whatsoever, to lawfully associate with others who share similar beliefs, to petition lawfully constituted authority for a redress of perceived grievances, and to participate in the electoral process."

The legislature, however, further finds that the State of California is in a state of crisis that has been caused by violent street gangs whose members threaten, terrorize, and commit a multitude of crimes against the peaceful citizens of their neighborhoods. "These activities, both individually and collectively, present a clear and present danger to public order and safety and are not constitutionally protected. The interests of the community are not invariably less important than the freedom of individuals," Brown wrote. "Indeed, the security and protection of the community is the bedrock on which the superstructure of individual liberty rests."

Despite hundreds of media reports and articles written every time a new injunction is filed that discusses how gang injunctions take away a God-given right to associate with whomever we choose, there is no general right of association granted in the U.S. Constitution. The right to association is limited to intimate associations according to the *Acuna* case. The U.S. Supreme Court defined an intimate association as those with "deep attachments and commitments to the individuals with whom one shares not only a special community of thoughts, experiences, and beliefs but also distinctively personal aspects of one's life." The Supreme Court has evaluated the purpose of the association in determining whether the association is intimate. Thus, familial associations are intimate associations protected by the Constitution. By contrast, organizations such as clubs are not. Street gangs do not fall within the Supreme Court's definition of intimate associations, as they are neither composed of a small number of people, selective in membership, or established for an intimate purpose.

Street gangs commonly are composed of 10 to several hundred members, each having varying degrees of involvement in gang activities and not all of whom even know each other, making it difficult for them to claim they are an intimate association. The court further defined relationships having an intimate or intrinsic value as those associations that are directly related to political, social, economic, educational, religious, and cultural ends. The court believed that while the association of Varrio Sureno Trece gang members in Rocksprings may provide some personal enrichment to all or some of the members, it did not fall within the protection of the First Amendment because it was not of the type of intimate or intrinsic relationship traditionally recognized by the Supreme Court as being protected by the First Amendment.

The VST gang did not associate for any political or religious objective within the Rocksprings neighborhood. Rather, the gang members clearly seemed to associate for the sole purpose of committing crimes and terrorizing the community, which is not a constitutionally protected activity. The right to free association under the First Amendment includes no cognizable right for gang members to congregate in the streets, even if they congregate peaceably.

Because this large and flexible membership is not limited to an intimate group of individuals, the congregation of street gangs is not protected as an intimate association (*People v. Acuna*, 1997). Regardless of the psychological reasons for the formation of gangs, the fact remains that gangs do not operate for any legitimate or intimate purpose. Even the opponents of gang injunctions typically cannot deny the illegal nature of a gang's activities. Thus even if gang members are satisfying subconscious needs for love, protection, or excitement, gang activity remains overtly illegal. As such, they are not intimate associations as defined by the Supreme Court. Therefore street gangs have no legitimate purpose and exist solely for the purpose of committing crime. Each gang member, in joining his or her fellow gang members in the gang's territory, knowingly and with intent furthers the gang's criminal purpose by providing additional strength to the presence of the gang, giving them greater control over their turf and adding significantly to the gang problem in the community.

As a result of the above case, most injunctions contain statements such as "Because of the defendant's behavior, residents in the safety zone have suffered great emotional distress in the form of fear, intimidation, anxiety, and invasion of privacy. Unless and until the activity is restrained, it will continue to cause great irreparable injury to the residents' safety, peace, and tranquility within the safety zone."

ISSUE OF FREE SPEECH

The First Amendment states, in part, that Congress shall make no law respecting an establishment of religion, or prohibiting the free exercise thereof, or abridging the freedom of speech or of the press, or the right of the people to peaceably assemble and petition the government for a redress of grievances (U.S. Constitution, Bill of Rights, First Amendment). Almost everyone knows that the First Amendment contains the right to freedom of speech. That means you can express an opinion without fear of censorship by the government, even if that opinion is an unpopular one.

However, it does not mean you can say anything you want, whenever you want. For instance, fighting words or words that cause distress or incite violence are not protected speech. A restriction on speech is valid if it is narrowly tailored to a compelling state interest. For example, one cannot board an airplane and say he or she has a bomb or yell "Fire!" in a movie theater because that speech now places others in danger and causes fear and panic in the community. An examination of the First Amendment indicates that an expressive element of a communication is a prerequisite to First Amendment protection. By contrast, any communication or conduct that does not contain a cognizable idea is not entitled to First Amendment protection.

The absence of an expressive message in gang hand gestures and clothing places them beyond the scope of the First Amendment (*People ex rel. Gallo vs. Acuna*, 1997). The gangs typically argue that gang hand gestures and clothing involve the communication of expressive ideas because both gang hand gestures and gang clothing convey a signal to other gang members that should be protected. Gang hand gestures and clothing do not involve a meaningful idea in the view of the courts. A street gang does not seek to advance any religious, political, social, cultural, or economic values. On the contrary, the gang's primary purpose is criminal and devoid of expressive value.

Just as all other gang activities are directed toward illicit purposes that are devoid of social value, gang hand gestures and clothing are usually directed toward these purposes as well. When a gang member wears gang clothing and uses gang hand gestures, he or she is contributing to and aiding the gang in their goal of control over the neighborhood, and it typically communicates that the neighborhood belongs to the gang. As applied to street gangs, a democratic duty to tolerate gang hand gestures and clothing would arise if their use expressed any meaningful idea that did not promote illegal activity. As noted above, however, gang hand gestures and clothing only further the illicit activities of the gang. Therefore a restriction on gang hand gestures and clothing does not implicate the legal duty to tolerate diverse ideas, nor does such a restriction preclude any gang member from expressing meaningful views (Herd, 1998).

Opponents have argued that restricting gang clothing also has a negative impact on community members that are not members of the gang but that wear similar clothing. As some gang injunctions are drafted, youth wearing specific clothing or logos are not subject to arrest unless they have been identified as gang members and served with the injunction. Nongang youth that happen to wear such clothing are not subject to the injunction. It is widely accepted, however, that the police have a duty to warn the nongang youth of the local gang in the area and educate them as to potential dangers that particular articles of clothing may present. Rivals may think they are a member of the gang even though they are not, making them more likely to be an innocent victim of gang violence, but they will not be restricted from wearing such clothing and are not subject to arrest for doing so. The use of gang hand gestures and clothing, as well as all other gang activities, stems from the destructive desire to dominate a neighborhood and intimidate the other inhabitants of that neighborhood, making them not constitutionally protected.

CASE LAW: *IN RE ENGLEBRECHT,* 67 CAL. APP. 486, 1998

In 1997, the district attorney's office and the Oceanside Police Department filed a civil lawsuit against 28 members of the Posole gang and obtained a permanent injunction (*People v. Varrio Posole Locos*, 1997). One of the gang members, David Englebrecht, challenged the injunction and went to court. It was the first gang injunction civil trial in the nation, and the prosecution prevailed. However, the ACLU filed an appeal on behalf of Englebrecht. The court of appeals sided with the San Diego County District Attorney's Office in its May 2001 decision (*People v. Englebrecht*, 2001).

In July 1998, the California Court of Appeals ruled that prosecutors must first prove through clear and convincing evidence that an individual is a gang member before using a gang injunction to restrict his or her right to engage in otherwise legal activities. Despite not being a gang member according to his defense, David Englebrecht, a man described as a 26-year-old father of three, was placed under a civil injunction designed to combat a local gang (Soto, 2001a). Under the injunction, Englebrecht was prohibited from making loud noises, whistling, wearing certain clothing, using certain words or hand gestures, or being seen in public with other alleged gang members within an approximately 1 square mile area of Oceanside (*In Re Englebrecht*, 67 Cal. App. 486, 1998).

"Prosecutors will no longer be able to use flimsy evidence to brand young Latino men with the label gang member," said Candace Carroll, an ACLU volunteer lawyer. "Under this injunction, Mr. Englebrecht was prohibited from going to outdoor parties in his neighborhood, speaking with some of his relatives and boyhood friends on the street, even shouting to his children in a local park. With so much at stake, the Constitution requires the government to meet a very high standard of proof." Englebrecht challenged his inclusion on a list of 28 persons restrained by the Posole gang injunction imposed by the San Diego Superior Court.

The superior court denied that challenge, but one year later Englebrecht was able to convince the court to take him off the list due to no gang contacts during the year. This is a very common provision in some injunctions, often called an opt-out. The Posole injunction did not have a specified provision allowing gang members a way off the injunction, but the district attorney allowed Englebrecht off the order when he went a year without being contacted by the police in the target area. Englebrecht was later rearrested for his involvement in a gang-related shooting, and he was sent to prison for his involvement in the case.

On May 9, 2001, in a case called *People v. Englebrecht*, the Fourth District Court of Appeals upheld a trial court's ruling that gang injunctions are constitutional. The case also established that gang members can keep their pagers after the state appeals court decided the devices cannot be included in future injunctions. An absolute ban on a common, legal communication device goes too far, even though injunctions intended to rid neighborhoods of gang activity have been upheld by the state Supreme court. "Pagers and beepers are not only used for illicit reasons, but have countless lawful, legitimate, and everyday uses," said Justice Judith Haller in the 3–0 ruling (The Associated Press, 1998). The court determined it might be possible to meet the court's concerns by proving a closer connection between pagers and gang activity deemed necessary in future injunctions. The court upheld the central terms of an injunction issued in December of 2007 by San Diego County Superior Court Judge John Einhorn, prohibiting members of Varrio Posolo Locos from meeting with any other member in an east Oceanside neighborhood.

One man named in the injunction, David Englebrecht, Jr., was found in contempt by Einhorn in April after being seen with two gang members in the neighborhood, the court said. He was sentenced to five days in jail and fined $1,000 but has remained free during his appeal. Deputy Public Defender Dawn Ella Gilzean said that Englebrecht denies he is an active gang member. The court said Englebrecht could be held in contempt for associating with other gang members but not for carrying a pager found on him. Lovett, who represented the prosecution in the appeal, said the ruling shouldn't hamper the effort to move gangs out of neighborhoods. He said it might be possible to meet the court's concerns by proving a closer connection between pagers and gang activity.

He also said another part of the injunction, still in effect, bars gang members from acting as lookouts or using any method, whistles, hand signals, or pagers to warn one another about police.

CASE LAW: *IRAHETA V. SUPERIOR COURT OF LA*, 70 CAL. APP. 4TH 1500, 1999

In 1999, the *Iraheta* case addressed the issue of the right for gang members to have appointed council to fight a civil gang injunction (*Iraheta v. Superior Court of Los Angeles*, 1999). The people filed a civil lawsuit seeking an injunction to abate a public nuisance, naming as defendants the 18th Street gang, including 92 named individuals and 200 DOEs. The complaint, which sought a preliminary and permanent injunction, alleged that petitioners and the other defendants as members of the 18th Street gang were actively contributing to the nuisance in two target areas. After the preliminary injunction was issued, the Los Angeles County Public Defender's Office filed a motion asking the superior court to appoint counsel for petitioners for the trial, which would determine whether a permanent injunction would be issued. The public defender pointed out that the petitioners are indigent and could not afford to pay for counsel, and argued that due to the unique and extraordinary circumstances of the case, petitioners should have the right to court-appointed counsel. The superior court denied the petitioners' request.

Generally, the right to counsel exists only where a defendant's physical liberty may be lost. The Fourteenth Amendment to the U.S. Constitution and Article I, Section 7, Subdivision (a) of the California Constitution ensure that an individual may not be deprived of life, liberty, or property without due process of law. Central to this constitutional right is the guarantee that "absent a countervailing state interest of overriding significance, persons forced to settle their claims of right and duty through the judicial process must be given a meaningful opportunity to be heard" (*Salas v. Cortez* (1979) 24 Cal. 3d 22, 26–27).

This has been held to include the right of a defendant to appointed counsel in civil actions, but only in restricted circumstances. Generally, "the right to counsel has been recognized to exist only where the defendant may lose his/her physical liberty if he/she loses the case."

In 1999, a California State Assembly bill was introduced to overturn *Iraheta*. Indigent defendants are entitled to lawyers in criminal cases, but since the injunctions are civil proceedings, some of those against whom they are sought now must confront them without legal counsel. Many feel alleged gang members in injunction cases routinely are being victimized by little or no legal representation, and that authorities are using the threat of greater penalties to coerce innocent defendants into pleading guilty to crimes. The bill, SB 167, sought to reduce the alleged victimization of the accused gang members and overturn the appellate court decision that rejected publicly funded counsel for gang members; the legislation was supported by public defenders who had petitioned for the right to represent members of the 18th Street Rampart gang in Los Angeles. Public defenders say providing counsel will prevent civil actions that are stacked against defendants. But prosecutors contend the legislation will turn every gang injunction hearing into a lengthy criminal trial and set a precedent for extending the right to counsel to a whole range of civil injunction proceedings like evictions, small claims actions, and workers' compensation cases.

The Second District Court of Appeal, in *Iraheta v. Superior Court*, ruled that gang members do not have a right to appointed counsel because they are only threatened with loss of liberty in a future contempt prosecution for failure to comply. If they do fail to comply they have the right to public counsel upon arrest.

YOLO APPEAL GOES TO COURT

On February 3, 2005, the permanent injunction against the Broderick Boys gang was granted. The ACLU filed an appeal in the Third District Court of Appeals based on the assertion that the district attorney won the case by default because the gang was not sufficiently advised of the proceedings against them, violating due process for the gang and its members.

The Broderick Boys gang reportedly had 350 members when the case was filed, of which 50 were named in the preliminary injunction (not as defendants but as supporting evidence of the gang and their nuisance activity). Of the 50 named persons only one member, Billy Wolfington, was served notice of the case. The ACLU claims this tactic of serving one member was calculated to ensure a default by the gang (*People v. Broderick Boys*, 2004). The first notice the gang members received was that they were in default and the injunction against them was granted. On July 28, 2005, appellants filed a motion under Code of Civil Procedure Section 473(d), seeking to set aside the default and default judgment as void, having been entered without affording the notice and opportunity to be heard required by the due process clause of the U.S. Constitution. On November 22, 2005, the trial court denied the motion.

The court concluded that because appellants "were not parties to the action and do not purport to be authorized representatives of the sole defendant Broderick Boys," they lack standing to raise the constitutional issue of whether the injunction was entered with adequate notice and an opportunity to be heard. Appellants could have their due process claim adjudicated only by admitting gang membership and claiming to act on behalf of the Broderick Boys (thus establishing a key element of the state's case) or by seeking a separate adjudication, and presumably losing on the gang membership issue. None of the defendants filed an order of declaratory relief, an order asking to be removed from the order they were served with. Filing such an order would of course put their gang membership documentation on display and would likely have proven their membership in the gang, which would make the order applicable to them. The prosecution contended that the four appealing members failed to even acknowledge that they were members of the enjoined gang, and therefore lacked standing to fight the order, as they were not officially parties to the action. The prosecution contended that the appeal was invalid, as only parties to an action can contest it, and the four appellants denied being members of the gang and were, therefore, not parties to the action.

On May 25, 2006, the ACLU appealed that ruling and asked the court to hold that they have standing to move to set aside the default judgment arguing the injunction is void, having been issued without adequate notice and an opportunity to be heard. The state's tactic in serving only a single alleged member of the Broderick Boys was clearly designed to avoid providing the targets of the injunction with any notice of this action until after the trial court had issued. There is no case or judicial precedent holding that service on and notice to a single gang member, occupying no position of leadership or authority in the gang, can confer jurisdiction over the gang and its 350 alleged members. The prosecution contended, however, that immediately after being served, the police observed Wolfington approach and talk to other Broderick Boy gang members, presumably spreading the word about the pending case that would have a significant impact on the gang.

On April 23, 2007, the Third District Court of Appeals overturned the two-year-old Broderick Boys injunction, saying there wasn't enough official notice given to suspected gang leaders. The court held that the injunction could not stand because the Yolo County district attorney failed to give adequate notice to those who would be affected by it. When it was first instituted in early 2005, the injunction was only served on one alleged gang member who had no apparent leadership role. At the same time, justices agreed there is evidence of gang problems in West Sacramento, an indication that another injunction would pass legal muster if those affected were properly notified. In a 30-page ruling issued, the court said the Yolo County District Attorney's Office failed to properly notify members of the Norteño-affiliated Broderick Boys when it first served the injunction in early 2005. On appeal the court concluded the plaintiff failed to provide adequate notice of the action and reversed the order, denying the motion to set aside the default judgment. (See *People ex rel. Reisig v. Broderick Boys* (2007), 149 Cal. App. 4th 1506, 1512–1516, 1528–1529 [59 Cal. Rptr. 3d 64].)

On remand, the plaintiff filed a first amended complaint naming as the defendant the "Broderick Boys aka BRK aka BSK aka Norteño aka Norte aka XIV" (Broderick Boys) as well as 23 named individuals and DOEs 1 through 400. The named defendants are Timothy Acuna (Cartoon), Thomas Cedillo, Robert Cortez, Victor Dazo, Jr. (Little Vic), Alex Estrada (Otter), Ramon Esquilin (Kiko), Victor Ferreira (Hugo), Jesse Garcia (Smokey), Michael Hernandez (Snoopy), Rainey Martinez, William McFadden (Billy), Robert Montoya (Little Rob), Michael Morales, Rudy Ornelas, Guillermo Duke Rosales (Duke), Robert Sanchez (Rabbit), Paul Savala (Savage), Rudy Tafoya (Rude Dog), Abel Trevino (Gangster), Felipe Valadez, Jr. (Shug), Billy Wolfington (Bouncer), Tyson Ybarra, and William Ybarra, Jr. (Shylos). The first amended complaint contains a single cause of action alleging a public nuisance in an area described as follows: "located in the City of West Sacramento, bounded by Harbor Boulevard to the West, the Sacramento River to the North and to the East (but not including the area previously known as the Lighthouse Marina and Golf Course) and by Highway 50/Business Loop 80 and State Route 275 to the South" (the safety zone).

On July 27, 2007, the plaintiff moved for a preliminary injunction, supported by copies of the criminal records of the named defendants and the declarations of 48 police officers, including that of Investigator Villanueva, a gang expert. These declarations described various crimes committed by the gang. In opposition to the plaintiff's motion, defendants presented their own declarations from approximately 100 residents and others familiar with the safety zone. Most of these declarants indicated they had not seen gang activity in the safety zone and did not believe there was a gang problem requiring an injunction. Two declarants indicated they had not seen any groups of gang members patrolling the streets in the safety zone, and others expressed the belief that the only ones engaging in harassment in the area were the police.

Yolo Appeal Decision (Case CV CV 04-002085), March 8, 2010 (182 Cal. App. 4th 866; 106 Cal. Rptr. 3d 560; 2010 Cal. App. LEXIS 301)

Plaintiff, the district attorney of Yolo County, initiated this action against the Broderick Boys, an alleged criminal street gang, and 23 of its members to enjoin as a public nuisance their activities in a 2.98-square-mile area of the City of West Sacramento. The trial court granted the plaintiff's motion for a preliminary injunction and the defendants' appeal. We conclude sufficient, credible evidence supports the trial court's conclusion the Broderick Boys is a criminal street gang whose activities have created a public nuisance in the designated area. However, we further conclude two provisions of the preliminary injunction, one dealing with controlled substances and the other dealing with the consumption of alcoholic beverages, are unenforceable.

We therefore reverse as to those provisions but otherwise affirm the order. The original complaint in this action was filed on December 30, 2004, against the Broderick Boys and DOEs 1 through 400 and obtained a preliminary injunction by default. Later, plaintiff dismissed the DOE defendants and obtained a permanent injunction against the Broderick Boys alone, also by default. Several individuals moved to set aside the judgment, but the trial court denied the motion. On appeal to this court, we concluded plaintiff failed to provide adequate notice of the action and reversed the order denying the motion to set aside the default judgment.

The nonassociation provision applies only within the safety zone and only in public places other than schools and churches. Although it places an incidental burden on familial relationships, such burden is necessary under the circumstances in order for the injunction to be effective. The injunction does not burden associational rights more than is necessary to serve the significant governmental interests at stake.

GANG ABATEMENT AND PREVENTION ACT OF 2007

The Gang Abatement and Prevention Act of 2007 was introduced by Senator Dianne Feinstein in January 2007, and subsequently passed the following October. Its companion bill, the Gang Prevention, Intervention, and Suppression Act (H.R. 3547), sponsored by Representative Adam Schiff, expanded the penal code regarding criminal street gangs, resulting in what many feel is an overreaching definition of both gangs and gang-related crimes. Additionally, these bills create a new section of penalties pertaining to gang crimes, increasing the enhanced sentences that are already in place. Both bills are referred to as the Gang Abatement Act. A report released in July 2007 by the Justice Policy Institute argues that implementing gang intervention programs like those that exist in New York are less costly than gang injunction programs. They have criticized this legislation, which would create a national gang member database and earmark $700 million for enforcement efforts, not prevention programs.

The Gang Abatement Act is focused mainly on suppression and enforcement tactics increasing law enforcement, prosecution capabilities, and sentence lengths. The law defines a *criminal street gang* as a formal or informal group, organization, or association of five or more individuals: (1) each of whom has committed at least one gang crime, and (2) who collectively commit three or more gang crimes (at least one of which is a serious violent felony), in separate criminal episodes. It defines a *gang crime* as a federal criminal offense punishable by imprisonment for more than one year or a state felony offense punishable by imprisonment of five years or more, involving: (1) physical force against another, burglary, arson, kidnapping, or extortion; (2) obstruction of justice or tampering or retaliating against a witness, victim, or informant; (3) drug trafficking; (4) illegal possession of firearms or explosives, racketeering, money laundering, or interstate transportation of stolen property; (5) harboring illegal aliens; or (6) aggravated sexual abuse, exploitation, or other sex crime.

It imposes criminal penalties on individuals who: (1) knowingly commit, or conspire, threaten, or attempt to commit, a gang crime in furtherance of a criminal street gang; (2) recruit persons to participate in a criminal street gang; and (3) commit other violent crimes in furtherance of a criminal street gang. It provides for criminal forfeiture of property used in the commission of a gang crime. After a review of the act, the following sections appear to be applicable to the use of civil remedies to curb gang activities:

Section 202: Amends the Controlled Substances Act to impose criminal penalties on individuals who commit murder and other violent crimes during and in relation to a drug trafficking crime.

Section 203: Expands restrictions on the release of persons charged with using firearms in a drug trafficking crime or a crime of violence.

Section 204: Establishes a 10-year limitation period for prosecutions of any noncapital felony crime of violence, including any racketeering activity or gang crime that involves any crime of violence.

Section 205: Directs the judicial conference of the United States to study changing the Federal Rules of Evidence to allow the admission into evidence the statements of a witness who is unavailable to testify due to a party's wrongdoing.

Section 206: Increases criminal penalties for possession of firearms by felons with one or more prior convictions for a violent felony or serious drug offense. It directs the U.S. Sentencing Commission to amend federal sentencing guidelines to reflect increases in penalties for possession of firearms by felons with multiple felony convictions.

Section 208: Amends the federal criminal code to: (1) redefine the crime of carjacking and increase penalties for such crime, (2) redefine and increase penalties for transfers of firearms to commit a crime of violence or drug trafficking, (3) apply criminal association restrictions to members of criminal street gangs, and (4) increase criminal penalties for conspiracy to commit a criminal offense or to defraud the United States.

Section 209: Authorizes the attorney general to conduct media campaigns in any area designated as a high-intensity gang activity area to educate residents of such area about changes in criminal penalties made by this act.

Section 212: Establishes as a predicate for a wiretap authorization violations of the Controlled Substances Act relating to murder and other violent crimes in furtherance of a drug trafficking crime and certain criminal street gang activity.

Section 214: Prohibits travel in interstate or foreign commerce, or use of the mail, to tamper with or retaliate against a witness, victim, or informant in a state criminal proceeding.

Section 301: Authorizes the attorney general to designate state high-intensity gang activity areas and provide assistance to such areas in combating gang activity. Establishes criteria for the designation of a high-intensity gang activity area. Requires the attorney general to submit a report to Congress, the director of the Office of Management and Budget (OMB), and the Domestic Policy Council on gangs in high-intensity gang activity areas. Authorizes the attorney general and the director of the Administrative Office of the U.S. Courts to hire additional personnel, including 94 assistant U.S. attorneys, to assist in anti-gang initiatives. Directs the Office of Justice Programs to establish a National Gang Research, Evaluation, and Policy Institute to design anti-gang programs, conduct research, and evaluate existing anti-gang programs.

Section 302: Authorizes the Office of Justice Programs of the Department of Justice (DOJ) to make grants to states, local, and tribal governments, and private entities to develop community-based programs that provide crime prevention, research, and intervention services designed for gang members and at-risk youth. Requires grant recipients to submit annual reports to the attorney general on their activities and their strategic plans.

Section 303: Authorizes the attorney general to expand the Project Safe Neighborhoods program to require each U.S.

attorney to: (1) identify, investigate, and prosecute significant criminal street gangs operating within his or her district; (2) coordinate the identification, investigation, and prosecution of criminal street gangs among federal, state, and local law enforcement agencies; and (3) hire additional personnel to support the expansion of the program.

Section 304: Authorizes the attorney general to expand the Safe Streets Program of the Federal Bureau of Investigation (FBI) to support criminal street gang enforcement teams. It directs the attorney general to: (1) establish a National Gang Activity Database to disseminate information to law enforcement agencies about gang activities and gang members, and (2) provide funding to the Regional Information Sharing Systems to use RISSNET (secure intranet) to connect existing gang information systems with the National Gang Activity Database.

Section 305: Amends the Violent Crime Control and Law Enforcement Act of 1994 to provide grants to assist prosecutors and law enforcement agencies in identifying gang members and violent offenders.

Section 306: Amends the Juvenile Justice and Delinquency Prevention Act of 1974 to direct the administrator of the Office of Juvenile Justice and Delinquency Prevention to expand the number of sites receiving juvenile delinquency reduction grants from 4 to 12.

Section 307: Authorizes the attorney general to make grants to public or nonprofit private entities (including faith-based organizations) to carry out projects involving innovative approaches to combat gang activity.

Section 308: Establishes in the U.S. Marshals Service a Short-Term State Witness Protection Section to provide protection for witnesses in state and local trials involving homicide or other major violent crimes. Authorizes the attorney general to make grants to prosecutor's offices to identify witnesses in need of protection.

Section 309: Allows nonreimbursable federal payments to states for the costs of investigating and prosecuting crimes of violence committed by a criminal street gang.

Section 310: Specifies that the federal Witness Relocation and Protection Program includes witnesses in cases involving criminal street gangs, serious drug offenses, and homicide, as well as organized criminal activity.

Section 404: Establishes the National Commission on Public Safety through Crime Prevention. Directs the commission to: (1) conduct a study of the effectiveness of crime and delinquency prevention and intervention strategies, organized around specified subcategories (i.e., family and community settings, law enforcement settings, and school settings); (2) make recommendations to the director of the National Institute of Justice for the dissemination of innovative crime prevention and intervention strategy grants; and (3) report to the president, Congress, and other federal and state officials on its findings and conclusions.

ORANGE VARRIO CYPRESS CASE 30-2009-00118739, FILED MAY 14, 2009

The ACLU filed a class action lawsuit in response to what they believed to be unlawful tactics by the Orange County district attorney that they felt violated both due process and the California Constitution. The ACLU argued that when the DA's office brought a civil nuisance abatement lawsuit against 115 members of the OVC gang, and then when 62 members showed up in court to contest the allegation they were gang members, the DA dropped them from the lawsuit. So what's the problem? Well, having done that, the DA turned around and served them with an injunction as gang members, meaning any of them can be arrested for violating the orders. The ACLU argued that due process is the cornerstone of our public policy, and they intend to hold the DA and Orange PD responsible for their actions.

The ACLU and the media portrayed members of the gang as victims of police harassment and specifically discussed one of the 115 gang members that were served. The ACLU said one of the targets of the injunction, Miguel Lara, was a 20-year-old freshman at Santiago Valley College who was studying criminal justice and looked less like a gang banger than a typical college kid. He claims police added him to the list in retaliation for his participation in an anti-gang protest. Lara told the media and the ACLU, "The cops are retaliating and don't want us to fight the right way, legally. They want us to step down and we won't allow that."

A review of Mr. Lara, described as a college student being unfairly targeted by the police, showed that he did in fact have more than 20 separate police contacts over a period of seven years leading up to being added to the OVC gang injunction. The sheer volume of contacts (20) shows a continuing pattern of criminal gang activity according to the police. Mr. Lara also stated in his ACLU deposition that he does go by the moniker "Wicked," not a typical nickname taken by your average college student.

On May 16, 2002, Mr. Lara admitted that he had been jumped into the gang. On April 6, 2007, Mr. Lara was involved in a fight in which he threw a bottle, striking another person with it. Following this assault, Mr. Lara and his friends made threats against the mother of the victim he assaulted with the bottle, in which they yelled, "OVC gang" and "We are going to kill you bitch." This conduct is why the police feel people like Mr. Lara are part of the gang problem in the community, and why the police feel the ACLU and the media portray these gang members as helpless innocent victims of the police, while the police are the ones terrorizing the community.

Miguel Lara has a tattoo on his left hand, three dots—a very common tattoo among the Hispanic gang community. The three dots represent "mi vida loca" or "my crazy life." This tattoo is not gang specific; however, it is a common indicator used in the Hispanic gang subculture. When asked about this tattoo in his deposition, Mr. Lara claimed his Fifth Amendment privilege against self-incrimination and did not want to discuss the meaning of this tattoo.

While the DA's office did drop several individuals from the nuisance lawsuit, the DA acknowledged that those individuals could still be arrested for violating the gang injunction if Orange PD provide evidence that the individual is an active participant in the gang. However, those individuals dropped from the case will not have a civil case judgment against them on their permanent record. The easiest way to avoid being prosecuted on the injunction is to cease membership in the gang, which is what the Orange County DA wanted them to do in the first place.

GANG ABATEMENT AND PREVENTION ACT OF 2009

This act amends the federal criminal code to impose penalties on individuals who knowingly commit a gang crime or other violent crime in furtherance of a criminal street gang or who recruit persons to participate in a gang. This act expands the prohibition against committing violent crimes in aid of racketeering activity to include gang-related racketeering activity, and increases the criminal penalties for threats, attempts, or conspiracies to commit crimes of violence. This act also amends the Controlled Substances Act to impose criminal penalties on individuals who commit violent crimes in relation to a drug trafficking crime.

The act in essence increases penalties against gang members by doing things like expanding restrictions on the release of persons charged with using firearms in a drug trafficking crime or a crime of violence, and establishing a 10-year limitation period for prosecutions of any noncapital felony crime of violence.

This act authorizes the attorney general to designate and assist state high-intensity gang activity areas in combating gang activity. It directs the Office of Justice Programs to establish a National Gang Research, Evaluation, and Policy Institute to design and evaluate anti-gang programs. It also authorizes the Office of Justice Programs of the Department of Justice (DOJ) to develop grants for community-based programs that provide crime prevention, research, and intervention services for gang members and at-risk youth.

This act also amends prior acts. It amends the Violent Crime Control and Law Enforcement Act of 1994 to provide grants to assist prosecutors and law enforcement agencies in identifying gang members and violent offenders. It amends the Juvenile Justice and Delinquency Prevention Act of 1974 to direct the administrator of the Office of Juvenile Justice and Delinquency Prevention to expand the number of sites receiving juvenile delinquency reduction grants.

It authorizes the attorney general to develop grants for carrying out projects involving innovative approaches to combat gang activity. It amends the Office of National Drug Control Policy Reauthorization Act of 1998 to require the director of National Drug Control Policy to promote prevention of youth heroin use. It establishes the National Commission on Public Safety through Crime Prevention to study the effectiveness of crime and delinquency prevention and intervention strategies in accordance with the Precaution Act (Prevention Resources for Eliminating Criminal Activity Using Tailored Interventions in Our Neighborhoods Act of 2009).

YOLO COUNTY DECISION (CASE CV CV 04-002085), MARCH 29, 2011

The Yolo County district attorney filed a complaint on December 30, 2004, and a first amended complaint on July 17, 2007, seeking to abate a public nuisance through a gang injunction applicable to the safety zone pursuant to Civil Code § 3479–3480. The safety zone is a 2.98-square-mile area located in the City of West Sacramento, bounded by Harbor Boulevard to the west, the Sacramento River to the north and the east (but not including the area previously known as the Lighthouse Marina and Golf Course), and by Highway 50, Business Loop 80, and State Route 275 to the south. The safety zone extends 100 yards to the outside of its boundaries.

The first amended complaint named as defendants the Broderick Boys a/k/a BRK a/k/a BSK a/k/a Norteño a/k/a Norte a/k/a XIV (Broderick Boys) and 23 individual defendants.

On December 19, 2007, judgment was entered on the first amended complaint against defendants Victor Dazo, Jr., Ramon Esquilin, Michael Hernandez, Rainey Martinez, William McFadden, Robert Sanchez, Paul Savala, Abel Trevino, and Tyson Ybarra. The trial on the permanent injunction served as a "prove up" hearing for these defendants.

The plaintiff's application for injunctive relief had the benefit of appellate review several times before trial on the merits. The trial court granted interim relief on the original complaint, entered defaults, and issued a permanent injunction on February 3, 2005. Defendants appealed the injunction, challenging the plaintiffs' method of serving the complaint; the court of appeals reversed with directions to set aside the void judgment granting the injunction.

On March 8, 2010, the court of appeals affirmed the order granting preliminary injunction except for two provisions: paragraph (I)(e) regarding controlled substances, and paragraph (I)(f) regarding alcohol, which provisions it invalidated as overbroad. The court of appeals noted that "nothing in this opinion is intended to suggest that plaintiff may not move the trial court to amend as appropriate paragraphs (l)(e) or (l)(f) of the preliminary injunction" to cure the overbroad language.

Trial on the permanent injunction commenced July 12, 2010, and ended December 15, 2010. The parties were permitted to submit a posttrial briefing in late January 2011, and the court took the matter under submission in February 2011. The evidence in the court trial included over 286 potential witnesses, a view of the entire safety zone by the court and counsel, 806 exhibits, and 54 trial days. After each side had rested, the court took the matter under submission, and invited parties to submit posttrial briefs.

For various reasons, the court found less credible the testimony of these defense witnesses as to the nonexistence of the Broderick Boys gang. These reasons included the witnesses' relationships to named defendants and their apparent motive to minimize the defendants' actions, their lack of personal knowledge regarding certain events, their use of the phrase "I don't recall," and gaps in their knowledge or recollection.

Some residents testified that they feared a reduction in their property values if the permanent injunction was to issue. Their fear seemed genuine, though the court found it unsubstantiated, because there was no competent evidence presented of the preliminary injunction causing a reduction in home values to support their assertions.

Other residents testified that they believed the West Sacramento Police Department had, in the past, selectively enforced the preliminary injunction against Hispanics. However, there was no credible, competent evidence to support their testimony.

The court found all the expert opinions very helpful in some areas, and less than persuasive in others. Of particular note was the testimony of Professor James Hernandez, who testified for the defense regarding the duration of youth involvement in gangs as "an affiliation that is elastic," typically lasting only a few years in young adulthood. Thereafter, according to Professor Hernandez, youth often (but not always) age out of the gang as they transition into adulthood. The expert testimony was less credible where the expert opinion was based on work done over 20 years ago, or where the expert repeatedly declined to identify the facts on which he relied to support his opinion that there was no gang, or where the expert applied a sociological definition of criminal street gang that was not consistent with the definition in the penal code.

Findings of Fact and Conclusions of Law

Having considered all matters submitted in the papers, all admissible evidence, and the file in this case, and the applicable law, and having considered the testimony in court and, sitting as the trier of fact, having assessed the credibility of the witnesses, the court finds by clear and convincing evidence, and concludes as follows:

The court shall enter a "Judgment Granting Injunction After Trial ('Judgment')" consistent with the terms of the preliminary injunction, the evidence at trial, and the opinion of the Third District Court of Appeal in *Broderick Boys IL supra.*

Injunctions are equitable remedies. As such, the court retains jurisdiction to modify, dissolve or extend the injunction as equity requires. Civil Code section 3424. This injunction will expire without further action on the seventh anniversary of the entry of the Judgment Granting Injunction After Trial, unless an interested party petitions the court to modify its scope or duration. Any petition for modification would have to demonstrate either a material change in circumstances that would compel the court to a different conclusion, that the law upon which the injunction was granted has changed, or that the interests of justice compel modification. Civil Code section 3424. After seven years of litigation, two appeals, a six-month trial, over 800 exhibits, and extensive post-trial briefing, the court is satisfied that the parties have fully presented the evidence and argument relevant to the injunction at this time. For the benefit of laypersons reading this Statement of Decision, a "preliminary injunction" is a temporary remedy that issues prior to trial. After trial, if plaintiff succeeds, the court issues what is often called a "permanent" or "final" injunction, although such injunctions are, as here, not necessarily permanent but of finite term.

Active members: An "active member" of Broderick Boys is a person who participates in or acts in concert with Broderick Boys. The participation or acting in concert must be more than nominal, passive, inactive or purely technical. The following factors may be used to determine whether an individual is an "active member" of Broderick Boys:

a. whether the subject admits to being a member of Broderick Boys;
b. whether the subject has tattoos that are only associated with Broderick Boys;
c. whether the subject has been arrested while participating with active members of Broderick Boys; or
d. whether a reliable informant provides information that the subject is an active member of Broderick Boys.

Clothing, accessories, photographs and close association with known gang members may be relevant to whether a person is an active gang member, but these factors alone are insufficient to validate a subject as an "active member" of Broderick Boys for purposes of this injunction.

Term: This injunction shall expire on its own terms seven years after entry of this judgment against defendant Broderick Boys.

DUE PROCESS CASE: *MANUEL VASQUEZ, ET AL. V. TONY RACKAUKAS, ET AL.* (SACV 09-1090-VBF), APRIL 1, 2011

A significant decision relating to the due process procedures of gang injunctions was decided in April 2011.

The court found for the plaintiffs (the four accused OVC gang members) and against the defendants (the Orange County district attorney and the City of Orange Police Department) on the claims against each defendant pursuant to 42 USC Section 1983, procedural due process under the Fourteenth Amendment, and procedural due process under California Constitution Article I, Section 7. The plaintiffs prevailed in their challenge to the defendants' action of enforcing the gang injunction against plaintiffs after dismissing them from the state court suit prior to judgment. This court ruled that "procedural due process required a pre-deprivation hearing in the circumstances presented in this case," meaning, this court found that the four accused gang defendants should have been given a hearing prior to inclusion in the injunction in this case according to this court, because when they appeared in state court to defend themselves, they were voluntarily dismissed by the Orange County District Attorney's Office, and added back to the case following imposition, denying them their due process.

The State Case Synopsis

On February 1, 2009, the OCDA, on behalf of the people of the State of California, filed in the superior court of California for the County of Orange (OCSC) a complaint for preliminary and permanent injunction to abate a public nuisance (*People v. Orange Varrio Cypress Criminal Street Gang, et al.*). The OCDA sued not only the Orange Varrio Cypress criminal street gang (OVC) but also 115 individuals and 150 DOEs alleged to be active members or associates.

On February 23, 2009, the OCDA filed an *ex parte* application to serve OVC under California Civil Procedure Code § 416.40(c). The OCDA requested and obtained permission to serve the gang via a named defendant, Patrick DeHerrera, whom the OCDA alleged was an OVC member.

On or about February 24 and 25, 2009, OPD officers served the summons, complaint, and supporting papers totaling at least 500 pages on numerous individuals named in the state court complaint. Ultimately, 34 defendants (all adults)—including plaintiffs Lara and Vasquez—filed an answer or a general denial in response to the complaint.

On May 12, 2009, the OCDA filed a request for dismissal against 62 individuals. This group included the 34 adults who responded to the complaint by filing either a general denial or an answer, and approximately 26 unrepresented juveniles. The dismissal was entered on May 12, 2009.

On May 14, 2009, the OCSC granted the OCDA's request for default and judgment, signing the order for permanent injunction (the order) against OVC and individuals who had not filed a response to the complaint and had default entered against them. The facts found in this section have not materially changed from the facts found in the court's ruling on the plaintiffs' motion for preliminary injunction and are supported by the evidence introduced at trial and through the plaintiffs' request for judicial notice. The order for permanent injunction applied to the OVC and to all members of the gang, whether or not named in the original lawsuit and to all "participants, agents, associates, servants, employees, aiders, and abettors whose membership, participation, agency, association, service, employment, aid or abetment is more than nominal, passive, inactive, or purely technical and all persons acting under, in concert with, for the benefit of, at the direction of, or in association with the OVC criminal street gang in any manner that is more than nominal, passive, inactive, or purely technical." The terms of the order for permanent injunction applied to a limited gang operation area in the safety zone in the City of Orange.

In early June, the OCDA, by and through the OPD, began to serve the order for permanent injunction. As of late September 2009, 94 individuals were served with the order for permanent injunction. These individuals include at least 22 individuals, including plaintiffs, who had been named in the litigation against OVC and its members but were voluntarily dismissed by the OCDA.

On July 10, 2009, the OCSC granted plaintiff Gabriel Bastida's request to vacate the default entered against him and to be permitted to contest the allegations against him. In late April 2009, the OCDA had sought and obtained entry of default against Mr. Bastida. In mid-May 2009, Gabriel Bastida had filed a request to vacate the default and a general denial, requesting that he be allowed to present a defense at trial and contest the allegations against him.

On July 16, 2009, the OCDA dismissed the case against Gabriel Bastida.

On August 13, 2009, defendant OPD served Gabriel Bastida with the gang injunction.

The Federal Case

On September 23, 2009, the plaintiffs Michael Vasquez, Miguel Lara, Gabriel Bastida, and Randy Bastida (plaintiffs) filed their complaint for declaratory and injunctive relief and petition for writ of habeas corpus against the defendants. The complaint has two causes of action for procedural due process violations: the first is a 42 USC Section 1983 claim under the Fourteenth Amendment of the U.S. Constitution, and the second is a claim under the California Constitution, Article I, Section 7.

The plaintiffs sought to enjoin defendants and their directors, officers, agents, and employees from enforcing the terms of the permanent injunction order against them issued in *People v. Orange Varrio Cypress Criminal Street Gang, et al.*, Orange County Superior Court, 30-200900118739, and those similarly situated "without first providing them with a full constitutionally-adequate hearing."

The core issue of the case was the plaintiffs challenging the defendants' tactics in subjecting them to a gang injunction, obtained via default against the gang to which they allegedly belonged, after dismissing the plaintiffs from that suit.

On September 29, 2009, the court denied the plaintiffs' *ex parte* application for a temporary restraining order, but set an order to show cause regarding a preliminary injunction hearing for November 5, 2009.

On November 17, 2009, the court denied plaintiffs' motion for preliminary injunction.

On September 27, 2010, the court denied the parties' cross motions for summary judgment.

In April 2011, the federal court heard the case and made a finding. The court found that the plaintiffs were not given predeprivation hearings, especially in light of the dismissals requested by the defendants. In sum, the constitutional rights of the four accused OVC gang members were violated. Procedural due process requires a predeprivation hearing in the circumstances of this case, especially where the class of individuals deprived of rights is vaguely defined and difficult to discern, where the prohibited conduct is indefinite or unclear, and where the defendants interfere with the plaintiffs' ability to engage in common day-to-day lawful activities. Deprived of a hearing by the dismissal, the plaintiffs were not given notice of and access to evidence, or the opportunity to confront and to be heard as required by due process. Nor were the plaintiffs given the right to have a neutral decision maker decide whether they were active participants in the OVC.

In this case, postdeprivation hearings cannot cure the lack of process. Intervention in the state action, postarrest contempt proceedings, and the removal procedure are not adequate postdeprivation remedies in this case. The risk of erroneous deprivation is substantial. Here, the government has no interest in failing to provide a predeprivation hearing. The defendants did not show that a need for prompt action justified a lack of due process. In sum, the defendants failed to provide adequate due process. Additional safeguards are required in this case, particularly some kind of hearing—notice and the opportunity to be heard—before the state deprives a person of liberty. At the time of this synopsis, it is not clear if the defendants intend to file an appeal to this decision and what the full impact of this case will be on future and current injunctions filed in the state courts in multiple states.

18

Gang Abatement Program Elements

The nuisance abatement statutes on the books in most states can be useful additions to the various methods law enforcement applies to stem the tide of gang activity. Removing the availability of places for gangs to gather can be very effective in disrupting the gang culture, thus making their activities less organized and more manageable for law enforcement. A nuisance suit under these laws can be brought against the person who owns the property in question, the gang members, or both.

In a successful suit, the court can enjoin the gang members from engaging in criminal activity and can issue appropriate orders to prevent the continued use of the property for gang activity. Any violations of these court orders can result in civil contempt charges for the offending defendant that can include fines or jail time or both. Additionally, violation of the court order can mean criminal liability. In short, as a property owner you can be sued for failing to take steps to remove the criminal element from your property in the event someone is hurt or killed, and it could have been or should have been prevented.

In November 1996, the Chicago Police Department (CPD) implemented a multiagency program designed to combat increasing criminal gang and narcotics activity in Chicago. This program serves as an example of what abatement programs can accomplish. The program was a joint effort of the CPD, Chicago Department of Law, Chicago Department of Buildings, and other city departments. The mission of the program was to tackle gang and drug problem buildings, known as non-owner-occupied multiunit dwellings.

The program targeted multiunit dwellings because they were believed to foster gang and drug crime; this is true in Chicago and many other large metropolitan areas. According to the police, certain buildings act as magnets for illegal activity, including gang and narcotics crime. Compounding the problem is a lack of cooperation from building owners and managers at many locations. This lack of attention to structural deterioration, inadequate screening of potential tenants, failure to monitor who has access to the location, and failure to take action against tenants who are known to engage in criminal activities all serve to feed the cycle of crime and disorder that gangs thrive on. Without a program or policy to deal with this issue, building owners or managers will not be forced to manage their properties in a manner that contributed to the vitality rather than the decay of the neighborhood. The strategy is to engage building owners as proactive partners in corrective measures and presents powerful deterrents against those owners who are unresponsive.

Once a problem location is identified via complaints and analysis, the police and other city departments, such as code compliance, building inspectors, and fire inspectors, conduct inspections for code violations, provide information and recommendations for improving the properties, and conduct administrative proceedings to bring landlords into compliance. Some cases are assigned to city attorneys for prosecution under the city or county nuisance abatement ordinances, allowing the city to hold landlords accountable for some criminal activities of their tenants.

Many other cases do not go to court; they are able to be handled through an administrative process rather than a formal, legal one. Administrative remedies include requiring landlords to appear at administrative hearings, sending notifications of violations to building owners, and recommending landlord training classes to code violators. These are options if voluntary abatement measures are not successful. This gives city attorneys some flexibility in finding solutions to nuisance abatement cases.

The program in Chicago has attempted to coordinate the efforts of inspectors and increase the sharing of information by creating teams that conduct inspections together. Each team consists of conservation, electrical, plumbing, fire, and revenue inspectors. Individual inspectors do not participate in every inspection, but are available on an as-needed basis, depending on the type of code violations expected by the task force. This increased level of coordination was a drastic change over past inspection programs. This program and others also have proposed steps that can be taken to help address problem locations.

STEP 1: SELECT ADDRESSES FOR INSPECTION

The inspection process begins with the identification, or targeting, of dwelling units for inspection. Targeting activities are usually initiated a few weeks before any actual case activity will take place;

in some cases a location can have a history of years of problems. Inspectors will select districts and beats for inspections, and tour these areas with police personnel looking for physical (and other) evidence of code or criminal violations at specific addresses. Lists of buildings and locations are completed and inspectors fill out "abatement checklists" for candidate buildings covering physical and other evidence of crime or nuisance problems (damage to property, gang graffiti, poor lighting, litter, etc.).

Potential targets can be identified from other sources as well. The police may suggest dwelling units for inspection based on information gathered at community meetings, from residents, or during the normal course of daily police work in the neighborhoods. In essence, any public official or city employee who is an integral part, or linked to the project, and any citizen who is connected to the police may suggest a dwelling unit as a target for inspection. Nominated (or targeted) dwelling units must meet certain threshold criteria relating to gangs and narcotics violations to be inspected. The main threshold criteria varied from the minimum required by the ordinance (two misdemeanors in the past six months or one felony) to up to five prior arrests for each dwelling unit (misdemeanors or felonies), with "hits" being for specific offense types associated with gang activity or drug trafficking. This was determined through inspection or by reviewing arrest reports and police calls for service at the location.

STEP 2: CONDUCT INSPECTIONS

Once officials develop a list of dwelling units to be inspected, inspection teams attempt to visit each address and conduct inspections. The teams typically include general building inspectors, electrical inspectors, and plumbing inspectors working in connection with the police. Depending on the dwelling unit, prior information known about the dwelling unit, or anticipated problems, other officials, such as police officers, fire inspectors, health inspectors, and housing authority representatives, or other specialists, may join the inspection team.

The inspection process at any one dwelling unit follows a routine. Generally, the team attempts to contact the landlord first, to notify him or her of the inspection and request admission to the property. When a landlord, building manager, or owner cannot be located, or uncooperative owners are encountered, the team attempts to contact individual tenants to gain admission. An inspection team's success at gaining entry on the first attempt varies considerably. Most times access is gained on the first visit; however, sometimes a few revisits to the address are required before entry is obtained.

In some instances a discussion with an owner, landlord, or tenant is not possible. In those cases, the team does the best it can to inspect the dwelling unit from the outside and along the perimeter of the property. In some cases the teams encounter significant resistance; this may require an inspection warrant, which can be sought when there is reasonable cause to believe that any premises is being maintained in violation of this section. Any judicial officer may, upon the petition of the prosecuting attorney, issue an inspection warrant for the premises. This process varies by state.

The general aim of the inspection is to determine whether evidence exists of city building code violations on the property and, when such evidence is found, to document it through reports, and photographs where appropriate. Two related goals of the inspections include compilation of an organized, legible case file for review with enough information to give the prosecution a viable case for court, and contact with property owners and landlords to provide advice and inform them of information and resources available to them to better manage and screen tenants, fix properties, and avoid future problems.

A less formal but often articulated goal of inspections directly relates to the informal mechanisms through which many other community policing initiatives operate, the public inspection itself that lets landlords and neighbors know that community (or official) action is being taken at dwelling units that are known to have crime (gang and drug) problems.

STEP 3: PREPARE CASE INFORMATION

Following an inspection conducted at a dwelling unit (and often, repeated attempts to conduct the inspection), inspectors prepare reports including evidence, a list of citation violations, forms, checklists, photos, and recommendations for further action. This information, compiled in packets, is reviewed by city attorneys for further action. In most cases, the time between the inspection and court action can be from a couple of weeks to several months, depending on the backlog of cases and available resources. The information collected on each case should include the following: case identification number, property location (such as the address, police beat, and district), dates of inspection and subsequent reinspection, date when case packet was received from the Department of Buildings, date the work was assigned to an attorney, date a notice of violation was sent to a property owner, and date of a resolution meeting. Finally, the case management file should provide information on the case origin (whether it originated from the task force, a city attorney, or another source), the basis for the case against a property (e.g., narcotics, gangs, building code violations, etc.), and the status of the case.

STEP 4: CASE PROCESSING

In a process similar to the perhaps more familiar felony review of arrests by prosecutors, attorneys review the inspection case packets to determine the quality of the case. (Are there true citation violations? Have threshold criteria for cases under the new nuisance abatement ordinance been met? Is the case information organized, legible, and complete?) A case may be rejected (threshold criteria not met, no true code violations, insufficient evidence, etc.) or accepted. Rejected cases may be reinspected or reworked and still pursued as routine code violations, or they may be abandoned. For each accepted case, attorneys have four general courses of action they can pursue. These typically include:

1. Send a notification of violation (NOV) letter to the landlord or property owner and pursue the course of voluntary compliance.
2. Require the landlord or owner to attend the Landlord Training Program, a special seminar on property improvement, tenant screening and management, etc.
3. Pursue the code violations through a special administrative hearing that includes possible imposition of fines and other sanctions.
4. Use civil (chancery) or other court hearings, the most formal sanction possible. These are typically used in cases of repeated criminal (gang and drug) violations, and refusal by the landlord or owner to pursue any other means to resolve the case.

STEP 5: REINSPECTION, CASE CLOSING, AND ASSESSMENT

Most inspection cases are resolved through voluntary compliance after a notification of violation. Reinspection of dwelling units in the process of compliance or nearing case completion is a key component of the process. Inspectors should revisit most of the addresses they originally cite, regardless of whether they are accepted or rejected by the prosecutors. It is typically the prosecutors, however, who determine when a case has been completed successfully or unsuccessfully under the project and, more importantly, under the law.

One key element of an ongoing injunction or abatement project is including an evaluation and assessment component against which to compare individuals, cases, or activities. In the future, a model case initiation, processing, and termination process should be developed, with input from all agencies involved; published and distributed; and utilized as an ongoing assessment and evaluation tool.

ABATEMENT LAWS BY STATE EXAMPLES

Arkansas

Section 5-74-109 addresses the issue of a premises or real property that is being used by criminal gangs:

> Any premises, building, or place used to facilitate the commission of a continuing series of three (3) or more criminal violations of Arkansas law is declared to be detrimental to the law-abiding citizens of the state and may be subject to an injunction, a court-ordered eviction, or a cause of action for damages as provided for in this subchapter. When there is reason to believe a common nuisance under subsection (b) of this section is kept or maintained, or exists in any county, the prosecuting attorney of the county in the name of the state, or the city attorney of any incorporated city, or any citizen of the state or a resident of the county in his or her own name, may enjoin permanently the person conducting or maintaining the nuisance and the owner, lessee, or agent of the building or place in or upon which the nuisance exists from directly or indirectly maintaining or permitting the nuisance. If the existence of the nuisance is established in the action, an order of abatement shall be entered as part of the judgment in the case, and the plaintiff's costs in carrying out the order are a lien upon the building or place. The order shall provide for any appropriate equitable relief as determined by the court to be necessary to abate the nuisance and may further provide, if determined to be the least restrictive alternative available to effectively accomplish the abatement, for the effectual closing of the building or place for such period of time as determined to be necessary by the court as adequate to abate the nuisance.

California

Section 186.22a states:

> Every building or place used by members of a criminal street gang for the purpose of the commission of the offenses listed in subdivision (e) of Section 186.22 or any offense involving dangerous

or deadly weapons, burglary, or rape, and every building or place wherein or upon which that criminal conduct by gang members takes place, is a nuisance which shall be enjoined, abated, and prevented, and for which damages may be recovered, whether it is a public or private nuisance. Whenever an injunction is issued pursuant to subdivision (a), or Section 3479 of the Civil Code, to abate gang activity constituting a nuisance, the Attorney General or any district attorney or any prosecuting city attorney may maintain an action for money damages on behalf of the community or neighborhood injured by that nuisance. Any money damages awarded shall be paid by or collected from assets of the criminal street gang or its members that were derived from the criminal activity being abated or enjoined. Only persons who knew or should have known of the unlawful acts shall be personally liable for the payment of the damages awarded. In a civil action for damages brought pursuant to this subdivision, the Attorney General, district attorney, or city attorney may use, but is not limited to the use of, the testimony of experts to establish damages suffered by the community or neighborhood injured by the nuisance. The damages recovered pursuant to this subdivision shall be deposited into a separate segregated fund for payment to the governing body of the city or county in whose political subdivision the community or neighborhood is located, and that governing body shall use those assets solely for the benefit of the community or neighborhood that has been injured by the nuisance.

Florida

Section 823.05 addresses places used by gangs that may be abated or enjoined:

> Whoever shall erect, establish, continue, or maintain, own or lease any building, booth, tent or place which tends to annoy the community or injure the health of the community, or become manifestly injurious to the morals or manners of the people shall be deemed guilty of maintaining a nuisance, and the building, erection, place, tent or booth and the furniture, fixtures, and contents are declared a nuisance. All such places or persons shall be abated or enjoined. As used in this section, the terms "criminal gang," "criminal gang member," "criminal gang associate," and "criminal gang-related activity" have the same meanings. A criminal gang, criminal gang member, or criminal gang associate who engages in the commission of criminal gang-related activity is a public nuisance. Any and all such persons shall be abated or enjoined. The use of a location on two or more occasions by a criminal gang, criminal gang members, or criminal gang associates for the purpose of engaging in criminal gang-related activity is a public nuisance.

Georgia

Section 16-15-7 states:

> Any real property which is erected, established, maintained, owned, leased, or used by any criminal street gang for the purpose of conducting criminal gang activity shall constitute a public nuisance and may be abated. Any person who is injured by reason of criminal gang activity shall have a cause of action for three times the actual damages sustained and, where appropriate, punitive damages; provided, however, that no cause of action shall arise under this subsection as a result of an otherwise legitimate commercial transaction between parties to a contract or agreement for the sale of lawful goods or property or the sale of securities. Such person shall also recover attorney's fees in the trial and appellate court and costs of investigation and litigation reasonably incurred.

Illinois

Section 720 ILCS 5/37-1 states:

> Any building used in the commission of offenses prohibited or used in the commission of an inchoate offense relative to any of the aforesaid principal offenses, or any real property erected, established, maintained, owned, leased, or used by a street gang for the purpose of conducting street gang related activity as defined in Section 10 of the Illinois Street gang Terrorism Omnibus Prevention Act is a public nuisance. A person convicted of knowingly maintaining such a public nuisance commits a Class A misdemeanor. Each subsequent offense under this Section is a Class 4 felony. Any person who is injured by reason of street gang related activity shall have a cause of action for 3 times the actual damages sustained and, if appropriate, punitive damages; however, no cause of action shall arise under this subsection. The cause of action created by this Act shall lie against any street gang in whose name, for whose benefit, on whose behalf, or under whose direction the act was committed; and (2) any gang officer or director who causes, orders, suggests, authorizes, consents to, agrees to, requests, acquiesces in, or ratifies any such act; and (3) any gang member who, in the furtherance of or in connection with, any gang-related activity, commits any such act; and (4) any gang officer, director, leader, or member.

Indiana

Section 32-21-6-3 defines *psychologically affected property*:

> Psychologically Affected Property which includes real estate or a dwelling that is for sale, rent, or lease to a criminal gang (as

defined in IC 35-45-9-1); or the illegal manufacture or distribution of a controlled substance.

Iowa

Section 657.2 defines *nuisance location* as

> houses of ill fame, kept for the purpose of prostitution and lewdness, gambling houses, places resorted to by persons participating in criminal gang activity, or places resorted to by persons using controlled substances, or houses where drunkenness, quarreling, fighting, or breaches of the peace are carried on or permitted to the disturbance of others.

Kansas

Section 22-3901 states:

> The following unlawful activities and the use of real or personal property in maintaining and carrying on such activities are hereby declared to be common nuisances: Any felony committed for the benefit of, at the direction of, or in association with any criminal street gang, with the specific intent to promote, further, or assist in any criminal conduct by gang members. As used in this subsection, "criminal street gang" means any organization, association, or group, whether formal or informal: (1) Consisting of three or more persons; (2) Having as one of its primary activities the commission of one or more person felonies, person misdemeanors, felony violations of the uniform controlled substances act, K.S.A. 65-4101 et seq.; (3) Which has a common name or common identifying sign or symbol; and (4) Whose members, individually or collectively engage in or have engaged in the commission, attempted commission, conspiracy to commit, or solicitation of two or more person felonies, person misdemeanors, felony violations of the uniform controlled substances act, K.S.A. 65-4101 et seq.

Louisiana

Section 15:1405 states:

> Every private building or place used by members of a criminal street gang for the commission of a pattern of criminal gang activity is a nuisance and may be the subject of an injunction or cause of action for damages. Any person may file a petition for injunctive relief with the appropriate court seeking eviction from or closure of any premises used for commission of a pattern of criminal gang activity by a criminal street gang. Upon proof by the plaintiff that the premises are being used by members of a criminal street gang for the commission of a pattern of criminal gang activity, the court may order the owner of record of the premises to remove or evict

> the persons from the premises and order the premises sealed, prohibit further use of the premises, or enter such order as may be necessary to prohibit the premises from being used for the commission of a pattern of criminal gang activity.

Minnesota

Section 617.92 states:

> The continuous or regular use of a place by a lessee or tenant to engage in or allow gang activity by a criminal gang that is knowingly permitted by the owner or a person who is responsible for maintaining the place on behalf of the owner is a public nuisance. A person who continuously or regularly engages in gang activity as a member of a criminal gang may be made a defendant in a suit. If the public nuisance involves the use of a place the owner or a person who is responsible for maintaining the place on behalf of the owner may be made a defendant in the suit pursuant to the procedures applicable to owners. If the court finds, by a preponderance of the evidence, that a criminal gang constitutes a public nuisance, the court may enter a temporary or permanent order.

Mississippi

Section 97-44-15 states:

> Every private building or place used by members of a criminal street gang for the commission of illegal activity is a nuisance and may be the subject of an injunction or cause of action for damages or for abatement of the nuisance as provided for in this chapter. Any person may file a petition for injunctive relief with the appropriate court seeking eviction from or closure of any premises used for commission of illegal activity by a criminal street gang. Upon clear and convincing proof by the plaintiff that the premises are being used by members of a criminal street gang for the commission of illegal activity, the court may order the owner of record or the lessee of the premises to remove or evict the persons from the premises and order the premises sealed, prohibit further use of the premises, or enter such order as may be necessary to prohibit the premises from being used for the commission of illegal activity by a gang and to abate the nuisance. The cause of action created by this chapter shall lie against: Any street gang in whose name, for whose benefit, on whose behalf or under whose direction the act was committed; and Any gang officer or director who causes, orders, suggests, authorizes, consents to, agrees to, requests, acquiesces in or ratifies any such act; and Any gang member who, in the furtherance of or in connection with, any gang-related activity, commits any such act; and Any gang officer, director, leader or member.

Missouri

Section 578.430 states:

> Any room, building, structure or inhabitable structure as defined in section 569.010, which is used by a criminal street gang in a pattern of criminal street gang activity shall be deemed a public nuisance. No person shall keep or maintain such a public nuisance. The attorney general, circuit attorney or prosecuting attorney may, in addition to any criminal prosecutions, prosecute a suit in equity to enjoin the public nuisance. If the court finds that the owner of the room, building, structure or inhabitable structure knew that the premises were being used for criminal street gangs in a pattern of criminal street gang activity, the court may order that the premises shall not be occupied or used for such period as the court may determine, not to exceed one year. All persons, including owners, lessees, officers, agents, offenders or employees, aiding or facilitating such a nuisance may be made defendants in any suit to enjoin the nuisance.

North Carolina

Section 14-50.24 states:

> Any real property that is erected, established, maintained, owned, leased, or used by any criminal street gang for the purpose of conducting criminal street gang activity shall constitute a public nuisance and may be abated. The provisions of this section shall not apply to real property used for criminal street gang activity where the owner or person who has legal possession of the real property does not have actual knowledge that the real property is being used for criminal street gang activity.

Ohio

Section 2923.43 defines a *criminal gang premises* that constitutes a nuisance as

> any building, premises, or real estate, including vacant land, that is used or occupied by a criminal gang on more than two occasions within a one-year period to engage in a pattern of criminal gang activity constitutes a nuisance subject to abatement. A criminal gang that uses or occupies any building, premises, or real estate, including vacant land, on more than two occasions within a one-year period to engage in a pattern of criminal gang activity is guilty of maintaining a nuisance and shall be enjoined as provided in sections 3767.03 to 3767.11.

South Carolina

Section 16-8-270 states a civil cause of action is

> Created in favor of the state of South Carolina, a county, municipality, or another political subdivision, that sustains any damage, impairment, or injury proximately caused by a pattern of criminal gang activity as defined in this article, or the commission of a criminal act for the purpose of benefiting, promoting, or furthering the interests of a criminal gang. The cause of action created by this section may be brought against a criminal gang, a criminal gang member, or any other person who intentionally directs, participates, conducts, furthers, or assists in the commission of a pattern of criminal gang activity, or any other person who commits a criminal act or delinquency for the purpose of benefiting, promoting, or furthering the interests of a criminal gang.

Tennessee

Section 29-3-101 defines a *nuisance* as

> that which is declared to be a nuisance by other statutes, and, in addition, means: A criminal gang, as defined by § 40-35-121(a), that regularly engages in gang related conduct. "Gang related conduct" occurs when one (1) or more criminal gang member or members regularly engages in the following: Intimidating, harassing, threatening, stalking, provoking or assaulting any person; Possessing weapons prohibited; Unlawfully damaging, defacing or marking any public or private property of another or possessing tools for the purpose of unlawfully damaging, defacing or marking any public or private property of another; Selling, possessing, manufacturing or using any controlled substance or drug paraphernalia or being under the influence of any controlled substance in public; Using, consuming, possessing or purchasing alcoholic beverages unlawfully; Criminal trespassing in violation of § 39-14-405.
>
> "Place" means and includes any building, room enclosure or vehicle, or separate part or portion thereof or the ground itself and all the property on which the nuisance is located that is under the ownership, management or control of the violator. Any person who uses, occupies, establishes or conducts a nuisance, or aids or abets therein, and the owner, agent or lessee of any interest in any such nuisance, together with the persons employed in or in control of any such nuisance by any such owner, agent or lessee, is guilty of maintaining a nuisance and such nuisance shall be abated.

Texas

Section 125.063 states:

> The habitual use of a place by a combination or criminal street gang for engaging in gang activity is a public nuisance. Any person who habitually associates with others to engage in gang activity as a member of a combination or criminal street gang may be made a defendant in the suit. Any person who owns or is responsible for maintaining a place that is habitually used for engaging in gang activity may be made a defendant in the suit.

Virginia

Section 48-7 states:

> Any person who shall knowingly erect, establish, continue, maintain, use, own, occupy, or lease any building, erection, place, or area used for the purpose of lewdness, assignation, prostitution, or activities of a criminal street gang, as criminal street gang is defined in § 18.2-46.1 in the Commonwealth is guilty of a nuisance, and the building, erection, place, or area, the ground itself, in or upon which such lewdness, assignation, prostitution, or criminal street gang activity is conducted, permitted, or carried on, continued, or exists, and the furniture, fixtures, musical instruments, and contents are also declared a nuisance, and shall be enjoined and abated as hereinafter provided.

Washington

Section 59.18.030 defines a *gang* as a group that

> (a) consists of three or more persons; (b) has identifiable leadership or an identifiable name, sign, or symbol; and (c) on an ongoing basis, regularly conspires and acts in concert mainly for criminal purposes. "Gang-related activity" means any activity that occurs within the gang or advances a gang purpose. Each tenant shall pay the rental amount at such times and in such amounts as provided for in the rental agreement or as otherwise provided by law and comply with all obligations imposed upon tenants by applicable provisions of all municipal, county, and state codes, statutes, ordinances, and regulations, and in addition shall not engage in any gang-related activity at the premises, or allow another to engage in such activity at the premises, that renders people in at least two or more dwelling units or residences insecure in life or the use of property or that injures or endangers the safety or health of people in at least two or more dwelling units or residences.

Wisconsin

Section 939.22 states:

> Any building or structure that is used as a meeting place of a criminal gang or that is used to facilitate the activities of a criminal gang, is a public nuisance and may be proceeded against under this section. If a nuisance exists, the city, town, or village where the property is located may maintain an action in the circuit court to abate the nuisance and to perpetually enjoin every person guilty of creating or maintaining the nuisance, the owner, lessee, or tenant of the building or structure where the nuisance exists and the owner of the land upon which the building or structure is located, from continuing, maintaining, or permitting the nuisance.

19

Graffiti Abatement

A significant issue that gang injunctions and gang abatement projects attempt to address is graffiti. The term *graffiti* includes any unauthorized inscription, word, figure, mark, or design that is written, marked, etched, scratched, drawn, or painted on real or personal property. Graffiti is the malicious defacing with graffiti or other inscribed material, and it damages or destroys any real or personal property not owned by the person doing the vandalism. These unauthorized inscriptions or graffiti vandalism is a major problem in many nations, including the United States. Graffiti is often referred to as the newspaper of the streets in the gang and tagger subculture. If that is true, law enforcement officers need to make sure they get the subscription so they can tell what is going on around them.

We need to understand all of the basic elements of graffiti, why it is used and what it means. It is a critical skill to understand the graffiti in your area, be able to read it, explain it, and document it so that the graffiti can be used against the gangs and crews and their individual members. Graffiti has many practical investigative tips; for example, it can help you identify the size and strength of the local gang, their monikers, pending or past crimes, ongoing rivalries, and boundaries. Gangs use graffiti to claim their turf, marking their neighborhoods with graffiti on fences, schools, sidewalks, walls, homes, and street signs. Graffiti is a very important element in the investigation of street gangs. In many ways, gang graffiti is a *code*, and like most codes, it's susceptible to analysis if you take the time and effort to do so.

VANDALISM IMPACT

The following paragraph is taken from the *People v. Hard Times* gang injunction and is a good overview of the concept behind the use of a gang injunction to attempt to address the issue of vandalism:

> Defendant seeks to proclaim its ownership of the Safety Zone, to bolster the notoriety of Hard Times, and to physically degrade the Safety Zone by the repeated application of gang graffiti on the interior and exterior walls of buildings, trees, fences and other

> property in the Safety Zone. The graffiti is meant to dissuade residents from complaining to the police department and to show the criminal street gang's power. Graffiti constantly appears on the walls of homes and buildings creating a nuisance in the area. Hard Times criminal street gang commits its graffiti vandalism by using spray paint cans and felt tip markers, as well as other techniques and devices. The property rights of the owners and their tenants are substantially impaired and interfered with because they are forced to repeatedly expend time, labor and money in a vain attempt to eradicate Defendant's gang graffiti. Moreover, it is injurious to the health of the residents, and their comfortable enjoyment of life and property are harmed, when Hard Times' gang graffiti attracts foreseeable and violent retaliation from rival street gangs.

The dollar amount spent on graffiti cleanup is enormous. In 2000 the national cost for graffiti cleanup exceeded $4 billion, which is widely seen as a very conservative estimate, as only a fraction of vandalism incidents are ever reported. To solve the problem the police try to work closely with the community and other city departments, such as public works and parks and recreation, and private property owners to address this issue.

The average cost of removing or painting over graffiti is $552 per incident in Los Angeles County, and the county spends over $30 million per year in graffiti cleanup costs. This is not unique to Los Angeles; every major city in America has similar issues, and graffiti vandalism is causing economic havoc and blight everywhere it is applied all across America. The money used to clean up the damage could be directed instead toward many more productive programs and possibly to put more police officers on the street or help with a wide range of social ills. When a business owner has to clean his business after taggers hit, he typically offsets his costs by charging higher prices for products. Aside from cost, graffiti just makes our cities look rundown and trashed. It lowers property values and causes fear in the community.

One of the more costly forms of vandalism is by way of etching or scribing one's name into glass, as on a commercial business or bus window. The associated replacement cost of many windows is typically between $20 and $30 per square foot depending on the grade of the glass, thickness, cut, and whether the glass is tempered or tinted. This canvas used by vandals can be up to 50 times more expensive than conventional graffiti painted on a concrete wall. This is difficult to prevent, as a number of hard objects can be used to etch glass, Leanne, or Lucite windows, or other surfaces, like elevator doors, anodized aluminum, polished aluminum, or stainless steel. On a positive note, technology and crime prevention concepts have been designed into many products to make the financial impact less costly. These techniques will be discussed later in the chapter.

In many cases governmental agencies are tasked with the cleaning up of graffiti. With budgets being cut, governments can ill afford to spend the millions of dollars spent each month just in Southern California. Graffiti comes from the Italian word *graffio*, meaning a crude inscription or drawing scratched, painted, or sprayed on a surface, such as a wall, with the intent of being seen by the passing public. The negative impact of graffiti on a community is significant, as graffiti vandalism instills feelings of fear and insecurity, often causing significant problems for local jurisdictions that need to keep the community clean, residents and businesses flee the area, and property values plummet. The presence of graffiti vandalism is an affront to all who live, work, and visit a community.

The only people that seem to enjoy looking at the graffiti around their community are the gang members and taggers that put the graffiti there. Graffiti is believed to have a direct nexus to other crimes in a neighborhood; when not quickly removed and left unchallenged, it oftentimes attracts more serious criminal activity. Graffiti creates fear, and as a result there is a loss in neighborhood pride and people begin to feel intimidated in their own neighborhoods. Graffiti lowers property values and negatively impacts local business, as people often see graffiti and react by viewing it as an unsafe place to be, taking their business elsewhere. In areas where gangs are allowed to destroy property at will, the physical environment supports the gang subculture and gives the local gang more power and more control over the target area.

According to Wilson's and Kelling's broken windows theory, if a window in a building is broken and left unrepaired, the rest of the windows will soon be broken, as this is taken as an indicator that the community does not have any interest in how the neighborhood looks. According to Wilson and Kelling, untended physical disorder, antisocial behavior, and nuisance activity all lead to the breakdown of social control and increase crime. As residents perceive that crime is rising, they often react by avoiding public spaces like parks, and their involvement in neighborhood events is significantly reduced.

As crime in a community increases, so does the fear of the local gang. This frequently causes those that have the means to move out of the area, leaving behind those who are either unable or unwilling to counter the presence of the local gang (Shaw and McKay, 1942). The remaining residents become even less likely to report crimes committed by the gang and less likely to provide information to the police. In this way, the community purposefully or inadvertently helps the gangs evade justice for the crimes committed against the community.

TAGGERS VS. GANGSTERS

By reviewing the existing research on graffiti, it is difficult to determine where graffiti got its start in America. If cavemen writing on cave walls counts, the first taggers were prehistoric. In more recent times, during World War II, the phrase "Kilroy was here" was written on tanks and military equipment throughout Europe and was later seen in the subway systems in New York. In the 1950s, following the war, street gangs used graffiti to mark their territory, promote the gang, promote themselves, and intimidate the community.

The first thing one should do when trying to determine if graffiti is tagger or gang related is to look at the letters, the overall design or symbols used. If it has "bubble letters," for example, and contains more than one color of paint or ink, or shows even a hint of skill, it's almost certainly not gang related. If it has sharp, angular stick letters done in one color of paint, it is probably gang related. Tagger graffiti is typically more colorful and more elaborate than gang graffiti. Tagger crews are loose affiliations, typically of young people, whose principal activity is graffiti. Some of these tagger crews will try to pass themselves off as party crews, or groups of young people that evolve around social functions like raves and house parties to avoid the scrutiny of police that their gang member friends typically receive.

Many times taggers carry the tools used for etching glass or mirror surfaces, such as spark plug porcelain, drill bits, screwdrivers with a sharpened tip, small rocks, or any other type of sharp instrument, or stickers that may have drawings or a tagging moniker written on them. These stickers are used to "slap tag"; they are slapped upon a surface and are difficult to remove and generally leave a residue. Many times taggers can be identified by paint or marker residue on their fingertips; they may carry artist notebooks that contain tagging or drawings, visit tagging websites on the computer, subscribe to tagging magazines, or have photographs of tagging in their possession. Taggers generally tag in or near their own neighborhoods and, like traditional gang members, associate with other people who exhibit these same traits.

Tagging has long been considered a stepping-stone to gang membership. The term *tag* is believed to originally stand for an early group of graffiti artists called the "Tuff Artist Group"; hence a tagger is a member of a graffiti group or crew. Taggers in many cases are not the same as gang members, although many taggers and their crews have turned into gangs over the years. A tagger is a person who adopts a nickname, known as a tag as opposed to a moniker. He or she writes his or her tag in as many places as possible, to be seen by as many people as possible. The more the tag is seen, and the more difficult locations it appears

(a)

(b)

FIGURE 19.1 Photos of graffiti on a truck and a train.

in, the more popularity and fame the individual tagger receives from his or her peers.

Trains and delivery trucks that travel long distances are popular targets, as taggers are all about the recognition they receive: the more people that see their tag the better. In the State of Louisiana, Section 14:56.4 says it shall be unlawful for any person to intentionally deface with graffiti immovable or movable property, whether publicly or privately owned, without the consent of the owner. *Deface* or *defacing* is the damaging of immovable or movable property by means of painting, marking, scratching, drawing, or etching with graffiti, which covers things like trains and trucks (Figure 19.1a and Figure 19.1b). Freeways are primary targets, as they are seen by all cars that pass (Figure 19.2a and Figure 19.2b).

(a)

(b)

FIGURE 19.2 Photos of graffiti on freeways.

Taggers have their own subculture, language, and dress that set them apart from street gangs. Their clothing tends to be very baggie to conceal spray paint and of brighter colors than the clothing worn by gangs. Many wear clothing designed specifically for taggers and emulate popular hip-hop culture. While some crews are all one ethnicity, taggers as a whole care less about the race of the person and more about how much and how often they can get the crew name up on walls, freeway signs, subway trains, buses, and other public places.

Tagger crew names are typically three letters, although they can range from two to five letter initials, which represent the full name of the crew. The numbers in a crew name can mean anything from a phone pad number (e.g., 787 for RTS, or Running the Show), to a number in place of a word (4 for *four*), to letter substitutions (1 = A, 2 = B, etc.), telephone area codes, penal codes, or a combination of any of these elements to add to the confusion. Examples include RCA or Ruthless City Artists, RTS or Running the Show, or SEK for South East Kings. There is a lot that can be learned about an individual based on moniker, and the same is true when looking at the name of a crew. Many taggers consider themselves just a group of writers, not vandals; they feel they have the talent of professional writers (or think they do) and as such incorporate the term *writer* into their name, for example, ATR or Able to Rite, KAR or Kalling al Riters, WMM or Writers Making Masterpieces, or TWTS or The Write to Survive.

Some crews honor their favorite method for applying graffiti, such as SKA or Spray Kan Artists, LOA or Living on Aerosol, KC or Krylon Criminals.

Many crews honor the destructive nature of their activity, such as TSU for Trash Shit Up, CUS or City under Siege, and LSD or Leaving Serious Damage.

Some names tell you what targets the crew prefers, for example, AOB or All Over Buses, RTDK or Rapid Transit District Killers, or IFT or Interstate Freeway Taggers.

Some tell you the ethnicity of the gang, such as MTK or Mexicans Taking Kontrol, or TMK or The Mexican Kings, or KAM for Krazy Ass Mexicans.

Some tell you the gender of the group, such as BWA or Bitches with Attitude, QCT or Queens Causing Trouble, and CFG or Crazy Fantasy Girls.

Some tell you their view of themselves, how they perceive the group, or level of violence, such as COS or Criminals Out Shooting, and WNA or Were No Angels.

Figure 19.3a is an example of how tagger crews and known gangs associate and align themselves; the RTS crew and the ESD or East San Diego gang associate with each other. Figure 19.3b is from the Sur Trece Juniors gang, applied to the front of a day care for all the kids to see.

Taggers as we know them today have made a significant transition from the early days. Crews have become more violent, and many have been classified as "tag bangers" by police. Once a tagger crew starts to claim a turf, jump members into the group,

(a)

(b)

FIGURE 19.3 Photos of graffiti on a daycare center and a wall.

actively attack rivals for entering their turf, and align with other gangs for protection, they are no longer a tagger crew. It is important to clarify that a tag banger *is* a gang member. From a law enforcement perspective, it is important to investigate taggers in the same manner as we do street gangs. The first thing many officers need to do is eliminate the mindset that "it is just tagging." Vandalism and property crimes take a back seat to violent crimes with many officers, but by not dealing with the graffiti problem in an aggressive manner, the overall gang problem will continue to get worse. It's also important to note that many street gang members have tagger friends and may even adopt a tag so they can claim to be "just" a tagger when stopped by police.

Increasingly, they are wannabe gangsters who use the mobility and guise of a tagger crew to take their crimes beyond the boundaries of their turf. They generally work under the cover of darkness, particularly when doing extensive murals and marking freeway signs and other public places where risk of exposure is high. However, they will deface property whenever they have the opportunity to do so. Taggers typically plan graffiti missions in advance and conduct prior surveillance of locations to check for security, cameras, and potential escape routes.

Gangs have placed a major emphasis on identifying themselves and their gang affiliation, and they use a variety of methods to communicate with each other and carry out their gang-related business, one of the most visual being graffiti. Graffiti illustrates the individual gang member's commitment to the gang and his or her claim to the neighborhood; it tells the world who he or she is and what he or she represents. Graffiti is also great evidence against gang members and has tremendous investigative significance for anyone that investigates gang members and gang crimes.

POLICE RESPONSE

Many law enforcement operations targeting gangs are designed to help address and protect the physical environment and limit social disorganization in the neighborhoods. When gang members are in possession of marker pens, spray paint cans, or other sharp objects capable of defacing private or public property, they are ready to damage property when they feel it is appropriate. As such, it is important for law enforcement to address such minor violations in order to limit the potential damage to public and private property and hinder the gang's ability to advertise themselves to the community. When the police apprehend gangsters spray painting, marking with marker pens, scratching glass windows of shops or public transit, applying stickers, or otherwise applying graffiti on any public or private property, including but not limited to the street, alley, residences, block walls, vehicles, or any other real or personal property, they are helping protect the environment of the neighborhood, in theory, and holding gang members responsible for even minor violations.

For example, a police agency may want to organize a "trap a tagger" operation, which may include selecting an area that is heavily targeted by vandals, finding a wall to paint clean as a tempting target, and conducting a surveillance. The key is to know the area well; taggers typically run on contact, so making sure you have sufficient officers to cut off escape routes is essential. Having video surveillance makes these cases easy to prove, and all of the witnesses are police officers, protecting the public by not utilizing citizen informants from the area.

FIGURE 19.4 Tagger drawing of vandals damaging a city bus.

Gangs use graffiti to identify themselves, identify their territory, and communicate messages such as threats, challenges, descriptions of criminal acts the gang committed, and gang rosters that let the community know who they are and how many members they have (Figure 19.4). Police officers do not want to make it easy for them to accomplish their mission, and they need to realize if apprehended doing damage, they will be arrested.

SUPPRESSION

Suppression is the involvement of law enforcement when criminal activity occurs and where arrest is the appropriate response. It targets gang leaders and hard-core members for aggressive suppression (full force of the law). It involves law enforcement, parole, probation, and prosecution working together, and removes dangerous and influential gang members from the community by effective use of gang intelligence, targeting, and vertical prosecution (wiretaps, informants, and enhancements).

GANG INJUNCTIONS

Many restrictions of gang injunctions are designed to help address and protect the physical environment and limit social disorganization in the target areas. Provisions of gang injunctions such as restricting the possession of marker pens, spray paint cans, or other sharp objects capable of defacing private or public property; and spray painting, marking with marker pens, scratching, applying stickers, or otherwise applying graffiti on any public or private property, including but not limited to the street, alley, residences, block walls, vehicles, or any other real or personal property, all help protect the environment in theory. Some injunctions contain wording that restricts damaging or vandalizing the property of another, both public and private property, including but limited to any vehicle, light fixture, door, fence, wall, gate, window, building, street sign, utility box, telephone box, trees, or power poles to help protect the physical environment.

In 1982, the Los Angeles city attorney and the Los Angeles police took a new approach to address the problem of gang graffiti. On July 22, 1982, a civil gang injunction was obtained against three gangs: Dogtown, Primera Flats, and the 62nd East Coast Crips. Seventy-two members of the three gangs were targeted with a civil gang injunction that had only restrictions aimed at reducing graffiti, including prohibiting graffiti on private property, on public property, and trespassing on private property with the intent to place graffiti. It also contained an order for the gang to clean up the graffiti that displayed the name of their gangs. The injunction required the 72 named defendants to do five hours of community service to clean graffiti. The theory behind the graffiti cleanup was based in part on the theories of Thrasher (1927) that indicated the result of the gang's graffiti was solidarity, group awareness, and strengthened attachment to a local territory. The graffiti attributed to the gangs covered storefronts, billboards, houses, and fences and allowed the gangs to control their territory.

PREVENTION TECHNIQUES

Vandalism prevention can be accomplished in several ways, by dealing with at-risk youth (prevention) who may become vandals, dealing with those that have already joined gangs or tagger crews (intervention), and holding vandals accountable for their actions (suppression). Gangs can be prevented by using all three common approaches. However, true vandalism prevention seeks to work in innovative and creative ways to enable young people to feel empowered in making safe and informed choices. This is often done by working with young people to raise their awareness of the risks of gang and tagger crew involvement, the consequences of engaging in criminal acts of vandalism, and developing exit strategies for those who are already involved in doing acts of vandalism.

Vandalism prevention includes the strategies, actions, and efforts used to dissuade youth from getting involved in gangs and tagger crews, violence, or antisocial behavior. The goal is to find those youth who are most likely to join a gang in the future and offer them alternatives and support to make better choices.

Examples include information campaigns, after-school and summer programs, truancy and dropout prevention, and prenatal and infancy support. Stopping them from joining in the first place will reduce gang membership and gang crime.

INTERVENTION WITH VANDALS

The strategies, actions, and efforts used to dissuade youth from continuing their involvement in a gang, violence, or anti-social behavior target active gang members and close associates. They require aggressive outreach, ongoing recruitment, and careful planning and coordination. A multidisciplinary intervention team provides assessment, intervention planning, and case management. Carrot = opportunities (educational/vocational); stick = accountability.

What motivates graffiti vandals? Some of them just want to damage property, but most get a thrill out of seeing their "art" or tags in places where lots of other people can see them too. If you can deny graffiti vandals this thrill, they'll go elsewhere next time, or they may reduce their involvement in vandalism activity, which may serve to start the process of breaking them away from vandalism.

Crime Prevention through Environmental Design (CPTED) is defined as the proper design and effective use of the built environment to reduce crime, disorder, and the fear associated with crime. This can include many different techniques, such as those outlined in the following sections.

Lock Up Aerosol Spray Paint Containers and Marker Paints

Over the past several years, graffiti vandalism has exploded across cities like San Diego, costing millions of dollars annually. Many individual citizens and community-based groups are working to stop the vandals and repair the damage they are causing. Law enforcement personnel report that many graffiti vandals claim to have stolen or "racked" the paint, markers, or etching tools used in their crimes. Vandals also claim that they have no problem buying spray paint from retail stores (Figure 19.5a and Figure 19.5b). The city's Responsible Retailer Program is a direct and practical response to this dilemma; retailers voluntarily step up employee education and internal security to deprive graffiti vandals of the legitimate products they misuse to commit property crimes.

The program is a combination of in-store activities designed to reduce retail theft of potential graffiti tools and stop the illegal sale of spray paint to customers under the age of 18. It includes training store employees, strategically placing signs at display and

(a)

(b)

FIGURE 19.5 Photos of spray paint locked up in store displays.

checkout points, and displaying graffiti tools in a prudent manner. Through awareness and strengthened self-policing, San Diego retailers can constrict the flow of products into the hands of those who use them in graffiti crimes. Further, by joining the program, participating retailers can curtail costly theft from their stores while demonstrating an active concern for the problems of the community in which they do business.

There are also laws that compel compliance, such as a municipal code from Los Angeles, which states:

> Every person who owns, conducts, operates or manages a retail commercial establishment selling aerosol containers or marker pens with tips exceeding four millimeters in width, containing anything other than a solution which can be removed with water after it dries, shall store or cause such aerosol containers or marker pens to be stored in an area viewable by, but not accessible to, the public in the regular course of business without employee assistance, pending legal sale or disposition of such market pens or paint containers. (L.A.M.C 47.11, Responsible Retailers Program)

California Penal Code Section 594.1 also addresses the sale, purchase, or possession of aerosol paint containers and mandates posting of notices by retailers:

> (a) It shall be unlawful for any person, firm, or corporation, except a parent or legal guardian, to sell or give or in any way furnish to another person, who is in fact under the age of 18 years, any aerosol container of paint that is capable of defacing property without first obtaining bona fide evidence of majority and identity. (b) It shall be unlawful for any person under the age of 18 years to purchase an aerosol container of paint that is capable of defacing property. (c) Every retailer selling or offering for sale in this state aerosol containers of paint capable of defacing property shall post in a conspicuous place a sign in letters at least three-eighths of an inch high stating: Any person who maliciously defaces real or personal property with paint is guilty of vandalism which is punishable by a fine, imprisonment, or both.

Glass Etching Cream/Product Display under Lock and Key

> Every person who owns, conducts, operates, or manages a retail commercial establishment selling glass etching cream, or any commercially available glass etching products, whether sold separately or in a kit in an area viewable by, but not accessible to, the public in the regular course of business without employee assistance, pending legal sale or disposition of such glass etching cream or glass etching product, is in violation of this section. No person who has not yet

FIGURE 19.6 Photos of graffiti etched into glass.

> attained the age of 18 years can purchase such items. Therefore this ordinance requires anyone who displays for sale glass etching cream, or any commercially available glass etching product, whether sold separately or in a kit, to display it under lock and key and allow its sale only to persons 18 years of age or older. (L.A.M.C 47.16)

Modern advances have made the damage from window etching less costly; now San Diego transit buses have a thin layer of plastic on both sides of the glass, which can be more easily replaced when vandals scratch their names in the glass, keeping transit cleaner for less money (Figure 19.6).

California Penal Code Section 594.2 addresses the possession of specified instruments with intent to commit vandalism or graffiti.

> Every person who possesses a masonry or glass drill bit, a carbide drill bit, a glass cutter, a grinding stone, an awl, a chisel, a carbide scribe, an aerosol paint container, a felt tip marker, or any other marking substance with the intent to commit vandalism or graffiti, is guilty of a misdemeanor. For the purposes of this section, "felt tip marker" means any broad-tipped marker pen with a tip exceeding three-eighths of one inch in width, or any similar implement containing an ink that is not water soluble. "Marking substance" means any substance or implement, other than aerosol paint containers and felt tip markers, which could be used to draw, spray, paint, etch, or mark.

Clean Up Graffiti Right Away—After It Has Been Documented

Gang members and taggers take the messages they read in graffiti seriously, and the longer graffiti is left up in a neighborhood, the greater the risk that the threats will be acted upon. Gang graffiti should be cleaned off property in the community quickly, but not before being documented and photographed by police whenever possible. The swift removal of the graffiti will let the gangs know that the community will not tolerate their vandalism, and that they care about the neighborhood they reside in. Graffiti costs millions of dollars a year in cleanup costs, lowers property values, affects businesses, and intimidates entire communities.

One important factor to consider when instructing citizens to clean graffiti is their personal safety. Many citizens have been the victim of violent crimes because they were cleaning graffiti off of their property. In some gang neighborhoods, graffiti is cleaned by the police so the gangs see that it is the police that are responsible for the graffiti being cleaned up and not the citizens. We do not want to make the process of cleaning graffiti a death sentence for a member of the community. All help reinforce the message that the gang is in control, and all are crucial aspects of a gang's day-to-day existence.

When graffiti is not cleaned up immediately, it will often multiply, as different gangs cross out their rivals' graffiti messages and add their own. This is the most important thing. The faster you remove the graffiti, the less of a thrill the vandal gets. There are products on the market, such as graffiti-proof paint, that make it easier to clean off the paint. Removing graffiti promptly is the best way to prevent it from occurring again. Conduct weekly inspections to help prevent graffiti on your property and in your community. Some cleanup jobs take just a few minutes; others can take all day, depending on the level of damage (Figure 19.7).

The police try to encourage property owners to use graffiti-resistant surface coatings. With advances in technology, products can stop spray paint and keep permanent marker and pen from penetrating the surface, making graffiti removal simple using

FIGURE 19.7 Typical wall in a neighborhood where graffiti is a daily occurrence. This wall has been cleaned many times, and the taggers and gangsters continue to apply graffiti. This is a great example of a tagger crew turned gang. The SE means South East, the C means Calle, and the gang is 32nd Street, which started out as the SKA (Spray Kan Artists) tagger crew. They are aligned under the Sureno gang umbrella shown by the number 13. The Ls means Locos, the Gst means Gangsters, and the individuals responsible are Chueks, Spider, ZoZo, and Loko. The gangsters help define the individual monikers by adding to lines between each name. The photo on the far right is a store owner that is taking a few minutes to remove fresh gang graffiti from the front of his store before he opens for the day.

water-based or other standard cleaning products. Use materials and surfaces that make graffiti vandalism difficult: apply a clear coat finish to protect painted and unpainted surfaces and use protective film coverings on windows. Use matching color paint or neutral colors like gray, white, or beige. Repaint the entire wall, making a straight line across the top with a color that matches the wall. This leaves no trace of graffiti and does not draw the attention of the vandals. This method is 10 times more effective than patching. When it is not possible to paint the entire wall, use a closely matched color blocked over the graffiti in neat, square shapes. The closer the color match, the more effective it is in preventing further vandalism.

The key is to be persistent. You may have to clean up the graffiti three times before the vandals realize it's not worth their effort. The vandals' objective is to have others see their tag name. Vandals are drawn to walls that are not cleaned immediately because it means their tag will be up longer and seen by more people.

It is also important to identify the method used by the vandal to apply the graffiti to the surface, and remember, the sooner you remove graffiti, typically the easier it is to clean. Before the removal method is selected, identify the surface to be cleaned. Smooth, hard surfaces are the easiest to clean, and rough, porous surfaces are the most difficult. Materials used to apply graffiti increase the difficulty of cleaning surfaces, which can include spray paint, grease pencils, felt-tipped pens, water-based paint, stickers, shoe polish, and even crayons.

Once the product used to apply the graffiti has been identified and the surface dynamics considered, a removal method can be chosen. Many times the easiest methods may work; try using soap, water, and a soft brush first to do the least amount of damage to the surface you are trying to clean. If that doesn't work, using a more powerful removal product that's appropriate for the application method and surface is recommended. In many cases graffiti can be cleaned using a removal product rather than painting over it. Removing graffiti is preferred since it is easier than painting and eliminates the difficulty of matching paint.

Educating Parents and the Community

Awareness is the key. Can you recognize taggers to be able to deal with them, and do you know what to do when you are the victim of graffiti vandalism? In many cases parents are unaware of their child's involvement in tagger crews. Many parents assume a "not my child attitude," which can be addressed by educating parents on the signs and symptoms of vandalism (Figure 19.8).

The City of Santa Ana California has a flyer to help parents answer the question: Is your child a tagger? Middletown Connecticut has a

FIGURE 19.8 PSAs on graffiti/tagger recognition.

program educating business owners on how to deal with graffiti, which is sponsored by a paint company.

Graffiti Reward Programs

Some cities offer a reward for information leading to the arrest and prosecution of suspects for tagging or graffiti-related vandalism. The City of Santa Clarita Graffiti Rewards Program is available to individuals or entities that report or identify any persons responsible for acts of graffiti vandalism within the city. The amount of the reward is based on the information provided and the action taken. A Graffiti Reward Program application along with approval from the Los Angeles County Sheriff's Department is required for each case before any reward funds will be distributed. Rewards are not awarded until each case has cleared the judicial system and sentencing has been established.

In states like Nevada, Section 244.3695 allows for the establishment of graffiti reward and abatement funds. "The Board of County Commissioners shall create a graffiti reward and abatement fund. The money in the fund must be used to pay a reward to a person who, in response to the offer of a reward, provides information that results in the identification, apprehension, and conviction of a person who violates a county ordinance that prohibits graffiti or other defacement of property."

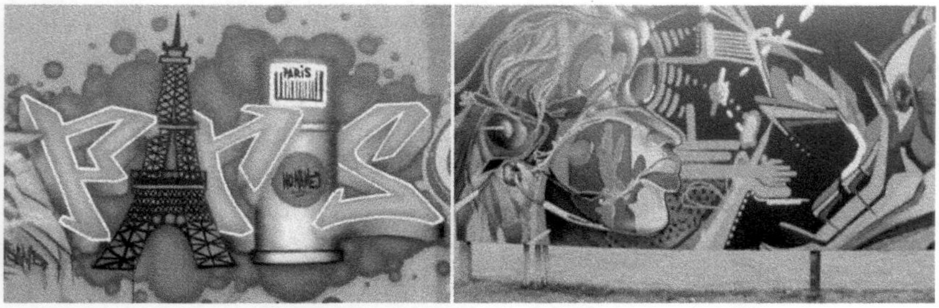

FIGURE 19.9 An example of the artistic side of the graffiti world; the city of Paris is illustrated. The photo on the right shows a woman's face in a futuristic theme. According to the administrator of the center, artwork like this may stay on the walls much longer than other works, which gives the artist more exposure within the local tagger/artist community. (Courtesy of Writerz Block.)

Legal Locations to Do Graffiti

Writer's Block, located at 5010 Market Street in San Diego, is a good example of a location where it is legal to do graffiti. It offers taggers an opportunity to legally practice their graffiti art in a place designed for just that purpose. I have visited this location several times and was surprised with the sophisticated artwork being created (Figure 19.9) The block consists of rows of hung sheets of plywood that fill up a couple of acres on the lot, and anyone has a chance to bring his or her own paint and create a design. It is a place for youths to gather after school and on weekends to create street art using cans of spray paint in a controlled, supervised, and most importantly, completely legal setting in which no private or public property is damaged.

Graffiti Hotlines

To help address many of these issues, many local jurisdictions have set up graffiti abatement hotlines, where citizens can call in and report vandalism and have it removed. San Diego's hotline receives over 4,000 calls per year; in addition to reporting the graffiti, callers can learn more about prevention. One of the complaints about these hotlines is the response time; there is often a lag time between a property owner calling about the graffiti and the actual removal of it. The length of delay should be a consideration for any jurisdiction planning on operating a hotline. Local jurisdictions must convince the callers that their complaint of vandalism will be a priority and cleaned off right away. If the jurisdiction does not have the resources to respond to complaints in a timely manner, the value of the hotline diminishes. Crews must be able to respond to individual service calls made to the graffiti hotline as well as focus on cleanup near schools, parks, and major intersections and transit routes to have the biggest impact. California Government Code 53069.3 is an example of a law that allows the use of public funds to remove graffiti. A city, county, or city and county may enact an ordinance to provide for the use of city or county funds to remove graffiti or other inscribed material from publicly or privately owned real or personal property located within the city, county, or city and county, and to replace or repair public or privately owned property within that city, county, or city and county that has been defaced with graffiti or other inscribed material that cannot be removed cost-effectively.

Vandalism and the Media/Antigraffiti Propaganda

A tagger's motivation is exposure, exposure, exposure; that is why when dealing with the media, try not to show examples of vandalism on a large scale in the community. Just like gangs, taggers use the Internet to display their work. If a wall is shown on the news, for example, do not disclose the exact location of recently cleaned areas, as this is often a challenge to taggers to immediately vandalize to send the community a message. This practice announces a clean canvas for the vandals, which is counterproductive.

The City of Santa Ana has a poster encouraging people to report vandals (Figure 19.10). The City of Burnaby encourages people to take back their community, and a graffiti busters sign tells taggers that graffiti is a crime; the taggers responded by adding the word *fun*, which is a great illustration of their attitude about damaging other people's property.

FIGURE 19.10 Anti-graffiti propaganda.

The Los Angeles County Sheriff's Department, and the Cities of Downey, La Mirada, Norwalk, Santa Fe Springs, Whittier, and Unincorporated Whittier launched the Aware Teens against Graffiti (ATAG), which is an innovative delinquency prevention program that targets first-time tagging and vandalism offenders between the ages of 9 to 15 and their parents. The weekend-long program focuses on the parents receiving an intensive two-day skill-building training, and the youth offenders participating in community service projects and group discussions while being supervised by law enforcement. The goal is to get the first-time offender through the system and encourage him or her to not reoffend.

VANDALISM PROSECUTION

Like all other gang and tagger cases, a gang expert will be needed. In 1993, the author had the opportunity to be part of a two-month undercover law enforcement operation that targeted tagger crews. Officers posed as an Australian movie production company called Star Productions doing a documentary on taggers. To advertise this, officers distributed posters and flyers throughout the tagger community asking for participation in a documentary (Figure 19.11).

FIGURE 19.11 Flyer from a undercover operation against taggers.

Taggers who came into the studio thought they were going to be in a film, and as such were asked to fill out an information sheet, submit to an interview, and show the film crew examples of their work in the studio and in the field. The operation resulted in the arrest of more than 40 taggers responsible for hundreds of acts of vandalism in the San Diego area. The key to this operation was aggregation of the individual incidents of vandalism, which caused the total dollar amount in damage to rise above the level that constitutes a felony.

In this operation I remember testifying against a tagger that called himself "Swor." I drove around and documented numerous incidents of vandalism that I attributed to the tagger we arrested. This is where a basic level of understanding about graffiti becomes very beneficial. In each case, this tagger was unique in how he wrote. Every time he wrote SwOr, a very uncommon method, it was clear that the start and end of each line was consistent, and the handwriting analysis was clear that each case was similar in every way.

Expert testimony can be extremely useful in graffiti vandalism prosecutions. Like gang expert testimony, it can be used to explain how graffiti vandals operate, their motivation, their terminology, and psychology. Further, this type of testimony can be used to prove damages when a damage amount is required by the offense or for the purpose of restitution.

AGGREGATION OF DAMAGES: GRAFFITI TRACKER DATABASES

This theory is that when offenders are caught putting up graffiti, they are not just charged with one count of vandalism; they can be held accountable for all of the other damage for which they are responsible. This has two main benefits. One, it sends a signal to the offenders that their vandalism is being tracked. Two, a city can seek restitution from offenders for all of the damage that they have committed, not merely a single incident. The system gives law enforcement personnel real-time, street-level intelligence that allows them to not only focus on the worst graffiti offenders and their damage, but also to monitor potential gang violence that is associated with the graffiti.

Several cities in California have found a way to exploit graffiti by establishing a tracking program that empowers law enforcement and prosecutors to use this form of street-level intelligence in court. The law allows for aggregation of damages for felony filings with a series of graffiti vandalism against different victims when there's one intention, one general impulse, and one plan. To make this a reality, many police departments have created databases to track incidents of graffiti. Utilizing a graffiti database graffiti tracker has some issues to be aware of, which include authenticating graffiti photos from the tracker system. Many times a city worker or contractor hired to clean the graffiti from a victim's property, or even a homeowner that has to clean his or her fence, takes a photo of the graffiti before removing it, calculating the cost of the damage, and then provides the photo to the police for investigation. These photos are then uploaded into the tracker system, where they can be compared to similar incidents of vandalism to try to solve a series of separate vandalism offenses.

The key to using these databases is having a standardized procedure set up in your public works or graffiti abatement operations to make sure the photos and the cases can be used. Another advantage of graffiti trackers is GIS mapping software. By mapping a suspect's graffiti, we can demonstrate a nexus between the geographic location of the graffiti and the location of the offender's residence. This has been used successfully in the course of securing search warrants of gang members' residences. During the course of the search it is common not only to find instruments of the crime but also additional graffiti at the offender's residence. This graffiti can then be matched in style to the graffiti stored in these tracker databases.

DAMAGE OR COST EXPERTS: PROOF OF AMOUNT OF DAMAGES

Many jurisdictions hire private contractors or citizen groups to assist the city with painting over graffiti, putting the city in the shoes of the victim (literally and figuratively, as the city is now absorbing the entire cost of the clean up). Experts can be used to prove amount of damages incurred and cost of repair. Certain penal code sections require specific monetary damages be proven as part of case in chief; hence these experts could be vital to successful prosecution. Many public agencies have individuals who can testify to costs of repair or cleaning items such as signs, walls, vehicles, etc. Often costs are greater than expected. For example, CALTRANS experts will testify the damage incurred when an overhead freeway sign is vandalized is $1,200, the cost to close travel lanes and for trucks, workers' salaries, and cleanup of the graffiti. In addition, many cities or community groups have graffiti cleanup groups charged with cleaning up graffiti and can testify to cost of damage.

ESTABLISHING A LACK OF PERMISSION

Figure 19.12 shows a sign on a San Diego transit bus that warns that vandalism is a crime, in an attempt to discourage acts of vandalism.

Evidence that the defendant does not own the property is required, and lack of permission is helpful but not critical. These issues can be solved easily in the defendant's interview when asked about the damage: "Did you own any of the properties in the photos I have shown you? Did you have permission from any of these property owners to tag in any of the locations in these photos (if so, which ones)?" Otherwise, ownership has to be disproved—through calling each owner to testify (of course, this does not apply to public property, but someone has to testify that it is public property) or obtaining certified copies of property deeds showing that the defendant was not the owner of the property at the time of the vandalism.

These trials will be time-intensive. However, juries should hate the tagger when they see how much damage he caused in the community vs. a random tag here or there. One can argue that with respect to those specific offenses relating to public property, mainly § 640.5 and 640.7, the permissive inference language of § 594 should control. That language currently reads that "with respect to real property, vehicles, signs, fixtures, or furnishings belonging to any public entity, as defined by §811.2 of the Government Code, and the Federal Government, it shall be a permissive inference that the person neither owned the property nor had the permission of the owner to deface, damage, or destroy the property." Lack of permission has been held not to be an element of the offense of vandalism; the argument can be made here that it is the defendant's burden to prove that he or she had permission to graffiti property not his or her own.

Permission is a key element; it must be clear that permission was not granted. For example, in New York, Section 145.60 states no person shall make graffiti of any type on any building, public

FIGURE 19.12 Photo from a San Diego City Bus

or private, or any other property, real or personal, owned by any person, firm, or corporation or any public agency or instrumentality, without the express permission of the owner or operator of said property. New Mexico Section 30-15-1.1 indicates graffiti consists of intentionally and maliciously defacing any real or personal property of another with graffiti or other material inscribed with ink, paint, spray paint, crayon, charcoal, or the use of any object without the consent or reasonable ground to believe there is consent of the owner of the property.

RESTITUTION

Restitution is often an issue once the case has been successfully prosecuted. These types of witnesses can be called to testify at a restitution hearing or be consulted on the amount of restitution to request. If a minor is personally unable to pay a fine levied for acts prohibited by this section, the parent of that minor shall be liable for payment of the fine. A court may waive payment of the fine, or any part thereof, by the parent upon a finding of good cause. In Washington, Section 4.24.330 states:

> An adult or emancipated minor who commits criminal street gang tagging and graffiti under section 306 of this act by causing physical damage to the property of another is liable in addition to actual damages, for a penalty to the owner in the amount of the value of the damaged property not to exceed one thousand dollars, plus an additional penalty of not less than one hundred dollars nor more than two hundred dollars, plus all reasonable attorneys' fees and court costs expended by the owner.

California Government Code 38773.2 allows for the collection of costs incurred and graffiti nuisance abatement liens.

> The legislative body of a city, county, or city and county may, by ordinance, establish a procedure to collect abatement and related administrative costs incurred in the summary abatement of any nuisance resulting from the defacement by a minor or other person of the property of another by graffiti or any other inscribed material. The ordinance shall require notice to the minor or other person prior to the recordation of a lien on the parcel of land owned by the minor or other person. The ordinance shall require notice to the parent or guardian having custody and control of the minor prior to the recordation of a lien on the parcel of land owned by the parent or guardian having custody and control of the minor.
>
> The notice shall be served in the same manner as a summons in a civil action pursuant to Article 3 (commencing with Section 415.10) of Chapter 4 of Title 5 of Part 2 of the Code of Civil

Procedure. A graffiti nuisance abatement lien shall be recorded in the county recorder's office in the county in which the parcel of land is located. From the date of recording, the lien shall have the force, effect, and priority of a judgment lien.

A graffiti nuisance abatement lien authorized by this section shall specify the amount of the lien; the name of the agency on whose behalf the lien is imposed; the date of the abatement order; the street address, legal description, and assessor's parcel number of the parcel on which the lien is imposed; and the name and address of the recorded owner of the parcel. If the lien is discharged, released, or satisfied, either through payment or foreclosure, notice of the discharge containing the information specified in subdivision (d) shall be recorded by the governmental agency. A graffiti nuisance abatement lien and the release of the lien shall be indexed in the grantor-grantee index. A graffiti nuisance abatement lien may be satisfied through foreclosure in an action brought by the city.

Notwithstanding Section 6103, Section 27383, or any other provision of law, the county recorder may impose a fee on the city, county, or city and county to reimburse the costs of processing and recording the lien and providing notice to the property owner. The city, county, or city and county may recover from the property owner any costs incurred regarding the processing and recording of the lien and providing notice to the property owner as part of its foreclosure action to enforce the lien.

As used in this law, "abatement and related administrative costs" include, but are not limited to, court costs, attorney's fees, costs of removal of the graffiti or other inscribed material, costs of repair and replacement of defaced property, and the law enforcement costs incurred by the city, county, or city and county in identifying and apprehending the minor or other person.

SUSPENSION OF LICENSE

Some jurisdictions have tied driver's licenses to vandalism cases, as a deterrent to vandalism by juveniles. In Arizona, for example, Section 28-3320 allows for the suspension of license for persons under 18 years of age if convicted for violation of any statute or ordinance involving graffiti. In Indiana Section 31-37-19-17 allows for the suspending of a child's operator's license, or invalidating the child's learner's permit, for one year beginning the date of the order if convicted of a graffiti violation.

ANTIGRAFFITI MURALS

In the District of Columbia, Section 1-325.101 establishes an Antigraffiti Mural Assistance Program Fund to identify and prioritize for the production of mural art locations in the District that have been targeted or are likely to be targeted for graffiti and are appropriate for mural art, and expend the monies solely in connection with the production of mural art, including training, supervising, and compensating the mural artists, at locations identified by the Department of Public Works.

REMOVAL OF GRAFFITI BY INMATES

In Georgia, Section 17-15A-4 allows for the free removal of graffiti by inmates in order to provide a form of compensation by the state to innocent victims of criminals.

> The Board of Corrections or any political subdivision of this state may authorize the use of labor by inmates from any penal institution or jail under its authority to remove or obliterate such unlawfully placed graffiti when such graffiti is visible from any public road or other public property. The Board of Corrections shall provide rules and regulations governing such use of labor by inmates from institutions under its jurisdiction. No graffiti removal program operated by any political subdivision of this state shall charge any fee to any property owner or operator for removal of graffiti from such property.

PROPERTY DAMAGE AND PARENTAL RESPONSIBILITY

In Hawaii, Section 577-3.5 states:

> The parents or legal guardians of a minor child shall be jointly and severally liable for graffiti damage caused by the minor to real or personal property, whether publicly or privately owned. As used in this section, *graffiti* means any unauthorized drawing, inscription, figure, or marking created by paint, ink, chalk, dye, or similar substances. In addition to any other lawful orders, if a minor is found under Chapter 571 to have committed an act constituting graffiti, the court may order the minor, the parents, or the legal guardians of the minor to pay the actual cost of having the damaged property repaired or replaced and may order the minor to perform community service. If the court orders payment for the actual cost of the damage, the court shall give due consideration to the financial resources of the minor, the parents, or the legal guardians of the minor to ensure that they will be able to pay the costs of the damage. If the court determines that the minor, the parents, or the legal guardians of the minor are unable to pay the actual cost of the damage, the court may order payment in an amount for which

they are able to pay or in a manner in which they are able to pay and may order the minor to perform community service work in an amount commensurate with the costs of the damage for which they are unable to pay.

DAMAGE OF PROPERTY USED FOR RELIGIOUS OR EDUCATIONAL PURPOSES

In Nevada, Section 206.125 addresses the special concerns associated with damage of property used for religious or educational purposes, for burial or memorializing dead or as a community center.

> A person who defaces, or otherwise damages any church, synagogue, or other building, structure, or place used for religious worship or other religious purpose; any cemetery, mortuary, or other facility used for the purpose of burial or memorializing the dead; any school, educational facility, or community center; any personal property contained in any institution, facility, building, structure, or place described in paragraph (a), (b), or (c) is guilty of a gross misdemeanor.
>
> In addition to any other penalty, the court shall order the person to pay restitution for the damage. A person who is paid money for restitution pursuant to subsection 1 shall use the money to repair or restore the property that was damaged.

In Wisconsin, Section 943.012 states:

> Anyone who intentionally causes damage to, intentionally marks, draws, or writes with ink or another substance on or intentionally etches into any physical property of another, without the person's consent and with knowledge of the character of the property, is guilty of a Class I felony if the property consists of one or more of the following: (1) Any church, synagogue, or other building, structure, or place primarily used for religious worship or another religious purpose; (2) Any cemetery, mortuary, or other facility used for burial or memorializing the dead; (3) Any school, educational facility, or community center publicly identified as associated with a group of persons of a particular race, religion, color, disability, sexual orientation, national origin, or ancestry or by an institution of any such group; or (4) Any personal property contained in any property under subs. (1) to (3) if the personal property has particular significance or value to any group of persons of a particular race, religion, color, disability, sexual orientation, national origin, or ancestry and the actor knows the personal property has particular significance or value to that group.

COMMUNITY SERVICE AS CONDITION OF PROBATION FOR OFFENSE INVOLVING GRAFFITI

In Oregon Section 137.131 allows for community service as condition of probation for offense involving graffiti.

> The court shall impose community service as a condition of a probation sentence when a person is convicted of criminal mischief and the conduct engaged in consists of defacing property by creating graffiti unless the sentence includes incarceration in a county jail or a state correctional institution. The community service must include removing graffiti, either those that the defendant created or those created by another, or both. If the defendant does not consent to donate labor as required by Section 137.128, the period of community service must be served under the supervision and control of the Department of Corrections.

DEFACING PRIVATE RESIDENCES, OFFICES, BUSINESSES, OR COMMERCIAL PROPERTY

In Rhode Island, Section 11-44-21.1 states:

> Every person who shall willfully, maliciously, or mischievously write upon, paint, or otherwise deface the private property or residence of another, any office building, business or commercial property, or public building, shall be guilty of a misdemeanor. For the first offense, said penalty shall not exceed a $500 fine and community service not exceeding 100 hours. Every person convicted of a second offense under this section shall be fined up to $1,000 and shall be required to perform up to 200 hours of community service.

20

Private Property Owners' Role and Liability, CPTED, and Crime-Free Multihousing

The police spend a lot of time working with property owners to address gang problems; a good example of this is dealing with apartment managers and property owners at apartment complexes and businesses where gangs like to congregate. There are a lot of things police officers can do to attack gangs, one of which is focusing attention on the places gangs like to hang out. In addition, there are a lot of things property owners can do to protect their property, reduce liability, and keep their tenants or customers safe.

A couple of the best examples of the police and the community working together are the Crime-Free Multihousing Program and Neighborhood Watch. Attracting good residents is the first step to building an apartment community. You need to begin by cleaning house, literally. It does not cost a lot of money to pick up garbage, broken glass, or other litter. Trimming trees and bushes does not have to be expensive either. Reputable applicants will come if they feel the management is operating the property responsibly. It is difficult to attract good residents if you have current residents loitering in the parking lots or common areas drinking alcohol or using drugs. People who display this kind of behavior will not only prevent good residents from moving in but will cause your best residents to leave.

CRIME-FREE MULTIHOUSING PROGRAM

You cannot build an apartment community free from gangs if you do not remove the obstacles that stand in your way. It is a good idea to visit the property at various times of the day and night to see how the residents behave. This is especially important for properties with off-site management or absentee landlords. Do not rely on independent management companies that contract their services. Many times, they are primarily concerned with occupancy levels and collecting the rent over dealing with problem tenants. Once you have attracted responsible applicants, be sure to sell them on the benefits of your particular property. While no property manager can guarantee a resident will not be affected by crime, a resident will take comfort in knowing the property has established a good rapport with local law enforcement. Good prospects will be happy to hear that management is a member of the Crime-Free Multihousing Program. Prospects with a history of drug or other illegal activity may simply say, "Thank you, there is another place I want to look at first." Be fair, but be firm in your residency requirements. It is your right. Once a resident shows interest in the property, let him or her know that all residents at the property have been required to sign the Crime-Free Lease Addendum and pass a criminal background check. While this is no guarantee, it does show that management is doing everything they can legally do to reduce the likelihood of criminal activity on the property.

The Crime-Free Multihousing Program is an international program that partners property owners, residents, and law enforcement personnel in an effort to eliminate crime in multihousing properties. The program is designed to reduce crime, drugs, and gangs on apartment properties. This program was successfully developed by the Mesa Arizona Police Department in 1992. The program spread like a wildfire in the 1990s and is now international, spreading to nearly 2,000 cities in 44 U.S. states, 5 Canadian Provinces, Mexico, England, Finland, Japan, Russia, Malaysia, Nigeria, Afghanistan, and Puerto Rico.

The program consists of three phases that must be completed by the property owner under the supervision of the local police department. Property managers can become individually certified after completing training in each phase and the property becomes certified upon successful completion of all three phases. Upon certification, the property owner will in theory have a safer property and will have the skills to manage the property and keep crime problems to a minimum. The police sell this concept by reminding the property owners they will have a stable, more satisfied tenant base, lower maintenance and repair costs, and increased property values if they screen tenants and remove those involved in criminal activity.

The police typically expect property owners to support police efforts to stop all illegal activities that occur on their premises. The police expect managers to call 911 when the managers or employees observe or suspect illegal activities occurring on their premises.

This of course does not always happen, and when it happens at a problem location, abatement may become an option if there is no other way to solve the problem. Property owners should comply with all city code requirements and bring said buildings into code compliance within a reasonable timeframe, if the building is not currently in compliance. Property owners and managers should implement reasonable means of security and do what they can to keep their tenants safe; when this does not happen the police try to force compliance. When gang members and drug dealers operate out of rental property, neighborhoods suffer and landlords pay a high price. That price may include a decline in property values, particularly when the activity begins affecting the reputation of the neighborhood; property damage arising from abuse, retaliation, or neglect; property damage from police raids; fire resulting from manufacturing or growing operations; civil penalties, including temporary closure of the property or even property seizure; loss of rent during the eviction and repair periods; and the loss of other valued tenants.

By being part of the Crime-Free Program, the owners can help to minimize the possibility of losses due to criminal activity on their property. This program is successful because it approaches crime on many fronts. Law enforcement cannot solve crime problems alone. Neither can the management or residents of rental properties. However, by working together, the end result has been the most successful approach to crimes in rental communities.

There are three ways gang activity comes into a rental community: (1) the gang members live there, (2) they visit friends there, and (3) they come to the property to commit crimes. The program addresses all three of these possibilities by implementing the principles of the program; property owners and managers not only reduce the likelihood of crime in the community, but they also reduce the number of visitors who come to the property with criminal intent (i.e., to purchase or sell drugs). For the opportunistic criminal, crime prevention through environmental design (CPTED) has been used to combat crimes that might occur in the parking lots or common areas. This includes assaults, robberies, drive-by shootings, and auto thefts.

Rental properties present a unique challenge for law enforcement. The typical Neighborhood Watch approach to residents in single-family homes is not easily adapted to rental communities. In single-family homes, owners generally have a large cash investment in the purchase of their home. Rising crime rates can lead to safety issues, lower property values, and a decreased quality of life. This motivates owners to be more concerned about crime in their neighborhoods and become proactive community members. Typically, single-family homeowners have a 30-year mortgage for their property and may be looking at long-term residency. The family home is the apex of their lives where they raise their family. For the most part, they have pride of ownership. When crime problems begin to appear, owners tend to organize Neighborhood Watch activities to protect the future interests of their families. In rental properties, the communities tend to be much more transient. Most often, residents sign a 6-month, 9-month, or 12-month lease for a rental property. In many cases, owners do not require leases, and residency is based on a month-to-month agreement. This enables an occupant to move easily if he or she feels crime has reached an intolerable level. It is easier to move away from crime than to confront it.

CRIME PREVENTION THROUGH ENVIRONMENTAL DESIGN (CPTED)

Removing the location for gang crime can be accomplished in a number of ways. Many times, physical changes to a location make it less desirable to a gang as a target because it requires significantly more effort or enhances the risk of apprehension. Sometimes, simply adding a light or a lock on a gate may be enough to make the gang member move on to an easier target. These strategies are part of a broader concept known as crime prevention through environmental design (CPTED). Removing the location can also refer to areas where gang bangers congregate. In general, most gangs have specific locations where they like to hang out. Many times they meet and plan crimes at these locations and use other places as safe havens after they have committed a crime. Having detailed information about these locations is critical to the gang investigator. Knowing where the gang likes to be and where they are likely to go, prior to and following a crime, increases the chances of capturing suspects and solving the crime. Understanding the physical layout of these gang hangouts can help cut off potential escape routes, and crime prevention techniques can be implemented to make the location a less desirable hangout for the future.

CPTED is based on the idea that situational factors such as the environment (poor lighting) can make crime more likely to occur at a particular time and place. CPTED measures can include added lighting, making the place less conducive for crime, cleaning the area, removing graffiti, addressing housing issues, etc. Many of these locations are well-known concentrated areas of a high level of gang crime. Many of these locations are identified as crime hot spots, which could mean that the location is poorly supervised and has poor place management, bad lighting, or other characteristics.

Changing some of those situational factors may help reduce levels of crime at that location.

Traditional local law enforcement typically operates on a reactive basis. That is, police wait for a call for service and react by arriving at the scene and, when appropriate, making an arrest. The emphasis in law enforcement circles today is to become more proactive to prevent crimes from occurring in the first place. Community policing is a proactive form of policing, while still encompassing reactive law enforcement. The community policing philosophy emphasizes identification and resolution of gang problems and conditions that cause gang crime rather than focusing exclusively on individual gang incidents.

The approach requires close cooperation between the citizens and police officers, and many view community-oriented policing as an attractive option for addressing fears that often are prevalent among minority communities. Your agency must sell its anti-gang program to community members so they will not consider it a form of repression against their respective neighborhoods and see it for what it is: a response the community deserves to protect it and remove violent offenders from the area.

A common application of nuisance abatement laws is to force owners to act against gang use of their buildings or face a governmental takeover. For example, landlords have been court-ordered to clean up graffiti, erect security gates, install lighting, remove abandoned cars, and evict known drug dealers. Such orders are commonly coordinated with community policing tactics to reinforce the owner's ability to act against gangs. Local building and housing codes can also be used against gang locations, compelling property owners to comply with fire, health and sanitation, and zoning requirements.

- Plant bushes in front of walls (make sure no windows or doors are too close). This makes it harder for people to get close to the wall.
- Erect fences between your business and public property. This helps people know where the boundaries are, and also makes it harder for graffiti vandals to get close enough to your walls. Create a barrier using vegetation or a fence to ward off potential graffiti vandals.
- If there are payphones and benches close to your business that encourage people to hang out, see about getting them removed (Figure 20.1a and Figure 20.1b).
- Use motion detector lights. Keeping the lights on all night makes it easier for people to see graffiti vandals. But, it also lets the vandals see what they are doing, and lets others see the graffiti when they are done. Also, if an area is usually dark, people will notice if it is suddenly lit up.

- Cameras can help, especially systems that activate by sensor and start recording when someone is on the property. These systems reduce the time needed to review footage, and more importantly can even alert you via text when it is activated. These systems are beneficial because you have instant knowledge of areas that have activity as it happens; there is no wasted manpower. These systems are also very

(a)

(b)

FIGURE 20.1 Graffiti on a payphone and a power box.

beneficial to use in connection with sting operations, so once triggered, officers can move into the area covertly and hopefully make an arrest.

- Remove large trees or bushes that block people's view of vandals. The best plant life for graffiti-prone areas is short bushes that keep people from getting too close to walls. Make sure you keep the bushes well trimmed. Move dumpsters to the ends of the alleys to reduce graffiti. Call dumpster companies and ask them to keep graffiti off dumpsters. (Their phone number is usually on the dumpster.)
- Use pebbles around the building to create noise when people are walking. But remember this will only make a difference if there is someone around to hear the noise, see what is happening, and do something about it.
- Lighting. Lighting by itself does not prevent crime. Lighting provides the opportunity for choice—the choice to walk forward because you can see clearly that the path is clear and free of danger. If the user can see a potential danger (person hiding, a gang of kids at the corner), he or she may choose to walk a different way. Lighting can illuminate a target as easily as it provides an opportunity for a legitimate user to see a potential threat or criminal. Lighting is a powerful tool the management and residents can use to control and reduce the fear and opportunity of crime. Unless you have formal or informal surveillance of an area, lighting may not prevent crime. In fact, good lighting without surveillance may actually encourage criminal activity in some cases.

Improve Surveillance

Surveillance is the first element of CPTED. Surveillance is the ability to look into an area, and the ability to look back out (Figure 20.2). It can be formal or informal. Formal surveillance is generally organized, while informal surveillance is naturally occurring. Among the objects that inhibit surveillance are overgrown trees and shrubs, fences, and poor lighting. The goal of surveillance strategies is to keep intruders under observation and undesirable behavior under control. To improve surveillance, trim trees and shrubs, use fencing appropriately, and utilize proper lighting techniques. There are three types of surveillance to consider: (1) natural, (2) mechanical, and (3) organized. The best plan will involve some combination of all three types of surveillance.

Natural surveillance is naturally occurring. As people are moving around an area, they will be able to observe what is going on around them, provided the area is open and well lit.

FIGURE 20.2 A New York Police Department Surveillance Camera.

Natural surveillance is typically free of cost, but observers may choose not to get involved in any situation that may pose a potential threat to themselves or others.

Mechanical surveillance employs the use of cameras, mirrors, and other equipment that allows an individual to monitor a remote area. Mechanical surveillance can involve the purchase of moderately inexpensive mirrors to the more expensive electronic devices, such as closed-circuit television (CCTV).

Organized surveillance includes security patrols and other groups of people who are organized to watch a targeted area. While this is the most effective deterrent to crime, it is also the least cost-effective. While it may be necessary to employ security patrols, once the patrols are discontinued, there is generally nothing left to show for your investment.

Improve Access Controls

Access control is the second element in CPTED. Because many criminals look for an easy escape, limiting access into an area and back out again is a great way to deter criminal activity. Access control can be demonstrated by having one way in and one way out of a location, such as a security post or the use of mechanical gates. Those who use alternative methods to enter an area look suspicious, risk detection, and sense an increased risk of apprehension. It is important to assess how the intended users are entering the property. It is equally important to assess how the nonintended users are entering the property as well. Inspect perimeter fencing for damage. Look for footprints in the dirt and gravel, and then check for wear patterns in grassy areas. Determining the weak points will be the first step in correcting the problem.

Increase Defensible Space

Maintenance is another key issue for territoriality. If a rental property is well maintained, it shows that management cares about and will defend the property against crime. A property that is not well maintained may indicate that management is not concerned about the property, and might overlook or ignore criminal activity. A property that is clean and well maintained is more likely to attract legitimate users. A property that is not well maintained is more likely to attract deviant users. If a property has several city or fire code infractions, a property manager may lose the ability to deal effectively with criminal activity. A person facing eviction may threaten to report the infractions to the city or county if the manager proceeds with the eviction process.

CRIME-FREE LEASES (SAMPLE): IT'S WORTH THE EFFORT

Property managers have differing views on how, or if, they should screen prospective residents. Some property managers have rigid guidelines established by their management company or owners. Other property managers may feel that calling references or checking prospective residents is not worth the effort. Many times they rely on their gut feelings when it comes to approving prospective tenants. Good screening procedures will result in getting better applicants, and may also prevent a discrimination case. Be certain to stay current with new laws pertaining to fair housing and consult with a qualified attorney before making changes to your policies.

The Crime-Free Lease Addendum was developed to give reasonable notice to new residents (at the time they enter into the rental agreement or when the Crime-Free Program is instituted) about activities or behaviors that contradict property rules, regulations, lease agreements, or state statutes. These agreements are typically available in several languages and can be an important tool for managers and landlords to protect their investments and help provide a secure living environment to residents.

If the contract is negotiated in another language and a translation of the contract is provided pursuant to CA Civil Code Section 1632, the addendum should be provided in that language too. The law in California lists Spanish, Korean, Chinese,

Vietnamese, and Tagalog as languages that are used in the state. It is recommended that managers negotiate contracts in English and (per that law) have residents bring their own adult interpreters. The language that follows is a sample only; it should be scrutinized for legal accuracy and correct translation prior to use in an actual lease.

> In consideration of the execution or renewal of a lease of the dwelling unit identified in the lease, owner and resident agree as follows:
>
> 1. Resident, any members of the resident's household, or a guest or other person under the resident's control shall not engage in criminal activity, including drug-related criminal activity, on or near the said premises. "Drug-related criminal activity" means the illegal manufacture, sale, distribution, use, or possession with intent to manufacture, sell, distribute, or use of a controlled substance (as defined in Section 102 of the Controlled Substance Act (21 USC 802)).
> 2. Resident, any member of the resident's household, or a guest or other person under the resident's control shall not engage in any act intended to facilitate criminal activity, including drug-related criminal activity, on or near the said premises.
> 3. Resident or members of the household will not permit the dwelling unit to be used for, or to facilitate, criminal activity, including drug-related criminal activity, regardless of whether the individual engaging in such activity is a member of the household or a guest.
> 4. Resident, any member of the resident's household or a guest, or another person under the resident's control shall not engage in the unlawful manufacturing, selling, using, storing, keeping, or giving of a controlled substance as defined in Health and Safety Code § 11350, et seq., at any locations, whether on or near the dwelling unit premises or otherwise.
> 5. Resident, any member of the resident's household, or a guest or another person under the resident's control shall not engage in any illegal activity, including prostitution, as defined in Penal Code § 647(b); criminal street gang activity, as defined in Penal Code § 186.20 et seq.; criminal threats, as prohibited in Penal Code § 422 PC; assault and battery, as prohibited in Penal Code § 240; burglary, as prohibited in Penal Code § 459; the unlawful use and discharge of firearms, as prohibited in Penal Code § 245; sexual offenses, as prohibited in Penal Code § 269 and 288, or any breach of the lease agreement that otherwise jeopardizes the health, safety, and welfare of the landlord, his agent, or other tenant or involving imminent or actual serious property damage.
> 6. *Violation of the above provisions shall be a material and irreparable violation of the lease and good cause for immediate termination of tenancy.* A single violation of any of the provisions of this added addendum shall be deemed a serious

violation and a material and irreparable noncompliance. It is understood that a single violation shall be good cause for termination of the lease. Unless otherwise provided by law, proof of violation shall not require criminal conviction, but shall be by a preponderance of the evidence.

7. In case of conflict between the provisions of this addendum and any other provisions of the lease, the provisions of the addendum shall govern.
8. This lease addendum is incorporated into the lease executed or renewed this day between owner and resident.

The Crime-Free Lease Addendum should be applied equally and fairly to all residents of an apartment community who have signed it. It should be signed by all new residents. If a resident is in the middle of a lease at the time the program is implemented, he or she can be asked to sign voluntarily. If he or she refuses during the lease term, the addendum may be made a mandatory part of the lease renewal process. If a month-to-month rental agreement is involved rather than a lease, the Crime-Free Lease Addendum can be enforced by a legally effective change in terms of the tenancy.

Lease agreements should also be clear that residents are responsible for members of the resident's household and guests (under their control) when it comes to illegal or noncompliant behavior on the property. It is important to stress to new residents that they should accompany their guests whenever possible to be certain they follow community rules. Guests should not be allowed into recreational or common areas unless they are with a resident of the property. Residents, members of the resident's household, or a guest (under the resident's control) should not be allowed to disturb the other resident's peaceful enjoyment of the premises. If complaints are received, the management should carefully document the information and send a warning letter or serve the appropriate notice.

Verify the Information Given

It is a good idea to verify names and phone numbers with a telephone book to be sure an applicant is not using a friend or relative to "front" for him or her, posing as an employer or property manager. Contact previous managers to inquire about an applicant's past behavior. This provides useful information when considering whether or not to rent to the applicant. Many managers are instructed to refrain from providing specific information about previous residents, but you are certainly allowed to ask! The focus would be on an applicant's history of nonpayment or other noncompliant behavior. It is a good idea to have a standard list of questions that will be asked for all applicants. These questions should also be carefully reviewed and followed closely whenever checking references. It is important to document the information received and names of references you contacted. The best protection against misunderstandings is to fax or email your list of relevant, objective questions and ask for a written response.

Be careful not to limit your questions only to the property manager who is currently renting to the applicant. He or she may be inclined to say anything to turn over a problem resident. Try to find a previous manager with no current interest in the applicant. He or she may be less inclined to misrepresent the applicant's previous behaviors and payment history.

To owners and managers with small properties: If you establish a written policy of checking on all applicants within a specified local area, it may take a little time, but you can learn a lot about an applicant by driving by his or her current address to see how he or she is caring for the property where he or she currently lives.

Communication Is the Key

Be certain to clearly communicate in writing your policy restricting subletting. The tenant should not be allowed to sublet, transfer, or assign a lease agreement, the premises, or any part thereof without the management's prior written consent. If the management gives written consent to sublet, such consent may include a provision that does not release the tenant from any liability. Only persons listed on the lease, and the tenant's temporary guest, shall be allowed to occupy the premises or any part thereof, without the management's prior written consent. A temporary guest shall be construed as someone who resides with the tenant for a short period of time (usually no longer than 10–14 days). Any type of drug activity or other illegal activity committed on or near the rental property should be investigated and management should consistently take reasonable and appropriate action against residents who violate the Crime-Free Lease Addendum.

Residents are responsible for members of the resident's household and guests (under their control) when it comes to illegal or noncompliant behavior on the property. It is important to stress to new residents that they should accompany their guests whenever possible to be certain they follow community rules. Guests should not be allowed into recreational or common areas unless they are with a resident of the property. Even if the property manager did not witness the disturbance, notice can still be served if the complainant is willing to testify in court. Let the judge decide.

THREE-PHASE PROGRAM

Property owners, managers, leasing staff, maintenance personnel, and others in the management team are encouraged by police to attend the entire training program so they fully understand what they can do to help keep gangs away.

This program is solution oriented. It is designed to be easy, yet very effective in reducing the incident of crime in rental property. The program utilizes a unique three-part approach that ensures the crime prevention goal while maintaining an approach that is very tenant-friendly. When each phase is completed, a certificate of completion is granted (Figure 20.3).

It is also recommended that police officers attend the training to understand the civil nature of rental communities, and to establish a rapport with managers of these communities. The theory is the program will give the managers more self-confidence in dealing with tenants, and enhance the belief that they have a choice in trying to live crime- and drug-free.

FIGURE 20.3 Riverside's Crime Free Multi-Housing Program Certificates and Sign.

An important fact to note is the police and managers are not always at odds; many share the same philosophy and have the same goals. Many property owners want the skills to avoid the problems noted above, and they want good, law-abiding, responsible tenants. The truth is that educating property owners about things like code violations at their properties can help reduce risk and liability and help protect the property owner's rights. The applicant screening process should start off with a rental agreement, one that is very clear and spells out the expectations of the tenant and the management. The program gives managers tips to strengthen rental agreements and tips on how to become a proactive property manager. The program also educates managers on things like the warning signs of drug and gang activity, the actions they should take if they discover their tenant or tenant's guests are conducting illegal activities at their property, the role of the police, and the proper legal eviction process.

Phase 1

After completion of the eight-hour training program, each participant will receive a certificate, which is signed by representatives of the police department, including the training coordinator. This green certificate should be framed and displayed in the leasing office, or in a prominent place where applicants will see it. Prospective residents should be informed as soon as possible that their property management is working with the sheriff's department to keep the community healthy. If there is no leasing office, a certificate can be displayed in a three-ring notebook with other materials used in the Crime-Free Multihousing Program. The manager or owner should show the notebook to prospective residents.

Additionally, participating managers should begin implementing the Crime-Free Lease Addendum, which is the backbone of the Crime-Free Multihousing Program. This addendum to the lease cites specific actions that will be taken by management if a resident, or someone under the resident's control, is involved in illegal or dangerous activity on or near the rental property. If the management is conducting a background check that includes credit and criminal information, the applicant should be informed before he or she turns in the application or pays any fees or deposits. It is advisable to get legal advice regarding the current requirements for "investigative" credit reports. Every prospective resident must be treated exactly the same as the others. It is important to develop office policies to ensure this.

Phase 1 discusses:

Prevention techniques
- Preparing the property so it does not attract crime
- Applicant screening procedures
- Defining rental agreements
- Crime-Free Lease Addendum
- Warning signs of illegal activity
- Actions to take if illegal activity is discovered

Proven management techniques
- Active management
- Spotting illegal activity
- Working with the police
- Proactive management

Property protection
- Crime prevention through environmental design (CPTED)
- Liability protection

Phase 2

In the second phase of the program a representative of the police department will inspect the property to assess physical security and general appearance of the property. If the property meets the agency's requirements, they will move on to phase 3.

In spite of laws and the risk of apprehension, some people are still criminally motivated. CPTED principles can be used to detect, deny, delay, and deter crime by using physical security devices and psychological signals to make an area less vulnerable to crime. This red certificate will certify that the property has met the minimum security requirements of the Crime-Free Multihousing Program. If the property does not meet the mandatory CPTED requirements, the management will be informed of needed changes and a follow-up inspection will be conducted.

Phase 3

In the third and final phase of the program, the police agency will conduct a "safety social" for residents. This will include information about general safety principles and crime prevention techniques. This will also give law enforcement the opportunity to explain the Crime-Free Multihousing Program to the residents of the community. Management is responsible for providing food, nonalcoholic drinks, and entertainment for this event. It is also recommended that property managers raffle door prizes as an added incentive to draw residents to the meeting.

It is necessary to conduct at least one meeting per year to maintain membership in the Crime-Free Multihousing Program. A certificate will be issued to the apartment community at the safety social to demonstrate to the residents that management is committed and has completed all three phases of the program.

Full Certification

Once fully certified, the property manager will receive a gold certificate. (This certificate is the only one that has an expiration date. It must be renewed each year after the subsequent safety social has been conducted.) After completion of the first safety social, the management can post the Crime-Free Multihousing Program signs on the property. It is recommended that one sign be posted at each entrance to the property where prospective residents will see them. The program logo can also be used in all advertisements.

THE CRIME-FREE HOTEL/MOTEL PROGRAM

This program certification is for hotel/motel properties no matter the size (Figure 20.4). This program is designed to be very easy

FIGURE 20.4 A Wichita Crime Free Business program sign.

and yet extremely effective at reducing criminal activity at hotels and motels, which are often used by gangs to conduct gang business, such as selling drugs, pimping and prostitution, and hiding from the police. Property managers or other designated employees would need to complete a short training session to learn about the program and basic crime prevention strategies.

The Crime-Free Hotel/Motel Program addresses these topics:

Understanding crime prevention
CPTED concepts
The registration process
Active property management
Combating crime problems
Police response to calls for service

An authorized representative of the police department will inspect the property to assess physical security and general appearance of the property. The security assessment will include looking at the locks, lighting, and landscaping. The property must meet the minimum CPTED requirements set forth in the inspection process to become a crime-free property. Upon successful completion of this phase, the manager will receive a certificate stating the property has met the minimum requirements of the Crime-Free Hotel/Motel Program. To be considered a fully certified crime-free property, the manager must follow certain guidelines, which include:

- Receive a positive photo identification of all guests
- Lighting, locks, and landscaping requirements (available from your crime prevention officer or Crime-Free Program administrator)
- Have screening procedures and cash policies in place
- Property key controls

The hotel or motel will receive full certification once the property has passed the CPTED review, submitted a completed Trespass Enforcement Request for the property, and at least one member of the staff has completed the required hotel/motel training course. A certificate in the name of the property will show that the property has passed the security assessment. This certificate will remain in effect for one year and will be renewed annually by the police department, after an audit has been conducted and the property has passed the annual CPTED evaluation. Individual certificates will be given to staff members after they have attended the required training. This certificate is good for three years and will still be valid, within those three years, if the staff members transfer properties.

Training Coordinators

The program begins with the training of law enforcement agency coordinators who will administer the program in their jurisdiction. Each Crime-Free Multihousing coordinator receives 24 hours of intensive training and becomes certified as an instructor of the program. The Crime-Free Program coordinators return to their cities and begin to provide training and certify apartment properties in their community. Fully certified properties have reported reductions in police calls for service up to 70% over previous years. The heart and soul of the program is in the correct implementation and use of the Crime-Free Lease Addendum.

Neighborhood Watch

Neighborhood Watch is a crime prevention program that stresses education and common sense (Figure 20.5). It teaches citizens how to help themselves by identifying and reporting suspicious activity in their neighborhoods. It also provides citizens with the opportunity to make their neighborhoods safer and improve the quality of life by focusing on observation and awareness as a means of preventing crime. The program employs strategies that range from simply promoting social interaction and watching out for each other to active patrols by groups of citizens.

Most neighborhood crime prevention groups are organized around a block or a neighborhood and are started with assistance from a law enforcement agency. Volunteers who donate their time and resources are typically at the center of such programs, since many do not have a formal budget or source of funding. Most Neighborhood Watches are located in areas that contain high percentages of single-family homes, little or no commercial establishments, and residents who have lived at their current address for more than five years. Just like the Crime-Free Multihousing Program, the Neighborhood Watch program uses street signs to show the presence of the program to potentially deter any would-be criminals.

FIGURE 20.5 Neighborhood Watch Signs.

All Neighborhood Watches share one foundational concept: bringing community members together to reestablish control of their neighborhoods, promote an increased quality of life, and reduce the crime rate in that area. If social disorganization is the problem and if traditional agents of social control no longer are performing adequately, we need to find alternative ways to strengthen informal social control and restore a sense of neighborhood in our communities; the same is true for single-family homes and apartment complexes. That's precisely what Neighborhood Watch strives to do. From the earliest attempts to deal with the neighborhood dynamics as it relates to neighborhood crime prevention, collective action by residents has proved one of the most effective strategies. The reason for this effectiveness is rather simple: involving community members in watch programs decreases opportunities for criminals to commit crime rather than attempting to change their behavior or motivation. While not all of the programs in place today go by the same name, they all accomplish the same goal: to bring community members together to fight crime.

Controlling Gangs

Situational crime prevention techniques for controlling problem behaviors of gangs and gang members and to increase the risks of detection:

- Increase guardianship of problem places through directed patrols.
- Increase formal surveillance of problem places through directed patrols.
- Use surveillance cameras.
- Reduce anonymity of offenders through field contacts.
- Increase natural surveillance, such as community reporting of gang behaviors and information.
- Collect graffiti reports via hotlines.
- Use confidential informants or sources.
- Improve lighting.
- Target chronic offenders.
- Target groups through enterprise investigations.
- Use detailed intelligence to improve investigations.
- Increase the effort to offend.
- Alter street patterns.
- Control weapons.
- Restrict spray paint sales.
- Reduce the rewards of offending.
- Disrupt street markets.
- Clean graffiti quickly.

- Prevent media reporting of gang and gang members' names.
- Increase penalties using gang enhancements.
- Link penalties or disposition to offense, e.g., community service such as cleaning graffiti, victim restitution.
- Improve prosecution of cases through better intelligence.
- Remove excuses or rule setting.
- Limit loitering.
- Abate nuisance properties.
- Use civil injunctions to restrict geographic areas.
- Enforce codes.
- Suspend driver's licenses.
- Monitor probationers and parolees for compliance.
- Establish or enforce truancy statutes.
- Establish or enforce juvenile curfews.

Premises liability factors:

- Prior gang crime on the premises (and throughout CHA property)
- Failure to use rudimentary access control policies
- Key control
- Inadequate/nonexistent security
- No enforcement of occupancy provisions
- Systemic gang problems within CHA properties
- Basic access control practices required
- Upgraded training for police assigned to CHA and private security assigned
- Clear understanding of responsibilities by security contractor and CHA
- Enforcement of CHA policies regarding vacant units
- Previous knowledge of the attackers causing trouble on premises
- Employees knew Gabby was in the Latin Kings
- Did not call the police—until after the stabbing or other crime
- Gang frequented the restaurant daily
- Gang members and affiliates worked for the restaurant
- Lack of security-related training
- Lack of personnel on duty
- Lack of supervision
- Lack of security procedures

Outcome:

- The case was settled prior to civil trial.

Learnings:

- Although the Burger King was in a rural vicinity, gang problems were prevalent.
- Attorneys in the case were unaware of the gang nexus or gang elements in the case.
- The gang attack was unprovoked.
- Most fast food establishments are trained only on robbery behaviors—most personnel have no clue how to react to gang violence on premises.

Contributing factors:

- Staff related to gang members
- No policy or procedures for gangs
- Restaurant was a known hangout for 4CH and associates
- Free meals/drinks served to keep teens at Arby's
- Oscar Peralta was an enforcer for the OAs

Premises liability factors:

- There was no notification of police despite the presence of threatening gang behavior and a weapon/
- Allowing gangs to loiter on premises is unwise.
- Management was untrained.
- No incident report of Friday night activities was prepared.
- Supervisors were not notified of the previous night's altercation.

Outcome:

- Plaintiff granted large award by jury.

Learnings:

- Gang retaliation for disrespecting can turn violent against those not directly involved.
- Train personnel on gang activity and have procedures to cope with gangs.
- Do careful background checking.
- Ensure that property does not become a known hangout.
- Supervisors need to audit locations at closing to ensure safe practices are followed.

EVICTION PROCESS

Three-Day Notices

Information regarding 3-day and 30-day notices is discussed at length by attorneys that train managers at seminars put on by the police in most jurisdictions. Please review the information provided by them, research the information at local law libraries, or purchase books on the subject. Employees of the sheriff's department cannot provide legal advice to the public but can direct you to the appropriate resources.

Failure to Pay Rent: Notice to Pay or Quit

This type of notice is used when the tenant has failed to pay his or her rent on time as specified in the rental agreement. If within three days after the notice has been properly served the tenant offers the entire amount demanded, the termination of tenancy is ineffective and the tenant can remain on the premises. If the tenant does not pay the demanded amount within the notice period, unlawful detainer proceedings may commence.

Violations of Rental Agreement/Property Damage to Premises: Notice to Perform Covenant or Quit or Notice to Quit

These notices are used for substantive rental agreement violations. There are two types: conditional and unconditional. The notice to perform or quit gives the tenant the option of staying if he or she corrects his or her behavior within the three-day period. If he or she does not, the tenancy is considered terminated, and the unlawful detainer process may be pursued.

Examples of when this notice is used include:

- The tenant has an unauthorized pet or occupant in violation of the lease.
- The tenant has failed to pay separate monetary charges, such as late charges, nonsufficient funds fees, or utility billings.
- The tenant has refused the landlord access to the premises when it is necessary to effect repairs.

The other three-day notice simply tells the tenant to move out in three days, without an option to correct his or her behavior. This unconditional surrender of the premises notice may be used when:

- The tenant has sublet all or part of the premises to a third person contrary to the rental agreement.

- The tenant is causing a legal nuisance by seriously interfering with the neighbor's ability to live normally in their homes (i.e., loud parties, hostile behavior).
- Illegal activities on the property (i.e., drug dealing).
- The tenant is causing a great deal of damage to the rental property (i.e., breaking windows, punching holes in walls, fire or water damage).

Thirty-Day Notices

Landlords and owners may prefer to use a 30-day notice in a month-to-month tenancy instead of a 3-day notice, if it is a situation in which the landlord does not have to prove their reason for eviction under the 30-day notice. In addition, a tenant who receives a three-day notice is more likely to defend the unlawful detainer in order to get revenge, vindicate his reputation, or gain additional time to move out of the premises. Using the 30-day notice gives the tenant time to rethink his position and allows him or her to move out under less pressure.

In the case of a month-to-month rental agreement rather than a lease, a landlord may terminate the tenancy by giving the tenant a 30-day written notice of termination of tenancy. Most state laws do not require that the notice state "cause" unless the property is in a rent control district. Federal subsidized housing programs (such as tax credit or Section 8) generally requires cause to be stated. Local ordinances may require cause (such as when a resident within the City of San Diego has lived in a property for two years or longer). Even if a statement of cause is not required, however, the landlord may not terminate the tenancy based on any federal, state, or local protected class (such as race, color, religion, sex, national origin, familial status, or handicap (federal classes; note that *handicap* is called *disability* in California), marital status, age, sexual orientation, ancestry, source of income, or any other arbitrary basis (CA classes).

Furthermore, a three-day notice violation requires significant documentation and credible testimony. Typically, a judicial officer will not order an eviction based on a three-day notice for minor rental agreement violations or property damage. In summary, evictions based on the three-day notice should only be pursued when the problem is serious and time is of the essence, or if there is no choice because the tenancy is pursuant to a lease rather than a month-to-month agreement.

The Unlawful Detainer Procedure

In California, the unlawful detainer proceedings may be commenced pursuant to Chapter 4 of the California Civil Code of

Procedure, commencing with § 1159. A lawsuit that is filed for possession of a real estate rental is called an eviction, or an "unlawful detainer" action. Because the landlord experiences a potential loss for each day he or she has to wait, unlawful detainers are entitled to priority over all civil actions except temporary restraining orders. Therefore, when an eviction is filed, the defendant (resident) has less time to respond to the court than he would if the lawsuit was for money only. If he or she fails to respond, the court can enter judgment without a trial. If a defendant responds in time, he or she is entitled to a trial. Even if the landlord wins at trial, there is a delay before possession of the premises is returned, due to paperwork requirements and because a defendant receives a final five-day notice that a lockout will occur on a particular date. Defendants can delay evictions with a number of legal tactics, but the average unlawful detainer in San Diego County runs approximately 21–45 days from the time of filing of the lawsuit to the date possession is returned.

Eviction Service and Procedures

Evictions can only occur after a landlord has received a judgment from the court and a writ of possession has been served or posted on the property. The purpose of a writ of possessions is to place with the rightful party possession of real property. Writs of possession usually arise as a result of a tenant's nonpayment of rent or a breach of the rental or lease agreement. After the process has been brought to the sheriff or police with the appropriate fee, you or your attorney of record will be sent a letter notifying you of the scheduled date of the eviction. You or your appointed agent will also receive a telephone call on the workday preceding the eviction to inform you of the exact time the officer will meet with you at the property. On the day of the eviction you may wish to change the locks at the residence while the police stand by for a reasonable time for this purpose. The landlord must provide access to the property in order to complete the eviction process. You should refer to Civil Code Sections 1983–1988 if you reside in California, or consult the laws in your state if questions arise regarding lawful disposition of possessions left on the property or any part of the eviction process.

BIBLIOGRAPHY

ABC News (2006, September 7). Proposed gang injunction ignites courtroom confrontation. Retrieved October 20, 2006, from www.abclocal.go.com/kfsn/story.

Akers, R. L. (1990). Rational choice, deterrence, and social learning theory: The path not taken. *Journal of Criminal Law and Criminology,* 653-676.

Akers, R. L. (1991). Self-control as a general theory of crime. *Journal of Quantitative Criminology,* 201–211.

Akers, R. L. (2002). Social learning theory and the explanation of crime: A guide for the new century. University of Florida Sociology Department.

Akiyama, *C. (2003).* Gangs, graffiti, and violence: A realistic guide to the scope and nature of gangs in America. *Criminal Justice Review,* 173-176.

Allan, E. (2002). *Policing by injunction: Problem-Oriented dimensions of civil gang abatement in the state of California.* Dissertation for the State University of New York at Albany.

Allen, R. (1998). People ex rel. Gallo v. Acuna: Abusing California's nuisance law to control gangs. *Western State University Law Review,* 257.

Alonso, A. (2003). Rocky Delgadillo will be attempting a civil gang injunction against the Rollin 60's Crips. Retrieved July 17, 2003, from www.streetgangs.com.

Altman, L. (2008). Ghost Town gang injunction map, defendants' names and press releases South Bay Crimes and Courts. October 15. http://www.insidesocal.com/crime&courts/2008/10/these-are-the-names-of.html Retrieved September 19, 2011.

American Civil Liberties Union (1997). False Premise/False Promise: The Blythe Street Gang Injunction and Its Aftermath. Los Angeles, CA: American Civil Liberties Union Foundation of Southern California. Retrieved November 3, 2006, from www.aclu-sc.org/blythe.html.

Amster, S. (2006). Los Angeles gang crimes and gang enhancement defense attorney. Retrieved September 4, 2006, from www.lacriminaldefenders.com/PracticeAreas/Gang-Crimes.asp.

Anderson, D. (2001, August 23). Gang Injunction: Is It Fair To Residents? *Precinct Reporter.*

Anderson, E. (1990). *Streetwise: Race, class, and change in an urban community*. Chicago: University of Chicago Press.

Andrews, D.A., Bonta, J. (1994). *The psychology of criminal conduct*, 2nd edition. Cincinnati: Anderson Press.

Aos, S., Phipps, P., Barnoski, R., Lieb, R. (1999). The comparative costs and benefits of programs to reduce crime: A review of National Research findings with implications for Washington State. Olympia, WA: Washington State Institute for Public Policy.

Arnette, J. L., Walsleben, M. C. (1998). Combating fear and restoring safety in schools. Bulletin. Washington, DC: U.S. Department of Justice, Office of Justice Programs, Office of Juvenile Justice and Delinquency Prevention.

Arnold, C. (1996). Due Process. Legal review. University of Calgary, Canada.

Arvizu, S. (2005, January 30). Oxnard solution is flawed. Ventura County Star.

Associated Press (2007, February 3). Judge issues injunction against Whittier gang. *Whittier Daily News*. Retrieved March 1, 2007 from www.ap.org.

Astvasadoorian, R. (1998). California's two-prong attack against gang crime and violence: The Street Terrorism Enforcement and Prevention Act and Anti-Gang Injunctions. *La Verne Law Review. Journal of Juvenile Law,* 19; 272-273.

Baccaglini, W. F. (1993). Project youth gang-drug prevention: A statewide research study. Rensselaer, NY State Division for Youth.

Baker, D. F. (2005, July 1). Injunction limits activities of 89 alleged Vista gang members. San Diego Union Tribune. Retrieved June 2006 from www.uniontribune.com.

Baldwin, J. (1979). Ecological and Areal Studies. In *Crime and Justice: An Annual Review.* Chicago: Univ. of Chicago Press.+

Bandura, A. (1977). Self-efficacy: Toward a unifying theory of behavioral change. *Psychological Review,* 84, 191–215.

Banks, S. (2006, April 28). Injunction has community feeling handcuffed. Separating family ties from implications of gang affiliation can be hard in Jordan Downs. *Los Angeles Times*. Retrieved June 1, 2006, from www.latimes.com.

Barboza, T. (2009). Injunction targets O.C. street gang. March 27. Los Angeles Times. http://latimesblogs.latimes.com/lanow/2009/03/injunction-targ.html Retrieved September 19, 2011.

Barlow, H. D. (1991). Explaining crimes and analogous acts. *Journal of Criminal Law and Criminology,* 82, 1; 229–230.

Barron, J. A. (2002). Constitutional Law in a Nutshell. The George Washington University School of Law.

Battin, S. R., Hill, K. G., Abbott, R. D., Catalano, R. F., Hawkins, J. D. (1998). The contribution of gang membership to delinquency beyond delinquent peers. *Criminology,* 36, 93–115.

Bustillo, Miguel (2000, January 13). Bill seeks legal aid for targets of gang orders. *Los Angeles Times.* Retrieved June 1, 2006, from www.latimes.com.

Baylis, M. (2005, October 12). Gang Injunction not suited to Santa Maria Police Say. Santa Maria Sun.

Beccaria, C. (1764). An Essay on Crime and Punishment.

Becerra, H. (1998, August 5). Gang members barred from meeting publicly. Los Angeles Times. Retrieved June 1, 2006, from www.latimes.com.

Becker, G. (1968). Crime and punishment: An economic approach. *The Journal of Political Economy,* 76, 169–217.

Bharath, D. (2010). Injunction issued against Garden Grove street gang. *Orange County Register.* January 28. http://articles.ocregister.com/2010-01-28/crime/24628399_1_gang-injunction-gang-clothes-gang-members Retrieved September 19, 2011.

Biskupic, J. (1999, June 11). Supreme Court Strikes Anti-Loitering Ordinance; Law aimed at gangs is called too vague. *Washington Post.*

Block, R., & Block, C. (1993). Street Gang Crime in Chicago. Research in Brief. Washington, DC: U.S. Department of Justice, Office of Justice Programs, National Institute of Justice. NCJ 144782.

Block, R., & Jones, E. (1999). Identifying and describing core areas of gang activity using GIS. Paper presented at the annual meeting of the American Society of Criminology, Toronto, Canada, November.

Block, R. (2000). Gang activity and overall levels of crime: A new mapping tool for defining areas of gang activity using police records. *Journal of Quantitative Criminology.* Vol. 16, 3; 369-371.

Boga, T. R. (1996). Gang Anti-loitering Laws Are Unconstitutional (From Gangs: Opposing Viewpoints, 132–139, 1996, David Bender and Bruno Leone, eds. See NCJ-159928).

Boga, T. R. (1994). Turf wars: Street gangs, local governments, and the battle for public space. *Harvard Civil Rights-Civil Liberties Law Review,* 29, 477.

Borunda, D. (2005, June). Gang activity flare up worries Central area neighborhood. *El Paso Times.*

Bowers, K., Johnson, S., Hirschfied, A. (2004) The Measurement of crime prevention intensity and its impact on levels of crime. *The British Journal of Criminology,* 44, 3; 419–420.

Boyum, D. (1994). *Alcohol and Other Drugs in Crime and Public Policy.* Institute for Contemporary Studies, San Francisco, CA: ICS Press.

Bradley, C. Q. (1998, September 1). L.A. attempts to curb gang activity with anti-loitering laws. First Amendment Center.

Branch, C. (1997). *Clinical Interventions With Gang Adolescents and Their Families.* Boulder, CO: Westview Press.

Braithwaite, J. (1989). *Crime, Shame, and Reintegration.* Cambridge, England: Cambridge University Press.

Brantingham, P. J., Brantingham, P. L. (1981). *Environmental Criminology.* Waveland Press.

Bratton, W. J. (1995). The New York City Police Department's civil enforcement of quality-of-life crimes. *Journal of Law and Policy,* 3, 447.

Brewer, D. D., Hawkins, J. D., Catalano, R. F., Neckerman, H. J. (1995). *Preventing Serious, Violent, and Chronic Juvenile Offending.* Thousand Oaks, CA: Sage Publications, 61–141.

Bridge, C. (2000, January 31). Gang injunction gunfight. *The Recorder.*

Brooks, H. (2001, June). Judge makes injunctions permanent. *North County Times.* Retrieved June 2006 from www.nctimes.com.

Brooks, R. (2007, February 2). San Bernardino County DA seeks gang-fighting tool. *The Press Enterprise.*

Brown, B., Cabral, E., Steenhausen, C. (2007) California's Criminal Justice System: A Primer. California Legislative Analyst's Office. Retrieved on April 23, 2007 from www.lao.ca.gov/2007/cj_primer.

Brown, S. E. (1982) Police patrol and the deterrence of crime. *Southern Journal of Criminal Justice,* 7, 2; 6–8.

Buerger, M.E. (1994). The limits of community. In *The Challenge of Community Policing: Testing the Promises,* D.P. Rosenbaum (Ed.). Thousand Oaks, CA: Sage Publications, 270-273.

Bufkin, J. (1997). Gangbangs and Drive-bys: Grounded culture and juvenile gang violence. *Social Pathology,* 3; 195–198.

Bulwa, D. (2006, October 23). San Francisco attorney wants to create gang-free zone, first in city would put 4 blocks of Hunters Point off-limits. *San Francisco Chronicle.*

Bulwa, D. (2007, June 22) City attorney aims to widen gang injunction. *San Francisco Chronicle.*

Bureau of Justice Assistance (1993). Problem-oriented drug enforcement: A community-based approach for effective policing. Washington, D.C.: U.S. Department of Justice, Office of Justice Programs, Bureau of Justice Assistance.

Bureau of Justice Assistance (1997a). Urban Street Gang Enforcement. Retrieved May 3, 2006, from www.ncjrs.gov/pdffiles/161845.pdf.

Bureau of Justice Assistance (1997b). Addressing Community Gang Problems: A Model for Problem Solving. Washington, D.C.: U.S. Department of Justice, Office of Justice Programs, Bureau of Justice Assistance.

Bureau of Justice Assistance (1998). Addressing Community Gang Problems: A Practical Guide. Washington, D.C.: U.S. Department of Justice, Office of Justice Programs, Bureau of Justice Assistance.

Bureau of Justice Assistance Bulletin (2006). Effective Gang Enforcement. Retrieved February 5, 2006, from www.ncjrs.gov/html/bja/gang/bja3.html.

Burgess, E. (1964). *Contributions to Urban Society.* Chicago: University Chicago Press.

Burnett, R. D. (1994). *Gangs and School. Understanding Contemporary Gangs in America: An Interdisciplinary Approach.* Upper Saddle River, NJ, Prentice Hall, 102.

Bursik, R. J. (1993). *Neighborhoods and Crime: The Dimension of Effective Community Control.* New York, NY: Lexington Books.

Bursik, R. (1988). Social disorganization and theories of crime. *Criminology,* 26, 519–521.

Byrne, J., Sampson, R. (1986). *The Social Ecology of Crime.* New York: Springer-Verlag.

Cabrera, Y. (1997, September 24). North Hills Neighborhood split on gang injunction: Crime prone area targeted, *Los Angeles Daily News.*

California Code of Civil Procedure, section 369.5 (Deering 2000).

California Code of Civil Procedure, section 731 (West 1997).

California Civil Code, sections 3479–80 (West 2005).

California Civil Code, section 3491 (West 2005).

California Code of Civil Procedure, section 369.5 (Deering 2004).

California Code of Civil Procedure, sections 525–527 (Deering 2004).

California Code of Civil Procedure, section 1209 (Deering 2004).

California Code of Civil Procedure, section 1218 (Deering 2004).

California Code of Civil Procedure, section 1222 (Deering 2004).

California Government Code, section 26507 (Deering 2004).

California Government Code, section 26528 (Deering 2004).

California Penal Code, section 166 (Deering 2004).

California Penal Code, section 186.20 et seq. (Street Terrorism Enforcement and Prevention Act), West 1997.

California Council on Criminal Justice (1989). State Task Force on Gangs and Drugs: Final Report. Sacramento, CA.

California Department of Motor Vehicles (2006). Driving without Auto Insurance. Retrieved October 2002, from www.dmv.ca.gov/vr/insurance_suspension.htm.

California Department of Justice (2003). Division of Criminal Justice Information Services, Crime and Delinquency in California, Federal Bureau of Investigation, U.S. Department of Justice, Uniform Crime Reports.

Campbell, D., Stanley, J. (1963). *Experimental and Quasi-Experimental Designs for Research.* Boston: Houghton Mifflin Company.

Capizzi, M., Cook, J. I., Schumacher, M. (1995). The TARGET model: A new approach to the prosecution of gang cases. *The Prosecutor,* Fall:18–21.

Capowich, G. E. (1995). *Evaluating Problem-oriented Policing: Process and Outcomes in Tulsa and San Diego* (executive summary). Alexandria, VA: Institute for Social Analysis.

Capowich, G. E., Roehl, J. A. (1994). Problem-oriented policing: Actions and effectiveness in San Diego. In *The Challenge of Community Policing: Testing the Promises,* Rosenbaum, D.P.(ed.). Thousand Oaks, CA: Sage Publications.

Carrillo, M. (2000). An Innovative Tool to Create Safe Communities. El Paso Police Special Projects Division Gang Injunctions Update.

Castorena, D. (1998a). SAGE Gang Injunction Cases. Unpublished report by the Hardcore Gang Division, Office of the District Attorney, County of Los Angeles.

Castorena, D. (1998b). The History of the Gang Injunction in California. Unpublished report by the Hardcore Gang Division, Office of the District Attorney, County of Los Angeles.

CBS News (2006, October 9). Injunctions Sought Against Highland Park Gangs. CBS News Service.

Chaiken, J. M. (1982). *Varieties of Criminal Behavior.* Santa Monica, CA: The RAND Corporation.

Chainey, S., Ratcliffe, J. (2005). *GIS and Crime Mapping*. London: John Wiley & Sons, Inc.

Cheh, M. M. (1991). Constitutional limits on using civil remedies to achieve criminal law objectives: Understanding and transcending the criminal-civil law distinction. *Hastings Law Journal*, 42, 1325.

Cheh, M. M. (1998). Civil remedies to control crime: Legal issues and constitutional challenges. In *Civil Remedies and Crime Prevention*, L.G. Mazerolle and J. Roehl. Monsey, NY: Criminal Justice Press, 45–66.

Christenson, W., Newman, S. (2004). Caught in the crossfire: Arresting gang violence by investing in kids. Fight crime invest in kids. Legislative Analyst's Office. Washington DC. Retrieved April 23, 2007 from www.fightcrime.org/reports/gangreport.pdf.

Christensen, L. (1999). Gang bangers: Understanding The Deadly Minds Of America's Street Gangs. Boulder, CO.: Paladin Press.

City News Service (1997a, May 20). Culver City gang faces injunction. Court order could curtail gang activity. Los Angeles.

City News Service (1997b, June 11). Injunction issued against Long Beach gang: court order filed against Crips to prevent life of crime. Los Angeles.

City News Service (1997c, June 11). Judge bans 18th Street gang: Issues injunction restricting gang activity in Jefferson Park.

City of Chicago v. Morales (1999). Supreme Court 119 S.Ct. 1849.

City of Commerce v. Chopper 12 (1996). Los Angeles Case No. BC155927 (Cal. Super. Ct. Los Angeles County).

City of Compton v. Tortilla Flats (1998). Los Angeles Case No. TC011598 (Cal. Super. Ct. Los Angeles County).

City of Inglewood v. Crenshaw Mafia (1996). Los Angeles Case No. YC028318 (Cal. Super. Ct. Los Angeles County).

City of Long Beach v. West Coast Crips (1997). Los Angeles Case No. NC021240 (Cal. Super. Ct. Los Angeles County).

City of Long Beach v. Westside Longos (1995). Los Angeles Case No. NC17601 (Cal. Super. Ct. Los Angeles County).

City of National City v. Old Town National City Gang (1998). San Diego Case No. SB007194 (Cal. Super. Ct. San Diego County).

City of Norwalk v. Orange St. Locos (1994). Los Angeles Case No. VC016746 (Cal Super. Ct. Los Angeles County).

City of Pasadena v. Denver Lanes (1995). Los Angeles Case No. GC015651 (Cal. Super. Ct. Los Angeles County).

City of Pasadena v. Villa & Krazy Boys (1996). Los Angeles Case No.GC017109 (Cal. Super. Ct. Los Angeles County).

City of Redondo Beach v. North Side Redondo 13 (1996). Los Angles Case No.YC026580 (Cal. Super. Ct. Los Angeles County).

City of San Diego v. Lincoln Park (1998). San Diego Case No. 725795 (Cal Super. Ct. San Diego County).

City of San Diego v. Lincoln Park (2005). San Diego Case No. 725795. Updated Filings modification of original order (Cal Super. Ct. San Diego County).

City of San Diego v. West Coast Crips (2006). San Diego Case No. GIC864852 (Cal Super. Ct. San Diego County).

Clarke, R. V. (1995). Situational crime prevention in *Building a Safer Society: Strategic Approaches to Crime Prevention*, Michael Tonry & Farrington, David (eds.). Chicago: The University of Chicago Press.

Clarke, R. V., Felson, M. (1993). *Routine Activity and Rational Choice. Advances in Criminological Theory*. New Brunswick, NJ: Transaction Books.

Clarke, R. V. & Eck, J (2003). *Becoming a Problem-Solving Crime Analyst. Jill Dando Institute of Crime Science*. London: University College London.

Cloward, R. A., Ohlin, L.E. (1960). *Delinquency and Opportunity: A Theory of Delinquent Gangs*. New York, NY: The Free Press.

Cloward, R. (1959). Illegitimate means, anomie and deviant behavior. *American Sociological Review*, 24, 164–176.

Cohen, A. K. (1960). *Delinquent Boys: The Culture of the Gang*. Glencoe, IL: The Free Press.

Cohen, M. A. (2000). Measuring the costs and benefits of crime and justice. National Institute of Justice.

Cohen, L. E., Felson, M. (1979). Social change and crime rate trends: a routine activity approach. *American Sociological Review*, 44, 588–608.

Cole, David (1997). No equal justice, race and class in the American criminal justice system. *Yale Law Journal*, 93 YALE L.J. 214.

Columbia Encyclopedia (2006). The Columbia Encyclopedia Injunction Defined, Sixth Edition. New York: Columbia University Press.

Conly, C. H. (1993). Street gangs: Current knowledge and statistics. Washington, DC: U.S. Department of Justice, Office of Justice Programs, National Institute of Justice.

Cook, P. J. (1986). The Demand and Supply of Criminal Opportunities. In *Crime and Justice: A Review of Research*. Chicago, University of Chicago Press.

Cornish, D., Clarke, R. (1986). Introduction in *The Reasoning Criminal*. Cornish, D. and R. Clarke (eds.). New York: Springer-Verlag. 1–16

Corpus Juris Secundum, S.v. "nuisances", section 110 (West 1997).

Costlow, T. (2002, May 20). A town fights gangs by obtaining right to sue them. *The Christian Science Monitor.*

Cramer, D. (2003). Advanced Quantitative Data Analysis, Understanding Social Research. Buckingham, UK: Open University Press.

Crank, J. (1993) Legalistic and order-maintenance behavior among police patrol officers. *American Journal of Police,* 1; 103-104.

Creswell, J. (2003). *Research Design: Qualitative, Quantitative, and Mixed Methods Approaches*. Thousand Oaks, CA: Sage Publications.

Cronkhite, C. (2005) Neighborhood Watch. *FBI Law Enforcement Bulletin.* 74, 5; 7–11.

Crowe, T. (2000). *Crime Prevention Through Environmental Design*, Second Edition. Boston: Butterworth-Heinemann.

Cruz, M. (2006). Injunctions eyed as tool. Officials continue to search for ways to combat gangs. *San Bernardino County Sun*.

Curry, G., Spergel, I. (1988). Gang homicide, delinquency, and community. *Criminology,* 26, 381–405.

Curry, G., Thomas, R. (1992). Community organization and gang policy response. *Journal of Quantitative Criminology,* 8, 357–374.

Curry, G., Ball, R. A.; and Fox, R. J. (1994). Research in Brief: Gang crime and law enforcement recordkeeping. Washington, DC: National Institute of Justice.

Curry, G., Ball, R. A., Decker, S. H. (1996). Research in Brief: Estimating the national scope of gang crime from law enforcement data. Washington, DC: National Institute of Justice. (NCJ 161477)

Curry, G. (1998). Female gang involvement. *Journal of Research in Crime and Delinquency,* 35, 100–118.

Curry, D., Decker, S., Egley, A. (2002) Gang involvement and delinquency in a middle school population. *Justice Quarterly,* 19, 2; 275–293.

Dahmann, J. (1981). *Operation Hardcore, A Prosecutorial Response to Violent Gang Criminality: Interim Evaluation Report*. Washington, DC: Mitre Corporation.

Davis, K. (2007, January 23). Expansion of gang injunctions sought. Escondido struggles with related crimes. *San Diego Union Tribune*. Retrieved February 2007 from www.uniontribune.com

Decker, S. H., Van Winkle, B. (1994). Slinging dope: The role of gangs and gang members in drug sales. *Justice Quarterly* 11, 583–604.

Decker, S. H., Van Winkle, B. (1996). *Life in the Gang: Family, Friends, and Violence*. New York, NY: Cambridge University Press.

Decker, S., Curry, D. (2000) Responding to gangs comparing gang member, police, and task force perspectives. *Journal of Criminal Justice,* 28, 2; 129–131.

Decker, S. H., Curry, D. G. (2001). *I'm Down for My Organization: The Rationality of Responses to Delinquency, Youth Crime and Gangs*. New York: Routledge.

Decker, S. H. (2002). *Policing Gangs and Youth Violence*. Newbury Park, CA: Wadsworth.

Decker, S. H., Curry, D. G. (2002) Gangs, gang homicides, and gang loyalty: Organized crimes or disorganized criminals. *Journal of Criminal Justice*, 30, 4; 343–345.

Decker, S. H., Curry, D. G. (2003). *Suppression Without Prevention, Prevention Without Suppression: Gang Interventions in St. Louis*. Newbury Park, CA: Wadsworth.

Delgadillo, R. (2006). Los Angeles City Attorney Gang Injunction Overview. Retrieved November 23, 2006, from www.lacity.org/atty/atycb1c2g.htm

DeMelo, D. M. (2005). Understanding Theory. Criminological Theory. Retrieved June 1, 2005 from www.home.comcast.net/~ddemelo/crime/crimetheory.html

Denno, D. W. & Schwarz, R. M. (1985). *Biological, Psychological, and Environmental Factors in Delinquency and Mental Disorder: An Interdisciplinary Bibliography*. Westport, CT: Greenwood Press.

Destro, R. A. (1997). Hostages in the 'Hoods: A Civil Rights Balancing Act. The Catholic University of America, Office of Public Affairs.

Destro, R. A. (1993). Gangs and civil rights. In *Gangs: The Origins and Impact of Contemporary Youth Gangs in the United States*, S. Cummings and D.J. Monti, (Eds.). Albany, NY: State University of New York Press. 277–304.

Do, A. (1993). City can't keep gang members apart, court rules. *The Orange County Register*, A01. Retrieved January 21, 2006, from www.lexis-nexis.com/universe.

Dolan, M. (1997, January 31). State court allows injunctions to restrict gangs, ruling stresses public concerns and lets communities ban legal activities of alleged gang members, such as on Blythe Street in Pomona. *Los Angeles Times*. Retrieved June 1, 2006, from www.latimes.com

Dolan, P., Peasgood, T. (2007) Estimating the economic and social costs of the fear of crime. *The British Journal of Criminology,* 47, 1; 121-122.

Dubin, R. (1959). Deviant behavior and social structure: Continuities in social theory. *American Sociological Review,* 24, 147–163

Durkheim, E. (1897/1997). *Suicide*. NY: Free Press. Retrieved June 1, 2005, from www.emiledurkheim.com

Eastern Group Publications (2005, April 5). L.A. Mayor's Plan: Gang Crackdown or Racial Profiling? News Report.

Eaton, A. J. (2007, February). City's first gang injunction inching along. Officials say it could be a year before tool to suppress gang violence is in place. *Compton Bulletin.*

Eck, J. E. (1995). *Crime and Place. Crime Prevention Studies 4*. Monsey, NY, Willow Tree Press.

Egan, E. A. (2006). Injunction Issued Against Urban Terrorists. Action Targets Dog Pound Gangsters. Fresno County District Attorney's Office. July 16. http://www.co.fresno.ca.us/uploadedFiles/Departments/District_Attorney/071608%20-%20Dog%20Pound%20Injunction.pdf Retrieved September 19, 2011.

Ehrenreich, B. (1997). Chained gang: Can the city attorney's injunction stop Pico-Union's 18th Street Gang? *LA Weekly*

Ehrenreich, B. (1999, July 7). Nation of Islam steps in to challenge gang injunction. *LA Weekly*. Retrieved June 1, 20006, from www.laweekly.com/news/news/crips-and-bloods-unite/6492/

Eitle, D., Gunkel, S., Van Gundy, K. (2004). Cumulative exposure to stressful life events and male gang membership. *Journal of Criminal Justice,* 32, 2; 95–96.

El Paso Times (2005, June 17). Gang Injunction Program in Texas. Retrieved February 4, 2006, from www.onrampelpaso.org/injunction.html

Elwood, M. (2007). *Critical Appraisal of Epidemiological Studies and Clinical Trials*, Third Edition. New York: Oxford University Press.

Epler, K. (2001, October 6). Second set of gang injunctions signed. *North County Times*. Retrieved June 2006 from www.nctimes.com

Esbensen, F. A., Huizinga, D. (1993). Gangs, drugs, and delinquency in a survey of urban youth. *Criminology,* 31, 565–589.

Esbensen, F. A. (1996). Gangs, drugs, and delinquency in a survey of urban youth. In *The Sociology of Juvenile Delinquency,* 2nd ed., R.J. Berger (Ed.). Chicago: Nelson-Hall. 69–87.

Esbensen, F. A., Winfree, L. T. (1998). Race and gender differences between gang and non-gang youth: Results from a multi-site survey. *Justice Quarterly,* 15, 505–526.

Esbensen, F., Osgood, D. (1999). Gang resistance education and training (great): Results from the national evaluation. *The Journal of Research in Crime and Delinquency*, 36, 2; 194–228.

Eslinger, B. (2006, November 23). Judge Ok's gang injunction, nixes curfew. *San Francisco Examiner*.

Evans, D. T.; Cullen, Francis. S.; Burton, Velmer. S., Dunaway, Gregory. R. & Benson, Michael. L. (1997). The social consequences of self-control: Testing the general theory of crime. *Criminology,* 35. 475–504

Fagan, J. E. (1989). The social organization of drug use and drug dealing among urban gangs. *Criminology,* 27, 633–669.

Fagan, J. E. (1990). Social process of delinquency and drug use among urban gangs. In *Gangs in America*, edited by C.R. Huff. Newbury Park, CA: Sage Publications, 183–219.

Fagan, J. E. (2003) Guns, science, and social policy. *Criminology & Public Policy,* 2, 3; 359–360.

Faris, R. (1930/1967). The development of the philosophy underlying the Durkheim School of Sociology. The University of Chicago Sociology Department.

Farish, L. (1998). *The First Amendment: Freedom of Speech, Religion, and the Press. Union County, N.J Springfield.*

Featherstone, R., Deflem, M. (2003). Anomie and strain: Context and consequences of Merton's two theories. *Sociological Inquiry,*73, 471–489.

Federal Bureau of Investigation (1997). Uniform Crime Reports 1996. Washington, DC: U.S. Department of Justice, Federal Bureau of Investigation.

Feinman, J. M. (2000). *Law 101: Everything You Need to Know About the American Legal System*. Rutgers School of Law. New York: Oxford University Press.

Feinstein, D. (2006) State of California Gang Prevention Effective Deterrence Act. Washington DC. Retrieved April 2007 from www.feinstein.senate.gov

Feldman, P. (1987a, November 6). Court rejects city attorney's bid to curb Westside gang's movements. *Los Angeles Times*. Retrieved June 1, 2006, from www.latimes.com

Feldman, P. (1987b, November 24). City attorney modifies plan to control street gang. *Los Angeles Times*. Retrieved June 1, 2006, from www.latimes.com

Feldman, P. (1987c, December 11). Judge raps city attorney's bid to neutralize gangs. *Los Angeles Times*. Retrieved June 1, 2006, from www.latimes.com

Felson, M. (1996) Preventing retail theft: An application of environmental criminology. *Security Journal,* 7, 1; 71–72.

Felson, M. (1997). Technology, business, and crime. in *Business and Crime Prevention*. Felson, M. & Clarke, R. V. Monsey, NY: Criminal Justice Press.

Felson, M. & Clarke, R. V. (1998). Opportunity Makes the Thief. Police Research Series, Paper 98. Policing and Reducing Crime Unit, Research, Development and Statistics Directorate.. London: Home Office. Accessed at www.homeoffice.gov.uk/rds/prgpdfs/fprs98.pdf

Ferrell, J. (1996). Youth, crime, and culture space. *Social Justice,* 23, 4; 21–23.

Finn, P., Healey, K. (1996). Preventing Gang- and Drug-Related Witness Intimidation. Washington, DC: U.S. Department of Justice, Office of Justice Programs, National Institute of Justice.

Finn, P., Hylton, M. (1994). Using Civil Remedies for Criminal Behavior: Rationale, Case Studies, and Constitutional Issues. Washington, DC: U.S. Department of Justice, Office of Justice Programs, National Institute of Justice.

Fischer, C. (1995). The subcultural theory of urbanism: A twentieth year assessment. *American Journal of Sociology* 101, 543–577

Fitzsimmons, E., Dobner, J. (2001). Escondido gangs focus of injunction effort. *San Diego Union-Tribune*, July 13, 2001. Retrieved June 2006, from www.lexis-nexis.com/universe.

Fleisher, M. S. (1995). *Beggars and Thieves: Lives of Urban Street Criminals*. Madison, WI: University of Wisconsin Press.

Flynn, D. (1998). Defining the "Community" in Community Policing. Washington, D.C.: Police Executive Research Forum. Retrieved June 1, 2006, from www.policeforum.org/cp.pdf.

Fox News (2006, June 15). Gang Injunction Granted against West Coast Crips in San Diego. Fox News. Retrieved June 20, 2006, from www.fox6.com/news/local/story.aspx

Fresno County Multi-Agency Gang Enforcement Consortium. (2009). Permanent Injunction Issued Against the VESR (Varrio East Side Reedley) Nortenos Criminal Street Gang. July 7. http://www.co.fresno.ca.us/uploadedFiles/Departments/District_Attorney/070709%20-%20Reedley%20VESR.pdf Retrieved September 19, 2011.

Fried, C., Reppucci, N. (2001).Criminal decision making: The development of adolescent judgment, criminal responsibility, and culpability. *Law and Human Behavior,* 25, 1; 45–47.

Freidman, W. (1998). Anti-Gang Ordinance. ABCNEWS.com

Freng, A. (1998). The gang intervention handbook. *Journal of Contemporary Criminal Justice,* 14, 1; 96–98.

Freng, A. (2000). Confronting gangs: Crime and community. *Criminal Justice Review,* 25, 1; 140–145.

Fritsh, E. J. (2003). Gang suppression through saturation patrol, aggressive curfew, and truancy enforcement: a quasi-experimental test of the Dallas Anti-Gang Initiative. 267-284 in S. Decker (Ed.) *Policing Gangs and Youth Violence*. Belmont, CA: Wadsworth.

Gaouette, N. (1997). L.A. to Gang Members: Don't Even Whistle. *The Christian Science Monitor*

Garvin, C. (2005). West Sac's Catch-22 Judge tosses suit against West Sac gang injunction but dodges constitutional issues. Newsreview.com

Gavan, P., Davey, J., Freeman, J. (2007). Policing alcohol-related incidents: a study of time and prevalence. *Policing,* 30, 1; 83.

Genelin, M. (1993). Gang prosecution: The hardest game in town. In *The Gang Intervention Handbook*, edited by A.P. Goldstein and C.R. Huff. Champaign, IL: Research Press, 417–426.

Gibson, S. (2005). Anti-gang strategy is called a success, But critics charge racism in West Sacramento's use of a court injunction. *Sacramento Bee*, March 23, 2005

Gilbertson, D. L. (2006). Confronting gangs: Crime and community. *Criminal Justice Review.* March 2006, 31, 1, 86–87.

Glazer, E. (1999). Thinking strategically, how federal prosecutors can reduce violent crime. *Fordham Urban Law Journal,* 26 Fordham Urb. L.J. 573

Goldberg, O. (2001). Pacoima gang latest targeted for injunction. *The Daily News of Los Angeles*.

Goldsmith, A. (2003). The void-for-vagueness doctrine in the Supreme Court, revisited : *American Journal of Criminal Law*

Goldstein, A. P. (1991). *Delinquent Gangs: A Psychological Perspective*. Champaign, IL: Research Press Company.

Goldstein, A., Huff, R. (1993). *The Gang Intervention Handbook.* Champaign, IL: Research Press Company.

Goldstein, A., Kodluboy, D. (1998). *Gangs in Schools: Signs, Symbols, and Solutions.* Champaign, IL: Research Press Company.

Goldstein, A. P. (2002). *The Psychology of Group Aggression.* Somerset, NJ: John Wiley & Sons Inc.

Goldstein, H. (1990). *Problem-oriented Policing.* New York: McGraw-Hill.

Goldstein, P. J. (1994). The drugs/violence nexus: A tripartite conceptual framework. *Journal of Drug Issues,* 14 No 4, 493–506.

Gordon, R. A. (2004) Antisocial behavior and youth gang membership: Selection and socialization. *Criminology.* Beverly Hills, 42, 1; 55–88.

Gottfredson, M., Hirschi, T. (1990). *A General Theory of Crime.* Stanford, CA: Stanford University Press.

Gottfredson, M., Hirschi, T. (1993) Rethinking the juvenile justice system. *Crime and Delinquency,* 39, 2; 262–272.

Gottlieb, D., Reeves, J (1962). *Adolescent Behavior in Urban Areas: A Bibliographic Review and Discussion of the Literature.* East Lansing, MI: Michigan State University of Agriculture and Applied Science.

Green, L. (1996). *Policing Places with Drug Problems.* Thousand Oaks, CA: Sage Publications.

Green, M. L., Roehl, J. (1998). Civil remedies and crime prevention: An introduction. In *Civil Remedies and Crime Prevention,* L. Green Mazerolle and J. Roehl (Eds.). Monsey, NY: Criminal Justice Press. 1–18.

Greenwood, P. W. (1996). *Diverting Children from a Life of Crime: Measuring Costs and Benefit.* Santa Monica, CA: RAND Corporation.

Griffin, M. L., Hepburn, J. R. (2006). The effect of gang affiliation on violent misconduct among inmates during early years of confinement. *Criminal Justice and Behavior,* 33, 4; 419–420.

Grinc, R. M. (1994). Angels in marble: Problems in stimulating community involvement in community policing. *Crime and Delinquency,* 40, 437–468.

Grogger, J. (2000). *The Effects of the Los Angeles County Gang Injunctions on Reported Crime.* Los Angeles, CA: Department of Policy Studies, University of California, Los Angeles.

Grogger, J. (2005). What we know about gang injunctions. *Criminology & Public Policy,* 4, 3, 637–642.

Gross, G. A. (2005, October 31). More than 100 accused gang members hit with injunction. *San Diego Union Tribune.* Retrieved June 2006 from www.uniontribune.com

Hagedorn, J. M. (1994). Neighborhoods, markets, and gang drug organization. *Journal of Research in Crime and Delinquency,* 31, 264–294.

Hagedorn, J. M. (2005). The global impact of gangs. *Journal of Contemporary Criminal Justice,* 21, 2; 153–154.

Hahn, J. K. (1992). Civil Gang Abatement: A Community Based Policing Tool of the Office of the Los Angeles City Attorney. Los Angeles City Attorney's Office

Hahn, J. K. (1988, February 5). Rethinking gangs rights versus our rights. *Los Angeles Times.* Retrieved June 1, 2006, from www.latimes.com

Hale, D. (2006, October 20). Gang Injunction: 300 Black Men Targeted. *Bay View Press.*

Harcourt, B. E. (2001). *Illusion of Order: The False Promise of Broken Windows Policing.* Cambridge, MA: Harvard University Press.

Harcourt, B. E. (1998). A critique of the social influence conception of deterrence, the broken windows theory, and order-maintenance policing New York style. *Michigan Law Review* 97, 91.

Harmon, D. (1998). US TX: Suspected Gang Members Get Restraining Order Subpoenas. *Austin American-Statesman*

Harries, K. (1980). *Crime and the Environment.* Springfield, IL: Charles C Thomas.

Hartlaub, P. (1997, October 12). Anti-Gang Injunction protested; North Hills neighbors march to show opposition. *Los Angeles Daily News.*

Hayden, T. (2005). *Street Wars, Gangs and the Future of Violence.* New York: New Press.

Hedlund, M. (2007, April 24). Cheers, Worries Over Broderick Boys Ruling. News 10, KXTV Sacramento. Retrieved May 1, 2007 from www.news10.net/display_story.aspx?storyid=27016&provider=top

Hemmens, C., Bennett, K. (1999). Juvenile curfews and the courts: Judicial response to a not-so-new crime control strategy. *Crime and Delinquency,* 45, 99–121.

Herd, B. (1998). Injunctions as a tool to fight gang-related problems in California after *People ex rel. Gallo v. Acuna:* A suitable solution? *Golden Gate University Law Review* 28, 629.

Hernandez, R. (2006). Gang injunction review being established. Retrieved March 2006 from www.InsideVC.com

Hernandez, R. (2006a, October 24). Judge OK's Southside Chiques injunction. *Ventura County Star.*

Herrera, D. (2005). Groundbreaking Civil Gang Injunction Program for S.F. City-Federal Partnership to Pursue Civil Remedies to Stem Gang Violence

Higgins, G. E., Ricketts, M. (2005). Self-Control Theory, Race, and Delinquency. *Journal of Ethnicity in Criminal Justice,* 3, 3; 5–6.

Hirschi, T. (1969). *Causes of Delinquency*. Berkeley: University of California.

Hirschi, T., Gottfredson, M. (1993). Commentary: Testing the general theory of crime. *Journal of Research in Crime and Delinquency,* 30, 47–54.

Hochstetler, A., Copes, H., DeLisi, M. (2002). Differential association in group and solo offending. *Journal of Criminal Justice,* 30, 6; 559–560.

Horowitz, R. (1987). Community tolerance of gang violence. *Social Problems,* 34, 5; 437–438.

Horwitz, J. (2007, February 5). Gang disruption plan. DA seeks to create unit to gain court injunctions. *San Bernardino Times.*

Houston, J. (1996). What works: The search for excellence in gang intervention programs. *The Journal of Gang Research,* 3, 1–16.

Howell, J.C. (1995). Guide for Implementing the Comprehensive Strategy for Serious, Violent, and Chronic Juvenile Offenders. Washington, DC: U.S. Department of Justice, Office of Justice Programs, Office of Juvenile Justice and Delinquency Prevention.

Howell, J. C., & Gleason, D. K. (1999). Youth Gang Drug Trafficking. Bulletin. Washington, DC: U.S. Department of Justice, Office of Justice Programs, Office of Juvenile Justice and Delinquency Prevention.

Howell, J. C.& Decker, S. H. (1999). The Youth Gangs, Drugs, and Violence Connection. Bulletin. Washington, DC: U.S. Department of Justice, Office of Justice Programs, Office of Juvenile Justice and Delinquency Prevention.

Howerton, A. (2006) Police response to crime: Differences in the application of law by race. *Journal of Ethnicity in Criminal Justice,* 4, 3; 51–53.

Huff, C. R. (1989). Youth gangs and public policy. *Crime and Delinquency,* 35, 524–537.

Huff, C. R. (1998). Comparing the criminal behavior of gang members and at-risk youths. Washington, DC: U.S. Department of Justice, Office of Justice Programs, National Institute of Justice.

Hughes, J. (2003, January 12). Police consider limiting gangs with safety zones. *The San Diego Union Tribune.* Retrieved June 2006 from www.uniontribune.com.

Hughes, L. A. (2005). Studying youth gangs: Alternative methods and conclusions. *Journal of Contemporary Criminal Justice,* 21, 2; 98–99.

Hunt, A. L. & Weiner, K. (1977). The impact of a juvenile curfew: Suppression and displacement patterns of juvenile offenses. *Journal of Police Science and Administration,* 5, 407–412.

Hunt, G. P., Laidler, K. J., Evans, K. (2002). The meaning and gendered culture of getting high: Gang girls and drug use issues. *Contemporary Drug Problems,* 29, 2, 375–517.

Hunt, G. P., Laider, K. J., Mackenzie, K. (2005). Youth gangs and drugs. *Journal of Ethnicity and Substance Abuse,* 4, 3; 99–101.

Ingram, J. (2006). Will Gang Injunctions Sweep California? Sacramento's Controversial New Way of Stopping Gangs May Be Coming to Your City. *Sacramento Press.*

In re Englebrecht (1998). California Court of Appeals, 67 Cal. App. 486.

Iraheta v. Superior Court of Los Angeles (1998). California Court of Appeals, 70 Cal. App.4th 1500.

Jacobus, P. (1994, June 18). Judge throws out Oakland suit against street gang. *San Francisco Chronicle.* Retrieved March 1, 2006, from www.lexis-nexis.com/universe.

Jacobius, A. (1996). Going gangbusters: Prosecutors fight gangs with injunctions banning conduct such as using beepers and applying graffiti. *American Bar Association Journal* 82, 24; 1–4.

Jansyn, L. R. (1966). Solidarity and delinquency in a street corner group. *American Sociological Review,* 31, 600–614.

Jiménez, J. L. (2007, January 28). Expanded 'safety zones' virtually blanket entire downtown in Escondido. *San Diego Union Tribune.* Retrieved February 2007 from www.uniontribune.com.

Johnson, B., Golub, A., Fagan, J. (1995) Careers in crack, drug use, drug distribution, and nondrug criminality. *Crime and Delinquency,* 41, 3; 275–296.

Johnson, D. (2000, February 22). Chicago council tries a new with anti-gang ordinance. *The New York Times.*

Jones, S. T. (1998, July 2). Liberty vs. Security. When the rights of individuals and communities clash, whose should prevail. Associated Press. Retrieved June 1, 2006 from www.ap.org.

Jones, M. B. (2000). The contagious nature of antisocial behavior. *Criminology,* 38, 25–46.

Jones, J. H. (2004, April 2). Lincoln Park area gang injunction is expanded. *San Diego Union Tribune.* Retrieved June 2006 from www.uniontribune.com.

Kahan, D. M. (1997). Social influence, social meaning, and deterrence. *Virginia Law Review,* 83, 349.

Kandel, J. (2004, June). Gangs unfazed by law. *Los Angeles Daily News*

Kantor, I. (1997) Gangs: A criminal justice approach. *Journal of Criminal Justice,* 25, 4; 335–338.

Kariak, P. (1995, June). Gang injunction protested. *Pasadena Star-News.*

Katz, C. M. (2006). *Policing Gangs in America.* Cambridge Studies in Criminology. New York: Cambridge University Press.

Katz, C., Maguire, E., Roncek, D. (2002) The creation of specialized police gang units. *Policing,* 25, 3; 472–507.

Keane, C., Gillis, A., Hagan, J. (1989) Deterrence and amplification of juvenile delinquency by police contact. *The British Journal of Criminology,* 29, 4; 336–338.

Keene, L. (2007, April 24). Yolo County gang injunction is overthrown. *Davis Enterprise.* Retrieved May 1, 2007 from lkeene@davisenterprise.net. www.umsl.edu/~keelr/200/ratchoc.html.

Keel, R. O. (1997). *Rational Choice and Deterrence Theory.*

Kelling, J. L. & Coles, C. M. (1996). *Fixing Broken Windows: Restoring Order and Reducing Crime in Our Communities.* New York: The Free Press.

Kelly, P. (2005, April 8). Oxnard gang injunction: DA Totten speaks about Chiques to Rotarians. *Santa Paula News.* Retrieved June 2005 from www.chiques-coalition.tripod.com/id13.html.

Kennedy, D. M. (1997, May). Pulling levers: Chronic offenders, high-crime settings, and a theory of prevention. *Valparaiso University Law Review,* 31, No. 2.

Keppel, G. (1991). *Design and Analysis: A Researcher's Handbook,* 3rd Edition. Englewood Cliffs, NJ: Prentice Hall.

Kersch, K. (2003). *Freedom of Speech: Rights and Liberties under the Law.* Santa Barbara, CA: ABS-CLI.

Klein, M. W. (1995). *The American Street Gang.* New York: Oxford University Press.

Klein, M. W., & Crawford, L. Y. (1967). Groups, gangs and cohesiveness. *Journal of Research in Crime and Delinquency,* 4, 63–75.

Klein, M. W. (1998). The problem of street gangs and problem-oriented policing. In *Problem oriented Policing: Crime-specific Problems, Critical Issues, and Making POP Work.* Washington, DC: Police Executive Research Forum, 57–86.

Klein, M. W. (1996). Street gangs and deterrence legislation. In *Three Strikes and Your Out Vengeance as Public Policy,* D. Shicher and D.K. Sechrest (Eds.). Thousand Oaks, CA: Sage Publications. 203–231.

Kleiman, M. (1999). Crime control policy in California, UCLA School of Public Policy and Social Research. *Valparaiso University Law Review,* 31; 554–555.

Knabe, D. (2005, May 20). Court gang injunction violators to serve full term of county jail sentence. County board of Supervisors Press Release.

Knox, G. W. (1991). *An Introduction to Gangs.* Barren Springs, MI: Vande Vere Publishing.

Knox, G. W. (1994). *National Gangs Resource Handbook: An Encyclopedic Reference.* Bristol, IN: Wyndham Hall Press.

Knox, G. W. (1998) Gangs and gang behavior. *Criminal Justice Review,* 23, 1; 104–106.

Knox, G. W. (1999, June). Trying to live "gang free" in Cicero, Illinois: A study of municipal gangs. *Journal of Gang Research,* 6, 4; 57–70.

Knox, G. W. (2005). National Gang Research Center Conference. Chicago Illinois Conference Notes.

Kornhauser, R. (1978). *Social Sources of Delinquency.* Chicago: Univ. of Chicago Press.

Krasnowski, M. (2001, May 23). Loved, hated and barely reviewed, gang injunctions become issue in L.A. mayor's race. Copley news service. Retrieved June 2005 from www.lexisnexis.com/universe.

Krohn, M. D. (1986). The web of conformity: A network approach to the explanation of delinquent behavior. *Social Problems,* 33, 581–593.

Kurki, L. (2000). Restorative and community justice in the United States. In *Crime and Justice: A Review of the Research,* Volume 27, 235-303. Chicago: The University of Chicago Press.

LaGrange, T. C., Silverman, R. A. (1999). Low self-control and opportunity: Testing the general theory of crime as an explanation for gender differences in delinquency. *Criminology,* 37, 41–72.

Laidler, K., Hunt, G. (1997). Violence and social organization in female gangs. *Social Justice,* 24, 4; 148–169.

Laidman, D. (2007) L.A. tweaks rules for injunctions against gangs. Copley News Service. www.knowgangs.com/news/may07/0513.php.

Lander, B. (1954). *Toward an Understanding of Juvenile Delinquency.* NY: Columbia Univ.

Langdon, J. (2010). Court affirms gang injunction: Upholds defendant's conviction. *Times Record News.* Oct. 7 http://www.timesrecordnews.com/news/2010/oct/07/court-affirms-gang-injunction/ Retrieved September 20, 2011.

Leovy, J. (2003, July 11). L.A. Seeks injunction against gang: Vowing to 'stamp out a reign of terror,' the city asks the court to curb activities of 31 people. *Los Angeles Times.*

Leovy, J. (2003b, August 29). City Targets Gang in Nickerson Gardens. *Los Angles Times*.

Levitt, S. D. (1998). The relationship between crime reporting and police: Implications for the use of Uniform Crime Reports. *Journal of Quantitative Criminology,* 14, 1; 61–65.

Levitt, S. D (2000). An economic analysis of a drug-selling gang's finances, 115 *Quarterly Journal of Economics,* 75, 769–775.

Levy, D. (1997, November 12). Injunction quashes L.A. Gang. *USA Today.*

Listokin, Y. (2005). Future-oriented gang members. Gang finances and the theory of present-oriented criminals. *The American Journal of Economics and Sociology,* 64, 4, 1073–1074.

Littlefield, D. (2003, September 13). Judge extends limits on gang; Injunction placed on the members of Center Street group. *San Diego Union Tribune*. Retrieved June 2006 from www.uniontribune.com.

Livingston, D. (1997). Police discretion and the quality of life in public places: Courts, communities, and the new policing. *Columbia Law Review,* 97, 551.

Loftin, C. (1986). Assaultive violence as a contagious social process. Bulletin of the *New York Academy of Medicine,* 62, 550-555.

Loh, L (2002, April 18). City seeks new court order to suppress 18th Street Gang. *Los Angeles Times*. Retrieved June 1, 2006, from www.latimes.com.

Lohr, S. L. (1998). Sampling: Design and Analysis. Department of Mathematics and Statistics Arizona State University. Retrieved June 2005 from www.math.la.asu.edu/~lohr.

Lopez, P. (2004, December 1). Gang targeted in injunction Parkside Bulldogs put on short leash; rules affect area near Roeding Park. *Fresno Bee*.

Lopez, R. J., Connell, R. (1999a, September). Police probe forces suspension of Rampart anti-gang injunctions. *Los Angeles Times*. Retrieved March 2006 from www.latimes.com.

Lopez, R. J. (1999, September 19). Rampart Probe May Put Gang Injunction at Risk. LAPD Officer's testimony fabricated. *Los Angeles Times*. Retrieved March 2006 from www.latimes.com.

Lopez, R. J. (1997). A Notorious Swath of Drugs and Violence. *Los Angeles Times*. Retrieved March 2006 from www.latimes.com.

Los Angeles City Attorney Gang Prosecution Section (1995). Civil gang abatement: a community based policing tool of the Office of the Los Angeles City Attorney.

Los Angeles Grand Jury Report (2004). A management review of the effectiveness of civil gang injunctions. Los Angeles County Civil Grand Jury Published Report. Los Angeles County.

Los Angeles Police Department (1995). Community Law Enforcement And Recovery (CLEAR).Retrieved March 1, 2006, from www.lapdonline.org/specialoperationssupportdivision/contentbasicview.

Los Angeles Times (1999a, May 30). Injunction Isn't Enough. *Los Angeles Times*. Retrieved March 2006 from www.latimes.com.

Los Angeles Times (1999b). Injunction Targets Culver City Gang. *Los Angeles Times*. Retrieved March 2006 from www.latimes.com.

Los Angeles Times (2002, February 26). Area Put Off-Limits to Valley Gang Members. *Los Angeles Times.* Retrieved March 2006 from www.latimes.com.

Los Angeles Times (2007, April 11) Make gang injunctions fair. As City Atty. Rocky Delgadillo formalizes rules for injunctions, he should examine how easy it is to get on the list and how hard it is to get off. *Los Angeles Times.* Retrieved March 2006 from www.latimes.com/news/opinion/editorials/la-ed-injunction.

Los Angeles District Attorney (2003, August 28). D.A.-City Attorney Seek Injunction Against Street Gang in Nickerson Gardens Area. Press Release.

Lota, L. (1997, August 29). Judge Puts More Heat on 18th Street Gang: Second Injunction Against Notorious Gang Granted. The Associated Press Los Angeles. Retrieved June 1, 2006 from www.ap.org.

Lynskey, D. (1998). Gangs in America. *Journal of Contemporary Criminal Justice,* 14, 1; 91–93.

Manolatos, T. (2007, February 5). Out of prison and looking for a fresh start, gang member finds old turf off-limits. *San Diego Union Tribune*. Retrieved March 2007 from www.uniontribune.com.

Marrow, A. F. (1969). *The Practical Theorist: The Life and Work of Kurt Lewin.* New York: Basic Books, Inc.

Marshall, S. (2001). Suspected gang member speaks out. *North County Times.* Retrieved June 2006 from www.nctimes.com.

Marshall, S. (2007, February). Judge grants second Escondido gang injunction. *North County Times.* Retrieved March 2007 from www.nctimes.com.

Mason, P. (2005). Innovate to intercept: Dealing with dealers. *Drugs and Alcohol Today,* 5, 2; 42–44.

Mateljan, F. (2003). City Attorney Delgadillo Secures Permanent Injunction Against KAM Criminal Street Gang. Press Release. Los Angeles City Attorney's Office.

Mateljan, F. (2006, June 1). Los Angeles City Attorney Press Release, Police Chief Bratton Announce Gang Injunction Against Black P Stones. Los Angeles City Attorney Office.

Matsueda, R. L. (1988). The current state of differential association theory. *Crime & Delinquency,* 34, 277–306.

Matza, D. (1964a). *Delinquency and Drift.* New York: John Wiley and Sons, Inc.

Matza, D. (1964b). *Becoming Deviant.* Englewood Cliffs, NJ: Prentice-Hall, Inc.

Maxfield, M. (1999) The National Incident-Based Reporting System: Research and policy applications. *Journal of Quantitative Criminology*, 15, 2; 119–122.

Maxson, C. L., Woods, K. J., Klein, M. W. (1996). Street gang migration: How big a threat? *National Institute of Justice Journal,* 230, 26–31.

Maxson, C. L. (1995). Street gangs and drug sales in two suburban cities. Research in Brief. Washington. DC: U.S. Department of Justice, Office of Justice Programs, National Institute of Justice.

Maxson, C. L. & Allen, T. (1997). An Evaluation of the City of Inglewood's Youth Firearms Violence Initiative. Los Angeles, CA: Social Science Research Institute, University of Southern California.

Maxson, C. L., Hennigan, K., Sloane, D. (1997). An Assessment of the Community Impact of Civil Gang Injunctions. Unpublished proposal to the National Institute of Justice, Investigator-Initiated Research Program.

Maxson, C. L. (1998, October). Gang members on the move. Juvenile Justice Bulletin. Washington, DC: U.S. Department of Justice, Office of Justice Programs, Office of Juvenile Justice and Delinquency Prevention.

Maxson, C. L., Hennigan, K. & Sloane, D. (2003). For the Sake of the Neighborhood: Civil gang injunctions as a gang intervention tool in southern California. In, S. H. Decker (Ed.) *Policing Gangs and Youth Violence.* Newbury Park, CA: Wadsworth.

Maxson, C. L. (2005). Its getting crazy out there: Can a civil gang injunction change a community? *Journal of Criminology and Public Policy,* 4, 3, 577–606.

Mayberry, C. (2001). Community celebrates park's rebirth: New beginning for Perry Park.

McBride, W. D., Jackson, R. K. (1985). *Understanding Street Gangs*. Plackerville, CA: Custom Publishing.

McClellan, E. (1998). *People ex rel. Gallo v. Acuna:* Pulling in the nets on criminal street gangs. *San Diego Law Review,* 35, 343.

McGabey, R. M. (1986). Economic conditions, neighborhood organizations, and urban crime. In *A.J. Reiss, Jr. and M. Tonry (Eds.). Communities and Crime,* Chicago: University of Chicago Press. 231–270.

McGloin, J. (2005). Policy and intervention considerations of a network analysis of street gangs. *Criminology & Public Policy,* 4, 3, 607–636.

McGreevy, P. (2006a, March 23). LA uses injunctions to fight thugs, but those who go straight find it hard to get off the list. *Los Angeles Times*. Retrieved March 2006 from www.latimes.com.

McGreevy, P. (2007a, January 30). Gang-injunction violators may serve full jail terms. *Los Angeles Times.* Retrieved March 2006 from www.latimes.com.

McGreevy, P. (2006b, June 2). L.A. city atty. seeks injunction against gang (Black P Stones). *Los Angeles Times.* Retrieved March 2006 from www.latimes.com.

McGreevy, P. (2007c, February 28). Judge grants an injunction against L.A. street gang (Highland Park). *Los Angeles Times*. Retrieved March 2006 from www.latimes.com.

McGreevy, P., Banks, S. (2007, April 17). L.A. gang injunction program overhauled. The process is revised amid complaints that none of the 11,000 people on the list in the last two decades have been able to get off it. *Los Angeles Times*. Retrieved May 1 from www.latimes.com.

McGreevy , P., Winton, R. (2007, January 10). L.A. shifts tactics against gangs. The city will focus on the worst ones regardless of size and use 'stay-away' orders against leaders. *Los Angeles Times.* Retrieved March 2006 from www.latimes.com.

McKenzie, R. D. (1924). The ecological approach to the study of the human community. *American Journal of Sociology,* 30, 287–301.

Meadows, R. J (2006). *Understanding Violence and Victimization,* 4th Edition. Upper Saddle River, NJ: Prentice Hall.

Meares, T. (2005). Gangs and gang related crime. *Journal of Criminology and Public Policy,* 4, 3, 575–576.

Merton, R. K. (1938). Social structure and anomie. *American Sociological Review* 3, 672–82.

Merton, R. K. (1959). Social conformity, deviation, and opportunity-structures: A comment on the contributions of Dubin and Cloward. *American Sociological Review,* 24, 177–189.

Merton, R. K. (1968). *Social Theory and Social Structure*. New York: Free Press.

Messner, S. F. (1984). The "Dark Figure" and composite indexes of crime: Some empirical explorations of alternative data sources. *Journal of Criminal Justice,*12, 5; 435–438.

Messner, S., Rosenfeld, R. (1994). *Crime and the American Dream*. Belmont, CA: Wadsworth.

Metropolitan News Enterprise (2002, October 8). Delgadillo Says He Is Seeking Gang Injunction to Give Area Hope. www.metnews.com

Mignon, S., Holmes, W. (1995) Police response to mandatory arrest laws. *Crime and Delinquency,* 41, 4; 430–443.

Miles, M. B. (1994). *Qualitative Data Analysis: An Expanded Sourcebook.* 2nd Ed. Thousand Oaks, CA: Sage Publications.

Miller, W. B. (1958). Lower class culture as a generating milieu of gang delinquency. *Journal of Social Issues,* 14, 5–20.

Miller, W. B. (1959). Implications of urban lower-class culture for social work. *The Social Service Review,* 33, 219–236.

Miller, W. B. (1982). Crime by Youth Gangs and Groups in the United States. Washington, DC: U.S. Department of Justice.

Mims, W. (2006). SB 1217 Gangs; punishment for activity taking place in school, etc., *penalty. Arizona State Senate Bill.*

Moore, J.W. (1990) Gangs, drugs, and violence. In *Drugs and Violence: Causes, Correlates, and Consequences, M. De La Rosa, E.Y. Lambert, and B. Gropper (Eds.).* National Institute on Drug Abuse, 160–176.

Moore, J. W. (1978). *Homeboys: Gangs, Drugs and Prison in the Barrios of Los Angeles.* Philadelphia, PA: Temple University Press.

Moore, M. H. (1984). *Dangerous Offenders: The Elusive Target of Justice.* Cambridge, MA: Harvard University Press.

Moreno, T. (2005). Lessons from a Gang Cop. Los Angeles Police Department.

Moreland, J. (2002, December). Oceanside police pursue two more gang injunctions. *North County Times.* Retrieved June 2006 from www.nctimes.com.

Moreland, J. (2005, July 2). Judge grants preliminary Vista gang injunction. *North County Times.* Retrieved June 2006 from www.nctimes.com.

Mowatt, R. (1995, August 21). The injunction pits public safety against private freedoms. *San Jose Mercury News.* Retrieved June 2006 from www.mercurynews.com.

Mrozek, T. (1993, August 26). Unusual anti-gang injunction leads to conviction of man for having a pager. *Los Angeles Times.* Retrieved March 2006 from www.latimes.com.

Murphy, W. P. (2000). The effect of supervision programs on street gangs. Unpublished San Diego State University Masters Thesis.

National Drug Intelligence Center (1995). NDIC Street Gang Symposium. No. 94-M0119-002A. Johnstown, PA, November 2-3, 1994. Johnstown, PA: U.S. Department of Justice, National Drug Intelligence Center.

NBC News (2007, January 18). Injunction To Be Filed Against 204th Street Gang, NBC News. Retrieved June 2006 from www.nbc.com.

Newman, O. (1972). *Defensible Space: Crime Prevention Through Urban Design.* New York: Macmillan.

Nelson, J. (2005, December 8). San Bernardino targets PPHG gang. *San Bernardino Times.*

Newton, G. D., Zimring, F. E. (1969). Firearms and Violence in American Life: A Staff Report to the National Commission on the Causes and Prevention of Violence. Washington, DC: U.S. Government Printing Office.

New York Times (1983, February 13). Los Angeles gangs heeding court order to erase graffiti. *The New York Times.*

Nix, D. (2002a, March 23). Gang members fight action. *The Daily Breeze.* Retrieved June 2005 from www.dailybreeze.com.

Nix, D. (2002b). Judge's decision against gang members will stand. *The Daily Breeze.* Retrieved June 2005 from www.dailybreeze.com.

Nix, D. (2002c). Judge denies gang injunction. Men believed to be members of Eastside Wilmas say they no longer have such affiliations. *The Daily Breeze.* Retrieved June 2005 from www.dailybreeze.com.

Nye, I. (1958). *Family Relationships and Delinquent Behavior.* New York: John Wiley & Sons, Inc.

NYGC - National Youth Gang Center (2006). *National Youth Gang Survey.* Institute for Intergovernmental Research. Retrieved April 23, 2007 from www.iir.com/nygc/nygsa.

O'Brien, R. M. (1996). Police productivity and crime rates. *Criminology,* 34, 2; 183–208.

O'Deane, M. (1993). Will they ever run out of spray paint. *Law Enforcement Quarterly.* San Diego County District Attorney's Office. November Issue.

O'Deane, M. (2001). Combating the Alliance Between Mexican Drug Trafficking Organizations and United States Gang Members. Unpublished Undergraduate Thesis, National University.

O'Deane, M. (2002). Overview of Gangs in America. Gangs in America Course Workbook.

O'Deane, M. (2006). Gang Investigations Manuscript. Course Text pending publication by Paladin Press.

Office of Criminal Justice Programs (2001). Gang Violence Suppression Program. Office of the Los Angeles District Attorney. Office of the District Attorney, County of Los Angeles.

Office of Juvenile Justice and Delinquency Prevention (1997). National Youth Gang Survey. Washington, DC: Office of Juvenile Justice and Delinquency Prevention, Office of Justice Programs, U.S. Department of Justice.

Office of Juvenile Justice and Delinquency Prevention (2000). National Youth Gang Survey. Washington, DC: Office of Juvenile Justice and Delinquency Prevention, Office of Justice Programs, U.S. Department of Justice.

O'Reilly, B. (2004, June 16). A Judge's Order has Gang Members Outraged. The O'Reilly Factor. Fox News Network Interview of two Ventura Colonia gang members.

Osborne, K. (2005, June 9). Public nuisance laws may be used against city gangs. *Cincinnati Ohio Post.* 06-09-2005. Retrieved March 2006 from www.news.cincypost.com/apps/pbcs.dll

Pacheco. R. (2008). Pacheco, Henry Announce Gang Injunction: Barrio Dream Home Criminal Street Gang Served with Civil Lawsuit. County of Riverside District Attorney. June 12. http://www.rivcoda.org/News/PressReleases/061208.html Retrieved September 19, 2011.

Padilla, F. (1992). *The Gang As an American Enterprise*. New Brunswick, NJ: Rutgers University Press.

Park, R. E., Burgess, E. W., McKenzie, R. D. (1925). *The City: Suggestions for Investigation of Human Behavior in the Urban Environment.* Chicago: University of Chicago Press.

Paternoster, R., Bushway, S. (2001). Theoretical and empirical work on the relationship between unemployment and crime. *Journal of Quantitative Criminology,* 17, 4; 391–393.

Pennell, S. (1994). Down for the Set: Describing and Defining Gangs in San Diego. San Diego, CA: Criminal Justice Research Division, Association of Governments.

People v. 18th St. Gang Alsace (1997). Los Angeles Case No. BC1679159 (Cal. Super. Ct. Los Angeles County).

People v. 18th St. Gang Pico/Union (1997). Los Angeles Case No. BC175684 (Cal. Super. Ct. Los Angeles County).

People v. 18th Street Pico Union (2002). Los Angeles Case No. BC272030 (Cal. Super. Ct. Los Angeles County).

People v. 18th St . Gang Shatto Park (1998). Los Angeles Case No. BC190334 (Cal Super. Ct. Los Angeles County).

People v. 18th Street Pico Union Gang (1997). Declarations in Support of the Plaintiff's Motion for Injunctive Relief to Abate a Public Nuisance, No. BC175684 (Cal. Super. Ct. Los Angeles County).

People v. 18th Street Hollywood (2003). Los Angeles Case No. BC305434 (Cal. Super. Ct. Los Angeles County).

People v. 18th Street Wilshire (2004). Los Angeles Case No. BC313309 (Cal. Super. Ct. Los Angeles County).

People v. 18th St CLCS & 9 Additional Gangs (2005). Los Angeles Case No. BC332713 (Cal. Super. Ct. Los Angeles County).

People v. 38th Street Newton (2004). Los Angeles Case No. BC319166 (Cal. Super. Ct. Los Angeles County).

People v. 42nd St. Gangster Crips (2004). Los Angeles Case No. BC326016 (Cal. Super. Ct. Los Angeles County).

People v. 7th Street Gang (1997). San Bernardino Case No. SCVSS42552 (Cal. Super. Ct. San Bernardino County).

People v. Acosta (1992). Los Angeles Case No. EC010205 (Cal. Super. Ct. Los Angeles County).

People v. Acuna (1993). Santa Clara Case No. 729322 (Cal. Super. Ct. Santa Clara County).

People v. Acuna (1995). California Court of Appeals, 40 Cal. Rptr. 2d 589.

People v. Acuna (1997). California State Supreme Court, 929 P.2d 596, cert. denied sub nom. Gonzalez v. Gallo, 117 S.Ct. 2513.

People v. Amaya (1993). Orange County Case No. 713223 (Cal. Super. Ct. Orange County).

People v. Avenues Gang (2002). Los Angeles Case No. BC287137 (Cal. Super. Ct. Los Angeles County).

People v. Big Hazard (2005). Los Angeles Case No. BC335749 (Cal. Super. Ct. Los Angeles County).

People v. Black P Stones (2006). Los Angeles Case No. BC352951 (Cal. Super. Ct. Los Angeles County).

People v. Broderick Boys (2004). Yolo County Case No. CV04-2085 (Cal. Super. Ct. Yolo County).

People v. Brown Nation (1997). Los Angeles Case No. VC 24170 (Cal. Super. Ct. Los Angeles County).

People v. B Street Boys (1994). Alameda County Case No. 735405-4, (Cal. Super Ct. Alameda County).

People v. Blythe Street Gang (1993). Los Angeles County Case No. LC20525 (Cal. Super. Ct. Los Angeles County).

People v. Bounty Hunter Bloods (2003). Los Angeles County Case No. BC301433 (Cal. Super. Ct. Los Angeles County).

People v. Canoga Park Alabama (2002). Los Angeles County Case No. BC267153 (Cal. Super. Ct. Los Angeles County).

People v. Center Street Gang (2003). San Diego County Case No. GIN032007 (Cal. Super. Ct. San Diego County).

People v. Chankla Bulldogs (2003). Fresno County Case No. 03CECG02881 (Cal. Super. Ct. Fresno County).

People v. Chopper City, Eddy Rock, and Knock Out Posse (2007) San Francisco County Case No. CGC07-464493 (Cal. Super. Ct. San Francisco County).

People v. Culver City Boys (1999). Los Angeles County Case No. SC056980 (Cal. Super. Ct. Los Angeles County).

People v. Delman Heights Bloods (2003). San Bernardino County Case No. SCVSS107068 (Cal. Super. Ct. San Bernardino County).

People v. Diablos Gang (2001). San Diego County Case No. GIN013906 (Cal. Super. Ct. San Diego County).

People v. Diablos Gang (2006). San Diego County Case No. GIN057995 (Cal. Super. Ct. San Diego County).

People v. Dogtown & Primera Flats (1982). Los Angeles County Case No. C418875 (Cal. Super. Ct. Los Angeles County).

People v. Eastside & Westside Wilmas (2001). Los Angeles County Case No. NC030080 (Cal. Super. Ct. Los Angeles County).

People v. Eastside Longos (2001). Los Angeles County Case No. NC030660 (Cal. Super. Ct. Los Angeles County).

People v. East Side Piru/Skyline (2004). San Diego County Case No. GIC827117 (Cal. Super. Ct. San Diego County).

People v. East Side Riva (2007). Riverside County Case No. RIC478810 (Cal. Super. Ct. Riverside County).

People v. East Side Victoria (2006). San Bernardino County Case No. VCVVS042664 (Cal. Super. Ct. San Bernardino County).

People v. Englebrecht (2001). California Court of Appeals, 88 Cal. App. 4th 1236.

People v. Five Time Hometown Crips (2003). San Bernardino County Case No. SCVSS080319 (Cal. Super. San Bernardino County).

People v. Fontana Headhunters (1996). San Bernardino County Case No. SCV30441 (Cal. Super. Ct. San Bernardino County).

People v. G Mobb (2004). Sacramento County Case No. 04AS02821 (Cal. Super. Ct. Sacramento County).

People v. Geer & Schoolyard Crips (2006). Los Angeles County Case No. BC349468 (Cal. Super. Ct. Los Angeles County).

People v. Gonzalez (1996). California Court of Appeals, 910 P.2d 1366.

People v. Grape Street Crips (2005). Los Angeles County Case No. BC330087 (Cal. Super. Ct. Los Angeles County).

People v. Green (1991). California Court of Appeals, 278 Cal. Rptr. 140.

People v. Harbor City/Harbor City Crips (1999). Los Angeles County Case No. NC026769 (Cal. Super. Ct. Los Angeles County).

People v. Harpys Gang (1998). Los Angeles County Case No. BC192678 (Cal Super. Ct. Los Angeles County).

People v. Hoovers (2005). Los Angeles County Case No. BC330272 (Cal. Super. Ct. Los Angeles County).

People v. Hoovers (2006). Los Angeles County Case No. BC341872 (Cal. Super. Ct. Los Angeles County).

People v. Insane Crips (2003). Los Angeles County Case No. NC033946 (Cal. Super. Ct. Los Angeles County).

People v. Junior Mafia (2006). Los Angeles County Case No. VC047440 (Cal. Super. Ct. Los Angeles County).

People v. Krazy Ass Mexicans (2002). Los Angeles County Case No. BC282629 (Cal. Super. Ct. Los Angeles County).

People v. Langdon Street (1999). Los Angeles County Case No. LC048292 (Cal. Super. Ct. Los Angeles County).

People v. Lennox-13 (1996). Los Angeles County Case No. YC027006 (Cal. Super. Ct. Los Angeles County).

People v. Linda Vista 13 (2000). San Diego County Case No. GIC745162 (Cal. Super. Ct. San Diego County).

People v. Logan Red Steps (2002). San Diego County Case No. GIC798708 (Cal. Super. Ct. San Diego County).

People v. Mara Salvatrucha (1998). Los Angeles County Case No. BC187039 (Cal. Super. Ct. Los Angeles County).

People v. Mara Salvatrucha Hollywood (2004). Los Angeles County Case No. BC311766 (Cal. Super. Ct. Los Angeles County).

People v. Nestor Gang (2002). San Diego County Case No. GIS9068 (Cal. Super. Ct. San Diego County).

People v. Norteños (2007). San Francisco County Case No. CGC07-464492 (Cal. Super. Ct. San Francisco County).

People v. Oakdale Mob (2006). San Francisco County Case No. CGC06456517 (Cal. Super. Ct. San Francisco County).

People v. Old Town National City (2005). San Diego County Case No. GIS26223 (Cal. Super. Ct. San Diego County).

People v. Orange Cove Bulldogs & Orange Cove Sur (2006). Fresno County Case No. CV06CECG02815 (Cal. Super. Ct. Fresno County).

People v. Original Bloods (1998). San Joaquin County Case No. CV05505 (Cal. Super. Ct. San Joaquin County).

People v. Olive Street (2006). Los Angeles County Case No. KC047752 (Cal. Super. Ct. Los Angeles County).

People v. Oxnard Colonia Chiques (2004). Ventura County Case No. CIV226032 (Cal. Super. Ct. Ventura County).

People v. Pacoima Project Boys (2001). Los Angeles County Case No. PC027254Y (Cal. Super. Ct. Los Angeles County).

People v. Playboy Gangster Crips (1987). Los Angeles County Case, Statement of Decision, No. WEC118860 (Cal. Super. Ct. Los Angeles County).

People v. Playboys (2006). Los Angeles County Case No. BC351990 (Cal. Super. Ct. Los Angeles County).

People v. Project Crips (2003). San Bernardino County Case No. SCVSS109373 (Cal. Super. Ct. San Bernardino County).

People v. Rolling Sixty Crips (2003). Los Angeles County Case No. BC298846 (Cal. Super. Ct. Los Angeles County).

People v. Santa Nita (2006). Orange County Case No. 06CC06903 (Cal Super. Ct. Orange County).

People v. Southside Montebello (2004). Los Angeles County Case No. BC324344 (Cal. Super. Ct. Los Angeles County).

People v. Sur Crazy Ones (1999). San Bernardino County Case No. SCVSS58315 (Cal. Super. Ct. San Bernardino County).

People v. Vagos Surenos (1998). Monterey County Case No. 115095 (Cal. Super. Ct. Monterey County).

People v. Varrio Hawaiian Gardens (2007). Los Angeles County Case No. BC375773 (Cal. Super. Ct. Los Angeles County).

People v. Varrio Horseshoe Gang et. al. (1998). Santa Clara County Case No. CV775225 (Cal. Super. Ct. Santa Clara County).

People v. Varrio Mesa Locos (1999). San Diego County Case No. N82223 (Cal. Super. Ct. San Diego County).

People v. Varrio Nueva Estrada (2004). Los Angeles County Case No. BC319981 (Cal. Super. Ct. Los Angeles County).

People v. Varrio Posole Locos (1997). San Diego County Case No. 76652 (Cal. Super. Ct. San Diego County).

People v. Varrio Posole Locos (2003). San Diego County Case No. GIN033214 (Cal. Super. Ct. San Diego County).

People v. Varrio San Marcos (1998). San Diego County Case No. N078777 (Cal. Super. Ct. San Diego County).

People v. Venice 13 Gang (2000). Los Angeles County Case No. SC060375 (Cal. Super. Ct. Los Angeles County).

People v. Venice Shoreline Crips Gang (1999). Los Angeles County Case No. SC057282 (Cal. Super. Ct. Los Angeles County).

People v. Verdugo Flats Gang (2003). San Bernardino County Case, No. SCVSS092975 (Cal. Super. Ct. San Bernardino County).

People v. Vista Homeboys (2005). San Diego County Case No. GIN044867 (Cal. Super. Ct. San Diego County).

People v. Westside Gang (2001). San Diego County Case No. GIN013907 (Cal. Super. Ct. San Diego County).

People v. Westside Gang (2006). San Diego County Case No. GIN057994 (Cal. Super. Ct. San Diego County).

People v. Westside Longos (2004). Los Angeles County Case No. NC035222 (Cal. Super. Ct. Los Angeles County).

People v. West Trece Gang (1993). Orange County Case No. 713223 (Cal. Super. Ct. Orange County).

People v. White Fence (2006). Los Angeles County Case No. BC353596 (Cal. Super. Ct. Los Angeles County).

People v. Whittier Varrio Locos (2006). Los Angeles County Case No. BC363464 (Cal. Super. Ct. Los Angeles County).

Perata, D. (1998, February 23). State Assembly Committee on Public Safety Bill 2585.

Petersen, R. D. (2004). *Understanding Contemporary Gangs in America: An Interdisciplinary Approach.* Upper Saddle River. NJ: Prentice Hall.

Peterson, D., Taylor, T., Esbensen, F. A. (2004). Gang membership and violent victimization. *Justice Quarterly.* 21, 4, 793–816.

Petersen, R. (2000). Definitions of a gang and impacts on public policy. *Journal of Criminal Justice,* 28, 2; 139–140.

Piquero, A., Bouffard, J. (2007) Something old, something new: A preliminary investigation of Hirschi's redefined self-control. *Justice Quarterly,* 24, 1; 1–28.

Polk, K. (1969). Class, strain and rebellion among adolescents. *Social Problems,*17, 214-24.

Polk, K., Schafer, W. (1972). *Schools and Delinquency*. Englewood Cliffs, NJ: Prentice-Hall.

Quan, D. (2007, June 12) Riverside County District Attorney is Drafting Injunction. *The Press-Enterprise*

Rackauckas, T. (2006, July 17). Gang injunction remarks by District Attorney Tony Rackauckas. Orange County District Attorney's Office.

Rackauckas, T. (1999). Annual Report, Gang Unit and Tri-Agency Resource, Gang Enforcement Teams (TARGET). Santa Ana, CA: Orange County District Attorney's Office.

Reckless, W. (1943). *The Etiology of Delinquent and Criminal Behavior*. Chicago: The University of Chicago Press.

Reckless, W. (1950). *The Crime Problem.* Chicago: The University of Chicago Press.

Reed, S. (2005). Court Extends East Side Gang Injunction. San Antonio Texas, Bexar County District Attorney Office.

Regini, L. A. (1998, February). Combating Gangs: The Need for Innovation. FBI Law Enforcement Bulletin, 67, 2, 25–32

Reiss, A., Tonry, M. (1986). *Communities and Crime*. Chicago: The University of Chicago Press.

Reiss, A. J. (1951). Delinquency as the failure of personal and social control. *American Sociological Review,* 16, 196–207.

Reiss, A., Rhodes, A. (1963). Status deprivation and delinquent behavior. *Sociological Quarterly,* 4, 135–149.

Reppetto, T. (1976). Crime prevention and the displacement phenomenon. *Crime and delinquency,* 22, 166–167.

Revolutionary Worker (2003, October 26). Watts: Under the Gun. How the so-called war-on-gangs is stripping the rights of a whole community. Revolutionary Worker #1217, October 26, 2003, posted at www.rwor.org.

Reyes, D. (2006). Judge signs injunction against Anaheim gang members about 90 members are being served. *Orange County Times*, November 18, 2006.

Reza, H. G. (2006). O.C. Gang's Movements are limited by Injunction. *Los Angeles Times,* Saturday Home Edition, July 15, 2006.

Ricciardulli, A. (2006). The Nitty Gritty of Gang Injunctions. MCLE Study.

Rivera, S. (2005). East L.A. Residents protest gang injunction. Eastern Group Publications, News Report, Sep 01, 2005.

Rivera, S. (2005). LA Implements gang injunction against Big Hazard. Eastern Group Publications, News Report, Aug 23, 2005.

Roberts, D. (1999). Forward: Race, vagueness, and the social meaning of order-maintenance policing. *The Journal of Criminal Law & Criminology,* 89: 775–836.

Robinson, A. (2007). City may seek court ban on gang activity. Strategy would identify Costa Mesa gang members and forbid specific gang-related behaviors. *Daily Pilot*, January 4, 2007.

Robinson, W. (1950). Ecological correlation and the behavior of individuals. *ASR* 15:351–57.

Rojas, M. (2000, February 10). City seeks injunction against Venice 13. *Los Angeles Times*. Available at www. latimes.com. February 10, 2000.

Roman, J. (2004) Can cost-benefit analysis answer criminal justice policy questions, and if so, how? *Journal of Contemporary Criminal Justice,* 20, 3; 257–260.

Romero, F. (2005, January 30). There's a better way to deal with gangs. *Ventura County Star*. Retrieved March 1, 2006, from www.lexis-nexis.com/universe.

Roneck, D. (2000). Schools and Crime. Analyzing Crime Patterns Frontiers of Practice. Thousand Oaks CA: Sage Publications.

Rooks, A. (2006). Court cements Lompoc gang injunction. *Santa Maria Sun.*

Rosenberg, K. (2006a, September 13). Gang Injunction first in county, Restricts ESV members by establishing safety zone. *The Daily Press.*

Rosenberg, K. (2006b, September). Five arrested in Old Town while gang injunctions are served. *Daily Press.*

Rosenberg, K. (2006c, October 1). Gang injunctions: Will they work?: Expert says method is not most effective means of tackling problem; may have driven gangs here. *Daily Press.*

Rosenfeld, R., Messner, S. (1995). Crime and the American Dream. *Criminological Theory*: 141–150.

Rosenthal, L. (2000) Gang loitering and race. *Journal of Criminal Law & Criminology,* 91, 1: 99–160.

Rubin, G. (2007). Drastic measures urged to rid area of gangs. Lancaster gang injunction would restrict dress, behavior. *Daily News.*

Rubio, M. (2006).Supervisor Rubio Launches Victims of Gang Violence Act of 2006. Kern County.

Rush, G. (2000). *Gangs, Graffiti, and Violence: A Realistic Guide to the Scope and Nature of Gangs in America.* Wadsworth Publishing.

Russell, W. (2004). Injunction targets gang as a whole. *Long Beach Press Telegram.* Retrieved June 2005 from www.presstelegram.com.

Sadovi, C. (2006). Flaunting wealth on the street is a must. *Chicago Sun Times.* Retrieved December 2006 from www.suntimes.com.

Sampson, R., Raudenbusch, S., Earls, F. (1997). Neighborhoods and violent crime: A multilevel study of collective efficacy. *Science,* 227, 918–924.

Sampson, R. J., Raudenbush. S. W. (1999). Systematic social observation of public spaces: A new look at disorder in urban neighborhoods. *American Journal of Sociology,* 105, 603–651.

Sampson, R.J., Groves, B.W. (1989). Community structure and crime: Testing social-disorganization theory. *American Journal of Sociology,* 94, 774–802.

San Bernardino District Attorney (2007, February 15). District Attorney announces formation of Gang Injunction Unit. *The Daily Press.* Retrieved March 2007 from www.dailypress.com.

Sanders, W. (1994). *Gangbangs and Drive-Bys: Grounded Culture and Juvenile Gang Violence.* New York: Aldin de Gruyter.

San Diego District Attorney (2000). Gang Enforcement training for law enforcement. Gang prosecution unit.

San Diego Union Tribune (1997). Novel crime control: Activity ban will dilute gang's power. Retrieved June 2006 from www.uniontribune.com.

San Diego Union Tribune (2001a). Escondido using injunction to squash gang problem. Retrieved June 2006 from www.uniontribune.com.

San Diego Union Tribune (2002, November 1). Logan Heights gang members prohibited from congregating: City obtains temporary restraining order against Red Steps Gang. Retrieved June 2006 from www.uniontribune.com.

Savitz, L., Rosen, L. *(1980)* Delinquency and gang membership as related to victimization. *Victimology,* 5, 2; 152-153.

Schroeder, E. (1999, September 21). ACLU-SC Voices Support For District Attorney's Decision to Halt 18th Street Gang Injunction. Retrieved March 1, 2006, from www.aclu-sc.org/News/Releases/1999/100283.

Sebba, L. (1996). *Third Parties, Victims and the Criminal Justice System.* Columbus, OH: Ohio State University Press.

Sense, J. L. (1997). L.A. tries to hold back 18th Street Gang with tough measures. *Agence France-Presse.*

Shah, A. (1998c). Judge issues injunction to curb crime. *Austin American-Statesman.* Retrieved March 1, 2006, from www.lexis-nexis.com/universe.

Sharfstein, D. (1997, June). Gang Busters, Enjoining the Boys in the Hood, American Prospect review of the Inglewood Crenshaw Mafia Injunction.

Shaw, C. R., McKay, H. D. (1942). *Juvenile Delinquency and Urban Areas: A Study of Rates of Delinquency in Relation to Differential Characteristics of Local Communities in American Cities.* Chicago: University of Chicago Press.

Sherman, L. W. (1990). Police crackdowns: Initial and residual deterrence. *Crime and Justice: A Review of Research,* 12, 1–48.

Shoemaker, D. J. (1996). *Theories of Delinquency.* New York, NY: University Press.

Short, J. F., Strodtbeck, F. L. (1974). *Group Process and Gang Delinquency.* Chicago: University of Chicago Press.

Short, J. F. (1996). Gangs and adolescent violence. Boulder, CO: Center for the Study and Prevention of Violence.

Short, J. F. (1963). Street corner groups and patterns of delinquency: A progress report. *American Catholic Sociological Review,* 28, 13–32.

Siegel, L. (2004). *Criminology: Theories, Patterns, & Typologies, 8th ed.* Belmont, CA: Wadsworth/Thomson Learning.

Singer, M. (2006, January 12). Injunction in the New Year. Both sides of the issue look at Oxnard's gang injunction going into new year. *Ventura County Star.*

Skipper, J. (1997). The civil injunction, a case study in the successful use of temporary restraining against street gangs in Redondo Beach, California. The FBI Law Enforcement Bulletin.

Skogan, W. G. (1988). Community organizations and crime. In *Crime and Justice: A Review of Research,* Vol. 10, Tonry, M. and Morris, N. (Eds.). Chicago, IL: The University of Chicago Press. 39–78.

Skogan, W. G. (1990). *Disorder and Decline: Crime and the Spiral Decay in American Neighborhoods.* New York: The Free Press.

Skogan, W. G. (1981). *Coping with Crime: Individual and Neighborhood Reactions*. Beverly Hills, CA: Sage Publications.

Southern California Public Radio. (2011). Judge rejects challenge to LA graffiti crew injunction. May 27. http://www.scpr.org/news/2011/05/27/26971/judge-rejects-challenge-la-graffiti-crew-injunctio/Retrieved September 20, 2011.

Southern California Public Radio. (2011). Ruling favors suspected Orange County Varrio Cypress gang members. May 11. http://www.scpr.org/news/2011/05/11/26614/ruling-favors-suspected-orange-county-varrio-cypre/ Retrieved September 19, 2011.

Soto, O. R. (2001a, May 12). Appeals court raises bar for anti-gang injunction. *San Diego Union-Tribune*.

Soto, O.R. (2001b, July 14). Judge imposed restrictions on gang members. *San Diego Union Tribune*. Retrieved June 2006 from www.uniontribune.com.

Spergel, I. A. (1966). *Street Gang Work: Theory and Practice*. Reading, MA: Addison-Wesley.

Spergel, I. A. (1984). Violent gangs in Chicago. *In Search of Social Policy*, 58, 199–225.

Spergel, I. A. (1990). Youth gangs: Continuity and change. In *Crime and Justice: A Review of Research, Vol. 12*, M. Tonry and N. Morris (Ed.). Chicago: University of Chicago Press, 171–275.

Spergel, I.A. (1995). *The Youth Gang Problem*. New York, NY: Oxford University Press.

Spergel, I. A., Curry, G. D. (1990). Strategies and perceived agency effectiveness in dealing with the youth gang problem. In *Gangs in America*, C.R. Huff (Ed.). Newbury Park, CA: Sage Publications, Inc., 288–309.

Stark, R. (1987). Deviant places: A theory of the ecology of crime. *Criminology*, 25, 893–909.

Stewart, G. (1998). Black codes and broken windows: The legacy of racial hegemony in gang civil injunctions. *Yale Law Journal*, 107, 2249.

Stone, G. (2005). Constitutional Law Review

Stronider, K. (2002). Anti-gang ordinances after *City of Chicago v. Morales*: The intersection of race, vagueness doctrine, and equal protection in the criminal law. *American Criminal Law Review*, 39, 1, 101–146.

Sutherland, E. (1924). *Principles of Criminology*, 4th ed. Philadelphia: Lippincott.

Sweeney, J. (1999, June 3). Injunction Highlights Culver City Gangs. *Culver City News*.

Sykes, G. M., Matza, D. (1957). Techniques of neutralization: A theory of delinquency. *American Sociological Review*, 22, 664–670.

Sylianou, S. (2003) Measuring crime seriousness perceptions: What have we learned and what else do we want to know. *Journal of Criminal Justice*, 31, 1; 37–39.

Taylor, R. (2001). The Ecology of Crime, Fear, and Delinquency: Social Disorganization versus Social Efficacy. In R. Paternoster & R. Bachman (Eds) *Explaining Criminals and Crime*. Los Angeles: Roxbury.

Terry, C., Ruiz, I. (1998) The making of a gang leader. *Alternatives to Incarceration*, 4, 3; 17–19.

Thabit, W. (2005). *Social Disorganization Theories and Crime: How Did East New York become a Ghetto?* New York: New York University Press.

The Associated Press (1998, April 14). Injunction targets Hollywood gang: Authorities say "Mara Salvatrucha" gang terrorizes residents. Los Angeles. Retrieved June 1, 2006 from www.ap.org.

The Associated Press (1998, October 28). California appeals court strikes down ban on carrying pagers. Retrieved June 1, 2006 from www.ap.org.

The Sheriff's Blogger. (2010). Garden Grove Gets Gang Injunction. January 28. http://capistranoinsider.typepad.com/the_sheriffs_blogger/2010/01/garden-grove-gets-gang-injunction.html Retrieved September 19, 2011.

The Winds (1997, July). Street Gangs Used to Divide and Conquer, 18 Street Gang of East Los Angeles and the Constitution. Retrieved August 1, 2006, from www.thewinds.org/1997/07/gangs.html.

Thompson, D. W., Jason, L. A. (1998). Street gangs and preventive interventions. *Criminal Justice and Behavior*, 15, 323-333.

Thompson, L. (2007, March 7). Ganging up on City Hall. *LA Weekly*. Retrieved April 23, 2007 from www.laweekly.com/news/news/ganging-up-on-city-hall/15863.

Thornberry, T. P., Krohn, M. D., Lizotte, A. J., Chard-Wiercheim, D. C. (1993). The role of juvenile gangs in facilitating delinquent behavior. *Journal of Research in Crime and Delinquency*, 300, 55–87.

Thornberry, T. P., Burch, J. H. (1997). Gang members and delinquent behavior. Juvenile Justice Bulletin. Washington, DC: U.S. Department of Justice, Office of Justice Programs, Office of Juvenile Justice and Delinquency Prevention.

Thornberry, T. P. (1987). Toward an interactional theory of delinquency. *Criminology*, 25, 863–891.

Thrasher, F. M. (1927/1963). *The Gang: A Study of 1,313 Gangs in Chicago*. Chicago: University of Chicago Press.

Thrasher, F. M. (1933). Juvenile delinquency and crime prevention. *Journal of Educational Sociology*, 6, 500–509.

Toby, J. (1957). Social disorganization and stake in conformity. *Journal of Criminal Law & Criminology,* 48, 12–17.

Tompkins, D. L. (1966). *Juvenile Gangs and Street Groups: A Bibliography.* Berkeley, CA: University of California, Institute of Governmental Studies.

Trevino, J. (2001, May 23). Politics in the Street: The Debate That Matters on Gang Injunctions. *LA Weekly.*

Tukey, J. W. (1977). *Exploratory Data Analysis.* Reading, MA: Addison-Wesley.

Urrea, Y. (2005). Oceanside gang injunction extended. *North County Times.* Retrieved June 2006 from www.nctimes.com.

Valdez, A. (2005). *Gangs: A Guide to Understanding Street Gangs*, 4th Ed. San Clemente, CA: Law Tech Publishing.

Valdez, A. (2000) Juvenile gangs. *International Journal of Offender Therapy and Comparative Criminology,* 44, 5; 635–638.

Valentine, B. (1995). *Gang Intelligence Manual: Identifying And Understanding Modern-Day Violent Gangs In The United States.* Boulder, CO: Paladin Press.

Van Derbeken, J. (2006, October 27). San Francisco, ACLU works to gang injunction plan. http://articles.sfgate.com/2006-10-27/bay-area/17317598_1_gang-members-street-gang-injunction.

Venkatesh, S. A. (1997). The social organization of street gang activity in an urban ghetto. *American Journal of Sociology,* 103, 82–111.

Villa, D. (2004, August 1). Colonia Civil Rights Coalition organized to fight injunction. *Ventura County Star.*

Villaraigosa, A. (1992, January 20). For safe parks, put gangs on the peace path. *Los Angeles Times.*

Vigil, D. (1993). The established gang. In *Gangs: The Origins and Impact of Contemporary Youth Gangs in the United States*, S. Cummings and D.J. Monti (Eds.). Albany, NY: State University of New York Press, 95–112.

Vigil, J. D. (1988). *Barrio Gangs: Street Life and Identity in Southern California.* Austin, TX: University of Texas Press.

Walker, G. (2005, October 26). City begins work on gang injunction: Officials believe injunctions may be key to curbing gang violence. *The Compton Bulletin.* Retrieved January 2006 from www.thecomptonbulletin.com/news02.

Walker, S., Spohn, C., Delone, M. (2000). *The Color of Justice: Race, Ethnicity and Crime in America*, 2nd ed. Belmont, CA: Wadsworth.

Wall Street Journal (2003, July 18). Opinion, Commenting about the NAACP July 14 Convention in Miami with 2004 presidential candidates.

Walston, G. (1999). Taking the Constitution at Its Word: A Defense of the Use of Anti-Gang Injunctions . University of Miami Law Review.

Warr, M. (1996). Organization and instigation in delinquent groups. *Criminology,* 34, 11–37.

Watkins, D. (2006). Gang Investigations: A Street Cop's Guide. Sudbury, MA: Jones & Bartlett.

Weisburd, D. (2006). Does crime just move around the corner? A controlled study of spatial displacement and diffusion of crime control benefits. *Criminology,* 44.

Welborn, L. (2006, July 14). DA seeks injunction against OC street gang. *Orange County Register.*

Werdegar, M. M. (1999). Enjoining the Constitution: The use of public nuisance abatement injunctions against urban street gangs. *Stanford Law Review,* 51.

Whitmer, J., Anker, D. (1997). The history of the gang injunction in California. Appendix M in S.A.G.E.: Strategy Against Gang Environments: A Handbook for Community Prosecution. Office of the District Attorney, County of Los Angeles.

Wilcox, P. (1996). Burglary victimization, perceptions of crime risk, and routine activities: A multilevel analysis across Seattle neighborhoods and census tracts. *Journal of Research on Crime and Delinquency,* 33, 147.

Williams, F., McShane, M. (1998). *Criminology Theory: Selected Classic Readings.*, 2nd Ed. Cincinnati: Anderson Publishing Co.

William-Ross, L. (2011). Judge Rejects Challenge to Injunction Against Tagging Group 'Metro Transit Assassins.' LAist. May 28. http://laist.com/2011/05/28/judge_upholds_injunction_against_ta.php Retrieved September 20, 2011.

Winton, R. (2004). Gang Crackdown Sought in Pomona. *Los Angeles Times.*

Wilson, J. Q. (1975). *Thinking About Crime.* New York: Basic Books.

Wilson, J. Q., Kelling, G. L. (1982). Broken windows: The police and neighborhood safety. *Atlantic Monthly,* 29–38.

Wilson, P. (1988) Preventing vandalism and graffiti. *Journal of Security Administration,* 11, 2; 28–29,

Wilson, W. J. (1985). Cycles of deprivation and the underclass debate. *Social Service Review,* 59, 541–559.

Wilson, W. J. (1991). Studying inner-city social dislocations: The challenge of public agenda research. *American Sociological Review,* 56, 1–14.

Wolcott, H. J. (1999, August 23). History of fights at fair makes gang fair game. *Los Angeles Times.*

Wolfgang, M. E. (1982). Criminal Violence and Race: A Selected Bibliography. Washington, DC: National Institute of Justice, US Dept. of Justice by the Center for Studies in Criminology and Criminal Law, University of Pennsylvania.

Wolfgang, M. E., Weiner, N. (1982). Domestic Criminal Violence: A Selected Bibliography. Washington, DC: US Dept. of Justice, National Institute of Justice.

Wortley, R. (2003) Measuring police attitudes toward discretion. *Criminal Justice and Behavior,* 30, 5; 538–540.

Xinhua News (2007). Los Angeles unveils new anti-gang injunctions. The People's Daily Online. Retrieved May 1, 2007 from english.people.com.cn/200704/17/eng20070417.

Yablonsky, L. (1962). *The Violent Gang.* New York, NY: Macmillan.

Yeager, M. (1998). *People ex rel. Gallo v. Acuna:* Cities allowed a new weapon in their arsenal for the crackdown on gangs. *Whittier Law Review* 19, 595.

Yoo, C. S. (1994). The constitutionality of enjoining criminal street gangs as public nuisances. *Northwestern University Law Review* 89, 212.

Zahniser, D. (2006, March 22). Hahn vs. Hahn, Janice tries to invoke reason in her brother's gang injunctions. *Los Angeles Times.*

Zedlewski, E. W. (1983). Deterrence findings and data sources: A comparison of the Uniform Crime Reports and National Crime Surveys. *The Journal of Research in Crime and Delinquency,* 20, 2; 262–264.

Zevitz, R. G., Takata, S. R. (1992). Metropolitan gang influence and the emergence of group delinquency in a regional community. *Journal of Criminal Justice,* 20, 93–106.

Zimring, F.E. 1996. Special Issue. Kids, guns, and homicide: Policy notes on an age-specific epidemic. *Law and Contemporary Problems* 59, 25–38.

Index

E

F

P

T

U

V

W

X

Z

For Product Safety Concerns and Information please contact our EU representative GPSR@taylorandfrancis.com
Taylor & Francis Verlag GmbH, Kaufingerstraße 24, 80331 München, Germany

www.ingramcontent.com/pod-product-compliance
Ingram Content Group UK Ltd.
Pitfield, Milton Keynes, MK11 3LW, UK
UKHW050056200926
475702UK00019B/2873
9781138374553